ELECTIONS IN THE AMERICAS
A DATA HANDBOOK

Elections in the Americas continues the series of election data handbooks published by Oxford University Press. Together with *Elections in Asia and the Pacific* and *Elections in Africa*, this is a highly reliable resource for historical and cross-national comparisons of elections and electoral systems world-wide.

Elections in the Americas

A Data Handbook

VOLUME I

North America, Central America, and the Caribbean

Edited by

DIETER NOHLEN

OXFORD

UNIVERSITY PRESS

OXFORD
UNIVERSITY PRESS

Great Clarendon Street, Oxford OX2 6DP

Oxford University Press is a department of the University of Oxford
It furthers the University's objective of excellence in research, scholarship,
and education by publishing worldwide in

Oxford New York

Auckland Cape Town Dar es Salaam Hong Kong Karachi Kuala Lumpur
Madrid Melbourne Mexico City Nairobi New Delhi Shanghai Taipei Toronto

With offices in

Argentina Austria Brazil Chile Czech Republic France Greece
Guatemala Hungary Italy Japan South Korea Poland Portugal
Singapore Switzerland Thailand Turkey Ukraine Vietnam

Published in the United States
by Oxford University Press Inc., New York

British Library Cataloguing in Publication Data
Data available

Library of Congress Cataloging in Publication Data
Data available

ISBN 0-19-928357-5 Vol-I
ISBN 0-19-928358-3 Vol-2
ISBN 0-19-925358-7 (2-Volume set)

Typeset by the Editor
Printed in Great Britain
on acid-free paper by
Biddles Ltd., King's Lynn

Preface

This two-volume work is the third installment in the series of election data handbooks published by Oxford University Press. Five years after the publication of the first title, *Elections in Africa* and three years after the publication of *Elections in Asia and the Pacific*, I now present the first compendium of electoral data that includes all American countries, from the introduction of universal male suffrage to the present day. The final part of the series *Elections Worldwide*, covering elections in Europe, is currently underway.

The basic idea of these handbooks—systematic and historically complete documentation of elections in all countries worldwide—is almost 40 years old. The idea was born in the early 1960s, when Dolf Sternberger and Bernhard Vogel embarked on an extensive research project on the election of parliaments at the University of Heidelberg (*Wahl der Parlamente und anderer Staatsorgane*). Since then, several research projects on elections and electoral systems have been carried out in Heidelberg, including empirical and theoretical publications covering the entire world. In 1978 a voluminous work on Africa was published under the subtitle *Politische Organisation und Repräsentation in Afrika* (Political Organization and Representation in Africa). In the same year I finished *Wahlsysteme der Welt* (Electoral Systems of the World), internationally better known in its Spanish version (*Sistemas electorales del mundo,* 1981). In the late 1980s an international research team under my direction began working on parliamentary and presidential elections in Latin America and the Caribbean. The main result concerning electoral data was published in 1993 in German (*Handbuch der Wahldaten Lateinamerikas und der Karibik*) and in Spanish (*Enciclopedia Electoral Latinoamericana y del Caribe*). A new project on elections and democratization in Africa and Latin America started in 1996. This project provided an ideal framework to revive the old idea of a worldwide compendium of electoral data.

The first book in this new series was *Elections in Africa* (1999), edited by Dieter Nohlen, Michael Krennerich, and Bernhard Thibaut, followed by *Elections in Asia and the Pacific* (2001), edited by Dieter Nohlen, Florian Grotz, and Christof Hartmann.

Elections in the Americas is based on our previous work *Handbuch der Wahldaten*. But even so, most of the articles required a lot of time and energy in their elaboration: Collecting the relevant information, fitting the quantitative and qualitative data into a strict series of guidelines and often recalculating national data according to our standards. The editorial team demanded a great deal of patience from the authors, who had to answer never-ending questions. Such a work produces an apparently paradoxical outcome: The more time spent on enhancing an article, the clearer and simpler it finally appears to the reader.

I am deeply grateful to the 31 contributors from more then ten different countries for their cooperation, patience, and encouragement. We have learnt a lot from them in these three years and their empathy with this project has become a decisive stimulus for us.

I am also especially grateful to those individuals and organizations that made this book possible. First of all, I owe much to my editorial team in Heidelberg: Matthias Catón, Philip Stöver, and Matthias Trefs have tirelessly edited the articles and collected and standardized the relevant information. Katrin Falk, Julia Leininger, Arthur Mickoleit, Florian Rehli, and Johannes Schwehm helped in different phases of the project and Dominique Le Cocq provided most valuable help in revising the English version.

I would also like to thank the *Institut für Politische Wissenschaft* (Institute of Political Science) at the University of Heidelberg for accommodating the project, the International Foundation for Electoral Systems (IFES) in Washington, the *Instituto Interamericano de Derechos Humanos* (IIDH; Inter-American Institute for Human Rights) in Costa Rica, especially its Center for Electoral Assistance and Promotion (CAPEL), and the International Institute for Democracy and Electoral Assistance (IDEA) in Stockholm. I am also indebted to the *Deutsche Forschungsgemeinschaft* (DFG; German Research Foundation), which supported the production of the typescript financially.

Finally, I thank Dominic Byatt and Claire Croft at Oxford University Press for their encouragement and professional support. Working with them has been a pleasure.

Heidelberg, February 2005   Dieter Nohlen

Contents

Notes on the Editor and the Contributors

Editor

DIETER NOHLEN is professor of political science at the University of Heidelberg and a well-known expert on electoral systems, political development, and democratization with a focus on Latin America. He received the Max Planck prize for internationally outstanding research in 1991, and the University of Augsburg prize for research on Spain and Latin America in 2000. His numerous books include *Wahlsysteme der Welt* (1978; Spanish edition 1981), *Elections and Electoral Systems* (1996), *Wahlrecht und Parteiensystem* (4th edn. 2004), *Sistemas electorales y partidos políticos* (3rd edn. 2004). He is editor of a seven-volume encyclopedia *Lexikon der Politik* (1992–1998), and co-editor of *Tratado de Derecho Electoral Comparado de América Latina* (1998; 2nd edn. 2005) as well as of an eight-volume *Handbook of the Third World* (3rd edn. 1991–1994), and a two volume encyclopedia of political science, *Lexikon der Politikwissenschaft* (2nd edn. 2004, Spanish edn. 2005). [E-mail: dieter.nohlen@urz.uni-heidelberg.de]

Contributors

CHRISTIAN BAUKHAGE holds a Master degree in political science and history from the University of Heidelberg (2003), where he has also been working as a research associate. His research focuses on the role of micro-states in international organisations, conflicts in Sub-Saharan Africa and the process of European integration. He is currently working for the German Ministry of Foreign Affairs. [E-mail: chbaukhage@gmx.de]

PETRA BENDEL is the managing director of the Central Institute for Area and Regional Studies at the University of Erlangen-Nuremberg in Germany and has worked on subjects focusing on both Latin America and Europe. She has published and edited several books, such as: *Central America. Peace, Development and Democracy?* (1993), *Party Systems in Central America* (1996), *The MERCOSUR* (1999), *Between Democratisation and Dictatorship* (2000), *In the Shadow of Terrorism, about*

9/11 (2002), *Social Injustice in Latin America* (2003), and *Democracy and State* (2003). [E-mail: pabendel@phil.uni-erlangen.de]

JULIO BREA FRANCO is associate professor at the University of South Florida and author of numerous books, essays and articles about constitutional, electoral and parliamentary law and political science. He is considered the best expert on the Dominican electoral system and he has vast experience in the organization of national elections. He has taught at the most prestigious universities of the Dominican Republic and currently works as a consultant. [E-mail: bfa@tampabay.rr.com]

MATTHIAS CATÓN (M.A.) is an assistant lecturer at the University of Heidelberg's Institute of Political Science, where he has also been working as a research associate. He focuses on electoral systems and party systems and is currently working on his Ph.D. thesis on contextual conditions of electoral systems. [E-mail: matthias@caton.de]

KATRIN FALK is a graduate student at the University of Heidelberg's Institute of Political Science. [E-Mail: katrinfalk@gmx.de]

BERND HILLEBRANDS is a management consultant working for international companies. He holds a Bachelor degree in theology, as well as a Master degree in political science and philosophy from the University of Heidelberg. In his research he focused on elections and party systems in the Commonwealth Caribbean and published numerous articles. [E-mail: office@hillebrands.com]

MICHAEL KRENNERICH works as a political consultant, among others for the Council of Europe. He holds a Ph.D. (1996) in political science, philosophy and public law from the University of Heidelberg and has worked as a research fellow a the same university as well as at the Institute for Iberoamerican Studies in Hamburg. He has been engaged in consulting activities in the field of electoral reforms in Latin America, Africa, Asia and Eastern Europe. He is author of a book on elections and civil wars in Central America (1996) and has co-edited *Elections in Africa. A Data Handbook* (1999) as well as two books on political violence (2000) and on social injustice (2002) in Latin America. [E-mail: krennerich-bendel@t-online.de]

RALF LINDNER has a degree in political science and economics from the University of Augsburg (Germany), completed graduate work at the

University of British Columbia (Vancouver, Canada) and post-graduate studies at Carleton University (Ottawa, Canada). He is a Ph.D. candidate at the department of political science at the University of Augsburg. His research interests include the theory and practice of advisory commissions, political parties, electoral behavior and federalism. His current research focuses on the impact of new information and communication technologies on the structures and processes of interest representation. His publications include contributions to a forthcoming volume on Canadian Royal Commissions (*Politik beraten und gestalten*, ed. by Rainer-Olaf Schultze and Tanja Zinterer, Opladen). [E-mail: ralf.lindner@phil.uni-augsburg.de]

RICHARD ORTIZ ORTIZ is a Ph.D. candidate at the University of Heidelberg where he studied political science, sociology and public law. He holds a Ph.D. in law from the Catholic University of Ecuador. Currently he is conducting research on the political stability in the Andean countries. [E-mail: richard-ortiz@gmx.de]

RAINER-OLAF SCHULTZE studied at the University of Heidelberg and at Harvard University. He is a professor of political science and managing director of the Institute for Canadian Studies at the University of Augsburg (Germany), as well as chairman of the board of the Foundation of Canadian Studies in German Speaking Countries. Schultze is a well-known specialist in comparative political analysis and political sociology with a focus on interest representation, political behavior and federalism in European and North American democracies. He is co-editor of the seven-volume *Lexikon der Politik* (Munich: Beck 1992–1998); of *The Politics of Constitutional Reform in North America* and of *Conservative Parties and Right-Wing Politics in North America*. [E-mail: rainer-olaf.schultze@phil.uni-augsburg.de]

JOHANNES SCHWEHM (M.A.) is an assistant lecturer at the University of Heidelberg's Institute of Political Science. He is an expert in political theory and international relations and is currently working on his Ph.D. thesis on governance beyond the nation state. [E-mail: jschwehm@web.de]

ALEXANDER SOMOZA (M.A.) is a research associate at the Free University Berlin. He studied political science at the University of Heidelberg. [E-mail: asomoza@zedat.fu-berlin.de]

PHILIP STÖVER has a Master degree in political science of the University of Heidelberg, where he currently is a research associate, lecturer, and Ph.D. candidate. In addition to elections and electoral systems his main field of research is the comparative analysis of the evolution of state structures in the context of European integration. [E-mail: philip.stoever@urz.uni-heidelberg.de]

JAN SUTER received his Ph.D. from the University of Basel, Switzerland. His thesis on the social and political history of El Salvador in the early 20th century was selected for a collection of outstanding research by the International Economic History Association in 1998. In addition to this work, Suter has published two books and numerous articles on the political and social history of Central America and the Caribbean. [E-mail: jand.suter@bluewin.ch]

MATTHIAS TREFS (MSc) received his Master's degree in comparative politics from the London School of Economics. He is currently working as a research associate, lecturer, and Ph.D. candidate at the Institute of Political Science at the University of Heidelberg. His research interests include electoral systems, parties, and party systems, particularly with regard to factions. [E-mail: trefs@uni-hd.de]

FÉLIX ULLOA holds law degrees from la *Universidad Complutense de Madrid*, and from the *Universidad de El Salvador*. He completed his post-graduate studies at the *Institut International d'Administration Publique* in Paris and at the Hubert H. Humphrey Institute of Public Affairs at the University of Minnesota. From 1994 to 1999, he served as a magistrate of the Supreme Electoral Tribunal. He has taught at several universities in El Salvador and has also served as president of the Institute of Law of El Salvador. Ulloa has worked for a number of projects of the OAS, IFES, IDEA, the Carter Center and NDI. He is currently the field director of the NDI project in civic education in Haiti. [E-mail: yaxpac51@hotmail.com]

ANDREAS M. WÜST is research fellow at the Mannheim Center of European Social Research (MZES) and lecturer in political science at the University of Heidelberg. His research focuses on elections, survey methodology and migration policies. Recent publications include his thesis on the electoral behaviour of naturalized citizens in Germany (*Wie wählen Neubürger?*, published in 2002) and an edited book on

Germany's well-known monthly political survey (*Politbarometer*, published in 2003). [E-Mail: mail@awuest.de]

CLAUDIA ZILLA has an M.A. in political science and is a Ph.D. candidate at the University of Heidelberg. She has a scholarship from the Konrad Adenauer Foundation and works as a researcher and lecturer at the University of Heidelberg's Institute of Political Science. Zilla has worked as an assistant for the 'Master in European Political Studies' program, a degree offered by the University of Heidelberg at its branch in Santiago de Chile. Her areas of specialization are Latin American politics, political institutions and research methods in social science. [E-mail: claudiazilla@yahoo.de]

DANIEL ZOVATTO GARETTO is the regional representative for Latin America at the International Institute for Democracy and Electoral Assistance (International IDEA) based in Stockholm, Sweden. From 1986 to 1996 he was executive director of the Center for Electoral Promotion and Assistance (CAPEL) of the Inter-American Institute of Human Rights, based in San José, Costa Rica. Between 1994 and 1996 he also held the position of deputy executive director at the same institution. He graduated from the School of Law and Social Sciences, National University of Cordoba, Argentina. He holds numerous post-graduate degrees, among others from the Diplomatic School of the Ministry of Foreign Affairs, Madrid and from Harvard. He also has a Ph.D. in international law from the *Universidad Complutense de Madrid*. He has been a visiting professor at several universities worldwide, a frequent contributor to many Latin American newspapers and scientific journals and a consultant for several international organizations and agencies. [E-mail: zovatto_idea@hotmail.com]

The data in this handbook are presented in the same systematic manner for all countries in order to provide electoral statistics in line with internationally established standards of documentation. The tables are organized in ten parts:

2.1 Dates of National Elections, Referendums, and Coups d'Etat: Table 2.1 provides an overview of the dates of elections to national political institutions, referendums as well as interruptions of the constitutional order by *coups d'état* since national independence. Where necessary, the dates of indirect elections are indicated by footnotes. The signs xx/xx indicate that no information could be found regarding the exact polling date.

2.2 Electoral Body: Table 2.2 provides a comparative overview of the evolution of the electoral body, and records the data on population size, registered voters and votes cast. The figures of registered voters and votes cast are drawn from the relevant Tables 2.5, 2.6, 2.7, and 2.9. Population data have been generally rounded and their sources are named in a relevant footnote. Where electors have multiple votes, the column for 'votes cast' documents the numbers of 'ballots cast'. A long dash (—) indicates that no information was available. All percentages are based on the figures given in the respective columns of this table.

2.3 Abbreviations: The abbreviations and full names of the political parties and alliances that appear in Tables 2.6, 2.7, and 2.9 follow an alphabetical order. Party mergers, splinters or successions are generally indicated in a footnote. Party names are given in their original language and the English translation is provided in parentheses. The abbreviations used in the tables are the ones commonly used in the country or in the international reference texts. In the few cases where no abbreviation is mentioned in electoral documents or reference texts, the authors may have used own abbreviations.

2.4 Electoral Participation of Parties and Alliances: The data regarding the participation of parties and alliances in all direct national elections are presented in a chronological order; they include the year of the elections and the number of elections contested. Only parties recorded in Tables 2.6, 2.7, and 2.9 appear in this table. If a party contested an election as part of an alliance, its participation is counted both with regard to the party and to the alliance.

2.5; 2.6; 2.7; 2.9 Distribution of Votes in National Referendums, Elections to Constitutional Assembly, Parliamentary and Presidential Elections: In these tables we try to provide exhaustive documentation of electoral participation, both in total numbers and in percentages, for every general election held since the introduction of male universale suffrage. The percentages refer to votes cast as a percentage of registered voters, invalid and valid votes as a percentage of votes cast and party votes as a percentage of valid votes. For the purpose of this handbook invalid votes are those that enter the ballot box but are disqualified out of different possible reasons, and therefore do not affect the electoral outcome. Regarding national referendums, their purpose is indicated in a footnote. According to international standards the book uses the term 'referendum' for both plebiscites and (constitutional) referendums. Parties that received less than 0.5% of the vote were subsumed in a residual category ('others'). The category of 'independents' includes all the candidates that did not run on a party label. A long dash (——) indicates the lack of exact data. A short dash (–) indicates that the information did not apply in this case, because the party did not participate in that election.

2.8 Composition of Parliament: This table illustrates the distribution of directly elected seats per party/ alliance as the result of the election. Subsequent changes in party affiliation are not documented. All parties and alliances that won at least one seat in the respective body are listed. In addition, the numbers of appointed or indirectly elected members are documented in footnotes. A short dash (–) indicates that the information was not applicable, because the party did not hold in that term. Optional subsections provide differentiated accounts of bicameral chambers and segments of electoral systems (in case of combined systems).

2.9 Presidential Elections: see 2.5.

2.10 List of Power Holders: Table 2.10 provides information on the succession in the executive. For presidential systems only the head of state (corresponding also to the head of government) is given. For semi-presidential and parliamentary systems both the head of state and the head of government are provided. The remarks describe the circumstances surrounding the accession to and resignation from office.

ELECTIONS AND ELECTORAL SYSTEMS IN THE AMERICAS
North America, Central America, and the Caribbean

by Dieter Nohlen[*]

This data handbook on *Elections in the Americas* is part of a wider project covering electoral data worldwide. While political scientists have been accustomed to finding information on elections ordered by country based on their economic, social and political levels of development (for example Mackie/ Rose 1991), the collection of data in this handbook follows continental lines. This is the third installment in the series, following volumes focusing on Africa in 1999 and on Asia and the Pacific (two volumes) in 2001.

Similar to the previous publications, this volume first presents the constitutional and other legal conditions of elections, from the introduction of male universal suffrage or political independence to the present day as well as the rules that actually govern the electoral processes; and second, the results of national elections to elect presidents and parliaments, including information on electoral participation and data on referendums. Basic information is provided on political institutions and the distribution of power, based on political preferences expressed in form of votes for political parties or candidates standing for political alternatives.

One of the main objectives of this handbook is to apply systematic criteria and homogeneous concepts to the information that has been collected. Official and non-official reports on elections often lack this requirement for comparative analyses. For example, percentages in official statistics and electoral results sometimes refer to votes cast, sometimes to valid votes. In this handbook, they always refer to the same absolute unit, the valid votes. The concept of electoral systems is often used indistinctly to refer to all, or a number of, the aspects governing an electoral process. Here it refers precisely to the way voters express their political preference in form of votes and the way these votes are trans-

[*] For research assistance I cordially thank Matthias Catón, Philip Stöver, and Matthias Trefs.

ferred into executive posts such as presidencies or legislative mandates in form of parliamentary seats. The information given on different electoral systems is organized around analytical criteria and is intended to allow and further historical and international comparisons. The presentation of data is guided by a country-by-country approach. One purpose of the following chapters is to give an initial comparative and systematic overview of the information that is treated in more detail in the individual country studies.

This first volume of *Elections in the Americas* comprises chapters on North America (Canada, Mexico, and the USA), Central America, and the Hispanic Caribbean (Costa Rica, El Salvador, Guatemala, Honduras, Nicaragua and Panama as well as Cuba, the Dominican Republic and Haiti), the English speaking Caribbean (Antigua and Barbuda, Bahamas, Barbados, Belize, Dominica, Grenada, Guyana, Jamaica, St. Kitts and Nevis, St. Lucia, St. Vincent, Trinidad and Tobago), and the former Dutch colony Surinam. All in all, there are 26 countries plus Puerto Rico with its special status, whose electoral development will be traced comparatively.

1. The Sub-Regional Division of Countries and Approaches to Comparative Studies

Until now, research on comparative politics has not focused on this geographical group of countries as a consistent area and thus, they have not been analyzed in a systematic, comparative way. Studies comparing the United States with other countries of the regions have not been very popular. The USA has predominantly been treated alone, which is also true to a certain extent for Canada. The only exceptions are comparisons between these two countries. However, the most commonly used comparative perspective is *extra*-regional. Both countries have usually been compared with European countries, in particular with Great Britain. The United States and Canada have rarely been the subject of comparisons with Latin America, except for modernization theory as models of development. Comparisons with the small insular countries of the Caribbean practically do not exist. It is not only the enormous difference in size that makes such a project less feasible, but also the conception of the Caribbean as backyard of the USA. From an academic point of view, the conditions of these countries are generally too different to gain insight from a comparison. These considerations are also valid with regard to the Central American countries, which form a group of their own, joined by Panama only a few decades ago. When countries of the latter two groups have been compared, then mainly *intra*-regionally, following the area approach. It is only within the regions that we find the degree of similarity and dissimilarity appropriate or even necessary for comparative analysis using the method of difference, for example, in Central America, besides the similarities of all the countries in the area, Costa Rica represents a sharp contrast compared with the other four Central American countries. The most common approach followed is a general comparison of Latin American countries in Central America, Mexico, South America and the Hispanic and the Francophone Caribbean (see W. Little, in D. Potter et al. 1997). Caribbean countries of different language groups have rarely been compared. A remarkable exception is the study of Rueschemeyer, Huber Stephens and Stephens (1992). The authors compare in particular the Anglophone Caribbean and the former Spanish colonies. Little attention was paid to Suriname; as a former Dutch colony it is situated outside the dominant linguistic areas.

Despite the fact that functionalism has spread from the USA to the rest of the academic community, little attention has been paid to countries south of the Rio Grande regarding basic topics concerning comparative politics. One exception is a study on political parties and party systems in Mexico, Chile, and Uruguay by Giovanni Sartori (1976). My studies on electoral systems (Nohlen 1978, 1981) included Argentina, Brazil, Chile, Guyana, Columbia, Mexico, Uruguay Paraguay, Venezuela, and the British West Indies. Undoubtedly, the field of research for political science has expanded with the third wave of democratization. This is particularly the case for cross-national studies and the statistical data collections that cover all countries worldwide. The field of qualitative analysis has undergone a similar development. The classic comparison of countries in the Western hemisphere in particular has benefited from the consideration of so-called young democracies. In his work *Patterns of Democracies* (1999) Arend Lijphart considered not only the USA and Canada, but also the Bahamas, Barbados, Jamaica, and Trinidad and Tobago, i.e. the great and traditional democracies were analyzed alongside younger and smaller democracies. Potter et al. (1997) offered a mixture of the regional and country-by-country approach in their research about the three waves of democratization, aiming at a global comparison.

However, we do not intend to take a variable-oriented approach to comparative research in this volume. This handbook has been conceived as a source for databased comparative research. This introduction pro-

vides the reader with a comprehensive picture of the electoral development in the countries treated in the first volume of *Elections in the
Americas* by elaborating similarities and differences from a comparative
perspective. Thus, the following sections, first examine some characteristics of the respective regional groups and then consider variations
within these groups.

Taking these findings into account, developments within these groups
will be highlighted by means of comparison. The countries are grouped
as follows: (a) the USA and Canada, (b) Mexico, Central America and
the Hispanic Caribbean,[1] (c) the English-speaking Caribbean.

2. General Trends and Differences: Sub-Regional Aspects

One of the main objections to a comparison between the countries in
this study could be the claim that they are simply too different. However, a comparison is necessary precisely to come to this conclusion.
Furthermore, the function of comparisons aims to uncover similarities as
well as differences. We also make comparisons along regional settings
were it makes sense to do so. Even if the differences undoubtedly out-
number the similarities, cross-regional similarities can still be found.
Moreover, some of the differences are likely to be the manifestations of
a common underlying variable, which in turn can be analyzed. This is
indeed the reason of comparing.

2.1 Size, Power Relations, and Democracy

The most obvious difference between the countries is their size. North
America consists of three large countries, the countries in Central America are rather small and the Caribbean countries can be labeled as micro-
states. Notwithstanding other factors, these differences affect the political life of each country. Of course, size is more than territory: it includes
population and also resources and economic wealth, which in turn are
the results of industrialization and economic development (Dahl/ Tufte
1973: 95). Brought down to one basic indicator, it is the sum of factors
that is expressed by classifying a country's developmental status as high

---

[1] Being a part of Latin America, this group of countries will also be integrated into the comparative account of the electoral and democratic development in Southern America in the second
volume.

income, middle income and low income (see Table 1). Since Seymour M. Lipset's seminal study, economic development has frequently been used as a criterion for assessing whether a country can be democratized (Lipset 1959). The stable democracies of the USA and Canada are not the only high-income countries among the political systems treated in this volume. The Bahamas and Bermuda are also included in this category, and Antigua, Barbados and St. Kitts and Nevis can be classified as middle-income countries. This concentration of prosperous nations in the Anglophone part of the American continent points to a regional setting: all of these countries have a higher per capita income than their Latin American counterparts. Belize, Dominica, Grenada, Guyana and Saint Vincent fall below the average numbers for Latin America and the Caribbean, but only Guyana is near to the low-income limit. Among Central American and Latin American countries, only Costa Rica is ranked above this average value. Except for Panama, these countries are located very close to the low-income category. Nicaragua, Haiti, and Cuba are undoubtedly part of this low-income bracket. Lipset's hypothesis could be applied when comparing both regions and trying to explain Costa Rica's unique democratic development among the Latin American countries. This relationship, however, cannot be established in intra-regional comparisons in the Anglophone Caribbean. In this region, consolidation of democracy was independent from the very different economic development levels.

Size in a multi-dimensional sense is the crucial factor determining relations of power, which play an important role in the political development of the countries in question. The Caribbean countries and those of Central America are seen as the backyard of the United States. We have to be aware of the great significance of the USA in the region, which even affects internal political processes in the countries in this region. Since the beginning of the 20th century, the USA is so dominant that whatever it does or does not do has direct consequences on the region. From an historical perspective, it has to be remembered that Mexico lost half of its territory to the USA in the 19th century. US policies of interventionism, first to free the Americas from foreign rule, as with Cuba and Puerto Rico in 1898 in their fight for independence from Spain, later in order to defend US interests, were sometimes invited by political powers in their internal fight against contenders. The USA backed the separation of Panama from Colombia and the foundation of a new country that supported their interests in the channel project to connect the Pacific with the Atlantic. In the first decades after independence, elections were monitored by the USA. In other countries of the region, the

USA sometimes intervened to restore political order (Cuba, Dominican Republic, Haiti, Honduras, and Nicaragua), to foster administrative modernization and to initiate democratic developments. After a continuous process of Americanization, Puerto Rico opted for an association with the United States (status of Commonwealth) in 1952. But the USA also intervened when its interests or influence were at stake and supported or helped to establish authoritarian regimes (Cuba, Nicaragua). In the context of the global conflict between East and West, and after the Cuban revolution, the USA tried to prevent the establishment of other communist regime (intervention in Grenada, support for the *Contras* in Nicaragua and the Central American regimes fighting revolutionary national liberation movements). On the other hand, Latin American politics were influenced by the human rights movement supported by US President Jimmy Carter. This movement supported the civil society and was crucial for the success of internal challenges to authoritarian regimes.

British colonialism in the Caribbean lasted until the 1960s, while the Spanish speaking countries in Central American and the Caribbean were dominated by the USA since the turn of the 19th century. This hegemony reinforced the position of domestic elites who favored the interests of American corporations. Interventionism in many cases can be 'directly linked to the defense of specific US corporate interests' (Rueschemeyer/ Huber Stephens/ Stephens 1992: 261).

2.2 Historical Record of Elections and Democracy

The countries included in this volume represent the whole spectrum of socio-political contexts, in which elections take place. Moreover, they display the functions that elections can fulfill. The study includes large and small countries and even micro-states; highly and less populated countries; societies that can afford to regulate public affairs by face-to-face communication and others that have to rely on the media to establish contact between politicians and citizens; societies in which democracy can still be conceived in ways similar to those of ancient Athens or Rousseau while others need to be representative democracies; societies split along ethnic, linguistic or religious cleavages while others are relatively homogeneous in this regard; industrialized as opposed to less developed countries; states with a long democratic tradition and others with a mainly authoritarian past; countries with a nearly uninterrupted history of electing their political leaders and countries where elections have not played a major role in their political history. Is it possible to group these countries according to their different characteristics? Are there correlations between any of these characteristics?

Table 1: Some Indicators of Economic and Political Development

	Income category[a]	Independent since	Free Elections since	Freedom House Index[b]	Transparency International Index[c]
Antigua and Barbuda	umic	1981	—	6	—[d]
Bahamas	hic	1973	1967	2	—[d]
Barbados	umic	1966	1951	2	—[d]
Belize	mic	1981	1954	3	4.5
Canada	hic	1867	1920/1960	2	8.7
Costa Rica	mic	1821	1949	3	4.3
Cuba	lic	1902	1940–1952	14	4.6
Dominica	mic	1978	1951	2	—[d]
Domin. Republic	mic	1844	1962	5	3.3
El Salvador	lmic	1821	1982	5	3.7
Grenada	mic	1974	1984	3	—[d]
Guatemala	mic	1821	1985	8	2.4
Guyana	lmic	1966	1992	4	—[d]
Haiti	lic	1804	—	12	1.5
Honduras	lmic	1839	1989	6	2.3
Jamaica	mic	1962	1997	5	3.8
Mexico	mic	1821	1997	4	3.6
Nicaragua	lic	1838	1990	6	2.6
Panama	mic	1821	1989	3	3.4
Puerto Rico	hic	–	1952	—	—[d]
St. Kitts and Nevis	umic	1983	1952	3	—[d]
St. Lucia	mic	1979	1951	3	—[d]
St. Vincent and the Grenadines	mic	1979	1951	3	—[d]
Suriname	lmic	1975	1949	3	—[d]
Trinidad and Tobago	mic	1962	1946	6	4.6
United States	hic	1776	1965	2	7.5

[a] Data from the World Bank for 2000: hic = high-income country; lic = low-income country; lmic = lower middle-income country; mic = middle-income country; umic = upper middle-income country.
[b] Data taken from Freedom House 2004. Regarding political rights and civil liberties, 2 stands for free and 14 for not free.
[c] Data taken from Transparency International 2003.
[d] Country not included in the Transparency International Index.

Democratic development and tradition vary along the sub-regions into which we have divided the countries. One could get the impression that the individual dates of independence, which are indeed very different, matter. Seen in European dimensions, these dates span a period from before the French Revolution (USA) until after World War II (Belize). However, Haiti, Mexico and Central America (without Panama) had already reached political independence at the beginning of the 19th century without democratic transformations. Although attempts to establish constitutional regimes were made and elections were held, constitutional governments were short-lived and elections subject to fraud.

The elections were used to superficially legitimate power holders (*continuismo*). Later on, this led to constitutional provisions prohibiting direct re-election. Periods of democracy and electoral efficiency were the exception rather than the rule. Nevertheless, the fight against *continuismo* and fraud triggered important political dynamics. This is particularly obvious in the case of Mexico, where the movement against the repeated re-election of Porfirio Díaz triggered the Mexican Revolution. With the exception of Costa Rica, democracy was only established in the last decade of the 20th century in all the Latin American countries in this volume.

In contrast to the Spanish speaking countries, the Anglophone Caribbean only achieved political independence from the 1960s onwards. However, they were able to make use of the institutions of self-administration that had been established under colonial rule. Therefore democracy rarely failed. In the Commonwealth Caribbean, democracy is and has been the rule rather than the exception. Thus, the date of independence offers little explanation for the process of establishment and consolidation of democracy. If we follow Huntington's (1991) differentiation, the USA and Canada are part of the first wave of democratization, the Anglophone Caribbean are part of the second wave, and the Latin American sub-region (except for Costa Rica) part of the third wave.

A particularly interesting comparison can be made between the Hispanic countries of Central America, where authoritarianism has been the rule and democracy the exception, and the Anglophone Caribbean, where democracy has been the rule and authoritarianism the exception. This comparison of regime outcomes is all the more interesting since the socioeconomic starting position of both groups of countries was similar and consequently formed an adequate context for comparison. The common base of the economies of the two regions was the plantation culture, which was firmly integrated in the global markets. Dietrich

Rueschemeyer, Evelyne Huber Stephens and John D. Stephens (1992) argue that the antecedents of the different regime outcomes up to the third wave of democratization can be found in the different reactions to the Great Depression in the 1930s. Whereas in the Spanish speaking countries, the military took control of the state and used force to repress protests from the emerging labor unions and their allied political parties, the British colonial government undertook reforms. Protests were channeled and this marked the beginning of political life and the establishment of a growing civil society that demanded institutional reforms. In the British Caribbean, unions, middle-class organizations, and political parties were allowed to form and consolidate their organization. All this let to a 'certain degree of power balance within civil society and between civil society and the state [...]. Thus, when independence transferred political powers to local actors, the state of development of civil society and of the party system was favorable for the consolidation of democracy' (ibid. 259 and 266). In search of comparative evidence, political answers to an exogenous economic crisis are seen as the main explanation for the different historical outcomes.

2.3 Institutional Alternatives: Political System and Electoral System

Scholars consulting this handbook are sure to be familiar with some of the general differences between the countries that are considered here. One of these differences is the type of political system in terms of the alternative of presidential and parliamentary systems and the type of electoral system in terms of the alternative of majority and proportional representation. Countries in the Americas are roughly evenly distributed as regard the type of political system and electoral system. The USA followed Montesquieu's theory and installed a system of strict checks and balances. Together with the Constitution of Cadiz, which ignored the further development of parliamentarism in Great Britain, it served as a model for the Latin American countries. In contrast to that, Canada and the British Caribbean followed the Westminster model and established a parliamentary system according to the functions described by Walter Bagehot (in *The English Constitution*, 1867). As for parliamentary elections, about half of the countries switched from the traditional plurality system to PR in the wake of mass enfranchisement. Most of these countries were in Latin America. The result is a regionally diversified picture, which can only be seen as uniform if compared to a theoretical third case. This is the case because the systems deviate from Arend Lijphart's (1991) institutional recommendation to combine parliamentarism with PR. The former British countries combine parliamentary government with plurality, the Latin American countries presidentialism with PR. There are only two explicit exceptions: first, the USA, which does not fulfill any of Lijphart's options. The USA is the oldest representative democracy in the world. And second, Guyana: here, in fact, parliamentarism and PR are combined. Yet, it is a bad example for the advantages of this institutional setting. The introduction of PR followed external pressure with the aim of ousting the governing party from power. After this, Guyana turned into a dictatorship and it was not until the 1990s that democratic conditions returned.

One could be tempted to try to strike a balance between both types of system as regards the consolidation of democracy in Latin America and the Caribbean, as was considered during the debates in the 1990s. At this time, some researchers traced Latin America's difficulties in establishing and consolidating democracy back to presidentialism. As a consequence, they recommended the adoption of a parliamentary system (Linz/ Valenzuela 1994). In contrast, other political scientists saw presidentialism as a better solution taking into account historical traditions, political culture und the structure of party systems in Latin America. Consequently, they advocated its preservation and pleaded for reforms (Nohlen/ Fernández 1991, 1998). Indeed, a pure statistical approach leads to an unambiguous result: political stability in the Caribbean countries under parliamentarism, political instability in Central American countries under presidentialism. However, the claimed causal link between regime outcome and chosen institutional setting distorts the true causes of the different developments of democracy. These causes are found in various other factors, including the ones I have already mentioned relating to the colonial past. Rueschemeyer, Huber Stephens and Stephens (1992: 230) are right to highlight the structural and institutional underpinning of authoritarianism and democracy and to emphasize the legacy of democratic institutions left by British colonialism as a crucial variable, linked to the relative strength of civil society and the weak or non-existent military establishment. These factors strongly influenced the political culture and other variables that ensure the political institutions function adequately.

Generally speaking, there are three worlds of political culture in the sub-regions: first, a western, liberal, white, civil society-based, reform-gradualist political culture in the USA and Canada; second, a Catholic, authoritarian, oligarchic, clientelist society of violent conflicts and revolutionary movements and a state-based development in the Latin American sub-region; and third, a political culture of small-island politics, conservative, inward looking, with a strong sense of community, based on British traditions of strong personalist leadership in the English speaking Caribbean. These characteristics of political culture clearly influenced the functioning of political institutions in such a way that it is not the institutions themselves but rather the context in which they arise that ought to be the main focus in the search for explanatory factors.

In this regard, it has to be mentioned that the Latin American countries had already had the choice between presidentialism and parliamentarism even before the third wave of democratization. These options and their advantages and disadvantages have been discussed comprehensively in previous decades, as for example, during the establishment of a constitutional system after the Mexican Revolution (see Valadés 2003) or in parliamentary debates prior to the passing of the stable constitution of 1949 in Costa Rica (Gutierrez et al. 1983). In doing so, the theoretical advantages of parliamentarian systems were adequately appreciated (as they are by advocates of presidentialism in Latin America today) but at the same time, the political culture of Latin America was emphasized. This particular context relativizes the theoretical findings. Thus, it (still) seems unadvisable to introduce parliamentarism in Latin America.

2.4 The Democratization of Franchise

The expansion of franchise was a long and complex process, particularly because there is generally no automatic voter registration in the Americas. Thus, research has to go beyond formal electoral provisions. Our attention should turn towards the specific conditions or barriers that limited the use of the formally granted franchise. However, this can be a problem, as we do not always have the necessary information. This distorts the picture, when countries seemingly fare worse only because they provide that kind of information. For example, Chile's democratic development is often only thought to be completed with the 1970 elections (see Rueschemeyer/ Huber Stephens/ Stephens 1992: 206).

Other countries receive a better assessment because of a lack of relevant information. Furthermore, the existence of democracy in the USA—where the legal obstacles to vote were only fully removed in the 1960s—is not usually linked to the effective enfranchisement. Be that as it may, there are problems in calculating the enfranchised electorate not least because the points of reference differ: either the total population or the adult population. Because of the very different demographic developments of the countries, the point of reference is important. In this study we use the total population as the point of reference. If we look at the expansion of franchise in the Americas, the major steps were the introduction of male universal suffrage, then female enfranchisement, then the inclusion of illiterates, and finally the lowering of the voting age.

Table 2: Democratization of Franchise

	Introduction of universal suffrage		Average number of registered voters as % of the total population					
	Male	Female	1950s	1960s	1970s	1980s	1990s	since 2000
Antigua and Barbuda	1951	1951	18.7	24.0	40.9	39.9	73.5	–
Bahamas	1967	1967	–	–	31.7	39.9	47.7	48.3
Barbados	1950	1950	42.8	43.4	51.0	67.3	75.0	79.1
Belize	1954	1964	–	–	34.9	43.5	43.8	49.3
Canada	1898[a]	1918	57.4	54.6	63.3	69.2	71.0	73.6
Costa Rica	1913	1949	32.5	36.4	44.6	53.7	56.8	56.7
Cuba	1901	1934	47.9	–	–	–	–	–
Dominica	1951	1951	43.3	37.1	37.7	55.6	69.4	84.9
Dominican Republic	1865	1942	53.7	48.1	45.5	46.3	48.7	52.0
El Salvador	1883	1939	—	38.3	36.5	50.6	50.1	51.7
Grenada	1951	1951	41.9	39.7	54.6	54.1	72.9	81.5
Guatemala	1879[b]	1945[b]	20.7	20.5	24.9	33.3	37.9	36.5
Guyana	1953	1953	–	45.6	56.9	53.8	51.1	51.4
Haiti	1950	1950	–	–	–	40.5	50.4	49.8
Honduras	1894	1955	27.6	35.7	34.2	41.3	46.6	52.4
Jamaica	1944	1944	51.4	41.4	36.7	45.0	43.9	49.7
Mexico	1857	1953	25.9	33.2	42.6	44.5	52.2	61.1
Nicaragua	1893	1955	–	37.1	52.6	49.0	48.8	—
Panama	1904	1945	40.8	40.4	43.1	45.6	62.9	68.0
Puerto Rico	1898[b]	1936	38.7	39.5	48.5	61.8	61.7	64.3
St. Kitts and Nevis	1952	1952	–	38.9	37.1	51.9	73.2	83.3
St. Lucia	1951	1951	44.9	43.0	48.1	62.8	69.0	73.4
St. Vincent and the Grenadines	1951	1951	39.3	37.1	49.2	52.8	67.2	75.5
Suriname	1949	1948	–	–	42.8	52.8	62.9	61.8
Trinidad and Tobago	1946	1946	45.4	45.1	43.1	71.1	64.4	66.6
United States	1971	1971	62.7[c]	60.0[c]	67.7[c]	73.6[c]	74.3[c]	73.1[c]

[a] Except Québec and Nova Scotia.
[b] Bound to certain conditions, such as literacy.
[c] Data refer to the elegible electorate.

A further difference between the countries concerns the question of whether franchise is a right or a duty. While the Anglo-American tradition conceives suffrage as an individual right, the Latin American tradition sees franchise as a public duty (for details see below).

2.5 The Administration of Elections

Accounts and analyses of elections tend to neglect the administrative aspect of the electoral process, although this subject is of utmost importance to the electoral and democratic development. These aspects have been reconsidered bearing in mind recent experiences in countries of the third wave of democratization. Today, electoral administrative authorities are treated as institutions of governance (López Pintor 2000). This change of importance is rooted in the different political cultures in the countries in transition. These countries were characterized by distrust in political institutions, especially in the incumbent state authority. This suspicion was caused by a long history of rigged elections. Free elections first required the elaboration of the institutional prerequisites for free and fair elections and for the legitimacy of the electoral result, particularly in regard to the losers. Two agents have been particularly active in this process: First, international organizations such as the UN, the OAS, and the Carter Center, and above all the Inter-American Institute for Human Rights (IIDH) with its electoral division, the Center for Electoral Assistance and Training (CAPEL), 'which played an important role in the diffusion and consolidation of standards of electoral practice and therefore in the enhancement of electoral bodies' (López Pintor 2000: 99). In fact, extraordinarily efficient administrative bodies were created in a context generally lacking administrative competence and efficiency. And second, the civil society organizations that monitored elections and the compliance with legal standards.

The organizational models of the electoral authorities reflect different cultural and historical conditions. In most Caribbean countries, elections are generally organized by the government, which is given full responsibility for them (e.g. in Antigua and Barbuda, Grenada, and in Saint Vincent and the Grenadines) or acts under a supervisory collective authority (e.g. in the Bahamas, Dominica, Guyana, and Jamaica). In the USA, the government also runs the elections, but in a highly decentralized system. The Federal Election Commission was only established in 1975. In Central America, Costa Rica was the first country to establish an independent and permanent commission, defined by the constitution as the fourth constitutional power—a successful model of how to administer elections within a specific political culture. Later on, independent commissions with full responsibility for the elections were also introduced in all other Central American countries, in the Dominican Republic, in Belize, Haiti, Saint Lucia, Suriname and Trinidad and Tobago as well as in Canada. In Mexico, the establishment of such an independent commission and a court for judicial revision was crucial in the process of transition to democracy since 1996. There are further differences, for example, whether the parties play the central role in these bodies (as in most cases) or not (Costa Rica and Canada), whether they are permanent or not (as in Haiti), whether there is one, two or more independent bodies (as in Barbados).

2.6 Electoral participation

Are there any marked differences between the sub-regions, or does voter turnout differ within the regions depending on the individual countries? As for regional comparisons the issue of which elections are to be compared must be resolved because there are two types of elections in presidential systems: Presidential and parliamentary. If elections of the same type are compared, there is the risk that elections of different importance may be compared. Parliamentary elections in presidential systems are by no means as important as in parliamentary systems. A similar argument holds true for presidential elections in parliamentary systems, if they take place at all. In the more important elections, turnout is generally higher, a fact that can be proven by mid-term election data showing lower turnout rates. In the case of parliamentary elections in presidential systems, the degree of simultaneousness has to be taken into account: on the same day, on the same ballot, with a single vote (Nohlen 1987).

It also is important to distinguish whether voting is compulsory or not. In our case this is likely to have only relative importance, as even in countries with compulsory voting there is generally no sanction for failing to vote. In any case it is very difficult to measure the influence of one variable in this multi-causal relationship. Even with these theoretical considerations in mind, it seems that there are certain regional differences regarding participation rates. Contrary to the assumption that plurality leads to lower participation, in the Commonwealth Caribbean it is generally higher than in the Latin American countries with PR. Deviant cases are Costa Rica, Nicaragua, and Panama with a relatively high voter turnout and Saint Lucia, Trinidad and Tobago as well as Antigua and Barbados with comparatively low participation levels. As for Canada and the United States, Canada has relatively high turnout rates, whereas in the USA electoral participation is relatively low.

However, the findings by International IDEA (2002) have to be treated very cautiously. Its analysis includes elections of very different quality. Data refers to registered voters. Since the accuracy of the registration of the theoretically eligible population depends on the system of registration, a higher participation rate can be an epiphenomenon of a worse method of voter registration. Remarkably, parallel to improvements in electoral administration, participation rates declined in many countries. The Mexican case is particularly conspicuous. In 2003, turnout reached an all-time low of slightly more than 40% in the most accurate election in history. Although there is no strict causal relationship, these facts point to the difficulties in the search for any determinate factors that could explain the differences in electoral participation.

Moreover, when comparing regionally different cultures and societies, we have to be aware that the degree of electoral participation, whether similar or not, can have a different meaning. For an adequate evaluation the following aspects have to be considered:

(1) Levels of social equality. High levels of social inequality usually result in a greater bias against the political participation of socially deprived groups, regardless of voter turnout. Furthermore, if the level of social injustice is high, elections are not seen as an act of political empowerment by the majority of voters but rather as an opportunity to trade votes for material profit or favors. Thus, depending on the degree of social inequality, high electoral participation can be coupled with entirely different expectation of politics.

(2) The governmental or societal focus of the political culture. This variable primarily applies to the rate of voter turnout. The societal focus on political culture in the United States, so aptly described by Alexis de Tocqueville, is likely to explain the low voter turnout in nation wide elections. As societal or community-oriented participation can compensate for low state-oriented political participation, it may relieve a democracy of the necessity of high voter turnout. To be sure, governmental or societal focus of the political culture is an essential factor in the interpretation of voter turnout figures.

(3) Centrality of a representative system of government in relation to other decision-making areas. A significant factor in interpreting voter turnout is whether a society has other means of enforcing its interests against veto powers, for example through traditional (violent) political conflict or via representational systems which lack democratically represented political power.

(4) Confidence in the political institutions. It makes a big difference whether constitutionally guaranteed political participation is based on trust and a high level of political accountability, or whether distrust and low levels of vertical and horizontal accountability exist. Not only is the meaning of voter turnout strongly influenced by this factor, but also the quality and legitimacy of democracy as a whole.

With regard to the regions that we are to compare, Latin America is characterized by a comparatively high degree of social inequality, a state oriented political culture, a questioned centrality of the representative system as well as a comparatively strong distrust of political institutions and low accountability. Even if voter turnout is similar between countries, dissimilarities with regard to these variables may result in a totally different meaning of voter turnout.

Table 3: Electoral participation

	Turnout as % of registered voters[a]
Antigua and Barbuda	62.2
Bahamas	90.8
Barbados	67.9
Belize	79.8
Canada	74.0
Costa Rica	65.4
Cuba	65.9
Dominica	77.2
Dominican Republic	67.9
El Salvador	43.1
Grenada	68.5
Guatemala	49.0
Guyana	85.0
Haiti	–
Honduras	72.9
Jamaica	66.2
Mexico	59.0
Nicaragua	81.0
Panama	76.1
Puerto Rico	73.4
St. Kitts and Nevis	72.0
St. Lucia	61.3
St. Vincent and the Grenadines	72.1
Suriname	66.3
Trinidad and Tobago	64.4
United States	52.2

[a] Average turnout since 1945 for elections to unicameral parliaments or to the lower chamber.

2.7 Different Worlds of Electoral Systems

We have to differentiate between presidential electoral systems and those for allocating seats in a single chamber or bicameral parliament. With regard to presidential electoral systems only countries that feature a constitutional form of government, where the head of state and of the executive branch is elected by popular vote have to be considered. Except for the USA, presidentialism is only found in all Latin American countries of Central America and the Caribbean. This is why we will account for internal differences of the electoral systems in the respective chapter on this group of countries. At this point it suffices to note that about half the countries vote according to a two-round (runoff) majority system, the others, including the USA, use the plurality system. The USA is the only country in which the president is chosen indirectly by an electoral college.

It is not only the specific form of presidential elections that influences the results. Taagepera and Shugart (1989) explain the importance of the electoral system in the case of the 1970 presidential elections in Chile: The president was elected by absolute majority. If no candidate received such a majority, the parliament chose the president from the two candidates with the most votes. The result would have been different if plurality or a runoff system had been used. 'Allende was the least desirable of the three candidates for more than half of the voters. [...] The centrist candidate would presumably [have been] the second best choice of both leftist and rightist, and the country would [have had] a president at least semi acceptable to everybody' (ibid.: 1). The type of presidential electoral system is also considered important for the structure of the party system (see below, Chapter 4.7).

Parliamentary elections in America follow a general pattern with only a few exceptions. The USA, Canada and the Anglophone Caribbean, except for Guyana, vote according to plurality in SMCs, Central America and the Dominican Republic according to PR in constituencies of different magnitudes. Special cases are Haiti with a majority system, Guyana with pure PR, and Mexico with a segmented system, where 300 deputies are elected according to plurality in SMCs and 200 seats are allocated by PR.

Table 4: Types of Electoral Systems for the Lower House or the National Assembly

Plurality System	Segmented system	PR in MMCs	Pure PR
Antigua and Barbuda			
Bahamas			
Barbados			
Belize			
Canada			
		Costa Rica	
Dominica			
		Dominican Republic	
		El Salvador	
Grenada			
		Guatemala	
			Guyana
		Honduras	
Jamaica			
	Mexico		
		Nicaragua	
		Panama	
Puerto Rico			
St. Kitts and Nevis			
St. Lucia			
St. Vincent and the Grenadines			
			Suriname
Trinidad and Tobago			
United States			

2.8 Different Worlds of Party Systems

There is a strong concentration of party preferences on only a few parties and therefore most countries have a two-party system. Plurality electoral systems are not the only reason, although almost all countries using plurality have a two-party system. Also several countries with PR systems have a low number of effective parties. As a consequence, most Latin American countries in Central America and the Caribbean are characterized by a dual party system. This is all the more surprising for Central America since in most countries the new majority parties have emerged under PR during the transition to democracy. In multi-party systems, presidential elections often force parties to form alliances. This is particularly the case in systems using runoff elections. Thus, the structure of party systems theoretically facilitates changes in government, however, in practice change is very uncommon in the two-party dominated Commonwealth Caribbean. In 137 elections, the opposition was successful in only 40 cases. There are also very few alternations in government in Central America. In post civil-war elections, conservative parties tended to be more successful than former revolutionaries (see the chapters on El Salvador, Guatemala, and Nicaragua in this book). In contrast, in Mexico a stable three-party system emerged during the transition to democracy. The conflict between president and parliament, however, paralyzes governance.

3. USA and Canada

In regard to the multiple dimensions of comparison that are possible on the basis of the countries covered in this study (e.g. between the United States and Central America), comparing the cases of the United States and Canada seems most reasonable. Even this comparison is limited, however, if we want go beyond a mere revelation of similarities and differences and try to obtain results that are theoretically useful. Canada and the USA are frequently compared with each other, especially by Canadians, focusing more on the day-to-day problems (for an exception see Lipset 1990). Yet, the more important point of concern seems to be contrasting the fundamental differences rather than the similarities. The countries are linked by their vast size, a long tradition of representative democracy, an uninterrupted series of elections, and a number of structural and institutional features.

3.1 Similarities of the Political Systems

The most striking feature is the political stability, which is manifest in the fact that the institutions have virtually remained unchanged since independence. Both are federal countries. Canada is divided into ten provinces and two territories; the US is divided into 50 states.

The federal structure is not only a result of the countries' size and of colonization but also of certain political objectives: separation and balance of powers have been a priority. In the case of the US, this intention is well documented in the Federalist Papers. In Canada, the different social developments led to a special federal structure. This is due to the need to articulate, channel, and integrate the regional conflicts. Three cleavages play a role in the elections: the ethnic and cultural conflict between Anglo- and Franco-Canadians, the socio-economic conflict between the rich and the poor provinces as well as between the center and the periphery. The heterogeneous social and political interests create an asymmetry which is then accommodated in the political process on the federal level (Schultze 1977; Agranoff 1999; Broschek and Schultze 2003).

The two North American democracies represent different types of political systems. The USA is a presidential system; Canada has a Westminster style parliamentary system. Two national institutions are elected in the USA: the president and the congress, and on numerous occasions the president lacked a majority in either one or both chambers of congress. In Canada, only the house of commons is elected; the government is elected by parliament and is therefore backed by it. However, parliamentary electoral systems in both countries are identical: plurality in SMCs. The federal structure also determines the allocation of seats: in the US, the 435 congressional seats are allocated among the states, in Canada among the provinces and territories. The electoral provisions (in the broad sense including all provisions concerning suffrage) of the United States and Canada differ in most respects.

3.2 Democratization of Franchise and Electoral Administration

Studies of franchise expansion often compare the United States and Western Europe; Canada is seldom taken into account (Bartolini 2000). A comparison of the legal and effective levels of franchise and of electoral participation is difficult with both Europe and Canada. This is due to the fact that electoral provisions are partially determined at the state or local level. Consequently, franchise expansion differed among the states. In addition, comparisons are difficult because voter registration follows different procedures, which has consequences for the effective suffrage and participation. In 27 US states women had been entitled to vote before universal suffrage was introduced by the 19th amendment in 1920. Canada introduced female suffrage in the same year, but women who served in the armed forces or who had close relatives who did, had been entitled to vote since 1917. In the US people have to register before election day to be able to vote in federal elections, which means

that there can be a large difference between the number of legally entitled voters and the number of actually registered voters. In Canada a national register of voters is established for each election by a nationwide
door-to-door registration process after each election. This register is also
updated regularly and is open to inspection by parliament and the political parties.

In the United States, despite the early introduction of universal suffrage, the effective vote expanded slowly because of the legal and administrative obstacles that were directed against Blacks. These obstacles
were only fully removed in the 1960s. While partisan gerrymandering is
still used, racial gerrymandering—i.e. redistricting to discriminate
against minorities—has been prohibited since the 1982 reform of the
Voting Rights Act. In the 1990s, the Supreme Court limited the possibilities of affirmative gerrymandering, which was to have secured the
election of minority representatives (see Rush 1998). In Canada, Native
Americans and citizens of Chinese or East Indian origin were not allowed to vote until the 1960s. The establishment of independent boundary commissions at the federal and the state level prevented partisan
gerrymandering.

In the USA, electoral legislation has mostly been the responsibility of
the states. Several constitutional amendments, federal laws (Federal
Voting Rights Act, National Voter Registration Act, Federal Election
Campaign Act), and decisions of the Supreme Court have, however,
considerably limited the states' autonomy—a development that was
pushed by the civil rights movement of the 1960s, which aimed at equal
suffrage for Blacks. Federal provisions, however, have not yet been established and the electoral offices in the states are dependent from the
executive and legislative bodies. Furthermore, elections are still organized autonomously by the states, which might explain the occurrence of
irregularities, as happened in Florida in the presidential elections of
2000, when George W. Bush was declared elected by a Supreme Court
decision and not through an undisputed result of counting votes. Only a
few aspects of the electoral administration, such as campaign financing,
are centralized. The responsibility for federal campaign financing issues
lies with the Federal Election Commission. In Canada, on the other
hand, the organization of federal elections is completely centralized, and
the administrative body is independent from the government. The Canada Elections Act is very detailed and has therefore become a model for
the organization and realization of free and fair elections in the young
democracies of developing countries.

3.3 Political Representation and Electoral Participation

Political representation has been adapted to the socio-economic and political reality and to territorial expansion in quite different ways. In the USA, two principles of representation have been implemented in parliament: representation according to population size in the House of Representatives and equal representation of the territories in the Senate. The House follows the principle of 'one person, one vote' and the Senate follows a territorial principle of 'one state, one vote'.

The Canadian system combines both principles in a specific way. In order to accommodate all regions and their vastly different populations and socio-economic and political conditions in a unicameral parliament the system guarantees a minimum number of constituencies to each federal unit. This leads to a certain inequality of representation, which can be measured through the weight of each vote. With the electoral reform of 1974, Canada officially adopted the principle of 'meaningful representation of provinces and territories' instead of equal representation. Malapportionment is only restricted at the provincial level, where the constituencies may not deviate from the average population size by more than 25%.

Turnout rates are also very different in Canada and the USA. In Canada, turnout is between 61.2 und 80.6%. Comparing the 18 Canadian national elections we can see a slight decrease since 1945 but in the 1990s turnout levels have consolidated at roughly 72.5%. In the US, turnout is much lower; it fluctuated between 89.7 (1968) and 48.5% (2000) in the 17 parliamentary elections from 1968 to 2000. The strong fluctuation is due to the fact that parliamentary elections are alternately held together with presidential elections (higher turnout) and as mid-term elections (lower turnout). Turnout at presidential elections is generally higher than for congress elections and varies less, but it is also decreasing. Only 51.2% of the registered voters participated in the 2000 presidential elections. Apart from the usual explanations of turnout, the rather societal orientation of political participation in the US is a key factor for low turnout (Skocpol/ Fiorinna 1999). This orientation has already been observed by Alexis de Tocqueville; recently communitarians are trying to revive it (see Putnam 1997).

The influence of different institutional factors on participation remains an open question. Local party strongholds in combination with plurality limit competition and paralyze participation. Yet, this occurs in both Canada and the USA. The effect of primaries on participation is not easy to assess. In stronghold areas they may be the elections in which voters really have a choice (see below, chapter 3.5).

3.4 Electoral System and Party System

The electoral system—and some phenomena related to it—is one of the few institutions that is identical in the USA and Canada. Both countries use plurality in SMCs and hold by-elections in case of vacancies. The structure of the party systems is, however, very different. Conventional assumptions about the effects of this electoral system are fulfilled in the USA. There is a two-party system and the presidency alternates between Republicans and Democrats. Majority in congress also shifts, albeit in longer intervals. Surprisingly, the relation between seats and votes is relatively proportional.

Canada has a multi-party system, despite the fact that the political culture is oriented around the British model of alternative government. In fact, the multi-party system sustains a one-party government. None of the parties is really a majority party because usually the winning party receives no more than 43% of the votes. The Liberal Party is closest to this type, although its dominance is more due to the absence of an alternative than to its own strength. Furthermore, the party does not always win an absolute majority of seats despite the plurality system: The winning party missed an absolute majority of seats in 11 of the 37 elections held between 1867 and 2004. In the three elections from 1993 to 2000, however, a manufactured parliamentary majority was won due to a disproportional result with a difference of up to 16.3 percentage points between vote shares and seat shares. In accordance with British tradition, even if no one party gains an absolute majority a coalition is not formed. The voters decide if the Liberals form a majority or a minority government and less on a change in power. This situation is legitimately called a system of single party dominance. The plurality system guarantees the Liberals' dominance. At the same time it strengthens regional and local strongholds, which intensifies the imbalances within the parties and the regionalized cleavages (Cairns 1968; Schultze and Schneider 1997). Generally, plurality in Canada correlates with phenomena that differ from those linked with the Westminster model. The theoretical assumptions that are usually associated with plurality are confirmed in only in a few aspects.

3.5 Primaries: Model USA

Primary elections, using plurality in most of the states, are a peculiarity of the USA. They are especially important for constituencies, where, due to strongholds, only the candidate of one party has a realistic chance to win. In this case the real choice is made in the primaries. It has to be noted that primaries fulfill ambivalent functions in the USA. Historically, they prevented the equal treatment of Blacks as determined in the 15th constitutional amendment. Parties, as private organizations, were not bound to the requirements of constitutional equality. Thus, the Black population of the Southern states could be excluded from Democratic primaries. This practice was forbidden in 1940 by the Supreme Court. The historically ambivalent role of primaries has not prevented them from becoming a model for many new democracies.

One advantage of the primaries is the possibility to nominate candidates even if they are not supported by the party organization. Primaries thus allow for more political competition. Since participation is much lower in primaries than in general elections, the democratizing function of primaries is controversial. Low participation works as a strong social bias in favor of middle and upper classes.

Primaries also reduce the importance of political content and programs both for the voters and the party system. They personalize politics and therefore enforce political symbolism. Consequently, they can fulfill contradictory functions, so that their significance must be evaluated separately within the context of the given socio-political situation.

3.6 USA and Canada: Some Remarks on Similarities and Dissimilarities

In principle, the thesis of the difference between the two countries has to be maintained. However, there are tendencies that suggest increasing similarity. These processes reflect general changes in both countries—like the development of the media society—and are due less to mutual imitation. The triangular relationship between politics, media, and voter, and the mediation of politics by the media have become increasingly similar in both countries. Furthermore, despite different institutional designs there are similarities in the political processes. In order to select candidates for important party offices or parliamentary seats, party leaderships in Canada use member polls similar to the selection of candidates via primaries. The organization of the executive is another example of increasing similarities. The position of the prime minister has been strengthened by an apparatus that centralizes government power in the core of the executive—comparable to the White House Office or the Executive Office in the US. Despite these processes of assimilation, clear differences due to national traditions remain. Developments adapt to or are affected by the preexisting patterns. Accordingly, the public selection of candidates is attenuated by the attempts of Canadian prime ministers to influence the nominations to ensure a conveniently composed parliament. In the USA this is prevented by the primaries. In Canada, the prime ministerial center of power is filled with independent, neutral officials, who are not exchanged after elections. In contrast, in the USA thousands of civil servants change after each presidential election. Canada has a mix of US influence and traditional structures. Sometimes, however, Canada is the model for the USA, e.g. in the area of campaign financing.

4. Mexico, Central America, and the Latin Caribbean (including Puerto Rico)

Elections have a long tradition in these Latin American countries, stemming from the era when the countries gained their independence from Spain (see Annino 1995). Yet, this tradition is characterized by fraud, the interruption of elected governments by authoritarian rule, and the use of elections for authoritarian aims. In the so-called façade democracies, elections are used to disguise the true power relations. In the eight elections in El Salvador between 1962/1966 and 1984, in the four Guatemalan elections between 1964 and 1982, and in the seven elections held under the Somoza regime in Nicaragua between 1937 and 1979, voters actually had no choice. In Panama those elections not monitored by the USA were manipulated and in 1989 the regime annulled the elections when the victory of the opposition became evident. All these cases demonstrate that elections are not a sufficient indicator for democracy. The analyses of the region confirm that when looking at elections we generally have to distinguish between competitive, semi-competitive, and non-competitive elections (Hermet/ Rose/ Rouquié 1978; Nohlen 1978). In the Latin American countries of Central America and the Caribbean we find all three types of elections and only in the last decades do we see a tendency towards really competitive elections. As mentioned above, these Latin American countries form part of the third wave of democratization with two exceptions: Costa Rica, which has been democratic since the late 1940s, and Cuba, which is still under communist rule. In view of the long authoritarian tradition and the series of fraudulent elections, free and fair elections are the most astonishing result of the political developments over the last 15 years.

Even if it is true that holding elections is not a sufficient criterion for a political system to be a democracy (Linz/ Stepan 1996), democracy—and democratization—is unthinkable without elections. With this in mind, it is evident that the different political points of departure and the different forces that triggered the democratic development of the region have not developed an alternative to democratizing the political systems through elections and to build up a representative democracy in line with Dahl's criteria, however fragile the democracy may still be. No matter if regimes were traditional authoritarian as in Honduras, revolutionary socialist as in Nicaragua or influenced by foreign countries as in Panama, elections have always played an important role in the process of democratization. The functions of competitive elections were even extended to the subregion. Elections were especially crucial in the process of pacification of Central American countries (Krennerich 1996). The elections of 1990 in Nicaragua, observed and monitored by the United Nations, were won by the opposition and were a crossroad for political development both in Nicaragua and in neighboring countries. In the following years, elections were held in El Salvador and Guatemala to overcome the violent conflicts between the government and revolutionary forces. The aim was to integrate the revolutionaries into the peaceful competition for power. Finally, the turn to plural democracy in Mexico was initiated by an electoral reform that established fair conditions and guaranteed free elections (see Nohlen on Mexico in this volume). The first free and fair elections in Mexico were held in 2000 and proved once again the democratic impact of elections: The election was won by the candidate of the main opposition party and 72 years of PRI hegemony were brought to an end. Elections became an important routine in the political process of the region (see Cerdas-Cruz et al. 1991; Rial/ Zovatto 1998; Payne et al. 2002).

Some scholars say that considering elections as crucial for democratic development means promoting electoralism, i.e. the reduction of democracy to elections. They also argue that in the cases of El Salvador and Guatemala, elections came too early in the process of pacification of these countries to permit a further development of non-violent and consensual approaches to politics (see for example Karl 1986 and 2000). Other scholars assert that in order to overcome authoritarianism, it would be better to develop liberal ideas and attitudes first to avoid illiberal democracies (Zakaria 1997). These are hypothetical considerations and mere counterfactual assumptions. Until now, people always demanded immediate free elections when authoritarian regimes fell, because they want a legitimate government based on the will of the majority.

4.1 Democratization of Franchise and Further Reforms

Legal electoral provisions have not been very effective: elections were generally controlled by the power holders, fraud was frequent and democracy was often interrupted by dictatorships. When working with the data collected in this book, scholars have to keep in mind the ups and downs of constitutional development and to distinguish between the different phases. In this context, the expansion of suffrage has to be considered in relation to the alternation of regime types. It posed a threat to oligarchic rule and foreign economic interests. The result was fraud, authoritarian regimes and elections without choice.

Universal male suffrage was introduced during the 19th century, with Costa Rica being the only exception. Female suffrage was only introduced in the middle of the 20th century. The exact dates differ from country to country and there were also differing minimum ages. Nicaragua was the only country to reduce the minimum age to 16 years. The other principles of suffrage, such as the secret vote, have developed very differently over time.

In accordance with the Latin American tendency, franchise in Central America is not considered a right, but a duty. Therefore, voting is compulsory in all countries with the exception of Nicaragua. Nevertheless, Honduras is the only country where abstention is sanctioned. Although the types of voter registration (see *infra*) and franchise (voluntary or obligatory) are important features of the electoral regime, their effect on voter turnout is not as great as may be supposed. Table 5 shows that there is no positive relation between them.

In the 1990s some attempts were made to reform the external voting system, i.e. suffrage for citizens living abroad. In Mexico and the Latin American States of Central America and the Caribbean this mainly concerns citizens who live in the USA. These Hispanic colonies exercise great pressure on national politicians to extend the franchise to them. The question is not easy to answer, as it touches the principle of congruence, according to which decisions should be made by those who are affected by its outcome. On one hand, Latin American citizens living abroad contribute greatly to the national income of their home countries with their transactions; on the other hand, their number is so high that they might determine the result of elections (for Mexico see Carpizo/ Valadés 1998). Under its special status as an associated state, Puerto Rico introduced external voting in 1977, Honduras followed in 2001. Panama introduced external voting in 1996 but abolished it in 2001 without having applied it. In Nicaragua, the reform of 2000 established suffrage for citizens living abroad, but putting it into practice requires an agreement between the Supreme Electoral Council and the parties. In the Dominican Republic, external voting will be applied for the first time in 2004.

Table 5: Features of Franchise in Latin American Countries

	Obligatory	With sanctions	Male since	Female since	From 18 years on since	Secret since	Average turnout in %[a]
Costa Rica	yes	no	1913	1949	1974	1893	65.4
Dominican Republic	yes	no	1880	1942	1873	—	67.9
El Salvador	yes	no	1883	1939	1950	1963	43.1
Guatemala	yes	no	1865	1945	1887	1946	49.0
Honduras	yes	yes	1894	1954	1981	1894	72.9
Mexico	yes	no	1857	1954	1973	—	59.0
Nicaragua	no	–	1893	1957	1979[b]	(1962) 1984	81.0
Panama	yes	no	1904	1945	1972	—	76.1

[a] For the lower chamber since 1945.
[b] 16 years; difficult to determine because of the practice of open electoral colleges.

4.2 Electoral Administration and Reform Processes

Improving the administration of elections is crucial to ensure that voting rights can be exercised effectively. The creation of an independent electoral body to organize the electoral process and the establishment of a trustworthy electoral register were the main concerns in the last decade. Costa Rica served as an example for the other Latin American countries of the region to show them how to design an electoral power that guarantees free and fair elections. Since the enactment of the 1949 Constitution in Costa Rica, the Supreme Court of Elections (*Tribunal Supremo de Elecciones*) has been fully independent and is officially recognized as the fourth state power. During the 1990s, the status, organizational structure and professionalism of the electoral administrative bodies improved considerably in all countries (see Nohlen/ Picado/ Zovatto 1998; Orozco Henríquez 2002). This development was fostered by international advice, training, and financing, especially by the Inter-American Institute for Human Rights and its electoral branch, the Center of Electoral Assistance and Promotion. This Center also served as secretariat for the Inter-American Union of Electoral Organizations (UNIORE), "which played an active role in encouraging the exchange of experiences and expertise among election officials in the region through reciprocal observation missions, professional courses, and sharing of expertise" (Kennedy/ Fischer 2000: 304).

Nicaragua and Mexico are excellent examples of this general trend and of the considerable importance of independent and professional electoral boards. In 1990, within an extremely polarized political climate and under very complex administrative conditions, the Nicaraguan Supreme Electoral Council (*Consejo Supremo Electoral*) maintained its independence despite politically motivated actions and ensured that the result of the election was recognized by all contenders, especially by the losing government and its supporters. In addition, international support, namely the UN mission and Jimmy Carter's presence on election day, were crucial for the acceptance of the electoral result. In Mexico, the establishment of the Federal Electoral Institute (Instituto Federal Electoral) in 1990 and the total independence from government which was granted in 1996 as well as the creation of the Electoral Court (*Tribunal Electoral del Poder Judicial de la Federación*) in the same year enabled the country to overcome a long tradition of rigged or allegedly rigged elections.

The ability to exercise suffrage depends on the voter registration. There are people living in the region who do not have any official documents to prove their identity. Apart from these individual cases, civil registers are often incomplete, which means that the electoral register cannot be based on them. In Nicaragua, for example, there was no permanent electoral register until 1996; people had to register for every election and identify themselves by an official document or two witnesses. A costly campaign had to be undertaken to draw up an accurate and reliable electoral register and to integrate ethnic minorities. Currently, registration is automatic in Costa Rica, El Salvador (since 2004), Honduras, Nicaragua, and Panama, while in the Dominican Republic, in Guatemala, and Mexico citizens have to register on their own initiative.

In the field of electoral administration the major institutional development in Latin America has taken place since the beginning of the third wave of democratization. It is recognized that the organization of elections may largely contribute to governance (López Pintor 2000). In countries of the region that have traditionally been susceptible to fraudulent elections, hardly any elections have been declared not free or unfair since the third wave of democratization (Pastor 1999). The fact that surveys show a widespread idea that elections are fraudulent is due less to the organization of the elections than to the general disappointment that parties do not keep their promises. This improvement in the electoral administration, however, is not ensured for the future. The political and institutional culture of the region does not firmly support independent electoral authorities and so they have to be defended against attempts to curtail their independence.

Nevertheless, procedural improvements do not prevent illegal practices at the local level. The traditional local power, poverty, clientelism and corruption are likely to pose constant legal problems. Due to the low ethical standard of civil servants and the general mistrust in political institutions constant efforts are required to keep democracy running. Also, elections are becoming very expensive: In 2003, Mexico spent 1.3% of the federal budget to organize elections.

It is important to point out the civil society's role in observing the elections. It controls the electoral processes in almost all countries now. The activities of civil society groups have largely contributed to the optimistic expectations concerning the democratic development of the region. The political culture of the region, however, cannot be simply divided into two spheres of ethics: opportunity determines values and behavior, and those who enter politics stick to the rules of the game. One of these rules is to postulate ethic standards publicly towards political contenders, while individually at the next opportunity, in public office, behavior serves the immediate and egoistic interests. Then, tradition is used to argue against a change in political culture: it is often said that things have always been done in a certain way and so they should remain as they are. Mexico is a good example: the party that was loudest in demanding free and fair elections was eventually unable to hold democratic primaries.

4.3 Elected Institutions

All countries of the region have presidential systems, and elections are therefore held for the executive and the legislature. In most countries, the two types of elections are held together: in Costa Rica, Guatemala,

Honduras, Nicaragua, Panama, and Mexico. In El Salvador, Haiti, and the Dominican Republic, the elections are held on different days.

The president is elected for a four-year term in Costa Rica, Guatemala, Honduras, and the Dominican Republic; for a five-year term in El Salvador, Haiti, Nicaragua, and Panama; and for a six-year term in Mexico. Consecutive re-election is prohibed in all countries except the Dominican Republic. There, re-election was only prohibited briefly between 1994 and 2003. All Central American parliaments are unicameral; Mexico, the Dominican Republic, and Haiti have bicameral legislatures.

4.4 Presidential Electoral Systems

An absolute majority of votes is required in El Salvador, Guatemala, Dominican Republic, and Haiti. If no candidate achieves this majority, a runoff election takes place between the two candidates with the most votes.

Plurality is used in Honduras, Panama, and Mexico. Candidates in Costa Rica and Nicaragua require a minimum of 40% and 45% of the valid votes; otherwise a runoff is held.

Table 6: Presidential Electoral Systems

	Duration of term in years	Re-election possible	Type of electoral system	Runoff
Costa Rica	4	after 2 terms	plurality (> 40%)	yes
Dominican Republic	5	yes	absolute majority	yes
El Salvador	4	no	absolute majority	yes
Guatemala	4	no	absolute majority	yes
Haiti	5	after 1 term	absolute majority	yes
Honduras	4	no	plurality	no
Mexico	6	no	plurality	no
Nicaragua	5	no	plurality (> 45%)	yes
Panama	5	no	plurality	no

4.5 Parliamentary Electoral Systems

All Central American countries and the Dominican Republic use proportional representation (PR) in MMCs to elect their unicameral parliaments or lower houses. PR was, however, introduced at different times:
in 1893 in Costa Rica, in 1946 in Guatemala, in 1957 in Honduras, in
1963 in El Salvador, in 1983 in Panama, and in 1984 in Nicaragua. If
we only look at competitive elections, PR is a relatively new phenomenon in Central America. Mexico is a special case; it uses a segmented
system to elect its chamber of deputies, in which 200 of the 500 seats
are distributed proportionally. For elections to the senate, Mexico uses a
majority system with minority representation and some proportional
elements. The Dominican Republic has maintained plurality in SMCs
for senate elections. Haiti is the only country on the continent to use a
system of absolute majority for both its chambers of parliament.

   With regard to the proportional systems in MMCs, it must be noted
that district magnitude is relatively low. Most seats are distributed in
small and medium-sized constituencies. Panama is unique in terms of
districting: 26 SMCs with plurality and 14 MMCs (see table 8).

Voters have one vote in Costa Rica, El Salvador, Honduras, and the
Dominican Republic. In the Dominican Republic, deputies and senators
are elected through the same vote. Voters have two votes in Nicaragua,
Guatemala, and Mexico. In Nicaragua, there is one vote for the national
list and one vote for a list at district level; in Guatemala, voters simultaneously elect a national list and the president; in Panama, voters have
one vote in the SMCs and as many votes as there are deputies to be
elected in the MMCs.

   The lists are closed and blocked in Costa Rica, El Salvador, Guatemala, Honduras, Nicaragua, and Mexico; closed with preferential vote
in the Dominican Republic; and open in the MMCs in Panama. As to the
electoral formula, the Hare quota combined with the method of the largest remainder is used in Costa Rica, El Salvador, Honduras. Nicara-
guans use the Hare quota and some special arrangements for binominal
districts and seats that are distributed at the national level. The d'Hondt
method is applied in Guatemala and the Dominican Republic.

Table 7: Parliamentary Electoral Systems

Country	Electoral system	Elected seats	Constituencies Number	Size(s)	Mean size	Form of candidacy	Ballot form	Electoral formula
Costa Rica	PR in medium and large MMCs	57	7	4–21	8.1	closed lists	single vote	Hare quota; largest remainder
Cuba	absolute majority system in SMCs	601	601	1		individual	single vote	absolute majority
Dominican Republic	PR in MMCs	120	47	2–8	4.0	semi-open, preferential	single vote for deputies and senators	d'Hondt
El Salvador	PR in MMCs with additional national list	84: 64 20	14 1	3–16 20	4.6	closed lists	single vote	Hare quota; largest remainder
Guatemala	PR in small and medium MMCs with additional national list	80: 64 16	23 1	— 17	2.8	closed lists closed lists	two votes: regional list and national list	d'Hondt
Guyana	pure PR	53	1	53		closed lists	single vote	Hare quota; largest remainder
Haiti	absolute majority system in SMCs	83	83	1		individual	single vote	absolute majority (runoff among top two candidates)
Honduras	PR in MMCs	128	18	—	7.1	closed lists	single vote	Hare quota; largest remainder

Country (continued)	Electoral system	Elected seats	Constituencies Number	Size(s)	Mean size	Form of candidacy	Ballot form	Electoral formula
Mexico	segmented system	500: 300 200	300 1	1 200		party candidates closed lists	one vote, both: personal and list vote	plurality Hare quota; threshold: 2% of national vote; largest remainder
Nicaragua	PR in MMCs with additional national list; One seat for the Ex-president, one for second voted pres. candidate	90: 70 20	17 1	1–19 20	4.2	closed lists at both levels	two votes: MMC-list vote national list vote	at both levels Hare quota; remaining MMC seats are allocated at national level with the following quota: national sum of residual votes divided by the sum of remaining seats; remaining national list seats are allocated under a quota calculated as the mean of 4 regional electoral quotas.
Panama	plurality in SMCs and PR in small and medium MMCs	71	40	1–6	3.2	SMC: individual; MMC: non-blocked lists	multiple vote (optional in MMC)	SMC: plurality; MMC: 3 steps: Hare quota; half Hare quota and highest number of personal votes

4.6 Electoral Reforms since the Beginning of the Third Wave of Democratization

Since redemocratization, electoral systems have been discussed as an important factor to improve political representation, participation and governance (see Nohlen 2004). The debate, however, is not an indicator for actual reforms. Closer attention is necessary to see if and which electoral reforms were carried out.

Contrary to other sources of information (see Colomer 2001) traditional electoral systems have generally been maintained for presidential elections. It was only in the Dominican Republic that the plurality system was replaced by absolute majority with runoff in 1996. Some countries have retained the plurality systems, such as Honduras (absolute majority before 1966), Nicaragua (since 1947, with a threshold of 45% since 1995), and Panama (since 1904). In other cases, the absolute majority system was modified with regard to the regulation to be applied if no one candidate wins an absolute majority. In El Salvador (1984) and Guatemala (1985), the decision by congress was replaced with a runoff election between the two top candidates. The logic of this system was not affected by this reform. There is no clear evidence that presidential systems have generally been transformed from plurality to absolute majority with runoff.

Table 8: Small-sized Constituencies

Number of members per constituency	Number of constituencies							Number of seats	
	1	2	3	4	5	Sub-total[a]	% of total[b]	Sub-total[c]	% of total[d]
Costa Rica	0	0	0	1	2	3	42.9	14	24.6
Dominican Republic	0	19	13	7	5	44	93.6	129	variable
El Salvador	0	0	8	2	2	12	80.0	42	50.0
Guatemala[e]	8	6	1	3	2	20	69.0	45	variable
Mexico[f]	300	0	0	0	0	300	98.4	300	60.0
Nicaragua[e]	1	5	6	1	0	13	72.2	33	35.9
Panama	26	7	1	3	2	39	97.5	65	variable

[a] Number of small-sized constituencies.
[b] Number of small-sized constituencies as a percentage of the total number of constituencies.
[c] Number of deputies elected in small-sized constituencies.
[d] Number of deputies elected in small-sized constituencies as a percentage of the total number of deputies.
[e] One group of deputies is elected by national list at national level.
[f] Segmented or parallel system.

Costa Rica is the one country in the region that has not changed its parliamentary electoral system at all. Reform proposals submitted by the National Electoral Court in 2002 (preferential vote, electronic vote, and external vote) were rejected by the National Assembly. The other extreme is Mexico, where the electoral system was reformed before each election in 1986, 1989, 1990, and 1993. It was only in 1996 that an electoral system was introduced that has a chance to be applied in more than one election. In the course of the reforms the plurality system in SMCs was transformed into a segmented system. However, the different reforms were implemented under authoritarian rule, during the process of gradually opening the system along Dahl's dimensions of democratic development: through more pluralism, i.e. better oppositional representation, and more participation, i.e. the guarantee of free and fair elections.

In the other countries of the sub-region, most changes made to electoral systems since the end of the 1970s concerned the number of seats in parliament. The number of deputies rose in the Dominican Republic in 1997 from 120 to 149, in El Salvador in 1988 from 60 to 84, and in Guatemala after continuous changes in 1998 from 80 to 113. In Honduras the size of parliament was increased from 82 to 134 in 1985 and reduced again to 128 in 1988. These changes required redistricting of constituencies and had an impact on their magnitude and thus on the proportionality of the electoral system.

Other reforms separated the vote for president and parliament (as in Honduras in 1992) or the ballots they were elected on (as in the Dominican Republic and Guatemala in 1990, in Honduras in 1993, and in Panama 1993). Some countries, such as El Salvador in 1982 and the Dominican Republic in 1994 separated the presidential from the parliamentary term, but this may enhance different majorities in presidency and parliament (as happened in El Salvador 2003/2004) and produce stalemates. Another reform focused on the introduction of a national constituency (El Salvador 1988). Furthermore, in Nicaragua some minor changes in the way seats are assigned did in fact substitute a purely proportional system with a system of PR in MMCs.

Major reforms concerned representation of women, as in Costa Rica, the Dominican Republic, El Salvador, Mexico, and Panama, where legal quota were introduced, ranking from 25% in the Dominican Republic to 40% in Costa Rica. Costa Rica, El Salvador, and Panama require parties to alternate men and women on the lists. Effective representation of women in Central American parliaments varies between one-third in Costa Rica and below 10% in El Salvador, Guatemala, Honduras, and Panama (see Peschard 1997: 180).

Table 9: Proportional Representation and Representation of Women by Quota

	PR since	Women quota since	Quota in %	Gender alternation on list
Costa Rica	1893	1997/ 2000	40	yes
Dominican Republic	1924	1997	25	no
El Salvador	1963	no[a]	–[a]	yes
Guatemala	1946	no	–	no
Honduras	1957	2000	30	no
Mexico	–	1996	30	no
Nicaragua	1984	no	–	no
Panama	1983	1997	30	yes

[a] FMLN has a 35% quota for women

4.7 The Effects of Electoral Systems

The effects of electoral systems on party systems depend on several factors, among them the structure and institutionalization of the party system itself. In presidential systems, presidentialism, the electoral system for the presidential election and the link between presidential and parliamentary elections are said to make a difference (Nohlen 1987; Shugart/ Carey 1992). It seems plausible that the most important election in a presidential system—the election of the president—affects the parliamentary elections and this effect is stronger the more closely linked the two types of elections are. The lowest degree of connection is when the two elections are merely held on the same day (concurrent elections). It is higher when there is a single ballot for president and parliament and it is highest when president and parliament are elected with a single vote.

In presidential elections—which are necessarily winner-takes-all elections—preferences tend to concentrate on those candidates with a realistic chance of winning and this may cause a similar effect on the parliamentary elections. This effect depends not only on the degree of simultaneity, but also on the electoral system. There are three assumptions in the academic debate: first, that the electoral system for presidential elections has an effect on the structure of the party system (Shugart/ Carey 1992; Jones 1995): 'A majority runoff formula encourages a larger number of parties to compete in the presidential race and obtain seats in the legislature than would be the case under a plurality system.' (Payne et al. 2002: 69). Second, that plurality structures the party system more strongly. The impact of presidential elections is especially strong 'when the presidential election is decided by plurality rather than by majority (which may require a runoff election)' (Lijphart 1994: 131). Third, that 'indirectly, by limiting the number of parties, presidentialism can also be hypothesized to reduce the degree of electoral disproportionality' (ibid.). Assessing the advantages of the respective electoral systems, Matthew S. Shugart and John Carey (1992), Mark P. Jones (1995), and Arend Lijphart (1994) prefer the plurality system due to the assumptions mentioned above. 'Over time, therefore the movement from plurality to a majority runoff system could end up worsening the problem of democratic governability by lowering the share of the first round vote typically received by the eventual victor, and by reducing the partisan congressional support for the president' (Payne et al. 2002: 69). In order to obtain an effective government, countries ought to elect their president using a plurality system. Other scholars emphasize the degree of political support that a candidate gains in a runoff with absolute majority (Sartori 1997). Josep Colomer (2002: 6) considers low political support for the elected candidate a menace for democratic governability. For this reason he prefers an absolute majority system because presidents elected via this system have a larger political basis. In the academic debate, the difference between plurality and absolute majority is often reduced to the alternatives of having a weakly legitimized president by popular support (the case of plurality system) or a president with little parliamentary support (the case of absolute majority system, which in theory contributes to a more fragmented parliamentary representation). But is this actually true?

In regard to presidential elections, in a total of 44 free and fair elections (Costa Rica: 13, Dominican Republic: 8; El Salvador: 5; Guatemala: 5; Honduras: 6; Mexico: 1; Nicaragua: 3; Panama: 3), 31 were governed by a plurality system (including 14 elections under a plurality system with a minimum quorum of votes) and 13 by the majority system. The winning candidates reached an absolute majority of the votes straight away in 22 cases. Plurality was applied in 18 of these cases, an absolute majority system in only four cases. Under plurality, an absolute majority was missed in 16 cases; under absolute majority this was the case ten times, nine of which required a subsequent runoff. Five of these runoff elections were held in Guatemala, where the party system is only weakly institutionalized. In seven cases the winner of the first round won, in two cases the candidate who came second in the first round finally became president.

Recapitulating, we see that under plurality more than half the elections ended with an absolute majority. In contrast, under an absolute majority system in two-thirds of the cases, this majority was only achieved in a runoff. Payne et al. (2002: 74) point out that the average share of votes for the winner in presidential elections with plurality exceed 50% in Costa Rica, Honduras, and Nicaragua, are slightly less than 50% in Panama, and 43.3% in the Dominican Republic. The average share of the winner in absolute majority systems is never higher than 50%. From this evidence it would seem that absolute majorities are more likely under plurality than under absolute majority systems. However, it has to be kept in mind that the choice of electoral system happens against the background of the structure of the given party system. Accordingly, Payne et al. (2002: 71) rightly emphasize that 'countries where many parties typically compete and present presidential candidates are precisely the ones that are most likely to adopt a majority runoff system'. This refers to the circular causality between electoral systems and party systems, one of the central results of my empirical analysis of this relationship (see Nohlen 2004).

In the lower house elections of some countries, PR has produced the expected moderate disproportionality between shares of votes and shares of seats. In Costa Rica and the Dominican Republic the highest disproportionality is 6.5 percentage points, in Honduras 4.6, and in Nicaragua 3.3. Disproportionality is very high in other countries: up to 16.4 percentage points in Guatemala and up to 25.6 in Panama. Constituency magnitude under PR and the fragmentation of the party systems are important factors. The larger the constituencies and the lower the number of parties, the more proportional the result will be. If we now turn around the causal assumption and take the degree of proportionality as our point of departure we see that high proportionality is by no means correlated with a fragmented party system.

If we compare the system for presidential elections, disproportionality and the structure of the party systems, we see that Costa Rica and Honduras use plurality, have a moderate degree of disproportionality and a two-party system. Guatemala, on the other hand, uses absolute majority with runoff, has a high degree of disproportionality and an unstable multi-party system. In Costa Rica and in Honduras the presidency alternates between two parties and the five Guatemalan presidents since 1985 were all supported by different party alliances. In Costa Rica a third party appeared in the 2002 elections and for the first time since 1913 the winner received less than 40% of the votes, so a runoff had to be held.

The other cases differ from this pattern of correlation: El Salvador has an absolute majority system and runoff, moderate disproportionality and the domination of one party in an ideologically polarized two-party system. Nicaragua uses plurality, has low disproportionality and a multi-party system. For presidential elections the parties rally around two camps. Panama uses plurality, has very high disproportionality and a multi-party system.

The Dominican Republic, in which the system for presidential elections was changed, has moderate disproportionality. The effects of different electoral systems on parliamentary representation can easily be retraced here because both chambers are elected with a single vote. In all of the seven elections to the senate (where plurality is used) one party won an absolute majority of seats, whereas this happened in only three of the elections to the house of deputies (where PR is used). In 1978, two different parties won a majority in the senate and the house of deputies. In 2002, the PRD with 42.2% of the votes only received 48.7% of the seats in the lower house but an overwhelming majority of 90.6% of the senate seats. Table 10 shows the development of the effective number of parties in the chamber of deputies for this group of countries.

Altogether, empirical evidence in Central America refutes the above-mentioned theoretical assumptions: Plurality is linked here with party concentration in parliament and with a high legitimacy of the presidents. The data supports the assumptions of those scholars who prefer plurality for presidential elections, even though the relationship between party systems and electoral systems is not linear or deterministic due to the circular linkage of the variables. For this sub-region, PR can be considered the dependent variable and the party system the independent one.

Table 10: Effective Number of Parliamentary Parties[a]

	1978–1985	1986–1991	1992–1997	1998–2000
Costa Rica	2.3	2.2	2.3	2.6
Dominican Republic	2.1	2.8	2.4	2.5
El Salvador	1.9	3.3	3.6	3.5
Guatemala	3.3	4.4	3.1	2.4
Honduras	2.1	2.0	2.1	–
Mexico	1.7	2.6	2.6	2.8
Nicaragua	–	2.1	2.8	–
Panama	3.1	–	4.3	3.4
Puerto Rico	1.9	1.8	1.0	2.0

[a] Calculated according to the proposal of Laakso and Taagepera 1979.

4.8 Democracy and Institutional Answers to its Critics

In the context of critique concerning political representation by political parties and representative democracy in general, which flourished in the 1990s and the beginning of the 21st century, three considerations and reform initiatives can be identified: (1) to open the nomination of candidates to parliamentary seats and public offices to independents or groups of civil society; (2) to enforce internal democracy of political parties; and (3) to introduce mechanisms of direct democracy.

With regard to electoral competition, political parties maintain their monopolist position in Costa Rica, El Salvador, Guatemala, Mexico, Nicaragua, and Panama, while independents may be nominated in the Dominican Republic and Honduras. In these two countries, however, the scope of party vote is especially deep. This is confirmed by the electoral results. In the Dominican Republic, in the parliamentary election of 2002, only 4.6% of the valid vote was won by parties other than the three main ones. In Honduras in 2001, the two main parties won 87.3% of the valid votes, and three other parties each received between 3.7 and 4.6% of the remaining votes. Political parties feel challenged by the civil society and they fight against proposals to introduce independent candidates. These fears seem exaggerated, especially as civil society groups would have to organize themselves in similar ways to the existing parties if they wanted to be successful in the long term.

There has been a general trend towards greater regulation of internal party democracy. Electoral authorities begun to take an interest in the internal life of parties after laws were passed that demanded parties follow democratic principles not only externally but also internally. Public scrutiny is becoming evident through the requirement to register parties and candidates with the electoral authorities. Both nomination of party leaders and candidates for public office are supposed to be democratic and attempts are being made to open up decision-making processes for ordinary party members. Internal elections and primaries play an increasing role; however, the presidential candidate is still generally nominated by traditional party organs. For parliamentary elections, openness is limited by the need to secure the efficiency of the parties, as defection of parliamentarians is a common problem. Furthermore, attempts to democratize internal affairs have so far been unable to prevent the general criticism of parties.

As far as direct democracy is concerned, many scholars doubt that the necessary conditions required for the system to be a success have been fulfilled in Latin America. Demands for direct democracy normally come from the civil society and are meant less as a form of participation complementary to representative democracy than as a radical critique of democracy itself. The possibilities for direct democracy have been increased recently (see Table 11). Costa Rica and Honduras introduced mechanisms of direct democracy in 2004. In practice, however, only Guatemala and Panama have held two referendums each on constitutional issues. They were all initiated by the government and three of them failed: in Panama in 1992 and 1998 and in Guatemala in 1999. Guatemalans only accepted a government proposal on constitutional reform in 1994. To date, direct democracy has had little influence in the sub-region.

Referendums in Latin America are not centered around the issue at stake but on the desire to pass a verdict on the government and politics in general. In some cases, referendums did not raise the degree of satisfaction with democracy. According to Daniel Zovatto (2005) mechanisms of direct democracy are distorting elements incapable of efficiently replacing the institutions of representative democracy, which are based on a party system strongly connected to society.

Table 11: Mechanisms of Direct Democracy

	Legislative initiative	Referendum/ Plebiscite	Recall
Costa Rica	yes[a]	yes[b]	no
Dominican Republic	no	no	no
El Salvador	yes[b]	yes	no
Guatemala	yes[b]	yes	no
Honduras	no	yes	no
Mexico	no	no	no
Nicaragua	yes[b]	yes[b]	no
Panama	no	yes	yes[b]
Puerto Rico	no	yes	no

Source: Zovatto 2005.
[a] Not at constitutional level.
[b] Has not been used to date.

5. The English-Speaking Caribbean and Suriname

Elections are crucial to political legitimacy in the English-speaking Caribbean—a region with an enviable record of civil liberties, political pluralism, and stable parliamentary democracy, especially when compared with Latin America. Democracy in the English-speaking Caribbean 'has proved to be more effective and durable than in any other sub-region in the developing world' (Payne 1995: 2). The only problematic cases—as far as democratic development is concerned—were Guyana before 1992, Grenada between 1979 and 1984, and Antigua and Barbuda under the rule of the Bird family, which lasted four decades. The sub-region is also interesting for an internal comparison, because we see a common pattern of development from which some countries differ in one way or the other, so that we can ask for the reasons that explain it. The area is ideally suited for the application of the most-similar-system strategy in comparative method. In the following sections we will first try to high-light those factors that enable us to understand the Caribbean democratic outcome. Subsequently, we will describe the main pattern of political development and analyze the type of government as well as the electoral provisions, in particular the electoral systems and their impact on party systems.

5.1 Geographical Conditions: Size and Democracy

The English speaking Caribbean contains areas of the former British co-lonial empire. It is a very widespread area ranging from Central Amer-ica (Belize) to Jamaica and the Eastern Caribbean islands to Guyana on the South American continent. Not all colonies sought independence.

Twelve countries became independent between 1962 and 1983. They are all rather small with the exception of Guyana. With the exception of Guyana, Trinidad and Tobago, and Jamaica the population in these countries is also low (see Table 11). This is an important issue because the size of states is likely to change the character of their politics, which in small countries seems more municipal or local. Dahl and Tufte (1973: 13–15) analyzed the relationship between size and democracy. Although they do not explain the success of democracy in the Commonwealth Caribbean, they offer a certain understanding of politics, especially the style of politics in small, mainly insular states. Dahl and Tufte purport that smaller democracies: (a) provide more opportunities for citizens to participate effectively in decisions; (b) make it easier for citizens to in-ternalize standards and values, therefore increasing voluntary compli-ance and reducing coercion; (c) are likely to be more homogeneous with respect to beliefs, values, and goals; (d) make it easier for citizens to perceive a relation between their own self-interest or understanding of the good and a public or general interest, the interest of others, or gen-eral conceptions of the good; (e) are more likely to generate loyalty to a single integrated community; (f) provide more opportunities for all citizens to gain the knowledge needed to make decisions using direct observation and experience. Citizens in a smaller democracy: (g) are likely to understand their political problems better than citizens in a larger democracy; and (h) are more likely to develop important civic relationships.

In accordance with these assumptions, empirical analysis of the Caribbean shows that the island societies are compact and homogeneous, that citizens show a strong sense of community, that political leadership is close to the people and more responsive to public opinion, but that the potential for personalist domination may be high. Immediately after independence union leaders exercised this domination, later it was increasingly the prime ministers, especially as the government's importance as an employer grew (see Thorndike 1991, Eldie 1994). This led to a parliamentary system with strong presidential characteristics, such as distinguished personalist and charismatic leadership (see Hillebrands 1993). Political styles with strong authoritarian components developed and were very different from those of Great Britain (see Edie 1994).

Table 12: Commonwealth Caribbean: Size, Population and Political Data

Country	Size (km^2)	Population	British colony since	First election by universal suffrage	Independent since
Antigua and Barbuda	440	65,000	1667	1951	01/11/1980
Bahamas	13,878	300,000	1717	1962	07/10/1973
Barbados	430	267,600	1627	1951	30/11/1966
Belize	22,965	256,000	1862	1954	21/09/1981
Dominica	751	71,000	1805	1951	03/11/1978
Grenada	344	100,900	1783	1951	07/02/1974
Guyana	214,969	856,000	1814	1953	26/05/1966
Jamaica	10,990	3,800,000	1655	1944	06/08/1962
St. Kitts and Nevis	269	41,000	1806	1952	19/09/1983
St. Lucia	616	163,300	1814	1951	22/02/1979
St. Vincent and the Grenadines	388	112,000	1763	1951	27/10/1979
Trinidad and Tobago	5,130	1,310,000	1802/ 1814	1946	31/08/1962

5.2 Historical and Political Characteristics

With regard to institutions and political culture, the English speaking Caribbean is a relatively homogenous area, due to the countries' common history as British colonies and also because they all followed the same path to independence: limited self-administration at first with partly nominated and partly elected institutions followed by universal suffrage. Most countries are also ethnically homogenous, with Trinidad and Tobago, Guyana, and Belize being the only exceptions. In these countries the process of independence was accompanied by violent disturbances.

The political process developed as external influences triggered a political awakening. Starting with working-class struggles in the context of the Great Depression in the 1930s, strong unions and workers' movements were created, which in turn formed the basis for the first political parties. These parties began to demand political participation, self-determination and finally independence. Great Britain reacted similarly to these demands and a slow process of disentanglement began, always within the British constitutional tradition. The Westminster model was institutionalized long before independence, in some cases as much as a century before (see Payne 1995: 58).

Democracy with respect to competition between political parties and inclusion (universal suffrage) preceded independence by 10 or 15 years, in some cases even 30 years. It is worth noting that the development of political culture in the Caribbean was closely linked to the colonial period, where the British political system was 'the only source and pattern that they know' (Spackman 1975). When independence was achieved, the new countries were able to incorporate a professional and well-developed bureaucratic apparatus, the civil service, which was inherited from the colonial period.

These all were favorable conditions to sustain the primacy of constitutionalism and the independence of the judiciary. Despite changes towards clientelist behavior after independence, the fight for power was limited to the democratic arena (see Mills 1990). The societies managed to maintain a system of representation capable of balancing the interests of different social sectors (see Kunsman 1963).

A common pattern can be observed in the development of the party systems. The labor parties followed social democratic ideals, insofar as they tried to improve the working and living conditions of the workers in the existing capitalist societies. These parties ruled since the introduction of universal suffrage until roughly one decade before independence.

Moderate leaders defected from these parties and founded parties on the center-right, which sometimes replaced the labor parties in power (see Table 15). These changes were generally peaceful and happened at the polls. Thorndike (1991: 117) states that if a government did not succeed in the quest for material and social improvement or if corruption exceeded the generally tolerated level, it was replaced.

Change was also facilitated by the death of the founders and leaders of the traditional labor parties. Despite latent doubts about capitalism, which was characterized by severe inequalities in the Commonwealth Caribbean, the conservatism of the population prevented the success of left-wing splinter groups.

The main factor that explains deviations from this common pattern of development is ethnic diversity or rather contrariness. In Guyana it influenced the institutional design with the introduction of proportional representation and in Trinidad and Tobago it facilitated the fragmentation of the party system along racial lines (see Catón in this volume). In contrast, the development of the party system in Belize was not greatly affected by ethnic diversity, as the country was more concerned with the issue of whether the country should seek a closer relationship to Central America. This was a demand made by the poorer Mestizos, whereas the Afro-Creole middle class favored integration with the West Indies. In addition, the Guatemalan threat to annex the territory was the reason that Belize only gained independence in 1981.

The breakdown of democracy in Grenada (see Baukhage and Hillebrands in this volume), violent conflicts in Trinidad and Tobago (see Catón in this volume), fraud in Guyana during more than two decades (see Trefs in this volume) and electoral irregularities in Jamaica in 1983 were exceptions to the success story of British style representative democracy in the Commonwealth Caribbean.

5.3 Elected Institutions: The Westminster Model

One of the most important characteristics of political development in the subregion is the Westminster model of parliamentary government. All countries in the region adopted this model after independence. Consequently, parliament is the only institution elected by popular vote, more precisely the lower house. Although eight of the English speaking Caribbean countries have a bicameral parliament, the members of the upper house are generally appointed by the British governor general on the advice of the prime minister, the opposition leader and at the governor general's own discretion. The appointed senate—which generally has a suspensive veto—is a variation of the Westminster model. Other variations are a codified constitution, courts with judicial review power and central banks with a certain degree of autonomy in monetary policy (see Lijphart 1999: 30).

The Westminster model was mainly followed in legislative executive relations, even with small parliaments. Currently, the number of parliamentary seats varies between 11 and 65. Of course, the size of the lower houses plays an important role, first with regard to political representation: The smaller a parliament, the more difficult it is for small parties to obtain a seat no matter what kind of electoral system is in force. Second, with regard to cabinet formation: in a parliamentary system, where cabinet members are also members of parliament, a relatively high proportion of legislators are cabinet members.

All English-speaking countries in the region maintained the British electoral system, i.e. plurality in SMCs. The only exception is Guyana, which introduced proportional representation in one nationwide constituency in 1964. This is an ideal example of political engineering (see Nohlen 1978: 244). The reason for the reform was to impede the victory of the Marxist People's Progressive Party (PPP), which drew its main support from the Indian population majority and had won 57.1% of the seats with 42.6% of the votes in the elections prior to the reform. Instead, the moderate People's National Congress (PNC), based on the Black population, was supposed to win the elections together with a coalition of small parties, which was exactly what happened after the reform.

This was the situation when Guyana became independent. The result was, however, that the winner of the 1964 elections, Forbes Burnham, continued to manipulate elections to establish a dictatorship. Ironically, he followed a cooperative concept by steering a socialist course. Democracy only came back in 1982 during the third wave of democratization. Although proportional representation remained in force, in 2001 ten regional constituencies with a total of 25 seats were established in addition to the nationwide constituency. Further reforms are still being discussed.

The former Dutch colony Suriname also has a proportional electoral system. Due to the fragmentation of the party system—which is characterized by ethnic heterogeneity and internal conflicts—several reforms took place within the realm of proportional representation. In 1987, the country introduced proportional representation with preferential vote in ten MMCs of variable magnitude.

Table 13: Commonwealth Caribbean: The Structure of Electoral Institutions

Country	Uni- or bicameral	Original size Lower House	Size in 2000–2004	Population in relation to seats
Antigua and Barbuda	bi	8 (1951)	17 (1999)	3,824
Bahamas	bi	38 (1972)	40 (2002)	7,500
Barbados	bi	24 (1951)	30 (2003)	8,920
Belize	bi	18 (1979)	29 (2003)	8,828
Dominica	uni	8 (1952)	21 (2000)	3,381
Grenada	bi	8 (1951)	15 (2003)	6,727
Guyana	uni	53 (1964)	65 (2001)	13,170
Jamaica	bi	32 (1944)	60 (2002)	63,333
St. Kitts and Nevis	uni	8 (1952)	11 (2000)	3,728
St. Lucia	bi	8 (1951)	17 (2001)	9,606
St. Vincent and the Grenadines	uni	8 (1951)	15 (2001)	7,467
Trinidad and Tobago	bi	9 (1946)	36 (2002)	3,639

5.4 Extension of Suffrage and Electoral Participation

Suffrage in the English-speaking Caribbean was extended slowly. Under colonial rule the legislative councils were at first appointed, then some of the members were elected by the male population and finally the councils were entirely elected. This last step generally took place together with either the introduction of universal suffrage or independence. Universal suffrage was first introduced in Jamaica in 1944, followed by Trinidad and Tobago in 1946. The other countries followed in the 1950s. The last country in the region to introduce suffrage for both men and women was the Bahamas in 1962. In all cases universal suffrage was established about ten years before independence (see Table 12). In the 1970s and 80s the voting age was lowered to 18 years.

Voter turnout in the sub-region is relatively high. In free and fair elections turnout has never fallen below 51.9%. In many cases it rose above 80% and sometimes even reached 95% or more (see Table 14). The average per country ranges from 61.2% in St. Lucia to 90.8% in the Bahamas. But, as Thorndike (1991: 114) observed, there are often wide variations around these figures.

Turnout generally decreased in the 1990s, after it had increased in the 1970s and 80s. As we have seen earlier, it is very difficult to explain fluctuations in voter turnout. We can assume that a stronger ideological polarization after independence favored a higher turnout. Growing unemployment, higher public debt, drug trafficking, and corruption caused disenchantment with democracy (see Payne 1995) and therefore turnout decreased.

5.5 The Effects of Electoral Systems

Most Caribbean countries have two-party systems. Generally, this is seen solely as an effect of the plurality electoral system, although SMCs have not always existed in many of the countries (Barbados, for example, had two-member constituencies until 1966). Dahl and Tufte (1973: 103) noticed that there is a high correlation between population size and the number of parties: fewer parties compete in small countries and even fewer manage to obtain seats.

This means additional conditions are necessary for plurality to have the effect that it is generally said to have, including the cleavage structure and the political culture of one-party government. The plurality system has never been questioned and new parties that could not replace old parties in the dualism of a two-party system had no chance to change the electoral system in order to secure their survival.

Party systems in the English-speaking Caribbean are highly concentrated. Nevertheless, the obvious correlation between plurality and a two-party system does not rule out that even under proportional representation only a small number of parties succeed. The only case with proportional representation, Guyana, is no exception to the general rule of two-party systems in the Caribbean. The number of effective parties in three cases is below 2.0 and in eleven cases between 2.0 and 2.5 (data for the last election). The inequalities in political representation are huge. From a total of 106 elections, in 55 cases the major party won 70% or more of the seats, in 33 cases it won 80% or more, in 19 cases it won 90% ore more and in 12 cases it won all seats (see Table 16). In a traditional understanding of democracy these huge majorities cause a loss of political control. There are only few cases where no party achieved an absolute majority of seats. In 1992, the Bahamian PLP won 55.1% of the votes, but only 32% of the seats; in Belize in 1993, the PUP won 51.2% of the votes and only 44.8% of the seats and in Dominica in 2000, the DLP only received the second highest amount of votes but won most of the seats. The Westminster plurality system used in the West Indies tends to produce what it is expected to do, namely a two-party system and enormous distortions in the political representation in form of huge majorities and a disconcerting bias.

Table 14: Commonwealth Caribbean: Voter Turnout 1951–2003

Elections	Antigua and Barbuda	Bahamas	Barbados	Belize	Dominica	Grenada	Guyana	Jamaica	St. Kitts and Nevis	St. Lucia	St. Vincent/ Grenad.	Trinidad and Tobago
1st	70.3	—	64.6	—	75.9	70.6	—	58.7	—	59.1	69.2	52.9
2nd	57.0	—	60.3	—	70.3	67.4	—	65.2	—	49.4	59.8	70.1
3rd	40.0	88.0	61.3	—	75.6	68.5	97.0	65.1	66.1	56.8	70.9	80.1
4th	—	89.9	79.3	89.9	76.9	55.5	85.1	66.1	70.3	—	77.1	88.1
5th	56.4	89.8	81.6	75.0	80.3	72.6	81.0	72.9	87.9	51.9	84.1	65.8
6th	95.0	87.9	74.1	72.6	81.6	77.1	82.3	82.2	72.0	53.2	82.6	33.2
7th	77.1	91.1	71.6	72.1	77.3	83.5	73.8	78.9	74.5	84.1	75.6	55.8
8th	61.1	98.5	76.7	90.1	80.2	65.3	80.4	85.2	77.7	68.1	63.2	56.4
9th	62.2	90.2	63.7	78.9	74.6	86.2	88.4	86.9	66.8	65.8	63.9	65.4
10th	—	—	60.9	—	66.6	68.4	91.7	2.7	66.4	60.7	88.8	65.7
11th	—	—	63.4	—	65.2	61.7	—	78.4	68.4	64.7	72.4	—
12th	—	—	56.8	—	60.2	56.5	—	60.3	64.2	62.8	—	—
13th	—	—	—	—	—	57.5	—	65.2	—	66.7	—	—
14th	—	—	—	—	—	—	—	59.1	—	52.3	—	—
Average	64.9	90.8	67.9	79.7	73.7	68.5	85.0	66.0	71.4	61.2	73.4	63.3

Table 15: Commonwealth Caribbean: Winning Parties and Alternation 1957–2003

Elections	Antigua and Barbuda	Bahamas	Barbados	Belize	Dominica	Grenada	Guyana	Jamaica	St. Kitts and Nevis	St. Lucia	St. Vincent/ Grenad.	Trinidad and Tobago
1st	ALP	PLP	BLP	PUP	Indep.	GULP	PPP	JLP	SKLP	SLP	Eighth Army	Indep.
2nd	ALP	PLP	BLP	PUP	Indep.	GULP	PPP	JLP	SKLP	SLP	Indep.	Indep.
3rd	ALP	PLP	DLP	PUP	Indep.	Coalition	PPP	PNP	SKLP	SLP	PPP	PNM
4th	ALP	PLP	DLP	PUP	DLP	GULP	PNC[a]	PNP	SKLP	SLP	PPP	PNM
5th	PLM	PLP	DLP		DLP	GNP	PNC	JLP	SKLP	UWP	PPP	PNM
6th	ALP	PLP	BLP	PUP	DLP	GULP	PNC	JLP	SKLP	UWP	SVLP	PNM
7th	ALP	FNM	BLP		DLP	GULP	PNC	PNP	Coalition	UWP	Coalition	PNM
8th	ALP	FNM	DLP	PUP	DFP	GULP	PNC	PNP	PAM	SLP	SVLP	PNM
9th	ALP	PLP 2002	DLP	PUP 2003	DFP	NNP	PPP	JLP	PAM	UWP	SVLP	NAR
10th	ALP	–	BLP	–	DFP	Coalition	PPP/C	JLP	SKLP	UWP	NDP	PNM
11th	ALP	–	BLP	–	DFP	NNP	PPP/ C 2001	PNP	SKLP	UWP	NDP	–
12th	–	–	BLP	–	UWP	NNP	–	PNP	SKLP	UWP	–	–
13th	–	–	–	–	–	NNP	–	PNP	–	SLP	–	–
14th	–	–	–	–	–	–	–	–	–	SLP	–	–
No. of Parties	2	2	2	2	3	4	3	2	3	3	5	2
Effective No.1999–2003	1,795	1,766	1,556	1,577	2,383	1,991	2,236	1,969	2,452	1,409	1,471	1,975

[a] Introduction of proportional representation, government by coalition against the majority party.

Table 16: Commonwealth Caribbean: Percentages of Votes and Seats of Winning Parties

Elections	Antigua and Barbuda	Bahamas	Barbados	Belize	Dominica	Grenada	Guyana	Jamaica	St. Kitts and Nevis	St. Lucia	St. Vincent/ Grenad.	Trinidad and Tobago
1st	87/100	—	55/63	—	100/100	64/75	—	41/96	85/100	50/63	70/100	30/11
2nd	87/100	—	49/63	—	100/100	46/75	—	43/53	54/63	47/63	60/63	49/33
3rd	85/100	59/76	56/58	—	100/100	—	—	51/56	65/70	66/88	49/63	40/54
4th	79/100	55/79	50/58	52/72	48/64	53/80	45/45	55/63	44/70	62/90	49/67	57/67
5th	58/77	57/74	57/75	54/74	65/90	54/60	56/57	50/58	51/78	52/60	49/56	52/67
6th	49/65	54/63	53/71	51/54	50/73	55/70	70/70	51/62	60/78	58/60	54/67	84/100
7th	58/77	44/67	52/63	49/75	49/76	59/87	78/77	56/70	56/56	54/59	50/46	54/67
8th	68/94	58/88	59/89	60/90	51/81	52/60	79/79	57/78	48/55	56/71	69/77	53/72
9th	64/88	52/73	50/64	53/76	57/71	58/93	54/53	59/85	44/55	56/88	54/85	66/92
10th	54/65	—	48/68	—	49/52	35/47	55/55	90/100	44/36	53/53	51/69	45/58
11th	53/71	—	65/93	—	36/52	32/53	53/52	57/75	49/64	53/53	66/100	—
12th	—	—	56/77	—	43/48	62/100	—	60/87	54/62	56/65	—	—
13th	—	—	—	—	—	48/53	—	56/83	—	61/82	—	—
14th	—	—	—	—	—	—	—	52/57	—	56/82	—	—

6. Elections and Electoral Systems: Design and Context

Until recently, comparative studies have paid relatively little attention to elections and electoral systems in Latin America and the Caribbean. This is probably due to the belief that elections in non-democratic countries or in countries where the rule of law is not guaranteed are not important and that their analysis is only justified when they are free and fair. This situation has changed with the third wave of democratization. My own study was based on this new focus (Nohlen 1993a; Nohlen/ Picado/ Zovatto 1998). On the one hand, almost all countries in the Western hemisphere have free and fair elections, on the other hand after research on transitions, the idea that actors influence political developments and that it is possible to shape democracy was conceivable. Today, there are many efforts to inform about elections and their development (see for example Cerdas et al. 1992, Rial/ Zovatto 1996, Payne 1995).

With the notion that democracy can be crafted (Di Palma 1990), both political institutions—among them elections—and the idea to increase governance and consolidate democracy through institutional design became crucial. Particularly with a view to the new democracies a lively debate developed in comparative politics about the best form of government and the best electoral system.[2] We can distinguish two main currents: one that compares abstract designs based on experiences from consolidated democracies and makes precise institutional recommendations (Linz, Lijphart, and in a certain way also Sartori), and another that follows an empirical-inductive path and takes the sociopolitical context of the new democracies and the existing institutions as the starting point for recommendations within the given circumstances (Mainwaring and Shugart, Nohlen, Shugart and Carey, Thibaut, Payne et al.). *Elections in the Americas* belongs to the second current. Institutions are important but their significance is limited. Following the neo-institutional approach they are influenced by the context; as a result, this context must be considered when recommending institutional reforms. Recommendations cannot be based on analyses of countries other than those the recommendations are intended for. On the contrary, when considering institutional designs those countries that have already tried to increase the importance of elections for decision-making should take the center

---

[2] For the debate on government systems see Lijphart 1994, Linz and Valenzuela 1994, Mainwaring and Shugart 1997, Nohlen and Fernández 1991, Nohlen and Fernández 1998, Sartori 1997, Shugart and Carey 1992, and Thibaut 1996. For the debate on electoral systems see Nohlen 2004, Payne et al. 2002, and Sartori 1997.

stage. The same is true for the effects of electoral systems. They can only be determined and to some extent predicted if the sociopolitical context is known. Furthermore, the analysis of elections in comparable cases gives an indication of the variables that have to be taken into account. *Elections in the Americas* offers this kind of information, which is crucial for comparatists and political engineers alike.

Bibliography

Alcántara, M. and Freidenberg, F. (eds.) (2004). *Partidos políticos de América Latina.* Mexico City: FCE.

Agranoff, R. (ed.) (1999). *Accommodating Diversity. Asymmetry in Federal States.* Baden-Baden: Nomos.

Annino, A. (ed.) (1995). *Historia de las elecciones en Iberoamérica, siglo XIX.* Buenos Aires: Fondo de Cultura Económica.

Barber, B. (1984). Strong Democracy. Participatory Politics for a New Age. Berkeley, Calif.: University of California Press.

Barczak, M. (2001). 'Representation by Consultation? The Rise of Direct Democracy in Latin America'. *Latin American Politics and Society* 43/3: 37–59.

Barrios, H. and Suter, J. (1996). *Politische Repräsentation und Partizipation in der Karibik.* Opladen: Leske + Budrich.

Bartels, L. M. (1988). *Presidential Primaries and the Dynamics of Public Choice.* Princeton, N.J.: Princeton University Press.

Bartolini, S. (2000). 'Franchise Expansion'. In R. Rose (ed.), *International Encyclopedia of Elections,* Washington, D.C.: CQ, 117–130.

Bendel, P. (1996). *Parteiensysteme in Zentralamerika. Typlogien und Erklärungsfaktoren.* Opladen: Leske + Budrich.

— (ed.) 1993. *Zentralamerika. Frieden, Demokratie, Entwicklung? Politische und wirtschaftliche Perspektiven in den 90er Jahren.* Franfurt/Main: Vervuert.

Bovens, M. (1998). *The Quest for Responsibility. Accountability and Citizenship in Complex Organizations.* Cambridge: Cambridge University Press.

Broschek, J. and Schultze, R.-O. (2003). 'Föderalismus in Kanada: Pfadabhängigkeiten und Entwicklungswege', in Europäisches Zentrum für Föderalismus-Forschung Tübingen (ed.), *Jahrbuch des Föderalismus 2003.* Baden-Baden, 333–366.

Butler, D. and Ranney, A. (eds.) (1994). *Referendums around the World. The Growing Use of Direct Democracy.* Washington, D.C.: AEI.

Cairns, A. C. (1968). 'The Electoral System and the Party System in Canada. 1921–1965'. *Canadian Journal of Political Science* 1: 55–80.

Cardoso, F. H. and Faletto, E. (1979). *Dependency and Development in Latin America*. Berkeley, Calif.: University of California Press.

Carpizo, J. (2000). *Nuevos estudios constitucionales*. Mexico City: Editorial Porrúa.

Carpizo, J. and Valadés, D. (1998). *El voto de los mexicanos en el extranjero*. Mexico City: UNAM.

Carrillo, M., Lujambio, A., Navarro, C., and Zovatto, D. (eds.) (2003). *Dinero y contienda político-electoral. Reto de la democracia*. Mexico City: FCE.

Cerdas-Cruz, R., Rial, J., and Zovatto, D. (eds.) (1992). *Una tarea inconclusa: Elecciones y democracia en América Latina 1988–1991*. San José: IIDH / CAPEL.

Clarke, C. (1991). *Society and Politics in the Caribbean*. Oxford: McMillan.

Colomer, J. M. (2001). *Instituciones políticas*. Barcelona: Ariel.

— (2002). 'Reflexiones sobre la reforma política en México'. *Este país. Tendencias y opinions* 137, 2–12.

Comisión Andina de Juristas (ed.) (1993). *Formas de gobierno. Relaciones ejecutivo-legislativo*. Lima: Comisión de Juristas.

Cox, C. G. (1997). *Making Votes Count. Strategic Coordination in the World's Electoral Systems*. New York: Cambridge University Press.

Dahl, R. A. (1956). *A Preface to Democratic Theory*. Chicago: University of Chicago Press.

Dahl, R. A. and Tufte, E. R. (1973). *Size and Democracy*. Stanford, Calif.: Stanford University Press.

Davis, J. W. (1997). *U.S. Presidential Primaries and the Caucus-Convention System. A Sourcebook*. Westport, Conn.: Greenwood.

del Castillo, P. and Zovatto, D. (eds.) (1998). *La financiación de la política en Iberoamerica*. San José: IIDH / CAPEL.

Diamond, L., Linz, J. J., and Lipset, S. M. (eds.) 1989: *Democracy in Developing Countries. Politics, Society, and Democracy in Latin America*. Vol. 4, Boulder, Colo.: Westview Press.

DiPalma, G. (1990). *To Craft Democracies. An Essay on Democratic Transitions*. Berkeley, Calif.: University of California Press.

Drake, P. W. and Silva, E. (ed.) (1986). *Elections and Democratization in Latin America, 1980–85*. San Diego, Calif.: University of California.

Dunn, C. (ed.) (1996). *Provinces. Canadian Provincial Politics*. Peterborough (Canada): Broadview.

Duverger, M. (1959). *Political Parties*. New York: John Wiley.

Edie, C. J. (1991). *Democracy by Default. Dependency and Capitalism in Jamaica*. Boulder, Colo.: Lynne Rienner.

— (1994): *Democracy in the Caribbean. Myths and Realities*. Westport, Conn.: Praeger.

Freedom   House   (2004).   *Freedom   in   the   World   2004*
<http://www.freedomhouse.org/research/freeworld/2004/table2004.pdf>
(as of 16/06/04).

Griner, S. and Zovatto, D. (eds.) (2004). *De las Normas a las Buenas Prácticas. El desafío del financiamiento político en América Latina.* San José: OEA/IDEA.

Grofman, B. and Lijphart, A. (eds.) (1986). *Electoral Laws and Their Political Consequences.* New York: Agathon.

Gutiérrez, C. J. et al. (1983). *Derecho Constitucional costaricense.* San José: Ed. Juricentro.

Heine, J. (ed.) 1991. *A Revolution Aborted. The Lessons of Grenada.* Pittsburgh, Pa.: University of Pittsburgh Press.

Hermet, G., Rose, R., and Rouquié, A. (eds.) 1978. *Elections without Choice.* London: McMillan.

Hillebrands, B. (1993). 'El desarrollo de la democracia Westminster en los micro-estados del Commonwealth caribe', in D. Nohlen (ed.) *Elecciones y sistemas de partidos en América Latina.* San José (Costa Rica): IIDH, 355–388.

Huntington, S. (1991). *The Third Wave. Democratization in the Late Twentieth Century.* Norman, Okla./ London: University of Oklahoma Press.

Instituto Interamericano de Derechos Humanos (ed.) (2000). *Diccionario Electoral.* 2 vols., San José/Costa Rica: IIDH.

International IDEA (1997). *Voter Turnout from 1945 to 1997. A Global Report on Political Participation* (2nd edn.). Stockholm: International IDEA.

— (2002). *Voter Turnout since 1945. A Global Report on Political Participation,* Stockholm: International IDEA.

Jaramillo, J. (1994). *Wahlbehörden in Lateinamerika.* Opladen: Leske + Budrich.

Jones, M. (1995). *Electoral Laws and the Survival of Presidential Democracies.* Notre Dame, Ind.: University of Notre Dame Press.

Karl, T. L. (1986). 'Imposing Consent? Electoralism vs. Democratization in El Salvador', in P. W. Drake and E. Silva (eds.). *Elections and Democratization in Latina America, 1980–1985.* San Diego, Calif.: University of California.

— (2000). 'Electoralism', in: R. Rose (ed.), *International Encyclopedia of Elections.* Wahington, DC: CQ, 95–96.

Katz, R. S. (1997). *Democracy and Elections.* New York: Oxford University Press.

Kennedy, J. R. and Fischer, J. W. (2002). 'Technical Assistance in Elections', in R. Rose (ed.), *International Encyclopedia of Elections.* Washington, D.C.: CQ Press, 300–305.

Krennerich, M. (1996). *Wahlen und Antiregimekriege in Zentralamerika.* Opladen: Leske + Budrich.

Kunsman, C. H. (1963). *The Origins and Development of Political Parties in the British West Indies.* Ph.D. thesis, Berkeley, Calif.

Laakso, M. and Taagepera, R. (1979). '"Effective" Number of Parties. A Measure with Application to West Europe'. *Comparative Political Studies*, 12/1: 3–27.

Lauga, M. (1999): *Demokratietheorie in Lateinamerika. Die Debatte in den Sozialwissenschaften.* Opladen: Leske + Budrich.

LeDuc, L., Niem, R. G., and Norris, P. (eds.) (1996). *Comparing Democracies. Elections and Voting in Global Perspective.* Thousand Oaks, Cal.: Sage.

Lijphart, A. (1991). 'Constitutional Choices for New Democracies'. *Journal of Democracy*, 2/1: 72-84.

— (1994). *Electoral Systems and Party Systems. A Study of Twenty-Seven Democracies, 1945–1990.* Oxford: Oxford University Press.

— (1999). *Patterns of Democracy.* New Haven, Conn./ London: Yale University Press.

— and Waisman, C. (eds.) (1996). *Institutional Design in New Democracies. Eastern Europe and Latin America.* Boulder, Col.: Westview Press.

Linz, J. J. and Stepan, A. (eds.) (1978). *The Breakdown of Democratic Regimes.* Baltimore, Md.: Johns Hopkins University Press.

— (1996). *Problems of Democratic Transition and Consolidation. Southern Europe, South America, and the Post-Communist Europe.* Baltimore, Md./ London: Johns Hopkins University Press.

Linz, J. J. and Valenzuela, A. (eds.) 1994. *The Failure of Presidential Democracy.* Baltimore, Md./ London: Johns Hopkins University Press.

Lipset, S. M. (1959). 'Some Social Requisites of Democracy. Economic Development and Political Legitimacy'. *American Political Science Review* 53: 69–105.

— (1960). *Political Man.* New York: Doubleday.

— (1990). *Continental Divide. The Values and Institutions of the United States and Canada.* New York et al.: Routledge.

López Pintor, R. (2000). *Electoral Management Bodies as Institutions of Governance.* New York: UNDP.

Lowenthal, A. F. (ed.) (1991). *Exporting Democracy. The United States and Latin America.* Baltimore: Johns Hopkins University Press.

Mackenzie, W. J. M. (1958). *Free Elections.* London: George Allan and Unwin.

Mackie, T. T. and Rose, R. (eds.) (1991). *The International Almanac of Electoral History* (3rd edn.). London: MacMillan.

Maingot, A. P. (1985). *Some Perspectives of Governing Elites in the English-Speaking Caribbean.* Claremont, Calif.: Claremont McKenna College.

Mainwaring, S. and Shugart, M. S. (eds.) (1997). *Presidentialism and Democracy in Latin America*. New York: Cambridge University Press.

Middlebrook, K. J. (ed.) (1998). *Electoral Observation and Democratic Transitions in Latin America*. La Jolla, Cal.: UCSD Center for US Mexican Studies.

Mills, D. J. (ed.): *A Reader in Public Policy and Administration*. Mona (Jamaica): The University of the West Indies.

Morgenstern, S. and Nacif, B. (eds.) (2002). *Legislatures and Democracy in Latin America*. New York: Cambridge University Press.

Nohlen, D. (1978). *Wahlsysteme der Welt*. Munich: Piper.

— (1981). *Sistemas electorales del mundo*. Madrid: Centro de Estudios Constitucionales.

— (1987). 'Presidencialismo, sistema electoral y sistema de partidos políticos en América Latina', in IIDH / CAPEL (ed.), *Elecciones y democracia en América Latina. Memoria del Primer Curso Anual Interamericano de Elecciones*. San José, 29–46.

— (ed.) (1993a). *Enciclopedia Electoral Latinoamericano y del Caribe*. San José (Costa Rica): IIDH-CAPEL.

— (ed.) (1993b). *Elecciones y sistemas de partidos en América Latina*. San José (Costa Rica): IIDH-CAPEL.

— (1996). *Elections and Electoral Systems*. New Delhi: McMillan.

— (2004). *Sistemas electorales y partidos políticos* (3rd edn.). Mexico City : Fondo de Cultura Económica.

— (2004) *Wahlrecht und Parteiensystem* (4th edn.). Opladen: Leske + Budrich.

— and Fernández, M. (eds.) (1991). *Presidencialismo versus parlamentarismo. América Latina*. Caracas: Nueva Sociedad

— (eds.) (1998). *El presidencialismo renovado. Instituciones y cambio politico en América Latina*. Caracas: Nueva Sociedad.

—, Picado, S, and Zovatto, D. (eds.) (1998). *Tratado de derecho electoral comparado de América Latina*. Mexico City: Fondo de Cultura Económica.

— et al. (eds.) (2005): *Tratado de Derecho Electoral Comparado de América Latina*. Mexico City: Fondo de Cultura Económica.

Norris, P. (ed.) (1999). *Critical Citizens. Global Support for Democratic Governance*. New York: Oxford University Press.

O'Donnell, G., Schmitter, P., and Whitehead, L. (eds.) (1986). *Transitions from Authoritarian Rule. Tentative Conclusions about Uncertain Democracies*. Baltimore, Md.: Johns Hopkins University Press.

Organización de los Estados Americanos (ed.) (1999). *Seminario internacional sobre legislación y organización electoral. Una visión comparativa*. Lima: Civil Transparencia.

Orozco Henríquez, J. J. (2001). *Sistemas de justicia electoral: Evaluación y perspectivas.* Mexico City: IFE et al.

Pastor, R. A. (1999). 'The Role of Electoral Administration in Democratic Transitions. Implications for Policy and Research'. *Democratization* 6/4: 1–27.

Payne, D. W. (1995). *Democracy in the Caribbean. A Cause for Concern.* Washington, D.C.: Center for Strategic and International Studies.

Payne, J. M. et al. (eds.) (2002). *Democracies in Development. Politics and Reform in Latin America.* Washington, D.C.: Johns Hopkins University Press.

Peschard, Jacqueline (1997). 'El sistema de cuotas en América Latina. Panorama general', in International IDEA (ed.) *Mujeres en el parlamento. Más allá de los números.* Stockholm: International IDEA, 173–186 <http://www.idea.int/gender/wip/PDF/Spanish/chapter_04a-CS-LatinAmerica.pdf> (as of 14/07/2004).

Planas, P. (1998). *Comunicación política y equidad electoral.* Lima: Universidad de Lima.

Potter, D. et al. (eds.) (1997). *Democratization.* Cambridge: Polity Press.

Prebisch, R. (1981). *Capitalismo periférico. Crisis y transformación.* Mexico City: Fondo de Cultura Económica.

Putnam, R. D. (1997). 'Bowling Alone. America's Declining Social Capital'. *Journal of Democracy*, 6/1: 65–78.

Rae, D. W. (1968). *The Political Consequences of Electoral Laws.* New Haven, Conn.: Yale University Press.

Reynolds, A. and Reilly, B. (1997). *The International IDEA Handbook of Electoral System Design.* Stockholm: International IDEA.

Rial, J. and Zovatto, D. (ed.) (1998). *Elecciones y democracia en América Latina 1992–1996. Urnas y desencanto.* San José: IIDH / CAPEL.

Rose, R. (ed.) (2000). *International Encyclopedia of Elections.* Washington, D.C.: CQ.

Rueschemeyer, D., Huber Stephens, E., and Huber, J. D. (1992). *Capitalist Development and Democracy.* Chicago: University of Chicago Press.

Rule, W. (2001). 'Political Rights, Electoral Systems, and the Legislative Representation of Women in 73 Countries. A Preliminary Analysis', in S. Nagel and A. Robb (eds.), *Handbook of Global Social Policy.* New York: Marcel Dekker, 73–92.

Rush, M. E. (ed.) (1998). *Voting Rights and Districting in the United States.* Westport, Conn.: Greenwood.

Sartori, G. (1976). *Parties and Party Systems. A Framework for Analysis.* Cambridge: Cambridge University Press.

— (1997). *Comparative Constitutional Engineering. An Inquiry into Structure, Incentives and Outcome* (2nd edn.). Houndmills/ London: MacMillan.

Schultze, R.-O. (1977). *Politik und Gesellschaft in Kanada*. Meisenheim a. Gl.: Hain.

Schultze, R.-O. and Schneider, S. (eds.) (1997). *Kanada in der Krise. Analysen zum Verfassungs-, Wirtschafts- und Parteiensystemwandel seit den 80er Jahren.*

Schultze, R. O. and Sturm, R. (eds.) (2000): *Constitutional Reform in North America*. Opladen: Leske + Budrich.

Shugart, M. S. and Carey, J. M. (1992). *Presidents and Assemblies. Constitutional Design and Electoral Dynamics*. Cambridge: Cambridge University Press.

Skocpol, T. and Fiorinna, M. (eds.) (1999). *Civic Engagement in American Democracy*. Washington, D.C.: Brookings Institution.

Spackman, A. (1975). *Constitutional Development of the West Indies 1922–1968. A Selection from the Major Documents*. St. Lawrence (Barbados): Caribbean University Press.

Taagepera, R. and Shugart, M. S. (1989). *Seats and Votes. The Effects and Determinants of Electoral Systems*. New Haven, Conn.: Yale University Press.

Thibaut, B. (1996). *Präsidentialismus und Demokratie in Lateinamerika. Argentinien, Brasilien, Chile und Uruguay im historischen Vergleich*. Opladen: Leske + Budrich.

Thorndike, T. (1991). 'Politics and Society in the South-Eastern Caribbean', in C. Clarke (ed.). *Society and Politics in the Caribbean*. Oxford: MacMillan, 110–130.

Transparency International (2003). *Transparency International Corruption Perceptions Index* <http://www.transparency.org/pressreleases_archive/2003/2003.10.07.cpi.en.html> (as of 03/06/04).

Tuesta Soldevilla, F. (ed.) 1996. *Simposio sobre reforma electoral*. Lima: IFES.

Valadés, D. (2003). *El gobierno de gabinete*. Mexico City: UNAM.

Zakaria, F. 1997: 'The Rise of Illiberal Democracy'. *Foreign Affairs* 76/6: 22–43.

Zovatto, D. (2005). 'Instituciones de democracia directa', in D. Nohlen et al. (eds.), *Tratado de derecho electoral comparado de América Latina* (2nd edn.). Mexico City: Fondo de Cultura Económica.

ANTIGUA AND BARBUDA

by Bernd Hillebrands and Johannes Schwehm

1. Introduction

1.1 Historical Overview

The political dynasty of the Bird family has dominated the politics of Antigua and Barbuda since the colony was granted internal self-government in the late 1950s. Vere Cornwell Bird and his son Lester Bird have won every election in Antigua and Barbuda since 1951, except the one in 1971. Like his father Vere, Lester governs in an authoritarian manner, disregarding the constitution (ignoring the judiciary branch in particular), and is involved in corruption and misuse of the electoral process. Elections are regarded as neither free nor fair.

Until 1956, the British colony of Antigua and Barbuda was administered by the colonial Leeward Islands Federation. When the political parties were forming, the workers' movement was an organized political force. In 1946, the Antigua Labour Party (ALP) was founded as the political committee of the Antigua Trades and Labour Union (ATLU), and was registered in 1940. Vere C. Bird was at the head of both organizations, and his charismatic leadership greatly influenced the history of the country until the mid-1990s.

When the British West Indies Federation was disbanded in 1962—it had been formed in 1958 by ten British island colonies to form a unit independent both economically and politically from Great Britain—Antigua and Barbuda was declared a seperate colony.

In February 1967, the colony was awarded the Associate Statehood from the British Kingdom, and in 1971 it was given autonomy in internal affairs (internal self-government). That same year, the Progressive Labour Movement (PLM) was founded, the only party in the country that managed to completely break away from the ALP's political domination. The PLM originated under the leadership of George Walter and Donald Halstead from the Antigua Workers Union (AWU), a union founded in 1967 by former leading members of the ATLU. In the mid-1960s the country suffered an economic crisis due to the decline in the sugar industry and violent conflicts. Subsequently, the ATLU and the ALP split up, and this division resulted in the political weakening of the latter. In 1968, Prime Minister Vere C. Bird was compelled to resign from his post as union leader. In the 1971 elections, the PLM gained a majority of 13 seats, putting an end to the period of one-party political domination (from 1946 to the end of the 1960s). Walter, former general secretary of the ATLU and founder of the AWU, became prime minister.

Walter's government (PLM) encountered serious economic difficulties, due to the increase in the price of oil in 1973/1974. The corruption scandals, in which important members of the government were involved, also discredited the PLM. Consequently, in the 1976 elections, Vere Bird, who had resumed his leading office in the ALP, was returned to power.

After the legislative elections of 1980, the newly victorious Prime Minister Bird began negotiations for the country's independence. The opposition party (PLM) and Barbuda's local administrative authorities rejected the separation from Great Britain. Barbuda accepted a common independence with Antigua, only after obtaining several rights regarding its internal administration from Bird's government. Antigua and Barbuda, to which the uninhabited island Redonda belongs, was declared independent on 1 November 1981. With independence a constitutional monarchy with Westminster-style parliament was established. The British Queen remained head of state with ample representative functions, and the governor general acted as her representative in the country.

The 1980s saw the emergence of many parties opposed to the ALP. However, in the elections of the 1980s and the 1990s, none of these new political forces were able to build an opposition alliance capable of bringing about a change of power at government level. Nonetheless, the ALP had to face constant power struggles within the party, which revolved in particular around the successor of Vere C. Bird. When he announced that he would not run in the 1994 election, his son Lester became ALP leader. Lester had taken his chance, after his older brother Vere jr, who was to succeed his father, was convicted of dealing in arms with the Medellín Drug Cartel. In the run up to the election in 1994, Lester presented himself as an agent of change and modernization and promised to fight corruption.

However, these promises remained unfulfilled, as the 1994 election proved. The elections were confirmed to be neither free nor fair. As Douglas W. Paine states '(1) the balloting system did not guarantee a secret ballot, (2) the voter registration process was deficient and open to manipulation by the ALP, and (3) the voter registry was inflated by up to 25% with names of people who had died or left the country' (Paine 1999: 18).

Lester Bird was re-elected in 1999. The ALP was able to win 12 out of 17 constituencies. The opposition, led by Baldwin Spencer and his United Progressive Party (UPP), lost one seat. However, the UPP, founded in 1992 as a coalition of three opposition parties (United National Democratic Party (UNDP), Antigua Caribbean Liberation Movement (ACLM), and PLM), only lost five constituencies by very small margins (a combined total of 554 votes). This shows that a different outcome to the elections, even a majority of seats for the UPP, could have been possible, if the campaign conditions—the government controls almost all newspapers as well as television and radio stations—and the elections had been free and fair. After the Bird government had given the false impression that the elections in 1994 had been monitored by the OAS and the Carter Center, whose efforts had been actually rejected, the elections of 1999 were monitored by a Commonwealth observer group, led by the former chief justice of Bangladesh, Muhammad Habibur Rahman. Due to continuing irregularities in the voter registry and the ballot system, the observers recommended (in accordance with some previous proposals of the electoral office of Antigua and Barbuda) the establishment of an independent electoral commission as well as a year-round registration period for electors. Such an electoral commission was established a few years later in 2002.

1.2 Evolution of Electoral Provisions

The 1967 Constitution introduced a bicameral system in Antigua and Barbuda: the members of the chamber of deputies were directly elected and the British governor general appointed those of the senate. After independence in 1981, the number of senators rose from 10 to 17.

For the 1951 elections to the chamber of deputies universal, equal, secret, and direct suffrage was established. But the fact that the ballots were numbered, that the numbers were not removed from the ballots before a vote was cast, and that the poll agent wrote the voter's registration number on the counterfoil, demonstrated that the secrecy of the vote was de facto undermined.

From 1951 on, the plurality system in single-member constituencies had been applied. In 1968, the number of parliamentary seats was increased from 13 to 17. Before the 1971 elections, four SMCs were transformed into two-member constituencies, in which additional elections took place in August 1968.

1.3 Current Electoral Provisions

Sources: The 1981 Constitution contains the electoral principles. Detailed electoral provisions are recorded in the Electoral Act of 1975. It was last amended in 1990.

Suffrage: The principles of universal, equal, secret, and direct suffrage are applied. Each citizen of the Commonwealth older than 18 with the right of residence in Antigua and Barbuda is entitled to active suffrage. The vote is not compulsory. New voters have to sign up during the first week of July, which is the shortest registration period in the whole of the Caribbean.

Elected national institutions: There is a two-chamber legislative, formed by the house of representatives, which is directly elected, and by the senate, which is made up of 17 senators appointed by the British governor general. Eleven are appointed on the advice of the prime minister, four on the advice of the leader of the opposition, one on the advice of the Barbuda Council and one at the governor general's own discretion. The parliamentary term runs for a maximum of five years. The prime minister can set an earlier date for the elections by dissolving parliament. If there are vacant parliamentary seats, by-elections are held within 120 days of the vacancy.

Nomination of candidates: Every citizen of the British Commonwealth older than 21 with a sufficient command of the English language, having resided at least one year in Antigua and Barbuda, is eligible to run for public offices. Clergy, certain civil servants and persons with functions related to the parliamentary electoral process, among others, cannot be elected.

Electoral system: Members of the house of representatives are elected by plurality in 16 SMCs.

Organizational context of elections: The responsibility for managing the elections rests with the constitutionally guaranteed office of the supervisor of elections and the newly established electoral commission.

The supervisor of elections is appointed by the governor general. His duties involve directing and supervising the administrative procedures of the election and to publicize important dates and information to the participating parties and the electors.

The electoral commission held its first meeting on 23 May 2002. It consists of five commissioners, all appointed by the governor general: the chairman and two other members are appointed on the advice of the prime minister, the other two on the advice of the opposition. In agreement with the supervisor of elections, the electoral commission has the task of managing all aspects of the electoral process, including the reform of the voter registry.

1.4 Commentary on the Electoral Statistics

The electoral data presented in the following tables were taken from Emmanuel (1992) and, for the elections held since 1980, from the official reports of the supervisor of elections. These data are considered partially deficient with regard to the voter registry, which observers claimed to be vastly inflated because the last time the voter registry was cleared of the deceased or those who have emigrated, was 1975. The percentages were calculated by the authors. Where no other source is specified, the demographic data correspond to the evaluations—halfway through the year—of the United Nations Organisation. Those electoral provisions that do not appear in the constitution were taken from secondary sources.

2. Tables

2.1 Dates of National Elections, Referendums, and Coups d'Etat

Year[a]	Presidential elections	Parliamentary elections	Elections for Constitutional Assembly	Referendums	Coups d'état
1951		20/12			
1956		01/11			
1960		29/11			
1965		29/11[b]			
1971		11/02			
1976		18/02			
1980		24/04			
1984		17/04			
1989		09/03			
1994		08/03			
1999		09/03			

[a] Data collection starts with the introduction of universal suffrage.
[b] Elections were continued on 15 December 1965 due to the withdrawal of three candidates three days before the original polling day.

2.2 Electoral Body 1951–1999

Year	Type of election[a]	Population[b]	Registered voters		Votes cast		
			Total number	% pop.	Total number	% reg. voters	% pop.
1951	Pa	46,000	6,886	15.0	4,843	70.3	10.5
1956	Pa	51,000	11,400	22.4	6,500	57.0	12.7
1960	Pa	55,500	6,738	12.1	2,559	38.0	4.6
1965	Pa	60,000	21,525	35.9	9,223	42.8	15.4
1971	Pa	65,500	30,682	46.8	17,309	56.4	26.4
1976	Pa	74,000	26,197	35.0	24,879	95.0	33.6
1980	Pa	75,000	28,906	36.6	22,280	77.1	29.7
1984	Pa	76,000	31,453	39.8	19,223	61.1	24.3
1989	Pa	82,000	36,876	43.4	22,390	60.7	26.3
1994	Pa	66,000	43,749	66.3	27,263	62.3	41.3
1999	Pa	65,000	52,385	80.6	33,320	63.6	51.3

[a] Pa = Parliament.
[b] 1970 population census: 65,525.

2.3 Abbreviations

ABDM	Antigua and Barbuda Democratic Movement
ACLM	Antigua Caribbean Liberation Movement
ADLP	Antigua Democratic Labour Party
AFP	Antigua Freedom Party
ALP	Antigua Labour Party
ANP	Antigua National Party
APP	Antigua People's Party
BDM	Barbuda Democratic Movement
BIM	Barbuda Independent Movement
BPM	Barbuda People's Movement
NDP	National Democratic Party
NRM	National Reform Movement
PLM	Progressive Labour Movement
UNDP	United National Democratic Party
UPM	United People's Movement
UPP	United Progressive Party

2.4 Electoral Participation of Parties and Alliances 1951–1999

Party / Alliance	Years	Elections contested[a]
ALP	1951–1999	11
ANP	1956	1
Post Union	1956	1
ADLP	1960	1
BDM	1960; 1989	2
ABDM	1965	1
APP	1971	1
PLM	1971–1984	4
ACLM	1980; 1989	2
UPM	1984	1
BIM	1989	1
BPM	1989–1999	3
UNDP[b]	1989	1
UPP[c]	1994–1999	2
AFP	1999	1
NRM	1999	1

[a] Only parliamentary elections have been held. Total number: 11.
[b] Union between UPM and NDP.
[c] New party formed by UNDP, ACLM, and remnants of PLM.

2.5. Referendums

Referendums have not been held.

2.6. Elections for Constitutional Assembly

Elections for constitutional assembly have not been held.

2.7 Parliamentary Elections 1951–1999

Year	1951		1956	
	Total number	%	Total number	%
Registered voters	6,886	–	11,400	–
Votes cast	4,843	70.3	6,500	57.0
Invalid votes	58	1.2	145	2.2
Valid votes	4,785	98.8	6,355	97.8
ALP	4,182	87.4	5,509	86.7
ANP	–	–	797	12.5
Post Union	–	–	49	0.8
Independents	603	12.6	–	–

Year	1960		1965	
	Total number	%	Total number	%
Registered voters	6,738	–	21,525	–
Votes cast	2,559	40.0	—	—
Invalid votes	56	2.2	—	—
Valid votes	2,503	97.8	9,223	—
ALP	2,128	85.0	7,275	78.9
BDM	151	6.0	–	–
ADLP	66	2.6	–	–
ABDM	–	–	1,859	20.2
Independents	158	6.3	89	1.0

Year	1971		1976	
	Total number	%	Total number	%
Registered voters	30,682	–	26,197	–
Votes cast	17,309	56.4	24,879	95.0
Invalid votes	397	2.3	280	1.1
Valid votes	16,912	97.7	24,599	98.9
PLM	9,761	57.7	12,268	49.9
ALP	6,409	37.9	12,056	49.0
APP	595	3.5	–	–
Independents	157	0.9	275	1.1

Year	1980		1984	
	Total number	%	Total number	%
Registered voters	28,906	–	31,453	–
Votes cast	22,280	77.1	19,223	61.1
Invalid votes	238	1.1	119	0.6
Valid votes	22,042	98.9	19,104	99.4
ALP	12,794	58.0	12,972	67.9
PLM	8,654	39.3	356	1.9
ACLM	259	1.2	–	–
UPM	–	–	4,401	23.0
Independents	335	1.5	1,375	7.2

Year	1989		1994	
	Total number	%	Total number	%
Registered voters	36,876	–	43,749	–
Votes cast	22,390	60.7	27,263	62.3
Invalid votes	141	0.6	147	0.3
Valid votes	22,249	99.4	27,116	62.0
ALP	14,207	63.9	14,763	54.4
UNDP	6,889	31.0	–	–
ACLM	435	2.0	–	–
BPM	304	1.4	367	1.3
BDM	150	0.7	–	–
UPP	–	–	11,852	43.7
Independents	193	0.9	123	0.4
Others[a]	71	0.3	11	0.1

[a] Others include for 1989: BIP; for 1994: WACS.

Year	1999	
	Total number	%
Registered voters	52,385	–
Votes cast	33,320	63.6
Invalid votes	223	0.7
Valid votes	33,097	99.3
ALP	17,521	52.6
UPP	14,713	44.5
BPM	418	1.3
Independents	355	1.1
Others[a]	90	0.3

[a] Others include: AFP: 57 votes (0.2%); NRM: 33 (0.1%).

Antigua and Barbuda

2.8 Composition of Parliament 1951–1999

Year	1951		1956		1960		1965	
	Seats	%	Seats	%	Seats	%	Seats	%
	8	100.0	8	100.0	10	100.0	10	100.0
ALP	8	100.0	8	100.0	10	100.0	10	100.0

Year	1971		1976		1980		1984	
	Seats	%	Seats	%	Seats	%	Seats	%
	17	100.0	17	100.0	17	100.0	17	100.0
PLM	13	76.5	5	29.4	3	17.7	0	0.0
ALP	4	23.5	11	64.7	13	76.5	16	94.1
UNDP	–	–	–	–	–	–	–	–
BPM	–	–	–	–	–	–	–	–
Independents	–	–	1	5.9	1	5.9	1	5.9

Year	1989		1994		1999	
	Seats	%	Seats	%	Seats	%
	17	100.0	17	100.0	17	100.0
ALP	15	88.2	11	64.7	12	70.6
BPM	1	5.9	1	5.9	1	5.9
UNDP	1	5.9	–	–	–	–
UPP	–	–	5	29.4	4	23.5

2.9 Presidential Elections

Presidential elections have not been held.

2.10 List of Power Holders 1981–2004

Head of State	Years	Remarks
Queen Elizabeth	1981–	Represented by governors general: Sir Wilfred E. Jacobs (01/11/1981–10/01/1993); Sir James Beethoven Carlisle (10/06/1993–)

Head of Government	Years	Remarks
Vere Bird	1981–1994	Vere Bird had already ruled the country before independence for almost four decades, from 1951–1994, except for the period of 1971–1976. Assumed office on 01/11/1981.
Lester Bird	1994–2004	Lester Bird was elected prime minister in 1994 and assumed office on 10/03/1994; re-elected in 1999.
Baldwin Spencer	2004–	Baldwin Spencer was elected prime minister on 24/03/2004.

3. Bibliography

3.1 Official Sources

Report on the General Elections During 1980 of Members to Serve in the House of Representatives. St. John's.
Report on the General Elections During 1984 of Members to Serve in the House of Representatives. St. John's.
Report on the General Elections During 1989 of Members to Serve in the House of Representatives. St. John's.
Report on the General Elections During 1994 of Members to Serve in the House of Representatives. St. John's.
Report on the General Elections During 1999 of Members to Serve in the House of Representatives. St. John's.
Representation of the People Act (1975). St. John's: Government Printer.

3.2 Books, Articles, and Electoral Reports

Alexis, F. R. (1984). *Changing Caribbean Constitutions*. Bridgetown (Barbados): Antilles Publications.
Emmanuel, P. A. M. (1979). *General Elections in the Eastern Caribbean. A Handbook*. Cave Hill (Barbados): University of the West Indies.

— (1992). *Elections and Party Systems in the Commonwealth Caribbean, 1994–1991*. Bridgetown (Barbados): CADRES.

Hill, K. (1988). 'El Registro Electoral de Antigua y Barbuda. Memoria de la Segunda Conferencia de la Asociación de Organismos Electorales de Centroamérica y el Caribe'. *El Registro Electoral en América Latina*. San José: IIDH-CAPEL, 13–27.

IDEA (2002) (ed.). *Voter Turnout Since 1945. A Global Report*. Stockholm.

Inter-Parliamentary Union (ed.) (various years). *Chronicle of Parliamentary Elections and Developments*. Geneva: IPU.

Kunsman Jr., C. H. (1963). *The Origins and Development of Political Parties in the British West Indies*. Ph.D. thesis, Berkeley, Calif.: University of California.

Midgett, D. (1983). *Eastern Caribbean Elections, 1950–1982*. Iowa City: University of Iowa.

Payne, D. W. (1994). *The 1994 Antigua & Barbuda Elections*. Election Report, CSIS Americas Program, Washington, D.C.

— (1999). 'The Failure of Governance in Antigua and Barbuda. The Elections of 1999'. *CSIS-Policy Papers on the Americas*. Washington, D.C.

Phillips, F. (1985). *West Indian Constitutions: Post-Independence Reform*. New York/London/Rome: Oceana Publications.

Spackman, A. (1975). *Constitutional Development of the West Indies 1922–1968. A Selection from the Major Documents*. St. Lawrence (Barbados): Caribbean University Press.

BAHAMAS
by Bernd Hillebrands and Johannes Schwehm

1. Introduction

1.1 Historical Overview

The process of political decolonization in the Bahamas ran parallel to the gradual extension of suffrage after 1959, and to the gradual transfer of power from British rule to an autonomous government. Internal self-government was granted in 1969, and the Bahamas finally gained independence in 1973, being one of the last British colonies to do so.

The longtime political preeminence of the white trade-oriented oligarchy ('Bay Street Boys'), which had been represented by the United Bahamian Party (UBP) since 1958, ended with the parliamentary elections of 1967. Despite its lower share of the vote, the UBP managed to win a clear majority of seats by means of gerrymandering. It obtained 19 seats, whereas its opponent, the Progressive Liberal Party (PLP), only won eight. The 1967 elections brought about a change in favor of the PLP. The PLP was led by the black lawyer Lynden O. Pindling, who remained in office for 25 years until 1992.

The PLP was founded by Pindling in 1953 and from the beginning it was closely linked to the union movement, receiving most of its support from the black underprivileged population (around 87%). When the death of one of its deputies led to early by-elections in 1968, the PLP lost its majority in parliament. On this occasion, constituencies were redistributed. The PLP then gained a solid majority of 29 seats compared to the seven seats won by the UBP (the remaining parties won two seats). The opposition subsequently accused the government of gerrymandering.

Towards the end of 1969, the leadership within the PLP became a controversial issue, and eventually led to a split in the party in 1971, with the creation of the Free Progressive Liberal Party (Free PLP). In the same year, the Free PLP formed an alliance with the UBP and founded the Free National Movement (FNM). The FNM sought to unify the traditional white upper class with the emerging white and black elites to build a new political force. In the elections following independence, the FNM was seen as the only really serious contender to be able to overcome the PLP's political dominance.

On 9 July 1973, the Commonwealth of the Bahamas was declared independent and a constitutional monarchy with a Westminster-style parliament was established. The British Queen remained as head of state, represented by the governor general. In the 1972 elections, the FNM strongly opposed immediate independence, fearing that a hasty process could negatively affect foreign investment and tourism, but the party was unsuccessful in its efforts.

In 1975, the Trades Union Congress (TUC) decided to form a coalition with the FNM as its members were no longer satisfied with the line followed by the PLP, the party they had previously supported. Criticism was directed in particular at Prime Minister Pindling's inefficiency in regard to social policy and his weak improvements in the area of unemployment. In 1976, the FNM suffered another split, when former UBP-sympathizers and the Bahamian Democratic Party (BDP) came together to try to represent the interests of the white upper class independently. In the face of these events, the TUC made a new pact with the PLP, this time ensuring that they would be able to have more influence over the PLP's policy. The BDP and the FNM wanted less state intervention in the economy and wanted the government to promote foreign investment in order to boost economic growth and create new jobs. The PLP on the other hand wanted the country to be economically self-reliant and wanted more state intervention in the most important branches of the economy (tourism, banking, agriculture and fishing).

As early as the 1977 elections, members of the government were suspected of being involved in corruption. Before the 1982 elections, Prime Minister Pindling's conduct was called into question, and he was accused of having accepted bribes from drug-traffickers, who used the Bahamas as an intermediate station for smuggled drugs en route to the USA and for money-laundering. Even though Pindling was suspected to be directly involved in these scandals, it did not affect his subsequent performance in the elections of 1982 and 1987, which he won. Even the change of government in the 1992 elections was attributed to the worsening economic situation (unemployment was at approximately 20%) rather than the government's involvement in corruption scandals. The landslide defeat of the PLP in 1992 (the PLP lost one half of its seats) brought an end to the party's, and Pindling's, 25-year leadership. Hubert Ingraham, the leader of the FNM, became the new prime minister. Ingraham had been a member of Pindling's government, but had resigned

from office in 1984 after having accused the government of being involved in corruption and drug trafficking. In the mid-90s, the Ingraham
administration, re-elected in 1997, focused successfully on economic
issues, such as creating new jobs, introducing a minimum wage, and
strengthening economic growth. The improvement in the economy was
achieved mainly by attracting foreign investment and by the recovery of
the tourist industry. In response to persistent political pressure from the
OECD ('Financial Action Task Force') and the USA, several laws were
passed in 2000, which were designed to deter money-laundering and to
increase transparency in the banking sector. Moreover, the Bahamas
signed a treaty with the USA that included the transfer of financial information. On 27 February 2002, the Bahamas held their first referendum since the country's independence. The referendum, which was one
of the FNM's major projects of the mid-90s, focused on several constitutional changes (such as the creation of an independent elections commission and the removal of some cases of gender discrimination from
the constitution). However, the constitutional review was rejected on
every single issue and, a few months later, the FNM lost the elections.
Perry Christie, leader of the PLP, became the new prime minister. It is
claimed that the PLP won such a decisive victory because the electorate
wanted to show that they rejected the referendum and express their an-
ger at the decline in the economy, which was due to a renewed crisis in
the tourism industry and the negative effects of the reforms in the financial sector.

Bahamas adopted the British plurality system even before independence. Despite some modifications concerning the number of constituencies the electoral system remained unaltered. It has facilitated the
emergence of a stable bipartism. The long predominance of the PLP was
first interrupted in 1992, when the FNM took over power for two legislative terms. In every election held since independence the winning
party did not only obtain an absolute majority of seats but also an absolute majority of votes (earned majorities).

1.2 Evolution of Electoral Provisions

The constitution of 1964 replaced the legislative council and the house
of assembly with the national assembly (members are elected by the
people), and the senate (members are appointed by the governor general). Hence, the bicameral system followed the Westminster-style tra-

dition of Britain, with the extraordinarily strong position of the prime minister.

Direct, universal, equal, and secret suffrage was introduced before the 1967 elections to the house of assembly. Until 1972, British citizens resident in the colony for a minimum of six months were also entitled to vote; this was abolished after independence and restricted to the citizens of the Bahamas.

Since the 1968 elections, the electoral system applied is the plurality system in single-member constituencies. Until this time there had been single, two, or three-member constituencies. The number of constituencies has been amended at various times (1982: 43; 1987: 49; 2002: 40).

1.3 Current Electoral Provisions

Sources: Several fundamental electoral principles are recorded in the constitution of 1974. The specific provisions are written down in the Electoral Law, which was last amended in 1992.

Suffrage: Suffrage is universal, equal, secret, and direct for the elections to the house of assembly. Every citizen of the Bahamas older than 18 years, who has resided in a constituency for at least three months, is entitled to vote. The mentally infirm, those serving prison sentences, and certain civil servants are not entitled to vote. Registration lists are revised every year. Voting is not compulsory.

Elected national institutions: There is a two-chamber legislature, consisting of the house of assembly and the senate. The house of assembly is directly elected for a five-year term. By-elections are held to fill vacant seats. The senate is made up of 16 members, appointed for five years by the governor general (nine on the advice of the prime minister, four on the advice of the opposition leader, and three on the advice of the prime minister after consultations with the opposition leader).

Nomination of candidates: Every Bahamian citizen older than 21 years, resident in the country for a minimum of one year, can be elected. Candidates for the house of assembly need the support of four voters, as well as a deposit of 400 US$, which is not returned if the candidate gains less than one-sixth of the votes cast in the constituency. Holders of certain public posts such as judges, the personal staff of the Ministry of

Tourism, and members of the armed forces cannot be elected. To be appointed as a senator, citizens must be at least 30 years old.

Electoral system: Plurality system is applied in 40 single-member constituencies.

Organizational context of elections: The Parliamentary Registration Department, headed by the parliamentary commissioner who is appointed by the governor general, is responsible for running elections. The commissioner and his deputies are responsible for registering voters and holding the elections. The Electoral Broadcasting Council (EBC) is headed by a chairman who is appointed by the governor general, but who is supposed to be independent of any authority. The function of the EBC is to ensure that the media reports fairly on the elections and that they are not biased towards one party. Therefore, the council acts as a board of review.

1.4 Commentary on the Electoral Statistics

The electoral data presented in the following tables have been taken from secondary sources. The percentages were calculated by the authors. Where no other source is specified, the demographic data correspond to the evaluations—halfway through the year—of the United Nations Organization. Electoral provisions that do not appear in the constitution were taken from secondary sources.

2. Tables

2.1 Dates of National Elections, Referendums, and Coups d'Etat

Year	Presidential elections	Parliamentary elections	Elections for Constitutional Assembly	Referendums	Coups d'état
1972		19/09			
1977		19/07			
1982		10/06			
1987		19/06			
1992		19/08			
1997		14/03			
2002		02/05		27/02	

2.2 Electoral Body 1972–2002

Year	Type of election[a]	Population[b]	Registered voters Total number	% pop.	Votes cast Total number	% reg. voters	% pop.
1972[c]	Pa	185,000	57,071	30.9	50,216[d]	88.0	27.1
1977	Pa	220,000	71,295	32.4	64,108[d]	89.9	29.1
1982	Pa	228,000	84,235	37.0	75,609[d]	89.8	33.2
1987	Pa	240,000	102,713	42.8	90,280[d]	87.9	37.6
1992	Pa	258,000	122,939	50.4	112,057[d]	91.1	43.4
1997	Pa	289,000	129,946	45.0	121,073	98.5	41.9
2002	Ref	300,000	144,758[e]	48.3	—	—	—
2002	Pa	300,000	144,758	48.3	130,536	90.2	43.5

[a] Pa = Parliament; Ref = Referendum.
[b] Population censuses: 1970: 175,192; 1980: 223,455; 1990: 255,095; 2000: 303,611.
[c] Electoral data were collected as of the last elections before independence (10/07/1973).
[d] Valid votes.
[e] Number of registered voters taken from the elections 2002, which were held three months after the referendum.

2.3 Abbreviations

BDP	Bahamian Democratic Party
BFA	Bahamian Freedom Party
CDP	Commonwealth Democratic Party
CLP	Commonwealth Labour Party
FNM	Free National Movement
LP	Labour Party
PLP	Progressive Liberal Party
SP	Survivors Party
VNSP	Vanguard Nationalist and Socialist Party
WP	Workers' Party

2.4 Electoral Participation of Parties and Alliances 1972–2002

Party / Alliance	Years	Elections contested[a]
CLP	1972	1
FNM	1972–2002	7
PLP	1972–2002	7
BDP	1977	1
VNSP	1977–1982	2
CDP	1982	1
WP	1982	1
LP	1987	1
BFA	1997–2002	2
SP	1997–2002	2

[a] Only the number of elections to the lower house is indicated. Total number: 7.

2.5 Referendums

Year	2002[a]		2002[c]	
	Total number	%	Total number	%
Registered voters[b]	144,758	–	144,758	–
Votes cast	—	—	—	—
Invalid votes	—	—	—	—
Valid votes	87,961	—	88,519	—
Yes	29,906	34.0	32,892	37.2
No	58,055	66.0	55,627	62.8

[a] Removal of gender discrimination from the constitution.
[b] Number of registered voters taken from the 2002 elections, which were held three months after the referendum.
[c] Creation of a commission to monitor the standards of teachers nationally.

Year	2002[a]		2002[b]	
	Total number	%	Total number	%
Registered voters[c]	144,758	–	144,758	–
Votes cast	—	—	—	—
Invalid votes	—	—	—	—
Valid votes	88,233	—	88,194	—
Yes	30,418	34.5	30,903	35.0
No	57,815	65.5	57,291	65.0

[a] Creation of an independent parliamentary commissioner.
[b] Creation of an independent election boundaries commission.
[c] Number of registered voters taken from the 2002 elections, which were held three months after the referendum.

Year	2002[a]	
	Total number	%
Registered voters[b]	144,758	–
Votes cast	—	—
Invalid votes	—	—
Valid votes	85,856	—
Yes	25,018	29.1
No	60,838	70.9

[a] The retirement age of judges will change from 60 (appellate court judges: 68) to 65 (appellate court judges 72).
[b] Number of registered voters taken from the 2002 elections, which were held three months after the referendum.

2.6 Elections for Constitutional Assembly

Elections for constitutional assembly have not been held.

2.7 Parliamentary Elections 1972–2002

Year	1972		1977	
	Total number	%	Total number	%
Registered voters	57,071	–	71,295	–
Votes cast	—	—	—	—
Invalid votes	—	—	—	—
Valid votes	50,216	—	64,108	—
PLP	29,628	59.0	35,090	54.7
FNM	19,736	39.3	9,995	15.6
CLP	254	0.5	–	–
BDP	–	–	17,252	26.9
Independents	598	1.2	1,716	2.7
Others[a]	–	–	55	0.1

[a] For the 1977 election, others include: VNSP.

Year	1982		1987	
	Total number	%	Total number	%
Registered voters	84,235	–	102,713	–
Votes cast	—	—	—	—
Invalid votes	—	—	—	—
Valid votes	75,609	—	90,280	—
PLP	42,995	56.9	48,339	53.5
FNM	31,097	41.1	39,009	43.2
Independents	1,292	1.7	2,820	3.1
Others[a]	225	0.3	112	0.1

[a] For the 1982 election, others include: VNSP: 181 votes (0.2%); WP: 31 (0.0%); CDP: 13 (0.0%). For the 1987 election: LP.

Year	1992		1997	
	Total number	%	Total number	%
Registered voters	122,939	–	129,946	–
Votes cast	—	—	120,710	92.9
Invalid votes	—	—	1,377	1.5
Valid votes	112,057	—	119,173	98.5
PLP	61,799	55.1	49,932	41.9
FNM	50,258	44.9	68,766	57.7
Independents	–	–	475	0.4

Year	2002		
	Total number		
Registered voters	144,758	–	
Votes cast	130,536	90.2	
Invalid votes	1,342	0.9	
Valid votes	129,194	89.2	
PLP	66,901	51.8	
FNM	52,807	40.8	
Independents	6,272	54.9	

[a] Others include: BDM: 414 votes (0.3%); BCP: 12 (0.0%); SUR: 10 (0.0%).

2.8 Composition of Parliament 1972–2002

Year	1972		1977		1982		1987	
	Seats	%	Seats	%	Seats	%	Seats	%
	38	100.0	38	100.0	43	100.0	49	100.0
PLP	28	76.3	31	79.0	32	74.4	31	63.3
FNM	10	23.7	1	5.3	11	25.6	16	32.7
BDP	–	–	6	15.8	–	–	–	–
Independents	–	–	–	–	–	–	2	4.1

Year	1992		1997[a]		2002	
	Seats	%	Seats	%	Seats	%
	49	100.0	40	100.0	40	100.0
PLP	16	32.7	6	22.5	29	72.5
FNM	33	67.3	34	87.5	7	17.5
Independents	–	–	–	–	4	10.0

[a] The seat allocation for the 1997 election took place after a by-election. The original distribution was 35 and 5, respectively.

2.10 List of Power Holders 1980–2004

Head of State	Years	Remarks
Queen Elizabeth	1973–	Represented by governors general: Sir John Warburton Paul (07/10/1973–07/31/1973); Sir Milo B. Butler (08/01/1973–01/22/1979); Sir Gerald Cash (01/22/1979–01/25/1988); Sir Henry Taylor (06/26/1988–01/01/1992); Sir Clifford Darling (01/02/1992–01/02/1995); Sir Orville Alton Turnquest (01/02/1995–11/13/2001); Dame Ivy Dumont (11/13/2001–).

Head of Government	Years	Remarks
Sir Lynden Pindling	1972–1992	Assumed office on 08/21/1972 after having won the last election before independence. Re-elected in 1977, 1982, and 1987, he ruled the country continuously the following 25 years.
Hubert Ingraham	1992–2002	Assumed office on 08/24/1992; re-elected in 1997.
Perry Christie	2002–	Assumed office on 05/03/2002.

3. Bibliography

3.1 Official Sources

Department of Statistics. *The Bahamas in Figures 1986/1987*. Nassau (Bahamas): Government Press.
The Government of the Bahamas. *Results of General Elections 1972, 1977, 1982 and 1987*. Nassau (Bahamas).
Electoral Act 1992. Nassau (Bahamas).

3.2 Books, Articles, and Electoral Reports

Alexis, F. R. (1984). *Changing Caribbean Constitutions*. Bridgetown (Barbados): Antilles Publications.
Craton, M. (1962). *A History of the Bahamas*. London: Collins.
Hughes, C. A. (1981). *Race and Politics in the Bahamas*. Queensland (Saint Lucia): University of Queensland Press.
International IDEA (2002) (ed.). *Voter Turnout Since 1945. A Global Report*. Stockholm: IDEA.
Inter-Parliamentary Union (ed.) (various years). *Chronicle of Parliamentary Elections and Developments*. Geneva: IPU.
Keesings Contemporary Archives, 21.–28.10.1972.
Phillips, F. (1985). *West Indian Constitutions: Post-Independence Reform*. New York/London/Rome: Oceana Publications.
Spackman, A. (1975). *Constitutional Development of the West Indies 1922–1968. A Selection from the Major Documents*. St. Lauwrence (Barbados): Caribbean University Press.
United Nations Population and Vital Statistics Report. Department of International Economic and Social Affairs (various years). *Statistical Papers, Series A*. New York: United Nations.

BARBADOS

by Bernd Hillebrands and Katrin Falk

1. Introduction

1.1 Historical Overview

Barbados' house of assembly was founded in 1639, which means that Barbados enjoys the third-oldest and uninterrupted tradition of parliamentary elections in the Commonwealth. However, as in the other colonies of the British West Indies, suffrage was restricted to the white population, in the case of Barbados until 1831 and property requirements remained in force until 1950.

Barbados' efficient bipartism was considered a model of its kind within the Caribbean Commonwealth and has to be considered in the context of the established electoral system—a plurality system in single-member constituencies. Since 1951, when universal suffrage was introduced, power has switched between the Barbados Labour Party (BLP) and the Democratic Labour Party (DLP). There has been a regular change of government every two or three electoral periods.

In 1941, the mass movement Barbados Progressive League, which had begun in 1938, founded the Barbados Workers' Union (BWU) and in 1946, the BLP. Sir Grantley Adams, one of the most remarkable political figures of the Caribbean region, was one of the founders of the BLP and joint leader of the party and the BWU. In 1947, Adams was appointed president of the regional union Caribbean Labour Congress. After the elections of 1951, deep-rooted conflicts emerged between Adams and the party's left wing. In this period, the party's chairmanship passed to Errol Barrow, who left the BLP in 1954 to found the DLP in 1955.

In the years leading up to independence on 30 November 1966, the metropolitan power had been conferring certain powers gradually to Barbados' local government. Thus, in 1950, ministries were created with limited competencies. In 1958, a government was established based on the British model, headed by a prime minister. Grantley Adams, former first minister for a few months, was appointed prime minister of the British West Indies Federation, also founded in 1958, with its seat of government in Port of Spain (Trinidad and Tobago). Adams returned to Barbados' political scene in 1962, after the federation had been dissolved.

The course of the British West Indies Federation, founded by ten British island colonies as a territorial unity both politically and economically independent from Great Britain, had significant consequences for Barbados' political development. Because of his function as prime minister, Grantley Adams could not serve the BLP as the decisive and charismatic leader they required. When the Federation finally fell (foreseen since the 1961 elections) Adams' prestige, together with that of the BLP, was damaged. The economic problems, the high rate of unemployment, and the split between the BLP and the BWU union (now supporting the DLP) also opened the way for the DLP to gain power under Errol Barrow. Between 1962 and 1965, the smallest island colonies of the Eastern Caribbean tried to form a federation with the support of the Barrow administration. Only after this attempt failed did Barbados seriously begin to fight for independence.

Grantley Adams led the BLP from 1946 until shortly before his death in 1972. His son Tom Adams succeeded him in this office. In the mid-1980s the BLP, for the second time, and the DLP—after the death of its central political figure—saw their political influence decrease. Tom Adams, the head of the government since 1976, died in 1985. Bernard St. John replaced him as the head of the party and was also appointed prime minister. The country's difficult economic situation together with St. John's lack of charisma in comparison with his rival candidate, Errol Barrow, are considered the main causes of the BLP's electoral defeat in 1986. Errol Barrow, the founder of the DLP, died in 1987, after only having served as prime minister for one year. He was succeeded by Erskine Sandiford, winner of the 1991 elections. The National Democratic Party (NDP), which was founded by former DLP members and was participating in a general election for the first time, did not win a seat. After a severe economic crisis at the start of the 1990s, which Sandiford's government responded to with austere measures, support for the DLP declined. After the shortest term of any government in Barbados, a no-confidence vote led to the dissolution of parliament in 1994. In the following general elections, the BLP came to power under Owen Arthur. The NDP won its first seat in the house of assembly. The popularity of the new government's economic policy was confirmed in the 1999 elections, in which the BLP secured the largest majority ever achieved in a general election in Barbados, winning 26 of the 28 seats. The remaining two seats were won by the DLP, while the NDP lost any influence it might have had before. The BLP was able to maintain a strong position in the 2003 election with 23 out of 30 seats (DLP: 7). The appearing difficulty of the NDP to gain a more endurable position in the house of assembly showed how in a homogenous context, as it exists in Barbados, a plurality system in single-member constituencies may contribute to the evolution of a two-party-system (at least regarding the parties represented in parliament).

1.2 Evolution of Electoral Provisions

The 1964 Constitution introduced a bicameral system in Barbados. There has been universal, equal, secret, and direct suffrage since the 1951 elections to the house of assembly. In 1964, the voting age for the elections to the house of assembly was reduced from 21 to 18. Up to and including the 1971 elections, all citizens of the Commonwealth older than 21, who had resided in Barbados for at least seven years before the election, were entitled to passive suffrage. After 1971, voters had to have Barbados citizenship and have resided in Barbados for at least seven years.

Until the 1966 elections, the electoral system applied was plurality in two-member constituencies, and each voter was entitled to two votes (multiple voting). Before the 1971 elections, the 12 constituencies were substituted by 24 single-member constituencies with one vote per voter. In 1980, the amendment of the Representation of the People Act increased the number of constituencies from 24 to 27, increased again in 1990 to 28 constituencies. The 2003 elections were held in 30 constituencies.

1.3 Current Electoral Provisions

Sources: The 1966 Constitution of Barbados and certain subsequent constitutional reforms contain the fundamental electoral principles. Other legislation includes the Electoral and Boundaries Commission (Review of Boundaries) Order, the Representation of the People Act, the General Elections (Allocation of Broadcasting Time) Regulations, the Election Offences and Controversies Act, the Election Offences and Controversies Rules, and the Parish Boundaries Act.

Suffrage: The principles of universal, equal, secret, and direct suffrage are applied. Each citizen of Barbados older than 18 is entitled to vote after having been registered. Members of the Commonwealth, who are older than 18 and who have resided in Barbados for at least three years before an election and who have lived in the constituency for at least three months beforehand, are also entitled to vote after registration. Neither registration nor voting are compulsory.

Elected national institutions: The bicameral legislative power is made up of the house of assembly, with 30 directly-elected members, and the senate, with 21 members appointed by the British governor general (seven in his own capacity, twelve on the advice of the prime minister, and two on the advice of the opposition leader). The parliamentarian term of office is five years. The prime minister can establish an earlier date for elections by dissolving parliament. By-elections are held if parliamentary seats become vacant. There are no other national institutions elected.

Nomination of candidates: Every citizen of Barbados who is 21 years or older and who has been resident for at least seven years in the country, can be elected to a public office. Each candidate requires the support of four electors (persons registered and eligible to vote) and a monetary deposit of $250, which is forfeited unless the candidate obtains one sixth of the votes cast in the constituency. Certain civil servants are excluded from the right to passive suffrage (for example, judges).

Electoral system: Plurality system in 30 single-member constituencies.

Organizational context of elections: The Electoral and Boundaries Commission ('Commission'), established on 1 April 1985, is the institution responsible for electoral registration, running elections in constituencies, electing members to the house of assembly, and reviewing the number and boundaries of constituencies and polling districts. It also checks written or recorded texts before they may be broadcasted. The Commission consists of a chairman, a deputy chairman, and three other members. The governor general appoints the chairman and two of the Commission members, on the recommendation of the prime minister after consultation with the leader of the opposition, and appoints the deputy chairman and the one remaining member on the recommendation of the leader of the opposition after consultation with the prime minister. They serve for a period of five years. Members can be re-appointed, but are not allowed to be minister, parliamentary secretary, a member of, or candidate for, elections to the house of assembly, a senator, or a public officer.

After consultation with the chief electoral officer who is the chief registering officer, the commission recruits a registering officer for each constituency and as many enumerators as necessary. The registration system is permanent and continuous.

The chief electoral officer is the chief supervisor of elections and is assisted by a deputy supervisor of elections (appointed by the governor general). After consultation with the chief supervisor of elections, the Commission may appoint a returning officer for each constituency responsible for running the polls, counting the votes, and declaring the elected candidate.

1.4 Commentary on the Electoral Statistics

The electoral data presented in the following tables were taken from official reports of the supervisor of elections for the years 1966, 1976, 1981, 1986, 1994, and 1999. These data are considered reliable. For the earlier parliamentary elections, and those of 1971 and 1991, official government and secondary sources were consulted, especially P. A. M. Emmanuel (1992). The percentages were calculated by the authors. Where no other source is specified, the demographic data correspond to the evaluations—halfway through the year—of the US Census Bureau (International Database).

2. Tables

2.1 Dates of National Elections, Referendums, and Coups d'Etat

Year[a]	Presidential elections	Parliamentary elections	Elections for Constitutional Assembly	Referendums	Coups d'état
1951		13/12			
1956		07/12			
1961		04/12			
1966		03/11			
1971		09/09			
1976		02/09			
1981		18/06			
1986		28/05			
1991		22/01			
1994		06/09			
1999		20/01			
2003		21/05			

[a] Data collection starts with the introduction of universal suffrage.

2.2 Electoral Body 1951–2003

Year	Type of election[a]	Population[b]	Registered voters		Votes cast		
			Total number	% pop.	Total number	% reg. voters	% pop.
1951	R	231,000	95,939	41.5	62,020	64.6	26.8
1956	R	235,000	103,290	44.0	62,274	60.3	26.5
1961	R	236,000	104,518	44.3	64,090	61.3	27.2
1966	R	236,000	99,988	42.4	79,691	79.7	33.8
1971	R	240,500	115,189	47.9	94,019	81.6	39.1
1976	R	248,000	134,241	54.1	99,463	74.1	40.1
1981	R	252,500	167,029	66.2	119,566	71.6	47.4
1986	R	258,500	176,739	68.4	135,562	76.7	52.4
1991	R	263,500	191,000	72.5	121,696	63.7	46.2
1994	R	267,000	206,642	77.4	125,822	60.9	47.1
1999	R	272,500	204,307	75.0	129,450	63.4	47.5
2003	R	276,500	218,811	79.1	124,177	56.8	44.9

[a] R = House of Representatives.
[b] Estimates on the basis of census results. Censuses were held in 1946, 1960, 1970, 1980, and 1990.

2.3 Abbreviations

BLP	Barbados Labour Party
BNP	Barbados National Party
CP	Congress Party
DLP	Democratic Labour Party
NDP	National Democratic Party
PPA	People's Political Alliance
PPM	Peoples' Progressive Movement
WPB	Workers Party of Barbados

2.4 Electoral Participation of Parties and Alliances 1966–2003

Party / Alliance	Years	Elections contested[a]
BLP	1951–2003	12
CP	1951	1
DLP	1956–2003	11
PPM	1961–1966	2
BNP	1966	1
PPA	1976	1
WPB	1986	1
NDP	1991–1994	2

[a] Only the number of the elections to the lower house is indicated. Total number: 12.

2.5 Referendums

Referendums have not been held.

2.6 Elections for Constitutional Assembly

Elections for constitutional assembly have not been held.

2.7 Parliamentary Elections 1951–2003

Year	1951 Total number	%	1956 Total number	%
Registered voters	95,939	–	103,290	–
Votes cast	62,020	64.6	62,274	60.3
Invalid votes	891	1.4	681	1.1
Valid votes	61,129	98.6	61,593	98.9
BLP	53,321	54.5	48,667	49.3
Conservatives	29,131	29.8	21,060	21.4
CP	5,228	5.3	–	–
DLP	–	–	19,650	19.9
PPM	–	–	1,695	1.7
Independents	10,212	10.4	7,552	7.7

Year	1961 Total number	%	1966 Total number	%
Registered voters	104,518	–	99,988	–
Votes cast	64,090	61.1	79,691	79.7
Invalid votes	263	0.4	—	—
Valid votes	63,827	99.6	146,054	—
BLP	40,096	36.8	47,610	32.6
DLP	39,534	36.3	72,384	49.6
Conservatives	24,015	22.1	–	–
BNP	–	–	14,801	10.1
PPM	–	–	598	0.4
Independents	5,263	4.8	10,661	7.3

Year	1971 Total number	%	1976 Total number	%
Registered voters	115,189	–	134,241	–
Votes cast[a]	94,019	81.6	99,463	74.1
Invalid votes	1,174	1.2	866	0.9
Valid votes	92,845	98.8	98,597	99.1
DLP	53,295	57.4	45,786	46.4
BLP	39,376	42.4	51,948	52.7
PPA	–	–	572	0.6
Independents	174	0.2	291	0.3

[a] Voters. The 1966 elections were held in twelve two-member constituencies, each voter being entitled to two votes.

Year	1981		1986	
	Total number	%	Total number	%
Registered voters	167,029	–	176,739	–
Votes cast	119,566	71.6	135,562	76.7
Invalid votes	1,065	0.9	903	0.7
Valid votes	118,501	99.1	134,659	99.3
BLP	61,883	52.2	80,050	59.4
DLP	55,845	47.1	54,367	40.4
WPB	–	–	40	0.0
Independents	773	0.7	202	0.2

Year	1991		1994	
	Total number	%	Total number	%
Registered voters	191,000	–	—	–
Votes cast	121,696	63.7	125,822	60.9
Invalid votes	1,344	1.1	659	0.5
Valid votes	120,352	98.9	125,163	99.5
DLP	59,900	49.8	47,979	38.3
BLP	51,789	43.0	60,504	48.3
NDP	8,218	6.8	15,980	12.8
Independents	445	0.4	700	0.6

Year	1999		2003	
	Total number	%	Total number	%
Registered voters	204,307	–	218,811	–
Votes cast	129,450	63.4	124,177	56.8
Invalid votes	820	0.6	286	0.2
Valid votes	128,630	99.4	123,891	99.8
BLP	83,445	64.9	69,294	55.9
DLP	45,118	35.1	54,746	44.2
Independents	67	0.1	137	0.1

2.8 Composition of Parliament 1951–2003

Year	1951		1956		1961		1966	
	Seats	%	Seats	%	Seats	%	Seats	%
	24	100.0	24	100.0	24	100.0	24	100.0
BLP	15	62.5	15	62.5	5	20.8	8	33.3
Conservatives	4	16.7	3	12.5	4	16.7	–	–
DLP	–	–	4	16.7	14	58.3	14	58.3
BNP	–	–	–	–	–	–	2	8.3

Year	1971 Seats 24	% 100.0	1976 Seats 24	% 100.0	1981 Seats 27	% 100.0	1986 Seats 27	% 100.0
DLP	18	75.0	7	29.2	10	37.0	24	88.9
BLP	6	25.0	17	70.8	17	63.0	3	11.1
NDP	–	–	–	–	–	–	–	–

Year	1991 Seats 28	% 100.0	1994 Seats 28	% 100.0	1999 Seats 28	% 100.0	2003 Seats 30	% 100.0
DLP	18	64.3	8	28.6	2	7.1	7	23.3
BLP	10	35.7	19	67.9	26	92.9	23	76.7
NDP	0	0.0	1	3.6	–	–	–	–

2.9 Presidential Elections

Presidential elections have not been held. Head of state is the Queen of the United Kingdom.

2.10 List of Power Holders 1966–2004

Head of State	Years	Remarks
Queen Elizabeth II	1966–	Represented by the following governors general: Sir John Stow (1966–1967), Sir Arleigh Winston Scott (1967–1976), Sir Deighton Ward (1976–1984), Sir Hugh Springer (1984–1990), Dame Ruth Nita Barrow (1990–1995), Sir Clifford Straughn Husbands (1996–).

Head of Government	Years	Remarks
Errol Walton Barrow	1966–1976	DLP; assumed office on 18/11/1966.
John Michael Geoffrey 'Tom' Adams	1976–1985	BLP; assumed office on 08/09/1976.
Bernard St. John	1985–1986	BLP; assumed office on 11/03/1985.
Errol Walton Barrow	1986–1987	DLP; assumed office on 29/05/1986.
Erskine Sandiford	1987–1994	DLP; assumed office on 01/06/1987.
Owen Seymour Arthur	1994–	BLP; in office since 07/09/1994.

3. Bibliography

3.1 Official Sources

Government of Barbados (without year). *Parliament. Laws of Barbados Relating to Parliament and Elections Thereto.* St. Michael (Barbados).

The Supervisor of Elections (without year). *Report on the General Election 1966.* Bridgetown (Barbados).

The Supervisor of Elections (without year). *Report on the General Election 1976.* Bridgetown (Barbados).

The Supervisor of Elections (without year). *Report on the General Election 1981.* Bridgetown (Barbados).

The Supervisor of Elections (without year). *Report on the General Election 1986.* Bridgetown (Barbados).

The Supervisor of Elections (without year). *Report on the General Election 1994.* Bridgetown (Barbados).

The Supervisor of Elections (without year). *Report on the General Election 1999.* Bridgetown (Barbados).

3.2 Books, Articles, and Electoral Reports

Alexis, F. R. (1984). *Changing Caribbean Constitutions.* Bridgetown (Barbados): Antilles Publications.

Barbados High Commission in London, the (ed.) (1991). *Results of the 1991 Barbados General Elections.*

Barriteau, E. (1981). 'The 1981 General Elections in Barbados. Some Comments'. *Bulletin of Eastern Caribbean Affairs*, 7/2: 38–46.

Dann, G. (1984). *The Quality of Life in Barbados.* London: Macmillan Publishers.

Duncan, N. (1994). Barbados: Democracy at the Crossroads, in C. J. Edie (ed.), *Democracy in the Caribbean. Myths and Realities.* London: Praeger, 75–92.

Emmanuel, P. A. M. (1979). *General Elections in the Eastern Caribbean. A Handbook.* Cave Hill (Barbados): University of the West Indies.

— (1992). *Elections and Party Systems in the Commonwealth Caribbean, 1944–1991.* Barbados: Caribbean Development Research Services.

Hoyos, F. A. (1963). *The Rise of West Indian Democracy. The Life and Times of Sir Grantley Adams.* Barbados: Advocate Press.

— (1974). *Grantley Adams and the Social Revolution. The Story of the Movement that Changed the Pattern of West Indian Society.* London: Macmillan Education.

— (1978). *Barbados. A History from the Amerindians to Independence.* London: Macmillan Education.

— (1987). *Barbados Comes of Age. From Early Strivings to Happy Fulfilment.* London: Macmillan Publishers.

— (1988). *Tom Adams. A Biography.* London: Macmillan Publishers.

Inter-Parliamentary Union (ed.) (various years). *Cronicle of Parliamentary Elections and Developments.* Geneva: International Centre for Parliamentary Documentation.

Kunsman Jr., C. H. (1963). *The Origins and Development of Political Parties in the British West Indies.* Ph.D. thesis, Berkeley: University of California.

Nuscheler, F. and Schultze, R. O. (1992). 'Barbados', in D. Nohlen and F. Nuscheler (eds.), *Handbuch der Dritten Welt, Vol. 2: Südamerika* (3rd edn.), Bonn: Dietz, 343–357.

Phillips, F. (1985). *West Indian Constitutions: Post-Independence Reform.* New York/London/Rome: Oceana Publications.

Spackman, A. (1975). *Constitutional Development of the West Indies 1922–1968. A Selection from the Major Documents.* St. Lauwrence (Barbados): Caribbean University Press.

United Nations Population and Vital Statistics Report, Department of International Economic and Social Affairs (various years). *Statistical Papers, Series A.* New York: United Nations.

Will, Marvin W. (1981). 'Mass Political Party Institutionalization in Barbados: Analysis of the Issues and Dynamics of the Post-Independence Period'. *Journal of Commonwealth and Comparative Politics*, 19/2: 134–156.

— (1989). 'Democracy, Elections and Public Policy in the Eastern Caribbean: The Case of Barbados'. *Journal of Commonwealth and Comparative Politics*, 27/3: 321–346.

BELIZE

by Bernd Hillebrands and Richard Ortiz Ortiz

1. Introduction

1.1 Historical Overview

Belize's modern history begins with the country's occupation by the British, when it was called British Honduras. The country did not become an independent parliamentary monarchy in the British Commonwealth until 21 September 1981, despite the fact that the 1964 Constitution had already established autonomy over the management of its internal affairs (internal self-government). This relatively long process of gaining independence can be explained, in part, by Guatemala's intention to annex the territory, even hinting at the possibility of an invasion. Great Britain maintained an armed presence in the country even after Guatemala had recognized Belize's independence in 1986. As early as 1982, Belize reached an agreement with the USA on military aid.

Belize is characterized by its ethnic diversity. In 2002, around 25% of the population was Black and Mulatto (Creoles), 49% was Mestizo, 11% Mayan, and 6% Garifunan. Small groups of Hindus, Arabs, and Chinese also made up part of the population. In comparative terms, however, the development of the party system was not greatly affected by this ethnic diversity. Notwithstanding this, the alignment with ethnic interests was a relevant factor in shaping party preferences.

The People's United Party (PUP), the first modern party in the colony, had its ideological and material basis in the union movement, which began in the mid-1940s. Soon after the PUP had been founded, it began to control the union movement politically. The PUP is the only party in the country that has existed continuously since the 1950s. Before 1984, the PUP dominated the electoral scene for more than 30 years and was the party in power when Belize gained independence in 1981. With the exception of the 1984 and 1993 elections, the PUP won all the elections from 1954 to 2003. From 1956 to 1996 the party was led by George Price, who was prime minister in 1961 and, when the 1964 Constitution changed the position's title, the premier. He was also the first head of government after independence.

A two-party system began to emerge with the foundation of the National Independence Party (NIP). This party was created in 1958 out of an alliance between two smaller parties and was conceived as opposition against the PUP. In 1973, the NIP's alliance with other political groups resulted in the foundation of the United Democratic Party (UDP), which did not assume power until 1984, headed by Manuel Esquivel.

The main differences between the PUP's and the UDP's stance concerned foreign policy. The PUP was anti-colonialist, defending national independence and a closer relationship with Central America. They received most of their support from the mestizo section of the population. The UDP was opposed to a hasty separation from the metropolis and was in favor of joining the British West Indies Federation. It represented the interests of the Afro-Creole people in particular, who belonged to the privileged middle-classes. These conflicts led to violent disturbances in the country, stirred up by the UDP eventually to a state of siege, before the declaration of independence in 1981.

In the general election of November 1979, the PUP ran on a platform endorsing independence. The UDP wanted instead to delay independence until the territorial dispute with Guatemala was resolved. Although the PUP won only 52% of the vote, it gained 13 of the 18 seats in the house of representatives and thus received a mandate for the preparation of an independence constitution. The national assembly passed the new constitution, the governor gave his assent on 20 September 1981, and Belize became independent the following day. Shortly after independence, faced with the Guatemalan threat and not knowing how long the British military might remain in Belize, Price's government was forced to tighten its links with the USA, a measure that received the support of the UDP.

Regarding the economic development of the country, the PUP, with leaders from the privileged middle-class, advocated equal opportunity and better living conditions, especially for the Afro-Creole urban lower classes. Price's proposal consisted basically of a mixed economic policy. The initial stances of the UDP and the PUP were fairly similar in this respect. But since 1984, during its time in government, the UDP limited state activity in the economic sector and boosted private economy. Infighting within the PUP is considered a basic factor contributing to the party's defeat.

After the 1989 elections, the PUP was returned to power, but only with a narrow majority of 15 parliamentary seats compared to 13 for the

UDP. This unprecedented majority ever since the beginning of internal self-governance highlighted the need for internal cohesion within the PUP. As was customary, Price appointed all the parliamentary members of his party as either ministers or interim ministers. Price's PUP government steered a course similar to his predecessor's: encouraging agricultural exports and expanding textile manufacturing. By 1992, Belize's economy was suffering due to the worldwide recession.

Confident about the 1993 elections, Price decided to call a general election before the end of his term. Shortly after this fateful decision, a series of events occurred in rapid succession that contributed to his government's defeat on 30 June. The UDP won the elections and Manuel Esquivel was sworn in again as prime minister.

The PUP won the 1998 elections and Said Musa became the new prime minister. Three political parties made up the house of representatives: the ruling UDP, with 15 seats; the NABR (National Alliance for Belize Right), which formed a coalition with the UDP, with one seat; and the opposition PUP with 13 seats. The People's Democratic Party was not represented in the house of representatives. Parliamentary elections were held on 5 March 2003 and the PUP repeated their electoral victory of 1998. The PUP won with 53.2% of the vote, compared with 45.6% for the UDP.

1.2 Evolution of Electoral Provisions

Belize's constitutional and political institutions are based on British traditions from the time when settlers brought with them the rights and immunities they had enjoyed in their native country. British common law included the tradition of recognizing the executive power of the Crown in settlements overseas, but the Settlement of Belize in the Bay of Honduras (renamed British Honduras in 1862 and Belize in 1973) enjoyed its own legislative competence. In 1871, however, it surrendered its legacy of self-government and abolished its elected legislature in order to obtain greater economic and political security as a Crown colony.

Resenting the pressure that had been brought to bear upon them to grant reserve powers, the unofficial members of the legislative council successfully lobbied for the inclusion of elected members, as had been offered when the council agreed to grant the governor reserve powers. In 1936, five of the seven unofficial posts of the twelve-member council became elected ones. In 1939, the council expanded to 13, the new member being an elected one. The mix of official and appointed members was changed several times before the council was replaced in 1954.

However, introducing elections for council members did not lead to mass political participation. Property requirements for voters and candidates effectively excluded non-white people from government. And until 1945, women could not vote before the age of 30, while men could vote when they turned 21. In 1947, the legislative council appointed a commission of enquiry to make recommendations for constitutional reforms. The commission issued its report in 1952 and recommended moving slowly ahead with reforms, paving the way for opening the political system to greater popular participation.

Universal, equal, secret, and direct suffrage was established for the elections to the legislative council in 1954. The new constitution also replaced the legislative council by a legislative assembly that had nine elected, three official, and three appointed members and established an executive council chaired by the governor. The nine members of the council were drawn from the legislative assembly and included the three official members, two appointed members, and four elected members chosen by the assembly. The governor was required to abide by the advice of the executive council but he still held reserve powers and controlled the introduction of financial measures into the legislature. In 1955 a quasi-ministerial government was established when three of the elected members of the executive council were given responsibility for overseeing three government ministries.

In 1959, British Honduras undertook another constitutional review and the reforms took effect in March 1961. As a result of the review, the composition of the legislative assembly and executive council changed. In the 25-member assembly, 18 members were now to be elected from single-member districts, five were to be appointed by the governor (three of these after consultation with the majority and minority party leaders), and two were to be official members. Assembly members served a term of four years. The eight-member executive council included the assembly's majority-party leader, who was appointed by the governor as first minister. Two council members were to be official members and five unofficial members were to be elected by the assembly. Five ministerial posts, including that of first minister, carried portfolios.

The constitution of 1 January 1964, which established full internal self-government, introduced a bicameral system. The members of the chamber of deputies were directly elected and the eight senators were appointed by the British governor.

1.3 Current Electoral Provisions

Sources: The constitution (21 September 1981) contains several fundamental principles, the individual provisions are recorded in detail in the
Electoral Law (*Representation of the People Ordinance*, 29 March
1978, last amendment 7 July 1998). The 1981 Constitution created a bicameral legislature (national assembly) consisting of a house of representatives and a senate. A governor general, appointed by the Queen of
England, serves as her representative and as the executive authority of
the government. The house of representatives consists of 29 members,
the senate of eight. The governor general appoints a prime minister, who
is a member of the house of representatives and is the leader of the political party or coalition that constitutes a majority in the house. The
term of office for members of the house of representatives may not exceed five years, and new elections must be held within three months of
the dissolution of the national assembly.

Suffrage: The principles of universal adult suffrage apply. The suffrage
is universal, equal, secret, and direct in the elections to the chamber of
deputies. All citizens have the right to vote, provided they are 18 years
old, a citizen of Belize, the Commonwealth or domiciled in the country
for at least one year before polling day, and are registered. The mentally
infirm, bankrupts, those who have committed electoral fraud, people
sentenced to death or who are serving prison sentences of more than one
year are disqualified from voting. The vote is not compulsory.

Elected national institutions: The national assembly is a bicameral legislature composed of an elected house of representatives and an appointed
senate. The 29 members of the house are popularly elected for a five-
year term. Vacancies arising between general elections are filled
through by-elections. The prime minister has the right to advise the governor general to dissolve the national assembly and so determine the
date of the next general election. Of the senate's eight members, five are
elected by the prime minister, two by the leader of the opposition, and
one by the governor general on the advice of the Belize Advisory Council. The senate is headed by a president who is a non-voting member appointed by the governing party.

Nomination of candidates: Qualifications for representatives and senators are similar: all citizens who are entitled to vote are also entitled to be candidates, under certain conditions. To be eligible for either chamber, a person must be a citizen of Belize, at least 18 years old, and have resided in Belize for at least one year immediately prior to his or her nomination (to the house) or appointment (to the senate). Members of the armed forces or the police force are excluded from serving in either chamber. People holding a government office or appointment are prohibited from membership in the house of representatives; they are prohibited from membership in the senate only if the position is connected with the conduct of elections or compilation of the electoral register. People who are party to any contract with the government or the public service must declare the nature of their contract publicly before the election in order to qualify for election to the house. Potential appointees to the senate must make such a disclosure to the governor general before their appointment. Sitting members of the national assembly are also prohibited from holding government contracts unless the house (or the governor general in the case of senators) waives the ban. Allegiance to a foreign state also leads to ineligibility.

Every Belizean citizen who has been resident for at least one year in the country before running as a candidate can be elected for public offices. Among others, the military and members of the police force, as well as those in charge of certain functions related to the electoral process, are prohibited from passive suffrage. The candidates have to make a deposit, which is forfeited if they obtain less than 10% of the votes cast in their constituency.

Electoral system: Plurality system in 29 SMCs.

Organizational context of elections: The constitution of Belize provides for an elections and boundaries commission composed of five members. The chairman and two members are appointed by the governor general on the advice of the prime minister and in consultation with the leader of the opposition. The governor general appoints the remaining two members on the advice of the prime minister and with the agreement of the leader of the opposition. Each member serves for a period of five years. The ministry for home affairs has jurisdiction over the commission, approving its budget and contracts.

The responsibilities of the elections and boundaries commission include registering voters and administering all elections and referenda. Additionally, it may propose new electoral divisions to the national assembly as long as each division has approximately an equal number of eligible voters.

The elections and boundaries commission designates a chief elections officer to be responsible for organizing and administering the registration process. He or she hires and trains the temporary registration officers and the temporary staff contracted to work in the regional offices, and supervises their work. They also receive the completed applications from the regional offices and enter them into the computerized voter registry. Disputes regarding the eligibility of applicants are forwarded to the chief elections officer, who decides whether or not to include those applicants on the registry.

1.4 Commentary on the Electoral Statistics

The electoral data presented in the following tables are taken from the reports of the Supervisor of Elections. These data are considered reliable. The percentages were calculated by the authors. Where no other source is specified, the demographic data correspond to the evaluations—halfway through the year—of the United Nations Organization. Those electoral provisions that are not recorded in the constitution come from secondary sources.

2. Tables

2.1 Dates of National Elections, Referendums and Coups d'Etat

Year[a]	Presidential elections	Parliamentary elections	Elections for Constitutional Assembly	Referendums	Coups d'état
1979		21/11			
1984		14/12			
1989		04/09			
1993		30/06			
1998		27/08			
2003		05/03			

[a] Data collection starts with the last election before independence (21 September 1981).

2.2 Electoral Body 1979–2003

Year	Type of election[a]	Population	Registered voters		Votes cast		
			Total number	% pop.	Total number	% reg. voters	% pop.
1979[b]	R	143,386[b]	50,091	34.9	44,971	89.9	31.4
1984	R	159,000	64,447	40.5	48,311	75.0	30.4
1989	R	178,000	82,556	46.4	59,954	72.6	33.7
1993	R	205,000	98,371	48.0	70,930	72.1	34.6
1998	R	238,000	94,173	39.6	84,876	90.1	35.7
2003	R	256,000	126,261	49.3	99,560	78.9	38.9

[a] R = House of Representatives (lower chamber).
[b] Figure based on the 1980 population census.

2.3 Abbreviations

CDP	Christian Democratic Party
PLF	People's Liberation Front
PUP	People's United Party
NABR	National Alliance for Belize Rights
TPP	Toledo Progressive Party
UDP[a]	United Democratic Party

[a] The UDP was founded in 1974 by the merger of the Liberal Party, the National Independence Party and the People's Development Movement.

2.4 Electoral Participation of Parties and Alliances 1979–2003

Party / Alliance	Years	Elections contested[a]
CDP	1984	1
PUP	1979–2003	6
NABR	1998	2
TPP	1979	1
UDP	1979–2003	6
UDP-NABR	1993	1

[a] Only the number of elections for the lower house is indicated. Total number: 6.

2.5 Referendums

Referendums have not been held.

2.6. Elections for Constitutional Assembly

Elections for constitutional assembly have not been held.

2.7 Parliamentary Elections 1979–2003

Year	1979		1984	
	Total number	%	Total number	%
Registered voters	50,091	–	64,447	–
Votes cast	44,971	89.9	48,311	75.0
Invalid votes	521	1.2	673	1.4
Valid votes	44,450	98.8	47,638	98.6
PUP	23,309	52.4	20,961	44.0
UDP	21,045	47.4	25,756	54.1
TPP	96	0.2	–	–
CDP	–	–	708	1.5
Independents	–	–	213	0.5

Year	1989		1993	
	Total number	%	Total number	%
Registered voters	82,556	–	98,371	–
Votes cast	59,954	72.6	70,930	72.1
Invalid votes	1,003	1.7	499	0.7
Valid votes	58,951	98.3	70,431	99.3
PUP	29,986	50.9	36,082	51.2
UDP	28,900	49.0	–	–
UDP-NABR	–	–	34,306	48.7
Independents	65	0.1	43	0.1

Year	1998		2003	
	Total number	%	Total number	%
Registered voters	94,173	–	126,261	–
Votes cast	84,876	90.1	—	—
Invalid votes	531	0.6	—	—
Valid votes	84,345	99.4	99,560	—
PUP	50,330	59.7	52,934	53.2
UDP	33,237	39.4	45,415	45.6
Others[a]	406	0.5	–	–
Independents	372	0.4	1,211	1.2

[a] PDP: 225 votes; NABR: 174; NTRCP: 7.

2.8 Composition of Parliament 1979–2003

Year	1979		1984		1989		1993	
	Seats	%	Seats	%	Seats	%	Seats	%
	18	100.0	28	100.0	28	100.0	29	100.0
PUP	13	72.2	7	25.0	15	53.6	13	44.8
UDP	5	27.8	21	75.0	13	46.4	16[a]	55.2

[a] In alliance with NABR (one seat).

Year	1998		2003	
	Seats	%	Seats	%
	29	100.0	29	100.0
PUP	26	89.7	22	75.9
UDP	3	10.3	7	24.1

2.9 Presidential Elections

Presidential elections have not been held. The Queen of the United Kingdom is the head of state.

2.10 List of Power Holders 1979–2004

Head of State	Years	Remarks
Queen Elizabeth II	1979–	Represented by the following governors general: Minita Gordon (1981–1993) and Sir Colville N. Young (since 17/11/1993).

Head of Government	Years	Remarks
George Price	1979–1984	Founding member and leader of PUP until 1996. He won an unbroken series of local and national elections until 1984. In 1961 he became first minister. The title changed to Premier in 1964 when London granted Belize internal self-government, and it changed to Prime Minister after independence.
Manuel Esquivel	1984–1989	He was a founding member of the UDP and leader of the party from 1982–1998. His sound fiscal management and encouragement of foreign investment in tourism and manufacturing helped to invigorate the country's economy. However, party wrangling, charges of corruption, and a series of contested party caucuses led to a surprising electoral defeat in 1989.
George Price	1989–1993	Second term. He steered a course similar to his predecessor's by encouraging agricultural exports and expanding textile manufacturing.
Manuel Esquivel	1993–1998	Second term. He quickly made good on several of his campaign promises by introducing free education at all levels and announced structural reforms to depoliticize the public service.
Said Musa	1998–	Leader of PUP since 1996. He has an ambitious plan to encourage economic growth while furthering social development.

3. Bibliography

3.1 Official Sources

Elections and Boundaries Commission, <www.belize-elections.org>.
'Results of General Elections'. *Belize Gazette*, 1 December 1979.
'Results of General Election'. *Belize Gazette*, 20 January 1985.
'Results of General Election'. *Elections and Boundaries Commission,* 7 September 1989.

'Results of General Election'. *Elections and Boundaries Commission*, 6 June 2003.

3.2 Books, Articles, and Electoral Reports

Belize Briefing (1989). 'Election Special'. *Belize Briefing* (London), 36: 1–7.
— (1989). 'PUP Wins Narrow Victory'. *Belize Briefing* (London), 37: 1–7.
Bolland, O. N. (1977). *The Formation of a Colonial Society. Belize from Conquest to Crown Colony.* Baltimore/London: The Johns Hopkins University Press.
— (1986). *Belize, a New Nation in Central America.* Boulder, Colo.: Westview.
Dobson, N. (1973). *A History of Belize.* London: Longman.
Edie, C. J. (ed.) (1994). *Democracy in the Caribbean. Myths and Realities.* London: Praeger.
Fernandez, J. A. (1989). *Belize: Case Study for Democracy in Central America.* Aldershot Hants (Great Britain): Avebury Gower.
Grant, C. H. (1976). *The Making of Modern Belize. Politics, Society, and British Colonialism in Central America.* Cambridge, Mass.: Cambridge University Press.
Illy, H. and Laceur, S. (1995). 'Belize', in D. Nohlen and F. Nuscheler (eds.). *Handbuch der Dritten Welt, Vol. 3* (3rd edn.). *Mittelamerika und Karibik.* Bonn: Dietz, 358–369.
Inter-Parliamentary Union (ed.) (various years). *Chronicle of Parliamentary Elections and Developments.* Geneva: International Centre for Parliamentary Documentation.
Hillebrands, B. (1994). 'Gewöhnung an häufige Machtwechsel? Die Parlamentswahlen von 1993 in Belize'. *Lateinamerika. Analysen, Daten, Dokumentation*, 25/25: 31–38.
Jones, M. (1995). 'A Guide to the Electoral Systems of the Americas'. *Electoral Studies*, 14/1: 5–21.
Nohlen, D. (1996). *Elections and Electoral Systems* (2nd edn.). New Delhi: McMillan.
— (2004). *Wahlrecht und Parteiensystem* (4th edn.). Opladen: Leske + Budrich.
Nohlen, D., et al. (ed.) (1998). *Tratado de derecho electoral comparado de América Latina.* Mexico City: Fondo de Cultura Económica.
Shoman, A. (1987). *Party Politics in Belize 1950–1986.* Belize City: Cubola.
Thorndike, T. (1983). 'Belizean Political Parties: the Independence Crisis and After'. *Journal of Commonwealth and Comparative Politics*, 21/2: 195–211.
Young, A. H. (1994). 'Belize: Challenges to Democracy', in C. J. Edie (ed.), *Democracy in the Caribbean.* Westport, Conn.: Praeger, 113–129.

CANADA

by Ralf Lindner and Rainer-Olaf Schultze[*]

1. Introduction

1.1 Historical Overview

Since Canada was granted independence from the British Empire in 1867, the liberal-democratic institutions of the former colony have displayed a remarkable stability. The Canadian political system is based on British heritage and developed without revolutionary transformations. Due to this evolutionary process, the basic structure of the polity—parliamentary democracy and federalism—remains virtually unchanged to the present day. The recognition of responsible government in Canada was, however, the result of a lengthy political struggle between parts of the settlers and the British administrators. In response to the growing demands for political representation, the government established elected legislative assemblies in the colony with the Constitution Act of 1791. Nevertheless, within this system of representative government, the assemblies' influence on the colonial administration was very limited. By the 1830s, a rudimentary two-party system had evolved, reflecting competing constitutional conceptions: the liberal reformers pushed for autonomy and responsible government, whereas the conservative constitutionalists essentially attended to the British interests and the administrative *élites* of the colony.

Politics in the pre-confederation era also reflected the central socio-political conflict in British North America. During the first decades of British rule, the linguistic-cultural antagonism between the French and Anglo settlers in the colony had become politically salient. After the French settlements were formally ceded to the United Kingdom in 1763, the British also acquired the problem of how to deal with the French-speaking, predominantly roman catholic population residing in the area

[*] The authors are grateful to Beate Winkler who assembled the election data for this article. We also would like to thank Elections Canada for providing the consolidated federal electoral legislation.

that was later called Québec. From the beginning, the governments'
policies towards the French *habitants* oscillated between contradictory
strategies of assimilation and accommodation. Yet, until responsible
government was finally achieved in 1848, the common socio-economic
interests of the agrarian majority of both ethnicities, who felt deprived
of their just political rights by the commercial and administrative *élites*
of the colony, acted as a quite powerful bonding agent between Franco-
and Anglophones. From that time, the dualism of the two national
groups gradually became a characteristic feature of Canadian politics.

Canada's development into a modern state formally began with the
ratification of the British North America Act by the British parliament.
The act united the four British colonies in North America (Ontario,
Québec, Nova Scotia, and New Brunswick) and formally acknowledged
the existence of the Dominion of Canada on 1 July 1867. Among the
numerous political and economic objectives that had led to the birth of
the new federation, the Canadian perception of a potentially expansion-
ist United States of America was clearly one of the most influential factors. In this sense, the founding of Canada was largely motivated in
defiance of US-American values. The new constitution established a
form of government very similar to that of the United Kingdom, repro-
ducing the central institutional arrangements and embedded values of
the Westminster System in Canada. However, other than the British example, political authority and jurisdiction were divided between central
government and the provinces along the lines of interstate federalism.
Today, Canada is subdivided into three semi-autonomous territories and
ten provinces, each operating their own responsible governments. Head
of state and formal executive is the British monarch, represented by the
governor general who mainly fulfils symbolic-ceremonial duties. The
bicameral legislature in Ottawa consists of the upper chamber, the senate, whose members are officially appointed by the Crown on the advice
of the Canadian prime minister. Despite the fact that the senate has formally retained a full set of legislative powers, its role is primarily consultative. The lower chamber, the house of commons, is directly elected
and therefore clearly dominates the legislative process. Formally, the
prime minister and his cabinet are dependent on the majority of the
house. However, due to his/her prerogative to dissolve parliament, the
functional necessity for party discipline and the fusion of executive and
legislative powers, the prime minister enjoys exceptional authority and
control over the policy-making process. Moreover, the principle of parliamentary supremacy is not only restrained by 'prime ministerial government': within the federal division of powers, the supreme court of

Canada has the ability to declare an act of parliament or an act of a provincial legislature *ultra vires*. Parliamentary supremacy is also limited by the entrenchment of individual and group rights in the Canadian Charter of Rights and Freedoms of 1982.

Since Confederation, Canada has experienced two long phases of political stability, which both have been characterized by far-reaching social consensus in central institutions and policies as well as relatively stable party systems. During the transitional phases following each stable period, new policy paradigms replaced the former orientations, and, correspondingly, the patterns of political participation changed.

The first phase (1867–1921) was characterized by the challenges of east west expansion and nation-building. The primary aim of the federal governments was to integrate the former British colonies politically as well as economically. In order to achieve this goal, the so-called First National Policy was initiated in 1878 by John A. Macdonald's Conservative government. This state-driven development strategy was conceived to foster the transcontinental Canadian market with massive public investments in infrastructure programs such as railway construction, and to encourage industrialization by means of protectionism and import substitution. This policy was an important key to Conservative dominance within the two-party system at the federal level, as it quite successfully accommodated the numerous conflicting social interests. Two main factors paved the way to the replacement of the Conservatives as the governing party in 1896: (1) The execution of Louis Riel in 1885, a Francophone *Métis* who was the head of an insurrection in Saskatchewan, outraged the Québécois, aggravating the collective feelings of being discriminated against by the Anglophone majority and provoking a major realignment in the province of Québec in favour of the Liberals. (2) The Liberal Party under Wilfrid Laurier abandoned free trade and started promoting protectionism, which was more in accordance with the popular First National Policy. World War I led to another polarizing conflict. Opposition to universal conscription and Canada's dutiful alliance with Great Britain during the war, which was particularly endorsed by the Conservative government, was mainly aired in Québec. As a consequence, the regional asymmetry of the federal party system was emphasized once more, reinforcing the Liberal stronghold in Québec, but weakening the party's standing in English-speaking parts of the country.

During the 1920s and 1930s, the pre-war pattern of the federal party system changed considerably. The traditional two-party system was replaced by a multi-party system, in which various 'third' parties became notable competitors. The growing social and economic dissatisfaction of the farmers in the western provinces and their perception that both Liberals and Conservatives were merely representatives of the industrial business interests of central Canada was the political foundation for the Progressive Movement. Since then, the political protest of the West has become an additional characteristic of Canadian politics, establishing a regional-economic cleavage next to the ethnic-cultural dimension within the party system. The general elections of 1930 and 1935 were dominated by the economic depression, which was especially devastating for the Canadian farmers. Similar to the development of the Progressive Party in the 1920s, two new parties emerged in the western provinces as protest movements as a result of the economic crisis: the Social Credit Movement (Soc. Cred.), a religious-oriented and paternalistic party, which had its main stronghold in Alberta, established itself on the conservative side of the political spectrum. After two politically quite successful decades mainly at the provincial level, the party was gradually supplanted by the Conservatives in the course of the 1950s and 1960s. The Cooperative Commonwealth Federation (CCF), since 1961 New Democratic Party (NDP), founded in 1932 as an association of various Marxist groups and farmers' organizations, was the answer of the left to the depression. This social-democratic party, representing the class cleavage, eventually became the most influential third party within the federal party system until the 1990s. However, due to the multiple fragmentation of the class cleavage within the Canadian context, the CCF/NDP was never able to capture more than about 20% of the popular vote at the federal level.

The depression of the early 1930s not only changed the composition of the federal party system, it also revealed the exhaustion of the First National Policy. After an extended phase of policy experimentation and ad hoc modifications, a new economic strategy was introduced in the early 1940s. This so-called Second Nation Policy was largely inspired by Keynesian economics and formed the basis of the modern Canadian welfare state.

The second long period of political stability (1935/45–1980/84) was marked by the expansion of the welfare state on the basis of the Second National Policy and the consolidation of the federal party system, with the Liberals and the (Progressive) Conservatives as the two leading parties. During the post-war era, the Liberals emerged as the 'natural party of government'. Nine of the 13 federal governments between 1945 and 1980 were headed by Liberal prime ministers. The Liberal dominance was largely based on the party's ability to gather sufficient electoral support in Québec as well as in the Anglophone provinces. Conversely, the Conservatives' performance in Québec never went beyond short-lived success. In 1958, the Tories and their charismatic leader John Diefenbaker were able to win majorities in all regions of Canada—including Québec. However, as early as 1963 the federal party system returned to the general pattern of the previous electoral phase. Nevertheless, after the 'Diefenbaker interlude' the Liberal dominance was somewhat weaker, as the electoral gap between the two major parties decreased. Consequently, the parliamentary strength of the Liberals was curtailed, which necessitated the formation of three Liberal minority governments during the 1960s and 1970s. As subsequent election outcomes illustrate, the Diefenbaker years significantly accentuated the regional disparities of the parties, consolidating the Liberal stronghold in central Canada and extending the Conservative support in the eastern and western parts of the country. With the growing cultural and political self-confidence of the Québécois in the 1960s, the independence issue and the threat of separatism became a central theme of Canadian politics. The federal governments sought to enhance national integration by implementing the official federal policies of bilingualism and multiculturalism.

In the late 1970s, the Liberal government under Prime Minister Pierre E. Trudeau faced increasing economic and political difficulties. The steep rise in unemployment due to the oil crisis and the international recession put the government under severe pressure. Similar to the situation in the 1930s, the economic potential of the Second National Policy had expired. After the nine-month interregnum of a weak Progressive Conservative (Prog. Con.) minority government in 1980, the Trudeau-Liberals returned to office and attempted to implement an ambitious economic strategy that was based on centralized interventionism and resource development. The so-called Third National Policy failed both economically and politically as it attracted fierce opposition from nearly every social group. This was particularly damaging for the Liberals, as they had hoped to utilize the economic strategy to reverse the trend of decentralization within the federal-provincial distribution of powers, which had continuously been weakening Ottawa during the previous 20 years. A cornerstone of the Liberal project to foster national integration was the patriation of the constitution and the enactment of the Charter of Rights and Freedoms (1982). After the unsuccessful but nevertheless polarizing 'sovereignty association' Referendum in Québec in 1980, Trudeau was determined to countervail the growing centrifugal tendencies in the federation by introducing a constitution which was to guaran-

tee far-reaching rights for all Canadians. However, after lengthy negotiations between Ottawa and the provinces, Québec rejected the constitutional compromise.

The first indicators that the second long phase of political stability
was coming to an end became apparent in the late 1970s/early 1980s.
After a transitional phase, a new consensus emerged in the economic
realm. However, due to fundamental changes in the party system in the
1990s, it remains uncertain as to whether Canada has entered a third
phase of political stability.

The 1984 general election produced a landslide victory for the Progressive Conservatives and their leader Brian Mulroney. During the following nine years of Conservative rule, a new economic paradigm was
gradually established. The traditional Canadian approach of shaping the
political economy by applying national development strategies was supplanted by the principles of market-orientation and liberalization (cf. the
1989 Free Trade Agreement with the USA). With his politics of national
reconciliation, Mulroney sought to remedy the unsolved constitutional
conflict. The first attempt failed in 1990 after the provinces Newfoundland and Manitoba refused to ratify the Meech Lake Accord. The second
proposal for constitutional reform, the Charlottetown Accord, was decided upon in a national referendum in 1992. Again, the reform failed,
but this time it was rejected by a majority of the Canadian voters.

The increasing dissatisfaction with the Canadian *classe politique* became even more evident in the 1993 general election. The federal party
system experienced a dramatic reshuffling of the patterns of popular
support. On the basis of a manufactured majority, the Liberal Jean Chré-
tien was elected prime minister. Both Conservatives and NDP suffered
most damaging losses. The changes of 1993 were linked to the appearance of two new competitors in the electoral arena: the separatist *Bloc
Québécois* (BQ), a new party which only fielded candidates at the federal level in Québec, captured nearly three quarters of the seats in the
province. The second new contender, the right-wing populist Reform
Party (Ref.) of Canada (between 2000 and 2003 Canadian Alliance,
CA), attained 19% of the vote and won seats predominantly in the western provinces. By and large, this overall pattern of electoral support was
repeated in the general elections of 1997 and 2000. After winning three
consecutive parliamentary majorities with pluralities of the popular vote,
the Liberals had to form a minority government as a result of the 38th
general election in 2004. To some extent, the ruling party's seat losses
were related to the consolidation of the two major right-of-centre parties, as the conservative competitors—the CA and the Progressive Con-

servatives—had formed the new Conservative Party of Canada in 2003. As a consequence of the amplified regionalization of the federal party system since the 1990s, no Canadian party can presently claim to represent all or at least most of the country's regions. The constant threat of national disintegration was put back on the top of the Canadian political agenda in 1995 after the separatist-oriented provincial government in Québec launched the second sovereignty referendum. The independence movement lost the plebiscite by an extremely narrow margin, winning 49.4% of the vote.

Due to the fact that the conflict between Québec and the rest of Canada remains unresolved, the ever-decreasing support for the traditional parties and their brokerage style of politics, together with the citizens' growing appreciation of new forms of participation, attempts to strengthen national cohesion are proving more complicated than ever.

1.2 Evolution of Electoral Provisions

Central elements of the electoral system, which were laid down in the British North America Act of 1867, are still in place today. Without significant variations, both levels of government have applied the single-member district and plurality electoral formula since Confederation. Only some provinces of the West have experimented with other forms in provincial elections (such as preferential voting systems). On the federal level, 'dual' constituencies have been used in some instances.

The evolution of the electoral provisions in Canada occurred in four major steps. (1) In the period prior to 1885, the franchise was limited to white males over the age of 21 who had to meet certain property and income qualifications in order to be eligible to vote. Due to the fact that no agreement could be reached about the regulations concerning the franchise at Confederation in 1867, the respective laws in each of the original provinces were in effect for federal elections. The secret ballot was introduced following the 1874 general election. (2) In 1885, parliament adopted the Electoral Franchise Act. With this act, the Conservative government wanted to reduce the influence of the Liberal provincial governments on the electoral procedures. However, the reform did little to unify the electoral provisions and continued to restrict the franchise on the basis of income and property qualifications. (3) In 1898, the Liberal government repealed the federal legislation, handing down the jurisdiction for electoral legislation to the provinces. In effect, this step removed most income and property qualifications (except in Québec and Nova Scotia) for the franchise. (4) The next significant expansion of the franchise was achieved between 1917 and 1920. The War-time Election Act of 1917, reasserting federal control over the franchise for federal elections, paved the way for female suffrage. Women who served or had close relatives in the forces were granted the right to vote under the act. Universal female suffrage was finally introduced with the 1920 Dominion Elections Act. Despite these important extensions, full universal suffrage was still not completely established. On the grounds of ethnic or racial origin, numerous groups, such as Canadians of Chinese or East Indian descent, were disenfranchised at various times. The right to vote was not extended to Canadians of Japanese origin, for example, until 1948. Aboriginal people were denied universal suffrage until 1960.

Compared to the expansion of the franchise, the right to be a candidate was far less controversial. After 1874, no income or property requirements applied. Since 1873, members of any provincial legislature or the senate are not eligible to stand as a candidate for the house of commons. Until 1970, numerous civil servants were also denied the right to stand for candidacy.

Due to the rapid growth of the country and its population shifts, the distribution of seats between the provinces proved to be a persistent source of political controversy. According to the British North America Act of 1867, the assignment of Commons seats to the provinces and territories had to meet the principle of proportionate representation. The senate, on the other hand, was created in order to represent citizens as members of a provincial community. Accordingly, the constitution requires that seats in the senate be assigned on a 'federal' principle of representation; that is, giving the less populous provinces greater representational—but not equal—weight. However, due to the lacking political legitimacy of the senate, this institution failed to adequately realize its original function within the bicameral parliament. As a consequence, the first chamber was forced to gradually water down the principle of representation by population in order to accommodate the demands of the less populous regions. As Manitoba, British Columbia, and Prince Edward Island joined the Confederation in the 1870s, political bargains entitled the new provinces to greater representation than they would have received under the proportionate rule. In order to protect provinces from the effects of declining relative populations, the Constitution of 1867 provided that a province would not lose seats until its population had declined relative to the total population of Canada by more than 5% since the previous census. In 1915, a constitutional amendment guaranteed a province no fewer seats in the house than it had senators (senate clause).

A new redistribution formula was implemented in 1947. Seats were assigned to the provinces by dividing their population by an electoral quota (which was obtained by dividing the total population of Canada by a fixed number of seats in the house). The 1915 senate clause still applied. During the following decades, the 1947 formula was amended several times, resulting in ever more complicated redistribution provisions. In 1985, the Representation Act set out a new redistribution formula which currently is in effect.

The drawing of the constituency boundaries is closely related to the allocation of seats to the provinces. Until 1964, the majority of the house of commons determined the boundaries of the electoral constituencies. Politically motivated malapportionment, manipulation, and gerrymandering during the readjustment of the boundaries had been rather the rule than the exception until World War I. The Electoral Boundaries Readjustment Act of 1964 instituted an independent and impartial process, introducing an electoral boundaries commission for each province. The act established the principle of comparable population in federal law for the first time. The act was amended in 1986.

In 1970, the Liberal government introduced several reforms of the electoral provisions. Voting age was lowered to 18, and legislation was passed in order to govern the election expenses of parties and candidates and regulate party financing. The next round of electoral reforms was initiated in the late 1990s. Largely based on the proposals of the 1991 report from a federal royal commission, the administration of the election process was modernized and additional restrictions for the funding of parties and candidates were introduced. Since the 1930s, nationwide door-to-door enumeration had been the basis for compiling preliminary voter lists. This massive logistical undertaking, at times involving more than 90,000 enumerators prior to each general election, was replaced by the establishment of a permanent voter list in 2000. The most recent reforms regarding the regime for the financing of federal elections entered force in 2004, thus enhancing the public financing component of the system, prohibiting corporate and trade union contributions to political parties, and expanding the regulation of financial activities of political entities to constituency associations as well as leadership and nomination contestants.

More far-reaching reform proposals regarding the first-past-the-post electoral formula have been on the political agenda several times. Critics argue that the traditional plurality system strengthens the regional basis of the federal party system because it tends to reward those parties that have established regional strongholds. In addition, with seven minority governments out of a total of 19 between 1945 and 2004, the ability of the plurality system to produce sound parliamentary majorities is not fulfilled adequately in the Canadian context. Due to a political culture which largely follows the territorial approach to representation, and due to vested interests of the political class, attempts to incorporate elements of proportional representation in Canada's electoral system have failed thus far. However, as some provinces currently seem to be moving towards mixed systems, successful transformations at the subnational level are likely to spark new debates on electoral reform and open up opportunities for a review of the electoral system (e.g. single transferable vote, fixed election dates etc.) at the federal level as well.

1.3 Current Electoral Provisions

Sources: Canada Act 1982 (U.K.) 1982 c. 11.; Canada Elections Act, S.C. 2000, c. 9.; Constitution Act, 1867, s. 51 and 51A.; Corrupt Practices Inquiries Act, R.S. 1985, c. C-45.; Disfranchising Act, R.S. 1985, c. D-3.; Dominion Controverted Elections Act, 1985, c. C-39.; Electoral Boundaries Readjustment Act, R.S.C. 1985, c. E-3.; Income Tax Act R.S.C. 1985 c. 1.; Referendum Act, S.C. 1992, c. 30.

Suffrage: The principles of universal, equal, direct, and secret suffrage are applied. Every Canadian citizen of 18 years of age or older is entitled to vote in a general election or in a by-election being held in the constituency in which the voter resides. Since 1982, the right to vote is constitutionally guaranteed by the Canadian Charter of Rights and Freedoms (section 3). Regulations concerning compulsory voting are not in effect. For Canadians living abroad or who are temporarily absent from their home constituency, special provisions apply. Under the Canada Elections Act certain individuals are excluded from the franchise: the chief and the assistant chief electoral officers, inmates of correctional institutions serving more than two years, and persons who have been concerned in any offence connected with the elections are prohibited from voting.

Elected national institutions: In the Canadian bicameral parliament, only the house of commons, currently consisting of 308 members (38th Parliament), is directly elected. The prime minister has the exclusive authority to advise the governor general to dissolve parliament and call an election. The maximum term is five years.

Nomination of candidates: Candidates must be eligible to vote in a general election and must be formally nominated. A candidate may run as a representative of a political party, or as an 'independent', or may choose to have no affiliation appearing on the ballot. The nomination requires the signature of 100 eligible voters in the electoral district and a deposit of CAN$ 1,000. The deposit will be fully refunded if the candidate receives at least 15% of the votes cast. There is no legal requirement that the candidates reside in the constituencies in which they are running. However, they must live in Canada. The possibility of re-election and the number of terms allowed are not restricted. The Canada Elections Act disqualifies individuals who are convicted of corrupt election practices during the period of five years after the date the person has been found guilty; certain legal officers of the Crown such as crown attorneys and federally appointed judges, members of the provincial legislatures or territorial assemblies, various election officials such as the chief and the assistant chief electoral officers, and the returning officers.

The chief electoral officer (CEO) must register any political party that files an application for registration. Registration requires the signatures of 100 electors who are members of the party. A party cannot be registered when the CEO is of the opinion that the name or the abbreviation of the party is likely to be confused with an already registered party. A party can be deleted from the registry if it fails to comply with the provisions and duties set out in the Canada Elections Act, such as communicating an annual fiscal return of the party's receipts and expenses to the CEO. Electoral district associations of registered parties are required to be registered separately, and to provide annual financial reports to the CEO.

Election financing: Both contributions to registered parties and individual candidates as well as their expenses are strictly regulated by the Canada Elections Act. The act states that registered parties, registered electoral district associations as well as leadership and nomination contestants of registered parties must submit annual fiscal and election expenses returns, including information such as the sources of money and the commercial value of goods and services provided for, and the names of each donor that made contributions exceeding CAN$ 200. In addition, leadership contestants are required to submit weekly interim reports of their contributions during the last four weeks of the contest.

Nomination contestants are only required to produce a financial report if they have accepted contributions of at least CAN$ 1,000 or have incurred nomination campaign expenses of at least CAN$ 1,000. The amounts which citizens or permanent residents can donate annually are restricted to a maximum of CAN$ 5,000 to each registered party and their affiliated entities (such as registered electoral district associations, candidates and nomination contestants), CAN$ 5,000 per leadership contest in aggregate to the contestants in a leadership race of a registered party, and CAN$ 5,000 per election to a candidate not endorsed by a registered party. Corporations, trade unions, and unincorporated associations are prohibited from making contributions to any registered political party or to any leadership contestant. However, they are allowed to contribute up to CAN$ 1,000 per year in the aggregate to the candidates, nomination contestants and registered electoral district associations of each registered party, and up to CAN$ 1,000 per election to a candidate who is not endorsed by a registered party. Corporations that do not carry on business in Canada, trade unions that do not hold bargaining rights for employees in Canada, Crown corporations, and corporations that receive more than 50% of their funding from the government of Canada are ineligible to make even these restricted contributions. Anonymous donations have to be forwarded to the CEO. Tax credits between 75 and 33.3% of the amount for political contributions are available to the taxpayer; the maximum total deduction is limited to CAN$ 650.

The expenses for a political party's election campaign should not exceed on aggregate the amount obtained by multiplying CAN$ 0.70 for each name appearing on the preliminary or revised lists of electors, whichever is greater, by the inflation adjustment factor published by the CEO each year. The candidates are also subject to a limit on their election expenses. The amount within each electoral district is the aggregate of CAN$ 2.07 for each of the first 15,000 voters on the preliminary lists of electors, CAN$ 1.04 for the next 10,000 names, and CAN$ 0.52 for each of the remaining electors. Increased spending limits apply for candidates running in sparsely populated electoral districts with less than ten electors per square kilometre. The Canada Elections Act also limits the expenses of nomination contestants to 20% of the maximum allowed for a candidate's election expenses in that electoral district during the immediately preceding general election.

Registered political parties that receive at least 2% of the valid votes cast nationally, or 5% of the valid votes cast in the electoral districts in which the party endorsed a candidate, are eligible for a quarterly allowance which, on the basis of a full year, will amount to CAN$ 1.75 per valid vote received by the party in the previous general election. A registered political party is subject to a reimbursement of 50% (60% for the first general election after the coming into force of this regulation on 1 January 2004) of its election expenses if it obtained at least 2% of the valid votes cast at the election, or 5% of the valid votes in the electoral districts in which the party put forward a candidate. Beginning 1 January 2005, parties that receive allowances will be required to submit a quarterly report on contributions and transfers into the party. In order to be eligible to a reimbursement of 60% of his or her actual election expenses, a candidate must have obtained a minimum of 10% of the valid votes cast in the constituency. Both expenses limits and quarterly allowances are annually adjusted for inflation.

The election advertising expenses of third parties, defined as individuals or groups other than a candidate, registered party or electoral district association of a registered party, are limited to CAN$ 150,000 during an election period in relation to a general election, of which no more than CAN$ 3,000 may be spent in any single riding. Third parties spending CAN$ 500 or more are required to register with the CEO during a campaign and to provide financial reports on their advertising expenses during the election period.

Every printed advertisement on behalf of a registered party or candidate must be authorized by the party or the candidate. The sponsors of any advertisement have to be indicated. Every broadcaster must make six and a half hours of broadcasting time available during prime time on its facilities in the period beginning on the issue of the writs and ending at midnight on the day before polling day at a general election. The allocation of paid broadcasting time must give equal weight to the percentage of the popular vote at the previous election of each registered party. In addition, the network operators must make a minimum of free broadcasting time available for each registered party. Again, the allotment of broadcasting time to each registered party is dependent upon the share of the popular vote at the previous election.

Media releasing the results of election opinion surveys have to provide information about the survey methodology, including the survey's sponsor, who conducted it, when it was held, the population from which the survey sample was drawn, the number of people contacted to participate, and the margin of error.

Electoral system: The national electoral system is based on the single-member plurality system ('first-past-the-post'). In each of the currently

308 constituencies (38th Parliament), a single member is elected. In order to fill vacancies in individual constituencies between general elections, by-elections must be held. The same basic rules apply for both types of elections.

Due to the regional disparities of the Canadian federation and its rapid population shifts, the principle of representation by population is modified by various provisions. The allocation of seats per province and in the territories is established using the following formula: (1) The Yukon Territory, the Northwest Territories, and the Territory of Nunavut are entitled to one seat each. (2) Based on 279 seats and the census population data of the ten provinces (excluding the territories), a national electoral quotient is established in order to indicate the average number of voters per seat. (3) The number of seats for each province is calculated on the basis of the quotient. (4) In order to guarantee minimum parliamentary representation for each of the provinces, two provisions are in effect: the senate clause, which was amended in the constitution in 1915, ensures that a province's seats in the house of commons should at least equal the number of senate seats allocated to that province; and the so-called grandfather clause of the Representation Act of 1985, which pegs minimum provincial representation at the 1974 level. According to these formulas, additional seats are allocated to the provinces. (5) To adjust provincial population increases, seats are added. The CEO is responsible for the application and calculation of the formula.

A readjustment of the electoral boundaries takes place after each nationwide decennial census. The governor general establishes impartial electoral-boundaries commissions for each province to assign new seats and redraw the constituency boundaries within their respective entities. According to the Electoral Boundaries Readjustment Act, the commissions are required to be composed of a chairperson who must be a provincial judge, appointed by the chief justice of that province, and two additional members, appointed by the speaker of the house of commons. The population size of any electoral district within a province should not deviate from the provincial quotient, which is obtained by dividing the population of the province by the number of members to be assigned, by more than 25%. However, exceptions are permitted on reasonable grounds in order to respect communities of identity or in order to maintain a manageable geographic size for districts in sparsely populated regions of the province. After an extensive process in which numerous political institutions and the public are invited to comment on the commissions' recommendations, the CEO drafts a representation order which sets down the boundary descriptions established by the commissions' final reports. The draft representation order is then laid out before the house of commons and turned to a parliamentary committee which deals with electoral matters. The committee must consider the matter of any objections and dispose of them. Finally, the CEO submits a representation order—with or without amendments—to the prime minister. By proclamation, the governor general declares the draft representation order to be in force.

Organizational context of elections: The conduct of federal elections and referendums is overseen by the CEO, who carries out the duties set down in the Canada Elections Act. The CEO, with the effective rank of deputy minister, is appointed by special resolution of the house of commons and remains in office until age 65.

For each constituency, the governor general appoints a returning officer (RO). The RO is responsible for managing and administering the election process in the respective electoral district and appoints numerous election officials, such as deputy returning officers, registration officers, revising agents, and the poll clerks for each of the polls within the riding. Registration officers and revising agents are recruited from lists of the registered parties whose candidates finished first and second in the last election in the electoral district. All appointments concerning the administration of the election process have to take place after the election writs are issued.

On the basis of the last nationwide door-to-door enumeration (April 1997), a national register of voters has been established. This preliminary list must be updated regularly from information that electors have expressively authorized to be given to the CEO and other reliable sources such as revised lists of voters from the last election, provincial enumerations, and various federal institutions. On 15 October of each year, the CEO must send an electronic copy of the list of electors to the elected members of parliament and, on request, to each registered party that presented a candidate in that electoral district in the previous election. Immediately after an election writ has been issued, the CEO sends the preliminary lists to each RO and a revision process is initiated. The ROs, aided by the revising agents, are responsible for the registration of applications of electors who wish to be included on the list, corrections, and possible deletions. The revision process terminates on the sixth day before polling day, after which a revised list of electors is issued. Those voters who have been left off the list of electors despite the revision process and who are eligible may register in person on polling day with the deputy returning officer in the polling station where the elector is qualified to vote.

General elections in Canada must be held on Mondays, unless the Monday is a holiday, in which case the day fixed for the poll must be Tuesday of the same week. The minimum time period between the time when the election writs are issued and polling day must be 36 days. On election day, various minor officials and party functionaries are present at each polling station in order to monitor the conduct of the poll and prevent irregularities.

Advance polls are available on specific dates and locations prior to polling day. Canadian citizens residing temporarily outside of Canada, members of the Canadian forces and public servants who are posted outside of Canada may vote by mail-in and special ballot.

The votes are counted immediately after the close of the polls. The deputy returning officer must proceed in the presence of the poll clerk and the candidates or their agents (or at least two electors if none of the candidates are represented).

Where, on the official addition, two or more candidates receive the same number of votes, or the number of votes separating the candidate receiving the highest number of votes and any other candidate is less than one-one thousandth of the votes cast, an automatic recount is initiated. If there are any alleged anomalies during the election, an independent judicial recount may be applied for. The recount is executed by a judge in the presence of the candidates or their agents. The applicant must deposit CAN$ 250 as a security for the costs.

In the polling stations, bilingual services must be available to the public in constituencies where 3% or more of the population is from an official language minority.

Referendums: The opinion of the electors on any question relating to the constitution of Canada may be obtained by the means of a referendum. In order to initiate a consultative referendum, the privy council proposes the text of the referendum question, which has to be approved by the house of commons. If the motion is adopted by parliament—with or without amendment—the CEO issues the writs of referendum. In regard to the conduct and administration of a referendum, most of the basic provisions for general elections are applied accordingly.

1.4 Commentary on the Electoral Statistics

Despite the pronounced federal nature of Canada and the essential role of the sub-national level in electoral politics, the statistics relating to the general elections since 1896 and particularly since the 1920s are remarkably well documented. Thus, the most commonly used sources and reference works, such as the contributions of Scarrow (1962), Beck (1968) or Feigert (1989) and especially the official publications of Statistics Canada (formerly the census and statistics office and the dominion bureau of statistics) and Elections Canada, display a high degree of coherence and accuracy. Up-to-date electoral data and comprehensive information on elections are available on Elections Canada's website <http://www.elections.ca>.

Two main factors have contributed to the overall precision of the data: (1) In 1920, parliament established the office of the chief electoral officer as an independent agency which is responsible for running and supervising federal elections. (2) In addition, the door-to-door enumeration, which was required prior to every general election between 1917 and 1997, ensured the existence of fairly precise voter lists and well-maintained statistical information about the electoral body.

Problems concerning the reliability and accuracy of the election data, especially those statistics relating to the popular vote, have to be taken into account for Canada's early electoral history. Inaccuracies during this era are caused by four main factors: (1) Election returns in some polls and ridings are missing, incomplete, or have not been reported. In particular, the figures concerning the federal elections of 1867 and during the 1870s have to be interpreted with caution. (2) In many instances, the party affiliations of the competing candidates were not, or only partially, recorded. Some of the resulting inconsistencies in the reported data between various sources are based on deviating interpretations of the party labels. These difficulties are mostly reflected by discrepancies in the categories 'other' and 'independent'. (3) In rare instances, the data in the period from 1896 to 1965 have been distorted by the existence of two-member constituencies in some provinces. Slight distortion of results has also been caused by occasional acclamations. (4) As the duty for running the federal elections fell into provincial jurisdiction from 1867 to 1885 and from 1898 to 1917, the provinces applied different voting qualifications, administrative standards, and procedures.

The data presented in Tables 2.2 and 2.5 are nearly exclusively based on official statistics provided by various publications of Statistics Canada and Elections Canada. The total numbers in the category 'votes cast' in Table 2.2 for the years 1867–1891 are taken from Scarrow (1962) and/or Beck (1968), who have provided the most comprehensive reference works for this early electoral period. If available, the figures in the categories 'registered voters', 'votes cast', 'invalid votes' and 'valid votes' of the Tables 2.5 and 2.7 have also been taken from official sources. The data in the category 'valid votes' in the federal elections 1867–1891 are based on Beck (1968). The reported election results in Tables 2.7 and 2.8 are generally taken from official sources, such as the various reports of the chief electoral officer, The Canada Year Book, and the Historical Statistics of Canada. As documentation of the national aggregate for the period 1867 until 1891 is disputed among the most commonly used data collections, returns for these elections are taken from Scarrow (1962) and Beck (1968).

2. Tables

2.1 Dates of National Elections, Referendums, and Coups d'Etat

Year	Presidential elections	Parliamentary elections[a]	Elections for Constitutional Assembly	Referendums	Coups d'état
1867		07/08–20/09			
1872		20/07–12/10			
1874		22/01			
1878		17/09			
1882		20/06			
1887		22/02			
1891		05/03			
1896		23/06			
1898				29/09[b]	
1900		07/11			
1904		03/11			
1908		26/10			
1911		21/09			
1917		17/12			
1921		12/06			
1925		29/10			
1926		14/09			
1930		28/07			
1935		14/10			
1940		26/03			
1942				27/04[b]	
1945		11/06			
1949		27/06			
1953		10/08			
1957		10/06			
1958		31/03			
1962		18/06			
1963		08/04			
1965		08/11			
1968		25/06			
1972		30/10			
1974		08/07			
1979		22/05			
1980		18/02		20/05[c]	
1984		04/09			
1988		21/11			
1992				28/08[b]	
1993		25/10			

Year (cont.)	Presidential elections	Parliamentary elections[a]	Elections for Constitutional Assembly	Referendums	Coups d'état
1995				30/10[c]	
1997		02/06			
2000		27/11			
2004		28/06			

[a] House of commons.
[b] National referendum.
[c] Provincial referendum (Québec).

2.2 Electoral Body 1867–2004

Year	Type of election[a]	Population[b]	Registered voters		Votes cast[c]		
			Total number	% pop.	Total number	% reg. voters	% pop.
1867	Pa	3,485,761	—	—	268,217	—	7.7
1872	Pa	3,547,236	—	—	318,342	—	9.0
1874	Pa	3,641,257	—	—	322,619	—	8.9
1878	Pa	4,268,364	—	—	533,941	—	12.5
1882	Pa	4,268,364	—	—	515,504	—	12.1
1887	Pa	4,833,239	—	—	722,722	—	15.0
1896	Pa	4,833,239	1,358,328	28.1	899,046	66.2	18.6
1896	Pa	5,323,967	1,358,328	25.5	899,046	66.2	16.9
1898	Ref	5,323,967	1,236,419	23.2	543,058	43.9	10.2
1900	Pa	5,323,967	1,167,402	21.9	950,763	81.4	17.9
1904	Pa	5,323,967	1,385,490	26.0	1,030,788	74.4	19.4
1908	Pa	7,200,136	1,463,591	20.3	1,174,709	80.3	16.3
1911	Pa	7,200,136	1,820,742	25.3	1,307,528	71.8	18.2
1917	Pa	7,591,971	2,093,799	27.6	1,885,329	90.0	24.8
1921	Pa	8,760,211	4,435,310	50.6	3,139,306	70.8	35.8
1925	Pa	8,776,352	4,608,636	52.5	3,168,412	68.7	36.1
1926	Pa	8,887,952	4,665,381	52.5	3,273,062	70.2	36.8
1930	Pa	8,887,952	5,153,971	58.0	3,922,481	76.1	44.1
1935	Pa	10,367,063	5,918,207	57.1	4,452,675	75.2	43.0
1940	Pa	10,429,169	6,588,888	63.2	4,672,531	70.9	44.8
1942	Ref	11,494,627	6,502,234	56.6	4,638,847	71.3	40.3
1945	Pa	11,494,627	6,952,445	60.5	5,305,193	76.3	46.2
1949[d]	Pa	11,823,649	7,893,629	66.8	5,903,572	74.8	49.9
1953	Pa	14,003,704	8,401,691	60.0	5,701,963	67.9	40.7
1957	Pa	16,073,970	8,902,125	55.4	6,680,690	75.0	41.6
1958	Pa	16,073,970	9,131,200	56.8	7,357,139	80.6	45.8
1962	Pa	18,238,247	9,700,325	53.2	7,772,656	80.1	42.6
1963	Pa	18,238,247	9,910,757	54.3	7,958,636	80.3	43.6

Year (cont.)	Type of election[a]	Population[b]	Registered voters		Votes cast[c]		
			Total number	% pop.	Total number	% reg. voters	% pop.
1965	Pa	18,238,247	10,274,904	56.4	7,796,728	75.9	42.8
1968	Pa	20,014,880	10,860,888	54.3	8,217,916	75.7	41.1
1972	Pa	21,568,311	13,000,778	60.3	9,974,661	76.7	46.3
1974	Pa	21,568,311	13,620,353	63.2	9,671,002	71.0	44.8
1979	Pa	22,992,604	15,234,997	66.3	11,541,000	75.8	50.2
1980	Pa	22,992,604	15,890,416	69.1	11,015,514	69.3	47.9
1984	Pa	24,343,181	16,775,011	68.9	12,638,424	75.3	51.9
1988	Pa	25,309,331	17,639,001	69.7	13,281,191	75.3	52.5
1992	Ref	27,296,859	18,598,931	68.1	13,888,999	74.7	50.9
1993	Pa	27,296,859	19,906,796	72.9	13,863,135	69.6	50.8
1997	Pa	27,296,859	19,663,478	72.0	13,174,788	67.0	48.3
2000	Pa	28,846,761	21,243,473	73.6	12,997,185	61.2	45.1
2004	Pa	30,007,094	22,466,621	74.9	13,683,570	60.9	45.6

[a] Pa = Parliament (house of commons), Ref = Referendum.
[b] 1867–1908: population of those areas that participated in the election. All population data are based on the census held before or after the respective election year. Between 1871 and 1911, censuses were held every ten years, and between 1911 and 1941 and from 1951 to 1996, they were held every five years.
[c] 1867–1917: valid votes.
[d] Census 1941 plus population established by 1945 Newfoundland census.

2.3 Abbreviations

BPC	*Bloc Populaire Canadien* (Canadian Popular Block)
BQ	*Bloc Québécois* (*Québécois* Block)
CA	Canadian Reform Conservative Alliance (Canadian Alliance)[a, b]
CCF	Cooperative Commonwealth Federation[c]
Con.	Conservative Party[d]
CPC	Conservative Party of Canada[b]
GP	Green Party
Lab.	Labour
Lab. Prog.	Communist Party/ Labour Progressive Party
Lib.	Liberal Party of Canada
NDP	New Democratic Party[c]
Prog. Con.	Progressive Conservative Party[d]
RC	*Ralliement des créditistes du Québec* (Union of *créditistes* of Québec)
Reconstn.	Reconstruction
Ref.	Reform Party[a]
Rhino	Rhinoceros Party
Soc. Cred.	Social Credit

[a] The Reform Party changed its name to Canadian Reform Conservative Alliance in 2000.

[b] The Canadian Alliance and the Progressive Conservative Party merged in 2003, creating the Conservative Party of Canada.
[c] The Cooperative Commonwealth Federation changed its name to New Democratic Party in 1961.
[d] The Conservative Party changed its name to Progressive Conservative Party in 1942.

2.4 Electoral Participation of Parties and Alliances 1867–2004

Party / Alliance	Years	Elections contested[a]
Conservative Party	1867–1940	19
Lib.	1867–2004	38
McCarthyites	1896	1
Patrons of Industry	1896	1
Lab.	1900–1940	11
Lab. Prog.	1921; 1930–1988	19
Progressive Party	1921–1930	4
CCF	1935–1958	7
Reconstn.	1935	1
Soc. Cred.	1935–1988	17
BPC	1945	1
Prog. Con.	1945–2000	18
NDP	1962–2004	14
RC	1965; 1968	2
Rhino	1979–1988	4
GP	1984–2004	6
Ref.	1988–1997	3
BQ	1993–2000	3
CA	2000	1
CPC	2004	1

[a] Elections to the house of commons. Total number: 38.

2.5 Referendums

Year	1898[a]		1942[b]	
	Total number	%	Total number	%
Registered voters	1,236,419	–	6,502,234	–
Votes cast	—	—	4,638,847	71.3
Invalid votes	—	—	50,327	1.1
Valid votes	543,058	—	4,588,520	98.9
Yes	278,487	51.3	2,945,514	64.2
No	264,571	48.7	1,643,006	35.8

[a] Issue: Prohibition of liquor.
[b] Issue: Releasing of government from its 1940 promise of no conscription for overseas military service.

Year	1992[a]			
	Total number	%		
Registered voters	18,598,931	–		
Votes cast	13,888,999	74.7		
Invalid votes	136,730	0.9		
Valid votes	13,752,269	99.0		
Yes	6,191,106	45.0		
No	7,561,163	55.0		

[a] Charlottetown Accord, issue: constitutional amendments.

Year	1980[a]		1995[a]	
	Total number	%	Total number	%
Registered voters	4,367,134	–	5,087,009	–
Votes cast	3,738,854	85.6	4,757,509	93.5
Invalid votes	65,012	1.7	86,501	1.8
Valid votes	3,673,842	98.3	4,671,008	98.2
Yes	1,485,861	40.4	2,308,360	49.4
No	2,187,991	59.6	2,362,648	50.6

[a] Held in Québec; issue: sovereignty.

2.6 Elections for Constitutional Assembly

Elections for a constitutional assembly have not been held.

2.7 Parliamentary Elections, House of Commons 1867–2004

Year	1867		1872	
	Total number	%	Total number	%
Registered voters	—	–	—	–
Votes cast	—	—	—	—
Invalid votes	—	—	—	—
Valid votes	268,217	—	318,342	—
Con.	134,269	50.1	159,006	49.9
Lib.	131,364	49.0	156,365	49.1
Others	2,584	1.0	2,971	0.9

Year	1874 Total number	%	1878 Total number	%
Registered voters	—	–	—	–
Votes cast	—	—	—	—
Invalid votes	—	—	—	—
Valid votes	322,619	—	533,941	—
Lib.	173,477	53.8	247,043	46.3
Con.	146,465	45.4	280,224	52.5
Others	2,677	0.8	6,674	1.2

Year	1882 Total number	%	1887 Total number	%
Registered voters	—	–	—	–
Votes cast	—	—	—	—
Invalid votes	—	—	—	—
Valid votes	515,504	—	722,722	—
Con.	261,293	50.7	362,632	50.2
Lib.	241,400	46.8	352,184	48.7
Others	10,613	2.1	2,730	0.4
Independents	2,198	0.4	5,176	0.7

Year	1891 Total number	%
Registered voters	—	–
Votes cast	—	—
Invalid votes	—	—
Valid votes	778,522	—
Con.	397,731	51.1
Lib.	366,817	47.1
Others	10,316	1.3
Independents	3,658	0.5

Year	1896 Total number	%	1900 Total number	%
Registered voters	1,358,328	–	1,167,402	–
Votes cast	—	—	—	—
Invalid votes	—	—	—	—
Valid votes	899,046	—	950,763	—
Con.	414,838	46.1	450,790	47.4
Lib.	405,185	45.1	487,193	51.2
Patrons of Industry	36,655	4.1	–	–
McCarthyites	17,532	2.0	–	–
Others	8,356	0.9	10,158	1.1
Independents	16,480	1.8	2,622	0.3

Year	1904 Total number	%	1908 Total number	%
Registered voters	1,385,490	–	1,463,591	–
Votes cast	—	—	—	—
Invalid votes	—	—	—	—
Valid votes	1,030,788	—	1,174,709	—
Lib.	536,370	52.0	592,596	50.4
Con.	478,729	46.4	550,351	46.9
Others	12,141	1.3	16,927	1.4
Independents	3,548	0.3	14,835	1.3

Year	1911 Total number	%	1917 Total number	%
Registered voters	1,820,742	–	2,093,799	–
Votes cast	—	—	—	—
Invalid votes	—	—	—	—
Valid votes	1,307,528	—	1,885,329	—
Con.	666,074	50.9	1,074,701	57.0
Lib.	623,554	47.7	751,493	39.9
Others	10,723	0.8	44,682	2.3
Independents	7,177	0.6	14,453	0.8

Year	1921 Total number	%	1925 Total number	%
Registered voters	4,435,310	–	4,608,636	–
Votes cast	3,139,306	70.8	3,168,412	68.7
Invalid votes	15,403	0.5	15,887	0.5
Valid votes	3,123,903	99.5	3,152,525	99.5
Lib.	1,272,660	40.7	1,256,824	39.9
Con.	945,681	30.3	1,465,331	46.5
Progressive Party	714,620	22.9	282,152	9.0
Lab.	71,321	2.3	55,330	1.8
Others	29,089	0.9	69,653	2.1
Independents	90,532	2.9	23,235	0.7

Year	1926		1930	
	Total number	%	Total number	%
Registered voters	4,665,381	–	5,153,971	–
Votes cast	3,273,062	70.2	3,922,481	76.1
Invalid votes	16,554	0.5	23,954	0.6
Valid votes	3,256,508	99.5	3,898,527	99.4
Lib.	1,500,302	46.1	1,761,352	45.2
Con.	1,474,283	45.3	1,903,815	48.8
Progressive Party	171,516	5.3	109,745	2.8
Lab.	48,352	1.5	29,315	0.8
Others	41,038	1.1	68,844	1.7
Independents	21,017	0.7	25,456	0.7

Year	1935		1940	
	Total number	%	Total number	%
Registered voters	5,918,207	–	6,588,888	–
Votes cast	4,452,675	75.2	4,672,531	70.9
Invalid votes	45,821	1.0	52,271	1.1
Valid votes	4,406,854	99.0	4,620,260	98.9
Lib.	1,975,841	44.8	2,381,443	51.5
Con.	1,305,565	29.6	1,416,230	30.7
CCF	387,056	8.8	393,230	8.5
Reconstn.	384,095	8.7	–	–
Soc. Cred.	180,301	4.1	123,033	2.7
Others	158,231	3.6	251,472	5.4
Independents	15,765	0.4	54,852	1.2

Year	1945		1949	
	Total number	%	Total number	%
Registered voters	6,952,445	–	7,893,629	–
Votes cast	5,305,193	76.3	5,903,572	74.8
Invalid votes	59,063	1.1	54,601	0.9
Valid votes	5,246,130	98.1	5,848,971	99.1
Lib.	2,146,330	40.9	2,897,662	49.5
Prog. Con.	1,435,747	27.4	1,736,226	29.7
CCF	816,259	15.6	782,410	13.4
Soc. Cred.	214,998	4.1	135,217	2.3
BPC	186,822	3.6	–	–
Communist Party	109,768	2.1	–	–
Others	51,297	1.0	175,459	3.0
Independents	284,909	5.4	121,997	2.2

Year	1953 Total number	%	1957 Total number	%
Registered voters	8,401,691	–	8,902,125	–
Votes cast	5,701,963	67.9	6,680,690	75.0
Invalid votes	60,691	1.1	74,710	1.1
Valid votes	5,641,272	98.9	6,605,980	98.9
Lib.	2,751,307	48.8	2,702,573	40.9
Prog. Con.	1,749,579	31.0	2,572,926	38.9
CCF	636,310	11.3	707,659	10.7
Soc. Cred.	305,551	5.4	436,663	6.6
Others	140,360	2.5	107,848	1.6
Independents	58,165	1.0	78,311	1.2

Year	1958 Total number	%	1962 Total number	%
Registered voters	9,131,200	–	9,700,325	–
Votes cast	7,357,139	80.6	7,772,656	80.1
Invalid votes	69,842	0.9	82,522	1.1
Valid votes	7,287,297	99.1	7,690,134	98.9
Prog. Con./ Con.	3,908,633	53.6	2,865,582	37.3
Lib.	2,447,909	33.6	2,861,834	37.2
CCF	692,398	9.5	–	–
NDP	–	–	1,036,853	13.5
Soc. Cred.	–	–	896,574	11.7
Others	223,630	3.1	22,946	0.3
Independents	14,727	0.2	6,345	0.1

Year	1963 Total number	%	1965 Total number	%
Registered voters	9,910,757	–	10,274,904	–
Votes cast	7,958,636	80.3	7,796,728	75.9
Invalid votes	64,560	0.8	83,412	1.1
Valid votes	7,894,076	99.2	7,713,316	98.9
Lib.	3,293,790	41.7	3,099,519	40.2
Prog. Con.	2,591,614	32.8	2,499,913	32.4
NDP	1,037,857	13.1	1,381,658	17.9
Soc. Cred.	940,703	11.9	282,454	3.7
RC	–	–	359,438	4.7
Others	24,876	0.3	38,848	0.5
Independents	5,236	0.1	51,486	0.7

Year	1968		1972	
	Total number	%	Total number	%
Registered voters	10,860,888	–	13,000,778	–
Votes cast	8,217,916	75.7	9,974,661	76.7
Invalid votes	91,920	1.1	307,172	3.1
Valid votes	8,125,996	98.9	9,667,489	96.9
Lib.	3,696,945	45.5	3,718,258	38.5
Prog. Con.	2,554,880	31.4	3,383,530	35.0
NDP	1,378,260	17.0	1,713,528	17.7
Soc. Cred.	–	–	737,972	7.6
RC	361,045	4.4	–	–
Others	98,725	1.2	58,600	0.6
Independents	36,141	0.4	55,601	0.6

Year	1974		1979	
	Total number	%	Total number	%
Registered voters	13,620,353	–	15,234,997	–
Votes cast	9,671,002	71.0	11,541,000	75.7
Invalid votes	165,094	1.7	85,298	0.7
Valid votes	9,505,908	98.3	11,455,702	99.3
Lib.	4,102,776	43.2	4,594,319	40.1
Prog. Con.	3,369,335	35.4	4,111,559	35.9
NDP	1,467,748	15.4	2,048,779	17.9
Soc. Cred.	481,231	5.1	527,604	4.6
Others	46,073	0.5	142,733	1.2
Independents	38,745	0.4	30,708	0.3

Year	1980		1984	
	Total number	%	Total number	%
Registered voters	15,890,416	–	16,775,011	–
Votes cast	11,015,514	69.3	12,638,424	75.3
Invalid votes	67,600	0.6	89,703	0.7
Valid votes	10,947,914	99.4	12,548,721	99.3
Lib.	4,853,914	44.3	3,516,486	28.0
Prog. Con.	3,552,994	32.5	6,278,697	50.0
NDP	2,164,987	19.8	2,359,915	18.8
Others	361,889	3.3	372,115	3.0
Independents	14,130	0.1	21,508	0.2

Year	1988				
	Total number	%			
Registered voters	17,639,001	–			
Votes cast	13,281,191	75.3			
Invalid votes	105,592	0.8			
Valid votes	13,175,599	99.2			
Prog. Con.	5,667,563	43.0			
Lib.	4,205,072	31.9			
NDP	2,685,308	20.4			
Others	594,776	4.5			
Independents	22,880	0.2			

Year	1993		1997	
	Total number	%	Total number	%
Registered voters	19,906,796	–	19,663,478	–
Votes cast	13,863,135	69.6	13,174,788	67.0
Invalid votes	195,464	1.4	188,824	1.4
Valid votes	13,667,671	98.6	12,985,964	98.6
Lib.	5,647,952	41.3	4,994,377	38.5
Ref.	2,559,245	18.7	2,513,070	19.4
Prog. Con.	2,186,422	16.0	2,446,705	18.8
BQ	1,846,024	13.5	1,385,821	10.7
NDP	939,575	6.9	1,434,509	11.0
Others	428,019	3.1	150,723	1.2
Independents	60,434	0.4	60,759	0.5

Year	2000		2004	
	Total number	%	Total number	%
Registered voters	21,243,473	–	22,466,621	–
Votes cast	12,997,185	61.2	13,683,570	60.9
Invalid votes	139,412	1.1	118,868	0.9
Valid votes	12,857,773	98.9	13,564,702	99.1
Lib.	5,252,031	40.8	4,982,220	36.7
CA	3,276,929	25.5	–	–
Prog. Con.	1,566,998	12.2	–	–
CPC	–	–	4,019,498	29.6
BQ	1,377,727	10.7	1,680,109	12.4
NDP	1,093,868	8.5	2,127,403	15.7
GP	104,402	0.8	582,247	4.3
Others	168,373	1.3	155,429	1.2
Independents	17,445	0.1	17,796	0.1

2.8 Composition of the House of Commons 1867–2004

Year	1867		1872		1874		1878	
	Seats	%	Seats	%	Seats	%	Seats	%
	180	100.0	200	100.0	206	100.0	206	100.0
Con.	108	60.0	104	52.0	67	32.5	142	68.9
Lib.	72	40.0	96	48.0	138	67.0	64	31.1
Others	–	–	–	–	1	0.5	–	–
Independents	–	–	–	–	1	0.5	–	–

Year	1882		1887		1891		1896	
	Seats	%	Seats	%	Seats	%	Seats	%
	211	100.0	215	100.0	215	100.0	213	100.0
Con.	139	65.9	126	58.6	121	56.3	88	41.3
Lib.	71	33.6	89	41.4	94	43.7	118	55.4
Patrons of Industry	–	–	–	–	–	–	2	0.9
McCarthyites	–	–	–	–	–	–	4	1.9
Others	1	0.5	–	–	–	–	–	–
Independents	–	–	–	–	–	–	1	0.5

Year	1900		1904		1908		1911	
	Seats	%	Seats	%	Seats	%	Seats	%
	213	100.0	214	100.0	221	100.0	221	100.0
Lib.	133	62.4	138	64.5	135	61.1	87	39.4
Con.	80	37.6	75	35.0	85	38.5	134	60.6
Others	–	–	1	0.5	1	0.4	–	–
Independents	–	–	–	–	–	–	–	–

Year	1917	
	Seats	%
	235	100.0
Con.	153	65.1
Lib.	82	34.9
Others	–	–
Independents	–	–

Year	1921		1925		1926		1930	
	Seats	%	Seats	%	Seats	%	Seats	%
	235	100.0	245	100.0	245	100.0	245	100.0
Lib.	116	49.4	99	40.4	128	52.2	91	37.1
Progressive Party	64	27.2	24	9.8	20	8.2	12	4.9
Con.	50	21.3	116	47.3	91	37.1	137	55.9
Lab.	2	0.8	2	0.8	3	1.2	2	0.8
Others	1	0.4	2	0.8	1	0.4	–	–
Independents	2	0.8	2	0.8	2	0.8	3	1.2

Year	1935		1940		1945		1949	
	Seats	%	Seats	%	Seats	%	Seats	%
	245	100.0	245	100.0	245	100.0	262	100.0
Lib.	173	70.6	181	73.9	125	51.0	190	72.5
Con./Prog. Con.	40	16.3	40	16.3	67	27.3	41	15.6
Soc. Cred.	17	6.9	10	4.1	13	5.3	10	3.8
CCF	7	2.9	8	3.3	28	11.4	13	5.0
Reconstn.	1	0.4	–	–	–	–	–	–
BC	–	–	–	–	2	0.8	–	–
Others	6	2.4	5	2.0	3	1.2	3	1.1
Independents	1	0.4	1	0.4	7	2.9	5	1.9

Year	1953		1957		1958		1962	
	Seats	%	Seats	%	Seats	%	Seats	%
	265	100.0	265	100.0	265	100.0	265	100.0
Lib.	171	64.5	105	39.6	49	18.5	100	37.7
Prog. Con.	51	19.2	112	42.3	208	78.5	116	43.8
CCF	23	8.7	25	9.4	8	3.0	–	–
Soc. Cred.	15	5.7	19	7.2	–	–	30	11.3
NDP	–	–	–	–	–	–	19	7.2
Others	2	0.7	2	0.7	–	–	–	–
Independents	3	1.1	2	0.8	–	–	–	–

Year	1963		1965		1968		1972	
	Seats	%	Seats	%	Seats	%	Seats	%
	265	100.0	265	100.0	264	100.0	264	100.0
Lib.	129	48.7	131	49.4	155	58.7	109	41.3
Prog. Con.	95	35.8	97	36.6	72	27.3	107	40.5
Soc. Cred.	24	9.1	5	1.9	–	–	15	5.7
NDP	17	6.4	21	7.9	22	8.3	31	11.7
RC	–	–	9	3.4	14	5.3	–	–
Others	–	–	1	0.4	–	–	–	–
Independents	–	–	1	0.4	1	0.4	2	0.8

Year	1974		1979		1980		1984	
	Seats	%	Seats	%	Seats	%	Seats	%
	264	100.0	282	100.0	282	100.0	282	100.0
Lib.	141	53.4	114	40.4	147	52.1	40	14.2
Prog. Con.	95	36.0	136	48.2	103	36.5	211	74.8
NDP	16	6.1	26	9.2	32	11.3	30	10.6
Soc. Cred.	11	4.2	6	2.1	–	–	–	–
Independents	1	0.4	–	–	–	–	1	0.4

Year	1988		1993		1997		2000	
	Seats	%	Seats	%	Seats	%	Seats	%
	295	100.0	295	100.0	301	100.0	301	100.0
Prog. Con.	169	57.3	2	0.7	20	6.6	12	4.0
Lib.	83	28.1	177	60.0	155	51.5	172	57.1
NDP	43	14.6	9	3.1	21	7.0	13	4.3
BQ	–	–	54	18.3	44	14.6	38	12.6
Ref./CA	–	–	52	17.6	60	19.9	66	21.9
Others	–	–	–	–	1	0.3	–	–
Independents	–	–	1	0.3	–	–	–	–

Year	2004	
	Seats	%
	308	100.0
CPC	99	32.1
Lib.	135	43.8
NDP	19	6.2
BQ	54	17.5
Independents	1	0.3

2.9 Presidential Elections

Presidential elections have not been held. Head of state is the monarch of the United Kingdom.

2.10 List of Power Holders 1867–2004

Head of State	Years	Remarks
Queen Victoria	1867–1901	Represented by governor general: Viscount Monck (1861–1869), Sir John Young (1869–1872), Earl of Dufferin (1872–1878), Marquis of Lorne (1878–1883), Marquis of Lansdowne (1883–1888), Baron Stanley of Preston (1888–1893), Earl of Aberdeen (1893–1898), Earl of Minto (1898–1901).
King Edward VII	1901–1910	Represented by governor general: Earl of Minto (1901–1904), Earl Grey (1904–1910).
King George V	1910–1936	Represented by governor general: Earl Grey (1910–1911), H.R.H. Duke of Connaught (1911–1916), Duke of Devonshire (1916–1921), Viscount Willingdon of Ratton (1926–1931), Earl of Bessborough (1931–1935), Lord Tweedsmuir of Elsfield (1935–1936).
King Edward VIII	1936	Represented by governor general: Lord Tweedsmuir of Elsfield (1936).
King George VI	1936–1952	Represented by governor general: Lord Tweedsmuir of Elsfield (1936–1940), Earl of Athlone (1940–1946), Viscount Alexander of Tunis (1946–1952).
Queen Elizabeth II	1952–present	Represented by governor general: Viscount Alexander of Tunis (1952), Vincent Massey (1952–1959), Georges Vanier (1959–1967), Roland Michener (1967–1974), Jules Léger (1974–1979), Edward Schreyer (1979–1984), Jeanne Sauvé (1984–1990), Ramon J. Hnatyshyn (1990–1995), Roméo LeBlanc (1995–1999), Adrienne Clarkson (1999–present).

Head of Government	Years	Remarks
John Alexander Macdonald	1867–1873	Con. Territorial consolidation, railway construction. Resigned due to railway scandal.
Alexander Mackenzie	1873–1878	Liberal. Institutional reforms. Electoral defeat.
John Alexander Macdonald	1878–1891	Con. First National Policy (developmental strategy, import substitution, trans-Canada railway, western settlement). Died in office.
John Joseph Caldwell Abbott	1891–1892	Con. Resignation (removed by Conservative caucus).
John Sparrow David Thompson	1892–1894	Con. Politico-religious dispute (Manitoba school question). Died in office.

Head of Government (continued)	Years	Remarks
Mackenzie Bowell	1894–1896	Con. Dispute on Manitoba school question. Resignation due to party-leadership problems.
Charles Tupper	1896	Conservative. Electoral defeat.
Wilfrid Laurier	1896–1911	Lib. Long phase of economic prosperity. Electoral defeat due to reciprocal trade agreement with the US and naval contributions to the Empire.
Robert Laird Borden	1911–1920	Con. Conscription crisis, war coalition (1917–1918). Resignation.
Arthur Meighen	1920–1921	Con. Emergence of the Progressive Movement. Electoral defeat.
William Lyon Mackenzie King	1921–1926	Lib. Dispute on tariffs and trade, agrarian protests. Two minority governments. Charges of maladministration. Requested dissolution in order to avoid vote of censure and resigns forthwith (improper constitutional practice).
Arthur Meighen	1926	Con. Interim prime minister. Minority government. Electoral defeat.
William Lyon Mackenzie King	1926–1930	Lib. Disputes on trade policy. Electoral defeat.
Richard Bedford Bennett	1930–1935	Con. Depression. Multi-party system emerges (CCF, Soc. Cred.). Electoral defeat.
William Lyon Mackenzie King	1935–1948	Lib. First phase of Second National Policy (Keynesian macro-economics, welfare state). Resignation.
Louis Stephen St. Laurent	1948–1957	Lib. Institutionalization of the welfare state. Electoral defeat.
John George Diefenbaker	1957–1963	Prog. Con. 'Diefenbaker interlude'. Minority governments 1957–1958 and 1962–1963. Electoral defeat.
Lester Bowles Pearson	1963–1968	Lib. Two minority governments. Resignation.
Pierre Elliott Trudeau	1968–1979	Lib. National integration through bilingualism, multiculturalism and 'just society'. Minority government 1972–1974. Electoral defeat.
Joseph Clark	1979–1980	Prog. Con. Minority government. Electoral defeat.
Pierre Elliott Trudeau	1980–1984	Lib. Patriation of the constitution, Charter of Rights and Freedoms, experiments with increased state-interventionism (policy programme of so-called 'Third National Policy'). Resignation.
John Napier Turner	1984	Lib. Electoral defeat.

Head of Government Years (continued)		Remarks
Martin Brian Mulroney	1984–1993	Prog. Con. Neo-conservative dismantling of the welfare state; market-driven continental economic strategy (FTA); politics of 'national reconcilia-tion' and constitutional reform failures (Meech Lake Accord, Charlottetown Accord). Resignation.
Avril Kim Campbell	1993	Prog. Con. Electoral defeat.
Jean Joseph Jacques Chrétien	1993–2003	Lib. Deficit reduction, continental market integration (NAFTA). Increased regionalization of the party-system (Ref./CA, BQ). Resignation.
Paul Edgar Philippe Martin	2003–	Lib. Minority government in 38th Parliament.

3. Bibliography

3.1 Official Sources

Census and Statistics Office (various publishers) (1906–1917). *The Canada Year Book* (1906–1917). Ottawa.

Chief Electoral Officer (various years). *Federal Electoral Legislation*. Ottawa: Elections Canada.

— (1996). *Canada's Electoral System. Strengthening the Foundation. Annex to the Report of the Chief Electoral Officer of Canada on the 35th General Election*. Ottawa: Elections Canada.

— (various years). *Official Voting Results*. Ottawa: Minister of Supply and Services Canada.

Dominion Bureau of Statistics (various publishers) (1918–1972). *The Canada Year Book* (1918–1972). Ottawa.

Elections Canada (various years). *Annual Reports of the Chief Electoral Officer*. Ottawa: Minister of Supply and Services Canada.

— (various years). *Electoral Insight* (various issues).

Pelletier, A. (1999). *Compendium of Election Administration in Canada*. Ottawa: Elections Canada.

Royal Commission on Electoral Reform and Party Financing (1991). *Reforming Electoral Democracy*, Final Report (vols. 1 & 2). Ottawa: Ministry of Supply and Services Canada.

— (1991). *Proposed Legislation*, Final Report (vol. 3). Ottawa: Ministry of Supply and Services Canada.

Statistics Canada (various years). *Census of Canada: Population*. Ottawa: Ministry of Supply and Services Canada.

— (1973–2002). *The Canada Year Book* (1973–2002). Ottawa.

— (1983). *Historical Statistics of Canada* (2nd edn.). Ottawa: Canadian Government Publication Centre.

3.2 Books, Articles, and Electoral Reports

Atkinson, M. M. (ed.) (1993). *Government Canada: Institutions and Public Policy*. Toronto: Hartcourt Brace Jovanovice.

Aucoin, P. (ed.) (1985). *Party Government and Regional Representation in Canada*. Toronto: University of Toronto Press.

Bakvis, H. (ed.) (1991a). *Canadian Political Parties. Leaders, Candidates and Organization*. Toronto: Dundurn Press.

— (ed.) (1991b). *Representation, Integration and Political Parties in Canada*. Toronto: Dundurn Press.

— (ed.) (1991c). *Voter Turnout in Canada*. Toronto: Dundurn Press.

Beck, J. M. (1968). *Pendulum of Power. Canada's Federal Elections*. Scarborough: Prentice Hall.

Blais, A. et al. (2002). *Anatomy of a Liberal Victory: Making Sense of the Vote in the 2000 Canadian Election*. Peterborough: Broadview Press.

Blake, D. E. (1985). *Two Political Worlds: Parties and Voting in British Columbia*. Vancouver: University of British Columbia Press.

Boyer, J. P. (1982). *Political Rights and the Legal Framework of Elections in Canada*. Toronto: Butterworths.

— (1992). *The People's Mandate: Referendums and a More Democratic Canada*. Toronto: Dundurn.

Brodie, J. and Jenson, J. (1988). *Crisis, Challenge and Change: Party and Class in Canada Revisited*. Ottawa: Carleton University Press.

Cairns, A. C. (1968). 'The Electoral and Party System in Canada, 1921-65'. *Canadian Journal of Political Science*, 1/1: 55–88.

Carty, R. K. et al. (2000). *Rebuilding Canadian Party Politics*. Vancouver: University of British Columbia Press.

Cassidy, M. (ed.) (1991). *Democratic Rights and Electoral Reform in Canada*. Toronto: Dundurn.

Clarke, H. D. et al. (1996). *Absent Mandate: The Politics of Discontent in Canada*. Toronto: Gage.

Clement, W. (ed.) (1997). *Understanding Canada. Building on the New Canadian Political Economy*. Montréal: McGill-Queen's University Press.

Cross, W. (ed.) 2002. *Political Parties, Representation, and Electoral Democracy in Canada*. Don Mills: Oxford University Press.

Dyck, R. (1991). *Provincial Politics in Canada*. Scarborough: Prentice Hall.

Elkins, D. J. and Simeon, R. (eds.) (1980). *Small Worlds: Provinces and Parties in Canadian Political Life*. Toronto: Methuen.

Feigert, F. (1989). *Canada Votes, 1935 – 1988.* Durham: Duke University Press.

Gagnon, A.-G. and Tanguay, A. B. (eds.) (1996). *Canadian Parties in Transition.* Scarborough: Nelson.

Jackson, J. J. and Jackson, D. (1998). *Politics in Canada. Culture, Institutions, Behaviour and Public Policy* (4th edn.). Scarborough: Prentice Hall.

Johnston, R. et al. (1992). *Letting the People Decide.* Montréal: McGill-Queen's University Press.

Landes, R. G. (1995). *The Canadian Polity. A Comparative Introduction.* Scarborough: Prentice Hall.

Lovink, J. A. A. (1970). 'On Analysing the Impact of the Electoral System on the Party System in Canada'. *Canadian Journal of Political Science,* 3: 479–516.

Milne, D. (1991). *The Canadian Constitution.* Toronto: Lorimer.

Milner, H. (ed.) (1999). *Making Every Vote Count. Reassessing Canada's Electoral System.* Peterborough: Broadview Press.

Nevitte, N. (1991). *The Decline of Deference. Canadian Value Change in Cross-national Perspective.* Peterborough: Broadview Press.

Nevitte, N. et al. (2000). *Unsteady State. The 1997 Canadian Federal Election.* Don Mills: Oxford University Press.

Pammett, J. H. and Doran, C. (eds.) (2001). *The Canadian General Election of 2000.* Toronto: Dundurn Press.

Scarrow, H. A. (1962). *Canada Votes: A Handbook of Federal and Provincial Election Data.* New Orleans: The Hauser Press.

Schultze, R.-O. (1977). *Politik und Gesellschaft in Kanada.* Meisenheim: Hain.

— (1996). 'Interessenrepräsentation und Westminster-Modell: Kanada – ein abweichender Fall?'. *Staatswissenschaften und Staatspraxis,* 7: 163–193.

Schultze, R.-O. and Schneider, S. (eds.) (1997). *Kanada in der Krise. Analysen zum Verfassungs-, Wirtschafts- und Parteiensystemwandel seit den 80er Jahren.* Bochum: Brockmeyer.

Seidle, F. L. (1993). *Equity and Community: The Charter, Interest Advocacy and Representation.* Montréal: Institute for Research on Public Policy.

Thunert, M. (1992). *Grundrechtspartiotismus in Kanada? Zur politischen Integrationsfunktion der Canadian Charter of Rights and Freedoms.* Bochum: Brockmeyer.

Weaver, K. R. (1997). 'Improving Representation in the Canadian House of Commons'. *Canadian Journal of Political Science,* 30/3: 473–512.

Whittington, M. S. and Van Loon, R. J. (1996). *Canadian Government and Politics. Institutions and Processes.* Toronto: McGraw-Hill Ryerson.

Young, L. and Archer, K. (eds.) (2002). *Regionalism and Party Politics in Canada.* Don Mills: Oxford University Press.

COSTA RICA
by Daniel Zovatto[*]

1. Introduction

1.1 Historical Overview

Costa Rica has the longest-established competitive democracy in Latin America. Since 1953, there has been an uninterrupted series of free and fair elections, with power usually switching between the *Partido Liberación Nacional* and the main opposition coalition or party. There have been few violations of civil and political liberties, and the values of democracy are firmly rooted in Costa Rican society. These features set Costa Rica apart from the other Central American countries.

Costa Rica, a distant, isolated, and poverty-stricken province under the captaincy-general of Guatemala, gained independence from Spain on 15 September 1821. In 1824, Costa Rica became a member of the Central American Federation. In the same year, the country's first constitution established a bicameral system with a relatively weak executive. The political actors were individuals rather than parties. The two principal political currents, liberalism and conservatism, had not yet formed clearly-defined parties or factions. During the Central American Confederation crisis in the 1830s, the dispute between liberals and conservatives intensified.

In the late 1830s, President Braulio Carrillo began to systematically strengthen the state, and encouraged the cultivation and exportation of coffee as the basis of Costa Rica's economy. Between 1842 and 1871 the country went through a period of political instability, during which six different constitutions were enacted and numerous changes of government took place. Costa Rica was declared a Republic in the 1848 Constitution.

---

[*] In the first place, the author is indebted to Bernhard Thibaut who wrote an earlier version of this article. Furthermore, the author would like to thank Silvia Pizarro and Ileana Aguilar for their invaluable assistance for this research.

Elections were part of the political process, but they were not the principal means for changing governments; rather, they served to legitimate
an incumbent government or its chosen successor. The 1871 Constitution modified the prevailing political organization and established a unicameral system with a stronger executive. Various administrative and
fiscal policies helped establish the pre-eminence of the state over other
powers, in particular the Church. This development was reinforced by
the *Leyes Liberales* (Liberal Laws) of the 1980s.

Towards the end of the 19th century, the patrimonial-oligarchic structure, based on the political and economic leadership of coffee producers,
was replaced by a liberal-oligarchic alliance. In the 1880s, the liberal
elite believed that the country would be strengthened by having a literate population and introduced public schooling for the whole country. In
the presidential elections of 1889, which are commonly considered to be
the start of democracy in Costa Rica, the incumbent government was
forced to accept its electoral defeat due to popular demonstrations. It
was in this context that the first political parties were born. In general
terms, Costa Rica's political system remained under the influence of two
parties, the liberal *Partido Republicano* (PR; Republican Party) and the
Partido Reformista, until approximately 1940–50. The first serious opposition to the dominant liberal organizations did not arise until 1923,
with the *Partido Reformista*, whose ideology was based on the social
doctrine of the Catholic Church. However, its influence did not last
long. The Communist Party, founded in 1931, acquired some relevance
in the banana regions.

During the 1940s, the country's politics became increasingly
polarized. The political crisis became acute after President Rafael Ángel
Calderón Guardia was inaugurated (1940–1944). To provide workers
with tangible benefits that might attract them to his cause, he formed an
alliance with the Communist Party. Using the republican majority in the
assembly, Calderón started an ambitious plan of social reforms, which
was influenced by Catholic social doctrine and set him at odds with the
liberal-conservative elite of coffee growers. His populist and increasingly authoritarian policies led to the opposition of reformist and anti-
communist groups, causing them to organize around the *Partido Unidad
Nacional* (PUN; National Unity Party) party, which was competing with
the Communists for control of organized labor.

Following the mid-term elections of 1946, the opposition successfully
gained effective control of the electoral tribunal as a condition for participating in the 1948 presidential elections. Calderón's refusal to accept
his defeat in that election led to a short but bloody civil war. At the end

of the conflict, Calderón and the communist leadership negotiated a surrender and were allowed to leave the country; the social democrat leader, José Figueres Ferrer, and his Army of National Liberation assumed control. Figueres signed an agreement with Otilio Ulate, the winner of the 1948 elections, which stated that the latter would assume office within eighteen months and that in the meantime the country would be ruled by a provisional organ, the *Junta Fundadora de la Segunda República,* led by Figueres. In the elections for the constituent assembly, which were influenced by the 1949 Constitution, Ulate's *Unión Nacional* gained a strong majority. The constituent assembly ratified most of the innovations decreed by the junta, but the Social Democrats nevertheless had to give up their hopes of a radical transformation of Costa Rica. Finally, the winner of the 1948 elections, Otilio Ulate Blanco, was appointed president by the junta.

The 1949 Constitution is still valid today. Although it basically followed the legislation of the 1871 Constitution, it introduced some important modifications: it reduced the power of the executive, reinforced the authority of the legislative, and instituted further organs of control, such as the *Tribunal Supremo de Elecciones* (Supreme Electoral Tribunal). Furthermore, the 1949 Constitution disenfranchised the armed forces, extended the social rights, and introduced women's suffrage.

The party system changed in 1951 with the emergence of a reformist party, the *Partido Liberación Nacional* (PLN; National Liberation Party), which was to play a dominant role in Costa Rica's political life. At the same time, the right-wing forces, which had grouped themselves around the *Partido Republicano*, started to divide into numerous groups. Ever since this time, coalitions and alliances between candidates of different parties have been common in Costa Rica: for instance, in 1983 the *Partido Unidad Social Cristiana* (PUSC; Social Christian Unity Party) managed to bring the right and center-right forces together.

In the second half of the 20th century, Costa Rica's political development served to consolidate the centripetal two-party system, characterized by moderate political competition between the PLN and the PUSC. The radical and regional parties were only of secondary importance. From 1970, the left was been a regular contender in elections, but remained a tiny minority, averaging well under 10% of the vote. This was the case until the elections of 2002, during which a third electoral force emerged that fragmented the traditional two-party system and caused the left to practically disappear from Costa Rica's electoral map.

Between 1982 and 2002, the PLN won the presidential elections in 1982 with 58.8% for candidate Luis A. Monge, in 1986 with 52.3% for

Oscar Arias, and in 1994 with 49.6% for José María Figueres Olsen. They also won the parliamentary elections in 1982 with 55.2%, in 1986 with 47.8%, and in 1994 with 44.6%. The PLN's opposition won the presidency in 1990, 1998, and 2002. Despite the serious challenges that confronted the country in the 1980s (economic problems as well as the revolutionary processes in the neighboring countries Nicaragua and El Salvador), the stability of Costa Rica's democracy has never been jeopardized.

The general election of 3 February 2002 marked an important deviation from previous electoral processes in Costa Rica. Before the elections were held, the Supreme Electoral Tribunal tried to introduce certain reforms to the electoral code, such as allowing independent candidates to participate in municipal elections; granting a preferential vote, which would give voters the opportunity to choose the first two slots on the lists of parliamentary candidates; using electronic voting, counting and tallying of ballots, plus the possibility of allowing Costa Ricans resident abroad to vote. These initiatives were rejected by congress. Their principle objections were that these reforms would be incompatible with the political constitution, which guarantees the party system and does not permit independent candidacies; that they would promote 'ungovernability' in the country by giving voters the possibility of voting for the candidate of their choice (currently voting is based on a closed list), and that there would be no certainty that electronic voting and voting from abroad would be totally secure and transparent.

For the first time in the country's history, none of the candidates from the majority parties gained the required 40% of the valid vote, which meant that a second electoral round was held on 7 April. In the first round, Abel Pacheco of the PUSC won 38% of the vote, Rolando Araya of the PLN won 32%, and an emerging third electoral force, the *Partido Acción Ciudadana* (PAC; Citizen Action Party), led by Ottón Solís (a former active militant of the PLN), won 26%. This was the first time in 30 years that a non-traditional party managed to become an electoral force with the real possibility of winning the presidency and of participating actively in the legislative balance of power.

The results of the parliamentary elections did not favor the new government and consequently affected its ability to represent the people and its capacity to promote initiatives on an individual basis. The PUSC won 19 seats (33.3%) followed by the PLN with 17 seats (29.8%), the PAC with 14 seats (24.7%), the *Partido Movimiento Libertario* (PLM; Libertarian Movement) with six seats (10.5%), and the *Partido Renovación Costarricense* with one seat (1.7%). This situation forced the government to seek alliances and a consensus when trying to obtain congress' approval for strategic bills.

The second round of elections took place on 7 April, and the ruling party, the PUSC, triumphed, gaining 58% of the votes (779,278). The PLN won the remaining 42% (563,202 votes). With regard to voter abstention, these elections continued the trend seen in the elections of 1998, in which voter participation, which historically hovered at 80 to 82%, fell to 70%. Thus, the abstention rate rose from 19% in the 1994 elections to 30.1% in 1998 and rose again to 31.2% (first round) and 39.8% (second round) in 2002.

1.2 Evolution of Electoral Provisions

In the 19th century, electoral provisions were basically included in the Costa Rican constitutions. After 1848, some aspects were also regulated by law: the Suffrage Law of 10 December 1848; the Electoral Law of 21 October 1862; the Electoral Laws of 20 June 1870; the Electoral Laws of 29 July 1889; the Electoral Laws of 11 November 1893; Decree No. 28 of 30 November 1908; the Electoral Law of 18 August 1913; Law No. 1 of 25 October 1919; the Restoration Law of 18 September 1919; Law No. 75 of 23 July 1925; Law No. 15 of 26 September 1936; the Electoral Code of 1946.

During the 19th century, voting rights were limited according to land ownership and educational criteria. The voting age was 18 years (1825 Constitution) and later 25 years (1844 and 1848 Constitutions). In 1869, the voting age was fixed at 21 years. Direct suffrage was introduced in the 1844 Constitution, but it was retracted for the 1847 elections. Voting has been indirect apart from during the 1844 elections. In 1913, the economic standing and educational requirements were eliminated and direct elections were reintroduced. The secret ballot was introduced in 1925, and compulsory voting was introduced in 1936. Women were enfranchised in 1949. Since the 1974 elections, the voting age has been lowered to 18.

Since the 1949 Constitution, parliamentary candidates are nominated by political parties. Candidates are required to have Costa Rican citizenship by birth or to have been resident in the country for at least ten years after naturalization. The minimum age for candidacy is 21.

Until 1825, the executive was a collegiate organ. The following constitutions in that century introduced a presidential system. Until 1913, the president was indirectly elected (by an electoral college or by par-

liament); an absolute majority was required, and a second round had to
be held if no candidate achieved such a majority. After 1913, the president was elected by plurality, and required 40% of the vote to win. Between 1825 and 1847 and after 1871, the presidential term of office was
four years; between 1859 and 1871, three years, and between 1847 and
1859, six years. In 1859, the re-election of the president was prohibited.
In 1871, it was established that the president could be re-elected after
four years, but this provision was not implemented until 1882. In 1949,
it was established that the president could be re-elected after eight years,
but this provision was eliminated in 1969. From this year on, re-election
was prohibited. However, in April 2003, after a long debate, the fourth
constitutional chamber ruled that subsection 1 of article 132 of the constitution, banning presidential re-election, was unconstitutional. It ruled
that this subsection violated the fundamental right to elect and be
elected. Former presidents are now able to run for presidency again
eight years after their first term in office. Since the 1949 constitution,
presidential candidates have been nominated by the political parties. The
minimum age is 30 years.

The electoral system used to elect parliament tended to produce proportional results, since the number of representatives to be elected in
each constituency, which corresponded to the provinces (or *comarcas*),
was established in relation to the demographic development. The Electoral Law of 1893 introduced the simple quota formula in constituencies
where more than two seats were contested; in those with two seats or
less, candidates had to attain an absolute majority (after 1913: plurality).
As of 1913, candidates were directly elected, and there had to be a
minimum of 43 representatives. The 1949 Constitution provided for minority representation and the establishment of the Supreme Electoral
Tribunal, a politically independent body to supervise the electoral process.

1.3 Current Electoral Provisions

Sources: 1949 Constitution; Electoral Code of 10 December 1952
reformed by various laws, most recent amendment on 23 July 2001; Organic Law of the Supreme Electoral Tribunal of 30 April 1965.

Suffrage: The principles of universal, equal, secret, and direct suffrage
are applied. Costa Rican citizenship is required (naturalized citizens can
only vote twelve months after acquiring this status). Minimum voting

age is 18. Voting is compulsory. However, the law does not provide for any action against those who do not vote.

Elected national institutions: The president and the two vice presidents are directly elected for a four-year term. Elections are held on the first Sunday of February. The re-election of the president is allowed after eight years. The *Asamblea Legislativa* (57 members or deputies) is directly elected for a four year term on the same day as the executive. Representatives can be re-elected after one legislative period and cannot contest presidential elections.

Nomination of candidates
- *presidential elections*: Presidential candidates are nominated by political parties. The minimum age for candidacy is 30 years.
- *parliamentary elections*: Parliamentary candidates are nominated by political parties. Candidates are required to have Costa Rican citizenship by birth or to have been resident in the country for at least ten years after naturalization. The minimum age for candidacy is 21.

Electoral system
- *presidential elections*: The president and vice presidents are elected by plurality, and the constitution requires a candidate to gain a minimum of 40% of the vote to win; if no candidate attains this share, a second round is held between the top two candidates.
- *parliamentary elections*: The seven MMCs (from four to 20 seats, according to the population censuses) correspond to the country's provinces. The representatives are elected on the basis of a closed and blocked party list, a different list to the one used for the presidential elections. Each voter is entitled to only one vote and the combination of different lists is not permitted. The seats are allocated using the simple quota formula. Seats remaining unfilled are distributed among parties in the order of their residual votes (but also including those parties that barely achieved the sub-quotient, their total vote being similar to a residual figure). Vacancies arising between general elections are filled by the next candidate on the party list to which the former member belonged; they are assigned by the supreme electoral tribunal.

Organizational context of elections: Elections are organized and supervised by the Supreme Electoral Tribunal.

1.4 Commentary on the Electoral Statistics

The Costa Rican electoral statistics are reliable and meet international standards. The data presented in the tables were obtained from the Supreme Electoral Tribunal (www.tse.go.cr). Some data were drawn from other official sources (*La Gaceta Official*, daily editions from 1913, 1917, 1923, 1928, 1936, 1940, and 1949). Further information about the elections from 1913 to 1949 were taken from secondary sources (Molina 2001a,b; Obregón 2000; Samper 1988). From the 1953 elections onwards, blank votes are included in the tables.

2. Tables

2.1 Dates of National Elections, Referendums, and Coups d'Etat

Year	Presidential elections	Parliamentary elections Total	Partial	Elections. for Constit. Assembly	Referendums	Coups d'état
1913	07/12	07/12	07/12			
1915			05/12			
1917	01/04	01/04	01/04			27/01
1919	07/12	07/12				
1921			02/12			
1923	02/12	02/12				
1925			06/12			
1928	12/02	12/02				
1930			09/02			
1932	14/02	14/02				
1934			11/02			
1936	09/02	09/02				
1938			13/04			
1940	11/02	11/02				
1942			08/02			
1944	13/02	13/02				
1946			10/02			
1948	08/02	08/02[a]		08/12		12/03[c]
1949	04/10[b]	04/10				
1953	26/07	26/07				
1958	02/02	02/02				
1962	04/02	04/02				
1966	06/02	06/02				
1970	01/02	01/02				
1974	03/02	03/02				
1978	05/02	05/02				
1982	07/02	07/02				
1986	02/02	02/02				
1990	04/02	04/02				
1994	06/02	06/02				
1998	01/02	01/02				
2002	03/02 (1st) 07/04 (2nd)	03/02 (1st) 07/04 (2nd)				

[a] Civil War. Congress elections were nullified.
[b] Vice-presidential elections.
[c] Civil war.

2.2 Electoral Body 1913–2002

Year	Type of election[a]	Population[b]	Registered voters Total number	% pop.	Votes cast Total number	% reg. voters	% pop.
1913	Pr	410,981	82,211	20.0	64,153	78.0	15.6
1913	Pa	410,981	82,211	20.0	64,599	78.6	15.7
1915	Pa	430,701	82,637	19.2	41,433	50.1	9.6
1917	Pr	454,995	91,079	20.0	63,066	69.2	13.9
1917	Pa	454,995	91,079	20.0	61,593	67.6	13.5
1919	Pr	463,727	84,987	18.3	49,099	57.8	10.6
1919	Pa	463,727	84,987	18.3	35,743	42.1	7.7
1921	Pa	476,581	90,149	18.9	27,394	30.4	5.7
1923	Pr	498,435	98,640	19.8	69,577	70.5	14.0
1923	Pa	498,435	98,640	19.8	82,717	83.9	16.6
1925	Pa	520,766	92,760	17.8	33,220	35.8	6.4
1928	Pr	492,541	116,983	23.8	73,085	62.5	14.8
1928	Pa	492,541	116,983	23.8	85,121	72.8	17.3
1930	Pa	565,427	105,592	18.7	32,429	30.7	5.7
1932	Pr	539,654	118,186	21.9	75,897	64.2	14.1
1932	Pa	539,654	118,186	21.9	75,827	64.2	14.1
1934	Pa	551,541	115,170	20.9	47,927	41.6	8.7
1936	Pr	591,862	129,701	21.9	89,290	68.8	15.1
1936	Pa	591,862	129,701	21.9	89,310	68.9	15.1
1938	Pa	623,414	124,289	19.9	88,004	70.8	14.1
1940	Pr	656,129	139,220	21.2	112,559	80.8	17.2
1940	Pa[c]	656,129	139,220	21.2	91,297	65.6	13.9
1942	Pa	672,043	142,047	21.1	105,081	74.0	15.6
1944	Pr	725,149	163,100	22.5	70,380	43.2	9.7
1944	Pa	725,149	163,100	22.5	—	—	—
1946	Pa	746,535	160,336	21.5	103,139	64.3	13.8
1948	Pr	825,378	176,979	21.4	99,369	56.1	12.0
1948	CA	825,378	176,979	21.4	84,010	47.5	10.2
1949	VPr[d]	850,659	158,210	18.6	69,238	43.8	8.1
1949	Pa	850,659	158,210	18.6	77,846	49.2	9.2
1953	Pr	898,329	293,678	32.7	197,489	67.2	22.0
1953	Pa	898,329	293,678	32.7	198,270	67.5	22.1
1958	Pr	1,099,962	354,779	32.3	229,543	64.7	20.9
1958	Pa	1,099,962	354,779	32.3	229,507	64.7	20.9
1962	Pr	1,302,829	483,980	37.1	391,406	80.9	30.0
1962	Pa	1,302,829	483,980	37.1	391,500	80.9	30.0
1962	Pa	1,302,829	483,980	37.1	391,500	80.9	30.0
1966	Pr	1,567,230	554,627	35.4	451,490	81.4	28.8
1966	Pa	1,567,230	554,627	35.4	451,475	81.4	28.8
1970	Pr	1,762,462	675,285	38.3	562,766	83.3	31.9
1970	Pa	1,762,462	675,285	38.3	562,678	83.3	31.9

Year (cont.)	Type of election[a]	Population[b]	Registered votes		Votes cast		
			Total number	% pop.	Total number	% reg. voters	% pop.
1974	Pr	1,945,894	875,041	45.0	699,340	79.9	35.9
1974	Pa	1,945,594	875,041	45.0	699,042	79.9	35.9
1978	Pr	2,098,531	1,058,455	50.4	860,206	81.3	41.0
1978	Pa	2,098,531	1,058,455	50.4	859,888	81.2	41.0
1982	Pr	2,403,781	1,261,127	52.5	991,679	78.6	41.3
1982	Pa	2,403,781	1,261,127	52.5	991,566	78.6	41.3
1986	Pr	2,709,944	1,486,474	54.9	1,216,300	81.8	44.9
1986	Pa	2,709,944	1,486,474	54.9	1,216,053	81.8	44.9
1990	Pr	3,029,746	1,692,050	55.8	1,384,326	81.8	45.7
1990	Pa	3,029,746	1,692,050	55.8	1,383,956	81.8	45.7
1994	Pr	3,301,210	1,881,348	57.0	1,525,979	81.1	46.2
1994	Pa	3,301,210	1,881,348	57.0	1,525,624	81.1	46.2
1998	Pr	3,558,697	2,045,980	57.5	1,431,913	70.0	40.2
1998	Pa	3,558,697	2,045,980	57.5	1,430,579	69.9	40.2
2002	Pr	4,019,723	2,279,851	56.7	1,569,418	68.8	39.0
2002	Pr[e]	4,019,723	2,279,851	56.7	1,372,943	60.2	34.2
2002	Pa	4,019,723	2,279,851	56.7	1,569,338	68.8	39.0

[a] CA = Constituent Assembly; Pa = Parliament; Pr = President; VPr = Vice-President.
[b] Source: Instituto Nacional de Estadística y Censos. For 1942 and 1946, the information was taken from Molina 2001b.
[c] There were no results available for Limon and Guanacaste.
[d] In the 1948 presidential elections, no vice presidents had been chosen. Therefore, these elections had to be held separately in 1949.
[e] Runoff.

2.3 Abbreviations

PD	*Partido Demócrata* (Democratic Party)
PDC	*Partido Democrático Cristiano* (Christian Democratic Party)
PLN	*Partido Liberación Nacional* (National Liberation Party)
PRD	*Partido Renovación Democrática* (Democratic Renovation Party)
PR	*Partido Republicano* (Republican Party)
PRN	*Partido Republicano Nacional Independiente* (Independent National Republican Party)
PUN	*Partido Unidad Nacional* (National Unity Party)
PUSC	*Partido Unidad Social Cristiana* (Social Christian Unity Party)
PAC	*Partido Acción Ciudadana* (Citizen Action Party)
PML	*Movimiento Libertario* (Libertarian Movement)

2.4 Electoral Participation of Parties and Alliances 1913–2002

Party / Alliance	Years[a]	Elections contested	
		Presidential[b]	Parliamentary[c]
1913–1948			
Agricultor Independiente	1913	0	1
Agrupación cartaginesa	1913	0	1
Civil	1913	1	1
PR	1913–1915; 1921–1934; 1948	4	10
PUN	1913; 1928; 1930; 1948	3	4
Coalición puntareneña	1915	0	1
Peliquista	1917	1	0
Acostista	1919	0	1
Acostista conciliador	1919	0	1
Constitucional acostista	1919	0	1
Constitucional obrero	1919	0	1
Obrero acostista	1919	0	1
Constitucional	1919–1921; 1930	1	3
Unión provincial	1919; 1925	0	2
PD	1919; 1942–1946	2	3
Agrícola reformado	1921	0	1
Agrícola verdadero	1921	0	1
Confraternidad Guanacasteca	1921	0	1
Constitucional agrícola	1921	0	1
Constitucional aguilista	1921	0	1
Constitucional carmonista	1921	0	1
Constitucional conciliador	1921	0	1
Constitucional popular	1921	0	1
Constitucional republicano	1921	0	1
Económico	1921	0	1
Esquivelista	1921	0	1
Fraternidad guanacasteca	1921	0	1
Jimenista de Cartago	1921	0	1
Regionalista Independiente	1921	0	1
Progresista	1921	0	1
Unión popular independiente	1921	0	1
Pueblo	1921	0	1
Republicano Independiente regional	1921	0	1
Republicano histórico	1921	0	1
Republicano histórico reformado	1921	0	1
Republicano reformado	1921	0	1

Party / Alliance (continued)	Years[c]	Elections contested	
		Presidential[a]	Parliamentary[b]
Agrícola Independiente	1921; 1925	0	2
Independiente	1921; 1925; 1930	0	3
Agrícola	1921–1925; 1930; 1948	1	5
Reformista	1923; 1925; 1930	1	3
Comercial obrero	1925	0	1
Agrupación popular	1925	0	1
Independiente de San José	1925	0	1
Pecuario	1925	0	1
Republicano briceñista	1925	0	1
Republicano Independiente	1925	0	1
Republicano popular	1925	0	1
Republicano labriego	1925	0	1
Republicano urbinista	1925	0	1
Unión limonense	1925	0	1
Nacional independiente	1925; 1934	0	2
Agrupación puntareneña	1930	0	1
Alianza de obreros y campesinos	1930	0	1
Antireeleccionista de oposición	1930	0	1
Antireelecionista Guanacaste	1930	0	1
Antirreeleccionista de oposición	1930	0	1
Antirreelecionista de Guanacaste	1930	0	1
Defensa limonense	1930	0	1
Jimenista	1930	0	1
Jimenista Republicano	1930	0	1
Pro-Limón	1930	0	1
Provincial josefino	1930	0	1
Republicano constitucional	1930	0	1
Renovación nacional	1930	0	1
Unión nacional provincial	1930	0	1
Unión nacional reformista	1930	0	1
Unión provincial de Heredia	1930	0	1
Unión provincial esquivelista	1930	0	1
PRN	1930–1940; 1948	3	6
Unión Republicana	1932	1	1
Nacionalista	1932–1934	1	2
Republicano agrícola	1934	0	1
Republicano alajuelense	1934	0	1

Party / Alliance (continued)	Years[a]	Elections contested Presidential[b]	Parliamentary[c]
Republicano nacional ricardista	1934	0	1
Acción socialista	1934	0	1
Agrícola civil	1934	0	1
Chaconista	1934	0	1
Independiente antireeleccionista	1934	0	1
Juventud antirreeleccionista	1934	0	1
Liga de obreros y agricultores	1934	0	1
Liga patriótica	1934	0	1
Nacional republicano	1934	0	1
Radical socialista	1934	0	1
Regeneración provincial alajuelense	1934	0	1
Unión guanacasteca	1934	0	1
Unión herediana	1934	0	1
Unión provincial alajuelense	1934	0	1
Republicano provincial	1934	0	1
Bloque de Obreros y Campesinos	1934–1942	2	4
Nacional	1936	1	1
Demócrata Independiente	1938	0	1
Independiente nacional	1938	0	1
Nacional demócrata	1938	0	1
Republicano nacional progresista	1938	0	1
Unión Mora y Turrubares	1938	0	1
Cortesista alajuelense	1942	0	1
Bloque de la victoria[d]	1944	1	0
Anticomunista	1946	0	1
Renovación provincial	1946	0	1
Acción Cívica	1948	0	1
Confraternidad Nacional	1948	0	1
Laborista	1948	0	1
Liberal	1948	0	1
Movimiento republicano popular	1948	0	1
Obrero	1948	0	1
Vanguardia popular	1948	0	1
Social demócrata	1948	0	1
Second Republic (since 1949)			
Constitucional	1949	0	1
Demócrata alajuelense	1949	0	1
Demócrata cortesista	1949	0	1
Unión cartaginesa	1949	0	1

Party / Alliance (continued)	Years[a]	Elections contested Presidential[b]	Parliamentary[c]
Socialdemócrata	1949	0	1
PD	1953–1958; 1966; 1974–1982;1998	5	7
PLN	1953–2002[e]	15	14
PR	1958–1962	0	2
Movimiento Democrático de Oposición	1958	1	1
Acción Democrática Popular	1958–1962	1	2
PUN	1949; 1953–1962; 1970	2	5
Independiente	1958; 1974–1998	6	8
Unión Cívica Revolucionaria	1958; 1966	0	2
Movimiento Depuración Nacional	1962	0	1
Acción Solidarista	1962	0	1
Alajuelense Democrático	1962	0	1
Renovación Nacional	1962	0	1
Unión Guanacaste Independiente	1962–1966; 1994–1998	0	4
Unificación Nacional	1966–1978	4	4
Frente Nacional	1970	1	1
Movimiento Revolucionario Costarricense	1970	0	1
Acción Socialista	1970–1974	2	2
PDC	1970–1974	2	2
Unión Agrícola Cartaginesa	1970–2002	0	9
Frente Popular Costarricense	1974; 1978	0	2
Nacional Independiente	1958; 1974–1978; 1990–1998	5	4
PRD	1974	1	1
PRN	1953; 1974; 1986	0	3
Socialista Costarricense	1974	1	1
Frente Popular Costarricense	1974; 1978	0	2
Movimiento Nacional Independiente	1978; 1982	1	2
Organización Socialista de los Trabajadores	1978	1	1
Auténtico Limonense	1978–1998	0	6
Auténtico Puntarenense	1978–1982	0	2
Concordia Costarricense	1978; 1982	0	2
Laborista Nacional	1978	0	1
Unidad[f]	1978–1982	2	2
Pueblo Unido[g]	1978–1990; 1998	5	5
Unión Republicana	1978	0	1
Acción del Pueblo	1982	0	1

Party / Alliance (continued)	Years[a]	Elections contested Presidential[b]	Parliamentary[c]
Acción Democrática Alajuelense	1982–1986; 1994–1998	0	4
Liberalismo Nacional Republicano Progresista	1982	0	1
Nacional Democrático	1986	0	1
Obrero Campesino	1982	0	1
Unión Parlamentaria de Cartago	1982	0	1
Acción del Pueblo	1982	0	1
Alianza Nacional Cristiana	1986–2002	5	5
Alianza Popular[h]	1986	1	1
Alajuelense Solidario	1986–1990	0	2
PUSC	1986–2002[e]	6	5
Unión Generaleña	1986–1998	2	4
Acción Laborista Agrícola	1990–1998	0	3
Agrario Nacional	1990–2002	0	4
Del Progreso	1990	1	1
Rev. de los Trabajadores	1990	1	1
Fuerza Democrática	1994–2002	3	3
Convergencia Nacional	1994–2002	0	3
Vanguardia Popular[i]	1994	0	1
Guanacaste Independiente	1994–1998	0	2
Nuevo Partido Democrático	1998	1	1
Cambio Ya	1998	0	1
Fuerza Agraria de los Cartagineses	1998–2002	0	2
Integración Nacional	1998–2002	2	2
Movimiento Libertario	1998–2002	2	2
Renovación Costarricense	1998–2002	2	2
Acción Ciudadana	2002	1	1
Cambio 2000	2002	1	1
Laborista agrícola	2002	0	1
Independiente Obrero	2002	0	1
Patriótico Nacional	2002	0	1
Unión General	2002	1	1

[a] Individual participation for the parliamentary elections in 1917, 1940 and 1944 has not been included.
[b] Total number: 10 (1913–1948), 13 (1953–2002).
[c] Total number: 32 (1913–2002).
[d] Coalition between *Bloque de Obreros y Campesinos* and *Republicano Nacional Independiente*.
[e] In 2002, the PUSC contested the presidential elections in the second electoral round with the PLN.
[f] Coalition between PRD and several conservative parties.
[g] Coalition between several left-wing parties.
[h] Coalition between the *Frente Amplio Democrático* and the *Vanguardia Popular*.
[i] Coalition between *Acción Democrática de Alajuela* and *Pueblo Unido*.

2.5 Referendums

Referendums have not been held.

2.6 Elections for Constitutional Assembly

1948	Total number	%	Seats	%
Registered voters	—	–		
Votes cast	—	—		
Invalid votes	—	—		
Valid votes	84,010	—		
			45	100.0
PUN	62,300	74.2	34	75.5
P. Constitucional	10,815	12.9	6	13.3
PSD	6,415	7.6	4	8.9
P. Confraternidad Nacional	2,439	2.9	1	2.3
P. Acción Cívica	844	1.0	0	0.0
Mov. Rep. Popular	749	0.9	0	0.0
Liberal	448	0.5	0	0.0

2.7 Parliamentary Elections 1913–2002

Year	1913		1915	
	Total number	%	Total number	%
Registered voters	82,211	–	82,637	–
Votes cast	64,599	78.6	41,443	50.2
Invalid votes	543	0.8	649	1.6
Valid votes	64,056	99.2	40,794	98.4
Republicano	27,094	42.3	27,341	67.1
Unión Nacional	19,747	30.8	–	–
Civil	17,215	26.9	–	–
Fusión	–	–	10,690	26.2
Agrupación cartaginesa	–	–	2,161	5.3
Coalición puntareneña	–	–	548	1.3
Others[a]	–	–	54	0.1

[a] Others include: *Agricultor Independiente* (54 votes).

Year	1917		1919	
	Total number	%	Total number	%
Registered voters	91,079	–	84,987	–
Votes cast	61,593	67.6	35,743	42.1
Invalid votes	—	—	190	0.1
Valid votes	—	—	35,724	99.9
Constitucional	—	—	26,751	74.9
Demócrata	—	—	3,014	8.4
Acostista	—	—	2,183	6.1
Constitucional	—	—	1,911	5.3
Unión provincial	—	—	1,123	3.1
Obrero acostista	—	—	616	1.7
Others[a]	—	—	126	0.4

[a] Others include: *Constitucional obrero* (106 votes); *Acostista conciliador* (20).

Year	1921		1923	
	Total number	%	Total number	%
Registered voters	90,149	–	98,640	–
Votes cast	27,394	30.4	82,717	83.9
Invalid votes	7	0.0	0	0.0
Valid votes	27,387	100.0	82,717	100.0
Agrícola	6,985	25.5	26,034	31.5
Constitucional	3,115	11.4	–	–
Confraternidad guanacasteca	3,081	11.2	–	–
Agrícola Independiente	1,754	6.4	–	–
Constitucional aguilista	1,551	5.7	–	–
Jimenista de Cartago	1,530	5.6	–	–
Unión popular Independiente	1,214	4.4	–	–
Constitucional agrícola	1,120	4.1	–	–
Regionalista Independiente	1,110	4.1	–	–
Republicano	1,001	3.7	42,568	51.5
Agrícola verdadero	650	2.4	–	–
Agrupación cartaginesa	620	2.4	–	–
Constitucional popular	598	2.2	–	–
Constitucional carmonista	521	1.9	–	–
Esquivelista	512	1.9	–	–
Fraternidad guanacasteca	508	1.8	–	–

Year (continued)	1921		1923	
	Total number	%	Total number	%
Constitucional republicano	367	1.3	–	–
Independiente	328	1.2	–	–
Progresista	266	1.0	–	–
Económico	197	0.7	–	–
Reformista	–	–	14,115	17.0
Others[a]	359	1.3	–	–

[a] Others include: *Republicano Independiente regional* (123 votes); *Republicano histórico* (117); *Pueblo* (55); *Provincial Josefino* (25); *Agrícola reformado* (16); *Jimenista republicano* (14); *Republicano reformado* (8); *Republicano histórico reformado* (1).

Year	1925		1928	
	Total number	%	Total number	%
Registered voters	92,760	–	116,983	–
Votes cast	33,220	35.8	85,121	72.8
Invalid votes	11	0.0	261	0.3
Valid votes	33,209	100.0	84,860	99.7
Republicano	13,202	39.8	39,662	46.7
Agrícola	7,320	22.0	–	–
Reformista	6,423	19.3	–	–
Republicano Urbinista	1,425	4.3	–	–
Republicano briceñista	1,283	3.9	–	–
Unión Provincial	833	2.5	–	–
Republicano Histórico	818	2.5	–	–
Unión Limonense	385	1.2	–	–
Agrícola legitimo	344	1.0	–	–
Republicano popular	313	0.9	–	–
Independiente	290	0.9	–	–
Agrupación popular	164	0.5	–	–
Unión Nacional	–	–	45,198	53.3
Others[a]	409	1.2	–	–

[a] Others include: *Republicano Independiente* (109 votes); *Nacional Independiente* (87); *Comercial obrero* (83); *Agrícola Independiente* (68); *Independiente de San José* (39); *Republicano Labriego* (14); *Pecuario* (9).

Year	1930		1932	
	Total number	%	Total number	%
Registered voters	105,592	–	118,186	–
Votes cast	32,429	30.7	75,827	64.2
Invalid votes	0	0.0	0	0.0
Valid votes	32,429	100.0	75,827	100
Unión Nacional	10,559	32.5	–	–
Republicano constitucional	3,481	10.7	–	–
Unión provincial Esquivelista	2,152	6.6	–	–
Unión provincial de Heredia	2,127	6.6	–	–
Unión Nacional Provincial	1,962	6.1	–	–
Republicano	1,588	4.9	17,302	22.8
Constitucional	1,340	4.1	–	–
Independiente	1,333	4.1	–	–
Independiente de Heredia	1,116	3.4	–	–
Jimenista republicano	1,085	3.3	–	–
Reformista	1,004	3.1	–	–
Renovación Nacional	885	2.7	–	–
Agrupación Puntareneña	810	2.5	–	–
Alianza de obreros y campesinos	744	2.3	–	–
Jimenista	637	2.0	–	–
Antirreeleccionista de Oposición	344	1.1	–	–
Unión Nacional Reformista	317	1.0	–	–
Unión provincial	288	1.0	–	–
Defensa limonense	256	0.8	–	–
Republicano Nacional Independiente	–	–	35,399	46.7
Unión Republicana	–	–	22,032	29.1
Nacionalista	–	–	1,094	1.4
Others[a]	401	1.2	–	–

[a] Others include: *Pro-Limón* (145 votes); *Antirreeleccionista de Guanacaste* (125); *Provincial josefino* (105); *Antirreeleccionista Guanacaste* (26).

Year	1934		1936	
	Total number	%	Total number	%
Registered voters	115,170	–	129,701	–
Votes cast	47,927	41.6	89,310	68.9
Invalid votes	184	0.4	0	0.0
Valid votes	47,743	99.6	89,310	100.0
Republicano Nacional Independiente	22,973	48.1	53,047	59.4
Republicano	4,126	8.6	–	–
Republicano provincial	2,848	6	–	–
Unión provincial alajuelense	2,640	5.5	–	–
Bloque de obreros y campesinos	2,395	5.0	5,448	6.1
Independiente antirreeleccionista	1,601	3.4	–	–
Unión Herediana	1,392	2.9	–	–
Nacionalista	1,335	2.8	–	–
Nacional republicano	1,141	2.4	–	–
Republicano agrícola	951	2.0	–	–
Regeneración provincial alajuelense	947	2.0	–	–
Liga de obreros y agricultores	923	1.9	–	–
Unión Guanacasteca	863	1.8	–	–
Agrícola Provincial	793	1.7	–	–
Nacional Independiente	656	1.4	–	–
Chaconista	626	1.3	–	–
Acción socialista	558	1.2	–	–
Republicano Nacional Ricardista	298	0.6	–	–
Nacional	–	–	30,815	34.5
Others[a]	677	1.4	–	–

[a] Others include: *Republicano alajuelense* (208 votes); *Agrícola civil* (169); *Liga Patriótica* (115); *Juventud antirreeleccionista* (96); *Radical socialista* (89).

Year	1938 Total number	%	1940 Total number	%
Registered voters	124,289	–	139,220	–
Votes cast	88,004	70.8	91,297	65.6
Invalid votes	127	0.1	—	—
Valid votes	87,877	99.9	—	—
Republicano Nacional	54,557	62.1	—	—
Bloque de Obreros y Campesinos	10,187	11.6	—	—
Republicano Independiente	6,453	7.3	—	—
Confraternidad guanacasteca	4,678	5.3	—	—
Republicano Provincial	3,921	4.5	—	—
Independiente Nacional	3,753	4.3	—	—
Republicano Nacional progresista	2,658	3.0	—	—
Unión Mora y Turrubares	721	0.8	—	—
Demócrata Independiente	610	0.7	—	—
Others[a]	339	0.4	—	—

[a] Others include: *Nacional Demócrata* (339 votes).

Year	1942 Total number	%	1944 Total number	%
Registered voters	142,047	–	163,100	–
Votes cast	105,081	74.0	—	—
Invalid votes	368	0.4	—	—
Valid votes	104,713	99.6	—	—
Republicano Nacional Independiente	66,256	63.3	—	—
Bloque de obreros y campesinos	17,060	16.3	—	—
Demócrata	9,628	9.2	—	—
Cortesista alajuelense	8,532	8.1	—	—
Confraternidad guanacasteca	2,554	2.4	—	—
Republicano Nacional Independiente	683	0.7	—	—

Year	1946 Total number	%	1949 Total number	%
Registered voters	160,336	–	158,210	–
Votes cast	103,139	64.3	77,846	49.2
Invalid votes	127	0.1	0	0.0
Valid votes	103,012	98.9	77,846	100.0
Republicano Nacional Independiente	52,044	50.5	–	–
Demócrata	42,860	41.6	–	–
Vanguardia Popular	5,577	5.4	–	–
Republicano	1,095	1.1	–	–
Anticomunista	521	0.5	–	–
Abstencionista	672	0.7	–	–
Unión Nacional	–	–	55,804	71.7
Constitucional	–	–	12,254	15.7
Social demócrata	–	–	5,169	6.6
Demócrata cortesista	–	–	1,931	2.5
Demócrata alajuelense	–	–	1,305	1.7
Unión Cartaginesa	–	–	1,383	1.8
Others[a]	243	0.2	–	–

[a] Others include: *Renovación Provincial* (243 votes).

Year	1953 Total number	%	1958 Total number	%
Registered voters	293,678	–	354,779	–
Votes cast	198,270	67.5	229,507	64.7
Blank votes	8,268	4.2	6,022	2.6
Invalid votes	13,872	7.0	16,969	7.4
Valid votes	176,130	88.8	206,516	90.0
PLN	114,043	64.7	86,081	41.7
PD	67,324	21.2	939	0.5
PRN Independiente	12,696	7.2	–	–
PUN	12,069	6.9	44,125	21.4
PR	–	–	46,171	22.4
P. Independiente	–	–	20,314	9.8
Unión Cívica Revolucionaria	–	–	6,855	3.3
Mov. Democrático de Oposición	–	–	1,417	0.7
Others[a]	–	–	614	0.3

[a] Others include: *P. Acción Democrática* (614 votes).

Year	1962		1966	
	Total number	%	Total number	%
Registered voters	483,980	–	554,627	–
Votes cast	391,500	80.9	451,475	81.4
Blank votes	8,186	2.1	8,090	1.8
Invalid votes	6,377	1.6	28,748	6.4
Valid votes	376,937	96.3	414,637	91.8
PLN	184,135	48.9	202,891	48.9
PR	126,249	33.5	–	–
PUN	50,021	13.3	–	–
P. Acción Democrática Popular	9,256	2.5	–	–
P. Acción Solidarista	3,358	0.9	–	–
P. Alajuelense Democrático	1,698	0.5	–	–
Unificación Nacional	–	–	178,953	43.2
Unión Cívica Revolucionaria	–	–	22,721	5.5
PD	–	–	8,543	2.1
Others[a]	2,220	0.6	1,529	0.4

[a] Others include in 1962: *Mov. Depuración Nacional* (1,192 votes); *Unión Guanacaste Indep.* (903); *P. Renovación Nacional* (125). In 1966: *Mov. Depuración Nacional* (1,529).

Year	1970		1974	
	Total number	%	Total number	%
Registered voters	675,285	–	875,041	–
Votes cast	562,678	83.3	699,042	79.9
Blank votes	10,873	1.9	12,967	1.9
Invalid votes	21,380	3.8	21,111	3.0
Valid votes	530,425	94.3	664,964	95.1
PLN	269,038	50.7	271,867	40.9
Unificación Nacional	190,387	35.9	164,323	24.7
P. Acción Socialista	29,133	5.5	29,310	4.4
Frente Nacional	16,392	3.1	–	–
PDC	13,489	2.5	13,688	2.1
PUN	6,105	1.2	–	–
Mov. Revolucionario Costarricense	3,279	0.6	–	–
Unión Agrícola Cartaginesa	2,394	0.5	8,074	1.2
P. Nacional Independiente	–	–	66,222	10.0
PRD	–	–	51,083	7.7
PRN	–	–	32,475	4.9
PD	–	–	14,161	2.1

Year (continued)	1970		1974	
	Total number	%	Total number	%
P. Socialista Costarricense	–	–	6,032	0.9
Frente Popular Costarricense	–	–	4,448	0.7
P. Independiente	–	–	3,282	0.5
Others[a]	208	0.0	–	–

[a] Others include: *P. Renovación Puntarenense* (208 votes).

Year	1978		1982	
	Total number	%	Total number	%
Registered voters	1,058,455	–	1,261,127	–
Votes cast	859,888	81.2	991,566	78.6
Blank votes	13,597	1.6	11,016	1.1
Invalid votes	25,731	3.0	24,560	2.5
Valid votes	820,560	95.4	955,990	96.4
P. Unidad	356,215	43.4	277,998	29.1
PLN	318,904	38.9	527,231	55.2
Pueblo Unido	62,865	7.7	61,465	6.4
Unificación Nacional	25,824	3.1	–	–
Frente Popular Costarricense	12,834	1.5	–	1.6
Unión Republicana	8,215	1.0	–	–
Unión Agrícola Cartaginés	7,887	1.0	7,235	0.8
Movimiento Nacional Indep.	6,673	0.8	34,437	3.6
P. Independiente	5,774	0.7	4,671	0.5
Organización Socialista de los Trabajadores	4,059	0.5	–	–
P. Concordia Costarricense	2,542	0.3	5,014	0.5
P. Nacional Democrático	–	–	11,575	1.2
P. Nacional Democrático	–	–	–	1.2
P. Acción Democrática Alajuelense	–	–	12,486	1.6
Others[a]	8,768	1.1	13,878	1.5

[a] Others include in 1978: PD (3,083 votes); *P. Auténtico Limonense* (2,954); *P. Auténtico Puntarenense* (1,729); *P. Laborista Nacional* (1,002). In 1982: *P. Acción del Pueblo* (3,546); PD (2,672); *P. Auténtico Limonense* (3,893); *P. Auténtico Puntarenense* (1,036); *Unión Parlamentaria de Cartago* (1,047); *P. Obrero Campesino* (976); *P. Liberalismo Nacional Republicano Progresista* (708).

Year	1986		1990	
	Total number	%	Total number	%
Registered voters	1,486,474	–	1,692.050	–
Votes cast	1,216,053	81.8	1,383,956	81.8
Blank votes	13,187	1.1	15,061	1.1
Invalid votes	30,667	2.5	32,723	2.4
Valid votes	1,172,199	96.4	1,336,172	96.5
PLN	560,694	47.8	559,632	41.9
PUSC	485,860	41.4	617,478	46.2
Pueblo Unido	31,685	2.7	44,161	3.3
Alianza Popular	28,551	2.4	–	–
Alianza Nacional Cristiana	19,972	1.7	22,154	1.6
Unión Agrícola Cartaginés	13,575	1.2	14,190	1.1
PRN	10,598	0.9	–	–
Unión Generaleña	4,402	0.4	32,292	2.4
P. Alajuelense Solidario	3,604	0.3	7,330	0.5
P. Nacional Independiente	–	–	10,643	0.8
P. del Progreso	–	–	7,733	0.6
Others[a]	13,258	1.1	20,559	1.5

[a] Others include in 1986: *P. Acción Democrática Alajuelense* (4,324 votes); *P. Auténtico Limonense* (3,813); *P. Independiente* (3,067); *P. Nacional Democrático* (2,054). In 1990: *P. Independiente* (5,566); *P. Auténtico Limonense* (4,901); *Acción Laborista Agrícola* (4,756); *P. Agrario Nacional* (4,594); *P. Revolucionario de los Trabajadores* (742).

Year	1994		1998	
	Total number	%	Total number	%
Registered voters	1,881,348	–	2,045,980	–
Votes cast	1,525,624	81.1	1,430,579	69.9
Blank votes	16,329	1.1	14,343	1.0
Invalid votes	33,702	2.2	32,709	2.3
Valid votes	1,475,593	96.7	1,383,527	96.7
PLN	658,258	44.6	481,933	34.8
PUSC	595,802	40.4	569,792	41.2
Fuerza Democrática	78,454	5.3	79,826	5.8
Unión Generaleña	25,420	1.7	12,583	0.9
Alianza Nacional Cristiana	21,064	1.4	9,176	0.7
Vanguardia Popular	20,026	1.4	–	–
Unión Agrícola Cartaginés	16,336	1.1	7,138	0.5
P. Agrario Nacional	13,589	0.9	7,497	0.5
P. Nacional Independiente	12,767	0.9	12,794	0.9

Year (continued)	1994		1998	
	Total number	%	Total number	%
P. Acción Democrática Alajuelense	11,630	0.8	6,614	0.5
P. Independiente	9,213	0.6	6,025	0.4
Acción Laborista Agrícola	3,859	0.3	16,955	1.2
Movimiento Libertario	–	–	42,640	3.1
P. Integración Nacional	–	–	34,408	2.5
Renovación Costarricense	–	–	27,892	2.0
P. Demócrata	–	–	17,060	1.2
Pueblo Unido	–	–	15,028	1.2
Nuevo Partido Democrático	–	–	12,476	0.9
P. Rescate Nacional	–	–	9,588	0.7
Others[a]	9,175	0.6	10,102	0.7

[a] Others include in 1994: *P. Auténtico Limonense* (5,468 votes); *P. Guanacaste Independiente* (2,843); *Convergencia Nacional* (864). In 1998: *Cambio Ya* (2,223); *Convergencia Nacional* (2,197); *P. Auténtico Limonense* (2,167); *Fuerza Agraria de los Cartagineses* (1,892); P. *Guanacaste Independiente* (1,623).

Year	2002	
	Total number	%
Registered voters	2,279,851	–
Votes cast	1,569,338	68.8
Blank votes	19,023	1.2
Invalid votes	28,461	1.8
Valid votes	1,521,854	97.0
Unidad Social Cristiana	453,201	29.8
Partido Liberación Nacional	412,383	27.1
Acción Ciudadana	334,162	22.0
Movimiento Libertario	142,152	9.3
Renovación Costarricense	54,699	3.6
Fuerza Democrática	30,172	2.0
Integración Nacional	26,084	1.7
Cambio 2000	12,992	0.8
Laborista Agrícola	10,890	0.7
Independiente Obrero	8,044	0.5
Patriótico Nacional	7,123	0.5
Agrícola Cartaginés	6,974	0.5
Others[a]	22,978	1.5

[a] Others include: *Alianza Nacional Cristiana* (6,825 votes); *Unión General* (5,883); *Rescate Nacional* (4,937); *Agrario Nacional* (2,595); *Fuerza Agraria de los Cartagineses* (1,390); *Convergencia Nacional* (1,348).

2.8 Composition of Parliament 1953–2002

Year	1953 Seats 45	% 100.0	1958 Seats 45	% 100.0	1962 Seats 57	% 100.0	1966 Seats 57	% 100.0
PLN	30	66.7	20	44.4	29	50.9	29	50.9
P. Independiente	–	–	3	6.7	–	–	–	–
Unión Cívica Revolucionaria	–	–	1	2.2	–	–	2	3.5
PUN	1	2.2	10	22.2	8	14.0	-	-
PD	11	24.4	–	–	–	–	–	–
PRN Independiente	3	6.7	–	–	–	–	–	–
PR	–	–	11	24.4	18	31.6	–	–
Unificación Nacional	–	–	–	–	–	–	26	45.6
Acción Democrática Popular	–	–	–	–	2	3.5	–	–

Year	1970 Seats 57	% 100.0	1974 Seats 57	% 100.0	1978 Seats 57	% 100.0	1982 Seats 57	% 100.0
PLN	32	56.1	27	47.4	25	43.9	33	57.9
PRD	–	–	3	5.3	–	–	–	–
Unificación Nacional	22	38.6	16	28.1	–	–	–	–
PDC	1	1.8	–	–	–	–	–	–
P. Nacional Independiente	–	–	6	10.5	–	–	–	–
PD	–	–	1	1.8	–	–	–	–
PRN	–	–	1	1.8	–	–	–	–
P. Unidad	–	–	–	–	27	47.4	18	31.6
Movimiento Nacional	–	–	–	–	–	–	1	1.8
P. Acción Socialista	2	3.5	2	3.5	–	–	–	–
Frente Popular Costarricense	–	–	–	–	1	1.8	–	–
Pueblo Unido	–	–	–	–	3	5.3	4	7.0
Unión Agrícola Cartaginés	–	–	1	1.8	1	1.8	–	–
Acción Democrática Alajuelense	–	–	–	–	–	–	1	1.8

Year	1986		1990		1994		1998	
	Seats	%	Seats	%	Seats	%	Seats	%
	57	100.0	57	100.0	57	100.0	57	100.0
PLN	29	50.9	25	43.9	28	49.1	23	40.4
PUSC	25	43.9	29	50.9	25	43.9	27	47.4
Pueblo Unido	1	1.8	1	1.8	–	–	–	–
Alianza Popular	1	1.8	–	–	–	–	–	–
Unión Agrícola Cartaginés	1	1.8	1	1.8	1	1.8	–	–
Unión Generaleña	–	–	1	1.8	–	–	–	–
Partido Agrario Nacional	–	–	–	–	1	1.8	–	–
Fuerza Democrática	–	–	–	–	2	3.5	3	5.2
Movimiento Libertario	–	–	–	–	–	–	1	1.8
Partido Integración Nacional	–	–	–	–	–	–	1	1.8
Partido Renovación Costarricense	–	–	–	–	–	–	1	1.8
Partido Acción Laborista Agrícola	–	–	–	–	–	–	1	1.8

Year	2002	
	Seats	%
	57	100.0
Unidad Social Cristiana	19	33.3
Partido Liberación Nacional	17	29.8
Acción Ciudadana	14	24.6
Movimiento Libertario	6	10.5
Renovación Costarricense	1	1.8

2.9 Presidential Elections 1913–2002

1913	Total number	%
Registered voters	82,211	–
Votes cast	64,153	78.3
Invalid votes	6	0.0
Valid votes	64,147	100.0
Máximo Fernández Alvarado (PR)	26,989	42.1
Carlos Durán Cartín (PUN)	19,818	30.9
Rafael Iglesias Castro (*Civilista*)	17,340	27.0

1917[a]	Total number	%
Registered voters	91,079	–
Votes cast	63,066	69.2
Invalid votes	249	0.4
Valid votes	62,817	99.6
Federico Tinoco (*P. Peliquista*)	62,817	100.0

[a] Fraudulent elections. Tinoco was the only candidate. However, the former president Rafael Iglesias Castro received 249 votes in Alajuela. These votes were registered as invalid votes.

1919	Total number	%
Registered voters	84,987	–
Votes cast	49,099	57.8
Invalid votes	7	0.0
Valid votes	49,092	100.0
Julio Acosta García (*P. Constitucional*)	43,832	89.3
José María Soto (PD)	5,260	10.7

1923	Total number	%
Registered voters	98,640	–
Votes cast	69,577	70.5
Invalid votes	10	0.0
Valid votes	69,567	100.0
Ricardo Jiménez Oreamuno (PR)	29,338	42.2
Alberto Echandi M. (*P. Agrícola*)	26,114	37.5
Jorge Volio Jiménez (*P. Reformista*)	14,115	20.3

1928	Total number	%
Registered voters	116,983	–
Votes cast	73,085	62.5
Invalid votes	845	1.2
Valid votes	72,240	98.8
Cleto González Víquez (PUN)	42,765	59.2
Carlos María Jiménez Ortiz (PR)	29,475	40.8

1932	Total number	%
Registered voters	118,186	–
Votes cast	75,897	64.2
Invalid votes	0	0.0
Valid votes	75,897	100.0
Ricardo Jiménez Oreamuno (PRN)	35,408	46.7
Manuel Castro Quesada (*Unión Republicana*)	22,077	29.1
Carlos María Jiménez Ortiz (PR)	17,316	22.8
Max Koberg Bolandi (*P. Nacionalista*)	1,096	1.4

1936	Total number	%
Registered voters	129,701	–
Votes cast	89,290	68.8
Invalid votes	1,441	1.6
Valid votes	87,849	98.4
León Cortés Castro (PRN)	52,924	60.2
Octavio Beeche Argüello (*P. Nacional*)	30,331	34.5
Carlos Luis Saénz (*Bloque de Obreros y Campesinos*)	4,594	5.3

1940	Total number	%
Registered voters	139,220	–
Votes cast	112,559	80.8
Invalid votes	2,643	2.3
Valid votes	109,916	97.7
Rafael A. Calderón Guardia (PRN)	92,849	84.5
Manuel Mora Valverde (*Bloque de Obreros y Campesinos*)	10,825	9.8
Virgilio Salazar Leiva (*P. Confraternidad Guanacasteca*)	6,242	5.7

1944	Total number	%
Registered voters	163,100	–
Votes cast	70,380	43.2
Invalid votes	0	0.0
Valid votes	70,380	100.0
Teodoro Picado Michalski (*Bloque de la Victoria*)	52,830	75.1
León Cortés Castro (PD)	17,550	24.9

1948[a]	Total number	%
Registered voters	176,979	–
Votes cast	99,369	56.1
Invalid votes	0	0.0
Valid votes	99,369	100.0
Otilio Ulate Blanco (PUN)	54,931	55.3
Rafael Angel Calderón Guardia (PRN)	44,438	44.7

[a] Fraudulent elections. The congress, whose president was Calderón, annulled the elections. This led to the 1948 civil war.

1953	Total number	%
Registered voters	293,678	–
Votes cast	197,489	67.2
Blank votes	4,391	2.2
Invalid votes	2,330	1.2
Valid votes	190,768	96.6
José Figueres Ferrer (PLN)	123,444	64.7
Fernando Castro Cervantes (PD)	67,324	35.3

1958	Total number	%
Registered voters	354,779	–
Votes cast	229,543	64.7
Blank votes	3,981	1.7
Invalid votes	4,013	1.7
Valid votes	221,549	96.5
Mario Echandi Jiménez (PUN)	102,851	46.4
Francisco J. Orlich B. (PLN)	94,788	42.8
Jorge Rossi Chavarría (*P. Nacional Independiente*)	23,910	10.8

1962	Total number	%
Registered voters	483,980	–
Votes cast	391,406	80.9
Blank votes	2,924	0.7
Invalid votes	5,020	1.3
Valid votes	383,462	98.0
Francisco J. Orlich Bolmarcich (PLN)	192,850	50.3
Rafael A. Calderón Guardia (PR)	135,533	35.3
Otilio Ulate Blanco (PUN)	51,740	13.5
Enrique Obregón Valverde (*P. Acción Democrático Popular*)	3,339	0.9

1966	Total number	%
Registered voters	554,627	–
Votes cast	451,490	81.4
Blank votes	3,825	0.8
Invalid votes	6,265	1.4
Valid votes	441,400	97.8
José Joaquín Trejos Fernández (*Unificación Nacional*)	222,810	50.5
Daniel Oduber Quirós (PLN)	218,590	49.5

1970	Total number	%
Registered voters	675,285	–
Votes cast	562,766	83.3
Blank votes	4,568	0.8
Invalid votes	18,153	3.2
Valid votes	540,045	96.0
José Figueres Ferrer (PLN)	295,883	54.8
Mario Echandi Jiménez (*Unificación Nacional*)	222,372	41.2
Virgilio Calvo Sánchez (*Frente Nacional*)	9,554	1.8
Lisímaco Leiva Cubillo (*P. Acción Socialista*)	7,221	1.3
Jorge Arturo Monge Zamora (PDC)	5,015	0.9

1974	Total number	%
Registered voters	875,041	–
Votes cast	699,340	79.9
Blank votes	5,023	0.7
Invalid votes	16,160	2.3
Valid votes	678,157	97.0
Daniel Oduber Quirós (PLN)	294,609	43.4
Fernando Trejos Escalante (*Unificación Nacional*)	206,149	30.4
Jorge González Martén (*P. Nacional Independiente*)	73,788	10.9
Rodrigo Carazo Odio (PRD)	61,820	9.1
Gerardo W. Villalobos Garita (PD)	18,832	2.8
Manuel Mora Valverde (*P. Acción Socialista*)	16,081	2.4
Jorge Arturo Monge Zamora (PDC)	3,461	0.5
José Francisco Aguilar Bulgarelli (*P. Socialista Costarricense*)	3,417	0.5

1978	Total number	%
Registered voters	1,058,455	–
Votes cast	860,206	81.3
Blank votes	5,374	0.6
Invalid votes	23,691	2.8
Valid votes	831,141	96.6
Rodrigo Carazo Odio (*P. Unidad*)	419,824	50.5
Luis Alberto Monge Álvarez (PLN)	364,285	43.8
Rodrigo Gutiérrez Sáenz (*Pueblo Unido*)	22,740	2.7
Guillermo Villalobos Arce (*P. Unificación Nacional*)	13,666	1.6
Gerardo W, Villalobos Garita (*P. Independiente*)	3,822	0.5
Jorge González Martén (*P. Nacional Independiente*)	3,323	0.5
Carlos Coronado Vargas (*Organización Socialista de los Trabajadores*)	1,868	0.2
Rodrigo Cordero Víquez (PD)	1,613	0.2

1982	Total number	%
Registered voters	1,261,127	–
Votes cast	991,679	78.6
Blank votes	4,862	0.5
Invalid votes	20,241	2.0
Valid votes	966,576	97.5
Luis Alberto Monge Álvarez (PLN)	568,374	58.8
Rafael Ángel Calderón Fournier (*P. Unidad*)	325,187	33.6
Mario Echandi Jiménez (*Movimiento Nacional*)	37,127	3.8
Rodrigo Gutiérrez Sáenz (*Pueblo Unido*)	32,186	3.3
Edwin Chacón Madrigal (*P. Independiente*)	1,955	0.2
Edwin Retana Chaves (PD)	1,747	0.2

1986	Total number	%
Registered voters	1,486,474	–
Votes cast	1,216,300	81.8
Blank votes	5,049	0.4
Invalid votes	26,029	2.1
Valid votes	1,185,222	97.4
Oscar Arias Sánchez (PLN)	620,314	52.3
Rafael Ángel Calderón Fournier (PUSC)	542,434	45.8
Rodrigo Gutiérrez Saénz (*Alianza Popular*)[a]	9,099	0.8
Alvaro Montero Mejía (*Pueblo Unido*)[b]	6,599	0.6
Alejandro Madrigal Benavides (*Alianza Nacional Cristiana*)	5,647	0.5
Eugenio Jiménez Sancho (*P. Independiente*)	1,129	0.1

[a] Coalition between the *Frente Amplio Democrático* and the *Vanguardia Popular*.
[b] Coalition between the *Partido Socialista Costarricense* and the *Partido de los Trabajadores*.

1990	Total number	%
Registered voters	1,692,050	–
Votes cast	1,384,326	81.8
Blank votes	5,393	0.4
Invalid votes	29,919	2.2
Valid votes	1,349,014	97.4
Rafael Calderón Fournier (PUSC)	694,589	51.5
Carlos Castillo (PLN)	636,701	47.2
Daniel Camacho (*Pueblo Unido*)	9,217	0.7
Fernando Ramírez (*Alianza Nacional Cristiana*)	4,209	0.3
Isaac Azofeifa (*P. del Progreso*)	2,547	0.2
Edwin Badilla (*P. Revolucionario de los Trabajadores*)	1,005	0.1
Rodrigo Cordero (*P. Independiente*)	746	0.1

1994	Total number	%
Registered voters	1,881,348	–
Votes cast	1,525,979	81.1
Blank votes	5,219	0.3
Invalid votes	30,663	2.0
Valid votes	1,490,097	97.6
José M. Figueres Olsen (PLN)	739,339	49.6
Miguel A. Rodríguez (PUSC)	711,328	47.7
Miguel Zúñiga Díaz (*Fuerza Democrática*)	28,274	1.9
Rafael Ángel Matamoros Mesén (*Alianza Nacional Cristiana*)	4,980	0.3
Jorge González Mesén (*P. Nacional Independiente*)	2,426	0.2
Norma Vargas Duarte (*Unión Generaleña*)	2,150	0.1
Holman Esquivel Garrote (*P. Independiente*)	1,600	0.1

1998	Total number	%
Registered voters	2,045,980	–
Votes cast	1,431,913	70.0
Blank votes	6,897	0.5
Invalid votes	36,318	2.5
Valid votes	1,388,698	97.0
Miguel A. Rodríguez (PUSC)	652,160	47.0
José M. Corrales (PLN)	618,834	44.6
Vladimir De la Cruz De Lemos (*Fuerza Democrática*)	41,710	3.0
Alejandro Madrigal Benavides (*Alianza Nacional Cristiana*)	3,545	0.3
Jorge González Martén (*P. Nacional Independiente*)	4,218	0.3
Walter Muñoz Céspedes (*Integración Nacional*)	19,934	1.4
Sherman Thomas Jackson (*Renovación Costarricense*)	19,313	1.4
Álvaro González Espinoza (*Demócrata*)	12,952	0.9
Norma Vargas Duarte (*Pueblo Unido*)	3,075	0.2
Marina Volio Brenes (*Rescate Nacional*)	2,681	0.2
Federico Malavassi Calvo (*Movimiento Libertario*)	5,874	0.4
Rodrigo Gutiérrez Schwanhäuser (*Nuevo Partido Democrático*)	3,025	0.2
Yolanda Gutiérrez Ventura (*P. Independiente*)	1,377	0.1

2002 (1st round)	Total number	%
Registered voters	2,279,851	–
Votes cast	1,569,418	68.8
Blank votes	7,241	0.3
Invalid votes	32,332	1.4
Valid votes	1,529,845	67.1
Abel Pacheco (PUSC)	590,277	38.6
Rolando Araya (PLN)	475,030	31.1
Ottón Solís Fallas (PAC)	400,681	26.2
Otto Guevara Gutt (PML)	25,815	1.7
Justo Orozco Álvarez (*Renovación Costarricense*)	16,404	1.1
Walter Muñoz Céspedes (*Integración Nacional*)	6,235	0.4
Vladimir De la Cruz De Lemos (*Fuerza Democrática*)	4,121	0.3
Walter Coto Molina (*Coalición Cambio 2000*)	3,970	0.2
Rolando Angulo Zeledón (*Unión General*)	2,655	0.2
Marvin Calvo Montoya (*Alianza Nacional Cristiana*)	1,271	0.1
Daniel Reynolds Vargas (*Patriótico Nacional*)	1,680	0.1
Pablo Angulo Casasola (*Rescate Nacional*)	905	0.0

2002 (2nd round)[a]	Total number	%
Registered voters	2,279,851	–
Votes cast	1,372,943	60.2
Blank votes	6,006	0.3
Invalid votes	27,457	2.0
Valid votes	1,339,480	58.7
Abel Pacheco (PUSC)	776,278	58.0
Rolando Araya (PLN)	563,202	42.0

[a] The second round had to be held because no candidate met the required minimum share of votes (40%) in the first round.

2.10 List of Power Holders 1824–2004

Head of State	Years	Remarks[a]
Supreme Chiefs of State		
Juan Mora Fernández	1824–1833	From 08/09/1824 to 09/03/1833 (provisional until 14 /04/1825).
Rafael José Gallegos Alvarado	1833–1834	From 09/03/1833 to 27/06/1834 (1st time).
Augustín Gutiérrez Lizaurzábal	1934	From 27/06/1934 to 19/07/1934.
Rafael José Gallegos Alvarado	1834–1835	From 19/07/1834 to 04/03/1835 (2nd time).
Juan José Lara Arias	1835	From 04/03/1835 to 18/03/1835 (provisional).
Manuel Fernández Chacón	1835	From 18/03/1835 to 05/05/1835.
Braulio Carrillo Colina	1835–1837	From 05/05/1835 to 01/03/1837 (1st time).
Joaquín Mora Fernández	1837	From 01/03/1837 to 17/04/1837 (provisional).
Manuel Aguilar Chacón	1837–1838	From 17/04/1837 to 27/05/1838.
Braulio Carrillo Colina	1838–1842	From 27/05/1838 to 11/04/1842 (2nd time).
Francisco Morazán Quesada	1842	From 12/04/1842 to 11/09/1842 (provisional).
Antonio Pinto Suárez	1842	From 11/09/1842 to 27/09/1842 (supreme commander of arms).
José María Alfaro Zamora	1842–1844	From 27/09/1842 to 23/11/1844 (1st time, provisional).
Francisco María Oreamuno Bonilla	1844–1846	From 23/11/1844 to 07/06/1846. Although he submitted his resignation on 17/12/1844, the chamber of deputies did not accept it. Thus, he remained the official president, but the de facto power lay in the hands of Rafael Moya Murillo (from 17/12/1844 to 30/04/1845) and José Rafael Gallegos Alvarado (from 01/05/1845 to 07/06/1846).
José María Alfaro Zamora	1846–1847	From 07/06/1846 to 08/05/1847 (2nd time, provisional).
José María Castro Madriz	1847–1848	From 08/05/1847 to 31/08/1848, when he became the first president of the new Republic.

Costa Rica 185

Head of State (cont.)	Years	Remarks[a]
Presidents		
José María Castro Madriz	1848–1849	From 31/08/1848 to 16/11/1849 (1st time).
Miguel Mora Porras	1849	From 16/11/1849 to 26/11/1849.
Juan Rafael Mora Porras	1849–1859	From 26/11/1849 to 14/08/1859. Former vice president. Re-elected three times.
José María Montealegre	1859–1863	From 14/08/1859 to 08/05/1863. Interim president until 29/04/1860.
Jesús Jiménez Zamora	1863–1866	From 08/05/1863 to 08/05/1866 (1st time).
José María Castro Madriz	1866–1868	From 08/05/1866 to 01/11/1868 (2nd time).
Jesús Jiménez Zamora	1868–1870	From 01/11/1868 to 27/04/1870 (2nd time). Provisional until 08/05/1869.
Bruno Carranza Ramírez	1870	From 27/04/1870 to 08/08/1870 as provisional chief.
Tomás Guardia Gutiérrez	1870–1876	From 10/08/1870 to 08/05/1876 (1st time). Provisional until 08/05/1872.
Aniceto Esquivel Sáenz	1876	From 08/05/1876 to 30/07/1876.
Vicente Herrera Zeledón	1876–1877	From 30/07/1876 to 11/09/1877.
Tomás Guardia Gutiérrez	1877–1882	From 11/09/1877 to 06/07/1882 (2nd time).
Saturnino Lizano Gutiérrez	1882	From 06/07/1882 to 20/07/1882.
Próspero Fernández Oreamuno	1882–1885	From 20/07/1882 to 12/03/1885.
Bernardo Soto Alfaro	1885–1890	From 12/03/1885 to 08/05/1890. Re-elected on 04/04/1886.
José Joaquín Rodríguez Zeledón	1890–1894	From 08/05/1890 to 08/05/1894.
Rafael Iglesias Castro	1894–1902	He assumed office on 08/05/1894. In 1898, he was re-elected in fraudulent elections after the prohibition of re-election in Art. 97 of the 1871 Constitution had been abolished. The elections took place under state of emergency and the republicans did not take part since they opposed the re-election.
Ascensión Esquivel Ibarra	1902–1906	Assumed office constitutionally on 08/05/1902.
Cleto González Víquez	1906–1910	Elected by parliament during the state of emergency. The opposition's candidate could not stand for elections, since he had been exiled. Assumed office constitutionally on 08/05/1906.

Head of State (cont.)	Years	Remarks[a]
Ricardo Jiménez Oreamuno	1910–1914	Assumed office constitutionally on 08/05/1910.
Alfredo González Flores	1914–1917	Although he had not run for presidency in the elections, he was appointed by congress on 08/05/1914, after the two candidates with the highest vote shares had resigned.
Federico Tinoco Granados	1917–1919	Army officer. Assumed power in a *coup d'état* on 27/01/1917. Elected in non-competitive elections on 1 April and declared elected by the national constitutional assembly on 11 April of that year. Removed from office in August 1919, went into exile.
Juan Bautista Quirós	1919	Army officer. Minister under Tinoco. Succeeded the latter for 22 days from 12/08 to 02/09. Fell due to North American pressure.
Francisco Aguilar Barquero	1919–1920	Appointed by *Junta de Notables* on 02/09/1919. On 17 September, he announced free elections which were held in December 1919.
Julio Acosta García	1920–1924	Assumed office constitutionally on 08/05/1920.
Ricardo Jiménez Oreamuno	1924–1928	Elected by parliament on 08/05/1924 because he did not gain the absolute majority in the elections held in December 1923.
Cleto González Víquez	1928–1932	Assumed office constitutionally on 08/03/1928.
Ricardo Jiménez Oreamuno	1932–1936	Elected by parliament on 01/05/1932, because he did not gain the absolute majority in the elections held in February 1932. Assumed office constitutionally on 08/05/1932.
León Cortés Castro	1936–1940	Assumed office constitutionally on 08/05/1936.
Rafael Ángel Calderón Guardia	1940–1944	Assumed office constitutionally on 08/05/1940.
Teodoro Picado Michalski	1944–1948	Assumed office constitutionally on 08/05/1944.
Santos León Herrera	1948	Interim President from 19/04/1948 to 08/05/1948.
José Figueres Ferrer	1948–1949	Founder of the Second Republic. On 08/05/1948, he assumed office as president of the *Junta Fundadora de la Segunda República*, which governed during 18 months after the opposition's victory in the civil war (from 08/03 to 19/04/1948).

Head of State (cont.)	Years	Remarks[a]
Otilio Ulate Blanco	1949–1953	Assumed office on 08/11/1949 as 'elected president' of the 1948 elections. After the opposition's victory in the 1948 civil war, Figueres and Ulate agreed on this transfer of power.
José Figueres Ferrer	1953–1958	Assumed office constitutionally on 08/11/1953.
Mario Echandi Jiménez	1958–1962	Assumed office constitutionally on 08/05/1958.
Francisco J. Orlich Bolmarich	1962–1966	Assumed office constitutionally on 08/05/1962.
José J. Trejos Fernández	1966–1970	Assumed office constitutionally on 08/05/1966.
José Figueres Ferrer	1970–1974	Assumed office constitutionally on 08/05/1970. Introduced suffrage for women.
Daniel Oduber Quirós	1974–1978	Assumed office constitutionally on 08/05/1974.
Rodrigo Carazo Odio	1978–1982	Assumed office constitutionally on 08/05/1978.
Luis Alberto Monge Alvárez	1982–1986	Assumed office constitutionally on 08/05/1982.
Oscar Arias Sánchez	1986–1990	Assumed office constitutionally on 08/05/1986.
Rafael A. Calderón Fournier	1990–1994	Former president Rafael Calderón Guardia's son. Calderón Jr. assumed office constitutionally on 08/05/1990.
José M. Figueres Olsen	1994–1998	Former president José Figueres Ferrer's son. Assumed office constitutionally on 08/05/1994.
Miguel A. Rodríguez	1998-2002	Assumed office constitutionally on 08/05/1998.
Abel Pacheco de la Espriella	Since 2002	Assumed office constitutionally on 08/05/2002.

[a] Between 1821 and 1824, the country was governed by various juntas. Since executive power during these years cannot clearly be attributed to one person or a small group, the names of the junta members have not been listed. Moreover, not all the dates for the transfers of power included in this table can be guaranteed. Nevertheless, traditionally, the president assumes office on 8 May.

3. Bibliography

3.1 Official Sources

Alcance a la Gaceta. No. 279, 07/12, 1923, 1–11.
Constitución Política de Costa Rica de 1871 (reprinted in 1944). San José.
Constitución Política de la República de Costa Rica de 1917, San José.
Dirección General de Estadística (1918). *Anuario Estadístico 1917. Volume XXI.* San Jose, Costa Rica: DGE.
— (1921). *Anuario Estadístico 1918. Volume XXIII.* San Jose, Costa Rica: DGE.
— (1922). *Anuario Estadístico 1921. Volume XXV.* San Jose, Costa Rica: DGE.
— (1924). *Anuario Estadístico 1923. Volume XXVII.* San Jose, Costa Rica: DGE.
— (1926). *Anuario Estadístico 1925. Volume XXIX.* San Jose, Costa Rica: DGE.
— (1930). *Anuario Estadístico 1928. Volume XXXII.* San Jose, Costa Rica: DGE.
— (1933). *Anuario Estadístico 1930. Volume XXXIV.* San Jose, Costa Rica: DGE.
— (1938). *Anuario Estadístico 1932. Volume XXXVI.* San Jose, Costa Rica: DGE.
— (1935). *Anuario Estadístico 1934. Volume XXXVIII.* San Jose, Costa Rica: DGE.
— (1941). *Anuario Estadístico 1936. Volume XL.* San Jose, Costa Rica: DGE.
— (1939). *Anuario Estadístico 1938. Volume XLII.* San Jose, Costa Rica: DGE.
— (1941). *Anuario Estadístico 1940. Volume XLIV.* San Jose, Costa Rica: DGE.
— (1945). *Anuario Estadístico 1944. Volume XLVIII.* San Jose, Costa Rica: DGE.
— (1950). *Anuario de la Dirección General de Estadística año 1949.* San Jose, Costa Rica: DGE.
General Statistics Bureau (1914). *Informe de la Dirección General de Estadística año 1913.* San Jose, Costa Rica: DGE.
Instituto Nacional de Estadística y Censos (2002). *Estadísticas de Población 2002* <http://www.inec.go.cr/> (as of 07/11/2002).
La Gaceta. No. 85, 15/04/1917, 414
La Gaceta. No. 48, 21/02/1928, 245.
La Gaceta. No. 49, 29/02/1928, 286–288.
La Gaceta. No. 49, 05/03/1932, 267–270.
La Gaceta. No. 56, 07/03/1936, 411–412.
La Gaceta. No. 63, 16/03/1940, 547–549.
La Gaceta. No. 239, 25/10/1949, 1954–1955.
Ministry of Economics and Finance (1949). *Anuario de la Dirección General de Estadística año 1948.* San Jose, Costa Rica: DGE.
Ministry of Economics, Industry and Trade (MEIC) – General Bureau of Statistics and Census (DGEC) (1955). *Anuario Estadístico 1953.* San Jose, Costa Rica: DGE.

MEIC-DGEC (1959). *Anuario Estadístico 1958*. San Jose, Costa Rica: DGE.
MEIC-DGEC (1963). *Anuario Estadístico 1962*. San Jose, Costa Rica: DGE.
MEIC-DGEC (1967). *Anuario Estadístico 1966*. San Jose, Costa Rica: DGE.
MEIC-DGEC (1971). *Anuario Estadístico 1970*. San Jose, Costa Rica: DGE.
MEIC-DGEC (1975). *Anuario Estadístico de Costa Rica 1974*. San Jose, Costa Rica: DGE.
MEIC-DGEC (1979). *Estadística Vital 1978*. San Jose, Costa Rica: DGE.
MEIC-DGEC (1985). *Anuario Estadístico de Costa Rica 1982*. San Jose, Costa Rica: DGE.
MEIC-DGEC (1997). *Anuario Estadístico de Costa Rica 1983-1987*. San Jose, Costa Rica: DGE.
MEIC-DGEC (1998). *Anuario Estadístico de Costa Rica 1988-1992*. San Jose, Costa Rica: DGE.
Ministry of Development, General Statistics Bureau (1917). *Anuario Estadístico 1915. Volume XIX*. San Jose, Costa Rica: DGE.
National Institute of Statistics and Census (2000). *Anuario Estadístico de Costa Rica 1993–1998*. INEC.
Nuestra Constitución Política (*Constitución Política de la República de Costa Rica*), *7/11/1949*, San José: Lehmann editores (1988).
Tribunal Supremo de Elecciones (1978). *Cómputo de votos y declaratorias de elección para Presidente y Vicepresidentes, Diputados a la Asamblea Legislativa, Regidores y Síndicos Municipales, Elecciones del 5 de febrero de 1978*. San José: TSE.
Tribunal Supremo de Elecciones (1986). *Cómputo de votos y declaratorias de elección – 1986*. San José: TSE.
Tribunal Supremo de Elecciones (without year). *Elecciones en cifras (1953–1986)*. San José: TSE.
Tribunal Supremo de Elecciones (1990). *Escrutinio de elecciones para Diputados celebradas el 4 de febrero de 1990*. San José: TSE.
Tribunal Supremo de Elecciones (1990). *Escrutinio de elecciones para Presidente y Vicepresidentes celebradas el 4 de febrero de 1990*. San José: TSE.
Tribunal Supremo de Elecciones (1994). *Escrutinio de elecciones para Presidente y Vicepresidentes celebradas el 6 de febrero de 1994*. San José: TSE.
Tribunal Supremo de Elecciones (1998). *Escrutinio de elecciones para Presidente y Vicepresidentes celebradas el 1 de febrero de 1998*. San José: TSE.
Tribunal Supremo de Elecciones (2002). *Resultados finales para la elección de Presidente y Vicepresidentes, en cifras absolutas y relativas*. <http://www.tse.go.cr/webapp/tseescrutinio.asp> (as of 07/11/02).

Tribunal Supremo de Elecciones (2002). *Resultados finales del escrutinio para la elección Presidente y Vicepresidentes en cifras absolutas y relativas, segunda vuelta.* <http://www.tse.go.cr/IIvuelta.html> (as of 07/11/2002).

Tribunal Supremo de Elecciones (2002). *Resultados finales para la elección de Diputados, en cifras absolutas y relativas.*

3.2 Books, Articles, and Electoral Reports

Aguilar Bulgarelli, O. (1980). *Costa Rica y sus hechos políticos de 1948* (2nd edn.). San José: EDUCA.
— (1983). 'Costa Rica: Evolución histórica de una democracia', in C. Zelaya et al. (eds.), *¿Democracia en Costa Rica? Cinco opiniones polémicas.* San José: Ed. Universidad Estatal, 35–93.
Alfaro Ramos, J. et al. (1980). *La evolución del sufragio en Costa Rica. Seminario de Graduación para optar al título de Licenciados en Derecho.* San José: University of Costa Rica, Law Faculty.
Ameringer, C. (1982). *Democracy in Costa Rica.* New York: Praeger.
Araya Pochet, C. (1983). 'Esbozo Histórico de la Institución del sufragio en Costa Rica'. *Center of Historic Research of Central America, University of Costa Rica. Research Progress Report No. 8.* San Jose, Costa Rica, 22.
Arias Sánchez, O. (1976). *¿Quién gobierna en Costa Rica?* San José: EDUCA.
Barahona, F. (ed.) (1988). *Costa Rica hacia el 2000.* Caracas: Nueva Sociedad.
Bell, J. P. (1972). *Crisis in Costa Rica. The 1948 Revolution.* Austin, Tex./London: University of Texas Press.
Bendel, P. (1998). 'Sistemas de partidos en América Latina: criterios, tipologías, explicaciones', in D. Nohlen and M. Fernández (eds.), *El presidencialismo renovado. Instituciones y cambio político en América Latina.* Caracas: Nueva Sociedad, 197–214.
Biesanz, R. et al. (1982). *The Costa Ricans.* Englewood Cliffs, N.J.: Prentice Hall.
Booth, J. A. (1984). 'Representative Constitutional Democracy in Costa Rica: Adaption to Crisis in the Turbulent 1980s', in S. C. Ropp and J. A. Morris (eds.), *Central America. Crisis and Adaption.* Albuquerque: University of New Mexico Press, 153–187.
— (1989). 'Costa Rica', in L. Diamond, J. J. Linz, and S. M. Lipset (eds.), *Democracy in Developing Countries, vol. 4: Latin America.* Boulder/London: Lynne Renner/Adamantine, 387–485.
Busey, J. L. (1958). 'Foundations of Political Contrast: Costa Rica and Nicaragua'. *Western Political Quarterly* (Salt Lake City), 11: 627–659.

— (1961). *Notas sobre la democracia costarricense*. San José: Editorial Costarricense.

Carvajal Herrera, M. (1978). *Actitudes políticas del costarricense*. San José: Editorial Costa Rica.

Castro Dobles, M. and González Acuña, A. L. (1995). *Partidos Políticos República de Costa Rica*. San Jose, Costa Rica: Supreme Electoral Tribunal and Civil Registry.

Cerdas, R. (1975). *La crisis de la democracia liberal en Costa Rica*. San José: EDUCA.

— (1986). 'The Costa Rican Elections of 1986'. *Electoral Studies*, 2/3, 311–312.

Chacón, N. (1975). *Reseña de nuestras leyes electorales*. San José: Imprenta LIL S.A.

Del Aguila, J. M. (1982). 'The Limits of Reform Development in Contemporary Costa Rica'. *Journal of Interamerican Studies and World Affairs*, 24/3, 355–374.

Delgaldo, J. G. (1980). *El Partido Liberación Nacional. Análisis de su discurso político-ideológico*. Heredia (Costa Rica): Ed. UNA.

Ernst, M. and Schmidt, S. (eds.) (1986). *Demokratie in Costa Rica. Ein zentralamerikanischer Anachronismus?* Berlin: Forschungs- und Dokumentationszentrum Chile/Lateinamerika (FDCL).

Escalante, A. C. et al. (1988). 'Democratización–modernización del Estado en Costa Rica', in G. De Sierra et al. (eds.), *Hacia un nuevo orden estatal en América Latina? Democratización/modernización y actores políticos*. Buenos Aires: Clacso, 219–315.

Fanger, U. (1984). 'Wahltradition als Element demokratischer Institutionenbildung in Costa Rica', in D. Nohlen (ed.), *Wahlen und Wahlpolitik in Lateinamerika*. Heidelberg: Esprint, 11–42.

Fanger, U. and Thibaut, B. (1995). 'Costa Rica', in D. Nohlen and F. Nuscheler (eds.). *Handbuch der Dritten Welt*. Bonn: Dietz.

Fernández, O. (1991). 'Las elecciones del 90 en Costa Rica', in R. Espinal et al. (eds.), *Análisis de los procesos electorales en América Latina. Memórias IV Curso Anual Interamericano de Elecciones*. San José: IIDH–CAPEL, 311–322.

Fuchs, J. (1991). *Costa Rica: Von der Conquista bis zur "Revolution". Historische, ökonomische und soziale Determinanten eines konsensualistisch–neutralistischen Modells in Zentralamerika*. Berlin: Schelzky und Jeep.

González Víquez, C. (1978). *El sufragio en Costa Rica ante la historia y la legislación*. San José: Editorial Costa Rica.

Hernández Valle, R. (1986). 'Costa Rica: Elecciones de 1986. Análisis de los resultados'. *Cuadernos del CAPEL*, 11: 9–71.

— (1990). 'Costa Rica: Elecciones generales del 4 de febrero de 1990'. *Boletín Electoral Latinoamericano*, 3: 9–16.

Instituto Centroamericano de Estudios Políticos (2002). *¡Al día!. Informe Electoral sobre las elecciones nacionales de Costa Rica del 3 de febrero del 2002*. Guatemala: INCEP.

— (2002). *¡Al día!. Informe Electoral del Instituto Centroamericano de Estudios Políticos sobre la segunda vuelta electoral de Costa Rica del 7 de febrero del 2002*. Guatemala: INCEP.

Jiménez Castro, W. (1977). *Análisis electoral de una democracia: estudio del comportamiento electoral político costarricense durante el período 1953–1974*. San José: Editorial de Costa Rica.

— (1982). 'Análisis electoral de una democracia: Los resultados electorales de 7 de febrero de 1982'. *Tiempo Actual*, 7/25: 19–40.

Junkins, R. J. (1988). 'Historical Sources in Costa Rica'. *Latin American Research Review*, 23/3: 117–127.

La Nación (2003). *Sala IV aprueba reelección presidencial*. <http://www.nacion.com/ln_ee/2003/abril/04/repres.html> (as of 05/04/2003).

Lehoucq, F. E. (1989). *Explaining the Origins of Democratic Regimes: Costa Rica in Theoretical Perspective*. San José: Ms.

López Vallecillos, I. (1985). 'Costa Rica, Democracia y elecciones'. *Estudios Centroamericanos*, 810–830.

Maislinger, A. (ed.) (1986). *Costa Rica. Politik, Gesellschaft und Kultur eines Landes mit ständiger aktiver und unbewaffneter Neutralität*. Innsbruck: Inn–Verlag.

McDonald, R. (1971). *Party Systems and Elections in Latin America*. Chicago, Ill.: Markham.

Molina Jiménez, I. (2001a). *Democracia y Elecciones en Costa Rica, dos contribuciones polémicas. Workbook of Social Sciences #120*. San José, Costa Rica: FLACSO, Costa Rican Headquarters.

— (2001b). 'Estadísticas electorales de Costa Rica (1897-1948). Una contribución documental'. *Dialogues, Electronic History Magazine, University of Costa Rica*, 2/3. <http://ns.fcs.ucr.ac.cr/~historia/bases/bases.htm> (as of 27/03/2002).

Nelson, H. D. (ed.) (1983). *Costa Rica. A Country Study*. Washington, D.C.: American University Area Handbook Series.

Obregón Quesada, C. (2000). *El proceso electoral y el Poder Ejecutivo en Costa Rica 1808-1998*. San Jose, Costa Rica: Editorial Universidad de Costa Rica.

Oconitrillo, E. (1982). *Un siglo de política costarricense. Crónica de 24 campañas presidenciales*. San José: Ed. Universidad Estatal a Distancia.

Peeler, J. A. (1985). *Latin American Democracies. Colombia, Costa Rica, and Venezuela*. Chapel Hill, N.C.: University of North Carolina Press.

— (1992). 'Elite settlements and democratic consolidation: Colombia, Costa Rica, and Venezuela', in J. Higley and R. Gunther (eds.), *Elites and Democratic Consolidation in Latin America and Southern Europe*. Cambridge: Cambridge University Press, 81–112.

Proyecto Estado de La Nación (2002). *Estado de la Nación en Desarrollo Humano Sostenible, 8th report 2001*, 252-265.

Rodríguez, M. A. (1991). 'La reforma electoral en Costa Rica', in H. de la Calle Lombana et al. (eds), *La reforma electoral en Latinoamérica. Memorias IV Curso Anual Interamericano de Elecciones*. San José: IIDH–CAPEL, 259–266.

Rojas Bolaños, M. (1986). *Lucha social y guerra civil en Costa Rica, 1940–1948*. San José: Ed. Alma Mater.

—. (1989a). '¿Democracia en Costa Rica?'. *Síntesis*, 8: 15–35.

— (1989b). 'El proceso democrático en Costa Rica', in M. Rojas Bolaños et al. (eds.), *Costa Rica: La democracia inconclusa*. San José: DEI, 15–67.

Rojas Ramírez, J. et al. (1987). *Enciclopedia Costa Rica, su historia, tierra y gentes, vol. 2*. San José: Ed. Océano.

Romero, C. M. (1984). 'Las transformaciones recientes del Estado costarricense y las políticas reformistas', *Estudios Sociales Centroamericanos*, No. 38, 41–53.

Rovira Mas, J. (1989). *Costa Rica en los años 80*. San José: Ed. Porvenir.

Salazar Mora, J. M. (1981). *Política y reforma en Costa Rica, 1914–1958*. San José: Ed. Porvenir.

Salazar Mora, O. (1986). *Tres décadas de Historia Electoral 1889–1919*. San Jose, Costa Rica: Center of History Research of Central America, University of Costa Rica.

Samper K. M. (1988). 'Fuerzas sociopolíticas y procesos electorales en Costa Rica, 1921–1936'. *Revista de Historia de la Universidad de Costa Rica*, special edition, 157–222.

Sánchez Machado, M. (1985). *Las bases sociales del voto en Costa Rica, 1974–1978*. San José: Uruk Editores.

Seligson, M. A. (1987). 'Costa Rica and Jamaica', in M. Weiner and E. Özbudun (eds.), *Competitive Elections in Developing Societies*. Washington, D.C.: American Enterprise Institute, 147–198.

Seligson, M. A. and Muller, E. (1987). 'Democratic Stability and Economic Crisis: Costa Rica, 1978–1983'. *International Studies Quarterly*, vol. 31, 301–326.

Seligson, M. A. and Gómez Barrantes, M. (1987). 'Elecciones ordinarias en tiempos extraordinarios: La economía política del voto en Costa Rica'. *Anuario de Estudios Centroamericanos*, 13/1: 5–24.

Sojo Martínez, A. (1986). 'La democracia política y la democracia económica. Una visión desde Costa Rica'. *Ciencias Sociales*, 31: 39–48.

Torres Rivas, E. et al. (1987). *Costa Rica. Crisis y desafíos*. San José: DEI.

Urcuyo, C. (1998). 'Costa Rica. Elecciones de 1994: Continuidad democrática', in J. Rial and D. Zovatto (eds.). *Elecciones y democracia en América Latina, 1992–1996*. San José: IIDH/CAPEL, 37–58.

Vega Carballo, J. L. (1986). *Hacia una interpretación del desarrollo costarricense. Ensayo sociológico*. San José: Ed. Porvenir.

— (1989). 'Partidos, desarrollo político y conflicto social en Honduras y Costa Rica. Análisis comparativo'. *Síntesis*, 8: 363–383.

Villegas Antillón, R. (1987). 'El Tribunal Supremo de Elecciones y el Registro Civil de Costa Rica'. *Cuadernos de CAPEL*, 18: 9–57.

Zelaya, C. et al. (1983). *¿Democracia en Costa Rica? Cinco opiniones polémicas*. San José: Ed. Universidad Estatal.

CUBA
by Jan Suter and Dieter Nohlen

1. Introduction

1.1 Historical Overview

Cuba gained its independence from Spain in 1902. Nevertheless, its sovereignty remained restricted. This was evident in the republic's first constitution, which was passed together with the Platt Amendment in 1901. It authorized the US to intervene in Cuban internal affairs. The 1901 Constitution established a representative democratic system, based on the separation of powers and elections through universal suffrage for men over 21. However, the democratic system and the elections as a means of self-government could not consolidate: Cuban political reality remained characterized by personalism and corruption. This was true in particular of the local oligarchy who dealt in sugar and the foreign companies, who together controlled the political, social and economic sectors by military coups and dictatorships.

Between 1906 and 1909 the US military intervened once again, after which a fragile two-party system was established, formed by Liberals and Conservatives. Although their programs did not differ greatly, the relationship between these two personalist and clientelist parties, who changed their names frequently, was marked by sharp antagonism. Violence became a common means of changing governments. In 1924 the liberal Gerardo Machado became president using fraudulent means and established a dictatorship. He was overthrown in 1933, in the midst of social and political conflict caused by the worldwide economic depression.

Ramón Grau San Martín introduced a nationwide social reform plan characterized by nationalist and populist features. However, it was not recognized by the United States. This, together with domestic opposition, facilitated the overthrow of the regime via a military coup. The provisional and de facto governments that followed remained under the tutelage and control of the army led by Fulgencio Batista. He used authoritarian methods to implement reform policies in order to change the

economic and political structure of the country. In 1934, the USA renounced the Platt Amendment. The Communist Party and the labor
movement (under the control of the Communist Party) were integrated
into Batista's reform plan. The interventionist power of the state was extended, and it became a corporate organization. The reform plan reached
its peak in 1940, when the new constitution was enacted and Grau San
Martín's opposition party, *Partido Revolucionario Cubano* (*Auténtico*)
(PRC(A); Cuban Revolutionary Party, Authentic) returned to the political life. Fulgencio Batista was elected in free elections, and thus the
power relations of the 1930s were confirmed. This seemed to help consolidate democratic procedures. In 1944 Grau San Martín won the elections and the change of government took place peacefully. After the
1948 elections, San Martín was replaced in government by Carlos Pío
Socarrás, a member of his own party. Both PRC(A) governments were,
however, notoriously corrupt, and resulted in the military seizing power
in 1952, led by Fulgencio Batista. He established a military dictatorship
that thwarted all political opposition.

Both political and social conflicts increased during the economic crisis that affected Cuba in the 1950s. As legal opposition was not possible, these conflicts took on a violent form. Finally, Batista lost US
support and was defeated by a combination of guerrilla and massive
mobilization in 1958.

During its early stage, the Cuban revolution was based on an alliance,
'*Movimiento 26 de Julio*' (26th of July Movement) between middle-
class liberal forces and Fidel Castro's guerrilla movement. Castro turned
out to be a very charismatic leader. Rapidly, the revolution brought
about a complete transformation of the state's structure. In the 1960s
Fidel Castro assumed full control of the state. His regime adopted Marx-
ism-Leninism as the official doctrine and formed an alliance with the
Soviet Union. Under these circumstances and US pressure, Cuba saw
itself becoming increasingly isolated from the rest of the Latin American countries.

Cuba's regime was institutionalized in the 1970s. In 1975, the organization of political cadres was left to the PRC, which held its first congress. The following year a new constitution and an electoral law were
passed. From this time onwards, the representatives at the different levels of the political system, including the National Assembly of People's
Power (NAPP), began to be elected according to the principle of the so
called 'people's power', which was embedded in what the regime called
a system of 'democratic centralism'. Nevertheless, there were never any
of the basic elements of liberal democracy contained within it, namely

free and competitive elections based on universal, free, secret, and direct suffrage.

However, it is important to note that the concept and functions of socialist elections are different to those of liberal democracy. Cuban elections since 1976 do not imply the legitimacy of the power holders and their control. Their first function was to support socialist development by mobilizing all social forces. They wanted to achieve this by strengthening the moral and political unity of the people based on the societal goals defined by the Communist Party. As unity is one of the basic fundaments of the regime, opposed to liberal pluralism, it is characterized by an extreme will for consent. Socialist non-competetive elections are an act to assure the consensus of the people for the socialist transformation of Cuban society, an act of re-articulation of this fundamental consensus, especially after periods of critical reflexions on the way Cuba is progressing to make the perfect socialist society, and to approve periodical rectifications. In the eyes of the regime, the unanimity expressed in the high rates of consent for the candidates standing for parliamentary offices provide the decisive criterion for the correctness of the decisions taken by the revolutionary leader, Fidel Castro. Obviously, dissent is against the spirit of this concept of democracy. Political participation is only considered legitimate within the channels offered by the regime. Furthermore, these forms of inclusiveness of the people in open assemblies at municipal level are often highlighted by regime defenders as a superior form of political participation.

The first socialist Cuban constitution, establishing this type of socialist democracy, was discussed in a massive dialog at grass-root-level, with the participation, as it is reported, of 6,216,000 persons. Modifications to the proposal were made to 60 of the 141 articles. The constitution was formally approved by the people in a referendum, celebrated on 15 February 1976. With 89.0% voter turnout, 97.7% of the votes were affirmative. In the elections held since 1976, more than 95% of the electorate participated and more than 97% voted for the official candidates. Electoral results refer to the electorate, to the turnout, to the percentage of voters approving the official candidates. They are rarely complete and consistent. The indirect electoral system from 1976 to 1992 makes accurate reporting virtually impossible. Since then, the electoral results resembled those of socialist Eastern Europe. In the first direct elections on 24 February 1993, the total amount of candidates was 589, exactly the number of seats to be allocated. According to the official results, the percentage of electoral participation amounted to 99.6% of the voters; 93.0% of the votes were valid, 4.0% were invalid and 3.0% were blank votes. According to the same governmental source, the electoral support for the uninominal candidacies was 88.4%. Only five candidates received less than 85% of the votes. There were also variations in the degree of support in the different provinces. According to the (unreliable) sources of the opposition, the percentage of invalid votes reached even 30%. In the 1998 elections, where 601 seats had to be filled, the number of registered voters totaled 8,064,205. The turnout was recorded at 7,931,229 voters, or 98.4% of the total registered. 1.7% of the ballots were annulled, 3.4% blank, so that 7,533,222 were reported valid votes, or 95.0% of the total vote cast. In the elections of 9 January 2003, when 609 seats had to be filled, 97.0% of the voters supported the official candidates.

One of the formal functions of the National Assembly of People's Power is to appoint the president of the Council of State for a new five-year term. This office is practically reserved for Fidel Castro.

The redemocratization process taking place in Latin America and, above all, the downfall of Communism in the Soviet Union and Eastern Europe at the end of the 1980s plunged the Cuban regime into a profound socio-economic and political crisis of legitimacy. In 1991, on the occasion of the first Ibero-American summit, it became evident that the Latin American countries made the normalization of economic and political relations with Cuba dependent on its political democratization. But the wind of change did not arrive at the Caribbean island. Despite the growing criticism on the absence of a liberal democratic system, Castro managed to defend the monocratic system without making any substantial progress toward a real liberalization of the regime. The only reform agreed to related to the way the members of the National Assembly of People's Power were elected. In accordance with the recommendations of the Fourth Congress of the Cuban Communist Party in 1991, by the new Electoral Law of 29 October 1992, indirect elections were replaced by direct ones. Furthermore, in the international field, the government made clear efforts to improve its relations with both Latin American and Third World countries. In short, the Cuban government tended toward the Chinese model of economic liberalization: opening to foreign investment on the one hand, and adhering to the socialist model and hampering any trace of substantial political liberalization on the other. This position led to discord with the United States, which intensified the economic blockade against Cuba and, within the framework of the Helms-Burton Law of 12 April 1996, threatened to penalize those countries which tried to strengthen their commercial relations with Cuba. The Latin American countries, Canada, and the European Union categorically rejected the U.S. sanction policy. When Pope John Paul II visited Cuba in January 1998 for the first time, he asked Castro for a conciliatory gesture, particularly for the release of political prisoners. Shortly afterwards, the Cuban government freed almost 300 dissidents. This concession obviously encouraged dissident groups, although the regime spokesman maintained that Cuba's decision did not mean that the island would yield to the political opposition. Interior dissident groups organized the Varela project. According to the constitutional provision that demands 11,000 signatures in order to call for a referendum, they collected signatures for a referendum to be held on the topic of a peaceful opening of the regime. In 2002, Oswaldo Payá, the coordinator of the project, received the Sakharov Prize for Freedom of Thought from the European Parliament. But the National Assembly of People's Power rejected the initiative as unconstitutional. Instead, it approved a reform of the constitution that declared the socialist regime as irrevocable.

1.2 Evolution of Electoral Provisions

The evolution of suffrage in Cuba must be divided into two periods, before and after the Revolution of 1959. Sources of the pre-revolutionary provisions are the constitution of 1901, which was fundamentally reformed in 1928, the Statute for the Provisional Government of Cuba (*Estatuto para el Gobierno Provisional de Cuba*) from 1933, the Constitutional Laws (*Leyes Constitutionales*) from 1934 and 1935, the constitution of 1940, and the Constitutional Law (*Ley Constitucional*) from 1952. The most important laws and electoral laws (*Códigos*) date from 11 August 1900, 23 December 1903, 11 September 1908, 8 August 1919, 10 July 1928, 2 July 1934, 15 April 1939, and 31 May 1943.

Before the revolution, the president of the republic and the members of the two chambers of congress (chamber of deputies and the senate) were elected in general elections. However, until 1940, the president and the senators were elected indirectly. The presidential term of office was four years and was increased to seven years in 1928. Re-election was only permitted until 1940. Originally, the term of office for senators was eight years and that of deputies four years. In 1928, the term for senators was increased to ten years, and that of the deputies to seven years. The constitution of 1940 reduced the term of both chambers to four years. Elections for president and congress were held on the same day, but half of the parliamentary mandates were renewed in mid-term elections.

As to the franchise, the constitution of 1901 established universal male suffrage. The Statute of Provisional Government from 1934 gave women the right to vote, so that they participated in the elections of 1936, 1938, and 1939 before female suffrage was constitutionally granted by the constitution of 1940. In the same year, suffrage became compulsory. The Electoral Law of 1919, however, had established that non-voting persons would loose their inscription in the permanent register of voters, created that same year, and would have to re-inscribe personally if they wanted to get the electoral identity card and their franchise again. Until 1940, the age for active suffrage was 21 years or above, since then 20 years. To be elected president, the age requirement originally amounted to 40 years, after 1940 it was reduced to 35 years. Nomination was free, with the exception of the constitutional reform of 1928, by which all parties except the Partido Liberal (PL; Liberal Party), the Partido Conservador Nacional (PCN; Conservative National Party), and the Partido Popular Cubano (PPC; Popular Cuban Party) were prohibited.

As to the electoral system, the president was elected by plurality in accordance with the constitution of 1940. Prior to this, since 1901, he was elected by an electoral college. The members of parliament were elected by plurality in MMCs, where the electors had a number of votes smaller than the number of candidates to be elected. In 1901, when the electoral law reduced the number of seats to 31, there was one MMC with 2 seats, one with with 3, one with 4 and one with 8 seats and two MMCs with 7 seats. The electors had a number of votes lower than the number of seats in the districts. While the province remained the territorial electoral unit, from 1940 on the electoral system changed. Proportional representation was introduced for the chamber of deputies. In MMCs the Hare quota was applied. Any remaining seats were given to the parties that gained half the quota. The number of seats in the chamber and the constituencies depended on the demographic situation: one deputy for 25,000 inhabitants (between 1901 and 1940) and one for 35,000 (and a remainder of 17,000) inhabitants according to the constitution of 1940. For the senate, since 1940, six senators were elected per province, four corresponding to the majority and two for the minority.

The post-revolutionary sources of electoral provisions are: the Fundamental Law (*Ley Fundamental*) from 1959, the constitution from 24 February 1976, the Law of Constitutional Reform of 12 July 1992, the

(Electoral) Law Nr. 1305 of 7 July 1976, the (Electoral) Law Nr. 37 of 15 August 1982, and the (Electoral) Law Nr. 72 of 29 October 1992.

The 1976 Constitution established universal, equal, and secret suffrage for citizens over 16. The minimum age required to be a representative of the National Assembly of People's Power is 18. Officers of the army and other security forces have the right to vote and to be elected. The 1982 Electoral Law established compulsory suffrage. The term of office for the National Assembly of People's Power is five years.

According to the 1976 Constitution, the elections to the National Assembly of People's Power were indirect. The elections to the municipal assemblies were the basis for the representation system controlled by the Communist Party. In these elections, each municipality was divided into several constituencies, in which one representative was elected by the direct vote. The proportion of voters per delegate varied considerably, and ranged from 100 to 3,000 inhabitants. The delegates of the provincial and national assemblies were elected indirectly by the municipal assemblies. For the national assembly, the proportion was one delegate per 20,000 inhabitants of a municipality or a fraction bigger than 10,000. At present, there is one delegate for each municipality, even if its population does not amount to 10,000 inhabitants.

Free candidacy existed only at the level of local elections. The electoral law established at least two candidates per constituency. Candidates for the national assembly were presented by an electoral committee comprised of members of Cuban social organizations and the Communist Party. In order to reflect the popular will expressed in direct local elections in the national assembly, the following rule was established: 50% of the members of the national assembly had to be delegates of the municipal assemblies. Likewise, two lists of candidates to the national assembly were submitted to the voters: one with members of the municipal assemblies and the other one with members of the Communist Party, personalities of the social organizations, etc. The latter was formed by the Communist Party's executive committee at the provincial level. In direct local elections, the delegates were elected through an absolute majority of the vote. If none of the candidates reached this majority, a second round was held between the candidates with the highest percentage of votes. The election was valid only if at least 50% of the registered electors took part. The reform of 29 October 1992, considered by its defenders as a major step in the further democratization of Cuban society, introduced the direct election of the National Assembly of People's Power. At the same time, the requirement of a turnout over 50% of the registered electorate was dropped.

1.3 Current Electoral Provisions

Sources: Constitution of 24 February 1976; Law of Constitutional Reform of 12 July 1992; Electoral Law of 29 October 1992.

Suffrage: The right to vote is granted to all Cuban citizens over 16 years of age, the right to be elected for those over 18 years. Active suffrage is considered a right and a duty that is voluntarily exercised. Electors can revoke a representative, if 20% of the registered electorate demands it.

Elected national institutions: National Assembly of People's Power, (in 2003) 609 members, elected in SMCs. A representative is elected for each 20,000 inhabitants or a fraction bigger than 10,000. Elections take place every five years. They are non-competitive.

Nomination of candidates: The only party permitted is the Cuban Communist Party. The voter is expected to give a vote of consent to the monopolist party. Franchise is universal and direct. The voter can choose between candidates, at least between two candidates within each constituency, but they stand for the same political orientation. The nomination is given to the electors themselves, and they exercise this right in public assemblies in each electoral constituency by voting on different proposals. Political competition between candidates or campaigning is not allowed. Voters are informed about the candidates by biographical notes, which are posted at the polling station.

Electoral system: The absolute majority system in SMCs is applied. If no candidate achieves 50% of the votes plus one, a runoff election will be held between the top two candidates. The voter can vote in favor of the official semi-open list of candidates, vote for one of the candidates, cast a blank vote, or a non-valid vote.

1.4 Commentary on the Electoral Statistics

Despite all efforts, collecting historical and recent electoral data was very difficult. There are no systematic official reports on Cuban elections. The figures presented were mainly taken from secondary sources, the format adopted for reporting electoral data was not consistent. Data are incomplete and not completely reliable.

2. Tables

2.1 Dates of National Elections, Referendums, and Coups d'Etat

Year	Presidential elections	Parliamentary elections	Elections for Constitutional Assembly	Referendums	Coups d'état
1900			15/09		
1901	31/12	31/12[a]			
1904		28/02[b]			
1905	01/12	01/12[a]			
1906					29/09[c]
1908	14/11	14/11[a]			
1910		01/11[b]			
1912	01/11	01/11[a]			
1914		01/11[b]			
1916	01/11	01/11[a]			
1918		01/11[b]			
1920	01/11	01/11[a]			
1922		01/11[b]			
1924	01/11	01/11[a]			
1926		01/11[b]			
1928	01/11		05/03		
1930		01/11[d]			
1932		01/11			
1933					12/08
1933					05/09
1934					15/01
1936	10/01	10/01			
1938		05/03[a]			
1939			15/11		
1940	14/07	14/07[a]			
1942		15/03			
1944	01/06	01/06[a]			
1946		01/06			
1948	01/06	01/06[a]			
1950		01/06			
1952					10/03
1954	01/11	01/11[a]			
1956		01/11[a]			
1958	01/11				

[a] Mid-term elections to allocate one half of the seats in the house of representatives and in the senate.
[b] Mid-term elections to allocate one half of the seats in the house of representatives.
[c] US military intervention.
[d] One part of the members of the house of representatives and of the senate are appointed following the so called '*Prórroga de Poderes*' (Reform of the 1928 Constitution).

2.2 Electoral Body 1900–1954

Year	Type of election[a]	Population[b]	Registered voters		Votes cast		
			Total number	% pop.	Total number	% reg. voters	% pop.
1900	CA	1,600,000	—	—	—	—	—
1901	Pr/C/S	1,680,000	335,699	20.0	213,166	63.5	12.7
1904	C[c]	1,880,000	—	—	—	—	—
1905	Pr/C[c]/S[c]	1,930,000	429,730	22.3	317,974	74.0	16.5
1908	Pr/C/S	2,090,000	466,745	22.3	331,455	71.0	15.9
1910	C[c]	2,220,000	512,652	23.1	352,424	68.7	16.9
1912	Pr/C[c]/S[c]	2,360,000	628,356	26.6	—	—	—
1914	C[c]/S[d]	2,510,000	—	—	—	—	—
1916	Pr/C[c]/S[c]	2,660,000	—	—	—	—	—
1920	Pr/C[c]/S[c]	3,000,000	515,353	17.2	—	—	—
1922	C[c]	3,170,000	—	—	—	—	—
1924	PrC[c]/S[c]	3,350,000	—	—	—	—	—
1928	CA/Pr	3,510,000	—	—	—	—	—
1930	S[c]/C[c]	3,650,000	—	—	—	—	—
1932	C[c]/S[d]	3,960,000	737,778	18.6	—	—	—
1936	Pr/C/S	4,110,000	1,675,813	40.8	1,123,848	67.1	27.3
1938	C[c]	4,230,000	1,697,651	40.1	749,737	44.2	17.7
1939	CA	4,250,000	1,940,434	45.7	—	—	—
1940	Pr/C/S	4,290,000	1,936,212	45.1	1,421,563	73.4	33.1
1942	C[c]	4,370,000	1,977,001	45.2	—	—	—
1944	Pr/C/S	4,850,000	2,330,021	48.0	—	—	—
1946	C[c]/S[c]	4,850,000	—	—	—	—	—
1948	Pr/C/S	5,164,000	2,506,734	48.5	1,972,705	78.7	38.2
1950	C[c]/S[c]	5,362,000	2,577,864	48.1	—	—	—
1954	C[c]/S	5,807,000	2,768,186	47.7	1,452,763	52.4	25.0

[a] C = Chamber of Deputies; CA = Constitutional Assembly; Pr = President; S = Senate.
[b] Censuses: 1899: 1,572,797; 1907: 2,048,980; 1919: 2,889,004; 1931: 3,962,344; 1943: 4,778,583; 1953: 5,829,029.
[c] Mid-term elections.
[d] Mid-term elections to fill up vacancies occurred during the legislative term.

2.3 Abbreviations

ABC	Full name unknown
AP	*Acción Progresista* (Progressive Action)
AR	*Acción Republicana* (Republican Action)
CLD	*Coalición Liberal Democrática* (Democratic Liberal Coalition)
CCN	*Conjunción Centrista Nacional* (National Centristic Association)
CND	*Conjunto Nacional Democrático* (Democratic National Association)
COI	*Coalición Oriental Independiente* (Independent Eastern Coalition)
CPN	*Coalición Progresista Nacional* (National Progressive Coalition)
CSP	*Coalición Socialista Popular* (Popular Socialist Coalition)
PAN	*Partido Agrario Nacional* (National Agrarian Party)
PAU	*Partido de Acción Unitaria* (Party of United Action)
PCN	*Partido Conservador Nacional* (National Conservative Party)
PD	*Partido Demócrata* (Democratic Party)
PDN	*Partido Demócrata-Nacionalista* (Democratic-Nationalist Party)
PDR	*Partido Democrático Republicano* (Republican Democratic Party)
PL	*Partido Liberal* (Liberal Party)
PL(H)	*Partido Liberal Histórico* (Historical Liberal Party)
PL(U)	*Partido Liberal Unionista* (Unionist Liberal Party)
PL(Z)	*Partido Liberal Zayista* (*Zayista* Liberal Party)
PLN	*Partido Liberal Nacional, Asbertista* (National Liberal Party, *Asbertista*)
PLP	*Partido Liberal Provincial, Oriente/Camagüey* (Provincial Liberal Party)
PM	*Partido Moderado* (Moderate Party)
PN	*Partido Nacional* (National Party)
PNC	*Partido Nacional Cubano* (Cuban National Party)
PNM	*Partido Nacional Moderado, Camaüey* (Moderate National Party, Camaüey)
PNR	*Partido Nacional Radical, Oriente* (Radical National Party, East)
PNRev	*Partido Nacional Revolucionario, Realista* (Revolutionary National Party, Realist)
PPC(O)	*Partido del Pueblo Cubano, Orthodox* (Party of the Cuban People, Orthodox)
PPC	*Partido Popular Cubano* (Cuban Popular Party)
PP	*Partido Progresista* (Progressive Party)
PR	*Partido Republicano* (Republican Party)
PRF	*Partido Republicano Federal* (Federal Republican Party)
PRC	*Partido Republicano Conservador* (Conservative Republican Party)
PRC(A)	*Partido Revolucionario Cubano, Auténtico* (Cuban Revolutionary Party, Authentic)
PRH	*Partido Republicano Histórico* (Historical Republican Party)
PSD	*Partido Social-Demócrata* (Social-Democratic Party)
PSP	*Partido Socialista Popular* (Popular Socialist Party)
PUC	*Partido Unionista Cubano* (Cuban Unionist Party)
UNa	*Unión Nacionalista 1927* (Nationalist Union 1927)
UR	*Unión Radical* (Radical Union)
URC	*Unión Revolucionaria Comunista* (Comunist Revolutionary Union)

2.4 Electoral Participation of Parties and Alliances 1901–1954

Party / Alliance	Years	Elections contested	
		Presidential[a]	Parliamentary[b]
Coalición Nacional Republicana	1901	1	—
PN	1901	1	1
PNC	1901; 1914	—	2
PR	1901; 1944–1950	2	4
PRF	1901	—	1
COI	1904	—	1
PLN	1904; 1912	1	2
PNM	1904	—	1
PNR	1904	—	1
PRC	1904	—	1
PRH	1904	—	1
PM	1905	1	1
Coalición Liberal[c]	1908	1	1
PCN	1908–1932	6	13
PL(H)	1908	1	1
PL(Z)	1908	1	1
Conjunción Patriótica[d]	1912	1	1
PL	1910–1954	10	21
PL(U)	1914–1918	—	1
PLP	1914–1918	—	2
Coalición Demócrata-Liberal-Nacionalista[e]	1920	1	1
Liga Nacional[f]	1920	1	1
PDN	1920	1	1
PPC	1920–1934; 1938	3	8
Coalición Liberal Popular[g]	1924	1	1
PP	1932	—	1
AR	1936; 1940	2	2
CCN	1936	1	—
CND	1936–1940	2	3
Coalición Tripartita[h]	1936	1	1
Liga CND-PUC	1936	1	0
PSD	1938	0	1

Party / Alliance (continued)	Years	Elections contested	
		Presidential[a]	Parliamentary[b]
PUC	1936–1938	1	2
UNa	1936–1940	2	3
ABC	1940–1946	2	4
CSP	1940	1	1
Frente de Oposición[i]	1940	1	1
PAN	1940	1	1
PDR	1940	1	1
PNRev	1940	0	1
PRC(A)	1940–1954	3	7
URC	1940–1942	1	2
PD	1942–1954	3	6
Alianza Auténtico-Republicana[j]	1944–1948	2	0
Coalición Socialista Democrática[k]	1944	1	0
PSP	1944–1950	2	4
CLD	1948	1	1
PPC(O)	1948–1950	1	2
Coalition among PRC(A), PD, and PL	1950	0	1
PAU	1950	0	1
AP	1954	1	1
CPN	1954	1	1
UR	1954	1	1

[a] Total number of presidential elections: 13.
[b] Only the number of elections for the lower house is indicated. Total number: 24.
[c] Coalition among PL(H) and PL(Z).
[d] Alliance among PCN and PLN.
[e] Coalition among PDN and PL.
[f] Alliance among PPC and PCN.
[g] Coalition among PL and PPC.
[h] Coalition among PL, UNa, and AR.
[i] Alliance among PRC(A), ABC, and AR.
[j] Alliance among PRC(A) and PR.
[k] Coalition among PD, PL, ABC, and PSP.

2.6 Elections for Constitutional Assemblies

1900	Total number	%	Seats	%
Registered voters	175,501	–		
Votes cast	131,627	75.0		
Invalid votes	—	—		
Valid votes	—	—		
			31	100.0
Coalición Republicana-Democrática (PR, UD)	—	—	18	58.1
PNC	—	—	9	29.0
Concentración Patriótica (PNC, Oriente)	—	—	4	12.9

1928	Total number	%	Seats	%
Registered voters	—	–		
Votes cast	—	—		
Invalid votes	—	—		
Valid votes	—	—		
			55	100.0
PL	—	—	29	52.7
PCN	—	—	21	38.2
PPC	—	—	5	9.1

1939	Total number	%	Seats	%
Registered voters	1,940,434	–		
Votes cast	—	—		
Invalid votes	—	—		
Valid votes	1,089,363	—		
			76	100.0
Frente gubernamental				
PUN	182,246	16.8	16	13.8
PUN	132,189	12.1	9	7.6
URC	97,944	9.0	6	5.2
CDN	77,527	7.1	3	2.6
PNRev	37,933	3.5	1	0.9
PPC	10,251	1.0	–	–
Frente de oposición				
PRC(A)	225,223	20.7	18	15.5
PDR	170,681	15.7	15	12.9
AR	80,168	0.7	4	3.4
ABC	65,842	6.0	4	3.4
PAN	9,359	0.9	–	–

2.7 Parliamentary Elections

Results for parliamentary election were not available.

2.8 Composition of Parliament

2.8.1 Lower Chamber (House of Representatives) 1901–1954

Year	1901		1904		1905		1908	
	Seats	%	Seats	%	Seats	%	Seats	%
	63	100.0	31	100.0	32	100.0	83	100.0
PN	27	42.8	–	–	–	–	–	–
PR	18	28.6	–	–	–	–	–	–
PRF	13	20.6	–	–	–	–	–	–
PNC	1	1.6	–	–	–	–	34	41.0
PRC	–	–	13	41.9	–	–	–	–
PLN	–	–	10	32.3	–	–	–	–
PNR	–	–	5	16.1	–	–	–	–
PNM	–	–	2	6.5	–	–	–	–
COI	–	–	1	3.2	–	–	–	–
PM	–	–	–	–	31	96.9	–	–
Coalición Liberal[a]	–	–	–	–	–	–	49	59.0
Independents	4	6.3	–	–	1	3.1	–	–

[a] Coalition among PL(H) and PL(Z).

Year	1910		1912		1914		1916[b]	
	Seats	%	Seats	%	Seats	%	Seats	%
	41	100.0	50	100.0	49	100.0	57	100.0
PCN	18	43.9	18	36.0	22	44.9	27	47.4
PL	23	56.1	24	48.0	15	30.6	27	47.4
PLN	–	–	8	16.0	–	–	–	–
Conjunción Patriótica[a]	–	–	26	52.0	–	–	–	–
PL(U)	–	–	–	–	9	18.4	4	7.0
PLP	–	–	–	–	2	4.1	2	3.5
PNC	–	–	–	–	1	2.0	–	–

[a] PCN and PLN contested in 1912 as members of the Conjunción Patriótica. The Conjunción's seats were distributed as follows: PCN: 18 (36%); PLN: 8 (16.0%).
[b] The figures, as reported by the secondary sources, are inconsistent. The given total number of seats (57) is lower than the number of seats allocated to the parties (60).

Year	1918 Seats 61	% 100.0	1920 Seats 59	% 100.0	1922 Seats 57	% 100.0	1924 Seats 53	% 100.0
PCN	33	54.1	–[a]	–	25	43.9	22	41.5
PL	20	32.8	–[b]	–	28	49.1	–[c]	–
PL(U)	6	9.8	–	–	–	–	–	–
PLP	2	3.3	–	–	–	–	–	–
Liga Nacional[a]	–	–	31	52.6	–	–	–	–
Coalición Demócrata-Liberal-Nacionalista[b]	–	–	28	47.5	–	–	–	–
PPC	–	–	–[a]	–	4	7.0	–[c]	–
PDN	–	–	–[b]	–	–	–	–	–
Coalición Liberal-Popular[c]	–	–	–	–	–	–	31	58.5

[a] PCN and PPC contested in 1920 as members of the Liga Nacional. The Liga's 31 seats were distributed as follows: PCN: 26 (44.1%); PPC: 5 (8.5%).
[b] PL and PDN contested in 1920 as members of the Coalición Demócrata-Liberal-Nacionalista. All 28 seats went to the PL.
[c] PL and PPC contested in 1924 as members of the Coalición Liberal-Popular. 27 seats (50.9%) went to the PL, 4 (7.5%) to the PPC.

Year	1930 Seats 59	% 100.0	1932 Seats 69	% 100.0	1936 Seats 162	% 100.0	1938 Seats 83	% 100.0
PL	28	47.5	35	50.7	–[a]		25	30.1
PCN	23	39.0	25	36.2	–	–	–	–
PPC	8	13.6	9	13.0	–	–	4	4.8
Coalición Tripartita[a]	–	–	–	–	90	55.6	–	–
CND	–	–	–	–	70	43.2	24	28.9
UNa	–	–	–	–	–[a]	–	22	26.5
AR	–	–	–	–	–[a]	–	–	–
PUC	–	–	–	–	2	1.2	2	2.4
PSD	–	–	–	–	–	–	6	7.2

[a] AR, PL, and UNa contested in 1936 as members of the Coalición Tripartita. The coalition's 90 seats were distributed as follows: PL: 35 (21.6%); UNa: 30 (18.5%); AR: 25 (15.4%).

Year	1940[a]		1942		1944		1946	
	Seats	%	Seats	%	Seats	%	Seats	%
	162	100.0	57	100.0	70	100.0	66	100.0
PL	23	14.2	21	36.8	18	25.7	11	16.7
CND	18	11.1	–	–	–	–	–	–
UNa	21	13.0	–	–	–	–	–	–
Frente de Oposición[a]	62	38.3	–	–	–	–	–	–
PRC(A)	–[b]		10	17.5	–	–	–	–
PDR	22	13.6	–	–	–	–	–	–
AR	–[b]	–	–	–	–	–	–	–
ABC	–[b]	–	2	3.5	4	5.7	3	4.5
URC	10	6.2	3	5.3	–	–	–	–
PD	–	–	21	36.8	17	24.3	10	15.2
PRC(A)	–	–	–	–	19	27.1	30	45.5
PR	–	–	–	–	8	11.4	7	10.6
PSP	–	–	–	–	4	5.7	5	7.6

[a] The figures, as reported by the secondary sources, are inconsistent. The given total number of seats (162) exceeds the number of seats allocated to the parties (156).
[b] In 1940, PRC(A), AR, and ABC contested as members of the Frente de Oposición. The Frente's 62 seats were distributed as follows: PRC(A): 34 (21.0%); AR:16 (9.9%); ABC: 12 (7.4%).

Year	1948		1950		1954	
	Seats	%	Seats	%	Seats	%
	70	100.0	66	100.0	130	100.0
PRC(A)	29	41.4	–[b]		16	12.3
PL	15	21.4	–[b]		24	18.5
PD	6	8.6	–[b]		15	11.5
PR	11	15.7	7	10.6	–	–
PSP	5	7.1	4	6.1	–	–
PPC(O)	4	5.7	9	13.6	–	–
PRC(A)/PD/PL	–	–	42	63.6	–	–
PAU	–	–	4	6.1	–	–
AP	–	–	4	6.1	60	46.2
UR	–	–	–	–	15	11.5

[a] The figures, as reported by the secondary sources, are inconsistent. The given total number of seats (66) is lower than the number of seats allocated to the parties (70).
[b] In 1950, PRC(A), PL, and PD formed a coalition. The coalition's 42 seats were distributed as follows: PRC(A): 28 (42.4%); PL: 8 (12.1%); PD: 6 (9.1%).

2.8.2 Upper Chamber (Senate) 1901–1954

Year	1901 Seats[a]	%	1905 Seats[a]	%	1908 Seats[a]	%	1912 Seats[a]	%
	24	100.0	12	100.0	24	100.0	13	100.0
PNC	11	45.8	–	–	–	–	–	–
PR	10	41.7	–	–	–	–	–	–
PM	–	–	12	100.0	–	–	–	–
Coalición Liberal[b]	–	–	–	–	24	100.0	–	–
PL(Z)	–	–	–	–	–[b]		–	–
PL(H)	–	–	–	–	–[b]		–	–
Conjunción Patriótica[c]	–	–	–	–	–	–	11	84.6
PCN	–	–	–	–	–	–	–[c]	–
PLN	–	–	–	–	–	–	–[c]	–
PL	–	–	–	–	–	–	2	15.4
Independents	3	12.5	–	–	–[b]		–	–

[a] Due to the system of partial renovation applied in parliament, its actual composition cannot be provided. This table indicates the composition of the chambers after each election, exclusively in relation to the seats allocation after each election.

[b] PL(Z), PL(H), and independent candidates contested in 1908 as members of the Coalición Liberal. The coalition's 24 seats were distributed as follows: PL(Z): 11 (45.8%); PL(H): 5 (20.8%); Independents: 8 (33.3%).

[c] PLN and PCN contested in 1912 as members of the Conjunción Patriótica. The Conjunción's 11 seats were distributed as follows: PCN: 7 (53.8%); PLN: 4 (30.8%).

Year	1914 Seats	%	1916 Seats	%	1920 Seats	%	1924 Seats	%
	1	100.0	12	100.0	13	100.0	12	100.0
PCN	1	100.0	8	66.7	–[a]	76.9	1	8.3
PL	–	–	4	33.3	2	15.3	7	58.3
PPC	–	–	–	–	–[a]	7.7	4	33.3
Liga Nacional[a]	–	–	–	–	11	84.6	–	–

[a] PCN and PPC contested in 1920 as Liga Nacional. The Liga's seats were distributed as follows: PCN: 10 (76.9%); PPC: 1 (7.7%).

Year	1930 Seats 24	% 100.0	1936 Seats 36	% 100.0	1940 Seats 36	% 100.0	1944 Seats 54	% 100.0
PCN	6	25.0	–	–	–	–	–	–
PL	18	75.0	–[a]	–	–[b]	–	–[c]	–
Coalición Tripartita[a]	–	–	24	66.7	–	–	–	–
AR	–	–	–[a]	–	–[d]	–	–	–
UNa	–	–	–[a]	–	–[b]	–	–	–
CND	–	–	12	33.3	–[b]	–	–	–
CSP[b]	–	–	–	–	22	61.1	–	–
PDR	–	–	–	–	–[b]	–	–	–
Frente de Oposición[d]	–	–	–	–	14	38.9	–	–
PRC(A)	–	–	–	–	–[d]	–	–[e]	–
ABC	–	–	–	–	–[d]	–	–[c]	–
AR	–	–	–	–	–[d]	–	–	–
Coalición Socialista Democrática[c]	–	–	–	–	–	–	30	55.6
Alianza Auténtico Republicana[e]	–	–	–	–	–	–	24	44.4
PD	–	–	–	–	–	–	–[c]	–
PSP	–	–	–	–	–	–	–[c]	–
PR	–	–	–	–	–	–	–[e]	–

[a] PL, AR, and UNa contested in 1936 as members of the Coalición Tripartita. The coalition's 24 seats were distributed as follows: PL: 10 (27.8%); UNa: 9 (25.0%); AR: 5 (13.9%).

[b] PDR, UNa, PL, PPC, CND, and URC contested in 1940 as Coalición Socialista Popular (CSP). The coalition's 22 seats were distributed as follows: PDR: 10 (27.8%); PL: 5 (13.9%); UNa: 5 (13.9%); CND: 2 (5.6%).

[c] PL, PD, ABC, and PSP contested in 1944 as members of the Coalición Socialista Democrática. The coalition's 30 seats were distributed as follows: PL: 13 (24.1%); PD: 10 (18.5%); ABC: 4 (7.4%); PSP: 3 (5.6%).

[d] PRC(A), ABC, and AR contested in 1940 as members of the Frente de Oposición. The Frente's 14 seats were distributed as follows: PRC(A): 8 (22.2%); ABC: 3 (8.3%); AR: 3 (8.3%).

[e] PRC(A) and PR contested in 1944 as members of the Alianza Auténtico-Republicana. The Alianza's 24 seats were distributed as follows: PRC(A): 17 (31.5%); PR: 7 (13%).

Year	1948		1954	
	Seats	%	Seats	%
	54	100.0	54	100.0
Alianza Auténtico-Republicana[a]	36	66.7	–	–
Coalición Liberal-Demócrata	18	33.3	–	–
Coalición Progresista-Nacional[c]	–	–	36	66.7
PRC(A)	–	–	18	33.3

[a] Alliance among PRC(A) and PR.
[b] Coalition formed by PL and PD.
[c] Coalition formed by AP, UR, PD, and PL.

2.9 Presidential Elections 1901–1954

1901	Total number	%
Registered voters	335,699	–
Votes cast	213,116	63.5
Invalid votes	—	—
Valid votes	—	—
Tomás Estrada Palma (independent)	158,970	—

1905	Total number	%
Registered voters	429,730	–
Votes cast	317,974	74.0
Invalid votes	—	—
Valid votes	—	—
Tomás Palma Estrada (PM)	306,874	—

1908	Total number	%
Registered voters	466,745	–
Votes cast	—	—
Invalid votes	—	—
Valid votes	331,455	—
José Miguel Gómez (Coalición Liberal: PL(Z)/PL(H))	201,199	60.7
Mario G. Menocal (PCN)	130,256	39.3

1912	Total number	%
Registered voters	628,356	–
Votes cast	—	—
Invalid votes	—	—
Valid votes	—	—
Mario G. Menocal (Conjunción Patriótica: PCN/indep.)	194,504	—
Alfredo Zayas (PL)	180,640	—

For the 1916 elections no detailed data were available. Mario G. Menocal was re-elected.

1920	Total number	%
Registered voters	515,353	–
Votes cast	—	—
Invalid votes	—	—
Valid votes	—	—
Alfredo Zayas (Liga Nacional: PPC/PCN)	148,278 [a]	—
José Miguel Gómez	124,739 [a]	—

a The votes of the Havana province, where Gómez gained majority, are excluded; the accurate definitive figures are not clear due to fraudulent maneuvers and to subsequent additional elections.

1924	Total number	%
Registered voters	—	–
Votes cast	—	—
Invalid votes	—	—
Valid votes	—	—
Gerardo Machado (Coalición Liberal-Popular: PL/PPC)	200,840	—
Mario G. Menocal	136,154	—

For the 1928 elections no detailed data were available. Gerardo Machado, candidate of the PL, PCN, and PPC, was re-elected.

1936	Total number	%
Registered voters	1,675,813	–
Votes cast	1,123,848	67.1
Invalid votes	—	—
Valid votes	—	—
Miguel Mariano Gómez (Coal. Tripartita: CND/AR/UNa)	343,289	—
Mario G. Menocal (CND)	256,606	—
Others[a]	–	–

a Carlos Manuel de Céspedes (CCN) withdrew.

1940	Total number	%
Registered voters	1,936,212	–
Votes cast	1,421,563	73.4
Invalid votes	—	—
Valid votes	—	—
Fulgencio Batista (Coal. Socialista Popular[a])	805,125	—
Ramón Grau San Martín (Frente de Oposición[b])	573,526	—
Reynaldo Márquez (PAN)	—	—

[a] Coalition formed by UCR, AP, PDR, CND and PL.
[b] Coalition formed by PRC(A), ABC and AR.

1944	Total number	%
Registered voters	2,330,021	–
Votes cast	—	—
Invalid votes	—	—
Valid votes	—	—
Ramón Grau San Martín (Alianza Auténtico-Republicana[a])	1,041,822	—
Carlos Saladrigas (Coal. Socialista Popular[b])	839,220	—

[a] Coalition of PR and PRC(A).
[b] Coalition of PSP and PPC.

1948	Total number	%
Registered voters	2,506,734	–
Votes cast	1,972,705	78.7
Invalid votes	—	—
Valid votes	—	—
Carlos Prío Socarrás (Alianza Auténtico-Republicana[a])	905,198	—
Ricardo Núñez Portuondo (Coal. Liberal-Democrática[b])	599,364	—
Eduardo Chibás (PPC(O))	324,634	—
Juan Marinello (PSP)	142,972	—

[a] Coalition of PRC(A) and PR.
[b] Coalition of PL and PDR.

1954	Total number	%
Registered voters	2,768,186	–
Votes cast	1,451,753	52.4
Invalid votes	—	—
Valid votes	—	—
Fulgencio Batista (Coal. Progresista Nacional: AP/UR/PDR/PL)	1,262,587	
Ramón Grau San Martín[a] [PRC(A)]	188,209	

[a] His candidacy was withdrawn.

1958: Andrés Rivero Agüero. Elected as the only candidate in fraudulent elections on 03/11/1958. Did not assume office due to the regime's downfall and to the success of the Socialist Revolution.

2.10 List of Power Holders 1902–2004

Head of State	Years	Remarks
Tomás Estrada Palma	1902–1906	Elected as the only candidate in the 1901 elections. Assumed presidency on 20/05/1902. Re-elected through fraudulent elections in 1905; this sparked violent uprising led by the *Partido Liberal* and the US military intervention. Deposed on 28/09/1906.
William H. Taft	1906	Appointed provisional governor and head of the military government by the president of the USA. Held office from 29/09/1906 to 13/10/1906.
Charles E. Magoon	1906–1909	Provisional governor and head of the military government appointed by the president of the USA. Held office from 13/10/1906 to 28/01/1909.
José Miguel Gómez Gómez	1909–1913	Elected in elections organized by the forces of occupation. Assumed office on 28/01/1909 and held it until 20/05/1913.
Mario G. Menocal Deop	1913–1921	Assumed office on 20/05/1913. His re-election in 1917 launched the Liberals' violent rebelion. Remained in office until 20/05/1921.
Alfredo Zayas Alfonso	1921–1925	Elections under the supervision of the US special envoy Enoch Crowder, who acted as a de facto head of government until 1923. Remained in office until 20/05/1925.

Head of State (cont.)	Years	Remarks
Gerardo Machado Morales	1925–1933	Established a dictatorial regime in 1928 by means of a constitutional reform and legal provisions (the so called *Prórroga de poderes*); had himself re-elected as the only candidate and extended his presidential term up to 1935.
Albert Herrera Franch	1933	Appointed provisional president after Machado's downfall. In legal terms, he did not assume presidency, due to the congress' failure to accept Machados' resignation. Resigned after one day in favor of Céspedes.
Carlos M. de Céspedes de Quesada	1933	Provisional president from 13/08 to 05/09/1933. Left office after the September Revolution.
Five-member Executive Comission	1933	Revolutionary junta (05–08/09/1933) formed by Ramón Grau San Martín, Porfirio Franco, José Miguel Irisarri, Sergio Carbó, and Guillermo Portela. Broke up after a few days in favor of a presidential government in order to facilitate diplomatic recognition by the US.
Ramón Grau San Martín	1933–1934	Held office from 10/09/1933 to 15/01/1934. Removed from office when the military denied its support, after the USA had denied his government diplomatic recognition.
Carlos Hevia de los Reyes Gavilán	1934	Appointed by Grau on 16/01/1934. Had to resign from his post (18/01/1934) when Batista's army denied its support.
Carlos Mendieta Montefur	1934–1935	Appointed president with the army's support. Overthrown by the military on 12/12/1935 after his economic and social policies failed to solve the crisis.
José A Barnet Vinageras	1935–1936	Appointed successor to Mendieta, governed with Batista's support until 20/05/1936.
Miguel Mariano Gómez Arias	1936	Elected in competitive elections, however with irregularities. Deposed by congress on 24/12/1936 when Batista withdrew his support.
Federico Laredo Brú	1936–1940	Vice president under Gómez, appointed constitutional substitute by the congress. Held office until 10/10/1940.
Fulgencio Batista y Zaldívar	1940–1944	Elected in free elections, after leaving his position as major in the army. Remained in office until 10/10/1944.

Head of State (cont.)	Years	Remarks
Ramón Grau San Martín	1944–1948	Defeated Saladrigas, the 'official' Batista-supported candidate, in the elections. The army did not participate in the process of power transfer. Held office until 10/10/1948.
Carlos Prío Socarrás	1948–1952	Elected to succeed Grau. Corruption and the pre-1933 excluding tendency reappeared in his government. Remained in office until 10/03/1952.
Fulgencio Batista y Zaldívar	1952–1958	Assumed power via a military coup. Elected president in 1954 as the only candidate and despite the complaints of broad sectors of society, a large part of which abstained, having been called by the opposition to do so. Held office until 31/12/1958.
Andrés Rivero Agüero	1958	Elected as the only candidate in fraudulent elections on 03/11/1958. Did not assume office due to the regime's downfall and to the success of the Socialist Revolution.
Manuel Urrutia	1959	Assumed presidential office, appointed by the representatives of the groups opposed to Batista. Resigned due to the influence of the revolution's leader, Fidel Castro, who held the prime ministerial office and due to disagreement with the official policy.
Osvaldo Dorticós Torrado	1959–1976	Appointed as Urrutia's successor, had limited power, due to Fidel Castro's pre-eminence in domestic policy.
Fidel Castro Ruiz	1976–	Elected by the national assembly, acts both as head of state and as president of the government (cabinet).

3. Bibliography

3.1 Official Sources

Academia de la Historia de Cuba (1952). *Constituciones de la República de Cuba.* Havana.
Archivo Nacional de Cuba. *Fondo Secretaría de la Presidencia, Fondo Especial, Fondo PRC(A)—Grau San Martín, Fondo PPC(O)—Eduardo Chibás.*
Borges, M. A. (1935). *Compilación ordenada y completa de la legislación cubana (1899–1934).* Havana.
Fitzgibbon, R. (1948). *The Constitutions of the Americas.* Chicago.
Third Congress of the Communist Party of Cuba (1986). Havana.
Schroeder, S. (1982*). Cuba. A Handbook of Historical Statistics.* Boston.

3.2 Books, Articles, and Electoral Reports

Aguilar, L. E. (1972). *Cuba 1933. Prologue to Revolution.* Ithaca, N.Y.: Cornell University Press
— (1986). 'Cuba, c. 1860–1934', in L. Bethell (ed.), *The Cambridge History of Latin America, Vol. V.* Cambridge: Cambridge University Press, 229–263.
Ameringer, C. D. (1985). 'The Auténticos and the Political Opposition in Cuba, 1952–1958'. *Hispanic American Historical Review*, 65: 327–351.
Annino, A. (1991). 'Cuba 1902–1990' (unpublished manuscript).
Benjamin, J. R. (1977). *The United States and Cuba. Hegemony and Dependent Development.* Pittsburgh: University of Pittsburgh Press.
Chongo Leiva, J. (1989). *El fracaso de Hitler en Cuba.* Havana: Editorial Letras Cubanas.
Duarte Oropesa, J. (1974). *Historiología Cubana.* Miami: Ediciones Universal.
Farber, S. (1976). *Revolution and Reaction in Cuba, 1933–1960. A Political Sociology from Machado to Castro.* Middletown, Conn.: Wesleyan University Press.
Guerra, R. et al. (eds.) (1952). *Historia de la Nación Cubana.* 10 Volumes. Havana: Editorial Historia de la Nación Cubana.
Guerrero Morales, B. (2000). 'Cuba frente a sus elecciones'. *Justicia Electoral*, 13: 53–62.
Instituto de la Historia del Movimiento Comunista y de la Revolución Socialista de Cuba anexo al Comité Central del Partido Comunista de Cuba (1987). *Historia del Movimiento Obrero Cubano 1865–1958.* Havana.

Le Riverend, J. (1984). 'Cuba. Del semicolonialismo al socialismo, 1933–1975', in P. González Casanova (ed.), *América Latina. Historia de medio siglo.* Mexico City, 39–86: Siglo Veintiuno Editores.

López Segrera, F. (1989). *Sociología de la colonia y la neocolonia cubana 1510–1959.* Havana: Editorial Ciencias Sociales.

Mateo, M. (1984). *Panorama Cronológico 1902–1925. De la instauración de la República mediatizada a la constitución del Partido Comunista.* Havana.

McDonald, R. H. and Ruhl, J. M. (1989). *Party Politics and Elections in Latin America.* Boulder, Colo.: Westview.

Nohlen, D. and Stahl, K. (1989). 'Kubas Kurs der Kurswechsel. Eine Bilanz der wirtschaftlichen, sozialen und politischen Entwicklung', in R. Rytlewsky (ed.), *Politik und Gesellschaft in sozialistischen Ländern. PVS-Sonderheft 20*, 489–509.

Pérez, L. A. (1976). *Army Politics in Cuba 1898–1958.* Pittsburgh, Pa.: University of Pittsburgh Press.

— (1978). *Intervention, Revolution, and Politics in Cuba, 1913–1921.* Pittsburgh, Pa.: University of Pittsburgh Press.

— (1983). *Cuba between Empires, 1878–1902.* Pittsburgh, Pa.: University of Pittsburgh Press.

— (1986). *Cuba under the Platt Amendment, 1902–1934.* Pittsburgh: University of Pittsburgh Press.

— (1996). *Cuba. Between Reform and Revolution* (2nd edn.). Oxford: Oxford University Press.

— (1990). 'Cuba c. 1930–1958', in L. Bethell (ed.), *The Cambridge History of Latin America, Vol. VII.* Cambridge: Cambridge University Press, 419–455.

Riera Hernández, M. (1955). *Cuba política 1899–1955.* Havana: Impresora Modelo.

Roca, S. (1982). 'Cuba', in R. J. Alexander (ed.), *Political Parties of the Americas, Vol. I.* Westport, Conn.: Greenwood Press, 325–344.

Ruiz, Ramón E. (1968). *Cuba. The Making of a Revolution.* Amherst, Mass.: University of Massachusetts Press.

Santos Jimenez, R. (1946). *Tratado de Derecho Electoral.* Havana.

Stahl, K. (1984). 'Die Institutionalisierung politischer Herrschaft in Cuba. Die Organe des Poder Popular', in D. Nohlen (ed.), *Wahlen und Wahlpolitik in Lateinamerika.* Heidelberg: Esprint, 245–261.

— (1987). *Kuba – eine neue Klassengesellschaft?* Heidelberg: Heidelberger Verlagsanstalt.

— (1996). 'Politische Institutionalisierung und Partizipation im postrevolutionären Kuba', in H. Barrios and J. Suter (eds.), *Politische Repräsentation und Partizipation in der Karibik*, Opladen: Leske + Budrich, 71–98.

Suárez Salazar, L. (1995). 'El sistema electoral cubano. Apuntes para una crítica', in Centro de Estudios sobre América (ed.), *La democracia en Cuba y el diferendo con los Estados Unidos*. Havana: Centro de Estudios sobre América, 190–215.

Suchlicki, J. (1988). *Historical Dictionary of Cuba*. Metuchen, N.J.: Scarecrow Press.

— (1990). *From Columbus to Castro*. Washington, D.C.: Brasseys.

Suter, J. (1996). 'Politische Repräsentation und Partizipation in Kuba', in H. Barrios and J. Suter (eds.), *Politische Repräsentation und Partizipation in der Karibik*, Opladen: Leske + Budrich, 11–70.

Thomas, H. (1971). *Cuba, or the Pursuit of Freedom*. London: Harper & Row.

DOMINICA
by Matthias Catón

1. Introduction

1.1 Historical Overview

Together with St. Lucia, St. Vincent and the Grenadines, and Grenada, the Commonwealth of Dominica belongs to the Windward Islands (Lesser Antilles). The former British colony gained independence in 1978 and since then has been a republic within the Commonwealth. Caribs lived on the island when Columbus discovered it in 1493. The Caribs themselves had exterminated the native Arawaks in the 14th century. Today, the population consists mainly of descendants of African slaves brought to the island in the 18th century, although some Caribs still remain.

Strong resistance from native inhabitants frustrated Spanish attempts to settle on Dominica. During the 17th and 18th century Dominica was the subject of a dispute between England and France, and control over the island changed hands several times. The Treaty of Paris granted the island to Britain in 1763 but the French invaded it again in 1778. Five years later it was again ceded to Britain. The island remained under British control until independence in 1978, despite French attempts to invade it in 1795 and 1805. It officially became a British colony in 1805.

The first legislative assembly was established as early as the 1760s, representing the white population. In 1831, the Brown Privilege Bill extended political and social rights to all free nonwhites; three Blacks were subsequently elected to the legislative assembly. Seven years later, following the abolition of slavery in 1834, Dominica had a black-controlled legislature under the leadership of George Charles Falconer. It was the first British colony with an assembly dominated by nonwhites.

The interests of the white planters differed completely from those of the Blacks, who were mainly small landholders and merchants. The planters' intensive lobbying led to the curtailment of local political rights. The situation began to be reversed in 1865 when Britain decided that one-half of the legislature was to be appointed by the Crown. In 1898 the legislative council decided to abolish the election of the remaining half of its members and re-established the crown colony system; all twelve members of the legislative council were subsequently nominated by the Crown, one half being members of the administration and the other half citizens of the colony. The governor and the administrator were also members of the legislative council.

Politically, Dominica was part of the Leeward Island Federation from 1871. The Federation shared one governor. The legislative council of Dominica sent two of its members to the legislative council of the Federation, which consisted of eight nominated members and eight representatives from the islands.

In 1924 elected members were reintroduced to the legislative council, but the official and nominated members retained their majority. In order to be elected, people had to possess land or have a certain amount of yearly income. Active suffrage was granted to men over 21 and women over 30 years of age. In addition, suffrage was bound to certain economic conditions of either a minimum income, land ownership, or tax payments. Universal suffrage for all citizens over 21 years was introduced in 1951.

After World War I, citizens founded the Representative Government Association to demand more representation. It won one-third of the popularly elected seats in the legislature in 1924 and one-half in 1936. As in many Caribbean islands, labor unrest formed part of the protests for representation in the 1930s.

Having been in the Leeward Island Federation for almost 70 years, Dominica became part of the Windward Islands in 1940, before joining the new West Indies Federation in 1958. This federation consisted of ten members and was founded to forge closer economic and political ties between the Caribbean islands. Many local politicians saw this as the first step towards an independent union. However, the West Indies Federation was dissolved only four years later, mainly because of the conflicts between regional leaders. After the federation's two largest members—Jamaica and Trinidad and Tobago—had opted for independence outside the federation the project failed. Dominica became an associate state of the UK and was granted full internal self-determination in 1967.

On 3 November 1978, Dominica became an independent republic within the British Commonwealth. It has a parliamentary system with a prime minister as the head of government and an indirectly-elected president as head of state. The country's economy relies largely on agricultural products, especially bananas, which make up approximately one-half of the exports. This makes Dominica vulnerable to fluctuations in the world market prices of bananas and also to the impact of hurricanes, which strike the island frequently.

Dominica lacked political parties during the first elections. The island's oldest party, the Dominica Labour Party (DLP), nominated candidates for the first time in 1961. It had been founded by Phyllis Allfrey in 1957 and was led by Edward LeBlanc when it won its first elections in 1961. LeBlanc became chief minister and later prime minister, when Dominica was granted internal self-determination in 1967. The DLP's conservative counterpart was the DUPP which was founded in 1961. Its leaders were R. H. Lockhart and Franklin Baron. However, the DUPP was dissolved only four years later and gave way to the Dominica Freedom Party (DFP) of Eugenia Charles.

In the 1960s and 1970s several minor parties were formed, among them the Peasant and Workers Movement (PWM), the All Island Industrial and Farmers Party (AIFP), the Dominica Democratic Party (DDP), the Caribbean Federal Party (CFP), and the Progressive Labour Party (PLP), none of which survived.

Between 1961 and 1975 the DLP was the dominant party and won all elections. By the end of the 1970s the party and its leaders were severely criticized for their performance. Prime Minister Patrick John resigned in 1979 following criticism of his economic policies, which were seen as largely ineffective in the fight against the island's underdevelopment, and a scandal involving a secret land deal. Internal conflicts within the DLP and a general strike secured the downfall of his government. An interim government was formed until the next elections in 1980. The DLP had already experienced a brief division in 1970, when two factions competed in the elections. After the resignation of John some party members defected again and founded the Dominica Democratic Labour Party (DDLP), which ran in the 1980 elections. In 1985 another faction appeared: the United Dominica Labour Party (UDLP). The DLP reunited in 1990.

The DFP won the 1980 elections and Eugenia Charles became the Caribbean's first female prime minister. Charles opened up the island's economy to attract tourism and some light manufacturing in order to lower its dependency on agricultural exports. Her policies were neo-liberal and pro-western. She survived two coup attempts by her predecessor John in 1981 and as a consequence the military was abolished. She was re-elected in 1985 and in 1990, before announcing her plans to retire in 1993. Brian Alleyne, Minister for External Affairs, became the leader of the DFP and her designated successor.

In 1992, the government introduced a controversial act to enable foreigners to buy Dominican citizenship for US$ 35,000 in investments. Protests—led mainly by the newly-found United Workers Party (UWP)—forced the government to alter its proposal. The issue was a main factor in the 1995 elections, which were won by the UWP. The party had been founded in 1988 and was only participating in elections for the second time. Its leader Edison James was elected prime minister.

In 2000 the DLP returned and won the largest share of seats in the house of assembly. For the first time in Dominican history, however, the winner fell short of an absolute majority. Hence, the DLP had to form a coalition and it chose to build an alliance with its former main rival, the conservative DFP. This major shift in the political landscape was possible because DLP Leader and newly-elected Prime Minister Roosevelt 'Rosie' Douglas had moved his party to the center. On 1 October 2000 Douglas died unexpectedly of a heart attack and Pierre Charles, DLP deputy leader and minister for communication, took over office; he was officially sworn in on 3 October.

Like most Caribbean countries that were once British colonies, Dominica based its own electoral system on Britain's. The plurality system was introduced before independence and remains unaltered. The electoral system facilitated the development of what was, for a long time, essentially a two-party system (DLP and DFP) and which has recently evolved into a three-party system with the rise of the UWP. The lack of ethnical or religious cleavages means that party competition is organized along a classical economic left-right axis with pro-labor parties on the left (DLP, UWP) and a more conservative party (DFP) on the right. Electoral volatility has generally decreased during the last six elections, although it rose again in 2000. Proportionality between vote shares and seat shares varies from election to election, sometimes reaching very high levels compared to other countries with plurality in SMC and sometimes reaching very low levels. The electoral system has not prevented changes in power nor has it blocked new parties from rising, as was proved by the UWP. Despite the fact that, on two occasions (1995 and 2000), the party which came second in terms of votes won more seats than the party which obtained the most votes, there has apparently not been much discussion about this bias, which is generally considered as one of the disadvantages of the plurality system.

1.2 Evolution of Electoral Provisions

In 1924, elected members were reintroduced to the legislative council. At this time, it was made up of the governor, the administrator, six official members, two nominated members, and four elected members. After Dominica's entry into the Windward Islands Federation in 1940 the council consisted of the governor, three official members, three nominated members, and five elected members. In 1951, the number of elected members rose to eight; two ex-officio and three nominated members remained. When the UK granted Dominica full internal self-determination in 1967, the number of elected members was increased to eleven and one of the two ex-officio seats was dropped. Initially, the qualifying age for voting was 21 but was lowered to 18 in 1971.

1.3 Current Electoral Provisions

Sources: The Commonwealth of Dominica Constitution Order of 1978, House of Assembly Elections Act of 1951 (amended in 1954, 1956, 1960, 1963, 1965, 1967, 1969, 1971, 1974, 1977, 1987, and 1990), House of Assembly Disqualification Act of 1967 (amended in 1967, 1980, 1990); Registration of Electors Act of 1974 (amended in 1975, 1977, 1979, and 1990).

Most of the electoral regulations are determined by the constitution. The House of Assembly Elections Act and the Registration of Electors Act contain regulations on how to run elections, responsibilities of electoral authorities, and so on.

Suffrage: The minimum voting age is 18 years, and suffrage is universal. Citizen's must register in order to vote. Mentally ill and people serving prison sentences are excluded from voting. Citizens living abroad remain registered for five years in the constituency where they last resided.

Elected national institutions: Dominica has a unicameral parliament, the house of assembly. Since 1973, 21 representatives are elected. They decide if an additional nine senators should be elected or appointed. If appointed, the prime minister selects five and the opposition leader four senators who are then appointed by the president. At any time, the prime minister and the leader of the opposition can demand that the president recall a senator they had chosen. Vacancies are filled by the same procedure as described above. If elected, the regional representatives vote for the senators. The maximum term of office for a member of the house of assembly is five years, but the president can call elections at any time at the demand of the prime minister or—if the office of prime minister is vacant—at his own discretion.

The president is elected by the house of assembly for a five-year term. If the prime minister and the leader of the opposition agree on a candidate, the speaker of the house declares him president without a formal election. Otherwise, parliament elects the president by secret ballot. If no candidate receives a majority from all the members of parliament, the process of nomination and election is repeated. The president can be reelected once.

The president in turn appoints the leader of the majority party as prime minister. He also appoints the ministers on the prime minister's recommendation. The prime minister and the cabinet can be removed by a parliamentary no-confidence vote.

Nomination of candidates
- *presidential elections*: The prime minister and the opposition leader first have to try to agree on a joint candidate. Only if they fail to do so can the prime minister, the opposition leader, or any group of at least three members of parliament nominate a candidate for president. Candidates for president have to fulfill the requirements to be representatives or senators (see below). In addition, they have to be Dominicans, at least 40 years old, and have been living in Dominica for at least five years prior to their nomination. The requirement of residency is waived if a candidate has to live outside Dominica because he works for the Dominican government or any international organization of which the country is a member. Also, parliament can waive the residency requirement for any other person by a majority of three-fourths. The office of president is incompatible with any other office or remunerated occupation.
- *parliamentary elections*: Candidates for representative or senator have to be Dominican citizens, at least 21 years old, resident in Dominica at the time of nomination or have been living in Dominica for at least twelve months prior to the nomination, and be able to speak and read English sufficiently well to participate in the parliamentarian proceedings. (The reading requirement does not apply to people hampered by physical disabilities.) In addition to these requirements, the following people are disqualified from running as a candidate: dependents of a foreign power or state, clergymen, bankrupts, those serving a prison

sentence of twelve months or more, or those with undisclosed contracts with the government. Each candidate has to deposit 500 Eastern Caribbean Dollars at the time of nomination. The deposit is refunded if the candidate is elected or receives at least one eighth of the votes in his or her constituency.

Electoral system: Representatives are elected by plurality in 21 SMCs. If a seat becomes vacant, by-elections must be held within three months.

Organizational context of elections: The Electoral Commission is responsible for voter registration and the conduct of elections. It consists of a chairman and four members who are all appointed by the president. Two members act on behalf of the prime minister and two on behalf of the opposition leader. The Chief Elections Officer directs the elections and the registration process. He is appointed by the president and is an ex officio member of the Electoral Commission, which can give him orders. The constituencies are determined and, if necessary, altered by the Constituency Boundaries Commission. It consists of a chairman and four members who are all appointed in the same manner as described above for the Electoral Commission.

Disputes concerning the validity of elections, disqualifications, and so on are decided by the High Court and subsequently by the Court of Appeal.

1.4 Commentary on the Electoral Statistics

Electoral data for the 1975 to 2000 elections were taken from official publications from Dominica's Electoral Office (*Reports on the House of Assembly General Elections*). This information is reliable. Data for the elections from 1951 to 1970 were taken from Emmanuel (1992). Population data are mid-year estimates by the United Nations.

2. Tables

2.1 Dates of National Elections, Referendums, and Coups d'Etat

Year	Presidential elections	Parliamentary elections	Elections for Constit. Assembly	Referen- dums	Coups d'état
1951		31/10			
1954		19/08			
1957		15/08			
1961		17/01			
1966		07/01			
1970		26/10			
1975		24/03			
1980		21/07			
1985		01/07			
1990		28/05			
1995		12/06			
2000		31/01			

2.2 Electoral Body 1951–2000

Year	Type of election[a]	Population[b]	Registered voters Total number	% pop.	Votes cast Total number	% reg. Voters	% pop.
1951	Pa	51,690	23,288	45.1	17,680	75.9	34.2
1954	Pa	54,290	23,835	43.9	16,746	70.3	30.8
1957	Pa	57,020	23,348	40.9	17,639	75.6	30.9
1961	Pa	60,830	22,838	37.5	17,571	76.9	28.9
1966	Pa	65,920	24,147	36.6	19,380	80.3	29.4
1970	Pa	70,300	25,899	36.8	21,122	81.6	30.0
1975	Pa	76,000	29,266	38.5	23,107	79.0	30.4
1980	Pa	73,000	38,452	52.7	30,842	80.2	42.2
1985	Pa	77,000	45,018	58.5	33,565	74.6	43.6
1990	Pa	83,000	50,557	60.9	33,693	66.6	40.6
1995	Pa	74,000	57,632	77.9	37,563	65.2	50.8
2000	Pa	71,000	60,266	84.9	36,264	60.2	51.1

[a] Pa = Parliament.
[b] Estimates are taken from the UN *Statistical Yearbooks*. Population data for 2000 are taken from the UN *Population and Vital Statistics Report*.

2.3 Abbreviations

AIFP	All Island Industrial and Farmers Party
CFP	Caribbean Federal Party
DDLP	Dominica Democratic Labour Party
DDP	Dominica Democratic Party
DFP	Dominica Freedom Party
DLMA	Dominica Liberation Movement Alliance
DLP	Dominica Labour Party
DPF[a]	Dominica Progressive Force
DPP[a]	Dominica Progressive Party
DUPP	(Full name unknown)
PLP	Progressive Labour Party
PWM	Peasant and Workers Movement
UDLP	United Dominica Labour Party
UWP	United Workers Party

[a] The DPF changed its name to DPP in 1990.

2.4 Electoral Participation of Parties and Alliances 1951–2000

Party / Alliance	Years	Elections contested
DLP	1961–2000	9
AIFP	1961	1
DDP	1961	1
DUPP	1961–1966	2
PWM	1961	1
DFP	1970–2000	7
CFP	1975	1
PLP	1975	1
DDLP	1980	1
DLMA	1980	1
DPF / DPP[a]	1985–1990	2
UDLP	1985	1
UWP	1990–2000	3

[a] The DPF changed its name to DPP in 1990.

2.5 Referendums

Referendums have not been held.

2.6 Elections for Constitutional Assembly

Elections for constitutional assemblies have not been held.

2.7 Parliamentary Elections 1951–2000

Year	1951		1954	
	Total number	%	Total number	%
Registered voters	23,288	–	23,835	–
Votes cast	17,680	75.9	16,746	70.3
Invalid votes	1,309	7.4	997	6.0
Valid votes	16,371	92.6	15,749	94.0
Independents	16,371	100.0	15,749	100.0

Year	1957		1961	
	Total number	%	Total number	%
Registered voters	23,348	–	22,838	–
Votes cast	17,639	75.6	17,571	76.9
Invalid votes	1,013	5.7	1,056	6.0
Valid votes	16,626	94.3	16,515[a]	94.0
DLP	–	–	7,848	47.5
DUPP	–	–	4,233	25.6
AIFP	–	–	1,333	8.1
PWM	–	–	487	2.9
DDP	–	–	125	0.8
Independents	16,626	100.0	2,539	15.4

[a] For unknown reasons there is a difference of 50 votes between the number of valid votes and the sum of all votes as listed here. Data were taken from Emmanuel (1992).

Year	1966		1970	
	Total number	%	Total number	%
Registered voters	24,147	–	25,899	–
Votes cast	19,380	80.3	21,122	81.6
Invalid votes	1,322	6.8	1,347	6.4
Valid votes	18,058[a]	93.2	19,775	93.6
DLP	11,735	65.0	9,877	49.9
DUPP	5,815	32.2	–	–
DFP	–	–	7,578	38.3
DLP faction	–	–	1,387	7.0
Independents	568	3.1	933	4.7

[a] For unknown reasons there is a difference of 60 votes between the number of valid votes and the sum of all votes as listed here. Data were taken from Emmanuel (1992).

Year	1975		1980	
	Total number	%	Total number	%
Registered voters	29,266	–	38,452	–
Votes cast	23,107	79.0	30,842	80.2
Invalid votes	1,769	7.7	247	0.8
Valid votes	21,338[a]	92.3	30,595	99.2
DLP	10,523	49.3	5,126	16.8
DFP	6,920	32.4	15,706	51.3
PLP	897	4.2	–	–
CFP	119	0.6	–	–
DDLP	–	–	6,034	19.7
DLMA	–	–	2,575	8.4
Independents	2,880	13.5	1,154	3.8

[a] This is the official total. It is one vote less than the sum of all parties' votes.

Year	1985		1990	
	Total number	%	Total number	%
Registered voters	45,018	–	50,557	–
Votes cast	33,565	74.6	33,693	66.6
Invalid votes	284	0.8	251	0.7
Valid votes	33,281	99.2	33,442	90.3
DFP	18,865	56.7	16,529	49.4
DLP	13,014	39.1	7,860	23.5
UDLP	558	1.7	–	–
DPF / DPP[a]	78	0.2	74	0.2
UWP	–	–	8,979	26.9
Independents	766	2.3	–	–

[a] The DPF changed its name to DPP in 1990.

Year	1995		2000	
	Total number	%	Total number	%
Registered voters	57,632	–	60,266	–
Votes cast	37,563	65.2	36,264	60.2
Invalid votes	376	1.0	460	1.3
Valid votes	37,187	99.0	35,804	98.7
DFP	13,317	35.8	4,858	13.6
UWP	12,777	34.4	15,555	43.4
DLP	11,064	29.8	15,362	42.9
Independents	29	0.1	29	0.1

2.8 Composition of Parliament 1951–2000

Year	1951		1954		1957		1961	
	Seats	%	Seats	%	Seats	%	Seats	%
	8	100.0	8	100.0	8	100.0	11	100.0
DLP	–	–	–	–	–	–	7	63.6
DUPP	–	–	–	–	–	–	4	36.4
Independents	8	100.0	8	100.0	8	100.0	0	0.0

Year	1966		1970		1975		1980	
	Seats	%	Seats	%	Seats	%	Seats	%
	11	100.0	11	100.0	21	100.0	21	100.0
DLP	10	90.9	8	72.7	16	76.2	–	–
DUPP	1	9.1	2	18.2	–	–	–	–
DLP faction	–	–	1	9.1	–	–	–	–
DFP	–	–	–	–	3	14.3	17	81.0
DDLP	–	–	–	–	–	–	2	9.5
Independents	0	0.0	0	0.0	2	9.5	2	9.5

Year	1985		1990		1995		2000	
	Seats	%	Seats	%	Seats	%	Seats	%
	21	100.0	21	100.0	21	100.0	21	100.0
DFP	15	71.4	11	52.4	5	23.8	2	9.5
DLP	5	23.8	4	19.0	5	23.8	10	47.6
UDLP	1	4.8	–	–	–	–	–	–
UWP	–	–	6	28.6	11	52.4	9	42.9

2.9 Presidential Elections

Direct presidential elections have not been held.

2.10 List of Power Holders 1978–2004

Head of State	Years	Remarks
Sir Louis Cools-Lartigue	1978–1979	03/11–16/01, interim president.
Frederick E. Degazon	1979	16/01–15/06, left Dominica on 11/06.
Sir Louis Cools-Lartigue	1979	15/06–16/06 acting president for Fredrick Degazon.
Jenner Bourne Maude Armour	1980	21/06–25/02/1980, acting president for Frederick Degazon.
Aurelius John B. L. Marie	1980–1983	President 25/02/1980–19/12/1983.
Clarence H. Augustus Seignoret	1983–1993	President 19/12/1983–25/10/1993.
Crispin Anselm Sorhaindo	1993–1998	President 25/10/1993–06/10/1998.
Vernon Lorden Shaw	1998–2003	President since 06/10/1998.
Nicholas Liverpool	2003–	President since 02/10/2003.

Head of Government	Years	Remarks
Patrick R. John	1974–1979	27/07/1974–21/06/1979, prime minister of an independent state since 03/11/1978, resigned.
Oliver J. Seraphine	1979–1980	Prime minister 21/06/1979–21/07/1980.
Dame Mary Eugenia Charles	1980–1995	Prime minister 21/07/1980–14/06/1995.
Edison C. James	1995–2000	Prime minister 14/06/1995–03/02/2000.
Roosevelt Douglas	2000	Prime minister 03/02–01/10, died in office.
Pierre Charles	2000–2004	Elected prime minister on 01/10/2000; acting until 03/10/2000. He died in office.
Roosevelt Skerrit	2004–	Elected prime minister 08/01/2004.

3. Bibliography

3.1 Official Sources

Government of Dominica (ed.) (1991). *Laws of Dominica. Revised Edition.* Roseau, Dominica: Law Revision Commission.

Report on the House of Assembly General Elections 1975. Roseau: Dominica, Electoral Office.

Report on the House of Assembly General Elections 1980. Roseau: Commonwealth of Dominica, Electoral Office.

Report on the House of Assembly General Elections 1985. Roseau: Commonwealth of Dominica, Electoral Office.

Report on the House of Assembly General Elections 1990. Roseau: Commonwealth of Dominica, Electoral Office.

Report on the House of Assembly General Elections 1995. Roseau: Commonwealth of Dominica, Electoral Office.

Report on the House of Assembly General Elections 2000. Roseau: Commonwealth of Dominica, Electoral Office.

3.2 Books, Articles, and Electoral Reports

Alexis, F. (1983). *Changing Caribbean Constitutions.* Bridgetown, Barbados: Antilles.

Andre, I. W. and Christian, G. J. (1992). *In Search of Eden. Dominica, the Travails of a Caribbean Mini-State.* Upper Marlboro, Md.: Pond Casse Press.

Baker, P. L. (1994). *Centring the Periphery. Chaos, Order, and the Ethnohistory of Dominica.* Montreal: McGill-Queen's University Press.

Borome, J. A. (1972). *Aspects of Dominican History.* Roseau, Dominica: Government Printing Division.

DeMerieux, M. (1992). *Fundamental Rights in Commonwealth Caribbean Constitutions.* Bridgetown, Barbados: Faculty of Law Library, University of the West Indies.

Emmanuel, P. A. M. (1992). *Elections and Party Systems in the Commonwealth Caribbean, 1944–1991.* St. Michael, Barbados: CADRES.

Higbie, J. (1993). *Eugenia. The Caribbean's Iron Lady.* London/ Basingstoke: MacMillan.

Hillebrands, B. (1993). 'Dominica', in D. Nohlen, *Handbuch der Wahldaten Lateinamerikas und der Karibik.* Opladen: Leske + Budrich, 251–257.

Honychurch, L. (1984). *The Dominica Story. A History of the Island.* Roseau, Dominica: Dominica Institute.

Midgett, D. (1983). *Eastern Caribbean Elections 1950–1982. Antigua, Dominica, Grenada, St. Kitts-Nevis, St. Lucia, and St. Vincent.* Iowa City, Iowa: Center for Development Studies, University of Iowa.

Myers, R. A. (ed.) (1987). *Dominica* (World Bibliographical Series). Oxford et al.: Clio.

Nuscheler, F. (1995). 'Dominica', in D. Nohlen and F. Nuscheler, *Handbuch der Dritten Welt, Vol 3. Mittelamerika und Karibik.* Bonn: Dietz, 370–380.

O'Loughlin, C. (1968). *Economic and Political Change in the Leeward and Windward Islands.* New Haven, Conn.: Yale University Press.

Payne, D. W. (1995). *Democracy in the Caribbean. A Cause for Concern.* (Policy Papers on the Americas VI, 3). Washington, D.C.: Center for Strategic and International Studies.

Phillips, F. (1985). *West Indian Constitutions. Post-Independence Reform.* New York/ London/ Rome: Oceana.

Spackman, A. (ed.) (1975). *Constitutional Development of the West Indies 1922–1968. A Selection from Major Documents.* St. Lawrence, Barbados: Caribbean University Press.

Will, W. M. (1991). 'A Nation Divided. The Quest for Caribbean Integration'. *Latin American Research Review,* 26 (2): 3–37.

DOMINICAN REPUBLIC
by Julio Brea Franco

1. Introduction

1.1 Historical Overview

The Dominican Republic is situated in the East of the Caribbean island of Hispaniola, with Haiti being its neighbor. It declared its independence from Spain in 1821, but was occupied by Haiti only two months later. Haiti's occupation ended in 1844. A new constitution established a presidential system and indirect and secret suffrage for men. The initial years of Dominican political life were tainted by recurring violence among the different sectors of the oligarchies, headed by caudillos who based their power on clientelist ties. The independence of the newly-born nation was constantly at risk due both to the constant threat from Haiti and the actions of certain oligarchic groups, which, in view of the fragile national situation, looked to foreign countries for protection.

In 1861, on the initiative of President Santana, the country became a Spanish colony again. However, a revolution soon broke out against the colonial system in 1863, which ended when Spain abandoned the island in 1865.

The 1865 Constitution re-established the Dominican Republic, but failed to bring about political stability or solve its vulnerability to external forces. This constitution granted men universal and secret suffrage. At this stage there was an ongoing confrontation between the two main factions of the oligarchies, the *Rojos* (Conservatives) and the *Azules* (Liberals); both with a strong personalist character. Until 1882, changes in power were brought about through elections. However, these elections merely functioned as a confirmatory instrument as their public nature meant they contravened the constitutional regulations. In 1882, General Ulises Heureaux established a dictatorship, and a period of tyranny and political instability followed. Heureaux was killed in 1899.

In 1905, the Dominican Republic transferred the administration of customs to the United States, in the hope of counteracting the pressure of the European creditors. The increasing internal conflicts led the

United States to demand full control of the Dominican financial and military sectors. In 1916, congress dismissed President Juan I. Jiménez, who had seemed ready to give in to North American pressure, and the United States responded by invading the country. The occupation lasted until 1924, after which a new search for a sovereign and democratic system began. Its failure became evident, however, in the *coup d'état* led by Major Rafael Trujillo in 1930, who inaugurated a markedly authoritarian regime backed by the United States. The system was based on the concentration of political and economic power in the figure of the dictator and the people close to him, as well as on the reinforcement of the traditional clientelist ties. The dictator also succeeded in gaining the support of the armed forces and the *Partido Dominicano* (PD; Dominican Party), founded as a single party in 1930. In 1939, the exile Juan Bosch created a left-wing opposition party, the *Partido Revolucionario Dominicano* (PRD; Dominican Revolutionary Party). It was not until 1961, however, that an internal opposition appeared in the country, with the conservative, catholic *Unión Cívica Nacional* (UCN; National Civic Union). This same year, Trujillo was assassinated in an attack supported by the CIA, and a period of great political instability followed.

After the fall of both Trujillo's successor, Joaquín Balaguer, and General Echevarría, the country experienced a brief period of political liberation. For the first time in the country's history, political parties acquired a significant role. Free and secret national elections were held in 1962: These established the position of the PRD and its candidate, Juan Bosch, with a landslide electoral victory giving them the presidency and two-thirds of the seats in both chambers of parliament. In 1963, a new constitution was drawn up to guarantee both civil and public rights, declare the pre-eminence of the civil authority over the armed forces and arrange the separation of the State and Church. But the reforming policy of President Juan Bosch generated scepticism both in Washington and among the leading oligarchies, culminating in the 1963 *coup d'état*. Infighting began among the military men in power, and they divided into 'constitutionalists', who wanted the 1963 Constitution to be re-established, and 'loyalists', with right-wing conservative convictions. In view of the uncertainties resulting from this conflict, and in the context of the Cold War after the Cuban revolution, the United States intervened again.

In 1966, after an election that excluded the 'constitutionalists', Joaquín Balaguer assumed office. He established an authoritarian regime, backed by the conservative sectors of the armed forces and the *Partido Reformista* (PR; Reformist Party). The new constitution drawn up in 1966 still acts as the standard legal basis for the electoral law and electoral system to the present day. It established universal, equal, secret, direct and compulsory suffrage for all electoral processes. The Balaguer era, however, was characterized by violations of human rights and civil liberties, as well as the repression of the opposition. The opposition's main representative, the PRD, did not participate in either the 1970 or in the 1974 elections. Competition was thus restricted to the pro-government party and some right and center-right parties. The 1970s also witnessed an increase in political violence, both on the part of leftist terrorist groups and of the death squads linked to the armed forces. In 1974, Juan Bosch founded a new opposition party, the *Partido de Liberación Dominicana* (PLD; Party of the Dominican Liberation).

In the late 1970s, the government of US President Jimmy Carter (1976–1980) pressed for human rights to be respected and for a transition to political pluralism. Thus, in 1978, free and competitive elections were held, contested by all the relevant political forces. The winner was the candidate of the opposition, Silvestre Antonio Fernández Guzmán. His party, the PRD, also won the majority in both chambers of congress. The armed forces refused to accept this victory, and even conducted a coup attempt. Under strong pressure from Washington, Guzmán finally assumed presidency, but the *Junta Central Electoral* (JCE; Central Electoral Authority) diminished the PRD's triumph in the parliamentary elections, by distributing the votes that had not been cast equally between the PRD and the PR. (The JCE was the main institution for electoral organization. It had accumulated wide-ranging powers since 1923 and was in charge of the whole electoral process, although it was in fact subordinate to the executive.) With the 1978 elections a period of very problematic elections began (five elections up to 1994). In the 1982 elections, victory went once more to the PRD. Its candidate, Salvador Jorge Blanco, was elected president with 46.7% of the votes (Balaguer received 39.2%). His government was marked by the economic crisis, the austere policies imposed by the IMF and the increasing social conflicts. In 1986, Balaguer was elected president with 41.4% of the vote. During what was then his fifth term of office he implemented populist policies in the economic sector. Balaguer and Bosch, the two great political figures of modern Dominican history, contested the 1990 elections. Balaguer took advantage of the split between PRD and one of its factions. This splinter group contested the elections under its new name, *Partido Revolucionario Independiente* (PRI; Independent Revolutionary Party), with its own presidential candidate. After a long vote count, the JCE declared Balaguer had won by a narrow margin (Balaguer won

35.5% of the votes compared with Bosch's 34.2%). This led to protests and accusations of fraud from the opposition. Balaguer's victory prompted a series of reforms in the electoral law in 1992, including: a rise in the number of members of the JCE, nominated by the three majority parties, although three out of five were backed by Balaguer; changes in the JCE's organizational structure and the elaboration of a new electoral roll. Despite these reforms, the 1994 elections were also branded fraudulent and their results questioned. The JCE proclaimed a narrow win for the PR (42.3%) versus the PRD (41.8%) and ratified Balaguer's presidency. Unlike the 1990 elections, the changes in the electoral organization, the higher vigilance of society and the international pressure, made it easier to investigate and identify irregularities. Even though adequate corrective measures were not applied, a political agreement was reached, the so-called *Pacto por la Democracia* (Pact for Democracy), which included a shortening of the presidential term of office by two years. Thus, in 1996, presidential elections were held, from which Balaguer abstained for the first time since 1966. Nevertheless, he continued to move the political strings in the background: after the first round of the presidential elections, his party, the PRD, and Juan Bosch's PLD united under the *Frente Patriótico* (Patriotic Front), supporting Leonel Fernández Reyna against the PRD's candidate, José F. Peña Gómez. In a particularly transparent and fair second round, Fernández was elected president. The composition of the legislative remained as it was in 1994, i.e. controlled by the PR and the PRD, whereas the president's PLD had only one out of the 30 senators and little more than 10% of the deputies.

The legislative backing of the president declined further after the 1998 parliamentary elections, which were clearly won by the PRD. The presidential elections of 2000 were then won by the PRD candidate Hipólito Mejia, and not by Danilo Medina, Fernández choice for succeeding him as president.

Mejia's tenure has been accompanied by an economic downturn, combined with rising public expenditure. He has also been criticized for his alleged autoritharian style. The PRD's vast majority in parliament allowed the president to reform the constitution and introduce presidential re-election.

1.2 Evolution of Electoral Provisions

To understand the evolution of Dominican electoral law one has to look back to 1923/24, when the first modern electoral law was introduced. During the first and second Republic (1845–1914), laws and regulations were constantly changed, a fact that reflects the general political instability during this time.

Throughout Dominican history there has been a total of ten different electoral laws. The current law has been revised 26 times from 1962 to date. Electoral provisions in the 1966 Constitution have also been changed twice.

The electoral law of 1923 was negotiated between the United States and local political forces. For the first time, a body was established to organize the elections, the *Junta Central Electoral* (JCE).

Universal male suffrage was established in 1865 (members of the police and armed forces have been excluded from voting since 1923). Economic conditions for voting were reestablished only for a brief period from 1879 to 1880. Female suffrage was introduced in 1942.

The minimum voting age was established at 21 years in 1844. In 1865, the age was lowered to 18 and increased again to 21 four years later. Since 1873, it has been established at 18 years of age.

As of 1844, the president was indirectly elected by absolute majority through an electoral college. If no candidate received an absolute majority, a second round was held between the three candidates with the most votes, followed by a third round between the top two candidates, if no candidate achieved an absolute majority in the second round either. Direct presidential elections were introduced in 1858, at first through a simple majority, but from 1877 onwards through an absolute majority and possible second and third rounds similar to the process before 1858. Between 1924 and 1994, simple majority was reintroduced.

The presidential term has always been four years, the only exceptions being the period from 1908 to 1924, when it was six years and between 1942 and 1962, when it was five years. Re-election was possible except for the 1996 and 2000 elections.

Members of the house of deputies were elected by plurality in SMCs between 1844 and 1914. From 1914 to 1924, the deputies were elected indirectly by provincial electoral colleges using the system of absolute majority. MMCs were introduced in 1924, but an important number of SMCs remained until 1962. Since then, all constituencies have been MMCs, usually with two or three deputies. The size of the constituencies was reduced again in 2002. Lists were open with multiple votes between 1924 and 1930. Since 1930, lists have been closed and blocked.

Since 1924, senators have been elected in SMCs using the method of plurality. The constituencies correspond to the development of the provinces and thus the number of senators has risen with the number of provinces: in 1924 there were twelve, today there are 31.

For most of the Dominican electoral history voters only had one vote; that is, they could not choose different parties for presidential, parliamentary and local elections. Separate votes for presidential and parliamentary elections were only possible in 1974, 1978, 1982 and 1990. Between 1996 and 2002 a type of electoral college was used for voting: voters had to appear at one of two dates (for example, either in the morning or afternoon) at a given time and wait for a couple of hours until all the voters were there and then vote at the same time. Given the impracticability of this procedure it was dropped in 2002.

1.3 Current Electoral Provisions

Sources: constitution of 28/11/1966, revised on 14/08/1994 and 20/07/2002; *Ley Electoral* No. 275-97 of 21/12/1997, *Ley de Registro Electoral* No. 55 of 1970; Laws 8-92 of 13/04/1992, 32-99 of 29/04/1999, 12-2000 of 06/04/2000 and Laws of 15/08/2002 and 10/12/2002.

Suffrage: All adults over 18 years can vote. Married people under this age limit may also vote. Members of the armed forces and the police are excluded from voting. Voting is compulsory, but no sanctions are applied. Citizens living abroad will be able to vote for the first time in 2004.

Elected national institutions: The elected offices at the national level are the president and the vice president and the members of the bicameral national congress, formed by the chamber of deputies and the senate. There are 32 senators and 150 deputies. The electoral term for these offices is four years. There is a different date for presidential and parliamentary elections. The president can be re-elected.

Nomination of candidates
- *presidential elections*: Candidates can be nominated either by political parties or by citizens' associations (so-called *Agrupaciones Políticas Accidentales*) that are especially created to nominate candidates for office.
- *parliamentary elections*: See the section on presidential elections above. In addition, 30% of candidates must be women. Parties may form list alliances.

Electoral system
- *presidential elections*: The president is directly elected by absolute majority. If no candidate obtains an absolute majority in the first round, a runoff is held between the two candidates who won the most votes.
- *parliamentary elections*: The deputies are elected using the system of proportional representation in MMCs, whose sizes range from one to eight. The constituencies generally correspond to the provinces plus the *Distrito Nacional*. The country's seven largest provinces are split into more than one constituency. There is one deputy per every 50,000 inhabitants or a fraction over 25,000, at least two deputies per province. The majority of the constituencies are small: 19 of two, 13 of three, seven of four, five of five, two of six and one of eight deputies. The candidates are presented in closed lists. Voters may cast a preferential vote for one candidate from the list they choose. The seats are allocated using the d'Hondt method.

The senate consists of 30 members. The senators are elected through plurality system in SMCs, which correspond to the 29 provinces plus the *Distrito Federal*. Voters have only one vote for both the senate and the chamber of deputies and hence cannot vote for different parties.

Organizational context of elections: The JCE is in charge of organizing the elections and also has judicial power in electoral matters. The JCE has nine members, including its president, who are chosen by the senate. Decisions made by the JCE can be appealed before the supreme court.

1.4 Commentary on the Electoral Statistics

The electoral results are published in the *Gaceta Oficial*. Most data have been taken from the *Gaceta* and other JCE publications, such as the *Archivo Administrativo*. The information published by the JCE is not always complete or necessarily accurate. Population data have been taken from the national censuses or are based on estimations made by the national statistical office (*Oficina Nacional de Estadística*) and the *Centro Latinoamericano de Demografía, Población y Desarrollo* (CELADE).

2. Tables

2.1 Dates of National Elections, Referendums, and Coups d'Etat

Year	Presidential elections	Parliamentary elections	Elections for Constitutional Assembly[a]	Referendums	Coups d'état
1924	15/03	15/03	15/03		
1927			01/06		
1929			01/06		
1930	16/05	16/05			23/02
1934	16/05	16/05	16/05		
1938	16/05	16/05			
1941			16/12		
1942	16/05	16/05			
1946			08/12		
1947	16/05	16/05			
1952	16/05	16/05			
1955			13/11		
1957	16/05	16/05			
1962	20/12	20/12	20/12		
1963					25/09
1966	01/06				
1970	16/05	16/05			
1974	16/05	16/05			
1978	16/05	16/05			
1982	16/05	16/05			
1986	16/05	16/05			
1990	16/05	16/05			
1994	16/05	16/05			
1996	16/05 (1st) 30/06 (2nd)				
1998		16/05			
2000	16/05				
2002		16/05			
2004	16/05				

[a] So-called *'Asambleas Revisoras de la Constitución'*. There are only data available on the first election in 1924.

2.2 Electoral Body 1924–2004

Year	Type of election[a]	Population	Registered voters Total number	% pop.	Votes cast Total number	% reg. voters	% pop.
1924	CA/G	1,012,000	147,228	14.5	—	—	—
1930	G	1,284,000	412,931	32.2	—	—	—
1934	G	1,440,000	286,937	19.9	—	—	—
1938	G	1,567,000	348,010	22.2	—	—	—
1942	G	1,742,000	—	—	—	—	—
1947	G	1,961,000	1,020,488	52.0	—	—	—
1952	G	2,227,000	1,224,550	55.0	—	—	—
1957	G	2,683,000	1,404,666	52.4	—	—	—
1962	G	3,437,000	1,646,973	47.9	1,066,295	64.7	31.0
1966	G	3,756,000	1,815,429	48.3	1,372,695	75.6	36.5
1970	G	4,289,000	2,044,619	47.7	1,297,843	63.5	30.3
1974	G	4,549,000	2,006,323	44.1	1,439,067	71.7	31.6
1978	G	5,112,000	2,283,784	44.7	1,731,095	75.8	33.9
1982	G	5,648,000	2,601,684	46.1	1,862,866	71.6	33.0
1986	G	6,542,000	3,039,347	46.5	2,195,648	72.2	33.6
1990	G	7,025,000	3,275,570	46.6	1,962,458	59.9	27.9
1994	G	7,552,000	3,598,328	47.6	3,150,838	87.6	41.7
1996	Pr (1st)	7,728,000	3,750,502	48.5	2,948,979	78.6	38.2
1996	Pr (2nd)	7,728,000	3,750,502	48.5	2,880,425	76.8	37.3
1998	Pa	7,904,000	4,129,554	52.2	2,183,707	52.9	27.6
2000	Pr	8,434,000	4,251,218	50.4	3,236,906	76.1	38.4
2002	Pa	8,678,000	4,647,839	53.6	2,371,591	51.0	27.3
2004	Pr	8,930,000	5,020,703	56.2	3,656,850	72.8	41.0

[a] CA = Constitutional Assembly; G = General Elections (i.e. presidential and parliamentary elections); Pa = Parliamentary Elections; Pr = Presidential Elections.

2.3 Abbreviations

14	*Agrupación Política 14 de junio* (Political Group of 14 June)
ANP	*Alianza Nacional Progresista* (Progressive National Alliance)
APD	*Alianza por la Democracia* (Alliance for Democracy)
ASD	*Alianza Social Demócrata* (Social Democratic Alliance)
ASDom	*Alianza Social Dominicana* (Dominican Social Alliance)
BIS	*Bloque Institucional Socialdemócrata* (Social Democratic Institutional Block)
BS	*Bloque Socialista* (Socialist Block)
CD	*Concertación Democrática* (Democratic Pact)
CP	*Confederación de partidos* (Confederation of Parties)

CPC	*Coalición Patriótica de ciudadanos* (Patriotic Coalition of Citizens)
FNP	*Fuerza Nacional Progresista* (Progressive National Force)
FR	*Fuerza de la Revolución* (Force of the Revolution)
LE/PLRD[a]	*La Estructura/Partido Liberal de la República Dominicana* (The Structure/Liberal Partido of the Dominican Republic)
MCN	*Movimiento de Conciliación Nacional* (Movement of National Reconciliation)
MIDA	*Movimiento de Integración Democrática* (Movement of Democratic Integration)
MIUCA	*Movimiento Independiente, Unidad y Cambio* (Independent Movement, Unity and Change)
MNJ	*Movimiento Nacional de la Juventud* (National Youth Movement)
MPS	*Movimiento por el Socialismo* (Movement for Socialism)
MSN	*Movimiento de Salvación Nacional* (National Salvation Movement)
MSolN	*Movimiento Solidaridad Nacional* (National Solidarity Movement)
PAC	*Partido Acción Constitucional* (Constitutional Action Party)
PACOREDO	*Partido Comunista de la República Dominicana* (Communist Party of the Dominican Republic)
PAD	*Partido por la Autentica Democracia* (Party for the Authentic Democracy)
PAN	*Partido Acción Nacional* (National Action Party)
PAR	*Partido Acción Revolucionaria* (Revolutionary Action Party)
PCD	*Partido Comunista Dominicano* (Dominican Communist Party)
PD	*Partido Dominicano* (Dominican Party)
PDC	*Partido Demócrata Cristiano* (Christian Democratic Party)
PDI	*Partido Democrático Institucional* (Institutional Democratic Party)
PDN	*Partido Democrático Nacionalista* (Nationalist Democratic Party)
PDP	*Partido Demócrata Popular* (Popular Democratic Party)
PLD	*Partido de la Liberación Dominicana* (Party of the Dominican Liberation)
PLE	*Partido Liberal Evolucionista* (Evolutionary Liberal Party)
PLN	*Partido Laborista Nacional* (National Labor Party)
PN	*Partido Nacional* (National Party)
PNA	*Partido Nueva Alternativa* (New Alternative Party)
PND	*Partido Nacional Democrático* (Democratic National Party)
PNRD	*Partido Nacionalista Revolucionario Democrático* (Democratic Revolutionary Nationalist Party)
PNVC	*Partido Nacional de Veteranos Civiles* (National Party of Civil Veterans)
PPC	*Partido Popular Cristiano* (Christian Popular Party)
PPD	*Partido del Pueblo Dominicano* (Party of the Dominican People)

PQD	*Partido Quisqueyano Demócrata* (Democratic *Quisqueyano* Party)
PR[b]	*Partido Reformista* (Reformist Party)
PRD	*Partido Revolucionario Dominicano* (Dominican Revolutionary Party)
PRDA	*Partido Revolucionario Dominicano Auténtico* (Authentic Dominican Revolutionary Party)
PRI	*Partido Revolucionario Independiente* (Independent Revolutionary Party)
PRN	*Partido Renacentista Nacional* (National Renaissance Party)
PRSC[b]	*Partido Revolucionario Social Cristiano/Partido Reformista Social Cristiano* (Social Christian Revolutionary Party/Social Christian Reformist Party)
PT	*Partido Trujillista* (*Trujillista* Party)
PTD	*Partido de los Trabajadores Dominicanos* (Party of the Dominican Workers)
PUN	*Partido de Unidad Nacional* (National Unity Party)
UCN	*Unión Cívica Nacional* (National Civic Union)
UD	*Unidad Democrática* (Democratic Unity)
UDC	*Unión Demócrata Cristiana* (Christian Democratic Union)

[a] LE changed its name to *Partido Liberal de la Republica Dominicana* (PLRD).
[b] PR and PRSC merged in 1985 under the label *Partido Reformista Social Cristiano* (PRSC).

2.4 Electoral Participation of Parties and Alliances 1924–2004

Party / Alliance	Years	Elections contested
ANP	1924	1
CPC	1924	1
CP	1930	1
PD	1934; 1938; 1942; 1947; 1952; 1957	6
PT	1942	1
PND	1947	1
PRD	1962; 1966;1978–2004	13
UCN	1962; 1966; 1978; 1982	4
PRSC	1962; 1966–1970; 1978; 1986;	6
ASD	1962; 1978; 1982; 1996; 2000; 2002	6
PNRD	1962; 1966	2
VRD	1962; 1966	2
PN	1962	1
PRDA	1962	1
PR-PRSC	1966; 1968–1982; 1990–2004	13
PLE	1966	1
PDC	1966	1

Party / Alliance (continued)	Years	Elections contested
14	1966	1
PAR	1966	1
MCN	1970–1978; 1986; 1994; 1998	6
MIDA	1970; 1978; 1982	3
MNJ	1970; 1974	2
PQD	1970; 1978–1994; 2000; 2002	8
PDP	1974; 1978; 2000; 2002; 2004	5
MSN	1978	1
PLD	1978–2004	11
PCD	1978–1986	3
PNVC	1982–1990; 2000; 2002	5
UPA	1982	1
PAN	1982	1
BS	1982, 1990	2
MPS	1982	1
PAC	1982–1990	3
LE-PLRD	1986; 1990	2
PPC	1986–1994; 2002; 2004	5
PDN	1986	1
UD	1986–1994; 2000	4
FNP	1986; 1990	2
PACOREDO	1990	1
PDI	1990; 1994	2
PPD	1990; 1994; 1998	3
PRI	1990; 1994; 1998–2004	6
PTD	1990; 1998; 2002	3
BIS	1994; 2000; 2002	3
PRN	1994; 1998–2002	4
MIUCA	1994; 2002	2
UNIDO	2000	1
APD	2002	1
FR	2002; 2004	2
PNA	2002; 2004	2
UDC	2002	1
PUN	2002	1
ASDom	2004	1
MSolN	2004	1
PAD	2004	1

2.5 Referendums

Referendums have not been held.

2.6 Elections for Constitutional Assembly

During the period considered, only so-called *Asambleas Constituyentes Revisoras* (Reviewing Constitutional Assemblies) existed. Their task was to amend given articles of the constitution in force. All the elections for such assemblies were held during Trujillo's dictatorship. This implied that candidates and assembly members belonged exclusively to the government party, the PD. No accurate information is available on the number of seats of these assemblies. For the period considered, the only 'authentic' constitutional assembly was that of 1924.

1924	Total number	%	Seats	%
Registered voters	147,228	–		
Votes cast	—	—		
Invalid votes	—	—		
Valid votes	103,281	—		
			33	100.0
ANP	72,094	69.8	25	75.8
CPC	31,187	30.2	8	24.2

2.7 Parliamentary Elections 1924–2002 (Upper and Lower Chamber)

In 1924, elections to the upper chamber coincided with the elections of the constitutional assembly. For results see section 2.6.

Year	1930[a]		1934[a, b]	
	Total number	%	Total number	%
Registered voters	412,931	–	286,937	–
Votes cast	—	—	—	—
Invalid votes	—	—	—	—
Valid votes	225,796	—	256,423	—
Confederación de Partidos	223,926	99.2	–	–
PD	–	–	256,423	100.0
Others	1,870	0.8	–	–

[a] No distinction is made between the election of deputies and the election of senators because the voters elect both types of representatives with the same vote.
[b] Non-competitive elections.

Dominican Republic

Year	1938[a]		1942[a]	
	Total number	%	Total number	%
Registered voters	348,010	–	—	–
Votes cast	—	—	—	—
Invalid votes	—	—	—	—
Valid votes	319,680	—	581,937	—
PD	319,680	100.0	581,937	100.0

[a] No distinction is made between the election of deputies and the elections of senators because voters elect both types of representatives with the same vote. Non-competitive elections. Probably fraudulent process.

Year	1947[a]		1952[a]	
	Total number	%	Total number	%
Registered voters	1,020,488	–	1,224,550	–
Votes cast	—	—	—	—
Invalid votes	—	—	—	—
Valid votes	840,340	—	1,098,816	—
PD	781,389	93.0	1,098,816	100.0
PND	29,765	3.5	–	–
PLN	29,186	3.5	–	–

[a] No distinction is made between the election of deputies and the election of senators because the voters elect both types of representatives with the same vote. Non-competitive elections. Probably fraudulent process.

Year	1957[a]		1962	
	Total number	%	Total number	%
Registered voters	1,404,666	–	1,646,973	–
Votes cast	—	—	1,066,295	64.7
Invalid votes	—	—	18,291	1.1
Valid votes	1,265,681	—	1,048,004	98.9
PD	1,265,681	100.0	–	–
PRD	–	–	592,088	56.5
UCN	–	–	315,371	30.1
PRSC	–	–	56,794	5.4
PNRD	–	–	36,972	3.5
ASD	–	–	18,726	1.8
VRD	–	–	18,586	1.8
PRDA	–	–	5,306	0.5
PN	–	–	4,161	0.4

[a] Non-competitive elections. Probably fraudulent process.

Year[a]	1966		1970	
	Total number	%	Total number	%
Registered voters	1,815,429	–	2,044,619	–
Votes cast	1,372,695	75.6	1,297,843	63.5
Invalid votes	27,291	1.5	59,638	2.9
Valid votes	1,345,404	98.5	1,238,205	97.1
PR	759,889	56.4	653,565	52.8
PRD	494,570	36.8	–	–
PRSC	30,660	2.3	63,697	5.1
UCN	16,152	1.2	–	–
VRD	13,855	1.0	–	–
PDC	9,376	0.7	–	–
PLE	6,540	0.5	–	–
MIDA	–	–	252,760	20.4
PQD	–	–	168,751	13.6
MNJ	–	–	53,571	4.3
MCN	–	–	45,861	3.7
Others	14,362[a]	1.1	–	–

[a] Others include: PAR: 5,489 votes (0.4%); Partido 14 de Junio: 4,834 (0.4%) and PNRD: 4,039 (0.3%).

Year	1974		1978	
	Total number	%	Total number	%
Registered voters	2,006,323	–	2,283,784	–
Votes cast	1,439,067	71.7	1,731,095	75.8
Invalid votes	404,878	20.2	85,530	3.7
Valid votes	1,034,189	79.8	1,645,565	96.3
PR-MNJ	929,112	89.8	–	–
PDP	62,682	6.1	5,667	0.3
PRD	–	–	838,973	50.1
PR	–	–	692,146	42.1
PLD	–	–	18,565	1.1
MIDA	–	–	13,317	0.8
UCN	–	–	13,316	0.8
ASD	–	–	11,056	0.7
PCD	–	–	10,751	0.7
MCN	–	–	7,743	0.5
MSN	–	–	7,727	0.5
PQD	–	–	5,984	0.4
Agrupaciones[a]	42,395	4.1	9,226	0.6

[a] So-called 'Agrupaciones políticas accidentales': Movimiento Municipal del Pueblo and Movimiento Voluntad Popular in 1974; Movimiento Popular Justicialista, Movimiento Revolucionario del Pueblo, Movimiento Municipal del Pueblo, Movimiento Restaurador Santiagués and Movimiento Unión Provincial Independiente in 1978.

Year	1982	
	Total number	%
Registered voters	2,601,684	–
Votes cast	1,862,866	71.6
Invalid votes	56,039	2.2
Valid votes	1,806,827	97.8
PRD	825,005	45.7
PR	656,904	36.4
PLD	174,464	9.7
PQD	35,185	1.9
PNVC	28,354	1.6
PAC	18,360	1.6
UPA	12,979	0.7
PCD	12,101	0.7
ASD	8,578	0.5
Others[a]	34,897	1.9

[a] Others include BS: 7,917 votes (0.4%); UCN: 7,896 (0.4%); MPS: 7,193 (0.4%); MIDA: 6,886 (0.4); PAN: 3,522 (0.2%) and several 'Agrupaciones': 1,483 (0.1%).

Year	1986		1990	
	Total number	%	Total number	%
Registered voters	3,039,347	–	3,275,570	–
Votes cast	2,195,648	72.2	1,962,458	59.9
Invalid votes	83,903	2.8	48,356	2.5
Valid votes	2,111,745	97.2	1,914,102	97.5
PRSC	877,380[a]	41.6	663,127[c]	34.6
PRD	828,209[b]	39.2	447,605[d]	23.4
PLD	387,881	18.4	625,929[e]	32.7
PRI	–	–	139,769	7.3
PPC	–	–	8,081[f]	0.4
Agrupaciones	–	–	11,052[g]	0.6
Others	18,275	0.9	18,539[h]	1.0

[a] Including votes for the PRSC's allies PQD and PNVC. The PRSC merged with the PR in 1985.
[b] Including votes for the PRD's allies PPC, MCN, UD and LE.
[c] Including votes for the PRSC's allies PQD, LE, PDI, PNVC and Agrupaciones MOFEI, Frente Amplio de Organizaciones Comunales-Futuro Verde, MSDO, FDE, MAIS and Morepma.
[d] Including votes for the PRD's allies BS and PTD.
[e] Including votes for the PLD's ally UD.
[f] Including votes for the PPC's ally, the Agrupación MIM.
[g] Includes Muica, MAR, Migrelu, MFP, MIS and Movimiento Independiente Meta.
[h] Others include FNP, PAC, PACOREDO and PPD.

Year	1994 Total number	%	1998 Total number	%
Registered voters	3,598,328	–	4,129,554	–
Votes cast	3,150,838	87.6	2,183,707	52.9
Invalid votes	182,556	5.8	90,021	4.1
Valid votes	2,968,282	94.2	2,093,686	95.9
PRD	1,244,441[a]	41.9	1,075,306[d]	51.4
PRSC	1,160,405[b]	39.1	351,347[e]	31.3
PLD	467,617	15.8	654,713	16.8
Others	95,819[c]	3.2	12,320[f]	0.6

[a] Including votes for the PRD's allies UD, PRI, BIS, PQD, ASD and PNCV.
[b] Including votes for the PRSC's ally PDP.
[c] Others include PDI, MCN, PPD and PRN.
[d] Including votes for the PRD's allies PPC, UD and BIS
[e] Including votes for the PRSC's ally PQD.
[f] Others include PDI, PPD, MCN and PRN.

Year	2002 Total number	%
Registered voters	4,647,839	–
Votes cast	2,371,591	51.0
Invalid votes	88,182	3.7
Valid votes	2,283,409	96.3
PRD	963,735[a]	42.2
PLD	657,658[b]	28.8
PRSC	556,431[c]	24.4
PRI	35,859[d]	1.6
PQD	29,969	1.3
FR	14,148[e]	0.6
PNVC	12,310	0.5
Others [f]	13,299	0.6

[a] Including votes for the PRD's allies ASD, PRN and UD.
[b] Including votes for the PLD's allies BIS and APD.
[c] Including votes for the PRSC's ally PPC.
[d] Including votes for the PRI's allies PDP and PTD (PTD partial alliance only).
[e] Including votes for the FR's ally MIUCA-PNA.
[f] Others include UDC: 4,946 votes (0.2%); PTD and allies: 2,792 (0.1%); MIUCA-PRN; PUN and the Agrupación MISAR.

2.8 Composition of Parliament

2.8.1 Lower Chamber (House of Representatives) 1924–2002

Year	1924 Seats	%	1930 Seats	%	1934 Seats	%	1938 Seats	%
	31	100.0	31	100.0	31	100.0	–	100.0
ANP	24	77.4	–	–	–	–	–	–
CPC	7	22.6	–	–	–	–	–	–
CP	–	–	31	100.0	–	–	–	–
PD	–	–	–	–	31	100.0	–	–

Year	1942 Seats	%	1947 Seats	%	1952 Seats	%	1957 Seats	%
	35	100.0	45	100.0	50	100.0	58	100.0
PD	35	100.0	45	100.0	50	100.0	58	100.0

Year	1962 Seats	%	1966 Seats	%	1970 Seats	%	1974 Seats	%
	74	100.0	74	100.0	74	100.0	91	100.0
PRD	49	66.2	26	35.1	–	–	–	–
UCN	20	27.0	–	–	–	–	–	–
PNRD	4	5.4	–	–	–	–	–	–
PRSC	1	1.4	–	–	–	–	–	–
PR	–	–	48	64.9	45	60.8	75	82.4
MNJ	–	–	–	–	15	20.2	11	12.1
MIDA	–	–	–	–	11	14.9	–	–
PQD	–	–	–	–	3	4.1	–	–
PD	–	–	–	–	–	–	3	3.3
MVP	–	–	–	–	–	–	1	1.1
MMP	–	–	–	–	–	–	1	1.1

Year	1978 Seats	%	1982 Seats	%	1986 Seats	%	1990 Seats	%
	91	100.0	120	100.0	120	100.0	120	100.0
PR	43	47.3	50	41.7	–	–	–	–
MNJ	–	–	–	–	–	–	–	–
PD	–	–	–	–	–	–	–	–
MVP	–	–	–	–	–	–	–	–
MMP	–	–	–	–	–	–	–	–
PRD	48	52.7	62	51.7	48	40.0	33	27.5
PLD	–	–	7	5.8	16	13.4	44	36.7
PAC	–	–	1	0.8	–	–	–	–
PRSC	–	–	–	–	56	46.6	41	34.2
PRI	–	–	–	–	–	–	2	1.6

Year	1994		1998		2002	
	Seats	%	Seats	%	Seats	%
	120	100.0	149	100.0	150	100.0
PRD	57	47.5	83	55.7	73	48.7
PLD	13	10.8	49	32.9	41	27.3
PRSC	50	41.7	17	11.4	36	24.0

2.8.2 Upper Chamber (Senate) 1924–2002

Year	1924		1930		1934		1938	
	Seats	%	Seats	%	Seats	%	Seats	%
	12	100.0	12	100.0	12	100.0	13	100.0
ANP	10	83.3	–	–	–	–	–	–
CPC	2	16.7	–	–	–	–	–	–
CP	–	–	12	100.0	–	–	–	–
PD	–	–	–	–	12	100.0	13	100.0

Year	1942		1947		1952		1957	
	Seats	%	Seats	%	Seats	%	Seats	%
	16	100.0	19	100.0	22	100.0	23	100.0
PD	16	100.0	19	100.0	22	100.0	23	100.0

Year	1962		1966		1970		1974	
	Seats	%	Seats	%	Seats	%	Seats	%
	27	100.0	27	100.0	27	100.0	27	100.0
PRD	22	81.5	5	18.5	–	–	–	–
UCN	4	14.8	–	–	–	–	–	–
PNRD	1	3.7	–	–	–	–	–	–
PR	–	–	22	81.5	21	77.8	23	85.2
MIDA	–	–	–	–	1	3.7	–	–
MNJ	–	–	–	–	5	18.5	4	14.8

Year	1978		1982		1986		1990	
	Seats	%	Seats	%	Seats	%	Seats	%
	27	100.0	27	100.0	30	100.0	30	100.0
PR	16	59.3	10	37.0	–	–	–	–
PRD	11	40.7	17	63.0	7	23.3	2	6.7
PRSC	–	–	–	–	21	70.0	16	53.3
PLD	–	–	–	–	2	6.7	12	40.0

Year	1994 Seats 30	% 100.0	1998 Seats 30	% 100.0	2002 Seats 32	% 100.0
PRD	15	50.0	24	80.0	29	90.6
PRSC	14	46.7	2	6.7	2	6.3
PLD	1	3.3	4	13.3	1	3.1

2.9 Presidential Elections 1924–2004

1924	Total number	%
Registered voters	147,228	–
Votes cast	—	—
Invalid votes	—	—
Valid votes	103,281	—
Horacio Vásquez (ANP)	72,094	69.8
Jacinto J. Peynado (CPC)	31,187	30.2

1930[a]	Total number	%
Registered voters	412,931	–
Votes cast	—	—
Invalid votes	—	—
Valid votes	225,796	—
Rafael L. Trujillo Molina (CDP)	223,926	99.2
En contra[b]	1,870	0.8

[a] Non-competitive elections.
[b] Negative vote. There is no detailed information available on how this vote was carried out.

1934[a]	Total number	%
Registered voters	286,937	–
Votes cast	—	—
Invalid votes	—	—
Valid votes	256,423	—
Rafael L. Trujillo Molina (PD)	256,423	100.0

[a] Non-competitive elections.

1938[a]	Total number	%
Registered voters	348,010	–
Votes cast	—	—
Invalid votes	—	—
Valid votes	319,680	—
Jacinto B. Peynado (PD)	319,680	—

[a] Non-competitive elections. Although he did not run for office, Rafael Trujillo maintained absolute control over the country.

1942[a]	Total number	%
Registered voters	492,627	–
Votes cast	—	—
Invalid votes	—	—
Valid votes	581,937	—
Rafael L. Trujillo Molina (PD)	581,937	100.0

[a] Non-competitive elections. Note that the official number of valid votes exceeds the number of registered voters.

1947[a]	Total number	%
Registered voters	—	–
Votes cast	—	—
Invalid votes	—	—
Valid votes	840,340	—
Rafael L. Trujillo Molina (PD)	781,389	93.0
Rafael A. Espaillat (PND)	29,765	3.5
Francisco Prats Ramírez (PLN)	29,186	3.5

[a] Essentially a non-competitive election.

1952[a]	Total number	%
Registered voters	–	–
Votes cast	1,098,816	—
Invalid votes	—	—
Valid votes	1,098,816	—
Héctor B. Trujillo Molina (PD)	1,098,816	100.0

[a] Non-competitive election. Although he did not run for office, Rafael Trujillo maintained absolute control over the country.

1957[a]	Total number	%
Registered voters	—	–
Votes cast	—	—
Invalid votes	—	—
Valid votes	1,265,681	—
Héctor B. Trujillo Molina (PD)	1,265,681	100.0

[a] Non-competitive election. Although he did not run for office, Rafael Trujillo maintained absolute control over the country.

1962	Total number	%
Registered voters[a]	1,646,973	–
Votes cast	1,073,245	65.2
Invalid votes	18,291	1.7
Valid votes	1,054,954	98.3
Juan Bosch (PRD)	628,044	59.5
Virgilio A. Fiallo (UCN)	317,327	30.1
Alfonso Moreno Martínez (PRSC)	54,638	5.2
Virgilio Maynardi Reyna (PNRD)	35,764	3.4
Juan Isidro Jiménez Grullón (ASD)	17,898	1.7
Others[b]	1,273	0.1

[a] As the Dominican electoral register was established only in 1974, the number given here is an estimation of the voting age population.
[b] PRDA candidate.

1966	Total number	%
Registered voters[a]	1,815,429	–
Votes cast	1,372,695	75.6
Invalid votes	27,291	2.0
Valid votes	1,345,404	98.0
Joaquín Balaguer (PR)	775,805	57.7
Juan Bosch (PRD)	525,230	39.0
Rafael F. Bonnelly (UCN)	39,535	2.9
Others[b]	4,834	0.4

[a] As the Dominican electoral register was established only in 1974, the number given here is an estimation of the voting age population.
[b] 14 candidates.

1970	Total number	%
Registered voters[a]	2,044,619	–
Votes cast	1,297,843	60.6
Invalid votes	59,638	4.6
Valid votes	1,238,205	95.4
Joaquín Balaguer (PR)	707,136	57.2
Francisco A. Lora (MIDA)	252,760	20.4
Elías Wessin y Wessin (PQD)	168,751	13.6
Alfonso Moreno Martínez (PRSC)	63,697	5.1
Jaime Manuel Fernández (MCN)	45,861	3.7

[a] As the Dominican electoral register was established only in 1974, the number given here is an estimation of the voting age population.

1974	Total number	%
Registered voters	2,006,323	–
Votes cast	1,518,297	75.7
Invalid votes	404,878	26.7
Valid votes	1,113,419	73.3
Joaquín Balaguer (PR)	942,726	84.7
Luis Homero Lajara Burgos (PDP)	170,693	15.3

1978	Total number	%
Registered voters	2,283,784	–
Votes cast	1,741,337	76.2
Invalid votes	85,530	4.9
Valid votes	1,655,807	95.1
S. Antonio Guzmán (PRD)	866,912	52.4
Joaquín Balaguer (PR)	711,878	43.0
Francisco A. Lora (MIDA)	27,095	1.6
Juan Bosch (PLD)	18,375	1.1
Narciso Isa Conde (PCD)	9,828	0.6
Alfonso Lockward (PRSC)	7,981	0.5
Luis Julián Pérez (MSN)	7,782	0.5
Luis Homero Lajara Burgos (PDP)	5,956	0.4

1982	Total number	%
Registered voters	2,601,684	–
Votes cast	1,886,769	72.5
Invalid votes	56,039	3.0
Valid votes	1,830,730	97.0
Salvador Jorge Blanco (PRD)	854,868	46.7
Joaquín Balaguer (PR)	706,951	38.6
Juan Bosch (PLD)	179,849	9.8
Elías Wessin y Wessin (PQD)	35,355	1.9
José Rafael Abinader (ASD)	9,208	0.5
Narciso Isa Conde (PCD)	18,481	1.0
Rafael F. Taveras (UPA)	15,250	0.8
Others[a]	10,768	0.6

[a] MIDA and PAN.

1986	Total number	%
Registered voters	3,039,347	–
Votes cast	2,195,455	72.2
Invalid votes	83,710	3.8
Valid votes	2,112,745	96.2
Joaquín Balaguer (PRSC)	877,378	41.6
Jacobo Majluta (PRD)	828,209	39.2
Juan Bosch (PLD)	378,881	18.4
Others[a]	28,277	1.3

[a] Others include Marino Vinicio Castillo (FNP): 6,684 votes (0.3%); Narciso Isa Conde (PCD): 5,021 (0.2%); Jorge Martínez Lavandier (PDN): 1,202 (0.1%) and others.

1990	Total number	%
Registered voters	3,275,570	–
Votes cast	1,982,889	60.5
Invalid votes	48,356	2.5
Valid votes	1,934,533	97.5
Joaquín Balaguer (PRSC)	678,065	35.5
Juan Bosch (PLD)	653,595	33.8
José F. Peña Gómez (PRD)	449,399	23.2
Jacobo Majluta (PRI)	135,649	7.1
Others[a]	17,815	0.9

[a] Others include candidates of FNP, PAC, PPC, PACOREDO, and PPD.

1994	Total number	%
Registered voters	3,598,328	–
Votes cast	3,163,396	87.9
Invalid votes	147,646	4.7
Valid votes	3,015,750	95.3
Joaquín Balaguer (PRSC)	1,275,460	42.3
José F. Peña Gómez (PRD)	1,253,179	41.6
Juan Bosch (PLD)	395,653	13.1
Jacobo Majluta (PRI)	68,910	2.3
Antonio Reynoso (MIUCA)	22,548	0.8

1996 (1st)	Total number	%
Registered voters	3,750,502	–
Votes cast	2,948,979	78.6
Invalid votes	45,120	1.5
Valid votes	2,903,859	98.5
José F. Peña Gómez (PRD)	1,333,925	45.9
Leonel Fernández (PLD)	1,130,523	38.9
Jacinto Peynado (PRSC)	435,504	15.0
José Rafael Abinader (ADS)	3,907	0.1

1996 (2nd)	Total number	%
Registered voters	3,750,502	–
Votes cast	2,880,425	76.8
Invalid votes	19,402	6.7
Valid votes	2,861,023	93.3
Leonel Fernández (PLD)	1,466,382	51.3
José F. Peña Gómez (PRD)	1,394,641	48.7

2000	Total number	%
Registered voters	4,251,218	–
Votes cast	3,236,906	
Invalid votes	42,090	
Valid votes	3,194,816	
Hipólito Mejia (PRD)	1,593,231	49.9
Danilo Medina (PLD)	796,923	24.9
Joaquín Balaguer (PRSC)	785,926	24.6
Others[a]	18,736	0.6

[a] Others include candidates of PNA, PTD, UNIDO, and PRN.

2004	Total number	%
Registered voters	5,020,703	–
Votes cast	3,656,850	72.8
Invalid votes	43,150	1.2
Valid votes	3,613,700	98.8
Leonel Fernández (PLD)	2,063,871	57.1
Hipólito Mejia (PRD)	1,215,928	33.7
Eduardo Estrella (PRSC)	312,493	8.7
Others[a]	21,408	0.5

[a] Includes, among others, candidates of FR, PNA, PRI, and PPC.

2.10 List of Power Holders 1924–2004

Head of State	Years	Remarks
Horacio Vásquez	1924–1930	Elected president. Assumed presidency constitutionally on 07/07/1924. Under the transitory provisions of the new constitutional text of 09/06/1927, the presidential term was extended until 16/08/1930.
Rafael Estrella Ureña	1930	Assumed presidency through a *coup d'état* on 02/03/1930.
Jacinto B. Peynado	1930	Interim president from 21/04/1930 and 16/08/1930.
Rafael L. Trujillo	1930–1938	Assumed presidency on 16/08/1930.
Jacinto B. Peynado	1938–1940	
Manuel de Jesús Troncoso de la Concha	1940–1942	Vice president; assumed presidency after Peynado's death on 07/03/1940.
Rafael L. Trujillo	1942–1952	
Héctor B. Trujillo	1952–1960	
Joaquín Balaguer	1960–1962	Vice president; assumed presidency when the president resigned on 03/08/1960. After the assassination of Rafael Trujillo on 30/05/1961 and several failed coup attempts a council of state was formed, made up of a president (Balaguer), two vice-presidents and four other members, with executive and legislative powers. Its mandate began on 01/01/1962.
Rafael F. Bonelly	1962–1963	First vice president of the council of state. Assumed the highest office after Balaguer's dismissal on 17/01/1962 due to a failed military uprising.
Juan Bosch	1963	President elected in competitive elections on 20/12/1962. Assumed presidency on 17/02/1963, date of his return from exile.
Triunvirato	1963–1965	Formed by Emilio de los Santos, Manuel E. Tavares Espaillat and Ramón Tapia Espinal. Came to power through the *coup d'état* of 26/09/1963, deposing President Bosch. When Santos resigned, Donald Reid Cabral entered the *Triunvirato*. Later Tavarez and Tapia resigned.
José Rafael Molina Ureña	1965	Interim president after the downfall of the *Triunvirato* on 25/04/1965.

Head of State (cont.)	Years	Remarks
Military Junta	1965	Headed by Bartolomé Benoit. Other members were Olgo Santana Carrasco and Enrique Casado Saladín. Established on 01/05, dissolved on 07/05.
Francisco Alberto Caamaño Deño	1965	
Gobierno de Reconstrucción Nacional	1965	Headed by Antonio Imbert Barreras. Other members were Carlos Grisolia Poloney, Alejandro Zeller Cocco, Bartolomé Benoit, and Julio Postigo. Appointed on 07/05/1965. On 10/08/1965 Julio Postigo resigned and was replaced by Leonte Bernard Vásquez.
Héctor García Godoy	1965–1966	Provisional president. Appointed on 03/09/1965.
Joaquín Balaguer	1966–1970	Constitutional president. Assumed office on 01/07/1966.
Manuel Ramón Ruiz Tejada	1970	President of the supreme court of justice. Assumed office as provisional president on 16/04/1970 after an agreement between the government party and the opposition, in order to allow Balaguer's new candidacy.
Joaquín Balaguer	1970–1978	Constitutional president, elections were only semi-competitive. Assumed office on 16/08/1970. Re-elected in semi-competitive elections in 1974.
Silvestre Antonio Guzmán	1978–1982	Constitutional president. Assumed office on 16/08/1978.
Jacobo Majluta	1982	Vice president. Assumed presidency after President Guzmán's suicide on 04/07/1982.
Salvador Jorge Blanco	1982–1986	Constitutional president. Assumed office on 16/08/1982.
Joaquín Balaguer	1986–1996	Constitutional president. Assumed office on 16/08/1986. Re-elected twice in 1990 and 1994. Accused of electoral fraud in both re-elections. In 1994, electoral fraud was confirmed by the JCE, yet the elections were not annulled. A political accord (*Pacto por la Democracia*) changed the constitution and limited the last term to two years.
Leonel Fernández	1996–2000	Constitutional president. The opposition candidate accused him of electoral fraud. Assumed office on 16/08/1996.
Hipólito Mejia	2000–2004	Constitutional president. Assumed office on 16/08/2000.
Leonel Fernández	2004–	Constitutional president

3. Bibliography

3.1 Official Sources

Constitución Política de la República Dominicana del 28 de noviembre de
1966, Santo Domingo: Corporan.
Junta Central Electoral (1985). *Ley No. 55 del Registro Electoral del 13 de
diciembre de 1985*, Santo Domingo: Nivar.
Junta Central Electoral (1985). *Resolución No. 6 del 29 de junio 1985, que
establece la boleta única*, Santo Domingo: Nivar.

3.2 Books, Articles, and Electoral Reports

Aguilar, J., Butten Varona, N., Campillo Pérez, J. et al. (1986). *Y nadie sabe
quien es su legislador. Coloquio Experiencias del sistema electoral.
Evaluación y perspectivas.* Santo Domingo: Universidad
APEC/Fundación Friedrich Ebert.
Báez Evertsz, F., Oleo Ramírez, F. (1985). *La emigración de dominicano a
Estados Unidos: Determinantes socio-económicas y consecuencias.*
Santo Domingo: Taller.
Barrios, Harald (1992). 'Konflikt um ein Wahlergebnis. Zu den Wahlen in
der Dominikanischen Republik 1990'. *Lateinamerika. Analysen–Daten–
Dokumentation* (Hamburg), no.18.
Barrios, H. and Suter, J. (1992). 'Dominikanische Republik', in D. Nohlen,
and F. Nuscheler (eds.), *Handbuch der Dritten Welt, vol. 3: Mittelameri-
ka und Karibik.* Bonn: Dietz, 373–396.
Black, J. K. (1987). *The Dominican Republic. Politics and Development in
an Unsovereign State.* Boston.
Brea Franco, J. (1983). *El sistema constitucional dominicano.* Santo
Domingo.
— (1984). *Introducción al proceso electoral dominicano.* Santo Domingo:
Taller.
— (1986). *La reglamentación jurídica de los partidos políticos en la
República Dominicana (Revista de Ciencias Jurídicas, Separata de
Doctrina).* Santo Domingo: Universidad Católica Madre y Maestra.
Butten Varona, N. *La problemática del registro electoral dominicano.* Santo
Domingo: Fundación Friedrich Ebert.
— (1983). *Temas electorales 1980–1982.* Santo Domingo: Editores
Asociados.
Campillo Pérez, J. (1982). *Origen y evolución de la Junta Central Electoral.*
Santo Domingo: Junta Central Electoral.

— (1986). *Historia electoral dominicana 1848–1986*. Santo Domingo: Junta Central Electoral.

Edie, C. J. (ed.) (1994). *Democracy in the Caribbean. Myths and Realities*. London: Praeger.

Espinal, R. (1990). 'Elecciones generales. República Dominicana, 16 de mayo de 1990'. *Boletín Electoral Latinoamericano (IIDH/CAPEL)*, 3: 41–46.

— (1991). 'Elecciones dominicanas de 1990'. *Memorias del IV Curso Anual Interamericano de Elecciones (IIDH/CAPEL)*.

Fernández Naranjo, C. (1986). *El Registro Electoral*. Santo Domingo: Junta Central de Elecciones.

Jiménez Grullón, J. (1982). *Sociología política dominicana 1844–1966*. Santo Domingo: Alfa y Omega.

Lozano, W. (1991). 'Las elecciones dominicanas de 1990 y la crisis del sistema populista', in C. Barba Solano, J. L. Barros Horcasitas, and J. Hurtado (eds.), *Transiciones a la democracia en Europa y América Latina*. México: Porrúa.

Nohlen, D. and Grupo de Investigación Heidelberg (1989). *Apuntes sobre democracia y representatividad en el sistema electoral dominicano*. Santo Domingo: Universidad APEC/Fundación Friedrich Ebert.

Nohlen, D., Picado, S., and Zovatto, D., (eds.) (1998). *Tratado de derecho electoral comparado de América Latina*. Mexico City: Fondo de Cultura Económica.

Oviedo, J. and Espinal, R. (1986). Democracia y proyecto socialdemócrata en República Dominicana. Santo Domingo: Taller.

EL SALVADOR

by Michael Krennerich

1. Introduction

1.1 Historical Overview

El Salvador, the smallest and most densely populated country in Central America, declared its independence from the Spanish viceroyalty in 1821. It then joined Mexico for a short time, before entering the Central American Confederation as an independent country, remaining a member until 1840.

Compared with the other Central American countries, El Salvador—then *Estado del Salvador*—adopted a constitution quite early on in its development (1824). This constitution provided for the separation of powers between a head of state (*Jefe de Estado*), a unicameral congress and a so-called representative council. The subsequent constitutions of 1841 and 1864 established a presidential system of government and a bicameral legislative.

The constitution of 1841 stated that the president and parliament were to be elected directly. However, like many other Latin American countries, political development of El Salvador was characterized by power struggles between the regional caudillos, who often resorted to violence as a means of solving political conflicts. The position of president changed hands frequently and irregularly.

In 1871, after Francisco Dueñas' conservative government came to an end, a new constitution was enacted. Its liberal traits were to be present in the many constitutions that were drafted in the following years (1871, 1872, 1880, 1883, 1885, and 1886). Such a high number of constitutions was not, however, due to substantial reforms in the political or social institutions, but to the maneuvers of political actors looking to secure a permanent position in power. The 1886 Constitution was the first one that remained in force for a longer period (until 1939). It provided for a presidential system and a one-chamber parliament.

The last decades of the 19th century saw the consolidation of a liberal oligarchic state. The introduction of coffee as an export product, the separation of the Church and State, and the privatization of communal lands, greatly affected the development of the Salvadorean society. The new coffee elite took control of political life, thereby creating a certain degree of stability, in contrast with the turbulent post-independence era. From 1903 to 1931, all presidents were formally elected. However, despite the universal male suffrage, in force since 1883, the elections had little political significance and the electoral competition was restricted to a small oligarchy.

The situation looked as if it was about to change in 1931, when the leader of the *Partido Laborista Salvadoreño*, Arturo Araujo, won the elections. But a military coup toppled Araujo that same year and brought the dictator Maximiliano Hernández Martínez to power (1932–1944). The *coup d'état* of 1931 and the fierce suppression of the peasant uprising (*La Matanza*, 1932) have become landmarks in the history of the country. In the following years the oligarchy and the military found a way of coexisting that remained in place until 1979: The oligarchy had control over the economy while the military assumed the presidency and guaranteed the established economic and social order.

However, as the country's economy developed, the interests of the oligarchy diversified, and this led to internal conflicts and clashes with the military (and even between different military factions). Conflicts between the conservative and the reform-oriented sections of the military led to successive *coups d'état* (in 1948, 1960, 1961, and 1979). However non-competitive or semi-competitive elections were still held regularly, and provided the stage for a façade democracy that was to last several decades. The 1950 and 1962 Constitutions were the basis of the institutional framework for this façade democracy. They maintained a presidential system with a one-chamber congress.

The party system was dominated by the official parties, namely the *Partido Revolucionario de Unificación Democrática* (PRUD; Revolutionary Party of Democratic Unification) in the 1950s and the *Partido de Conciliación Nacional* (PCN; National Reconciliation Party) in the 1960s and 1970s. The political and ideological presence of authorized opposition parties was at first very limited, but new opposition parties began to emerge during the 1960s. When the system of proportional representation (PR) was introduced in 1963, the *Partido Demócrata Cristiano* (PDC; Christian Democratic Party) became the PNC's main rival in the competition for the allocation of seats both in parliament and at the municipal level. Likewise, some left-wing parties began to contest the elections from the 1960s: the *PAR-nueva línea*, the *Movimiento Nacionalista Revolucionario* (MNR; Revolutionary National Movement), and the *Unión Democrática Nacionalista* (UDN; Nationalist Democratic Union). The *PAR-nueva línea* was prohibited after the 1967 elections.

During the 1970s the electoral climate was marked by violence, with growing state and parastate repression. The very idea that the Unión Nacional Opositora (UNO) opposition alliance, led by the Christian Democrats, could win the elections, seemed to justify the government's right to rig elections and repress the population.

As the country's political, social, and economic demands were not met, conditions became favorable for the establishment of revolutionary armed groups and popular anti-establishment organizations. Society was gradually polarized between the state and parastate violence on the one hand, and the revolutionary movements on the other. The military's fear of a revolution like the one in Nicaragua was one of the underlying reasons behind the coup of October 1979, especially after the strengthening of the leftist groups.

As a consequence of the 1979 coup, a civil-military junta came to power. This group included representatives from the reform-oriented opposition parties, but reactionary resistance forces soon led to a split in this reformist junta. In a climate of (para)state terror, the revolutionary forces joined under the *Frente Farabundo Martí de Liberación Nacional/Frente Democrático Revolucionario*; *Farabundo Martí* (FMLN/FDR; Front for National Liberation/Revolutionary Democratic Front).

The 1980s were characterized by a fierce civil war and a difficult process of democratization, which was undermined by the use of violence and the military's lack of civil control. By providing extensive economic and military aid the USA had a great influence over both events. After several military-Christian-Democratic juntas (1980–1982), a constitutional assembly was elected in 1982. Its members elected an interim president (Álvaro Alfred Magaña, 1982–1984) and enacted a new constitution in 1983, which provided for a presidential system and a one-chamber parliament.

In the 1980s, the electoral competition basically revolved around the PDC, the extremist right-wing party *Alianza Republicana Nacional* (ARENA; Nationalist Republican Alliance Party) and the former government party PCN. Leftist parties did not participate in the elections until 1989. The Christian Democrat José Napoleón Duarte won the presidential election in 1984, and was succeeded in 1989 by Alfredo Félix Cristiani of the ARENA party.

In January 1992, under the auspices of the UN, Cristiani's government and the FMLN agreed to end the civil war. The peace accord included the demobilization of the guerrilla forces and their integration into constitutional political life. This event became a milestone in the difficult process of democratization. Since then, ARENA and FMLN have been the two most important parties in El Salvador. The 1994 and 1999 presidential elections gave victory to ARENA, but the FMLN was the strongest party in the 2000 and the 2003 parliamentary elections.

1.2 Evolution of Electoral Provisions

El Salvador has enjoyed a long tradition of elections, although only some of them can be considered free and fair. In the 20th century, the electoral law of El Salvador was laid down in the constitutions of 1889, 1939, 1952, 1962, and 1983 (and their corresponding reforms), in the electoral laws of 1886, 1939, 1961, 1985, 1988, and 1993 (and their corresponding reforms), and in the transitional provisions of 1950, 1981, and 1984. The 1886 Constitution was reintroduced in 1945, after having undergone small amendments. The electoral law of 1959 was not applied in any elections.

The 1841 Constitution introduced direct suffrage, and the 1883 Constitution established universal suffrage for men, independent of property or educational criteria. Active suffrage was introduced for women in 1939. Since 1950 every Salvadorean over 18 is eligible to vote, irrespective of gender.

The presidential term of office has ranged from between four to six years and has been set at five years since 1962. Apart from during brief periods, the president has been prohibited from standing for immediate re-election.

Traditionally, the Salvadorean president has been elected by an absolute majority, except in the 1950s, when the system of plurality was applied. Until the end of the 1970s, if no candidate achieved the absolute majority, parliament had to decide. Since 1984 a runoff has been held between the top two candidates.

The parliamentary term is relatively short compared to other Latin American countries: in the 1950s, 1960s, and 1970s the term was only two years, and since 1982 deputies are elected for a period of three years. In the 1950s, the majority system was applied in multi-member constituencies (MMCs), combined with more rigid party lists and a single vote. Since the constitutional law was reformed in 1963, deputies are elected according to the PR system using the simple quota system (Hare quota) and the method of the largest remainder. This electoral system was also applied in the elections held during the 1980s, when the number of deputies rose from 52 to 60.

Since 1991, the system used is PR in MMCs with an additional national list: 64 deputies are elected in 14 MMCs (with three to 16 seats each) using the Hare quota (plus largest remainder). Furthermore, 20 deputies are elected in a nationwide constituency, also using the Hare quota (and largest remainder). The closed party lists and single vote system have been maintained, so each voter is entitled to one vote in parliamentary elections.

1.3 Current Electoral Provisions

Sources: The basic principles of the electoral law are laid down in the 1983 Constitution and in the 1993 Electoral Code, both of which have been reformed several times.

Suffrage: The principles of universal, equal, direct, and secret suffrage are applied. All citizens over 18 years registered in the electoral roll (elaborated by the *Tribunal Supremo Electoral*) are eligible to vote.

Elected national institutions: The president and the vice president are elected at the same time for a five-year term. The immediate re-election of the president is prohibited. Parliament is made up of 84 candidates elected for a three-year term.

Nomination of candidates
- *presidential elections*: Every citizen 30 years or older, who is born in El Salvador (or who has a Salvadorean parent) and has been in possession of his/her citizens' rights for at least six years prior to the elections, is eligible to run for president. Presidential candidates must be affiliated to an officially recognized political party.
- *parliamentary elections*: Every citizen 25 years or older, who is born in El Salvador (or who has a Salvadorean parent) and has been in possession of his/her citizens' rights for at least five years prior to the elections, is eligible for to run for parliament.

Electoral system

- *presidential elections*: The president and vice president are elected on a single ticket by absolute majority. If no candidate reaches this majority, a second round is held between the two top candidates.

- *parliamentary elections*: In parliamentary elections, PR is applied in MMCs with an additional national list: 64 deputies are elected in 14 MMCs of different size (eight of three, two of four, two of five, one of six, and one of 16 seats). In addition, 20 deputies are elected in one nationwide constituency. The lists are closed. Each voter is entitled to one vote. The seats are distributed using the simple quota system (Hare quota). If there are remaining seats to be allocated, the wasted votes are taken into consideration and the method of the largest remainder is applied.

Organizational context of elections: The *Tribunal Supremo Electoral* (TSE; Central Electoral Commission) is responsible for organizing and supervising the elections. It is a permanent body made up of five members who are elected by parliament. Three of the members are proposed by the three strongest parties in the presidential elections and two members are proposed by the *Corte Suprema de Justicia* and elected by a two-third majority in parliament. In practice, the TSE is highly influenced by political interests. The first post-war elections in 1994 were closely monitored by international and national observers.

1.4 Commentary on the Electoral Statistics

As far as possible, the following statistics were determined on the basis of official data from the *Consejo Central de Elecciones* or from the *Tribunal Supremo*. In the cases where no such data were available, the authors resorted to secondary sources, among which the journal *Estudios Centroamericanos* (ECA) proved especially helpful. This journal records the elections held since the 1980s.

But among the great array of secondary sources it is often possible to find very different data for the same election. This is partly due to the fact that on many occasions, provisional data were in use in the country before the final results were published, which usually took quite some time. In some cases, mistakes were made while copying the electoral data, and extended later to further sources. In a few cases, official data were incomplete or flawed. Especially problematic are the data on electoral turnout: for many elections, the official electoral rolls are not reliable; in addition, the number of voters with electoral cards (*carnet electoral*) has always been much lower than the number of registered voters.

Finally, the elections of the 1970s in particular are classed as fraudulent, and even the polls held during the incipient democratization process of the 1980s show irregularities, though to a lesser extent. The author has calculated the percentages in the following tables according to the standards of the data handbook.

2. Tables

2.1 Dates of National Elections, Referendums, and Coups d'Etat

Year	Presidential elections	Parliamentary elections	Elections for Constitutional Assembly	Referendums	Coups d'état
1931	11–13/01	11–13/01			02/12
1932		03–05/01[a]			
1935	xx/xx				
1944					07/05
1944					21/10
1945	14–16/01				
1948					14/12
1950	26–29/03		26–29/03		
1952		xx/03			
1954		xx/03			
1956	04/03	15/05			
1958		23/03			
1960		24/04			26/10
1961			17/12		25/01
1962	30/04				
1964		08/03			
1966		13/03			
1967	05/03				
1968		10/03			
1970		08/03			
1972	20/02	12/03			
1974		10/03			
1976		14/03			
1977	20/02				
1978		12/03			
1979					15/10
1982			28/03		
1984	25/03 (1st)				
1984	06/05 (2nd)				
1985		31/03			
1988		20/03			
1989	19/03				
1991		10/03			
1994	20/03 (1st)	20/03			
1994	24/04 (2nd)				
1997		16/03			
1999	07/03				
2000		12/03			
2003		16/03			

[a] Two electoral contests were planned (from 3 to 5 and from 10 to 12 January). The second poll was cancelled.

2.2 Electoral Body 1931–2003

Year	Type of election[a]	Population[b]	Registered voters Total number	% pop.	Votes cast Total number	% reg. voters	% pop.
1931	Pr	1,434,361	392,383	27.4	228,866[c]	58.3	16.0
1935	Pr	1,531,000	—	—	—	—	—
1945	Pr	1,742,000	—	—	313,694[c]	—	18.0
1950	Pr/CA	1,855,917	—	—	647,666	—	34.9
1952	Pa	1,952,000	—	—	700,979[c]	—	35.9
1954	Pa	2,075,000	—	—	—	—	—
1956	Pr	2,210,000	—	—	711,931[c]	—	32.2
1956	Pa	2,210,000	—	—	585,000[c]	—	26.5
1958	Pa	2,346,000	—	—	450,000[c]	—	19.2
1960	Pa	2,454,000	—	—	420,102[c]	—	17.1
1961	CA	2,510,984	795,805	31.7	345,582[c]	43.4	13.8
1962	Pr	2,649,000	—	—	400,118	—	15.1
1964	Pa	2,824,000	1,074,243	38.0	296,434[c]	27.6	10.5
1966	Pa	3,037,000	1,195,823	40.4	387,155[c]	32.4	12.7
1967	Pr	3,151,000	1,266,587	40.2	491,894[c]	38.8	15.6
1968	Pa	3,266,000	1,342,775	41.1	492,037	36.6	15.1
1970	Pa	3,441,000	1,494,931	43.4	622,570	41.6	18.1
1972	Pr	3,670,000	1,119,699	30.5	806,357	72.0	22.0
1972	Pa	3,670,000	1,119,699	30.5	634,651	56.7	17.3
1974	Pa	3,890,000	—	—	—[d]	—	—
1976	Pa	4,120,000	—	—	—[d]	—	—
1977	Pr	4,260,000	—	—	1,206,942	—	27.5
1978	Pa	4,350,000	1,800,000	41.4	849,208[c]	47.2	18.8
1982	CA	4,999,000	2,440,000[e]	56.1	1,660,393	68.0	33.2
1984	Pr (1st)	4,780,000	2,521,000[h]	52.7	1,419,503	56.3	29.7
1984	Pr (2nd)	4,780,000	2,581,000[f]	54.0	1,524,079	59.0	31.9
1985	Pa	4,819,000	2,623,000[f]	54.4	1,101,606	42.0	22.9
1988	Pa	5,107,000	1,950,000[g]	38.2	1,150,934	59.0	22.5
1989	Pr	5,207,000	2,513,000[g]	48.3	1,003,153	40.2	19.3
1991	Pa	5,279,389	2,582,000[g]	48.9	1,153,013	44.7	21.8
1994	Pr (1st)	5,642,035	2,822,000[g]	50.0	1,411,320	50.0	25.0
1994	Pr (2nd)	5,642,035	2,822,000[g]	50.0	1,246,220	45.5	22.1
1994	Pa	5,642,035	2,822,000[g]	50.0	1,453,229	51.5	25.8
1997	Pa	5,924,255	3,004,174[g]	50.7	1,176,887	39.2	19.9
1999	Pr	6,188,828	3,170,414	51.2	1,223,215	38.5	19.8
2000	Pa	6,319,427	3,264,724[g]	51.7	1,256,342	38.5	19.9
2003	Pa	6,600,000	—	—	1,398,719[c]	—	—

[a] CA = Constitutional Assembly; Pa = Parliament; Pr = President.
[b] The data for the years 1931, 1950 and 1961 are taken from the censuses results of 01/05/1930, 13/06/1950 and 02/05/1961. Other population censuses: 1,006,848 (1901) and 3,554,648 (1971). Other population data are taken from various sources, since 1991 from SIECA.
[c] Valid votes. The number of voters was not available.
[d] No official electoral results were published.
[e] The lists of registered voters were not reliable.
[f] Until 1983, all the electoral registers were elaborated on the basis of the identity card duplicates (*cédulas de identidad personal*, previous denomination: *cédula de vecindad*). But these were not reliable. The 1983 Constitution provides for the Central Electoral Council to produce them autonomously, following different procedures to any other public register. Yet, due to time problems the CEC could not elaborate a dependable electoral register until the 1984 and 1985 elections.
[g] Only some of the registered voters were in possession of an electoral card (*carnet electoral*), a basic requirement to vote. The number of voters with electoral cards was 1,650,000 (1988), 1,870,000 (1989), 2,180,000 (1991), 2,718,000 (1994), 2,748,000 (1994, second round of presidential elections), 2,679,055 (1997) and 3,007,233 (2000). The data for the year 2000 have been taken from the TSE's homepage and date from 10/02/00.

2.3 Abbreviations

AD	*Partido Acción Democrática* (Democratic Action Party)
AP	*Acción Popular* (Popular Action)
ARENA	*Partido Alianza Republicana Nacionalista* (Nationalist Republican Alliance Party)
CC	*Coalición por el Cambio* (Coalition for Change)
CD	*Convergencia Democrática* (Democratic Convergence)
CDU	*Centro Democrático Unido* (United Democratic Center)
FC	*Fuerza Cristiana* (Christian Force)
FE	*Movimiento Fuerza y Esperanza* (Movement Force and Hope)
FMLN	*Partido Frente Farabundo Martí para la Liberación Nacional* (*Farabundo Martí* Front for National Liberation)
FU	*Fuerza Cristiana* (Christian Force)
FUDI	*Frente Unido Democrático Independiente* (Independent Democratic United Front)
LIDER	*Liga Democrática Republicana* (Republican Democratic League)
MAC	*Movimiento Auténtico Cristiano* (Christian Authentic Movement)
MAS	*Movimiento Auténtico Salvadoreño* (Salvadorean Authentic Party)
MERECEN	*Movimiento Estable Republicano Centrista* (Centrist Republican Stable Movement)
MNR	*Movimiento Nacional Revolucionario* (Revolutionary National Movement)
MPSC	*Movimiento Popular Social Cristiano* (Social Christian Popular Movement)
MSN	*Movimiento de Solidaridad Nacional* (Movement of National Solidarity)
MU	*Movimiento de Unidad* (Movement of Unity)

MUDC	*Movimiento Unido Demócrata Cristiano* (Christian Democratic United Movement)
PAC	*Partido Auténtico Constitucional* (Constitutional Authentic Party)
PAISA	*Partido Auténtico Institucional Salvadoreño* (Salvadorean Institutional Authentic Party)
PAN	*Partido Acción Nacional* (National Action Party)
PAR	*Partido Acción Renovadora* (Renovating Action Party)
PCN	*Partido de Conciliación Nacional* (National Reconciliation Party)
PD	*Partido Demócrata* (Democratic Party)
PDC	*Partido Demócrata Cristiano* (Christian Democratic Party)
PID	*Partido Institucional Demócrata* (Democratic Institutional Party)
PL	*Partido Liberación* (Liberation Party)
PLD	*Partido Liberal Democrático* (Democratic Liberal Party)
PMR	*Partido Movimiento Renovador* (Renovating Movement Party)
POP	*Partido de Orientación Popular* (Party of Popular Orientation)
PPL	*Partido Popular Laborista* (Popular Labor Party)
PPR	*Partido Popular Republicano* (Republican Popular Party)
PPS	*Partido Popular Salvadoreño* (Salvadorean Popular Party)
PREN	*Partido Republicano de Evolución Nacional* (Republican Party of National Evolution)
PRUD	*Partido Revolucionario de Unificación Democrática* (Revolutionary Party of Democratic Unification)
PSD	*Partido Social Demócrata* (Social Democratic Party)
PUNTO	*Partido Pueblo Unido Nuevo Trato* (Party United People New Treatment)
UDN	*Unión Democrática Nacionalista* (Nationalist Democratic Union)
UNO	*Unión Nacional Opositora* (National Opposition Union)
UP	*Unidad Popular* (Popular Union)
UPD	*Unión de Partidos Democráticos* (Union of Democratic Parties)
USC	*Unión Social Cristiana* (Social Christian Union)

2.4 Electoral Participation of Parties and Alliances 1950–2003

Party / Alliance[a]	Years	Elections contested	
		Presidential	Parliamentary
PRUD	1950–1960	2	6
PAR[b]	1950; 1956; 1960–1961; 1964–1967; 1985–1989	4	7
PAC	1956; 1961	1	1
PAN	1956; 1961; 2000–2003	–	4
PCN	1961–2003	8	17
UPD[c]	1961	–	1
PDC[d]	1961; 1964–1974; 1977; 1982–2003	7	15
PREN	1966	–	1

Party / Alliance[a] (continued)	Years	Elections contested Presidential	Parliamentary
PPS[e]	1966–1972; 1978–1985; 1989	4	8
MNR[f]	1968–1974; 1977; 1989–1994	4	6
UDN[g]	1970–1974; 1977; 1991	2	4
FUDI	1972–1974	1	2
UNO[h]	1972–1974; 1977	2	2
AD	1982–1991	2	4
ARENA	1982–2003	4	8
POP	1982–1988	1	3
MERECEN	1984	1	–
PAISA[i]	1984–1989	2	2
CD[j]	1989–2000	3	4
MAC	1989–1994	2	2
UP[k]	1989	1	–
FMLN	1994–2003	2	4
MSN	1994–1997	1	2
MU	1994–1997	1	2
MAS	1997	–	1
PD[l]	1997–1999	1	1
PL	1997	–	1
PLD	1997; 2000	–	2
PRSC	1997	–	1
CDU[m]	1999–2003	1	2
LIDER	1999	1	–
PUNTO	1999	1	–
USC	1999–2000	1	1
PPL[l]	1999–2000	1	1
AP	2003	–	1
FU	2003	–	1
PMR	2003	–	1
PPR	2003	–	1
PSD[n]	2003	–	1

[a] Only those parties that have contested elections independently at least once are included in the table.
[b] Member of the UPD in 1961.
[c] Electoral alliance formed by PAR, PDC, and PSD.
[d] Member of the UPD in 1961 and of the UNO in 1972, 1974, and 1977.
[e] Member of the UPD in 1989.
[f] Member of the UNO in 1972, 1974 and 1977; of the CD in 1989 and 1991.
[g] Member of the UNO in 1972, 1974, and 1977.
[h] Alliance formed by the PDC, MNR, and UDN.
[i] Member of the UP in 1989.
[j] On 29/11/1987, the member parties of the *Frente Democrático Revolucionario* (FDR)—MNR and MPSC—merged with the PSD in the CD. In the elections held in 2000, the CD and the PSD formed the CDU.
[k] Electoral alliance formed by PAISA, PL, and PPS.
[l] Member of CDU in 1999.
[m] Alliance formed by CD, PD, PPL, MUDC, and FE in 1999, and by CD and PSD in 2000.
[n] In the elections held in 2000, the CD and the PSD formed the CDU.

2.5 Referendums

Referendums have not been held.

2.6 Elections for Constitutional Assembly

1950	Total number	%	Seats	%
Registered Voters	—	–		
Votes cast	647,666	—		
Invalid Votes	36,256	5.6		
Valid Votes	611,410	94.4		
			52	100.0
PRUD	345,139	56.4	38	73.1
PAR	266,271	43.6	14	26.9

1961	Total number	%	Seats	%
Registered Voters	789,805	–		
Votes cast	—	—		
Invalid Votes	—	—		
Valid Votes	345,582	—		
			54	100.0
PCN	207,701	60.1	54	100.0
UPD[a]	64,916	18.8	—	—
PAN	49,300	14.3	—	—
PAC	23,665	6.8	—	—

[a] Alliance formed by PAR, PDC, and PSD.

1982	Total number	%	Seats	%
Registered Voters	2,440,000	–		
Votes cast	1,660,393	68.0		
Invalid Votes	191,096[a]	11.5		
Valid Votes	1,469,297	88.5		
			60	100.0
PDC	590,644	40.2	24	40.0
ARENA	430,205	29.3	19	31.7
PCN	273,383	18.6	14	23.3
AD	112,787	7.7	2	3.3
PPS	44,900	3.1	1	1.7
POP	17,378	1.2	—	—

[a] This figure includes 130,740 invalid votes, 53,912 blank votes and 6,444 challenged votes.

2.7 Parliamentary Elections 1952–2003

Year	1952		1954	
	Total number	%	Total number	%
Registered Voters	—	–	—	–
Votes cast	—	—	—	—
Invalid Votes	—	—	—	—
Valid Votes	700,979	—	—	—
PRUD[a]	700,979	100.0	—	100.0

[a] The government party was the only contender.

Year	1956		1958	
	Total number	%[a]	Total number	%[a]
Registered Voters	—	–	—	–
Votes cast	—	—	—	—
Invalid Votes	—	—	—	—
Valid Votes	585,000	—	450,000	—
PRUD	552,000	94.4	450,000[a]	100.0
PAN	33,000	5.6	–	–

[a] The government party was the only contender.

Year	1960		1964	
	Total number	%	Total number	%
Registered Voters	—	–	1,074,243	–
Votes cast	—	—	—	—
Invalid Votes	—	—	—	—
Valid Votes	420,102	—	296,434	—
PRUD	368,545	87.7	–	–
PAR	51,557[a]	12.3	45,499	15.3
PCN	–	–	176,620	58.6
PDC	–	–	77,315	26.1

[a] The Central Electoral Council disqualified the PAR's candidacy in seven constituencies out of 14.

Year	1966		1968	
	Total number	%	Total number	%
Registered Voters	1,195,823	–	1,342,775	–
Votes cast	—	—	492,037	36.6
Invalid Votes	—	—	45,931	9.3
Valid Votes	387,155	—	446,106	90.7
PCN	207,586	53.6	212,661	47.7
PDC	120,645	31.2	193,248	43.3
PAR	26,661	6.9	–	–
PREN	22,960	5.9	–	–
PPS	9,303	2.4	22,748	5.1
MNR	–	–	17,449	3.9

Year	1970[a]		1972[a]	
	Total number	%	Total number	%
Registered Voters	1,494,931	–	1,119,699	–
Votes cast	622,570	41.6	634,651	56.7
Invalid Votes	94,463	15.2	109,698	17.3
Valid Votes	528,107	84.8	524,953	82.7
PCN	315,560	59.8	353,775	67.4
PDC	142,659	27.0	–	–
PPS	28,606	5.4	31,790	6.1
MNR	8,832	1.7	–	–
UDN	32,450	6.1	–	–
UNO[b]	–	–	119,194[c]	22.7
FUDI	–	–	20,194	3.8

[a] Massive electoral fraud.
[b] Alliance formed by PDC, MNR and UDN.
[c] The Central Electoral Council disqualified the UNO's candidacy in five constituencies out of 14, including San Salvador.

For the elections of 1974 and 1976, characterized by massive electoral fraud, official vote counting results were not published. For both elections, the distributions of seats is reported under 2.8. Boycotted by the opposition, the 1976 elections were contested only by the government party.

Year	1978		1985	
	Total number	%	Total number	%
Registered Voters	1,800,000	–	2,623,000	–
Votes cast	—	—	1,101,606	42.0
Invalid Votes	—	—	136,375[a]	12.4
Valid Votes	849,208	—	965,231	87.6
PCN	766,673	90.3	80,730[b]	8.3
PPS	82,535	9.7	16,344	1.7
PDC	–	–	505,338	52.4
ARENA	–	–	286,665[b]	29.7
PAISA	–	–	36,101	3.7
AD	–	–	35,565	3.7
Others	–	–	4,488[c]	0.5

[a] Includes 74,007 invalid votes, 57,690 blank votes and 4,678 challenged votes.
[b] ARENA and PCN formed an electoral alliance.
[c] Others include: PAR: 2,963 votes (0.3%); POP: 836 (0.1%); MERECEN: 689 (0.1%).

Year	1988		1991	
	Total number	%	Total number	%
Registered Voters	1,950,000[a]	–	2,582,000[a]	–
Votes cast	1,150,934	59.0	1,153,013	44.7
Invalid Votes	220,185[b]	19.1	101,532[c]	8.8
Valid Votes	930,749	80.9	1,051,481	91.2
PCN	78,756	8.5	94,531	9.0
PDC	326,716	35.1	294,029	28.0
ARENA	447,696	48.1	466,091	44.3
PAISA	19,609	2.1	–	–
AD	16,211	1.7	6,798	0.7
PAR	5,059	0.5	–	–
POP	1,742	0.2	–	–
PL	34,960	3.8	–	–
CD	–	–	127,855	12.2
MAC	–	–	33,971	3.2
UDN	–	–	28,206	2.7

[a] The number of voters with '*carnet electoral*' was only 1,650,000 in 1988 and 2,180,000 in 1991.
[b] This figure includes 107,355 invalid votes, 34,320 blank votes, 11,388 challenged votes and 64,510 unused votes, all of them included in the total number of votes (see Montes 1988).
[c] Includes 59,998 invalid votes, 34,508 blank votes and 7,026 challenged votes.

Year	1994		1997	
	Total number	%	Total number	%
Registered Voters	2,822,000[a]	–	3,004,174[a]	–
Votes cast	1,453,299	53.1	1,176,887	39.2
Invalid Votes	108,022[b]	7.4	57,284[c]	4.9
Valid Votes	1,345,277	92.6	1,119,603	95.1
ARENA	605,775	45.0	396,301	35.4
FMLN	287,811	21.4	369,709	33.0
PDC	240,451	17.9	93,545	8.4
PCN	83,520	6.2	97,362	8.7
CD	59,843	4.4	39,145	3.5
MU	33,510	2.5	25,244	2.2
MSN	12,827	1.0	7,012	0.6
MAC	12,109	0.9	–	–
MNR	9,431	0.7	–	–
PRSC	–	–	40,039	3.6
PLD	–	–	35,279	3.2
PD	–	–	13,533	1.2
Others[d]	–	–	2,434	0.2

[a] The number of voters with '*carnet electoral*' was only 2,718,000 in 1994 and 2,679,055 in 1997.
[b] Includes 77,062 invalid votes, 26,632 blank votes and 4,328 challenged votes.
[c] Includes 38,829 invalid votes, 14,893 blank votes and 3,562 challenged votes.
[d] Others include: PL: 2,302 votes (0.2%) and MAS: 132 (0.0%).

Year	2000			2003	
	Total number	%		Total number	%
Registered Voters	3,007,233[a]	–		—	–
Votes cast	1,256,342	38.5		—	—
Invalid Votes	46,073[b]	3.7		—	—
Valid Votes	1,210,269	96.3		1,398,718[c]	—
ARENA	436,169	36.0		446,233	31.9
FMLN	426,289	35.2		475,043	34.0
PCN	106,802	8.8		181,167	13.0
PDC	87,074	7.2		101,841	7.3
CDU	65,070	5.4		89,115	6.4
PAN	44,901	3.7		14,574	1.0
USC	23,329	1.9		–	–
PLC	15,639	1.3		–	–
PPL	4,996	0.4		–	–
PMR	–	–		26,299	1.9
PPR	–	–		22,785	1.6
AP	–	–		15,906	1.1
FC	–	–		15,573	1.1
PAN	–	–		14,574	1.0
PSD	–	–		10,203	0.7

[a] The number of voters with '*carnet electoral*'was only 3,007,233. The data have been taken from the TSE's homepage and date from 10/02/00.
[b] Includes 29,869 invalid votes, 13,500 blank votes and 2,704 challenged votes.
[c] There is a difference of 20 votes between the official number of valid votes (1,398,718) and the sum of the official number of party votes (1,398,738).

2.8 Composition of Parliament 1952–2003

Year	1952		1954		1956		1958	
	Seats	%	Seats	%	Seats	%	Seats	%
	54	100.0	54	100.0	54	100.0	54	100.0
PRUD	54	100.0	54	100.0	54	100.0	54	100.0

Year	1960		1964		1966		1968	
	Seats	%	Seats	%	Seats	%	Seats	%
	54	100.0	52	100.0	52	100.0	52	100.0
PRUD	54	100.0	–	–	–	–	–	–
PCN	–	–	32	61.5	31	59.6	27	51.9
PDC	–	–	14	26.9	15	28.8	19	36.5
PAR	–	–	6	11.5	4	7.7	–	–
PPS	–	–	–	–	1	1.9	4	7.7
PREN	–	–	–	–	1	1.9	–	–
MNR	–	–	–	–	–	–	2	3.8

Year	1970		1972		1974		1976	
	Seats	%	Seats	%	Seats	%	Seats	%
	52	100.0	52	100.0	52	100.0	52	100.0
PCN	34	65.4	39	75.0	36	69.2	52	100.0
PDC	16	30.8	–	–	–	–	–	–
PPS	1	1.9	4	7.7	–	–	–	–
UDN	1	1.9	–	–	–	–	–	–
UNO	–	–	8	15.4	15	28.8	–	–
FUDI	–	–	1	1.9	1	1.9	–	–

Year	1978		1985		1988		1991	
	Seats	%	Seats	%	Seats	%	Seats	%
	54	100.0	60	100.0	60	100.0	84	100.0
PCN	50	92.6	12[a]	20.0	7	11.7	9	10.7
PPS	4	7.4	–	–	–	–	–	–
PDC	–	–	33	55.0	22	36.7	26	31.0
ARENA	–	–	13[a]	21.7	31	51.7	39	46.4
AD	–	–	1	1.7	–	–	–	–
PAISA	–	–	1	1.7	–	–	–	–
CD	–	–	–	–	–	–	8	9.5
MAC	–	–	–	–	–	–	1	1.2
UD	–	–	–	–	–	–	1	1.2

[a] ARENA and PCN joined in an electoral alliance.

Year	1994		1997		2000		2003	
	Seats	%	Seats	%	Seats	%	Seats	%
	84	100.0	84	100.0	84	100.0	84	100.0
ARENA	39	46.4	28	33.3	29	34.5	27	32.1
FMLN	21	25.0	27	32.1	31	36.9	31	36.9
PDC	18	21.4	10	12.0	6	7.1	5	6.0
PCN	4	4.8	11	13.1	13	15.5	16	19.0
CD	1	1.2	2	2.4	–	–	–	–
MU	1	1.2	1	1.2	–	–	–	–
PRSC	–	–	3	3.6	–	–	–	–
PLD	–	–	2	2.4	–	–	–	–
CDU	–	–	–	–	3	3.6	5	6.0
PAN	–	–	–	–	2	2.4	–	–

2.9 Presidential Elections 1931–1999

1931	Total number	%
Registered Voters	392,383	–
Votes cast	—	—
Invalid Votes	—	—
Valid Votes	228,866	—
Arturo Araujo (Partido Laborista Salvadoreño[a])	106,777	46.7
Alberto Gómez Zárate (Partido Zaratista)	64,280	28.1
Enrique Córdova (Partido Evolución Nacional)	34,499	15.1
Antonio Claramount Lucero (Partido Fraternal Progresista)	18,399	8.0
Miguel Tomás Molina (Partido Constitucional)	4,911	2.1

[a] The *Partido Laborista Salvadoreño* enjoyed the support of the *Partido Nacional Republicano*.

1935	Total number	%
Registered Voters	—	–
Votes cast	—	—
Invalid Votes	—	—
Valid Votes	—	—
Maximiliano Hernández Martínez (Pro Patria)[a]	—	—

[a] Only one candidate contested.

1945	Total number	%
Registered Voters	—	–
Votes cast	—	—
Invalid Votes	—	—
Valid Votes	313,694	—
Salvador Castañeda Castro (Partido Agrario)[a]	312,754	99.7

[a] Other candidates (Antonio Claramount Lucero; Arturo Romero; Napoleón Viera Altamirano; José Cipriano Castro) withdrew from the elections, but received some votes nevertheless.

1950	Total number	%
Registered Voters	—	–
Votes cast	647,666	—
Invalid Votes	36,256	5.6
Valid Votes	611,410	94.4
Oscar Osorio (PRUD)	345,139	56.4
José Ascencio Menéndez (PAR)	266,271	43.6

1956	Total number	%[a]
Registered Voters	—	–
Votes cast	—	—
Invalid Votes	—	—
Valid Votes	711,931	—
José María Lemus (PRUD)	677,748	95.2
Rafael Carranza Anaya (PAC)[a]	22,659	3.2
Enrique Magaña Menéndez (PAR)[a]	11,524	1.6

[a] The Central Electoral Council disqualified the candidacies of José Alberto Funes (PID), Roberto Edmundo Cannessa (PAN) and José Alvaro Díaz (*Partido Demócrata Nacionalista*). It also forbade Carranza Anaya and Magaña Menéndez to withdraw their candidacies; nevertheless, the latter two boycotted the elections.

1962	Total number	%
Registered Voters	—	–
Votes cast	400,118	—
Blank Votes	19,337	4.8
Invalid Votes	11,980	3.0
Valid Votes	368,801	92.2
Julio Adalberto Rivera (PCN)[a]	368,801	100.0

[a] The candidate of the government party was the only contender

1967	Total number	%
Registered Voters	1,266,587	–
Votes cast	—	—
Invalid Votes	—	—
Valid Votes	491,894	—
Fidel Sánchez Hernández (PCN)	267,447	54.4
Abraham Rodríguez Portillo (PDC)	106,358	21.6
Fabio Castillo Figueroa (PAR)	70,978	14.4
Alvaro Magaña (PPS)	47,111	9.6

1972[a]	Total number	%
Registered Voters	1,119,699	–
Votes cast	806,357	72.0
Blank Votes	13,262	1.6
Invalid Votes	22,501	2.8
Valid Votes	770,594	95.6
Arturo Armando Molina (PCN)	334,600	43.4
José Napoleón Duarte (UNO)[b]	324,756	42.1
José Antonio Rodríguez Porth (PPS)	94,367	12.2
José Alberto Medrano (FUDI)	16,871	2.2

[a] Massive electoral fraud.
[b] Alliance formed by PDC, MNR and UDN.

1977[a]	Total number	%
Registered Voters	—	–
Votes cast	—	—
Invalid Votes	—	—
Valid Votes	1,206,942	—
Carlos Humberto Romero (PCN)	812,281	67.3
Ernesto Claramount Rozeville (UNO)[b]	394,661	32.7

[a] Massive electoral fraud.
[b] Alliance formed by PDC, MNR and UDN.

1984 (1st round)	Total number	%
Registered Voters	–	–
Votes cast	1,419,503	48.6
Invalid Votes	153,217[a]	10.8
Valid Votes	1,266,286	89.2
José Napoleón Duarte (PDC)	549,727	43.4
Roberto d'Aubuisson (ARENA)	376,917	29.8
José Francisco Guerrero (PCN)	244,556	19.3
René Fortín Magaña (AD)	43,939	3.5
Francisco Quiñónez Avila (PPS)	24,395	1.9
Roberto Escobar García (PAISA)	15,430	1.2
Juan Ramón Rosales y Rosales (MERECEN)	6,645	0.5
Gilberto Trujillo (POP)	4,677	0.4

[a] Includes 104,577 invalid votes, 41,736 blank votes and 6,924 challenged votes.

1984 (2nd round)	Total number	%
Registered Voters	–	–
Votes cast	1,524,079	–
Invalid Votes	119,713[a]	7.9
Valid Votes	1,404,366	92.1
José Napoleón Duarte (PDC)	752,625	53.6
Roberto d'Aubuisson (ARENA)	651,741	46.4

[a] Includes 81,017 invalid votes, 32,582 blank votes and 6,114 challenged votes.

1989	Total number	%
Registered Voters	1,834,000	–
Votes cast	1,003,153	54.7
Invalid Votes	64,075[a]	6.4
Valid Votes	939,078	93.6
Alfredo Félix Cristiani (ARENA)	505,370	53.8
Fidel Chávez Mena (PDC/AD)[b]	342,732	36.5
Rafael Morán Castañeda (PCN)	38,218	4.1
Guillermo Manuel Ungo (CD)[c]	35,642	3.8
Julio Adolfo Rey Prendes (MAC)	9,300	1.0
Hugo Barrera (UP)[d]	4,609	0.5
Ricardo Molina (PAR)	3,207	0.3

[a] Includes 51,182 invalid votes, 7,409 blank votes and 5,484 challenged votes.
[b] The AD supported the PDC's candidate and won 4,363 votes (0.5% of the valid vote).
[c] Aliance formed b MNR, MPSC and PSD.
[d] Alliance formed by PAISA, PL and PPS.

1994 (1st round)	Total number	%
Registered Voters	2,822,000[a]	–
Votes cast	1,411,320	50.0
Invalid Votes	103,663[b]	7.3
Valid Votes	1,307,657	92.7
Armando Calderón Sol (ARENA)	641,108	49.0
Rubén Ignacio Zamora Rivas (FMLN/CD/MNR)	325,582	24.9
Fidel Chávez Mena (PDC)	214,277	16.4
Roberto Escobar García (PCN)	70,504	5.4
Jorge Martínez (MU)	31,502	2.4
Edgardo Rodríguez Engelhard (MSN)	13,841	1.1
Rhina Victoria Escalante de Rey Prendes (MAC)	10,843	0.8

[a] Only 2,718,000 voters with '*carnet electoral*'.
[b] Includes 70,503 invalid votes, 28,311 blank votes and 4,849 challenged votes.

1994 (2nd round)	Total number	%
Registered Voters	2,822,000[a]	–
Votes cast	1,246,220	45.5
Invalid Votes	48,976[b]	3.9
Valid Votes	1,197,244	96.1
Armando Calderón Sol (ARENA)	818,264	68.3
Rubén Ignacio Zamora Rivas (FMLN/CD/MNR)	378,980	31.7

[a] Only 2,748,000 voters with '*carnet electoral*'.
[b] Includes 40,048 invalid votes, 5,461 blank votes and 3,469 challenged votes.

1999	Total number	%
Registered Voters	3,170,414	–
Votes cast	1,223,215	38.5
Invalid Votes	40,967[a]	3.3
Valid Votes	1,182,248	96.7
Francisco Guillermo Flores Pérez (ARENA)	614,268	52.0
Facundo Guardado (FMLN/USC)[b]	343,472	29.0
Rubén Ignacio Zamora Rivas (CDU)	88,640	7.5
Rodolfo Antonio Parker Soto (PDC)	67,207	5.7
Rafael Hernán Contreras Rodriguez (PCN)	45,140	3.8
Nelson Salvador García Córdova (LIDER)	19,269	1.6
Francisco Ayala de Paz (PUNTO)	4,252	0.4

[a] Includes 34,394 invalid votes, 3,594 blank votes and 3,079 challenged votes.
[b] FMLN and USC formed the so-called Coalition for Change (CC, *Coalición por el Cambio*).

2.10 List of Power Holders 1898–2004

Head of State	Years	Remarks
Tomás Regalado	1898–1903	Army officer; appointed provisional president by his troops on 13/11/1898; constitutional president since 01/03/1899.
Pedro José Escalón	1903–1907	Elected constitutional president by the national assembly. Assumed presidency on 01/03/1903.
Fernando Figueroa	1907–1911	Army officer; elected constitutional president by the national assembly. Assumed presidency on 01/03/1907.
Manuel Enrique Araujo	1911–1913	Elected constitutional president by the national assembly. Assumed presidency on 01/03/1911. Assassinated on 08/02/1913.
Carlos Meléndez	1913–1914	Governed as First *Designado* to presidency; resigned on 28/08/1914 in order to contest the presidential elections.
Alfonso Quiñónez Molina	1914–1915	Governed as *Designado* to presidency. End of the provisional tenure on 28/02/1915.
Carlos Meléndez	1915–1918	Elected constitutional president. Assumed presidency on 01/03/1915. Resigned on 21/12/1918 due to health problems.
Alfonso Quiñónez Molina	1918–1919	Governed in his capacity as vice president. End of provisional tenure on 28/02/1919.

Head of State (cont.)	Years	Remarks
Jorge Meléndez	1919–1923	Elected constitutional president. Assumed presidency on 01/03/1919.
Alfonso Quiñónez Molina	1923–1927	Elected constitutional president. Assumed presidency on 01/03/1923.
Pío Romero Bosque	1927–1931	Elected constitutional president. Assumed presidency on 01/03/1927.
Arturo Araujo	1931	Elected constitutional president. Assumed presidency on 01/03/1931. *Coup d'état* on 02/12/1931.
Directorio Militar	1931	Formed after the coup. Withdrew from government on 04/12/1931 after negotiating with Vice President and War Minister Hernández Martínez.
Maximiliano Hernández Martínez	1931–1934	Army officer; governed as vice president; confirmed by the congress on 07/02/1932. Resigned on 28/08/1934 in order to contest the elections.
Andrés Ignacio Menéndez	1934–1935	Army officer; *Designado* to presidency. End of the provisional tenure on 28/02/1935.
Maximiliano Hernández Martínez	1935–1944	Army officer; elected constitutional president (only candidate to the elections). Re-elected in 1939 and 1944 by the national constitutional assembly. Resigned under popular pressure on 08/05/1944.
Andrés Ignacio Menéndez	1944	Assumed office in his capacity as vice president. *Coup d'état* on 21/10/1944.
Osmín Aguirre y Salinas	1944–1945	Army officer; appointed by the military leaders.
Salvador Castañeda Castro	1945–1948	Army officer; elected constitutional president. Assumed presidency on 01/03/1945. *Coup d'état* on 14/12/1948.
Consejo de Gobierno Revolucionario	1948–1950	Formed after Castañeda's downfall. Resigned on 14/09/1950.
Oscar Osorio	1950–1956	Army officer; elected constitutional president. End of tenure on 14/09/1956.
José María Lemus	1956–1960	Army officer; elected constitutional president. *Coup d'état* on 26/10/1960.
Junta de Gobierno Cívico-Militar	1960–1961	Military-civil junta; formed after Lemus' downfall. Military coup on 25/01/1961.
Directorio Cívico-Militar	1961–1962	Military-civil; appointed by the coup's military leaders. On 25/01/1962 it gave over the power to a provisional government.
Eusebio Rodolfo Cordón Cea	1962	Appointed provisional president by executive decree.

Head of State (cont.)	Years	Remarks
Julio Adalberto Rivera Carballo	1962–1967	Army officer; elected constitutional president (single candidate to the elections). Assumed presidency on 01/07/1962.
Fidel Sánchez Hernández	1967–1972	Army officer; elected constitutional president. Assumed presidency on 01/07/1967.
Arturo Armando Molina	1972–1977	Army officer; elected constitutional president (massive electoral fraud). Assumed presidency on 01/07/1972.
Carlos Humberto Romero	1977–1979	Army officer; elected constitutional president (massive electoral fraud). Assumed presidency on 01/07/1977. Military coup on 15/10/1979.
Juntas militares-civiles	1979–1982	The first junta was formed by the army officers Jaime Abdul Gutiérrez and Adolfo Arnoldo Majano; since 18/10/1979 also by the civilians Ramón Mayorga Quiroz, Guillermo Manuel Ungo and Mario Andino. Since early in 1980, the various juntas were mainly comprised of conservative army officers and Christian Democrats.
Alvaro Alfredo Magaña	1982–1984	Interim president. Elected by the constitutional assembly. Assumed presidency on 02/05/1982.
José Napoleón Duarte	1984–1989	Elected constitutional president. Assumed presidency on 01/06/1984.
Alfredo Félix Cristiani Burkhard	1989–1994	Elected constitutional president. Assumed presidency on 01/06/1989.
Armando Calderón Sol	1994–1999	Elected constitutional president. Assumed presidency on 01/06/1994.
Francisco Guillermo Flores Pérez	1999–	Elected constitutional president. Assumed presidency on 01/06/1999.

3. Bibliography

3.1 Official Sources

'Código Electoral'(19.01.1988). *Diario Oficial*, 298/12. San Salvador.

Consejo Central de Elecciones (1950). 'Acta del Escrutinio Presidencial', in *Diario Oficial*, 148/92. San Salvador.

Consejo Central de Elecciones (without year). *Memoria de los labores realizados por el Consejo Central de Elecciones, durante el período comprendido entre abril de 1965 y marzo de 1968*. San Salvador.

Consejo Central de Elecciones (1982). *Memoria del Consejo Central de Elecciones*. San Salvador.

— (1982). *Ley Electoral Transitoria (1982), Decreto No. 994*. San Salvador.

— (1984). 'Cómputos oficiales, 25 de marzo de 1984, elecciones para presidente y vice–presidente de la república', in *Estudios Centroamericanos*, 39/426–427: 365. San Salvador.

— (1984). 'Cómputos oficiales, 6 de mayo de 1984, elecciones para presidente y vice–presidente de la república, in *Estudios Centroamericanos*, 39/426–427: 366. San Salvador.

— (1988). 'Elecciones de diputados, 20 de marzo de 1988', in *Estudios Centroamericanos*, 43, 473–474: 285. San Salvador.

— (1989). *Acta final de escrutinio realizado el 19 de marzo/89 por el Consejo Central de Elecciones para elegir Presidente y Vice–Presidente de la República de El Salvador*. San Salvador.

— (1991). *Código Electoral y sus reformas 1991*. San Salvador.

— (without year). *Ley Electoral y sus reformas hasta 1975*. San Salvador.

'Constitución Política de la República de El Salvador decretada por el Congreso Nacional Constituyente de 1886', in *Diario Oficial*, 21/185, 17.08.1886. San Salvador.

'Constitución Política de la República', in *Diario Oficial*, 126/15, 20.01.1939. San Salvador.

'Constitución Política de El Salvador', in *Diario Oficial*, 149/196, 08.09.1950. San Salvador.

Departamento de Relaciones Publicas, Casa Presidencial (1972). *El Salvador. Elecciones del 1972*. San Salvador.

Instituto Salvadoreño de Administración Municipal (1984). *Constitución Política de la República de El Salvador 1983*. San Salvador.

'Ley Electoral (1952). Decreto No.601, in Diario Oficial, 154/40, 27.02.1952. San Salvador.

'Ley Electoral (1985)', in *Diario Oficial*, 286/2, 04.01.1985. San Salvador

'Ley Electoral Transitoria (1950). Decreto No.464', in *Diario Oficial* 148/16, 21.01.1950. San Salvador.

'Ley Electoral Transitoria (1984)', in *Diario Oficial*, 282/31, 13.02.1984. San Salvador.
Ley Reglamentaria de Elecciones (1886). San Salvador.
'Ley Reglamentaria de Elecciones (1939). Decreto No.31', in *Diario Oficial*, 126/44, 24.02.1939. San Salvador.
'Ley del Registro Electoral (1986)', in *Diario Oficial*, 291/97, 26.05.1986. San Salvador.
Ministerio de Educación (1967). *Constitución Política y Códigos de la República de El Salvador*. San Salvador.
'Reformas a la Ley Reglamentaria de Elecciones (1944). Decreto No. 9', in *Diario Oficial*, 136/47, 25.02.1944. San Salvador.
Tribunal Supremo Electoral (1993). *Codigo Electoral 1993*. San Salvador.

3.2 Books, Articles, and Electoral Reports

Acevado, C. (1991). 'El significado político de las elecciones del 10 de marzo'. *Estudios Centroamericanos*, 46/509: 151–168.
Alcantara, M. (1994). 'Las "elecciones del siglo" salvadoreñas'. *Boletín Electoral Latinoamericano*, 11: 157–180.
Anderson, T. P. (1982). *El Salvador 1932*. San José: EDUCA.
Armstrong, R. (1982). 'El Salvador Beyond Elections'. *NACLA-Report on the Americas*, 16/2: 2–31.
Arriaza Meléndez, J. (1989). *Historia de los procesos electorales en El Salvador (1811–1989)*. San Salvador: ISEP.
Baloyra, E. (1982). *El Salvador in Transition*. Chapel Hill, N.C.
— (1995). 'Elections, Civil War, and Transition in El Salvador, 1982–1994. A Preliminary Evaluation', in M. A. Seligson and J. Booth (eds.), *Elections and Democracy in Central America Revisited*. Chapel Hill, N.C./ London: The University of North Carolina Press, 45–64.
Base de Datos Políticos de las Américas (1999). *El Salvador: Elecciones Legislativas 1985-1991/ Legislative Elections 1985-1991*. <http://www.georgetown.edu/pdba/Elecdata/ElSal/saleg85-91.html> (as of 05/06/2004).
Bendel, P. (1995). 'Partidos políticos y sistema de partidos en Centroamérica', in *Documentos de Trabajo, Serie Análisis de la Realidad Nacional* 95/4. San Salvador: Fundaungo.
Benítez Manaut, R. (1990). 'El Salvador. Un equilibrio imperfecto entre los votos y las botas'. *Secuencia* (Mexico City), 17: 71–92.
Blutstein, H. I. et al. (1971). *Area Handbook for El Salvador*. Washington, D.C.: Government Printing Office.
Bowdler, G. A. and Cotter, P. (1982). *Voter Participation in Central America, 1954–1981*. Washington, D.C.: University Press of America.

Browning, D. (1989). *Report on the Conduct and Context of the Presidential Election in El Salvador on 19 March 1989*. London: Her Majesty's Stationery Office.

Calderón, J. T. (1931). *Sufragio libre. Elecciones de Autoridades Supremas*. San Salvador.

Central American Information Office (CAMINO) (1982). *El Salvador 1982. Elections without Choice*. Cambridge, Mass.

CINAI (1984). 'Destapando la "caja negra". Condicionamientos del proceso electoral 1984'. *Estudios Centroamericanos* (San Salvador), 39/426–427: 197–218.

Close, D. (1991). 'Central American Elections 1989–90. Costa Rica, El Salvador, Honduras, Nicaragua, Panama'. *Electoral Studies*, 10/1: 60–76.

Colindres, Eduardo (1997). *El sube y baja de los partidos políticos. Resultados y consecuencias de las elecciones de 1997 en El Salvador*. San Salvador: KAS/FUCAD.

Córdova Macías, R. (1989). 'El Salvador. Análisis de las elecciones presidenciales de marzo de 1989'. *Presencia* (San Salvador), 2/5: 87–103.

— (1990). 'El Salvador. Análisis de las elecciones presidenciales y perspectivas políticas. Marzo de 1989'. *Polémica* (San José), 11: 2–18.

— (1992). 'Procesos electorales y sistema de partidos en El Salvador (1982–1989)', in *Documentos de Trabajo*. San Salvador: Fundaungo.

CUDI (1982). 'Las elecciones de 1982. Realidades detrás de las apariencias'. *Estudios Centroamericanos* (San Salvador), 37: 573–596.

Dutrenít, S. (1988). *El Salvador*. Mexico City: Alianza Editorial Mexicana.

Eguizábal, C. (1982). 'El Salvador 1961–1981. Poder militar y luchas civiles'. *Polémica* (San José), 4–5: 84–94.

— (1984). 'El Salvador. Elecciones sin democracia'. *Polémica* (San José), 14–15: 16–33.

— (1989). 'Los partidos políticos y el desarrollo de la democracia representativa en El Salvador (1948–1988)'. *Relaciones Internacionales* (Heredia, Costa Rica), 29: 19–27.

— (1991). 'Elecciones legislativas, municipales y para el Parlamento Centroamérica. El Salvador, 10 de marzo de 1991'. *Boletín Electoral Latinoamericano* (San José: IIDH–CAPEL), 5: 18–25.

— (1992). 'Parties, Programs, and Politics in El Salvador', in L. W. Goodman et al. (eds.), *Political Parties and Democracy in Central América*. Boulder, Col./ San Francisco/ Oxford: Westview Press, 135–160.

Estudios Centroamericanos (1991). 'Documentación: Las elecciones del 10 de Marzo'. *Estudios Centroamericanos*, 509: 204.

— (1994). 'Los resultados electorales'. *Estudios Centroamericanos*, 545/6: 364.

Gallardo, R. (1961). *Las Constituciones de El Salvador*. Madrid: Ediciones Cultura Hispánica.

García, J. J. (1989). 'El Salvador. Recent Elections in Historical Perspective', in J. A. Booth and M. A. Seligson (eds.), *Elections and Democracy in Central America*. Chapel Hill, N.C./ London: University of North Carolina Press.

García, J. Z. (1995). 'The Salvadoran National Legislature', in D. Close (ed.), *Legislatures and the New Democracies in Latin America*. Boulder, Col./ London: Lynne Rienner, 37–47.

Herman, E. S. and Brodhead, F. (1984). *Demonstration Elections. US-Staged Elections in the Dominican Republic, Vietnam and El Salvador*. Boston, Mass.

Hernández-Pico, J. et al. (1973). *El Salvador año político 1971–72*. Guatemala: Publicaciones de la Universidad Centroamericano José-Simeón Cañas.

Hispanic American Report (Stanford, Calif.). (various years).

Instituto Centroamericano de Estudios Políticos (INCEP) (ed.) (1997). *El Salvador. Elecciones Municipales y Legislativas 1997*. Guatemala.

Instituto de Relaciones Europeo-Latinoamericanas (IRELA) (1991). *Elections and Negotiations in El Salvador: Obstacles and Expectations*. Madrid: IRELA.

Instituto Nacional Republicano para Asuntos Internaciones (NRIIA) (1991). *Las elecciones de 1991 en El Salvador*. Washington, D.C.: NRIIA.

International Human Rights Law Group (1989). *Report on the 1989 Salvadoran Electoral Process*. Washington, D.C.

Jiménez C., E. et al. (1988). *El Salvador. Guerra, política y paz (1979–1988)*. San Salvador: CINAS/CRIES.

Karl, T. L. (1986). 'Imposing Consent? Electoralism vs. Democratization in El Salvador', in P. W. Drake and E. Silva (eds.), *Elections and Democratization in Latin America, 1980–85*. San Diego, Calif.: University of California: 9–36.

Krennerich, M. (1992). 'Die Wahlen in El Salvador vom 10. März 1991. Eine Analyse im Lichte der Wahlgeschichte'. *Lateinamerika. Analysen Daten, Dokumentation* (Hamburg), 18: 86–95.

— (1993). Competitividad de las elecciones en Nicaragua, El Salvador y Guatemala en una perspectiva histórica comparada, in D. Nohlen (ed.), *Elecciones y sistemas de partidos en América Latina*. San José: IIDH/CAPEL: 169–203.

— (1996). *Wahlen und Antiregimekriege in Zentralamerika. Eine vergleichende Studie*. Opladen: Leske + Budrich.

Krumwiede, H.-W. (1982). 'Zur innen- und außenpolitischen Bedeutung der Wahlen zur Verfassungsgebenden Versammlung in El Salvador vom 28.3.1982'. *Zeitschrift für Parlamentsfragen*, 4: 541–548.

La Nación (San José). 23/04/1950; 09/03/1956.

La Prensa Gráfica (San Salvador) (various years).

Las elecciones en El Salvador, in *Boletín de Ciencias Económicas y Sociales* (San Salvador), 5 (1982), 46–47: 301–320.

Latin American Bureau (1977). *Violence and Fraud in El Salvador*. London.

Lehoucq, F. E. (1995). 'The Election of 1994 in El Salvador'. *Electoral Studies*, 14/2: 179–183.

Lungo Uclés, M. (1990). *El Salvador en los 80. Contrainsurgencia y revolución*. San José: EDUCA–FLACSO.

McDonald, R. H. (1971). *Party Systems and Elections in Latin America*. Chicago: Markham.

Monteforte Toledo, M. (1972). *Centro América. Subdesarrollo y dependencia*. Mexico City: UNAM.

Montes, S. (1985). 'Las elecciones del 31 de marzo'. *Estudios Centroamericanos* (San Salvador), 40/438: 215–228.

— (1988). 'Las elecciones del 20 de marzo 1988'. *Estudios Centroamericanos* (San Salvador), 43/473–474: 175–189.

— (1989). 'Las elecciones presidenciales del 19 de marzo de 1989'. *Estudios Centroamericanos* (San Salvador), 44/485: 199–209.

Murillo, G. (1990). 'Análisis del proceso electoral salvadoreño del 19 de marzo de 1989', in *Transición democrática en América Latina. Reflexiones sobre el debate actual. Memoria del III Curso Anual Interamericano de Elecciones*. San José: IIDH–CAPEL.

National Democratic Institute for International Affairs (1989). *The 1989 Salvadorean Election. Challenges and Opportunities*. Washington, D.C.

Parlamento Latinoamericano (PARLATINO) and Instituto de Relaciones Europeo-Latinoamericanas (IRELA) (1997). *Manual de los partidos políticos de América Latina*. Madrid: IRELA.

Perry, W. (1984). *The Salvadorean Presidential Election*. Washington, D.C.: Center for Strategic and International Studies.

Pickering, T. R. (1984). *Elections in El Salvador, Address before the Corporate Round Table of the World Affairs Council*. Washington, D.C., 1 March 1984 (Department of State, Bureau of Public Affairs, Current Policy No. 554).

Pleitez, J. E. (1993). 'La confiabilidad del registro electoral'. *Cuadernos de IEJES*, 8: 105–119.

Roggenbuck, S. (1994). 'Die allgemeinen Wahlen in El Salvador vom 20. März 1994. Ein weiterer Schritt zur Festigung der Demokratie'. *KAS-Auslandsinformationen*, 6: 74–97.

Rosenberg, M. B. (1985). '¿Democracia en Centroamérica?'. *Cuadernos de CAPEL* (San José), 5.

Ruddle, K. and Gillette, P. (eds.) (1972). *Latin America Political Statistics. Supplement to the Statistical Abstract of Latin America*. Los Angeles, Calif.: University of California.

Ryan, J. J. (1997). 'Democratic Transition and Consolidation in a Polarized System. The Role of the Center in El Salvador'. *Party Politics*, 3/2: 169–188.

Samayoa, M. (1986). 'Legislación y procesos electorales en El Salvador', in Centro de Asesoria y Promoción Electoral (CAPEL–IIDH)/Instituto de Investigaciones Jurídicas (eds.), *Legislación electoral comparada*. San José: EDUCA: 109–132.

Samayoa, M. (1988). 'El nuevo Registro Electoral de la República de El Salvador', in *Memoria de la Segunda Conferencia de la Asociación de Organismos Electorales de Centroamérica y el Caribe*. San José: IIDH–CAPEL, 41–74.

Spence, J. and Vickers, G. (1994). *Toward a Level Playing Field? A Report on the Post-War Salvadoran Electoral Process*. Cambridge: Hemisphere Initiatives.

Torres-Rivas, E. (1991). 'Imágenes, siluetas, formas en las elecciones centroamericanas. Las elecciones de la década'. *Polémica* (San José), 14–15: 2–21.

Villaveces de Ordóñez, M. M. (1989). 'Elecciones presidenciales. El Salvador 19 de marzo de 1989'. *Boletín Electoral Latinoamericano* (San José: IIDH–CAPEL), 1: 5–9.

Washington Office on Latin America (WOLA) (1991). *A Step Toward Peace? The March 1991 Elections in El Salvador*. Washington, D.C.

Webre, S. (1979). *José Napoleón Duarte and the Christian Democratic Party in El Salvadorean Politics, 1960–1972*. Baton Rouge, La.: Louisiana State University Press.

Wells, H. (ed.) (1967). *El Salvador Election Factbook, March 5, 1967*. Washington, D.C.: Institute for the Comparative Study of Political Systems.

White, A. (1973). *El Salvador*. New York/ Washington, D.C.

Williams, P. J. and Walter K. (1997). *Militarization and Demilitarization in El Salvador's Transition to Democracy*. Pittsburgh, Pa.: University of Pittsburgh Press.

GRENADA

by Christian Baukhage and Bernd Hillebrands

1. Introduction

1.1 Historical Overview

Until 1958, the island of Grenada was a British Crown Colony and part of the *Windward Islands Federation*. From 1958 until 1962, Grenada was one of ten insular colonies that formed the *British West Indies Federation*, a short-lived attempt to create a union that would no longer be dependent economically or politically on the United Kingdom. As of 1950, the main turning points in Grenada's political development were the revolution of 1979 and the US-led invasion in 1983.

Universal suffrage was introduced in Grenada for the 1951 elections. For the first time, political participation was extended to the poor and underprivileged majority of the population. Simultaneously, these elections marked the beginning of Eric Gairy's ascent. As chairman of both the Grenada Manual and Mental Workers' Union (GMMWU) and the Grenada United Labour Party (GULP), Gairy managed to organize a political mass movement. As prime minister, he put through far-reaching social reforms. However, his government soon showed personalist and authoritarian traits, and corruption and clientelism became prominent aspects of his administration.

From 1957 until 1961, a three-party coalition opposed to Gairy controlled the parliamentary majority. This coalition lost power to the Grenada National Party (GNP), which was founded in 1955 and backed by the urban middle class and the land owners. In 1967, Gairy was returned to power. The same year, a new constitution was enacted in Grenada, and the island achieved autonomy in its internal affairs (Associated Statehood). The process of decolonization was completed with the declaration of independence within the British Commonwealth of Nations on 7 February 1974. The Queen remained head of state, represented by a governor general.

Meanwhile, Gairy's regime had become increasingly authoritarian. His secret police, the 'Mongoose Gang', threatened the opposition with violence, the government itself was accused of fraud in the 1976 parliamentary elections. Internationally, Gairy had become known mainly for his interest in UFO research.

On 13 March 1979, Gairy's regime was overthrown by an armed revolution, led by the New Jewel Movement (NJM). The coup was actively supported by a large part of the population and encountered little resistance from the armed forces or the police. The NJM had been formed in 1973 as an alliance between the Joint Endeavour for Welfare, Education and Liberation (JEWEL) and the Movement for Assemblies of the People (MAP). JEWEL emphasized the need for social reforms in the rural areas and was supported by a large number of the population. MAP was a more ideological organization inspired mainly by Tanzania's *Ujamaa* socialism. For the 1976 elections, the NJM formed a tactical anti-Gairy alliance with the conservative GNP and the United People's Party (UPP). These elections were branded fraudulent by the opposition and international observers.

The coup was led by the former leader of the opposition in parliament, Maurice Bishop. He subsequently became prime minister of the new People's Revolutionary Government (PRG). The PRG abolished the 1974 Constitution, not touching, however, the positions of the Queen and of the governor general.

Bishop was a charismatic leader. For the people, he represented a new hope, especially because of his hard work in the area of social reforms. The orthodox Leninist ideology, which dominated parts of the NJM, was barely made public. Furthermore, no substantive changes were introduced in the private sector. Economic policy remained directed by pragmatic decisions without being able to overcome the country's economic weakness. To secure its power domestically and internationally, the PRG had to increase spending on armed forces and police, and had to resort to political repression. Cuba, amongst other socialist states, became the most prominent supporter of the regime. Within the context of the East-West conflict, Grenada gained strategic importance as a possible base for Soviet and Cuban submarines and missiles. The building of an international airport in Point Salines led to confrontation with the USA, who saw this airport as a possible stopover for enemy aircraft.

An internal power struggle between Bishop and Vice Premier Benjamin Coard, ideologist of the NJM, culminated in the assassination of Bishop and some of his followers on 19 October 1983. A military council (Revolutionary Military Council) under the formal leadership of General Austin Hudson assumed power for a few days, but this coup was brought to an end on 25 October after an invasion by the USA and several Caribbean states. Large parts of the population welcomed the invasion as a means of bringing an end to violence and to the stagnation of the political process at the end of the Bishop era.

After the occupation, the British Governor General Paul Scoon appointed a transitional government, and the 1974 Constitution was reintroduced with few alterations. The US invasion can be seen as evidence for the fact that the Caribbean still belonged to the US sphere of influence, while European countries continually lost interest in this region.

Since former dictator Eric Gairy intended running in the upcoming 1984 elections, the US and numerous Caribbean prime ministers pushed for the creation of an anti-Gairy alliance. The new party, under the leadership of Herbert Blaize, was called the New National Party (NNP). While Gairy ran for office with his GULP, the former followers of Bishop founded the Maurice Bishop Patriotic Movement (MBPM). The NNP gained 14 seats in parliament and Blaize became prime minister. The Constitution Commission, which had been called up to review the 1974 Constitution, had almost no influence on political developments. Its report was published in 1985.

Conflicts within the NNP led to the split of the party. Shortly before his death on 19 December 1989, Blaize created his own party: The National Party (TNP). Blaize's successor as prime minister, Nicholas Brathwaite, a member of the National Democratic Congress (NDC), founded in 1984, had to rely on a coalition of NDC and TNP. Eric Gairy's GULP gained four seats while he himself was not elected. After four members of other parties had joined the NDC, Brathwaite governed with a stable majority of eleven seats. On 1 February 1995, Brathwaite, who had to resign as head of his party earlier because of internal differences, also resigned as prime minister. His successor was the new NDC-leader George Brizan.

Brizan had to accept defeat in the parliamentary election of June 1995. The NDC gained only five seats. Gairy's GULP, that attempted another political comeback, won two seats. The new prime minister, the former Labour and Communications Minister Keith Mitchell, could rely upon the NNPs majority of eight seats. Sir Eric Gairy died in 1997 without having regained political influence outside his party.

Early elections had to be called when Foreign Minister Ralph Fletcher and another minister accused Prime Minister Mitchell of corruption and joined the opposition. On 19 January 1999, the NNP gained a landslide victory of all 15 constituencies. No other party could enter the parliament. Mitchell was reelected as prime minister. However, in the course of that election period, one MP joined the GULP and thereby became leader of the opposition. Prior to the elections held on 27 November 2003, the new NDC leader Tillman Thomas accused the NNP of wasting public funds and mismanaging the economy. The NDC regained strength and won seven seats, while the NNP remained the strongest party with eight seats. Nevertheless, re-elected Prime Minister Mitchell had to deal with a tenuous one-seat majority, as well as with the NDC having filed a court motion calling for re-election because of alleged irregularities.

1.2 Evolution of Electoral Provisions

Universal, equal, direct, and secret parliamentary elections were held as early as 1951, when Grenada was still a colony. From the beginning, Grenada followed the Westminster type of electoral system. From 1979 until 1983, the constitution was suspended, therefore no regular elections were held during that period. Voting age was reduced from 21 to 18 for the 1976 elections. The number of SMCs has been increased from eight to ten in 1962, and to 15 in 1972. There has been no change in the number of constituencies since independence.

1.3 Current Electoral Provisions

Sources: Fundamental electoral principles are listed in the 1974 Constitution. The specific provisions are laid down in the 1958 Electoral Law.

Suffrage: Suffrage is universal, equal, direct, and secret. Voters have to be 18 years old and they have to be citizens of Grenada. Voting is not compulsory.

Elected national institutions: The house of representatives is the only political institution in Grenada in which the members are directly elected. Members of the upper house, the senate, are appointed. Of the 13 members of the senate, seven are appointed by the prime minister, three by the prime minister after consultation with interest groups and three by the leader of the opposition.

The prime minister is elected by the house of representatives. The house has 15 members. If there is a vacancy, by-elections are held in the respective constituency. The term of office is five years.

Nomination of candidates: Every Commonwealth citizen over 18 years of age is eligible to run in the elections to the house. A candidate has to have the support of a minimum of six citizens, and has to pay a deposit of 300 EC$, which is not refunded unless the candidate gains at least one-eighth of the valid votes in the respective constituency. Candidates are usually affiliated to one party, but independent candidates are also possible.

Electoral system: The plurality system applies. Members are elected in 15 SMCs.

Organizational context of elections: The administration of the elections—registration and voting—is under the control of the Supervisor of Elections. The Supervisor of Elections is a public officer, who is selected and appointed solely on the discretion of the governor general. The governor general is also the only person entitled to remove this officer. The Constituency Boundaries Commission (CBC) alone is responsible for constituency matters. It reviews the number and boundaries of the constituencies and issues reports—at least every five years—on the necessity of changes. This is supposed to ensure that constituencies remain approximately equal in size. These changes, however, have to be accepted by the parliament. The members of the CBC are the speaker of the house ex officio, two members appointed on the advice of the prime minister and two on the advice of the leader of the opposition. The latter four must not be members of parliament, and can be removed only by tribunal. Therefore, the CBC is under the control of the government, since three of the commission members are affiliated to the ruling party.

1.4 Commentary on the Electoral Statistics

The data for the 1951 to 1976 elections have been taken from Emmanuel (1992). The data for 1984, 1990, 1995, 1999, and 2003 elections are taken from the official reports of the Supervisor of Elections, as published on the internet. Percentages have been partly recalculated by the author. These sources are generally reliable, only the number of invalid votes in 1984 and 1990 elections differs depending on the date of the data collection. The most reliable figures have been included in the table. Population data come from the United Nations mid-year estimates.

2. Tables

2.1 Dates of National Elections, Referendums, and Coups d'Etat

Year	Presidential elections	Parliamentary elections		Elections for Constit. Assembly	Referen-dums	Coups d'état
		Lower Chamber	Upper Chamber			
1951		10/10				
1954		20/09				
1957		24/09				
1961		27/03				
1962		13/09				
1967		24/08				
1972		28/02				
1976		07/12				
1979						12/03
1983						14/10
1984		03/12				
1990		13/03				
1995		20/06				
1999		18/01				
2003		27/11				

2.2 Electoral Body 1951–2003

Year	Type of election[a]	Population[b]	Registered voters		Votes cast		
			Total number	% pop.	Total number	% reg. voters	% pop.
1951	R	79,000	33,389	42.3	23,566	70.6	29.8
1954	R	86,000	36,846	42.8	24,834	67.4	28.9
1957	R	93,000	37,738	40.6	25,839	68.5	27.8
1961	R	90,000	41,087	45.7	22,801	55.5	25.3
1962	R	91,000	31,766	34.9	23,060	72.6	25.3
1967	R	101,000	38,880	38.5	29,984	77.1	29.7
1972	R	96,000	41,529	43.3	34,679	83.5	36.1
1976	R	96,000	63,193	65.8	41,196	65.2	43.0
1984	R	89,088	48,158	54.1	41,506	86.2	46.6
1990	R	91,000	58,374	64.1	39,939	68.4	43.9
1995	R	92,000	71,413	77.6	44,090	61.7	47.9
1999	R	95,537	73,673	77.1	41,658	56.5	43.6
2003	R	100,895	82,278	81.5	47,488	57.7	47.1

[a] R = House of Representatives.
[b] Population data are mid-year estimates and taken from the United Nation's *Population and Vital Statistics Report* (various editions) and other sources.

2.3 Abbreviations

CDLP	Christian Democratic Labour Party
GFLP	Grenada Federated Labour Party
GNP	Grenada National Party
GOD	Good Old Democratic Party
GRP	Grenada Renaissance Party
GULP	Grenada United Labour Party
GULP/UL	Grenada United Labour Party/ United Labour
MBPM	Maurice Bishop Patriotic Movement
NDC	National Democratic Congress
NJM	New Jewel Movement
NNP	New National Party
PA	People's Alliance
PDM	People's Democratic Movement
PLM	People Labour Movement
PPM	(Full name unknown)
TNP	The National Party
UPP	United People's Party
URP	United Republican Party
WIFLP	West Indian Federal Labour Party

2.4 Electoral Participation of Parties and Alliances 1951–2003

Party / Alliance	Years	Elections contested[a]
GULP	1951–1995, 2003	12
GNP	1957–1972	5
PDM	1957	1
WIFLP	1957	1
PPM	1961	1
PA[b]	1976	1
CDLP	1984	1
GFLP	1984	1
MBPM	1984–1999	4
NNP	1984–2003	5
GOD	1990–2003	4
NDC	1990–2003	4
TNP	1990–1995	2
URP	1995	1
GULP/ UL[c]	1999	1
PLM	2003	1
GRP	2003	1

[a] Only parliamentary elections. Total number: 13.

[b] Coalition of GNP, NJM, and UPP.

[c] Coalition of GULP and Democratic Labour Party.

2.5 Referendums

Referendums have not been held.

2.6 Elections for Constitutional Assembly

There has been no constitutional assembly. The elected house of representatives had already been in place prior to the first election under independence, and adopted the 1974 Constitution.

2.7 Parliamentary Elections 1951–2003

Year	1951		1954	
	Total number	%	Total number	%
Registered voters	33,389	–	36,846	–
Votes cast	23,566	70.6	24,834	67.4
Invalid votes	2,819	12.0	2,358	9.5
Valid votes	20,747[a]	88.0	22,476	91.5
GULP	13,328	64.2	10,347	46.0
Independents	7,509	36.2	12,129	54.0

[a] The source states 90 valid votes less than the sum of all parties' votes.

Year	1957		1961	
	Total number	%	Total number	%
Registered voters	37,738	–	41,087	–
Votes cast	25,839	68.5	22,801	55.5
Invalid votes	1,129	4.4	1,041	4.6
Valid votes	24,710[a]	95.6	21,760	95.4
GULP	10,952	44.3	11,606	53.3
GNP	6,012	24.3	7,325	33.7
PDM	5,327	21.6	–	–
WIFLP	246	1.0	–	–
PPM	–	–	2,394	11.0
Independents	2,145	8.7	435	2.0

[a] The source states 28 valid votes more than the sum of all parties' votes.

Year	1962		1967	
	Total number	%	Total number	%
Registered voters	31,766	–	38,880	–
Votes cast	23,060	72.6	29,984	77.1
Invalid votes	1,953	8.5	985	3.3
Valid votes	21,107	91.5	28,999	96.7
GULP	9,705	46.0	15,827	54.6
GNP	11,341	53.7	13,172	45.4
Independents	61	0.3	–	–

Year	1972	
	Total number	%
Registered voters	41,529	–
Votes cast	34,679	83.5
Invalid votes	435	1.3
Valid votes	34,244[a] (34,289)	98.7
GULP	20,164	58.9
GNP	14,125	41.1

[a] The source states 45 valid votes less than the sum of all parties' votes.

Year	1976		1984	
	Total number	%	Total number	%
Registered voters	63,193	–	48,158	–
Votes cast	41,196	65.2	41,506	86.2
Invalid votes	399	1.0	483	1.2
Valid votes	40,797	99.0	41,023	98.8
GULP	21,108	51.7	14,721	35.9
PA	18,886	46.3	–	–
NNP	–	–	24,045	58.6
MBPM	–	–	2,039	5.0
Independents	803	2.0	104	0.3
Others[a]	–	–	114	0.3

[a] Others include: CDLP (104 votes); GFLP (10).

Year	1990			1995	
	Total number	%		Total number	%
Registered voters	58,374	–		71,413	–
Votes cast	39,939	68.4		44,090	61.7
Invalid votes	468	1.2		371	0.8
Valid votes	39,471	98.8		43,719	99.2
NDC	13,637	34.5		13,372	30.6
GULP	11,105	28.1		11,608	26.6
NNP	6,916	17.5		14,154	32.4
TNP	6,854	17.4		2,826	6.5
MBPM	938	2.4		694	1.6
Independents	15	0.0		982	2.2
Others[a]	6	0.0		83	0.2

[a] Others include in 1990: GOD (6 votes). In 1995: URP (67) GOD (16).

Year	1999			2003	
	Total number	%		Total number	%
Registered voters	73,673	–		82,278	–
Votes cast	41,658	56.5		47,488	57.7
Invalid votes	203	0.5		249	0.5
Valid votes	41,455	99.5		47,239	99.5
NNP	25,896	62.5		22,566	47.8
NDC	10,396	25.1		21,445	45.4
GULP/UL[a]	4,853	11.7		2,243	4.7
Independents	38	0.1		36	0.1
PLM	–	–		933	2.0
Others[b]	292	0.6		16	0.0

[a] 2003 elections: GULP.

[b] Others include in 1999: MBPM (260 votes); GOD (12). In 2003: GOD (10); GRP (6).

2.8 Composition of Parliament 1951–2003

Year	1951		1954		1957		1961	
	Seats	%	Seats	%	Seats	%	Seats	%
	8	100.0	8	100.0	8	100.0	10	100.0
GULP	6	75.0	6	75.0	2	25.0	8	80.0
GNP	–	–	–	–	2	25.0	2	20.0
PDM	–	–	–	–	2	25.0	–	–
Independents	2	25.0	2	25.0	2	25.0	0	0.0

Year	1962		1967		1972		1976	
	Seats	%	Seats	%	Seats	%	Seats	%
	10	100.0	10	100.0	15	100.0	15	100.0
GULP	4	40.0	7	70.0	13	86.7	9	60.0
GNP	60	60.0	3	30.0	2	13.3	–	–
PA	–	–	–	–	–	–	6	40.0

Year	1984		1990		1995		1999	
	Seats	%	Seats	%	Seats	%	Seats	%
	15	100.0	15	100.0	15	100.0	15	100.0
GULP	1	6.7	4	26.7	2	13.3	–	–
PA	–	–	–	–	–	–	–	–
NNP	14	93.3	2	13.3	8	53.3	15	100.0
NDC	–	–	7	46.7	5	33.3	–	–
TNP	–	–	2	13.3	–	–	–	–

Year	2003	
	Seats	%
	15	100.0
NNP	8	53.3
NDC	7	46.7

2.9 Presidential Elections

Presidential elections have not been held.

2.10 List of Power Holders 1974–2004

Head of State	Years	Remarks
Queen Elizabeth II	1974–	Represented by the following governors general: Sir Paul Scoon (1973–1992, acting prime minister after the 1983 invasion), Sir Reginald Palmer (1992–1996), Sir Daniel Williams (1996–).

Head of Government	Years	Remarks
Sir Eric M. Gairy	1974–1979	GULP; ousted by the NJM coup on 12/3/1979 and exiled, returned in 1983, died in 1997.
Maurice Bishop	1979–1983	NJM; coup on 12/3/1979; removed by a coup on 14/10/1983; murdered on 19/10/1983.
Benjamin Coard	1983	NJM; former vice premier, succeeded Bishop on 14/10/1983, stepped back the same day, but was the actually controlling the Military Council.
Hudson Austin	1983	President of the Revolutionary Military Council from 19/10/1983 to 31/10/1983.
Sir Paul Scoon	1983	Governor general, leader of the provisional government from 01/11/1983 to 08/12/1983.
Nicholas Brathwaite	1983–1984	NDC, head of the provisional government, appointed by the governor general for the period from 08/12/1983 to 04/12/1984.
Herbert Blaize	1984–1989	NNP, elected on 04/12/1984, founded his own splinter party, TNP, on 21/07/1989. Died in office on 19/12/1989.
Ben Jones	1989–1990	TNP, from 19/12/1989 to 13/03/1990.
Nicholas Brathwaite	1990–1995	NDC, from 13/03/1990 to 01/02/1995. Had to step back because of intra-party power struggle.
George Brizan	1995–1995	NDC, successor of Brathwaite both as NDC leader and as prime minister, from 01/02/1995 to 20/06/1995.
Keith Claudius Mitchell	1995–	NNP, elected on 20/06/1995, re-elected in early elections on 19/01/1999; re-elected on 27/11/2003.

3. Bibliography

3.1 Official Sources

Grenada Constitution Order 1973.

Cable and Wireless Grenada Limited (2002). *Grenada General Elections 1999.* <http://www.spiceisle.com/main/events/1999/elections/index.htm> (as of 18/11/02).
Cable and Wireless Grenada Limited (2002). *Past Election Results.* <http://www.spiceisle.com/main/events/1999/elections/past.htm> (as of 18/11/02).
Election Monitor (2004). <http://www.spieceisle.com> (as of 05/01/04).
The Supervisor of Elections (1984). *Report on the House of Assembly General Elections, December 3rd, 1984.* St. George's (Grenada).
The Supervisor of Elections (1995). *Grenada General Elections 1995.* St. Georges's (Grenada).
The Supervisor of Elections (1999). *Grenada General Elections January 18th 1999.* St. Georges's (Grenada).
United Nations Department of Economic and Social Affairs (various years). *Demographic Yearbook.* New York: United Nations.

3.2 Books, Articles, and Electoral Reports

Alexis, F. R. (1984). *Changing Caribbean Constitutions.* Bridgetown (Barbados): Antilles Publications.
Archer, E. (1985). 'Gairyism, Revolution, and Reorganisation: Three Decades of Turbulence in Grenada'. *Journal of Commonwealth and Comparative Politics*, 23/2: 91–111.
Brizan, G. (1984). *Grenada: Island of Conflict. From Amerindians to People's Revolution 1498–1979.* London: Zed Books.
Edie, C. J. (ed.) (1994). *Democracy in the Caribbean. Myths and Realities.* London: Praeger.
Emmanuel, P. A. (1979). *General Elections in the Caribbean. A Handbook.* Cave Hill Campus (Barbados): University of the West Indies.
— (1992). *Elections and Party Systems in the Commonwealth Caribbean 1944–1991.* St. Michael/Barbados: CADRES.
— (1993). *Governance and Democracy in the Commonwealth Caribbean: An Introduction.* Cave Hill Campus (Barbados): Institute of Social and Economic Research of the University of the West Indies.

Emmanuel, P. A., Brathwaite, F., and Barriteau, E. (without date). *Political Change and Public Opinion in Grenada 1979-1984. Occasional Paper No. 19*. Cave Hill Campus (Barbados): University of the West Indies.

Ferguson, J. (1990). *Grenada: Revolution in Reverse*. London: Latin American Bureau.

Gilmore, W. C. (1984). *The Grenada Intervention: Analysis and Documentation*. Berlin: Berlin Verlag.

Lewis, D. E. (1984). *Reform and Revolution in Grenada 1950 to 1981*. Havana: Ediciones Casa de las Américas.

Lewis, G. K. (1987). *Grenada: The Jewel Despoiled*. Baltimore, Md./ London: Johns Hopkins University Press.

Midgett, D. (1983). *Eastern Caribbean Elections, 1950-1982: Antigua, Dominica, Grenada, St. Kitts-Nevis, St. Lucia, St. Vincent*. Iowa City: University of Iowa.

Millette, R. and Gosine, M. (1985). *The Grenada Revolution: Why it Failed*. New York: Africana Research Publications.

Payne, D. W. (1999). *The 1999 Grenada Elections. Post-Election Report*. (without place): CSIS America Program.

Phillips, Sir F. (1985). *West-Indian Constitutions: Post-Independence Reform*. New York/ London/ Rome: Oceana Publications.

Sandford, G. and Vigilante, R. (1984). *Grenada: The Untold Story*. Lanham/ New York/ London: Madison Books.

Searle, C. (without date). *Grenada: The Struggle Against Destabilization*. London: Writers and Readers Publishing Cooperative Society.

Spackman, A. (1975). *Constitutional Development of the West Indies 1922-1968. A Selection from the Major Documents*. St. Lauwrence (Barbados): Caribbean University Press.

Sutton, P. (1999). 'Democracy in the Commonwealth Caribbean'. *Democratization*, 6/1: 67–86.

Thorndike, T. (1985). *Grenada: Politics, Economics, and Society*. London: Frances Printer.

Williams, D. (1994). 'Grenada: From Parliamentary Rule to People's Power', in C. J. Edie (ed.), *Democracy in the Caribbean: Myths and Realities*. Westport: Praeger, 93–112.

GUATEMALA

by Petra Bendel and Michael Krennerich

1. Introduction

1.1 Historical Overview

Guatemala declared its independence from Spain in 1821. During the next two years it remained a part of the Mexican Empire, and in 1823 it was a founder member of the Central American Federation. The first national constitution was enacted in 1825. It had a liberal character and established an executive with relatively weak powers and a unicameral legislature.

When the caudillo José Rafael Carrera (1839–1865) came to power, the so-called 'Thirty Year Regime' was established. Conservative and clerical, this regime was the culmination of the anti-liberal actions conducted in the past against the federation. Carrera, appointed president for life, decreed independence from the federation in 1839. It was not until 1851 that Guatemala enacted its first constitution independent of the federation, which came to be known as *Acta Constitutiva* and gave legislative functions to the president.

A series of alleged 'liberal' governments, which were in fact authoritarian, succeeded each other from 1871 to 1944. The elections held during these years were characterized by personalism. Political competition was restricted to liberal and conservative groups, but none of these groups managed to consolidate organizationally or, and changes in government were usually brought about by *coups d'état*. In 1871 Justo Rufino Barrios (1873–1885) established the so-called 'Liberal Reform'. This reform consolidated state power and transformed and modernized the socio-economic structure, boosted by such measures as the expropriation of both Church and indigenous lands. In 1879, a new constitution established the separation of State and Church as well as the separation of powers with a strong executive. Later, the authoritarian governments of Manuel Estrada Cabrera (1898–1920) and Jorge Ubico (1931–1944) followed. Ubico's government banned all the political parties opposed to his so-called democratic order and the workers' organizations. In 1944, Ubico, the 'last caudillo', was deposed by a coalition of diverse social forces.

A civil-military junta re-established the constitutional guarantees, thus facilitating the establishment of several political parties, some of them reform-oriented. However, in 1944, an attempt to manipulate the elections led to the so-called Guatemalan Revolution headed by the *Frente Unido de Partidos Arevalistas* (FUPA; United Front of *Arevalista* Parties). That same year, the FUPA's candidate, Juan José Arévalo, won the first free presidential elections.

The 1944 Revolution was a landmark in the country's political life. The 1945 Constitution introduced substantial reforms, such as the limitation of presidential authority and the right to form political parties and unions. One further reform was the extension of suffrage to literate women.

Arévalo's successor, Jacobo Arbenz, was elected in 1950. When he assumed office, he proposed a structural change based on expropriations and an agrarian reform. The strong opposition to this policy led to the 1954 counterrevolution, with Castillo Armas' *coup d'état* backed by the United States and the Guatemalan oligarchy. The constitutional guarantees were suspended again and the political parties and leftist organizations were banned. In 1956, a new constitution banned all communist activities, whether individual or collective, and established the protection of private property.

From 1966 to 1970 during Julio César Méndez Montenegro's government, the military and the agrarian oligarchy formed a power alliance which was to influence politics from 1954 to 1986. This created a façade democracy. During these years, the military became the most influential political actor. Elections were held, but they were fraudulent and took place in the context of systematic civil-right violations. Reform-oriented political parties were excluded by election reforms. Several military parties reflected the heterogeneous structure within the military, and newly-formed right-wing parties represented the industrial and commercial bourgeoisie as well as the traditional oligarchy. Elections and parties only represented different fractions within the oligarchical and military elite, and they served to present a democratic façade. At the same time as guerrilla groups were formed in the 1960s, the Counterinsurgency Doctrine was consolidated and realized by the military governments through repressive action and state terror. On the other hand, the insurgent movements intensified from the 1980s onwards.

The political liberalization began in 1982 with a military coup conducted by young army officers. In 1984, elections to the constituent assembly were held, which elaborated a new constitution. Finally, the 1985 presidential and parliamentary elections marked the beginning of a democratization process. The winner was the Christian Democrat Vinicio Cerezo Arévalo, the first constitutionally elected civil president in 20 years. Cerezo's government resisted several *coups d'état* conducted by military factions.

In 1990/1991, the conservative Jorge Serrano Elías was elected president. This was the first electoral transfer of power between two civil presidents in that century. After a failed coup organized by Serrano Elías himself in 1993, parliamentary elections were held in 1994, under the provisional, congress-appointed President Ramiro de León Carpio. Presidential elections were held again in 1995/1996, and they led to a change of government with Álvaro Arzú at the head—Arzú led the *Partido de Avanzada Nacional* (PAN), a group included in the so-called 'New Right'. In 1999, Alfonso Portillo, from the *Frente Republicano Guatemalteco* (FRG), won the presidency. The FRG was founded by ex-dictator Ríos Montt, who was barred from candidacy for constitutional reasons, but who served as president of the parliament. After the peace accords of 1996, the guerrilla forces in the *Unidad Revolucionaria Nacional Guatemalteca* organized as a political party and participated in an electoral alliance for the first time in the elections of 1999.

In the campaign period before the elections of November 2003, a political and judicial dispute arose regarding Ríos Montt's candidacy for president. According to the constitution, people who have illegally seized power cannot run for president. The Supreme Court, however, decided that this rule could not be applied because Montt's coup had taken place before the enactment of the constitution. Montt was allowed to run, but his FRG was defeated by the GANA, an alliance comprising the *Partido Patriota,* the *Movimiento Reformador*, and the *Partido de Solidaridad Nacional*. Eleven candidates ran for president and GANA candidate Óscar Berger Perdomo was elected in the runoff. His alliance won 31% of the parliamentary seats with around 25% of the votes. Despite a non-violence pact among all parties, violence and even killings related to the elections were reported.

The process of democratization remains tarnished by civil-rights violations, a weak rule of the law, the scarce representation of most of the political institutions, and the absence of policies to promote the political, social and economic integration of large sectors of the population, especially the indigenous groups.

1.2 Evolution of Electoral Provisions

Guatemala has been under authoritarian rule for most of its political history. Until the mid-1980s, therefore, most of its elections cannot be considered as free and fair. The legal framework for the elections was laid down in the constitution of 1879 and its reforms of 1903, 1921, 1927, 1935, in the constitutions of 1945, 1956, 1965, and 1985 with their amendments and the respective electoral laws, the most important of them being those of 1887, 1937, 1946, 1965, and of 1985.

Universal, direct, and secret suffrage was introduced successively: The 1879 Constitution provided for the direct vote for men, which, in the following decades, varied according to voting age, literacy and other voting conditions. Suffrage for literate women was introduced in 1945. From 1956 onward, secret ballot was provided.

The presidential term varied between four and six years. Traditionally, the Guatemalan president is elected by absolute majority. Initially, if no candidate achieved an absolute majority, the parliament would decide between the two most successful candidates. In the framework of the democratization process, however, a run-off between the two top-candidates was introduced, which took place for the first time in 1990/91.

With few exceptions, the parliamentary term corresponded to the presidential term. From 1887 on, members of the congress were elected in SMCs and MMCs. Later, reforms in the 1940s and 1950s led to a) the introduction of the Hare quota in MMCs and b) to the abolishment of the SMCs in favor of small MMCs. From 1965 on, closed lists and the d'Hondt method were used. Each voter had one vote.

In 1985, the voter was given two votes: one vote for the national list (being identical with the one for the presidential election) and one for the election of the candidates in the constituencies. Since then, the basic rules of the electoral system have not been changed substantially. Major changes referred to the size of the parliament (1985: 100 seats, 1990: 116, 1994 and 1995: 80, 1999: 113, 2003: 158), to the reduction of the presidential and parliamentary term of office (today: four years instead of five), as well as to the separation of votes for president/vice president and the national list for congress.

1.3 Current Electoral Provisions

Sources: The electoral rules are regulated by the 1985 Constitution, the 1985 *Ley Electoral y de Partidos Políticos* and their subsequent reforms.

Suffrage: The principles of universal, equal, direct, and secret suffrage are applied. All citizens over 18 years who are registered in the national register (*Registro de Ciudadanos*) are eligible to vote. Active members of the military and the police forces are not allowed to vote.

Elected national institutions: The president and the vice president are elected together for a four-year term. The re-election of the president is prohibited. The national congress consists of only one chamber and is elected for the same electoral period.

Nomination of candidates
- *presidential elections*: Every citizen 40 years of age or older who is a national by origin is eligible to run for president. Among others, *caudillos*, leaders of military coups or revolutions and members of the armed forces cannot run as candidates.
- *parliamentary elections*: Every citizen 18 years of age or older who is a national by origin is eligible to run for parliament. Members of military in active service are not allowed to be elected deputies.

Electoral system
- *presidential election*: The president and the vice president are elected together on a single ticket via absolute majority. If no ticket receives this majority, a runoff is held between the two tickets that received the highest percentage of the votes.
- *parliamentary elections*: Proportional representation in constituencies of different size. The national congress consists partly of deputies who are elected in a nationwide constituency (2003: 31 out of 158) and partly by deputies (2003: 127) who are elected in 23 constituencies, which correspond to the administrative divisions of the country (one constituency with one seat, two with two seats, seven with three seats, three with four seats, two with five seats, one with six seats, one with seven seats, one with eight seats, two with nine seats, one with ten seats, one with eleven seats, and one with 19 seats; average size: 5.5).
    Both at the national and at the constituency level, the lists are closed. Each voter has two votes: one vote for the election of the national list of

deputies and another one for the election of the district deputies. In both cases, the seats are distributed via the d'Hondt method.

Organizational context of elections: The Central Electoral Commission (*Tribunal Supremo Electoral*, TSE) is responsible for organizing and supervising the elections. It is a permanent body made up of five members who are elected by a two-third majority by parliament from 30 candidates. The members are nominated for a six-year term.

1.4 Commentary on the Electoral Statistics

As far as possible, the following statistics were established from official data. Often, however, secondary sources had to be consulted. Unfortunately, data on elections in Guatemala are hardly ever complete and sometimes even differ from source to source. The elections under military rule before the 1980s in particular were often manipulated. With regard to the parliamentary elections since 1985, in general, only the national lists are documented, whereas data for the constituency lists are missing or only available in disaggregated form.

2. Tables

2.1 Dates of National Elections, Referendums, and Coups d'Etat

Year	Presidential elections	Parliamentary elections	Elections for Constitutional Assembly	Referendums	Coups d'état
1926	1926				1926
1930					16/12
1931	1931				
1944	17–19/12	1944			20/10[a]
1950	10–12/11	16/12			
1953		16–18/01			
1954			18/10	10/10	28/06
1957	20/10[b]	20/10[b]			24/10
1958	19/01	19/01			
1959		16/12			
1961		03/12			
1963					31/03
1964			24/05		
1966	06/03	06/03			
1970	01/03	01/03			
1974	03/03	03/03			
1978	05/03	05/03			
1982	07/03	07/03			23/03
1983					08/08
1984			10/06		
1985	03/11 (1st) xx/12 (2nd)	03/11			
1990	16/11 (1st)	16/11			
1991	xx/01 (2nd)				
1993					
1994		14/08		30/01	
1995	12/11 (1st)	12/11			
1996	07/01 (2nd)				
1999	07/11 (1st) 26/12 (2nd)	07/11		16/05	
2003	09/11 (1st) 28/12 (2nd)	09/11			

[a] The so-called '*Revolución del 44*', is, strictly speaking, not to be interpreted as a *coup d'état*.
[b] Elections nullified.

2.2 Electoral Body 1926–2003

Year	Type of election[a]	Population[b]	Registered voters Total number	% pop.	Votes cast Total number	% reg. Voters	% pop.
1926[c]	Pr	1,560,000	—	—	324,352[d]	—	20.8
1931	Pr	1,810,000	—	—	305,841[d]	—	16.9
1944	Pr	2,390,000	310,000	13.0	302,456	97.6	12.7
1950	Pr	2,810,000	583,000	20.7	417,570	71.6	14.9
1954	Pr	3,180,000	689,985	21.7	485,531	70.4	15.3
1958	Pr	3,610,000	736,400	20.4	492,274	66.8	13.6
1958	Pa	3,610,000	736,400	20.4	343,883[d]	46.7	9.5
1959	Pa	3,720,000	756,000	20.3	337,496	44.9	9.1
1961	Pa	3,950,000	814,000	20.6	362,064	44.5	9.2
1964	CA	4,310,000	—	—	336,823	—	7.8
1966	Pr	4,600,000	944,170	20.5	531,270	56.3	11.5
1966	Pa	4,600,000	944,170	20.5	519,393	50.0	11.3
1970	Pr	5,200,000	1,190,449	22.9	640,684	53.8	12.3
1970	Pa	5,200,000	1,190,449	22.9	633,979	53.3	12.2
1974	Pr	5,900,000	1,568,724	26.6	727,174	46.4	12.3
1978	Pr	6,600,000	1,785,764	27.1	652,073	36.5	9.9
1982	Pr	7,400,000[e]	2,355,064	31.8	1,079,392	45.8	14.6
1984	CA	7,600,000	2,554,002	33.6	1,994,933	78.1	26.2
1985	Pr/Pa	7,960,000	2,753,572	34.6	1,907,771	69.3	24.0
1990	Pr	8,749,000	3,204,955	36.6	1,808,801	56.4	20.7
1994[f]	Pa	9,718,000[g]	3,480,198	35.8	731,357	21.0	7.5
1995	Pa	9,976,000	3,711,589	37.2	—	—	—
1995	Pr (1st)	9,976,000	3,711,589	37.2	1,737,033	46.8	17.4
1996	Pr (2nd)	9,976,000	3,711,589	37.2	1,368,828	36.9	13.7
1999	Ref	11,088,000	4,086,012	36.9	757,978	18.6	6.8
1999	Pa[h]	11,088,000	4,458,744	40.2	2,396,883	53.8	21.6
1999	Pr (1st)	11,088,000	4,458,744	40.2	2,397,212	53.8	21.6
1999	Pr (2nd)	11,088,000	4,458,744	40.2	1,799,928	40.4	16.2
2003	Pa[h]	13,909,000	5,073,282	36.5	2,936,936	57.9	21.1
2003	Pr (1st)	13,909,000	5,073,282	36.5	2,937,169	58.9	21.1
2003	Pr (2nd)	13,909,000	5,073,282	36.5	2,373,469	46.8	17.1

[a] CA = Constitutional Assembly; Pa = Parliament; Pr = President.
[b] The source of information changes in 1966.
[c] The collection of data starts in 1926, when the first election results for presidential elections are available.
[d] Only valid votes available.
[e] 1981 census: 6,054,227 inhabitants.
[f] Early parliamentary elections.
[g] According to the census of April 1994, Guatemala has 8,322,051 inhabitants; technical problems are possible, since other estimations show a 10% higher population. Our data for the 1990s refer to estimations of SEGEPLAN.
[h] Data refer to the nationwide constituency.

2.3 Abbreviations

AD	*Acción Democrática* (Democratic Action)
ANDE	*Asociación Nacional Democrática* (Democratic National Association)
AN	*Alianza Nacional* (National Alliance)
ANN	*Alianza Nueva Nación* (New Nation Alliance)
ANP	*Alianza Nacional Progresista* (Progressive National Alliance)
AP–5	*Alianza Popular Cinco* (Popular Alliance Five)
ARDE	*Partido Acción Renovadora Democrática* (Party Democratic Renewal Action)
ARENA	Full name unknown
CAMHINA	*Cambio Histórico Nacional* (National Historic Change)
CAN	*Central Auténtica Nacionalista* (Nationalist Authentic Center)
CAO	*Central Aranista Organizada* (Organized *Aranista* Center)
COZAUN	*Comité Zacapa Unido* (United *Zacapa* Committee)
CND	*Coordinadora Nacional Democrática* (Democratic National Coordination)
DCG	*Democracia Cristiana Guatemalteca* (Guatemalan Christian Democracy)
DIA	*Desarrollo Integral Auténtico* (Authentic Integral Development)
DSP	*Democracia Social Participativa* (Participative Social Democracy)
FAN	*Frente de Avance Nacional* (National Progress Front)
FCD	*Frente Cívico Democrático* (Democratic Civic Front)
FDP	*Fuerza Demócrata Popular* (Popular Democratic Force)
FDNG	*Frente Democrático Nueva Guatemala* (Democratic Front New Guatemala)
FND	*Frente Nacional Democrático* (Democratic National Front)
FNO	*Frente Nacional de Oposición* (National Front of the Opposition)
FPL	*Frente Popular Libertador* (Popular Liberating Front)
FRG	*Frente Republicano Guatemalteco* (Guatemalan Republican Front)
FUN	*Frente de Unidad Nacional* (National Unity Front)
FUPA	*Frente Unido de Partidos Arevalistas* (United Front of *Arevalista* Parties)
FUR	*Frente Unido de la Revolución* (United Front of the Revolution)
GANA	*Gran Alianza Nacional* (Great National Alliance)
LOV	*La Organización Verde* (The Green Organization)
MAS	*Movimento de Acción Solidaria* (Movement of Action in Solidarity)
MD	*Movimiento de los Descamisados* (Destitute People's Movement)
MDN	*Movimiento Democrático Nacionalista* (Nationalist Democratic Movement
MEC	*Movimiento Emergente de Concordia* (Emerging Movement of Harmony)

MLN	*Movimiento de Liberación Nacional* (Movement of National Liberation)
MPL	*Movimiento Patriótico Libertad* (Patriotic Movement Liberty)
MSPCN	*Movimiento Social y Político Cambio Nacional* (Social and Political Movement National Change)
OCAS	*Organización Campesina de Acción Social* (Rural Organization of Social Action)
PAA	*Partido Auténtico Anticomunista* (Anticommunist Authentic Party)
PAD	*Partido Auténtico Democrático* (Democratic Authentic Party)
PAN	*Partido de Avanzada Nacional* (National Vanguard Party)
PAR	*Partido Acción Revolucionaria* (Revolutionary Action Party)
PCN	*Partido de Conciliación Nacional* (Party of National Reconciliation)
PCSG	Full name unknown
PD	*Partido Demócrata* (Democratic Party)
PDC	*Partido Demócrata Central* (Central Democratic Party)
PDCN	*Partido Democrático de Cooperación Nacional* (Democratic Party of National Cooperation)
PDG	*Partido Demócrata Guatemalteco* (Guatemalan Democratic Party)
PDN	*Partido Democrático Nacionalista* (Nationalist Democratic Party)
PDP	*Partido del Pueblo* (People's Party)
PGT	*Partido Guatemalteco del Trabajo* (Guatemalan Labor Party)
PID	*Partido Institucional Democrático* (Democratic Institutional Party)
PIN	*Partido de Integridad Nacional* (National Integrity Party)
PL	*Partido Liberal de Guatemala* (Liberal Party of Guatemala)
PLAG	*Partido Liberal Anticomunista Guatemalteco* (Guatemalan Anticommunist Liberal Party)
PLG	*Partido Laborista Guatemalteca* (Guatemalan Labor Party)
PLN	*Partido Liberal Nacionalista* (Nationalist Liberal Party)
PLP	*Partido Libertador Progresista* (Progressive Liberating Party)
PNR	*Partido Nacional Renovador* (National Renewal Party)
PNR 44	*Partido Nacional Reivindicador del 44* (National Claiming Party of 44)
PNT	*Partido Nacional de Trabajadores* (National Workers' Party)
PP (1)	*Partido Populista* (Populist Party)
PP (2)	*Partido Progesista* (Progressive Party)
PR	*Partido Revolucionario* (Revolutionary Party)
PRA	*Partido Revolucionario Auténtico* (Authentic Revolutionary Party)
PRDN	*Partido de Reconciliación Democrática Nacional* (Party of National Democratic Reconciliation)
PREG	*Partido Reformador Guatemalteco* (Guatemalan Reformist Party)
PRG	*Partido de la Revolución Guatemalteca* (Guatemalan Revolution Party)
PRI	*Partido Reformista Institucional* (Institutional Reformist Party)
PRp	*Partido Republicano* (Republican Party)
PS	*Partido Socialista* (Socialist Party)
PSC	*Partido Social Cristiano* (Christian Social Party)
PSD	*Partido Social Demócrata* (Democratic Social Party)

PTD	*Partido de Trabajadores Democrático* (Democratic Workers' Party)
PU	*Partido Unionista* (Unionist Party)
PUA	*Partido de Unificación Anticomunista* (Party of Anticommunist Unification)
PUD	*Partido de Unidad Democrática* (Democratic Unity Party)
PULN	*Partido Unión Liberal Nacionalista* (Party Nationalist Liberal Union)
PUR	*Partido de Unidad Revolucionaria* (Revolutionary Unity Party)
REDENCION	*Reconciliación Nacional* (National Reconciliation)
RN	*Renovación Nacional* (National Renewal)
TRANS	*Transparencia* (Transparency)
UCN	*Unión del Centro Nacional* (National Center Union)
UD	*Unión Democrática* (Democratic Union)
UN	*Unión Nacional* (National Union)
UNE (1)	*Unión Nacional Electoral* (Electoral National Union)
UNE (2)	*Unidad Nacional de la Esperanza* (National Union of Hope)
UNO (1)	*Unión Nacional Organizada* (Organized National Union)
UNO (2)	*Unidad Nacionalista Organizada* (Organized Nationalist Union)
URNG	*Unidad Revolucionaria Nacional Guatemalteca* (Guatemalan National Revolutionary Union)
URS	*Unión Reformista Social* (Social Reformist Union)

2.4 Electoral Participation of Parties and Alliances 1926–2003

Party / Alliance	Years	Elections contested	
		Presidential	Parliamentary
Partido Unionista	1926	1	–
Partido Progresista	1926	1	–
Partido Liberal Progresista	1931	1	–
FND[a]	1944	1	–
FUPA[b]	1944	1	–
Partido Constitucional Democrático	1944	1	–
Partido Socialista Democrático	1944	1	–
FPL	1950	1	–
Frente Electoral[c]	1950	1	–
PCSG	1950	1	–
PP	1950	1	–
UNE (1)[d]	1950	1	–
MDN[e]	1957–1959	2	2
PRDN[f]	1957–1961	2	3

Party / Alliance (continued)	Years	Elections contested Presidential	Parliamentary
ANDE[f]	1958	1	–
DCG[e, g, h, i]	1958–1961; 1970–2003	10	1
Frente Anticomunista Nacional[f]	1958	1	–
MDN	1958–1959	1	2
PAA	1958–1959	0	2
PDN[f]	1958	1	–
PL[e]	1958	1	1
PLN[f]	1958	1	–
PLAG[f]	1958–1959	1	2
PR[j, k, l]	1958–1994	8	–
PRp[e]	1958	1	–
PTD	1958	0	1
PUA[e, m]	1958; 1984–1985	2	3
PULN	1958–1959	1	2
PNR–44	1959	0	1
PRA	1959	0	1
PRI	1959	0	1
PUR	1959	0	1
PAD	1961	0	1
MLN[n, o, p, q]	1961–1999	9	12
PID[n, j, r, k, s]	1966–1995	8	10
CAO[j]	1974–1978	1	2
PRA[g]	1978	1	–
FUN[r, m, s]	1982–1995	4	6
UNO (1)	1982	1	1
CAN[q]	1982–1995	4	6
PNR[h]	1982–1990	3	4
AD	1984; 1999	1	2
ANP	1984	0	1
CND[t]	1984	0	1
COZAUN	1984	0	1
FCD	1984	0	1
FDP[t]	1984–1985,1994–1995	2	4
FUR	1984; 1990	1	2
MEC[m]	1984–1990	2	3
PDCN[k]	1984–1990	2	3
PP	1984	0	1
OCAS	1984	0	1
UCN	1984–1999	4	6
PSD[u]	1985–1995	3	4
AP–5[u]	1990; 1995	2	2
FAN[p]	1990	1	1

Party / Alliance (continued)	Years	Elections contested Presidential	Parliamentary
FRG	1990–2003	3	5
MAS	1990–1994	1	2
PAN	1990–2003	4	5
PD	1990	1	1
PDG	1990; 1995	2	2
UNO (2)	1990	0	1
UD[v]	1994–2003	2	4
MD	1994–1995	1	2
PP (2)	1994–1995	1	2
PREG	1994–1995	1	2
PSC	1994–1995	0	2
AN	1995	1	1
CAMHINA	1995	1	1
DIA	1995–2003	3	3
FDNG[i]	1995–1999	2	2
MPL	1995	1	1
PCN	1995	1	1
PDP	1995	1	1
PLG	1995	0	1
PLP	1995–2003	2	3
URS	1995	0	1
ANN	1999–2003	0	2
ARDE	1999	1	1
ARENA	1999	1	1
LOV[v]	1999	1	1
UN	1999–2003	1	2
URNG	1999–2003	2	2
DSP	2003	1	1
GANA[w]	2002	1	1
MSPCN	2003	1	1
PU	2003	1	1
TRANS	2003	0	1
UNE (2)	2003	1	1

[a] Electoral alliance including PDC.

[b] Electoral alliance comprising FPL and RN.

[c] Electoral alliance comprising PAR, PIN, and PS.

[d] Electoral alliance comprising PUA, PUD, and REDENCION.

[e] In 1958, MDN, PUA, PL, PRp, and DCG contested in an electoral alliance.

[f] In 1958, PRDN, PDN, PLN, PLAG, *Frente Anticomunista Nacional*, and ANDE contested in an electoral alliance.

[g] In 1978, DCG and PRA contested in an electoral alliance.

[h] In 1982, DCG and PNR contested in an electoral alliance.

[i] In 1984, DCG and PNR contested in an electoral alliance.

[j] In 1978, PID, PR, and CAO contested in an electoral alliance.

[k] In 1985, PDCN and PR contested in an electoral alliance.

[l] In 1995, the *Partido Revolucionario* (PR) changed its name to FDNG.
[m] In 1985, PUA, MEC, and FUN contested in an electoral alliance.
[n] In 1970 and in 1974, MLN and PID contested in an electoral alliance.
[o] In 1985, MLN and PID contested in an electoral alliance.
[p] In 1990, MLN and FAN contested in an electoral alliance.
[q] In 1984, MLN and CAN contested in an electoral alliance.
[r] In 1982, PID, PR, and FUN contested in an electoral alliance.
[s] In the parliamentary elections of 1990, FRG, PID, and FUN participated in an electoral alliance only at the district level.
[t] In 1984, FDP and CND contested in an electoral alliance.
[u] In 1990, PSD and AP-5 contested in an electoral alliance.
[v] In 1999, UD and LOV contested in an electoral alliance.
[w] Coalition composed of the *Partido Patriótico*, the *Movimiento Revolucionario*, and the *Partido de Solidaridad Nacional*.

2.5 Referendums

Year	1994[a]	
	Total number	%
Registered voters	3,439,331	–
Votes cast	545,894	15.9
Invalid votes	97,107	17.8
Blank votes	7,982	1.5
Valid votes	440,805	80.7
Yes	370,044	83.9
No	70,761	16.1

[a] After the frustrated *coup d'état* of 25/05/1993 by President Jorge Serrano Elías, the newly elected government held a referendum on constitutional reforms. Among other aims, the government intended to abridge the parliamentary term.

Year	1999			
	Total number	%[a]		%[a]
Registered voters	4,080,398	–		
Votes cast	757,940	18.6		
	Question I[b]		Question II[c]	
Invalid votes	—	—	—	—
Valid votes	—	—	—	—
Yes	32,854	8.2	284,423	42.0
No	366,591	91.8	392,223	58.0

[a] Percentages calculated by the authors.
[b] Constitutional reform: definition of the nation and social rights (including the rights of the indigenous population, military service, workers' rights and the extension of the security system).
[c] Constitutional reform: reforms of the legislature.

Year	1999[a]			
	Total number	%[a]		%[a]
Registered voters	4,080,398	–		
Votes cast	757,940	18.6		
	Question III[b]		Question IV[c]	
Invalid votes	—	—	—	—
Valid votes	—	—	—	—
Yes	294,849	42.9	315,565	45.8
No	392,223	57.1	373,025	54.2

[a] Percentages calculated by the authors.
[b] Constitutional reform: reforms of the executive (redefinition of the military's role, among others).
[c] Constitutional reform: reforms of the judicial branch.

2.6 Elections for Constitutional Assembly

1964[a]	Total number	%	Seats	%
Registered voters	—	–		
Votes cast	336,823	—		
Invalid votes	43,383	12.9		
Valid votes	293,440	87.1		
			—	100.0
MLN	142,248	48.5	—	—
PR	122,374	41.7	—	—
MLN/PR[b]	28,818	9.8	—	—

[a] These two parties presented the same candidates.
[b] Alliance of MLN and PR factions.

1984[a]	Total number	%	Total number	%	Seats	%
Registered voters	2,554,002	–	2,554,002	–		
Votes cast	1,994,933	78.1	1,992,394	78.0		
Invalid votes	459,379	23.0	439,120	22.0		
Valid votes	1,535,554	77.0	1,553,274	78.0		
					88	100.0
DCG	326,064	21.2	261,207[b]	16.8	20	22.7
UCN	273,744	17.8	278,740	17.9	21	23.9
MLN/CAN	249,712	16.3	260,466	16.8	23	26.1
PR	146,092	9.5	179,199	11.5	10	11.4
PNR	133,680	8.7	126,021	8.1	5	5.7
PID	106,188	6.9	109,905	7.1	5	5.7
PUA	61,116	4.0	53,385	3.4	1	1.1
FUR	45,677	3.0	45,490	2.9	–	–
MEC	42,764	2.8	43,753	2.8	–	–
FUN	40,488	2.6	47,366	3.0	1	1.1
AD	28,347	1.8	36,747	2.4	–	–

1984[a] (cont.)	Total number	%	Total number	%	Seats	%
Registered voters	2,554,002	–	2,554,002	–		
Votes cast	1,994,933	78.1	1,992,394	78.0		
Invalid votes	459,379	23.0	439,120	22.0		
Valid votes	1,535,554	77.0	1,553,274	78.0		
					88	100.0
FCD	28,040	1.8	27,928	1.8	–	–
PDCN	25,238	1.6	18,544	1.2	–	–
PP	14,354	0.9	14,686	0.9	–	–
FDP/CND	14,050	0.9	13,376	0.9	–	–
DCG/PNR	–	–	14,762	1.0	1	1.1
OCAS	–	–	12,222	0.8	1	1.1
Others	–	–	9,497[c]	0.6	–	–

[a] Presentation of electoral data corresponds to the electoral system, which is held with a national list (first column) and the respective constituencies at the departmental level (second column).
[b] At the district level, DCG formed an alliance with the PNR.
[c] Others include: ANP: 6,766 votes (0.4%) and COZAUN: 2,731 (0.2%).

2.7 Parliamentary Elections 1958–2003

Year	1958		1959	
	Total number	%	Total number	%
Registered voters	736,400	–	756,000	–
Votes cast	—	—	337,496	44.9
Invalid votes	—	—	34,370	10.1
Valid votes	343,883	—	303,126	89.9
PRDN	127,195	37.0	78,763	25.8
PUA	112,105	32.6	–	–
PR	88,418	25.7	71,682	23.5
PL	3,785	1.1	–	–
MDN	3,674	1.1	67,615	22.2
PULN	2,955	0.9	2,734	0.9
PAA	2,451	0.7	3,212	1.1
PLAG	1,918	0.6	4,255	1.4
PTD	1,382	0.4	–	–
DCG	–	–	30,358	9.9
PUR	–	–	21,173	6.9
PRA	–	–	14,158	4.6
PNR	–	–	7,677	2.5
PRI	–	–	3,499	1.1

Year	1961		1966[a]	
	Total number	%	Total number	%
Registered voters	814,000	–	944,170	–
Votes cast	362,064	44.5	519,393	50.0
Invalid votes	63,247	17.5	82,848	16.0
Valid votes	298,717	82.5	436,545	84.0
PRDN/MDN/PUD	150,948	50.5	–	–
PR	81,500	27.3	192,366	44.1
MLN	25,102	8.4	–	–
DCG	20,957	7.0	–	–
PAD	20,310	6.8	–	–
PID	–	–	138,873	31.8
MLN	–	–	105,306	24.1

[a] The DCG's participation was prohibited; this party therefore called for null-voting.

Year	1970	
	Total number	%
Registered voters	1,190,449	–
Votes cast	633,979	53.3
Invalid votes	78,953	12.5
Valid votes	555,026	87.5
MLN/PID	231,528	41.7
PR	201,119	36.2
DCG	122,379	22.0

Data on the parliamentary elections of 1974, 1978, and 1982 are not available.

Year	1985[a]			
	Total number	%	Total number	%
Registered voters	2,753,572	–		
Votes cast	1,907,771	69.2	1,904,236	69.2
Invalid votes	228,771	12.0	239,488	12.6
Valid votes	1,679,000	88.0	1,664,748	87.4
DCG	648,803	38.6	575,785	34.6
UCN	339,695	20.2	342,742	20.6
PDCN/PR	231,423	13.8	225,246	13.5
MLN/PID	210,966	12.6	254,276	15.3
CAN	105,540	6.3	104,374	6.3
PSD	57,368	3.4	60,946	3.7
PNR	52,949	3.2	70,514	4.2
PUA/MEC/FUN	32,256	1.9	27,234	1.6
FCD	3,631	0.2	–	–

[a] Presentation of electoral data corresponds to the electoral system, which is held with a national list (first column) and the respective constituencies at the departmental level (second column).

Year	1990[a]		1994[a]	
	Total number	%	Total number	%
Registered voters	3,204,955	–	3,480,196	–
Votes cast	1,808,801	56.4	731,357[b]	21.0
Invalid votes	254,488	14.1	89,017	12.2
Valid votes	1,554,313	85.9	642,335	87.8
UCN	399,777	25.7	57,152	8.9
MAS	375,165	24.1	20,418	3.2
DCG	271,933	17.5	78,000	12.1
PAN	268,796	17.3	162,161	25.2
MLN/FAN	74,825	4.8	28,581	4.4
PSD/AP–5	55,819	3.6	13,635	2.1
PR	33,429	2.2	17,747	2.8
PDCN	32,325	2.1	–	–
MEC	16,894	1.1	–	–
PNR	11,052	0.7	–	–
FUR	7,957	0.5	–	–
PD	6,341	0.4	–	–
FRG	–	–	206,960	32.2
UD	–	–	19,734	3.1
PREG	–	–	13,007	2.0
CAN	–	–	9,690	1.5
FUN	–	–	6,501	1.0
PID	–	–	5,599	0.9
MD	–	–	3,150	0.5

[a] The electoral system provided for two votes, one for the national list and one for the constituencies at the departmental level. Only data for the national list (which, for 1990, are identical to the results of the first round of presidential elections) can be documented here. At the constituency level, PID/FUN/FRG participated in the elections, as well as UNO (2).
b Sum of valid and invalid votes does not correspond completely with total votes (difference of five votes).

Data on the parliamentary elections of 1995 are not available.

Year	1999[a]			
	Total number	%	Total number	%
Registered voters	4,458,744	–	4,458,744	–
Votes cast	2,396,883	53.8	2,395,627	53.7
Invalid votes	279,011[b]	11.6	268,249[c]	11.2
Valid votes	2,117,872	8.8	2,127,378	88.8
FRG	891,429	42.1	879,839	41.4
PAN	570,108	26.9	589,550	27.7
ANN	233,870	11.0	231,970	10.9
DCG	86,839	4.1	68,609	3.2
PLP	84,187	4.0	91,484	4.3
ARDE	63,824	3.0	76,994	3.6
FDNG	60,821	2.9	53,544	2.5
LOV/UD	48,184	2.3	48,398	2.3
UCN	42,921	2.0	40,069	1.9
MLN	22,857	1.0	21,656	1.0
Others	12,822[d]	0.6	25,265[e]	1.2

[a] Presentation of electoral data corresponds to the electoral system, which is held with a national list (first column) and the respective constituencies at the departmental level (second column). Constituency election results were only available in disaggregated form and had to be summed up.
[b] Annulled votes: 153,903; blank votes: 125,108.
[c] Annulled votes: 150,573; blank votes: 117,676.
[d] Including: AD: 8,644 votes (0.4%); ARENA: 4,178 (0.2%).
[e] Including: AD: 6,074 (0.3%); UCN/DCG: 6,480 (0.3%); DCG/FDNG: 5,792 (0.3%); UN: 3,222 (0.2%); ARENA: 1,868 (0.1); MLN/DCG: 1,829 (0.1%).

Year	2003[a]			
	Total number	%	Total number	%
Registered voters	5,073,282	–	5,073,282	–
Votes cast	2,936,936	57.9	2,511,372	
Invalid votes	384,562	13.1	318,828	
Valid votes	2,552,374	86.9	2,192,544	
GANA	620,121	24.3	504,010	23.0
FRG	502,470	19.7	486,019	22.2
UNE (2)	457,308	17.9	362,859	16.5
PAN	278,393	10.9	270,549	12.3
PU	157,893	6.2	133,663	6.1
ANN	123,853	4.9	59,891	2.7
URNG	107,276	4.2	93,980	4.3
DCG	82,324	3.2	78,523	3.6
DIA	75,295	2.9	67,456	3.1
UD	55,793	2.2	55,321	2.5
DSP	28,425	1.1	29,109	1.3
TRANS	27,740	1.1	21,421	1.0
MSPCN	18,005	0.7	15,265	0.7
UN	17,478	0.7	10,274	0.5
Others	–	–	4,204	0.2

[a] Presentation of electoral data corresponds to the electoral system, which is held with a national list (first column) and the respective constituencies at the departmental level (second column). Results at the departmental level were only available in disaggregated form and had to be summed up. The electoral data of the *Distrito Central*, an eleven-seat constituency, have not been available and are thus missing in regard to the total of the departmental level results.
[b] Others include: PLP: 2,868 votes (0.1%); UN-DIA-ANN: 1,336 (0.1%).

2.8 Composition of Parliament 1966–2003

Year	1966		1970[a]		1974[a]		1978[a]	
	Seats	%	Seats	%	Seats	%	Seats	%
	55	100.0	55	100.0	60	100.0	61	100.0
PR	29	52.7	19	34.5	10	16.7	14	23.0
PID	21	38.2	–	–	14	23.3	17	27.9
MLN	5	9.1	–	–	16	26.7	20	32.8
MLN/PID	–	–	31	56.4	–	–	–	–
CAO	–	–	–	–	6	10.0	3	4.9

[a] Data inconsistencies could not be clarified.

Year	1982[a]		1985		1990		1994	
	Seats	%	Seats	%	Seats	%	Seats	%
	66	100.0	100.0	100.0	116	100.0	80[b]	100.0
PID/PR/FUN	33	50.0	–	–	–	–	–	–
MLN	21	31.8	12[c]	12.0	–	–	0	0.0
CAN	3	4.5	1	1.0	0	0.0	0	0.0
UNO	2	3.0	–	–	0	0.0	–	–
DCG	–	–	51	51.0	27	23.3	13	16.3
PID	–	–	–[c]	–	–	–	0	0.0
PNR	0	0.0	1	1.0	0	0.0	–	–
UCN	–	–	22	22.0	41	35.3	8	10.0
PDCN/PR	–	–	11	11.0	–	–	–	–
PSD	–	–	2	2.0	–	–	0	0.0
MAS	–	–	–	–	18	15.5	0	0.0
PAN	–	–	–	–	12	10.3	24	30.0
FRG/PID/FUN	–	–	–	–	12	10.3	–	–
MLN/FAN	–	–	–	–	4	3.4	–	–
PSD/AP–5	–	–	–	–	1	0.9	–	–
PR	–	–	–	–	1	0.9	0	0.0
FRG	–	–	–	–	–	–	32	40.0
Others	7	10.6	–	–	–	–	3	3.8

[a] Since electoral data for the 1982 elections are not available, it is not always clear whether a party did not win any seat (usually indicated by '0') or did not contest elections ('–').
[b] In November 1993, the congress agreed to reduce the number of seats from 116 to 80. This led to an election in August 1994 in order to elect an interim congress of 80 members to serve until the November 1995 general elections.
[c] Electoral alliance, composed of MLN and PID.

Year	1995		1999		2003	
	Seats	%	Seats	%	Seats	%
	80	100.0	113	100.0	158	100.0
PAN	43	53.8	37	32.7	17	10.8
FRG	21	26.3	63	55.6	41	25.9
FDNG	6	7.5	0	0.0	–	–
DCG	3	3.8	2	1.8	–	–
UCN	2	2.5	0	0.0	–	–
DCG/UCN/PSD	2	2.5	–	–	–	–
UD[a]	2	2.5	1	0.9	2	1.3
MLN	1	1.3	0	0.0	–	–
ANN	–	–	9	8.0	6	3.8
PLP	0	0.0	1	0.9	–	–
GANA	–	–	–	–	49	31.0
UNE (2)	–	–	–	–	30	19.0
PU	–	–	–	–	7	4.4
URNG	–	–	–	–	2	1.3
DIA	–	–	–	–	1	0.6
Others	0	0.0	0	0.0	3	1.9

[a] Contested the 1999 election in an alliance with LOV.

2.9 Presidential Elections 1926–2003

1926	Total number	%
Registered Voters	—	–
Votes cast	—	—
Invalid Votes	—	—
Valid Votes	324,352	—
Lázaro Chacón (Partido Unionista)	287,412	88.6
Jorge Ubico Castañeda (Partido Progresista)	36,940	11.4

1931	Total number	%
Registered Voters	—	–
Votes cast	—	—
Invalid Votes	—	—
Valid Votes	305,841	—
Jorge Ubico Castañeda (Partido Liberal Progresista)[a]	305,841	100.0

[a] Single candidate only.

1944	Total number	%
Registered Voters	310,000	–
Votes cast	302,456	97.6
Invalid Votes	6,042	2.0
Valid Votes	296,414	98.0
Juan José Arévalo Bermejo (FUPA)	255,660	86.3
Adrían Recinos (FND/PDC)	20,949	7.1
Manuel María Herrera (PNT)	11,062	3.7
Guillermo Flores Avendaño (PSD)	8,230	2.8
Others[a]	513	0.2

[a] 13 candidates.

1950	Total number	%
Registered Voters	583,300	–
Votes cast	417,570	71.6
Invalid Votes	9,907	2.4
Valid Votes	407,663	97.6
Jacobo Arbenz Guzmán (Frente Electoral)[a]	266,778	65.4
Miguel Ydígoras Fuentes (UNE (1))[b]	76,180	18.7
Jorge García Granados (PP)	28,897	7.1
Víctor Manuel Giordiani (FPL)	15,664	3.8
Manuel Galich (FPL-Galich)	7,118	1.7
Clemente Marroquín Rojas (PCSG)	6,589	1.6
Others[c]	6,437	1.6

[a] Electoral alliance, composed of PAR, PIN and PS.
[b] Electoral alliance, composed of PUA, PUD and REDENCION.
[c] Including the following candidates: Arcadio Chévez Guillén (4,041 votes), Miguel Angel Mendoza (1,684) and Alejandro Valdizón (712).

1957[a]	Total number	%
Registered Voters	—	–
Votes cast	—	—
Invalid Votes	—	—
Valid Votes	—	—
Miguel Ortiz Passarelli (MDN)	241,335	—
Miguel Ydígoras Fuentes (PRDN)	173,365	—
Miguel Asturias Quiñónez	52,600	—

[a] Elections nullified due to protests against electoral fraud.

1958	Total number	%
Registered Voters	736,400	–
Votes cast	492,274	66.8
Invalid Votes	24,156	4.9
Valid Votes	468,118	95.1
Miguel Ydígoras Fuentes (PRDN/PDN/PLN/PLAG/Frente Anticomunista Nacional/ANDE)	190,972	40.8
José Luis Cruz Salazar (MDN/PUA/PL/PRp/DCG)	138,488	29.6
Mario Méndez Montenegro (PR)	132,824	28.4
José Enrique Ardón Fernández (PULN)	5,834	1.2

1966	Total number	%
Registered Voters	944,170	–
Votes cast	531,270	56.3
Invalid Votes	64,060	12.1
Valid Votes	467,210	87.9
Julio César Méndez Montenegro (PR)	209,204	44.8
Juan de Dios Aguilar de León (PID)	148,025	31.7
Miguel Angel Ponciano (MLN)	109,981	23.5

1970	Total number	%
Registered Voters	1,190,449	–
Votes cast	640,684	53.8
Invalid Votes	61,360	9.6
Valid Votes	579,324	90.4
Carlos Manuel Arana Osorio (MLN/PID)	251,135	43.3
Mario Fuentes Pieruccini (PR)	202,241	34.9
Jorge Lucas Caballero Mazariegos (DCG)[a]	125,948	21.7

[a] Supported by the illegal FURD.

1974[a]	Total number	%
Registered Voters	1,566,724	–
Votes cast	727,174	46.4
Invalid Votes	57,059	7.8
Valid Votes	670,131	92.2
Kjell Eugenio Laugerud García (MLN/PID)	298,953	44.6
Efraín Ríos Montt (FNO)[b]	228,067	34.0
Ernesto Paíz Novales (PR)	143,111	21.4

[a] Massive electoral fraud; the results are not trustworthy.
[b] Electoral alliance of different opposition parties, among them, the DCG.

1978[a]	Total number	%
Registered Voters	1,785,764	–
Votes cast	—	—
Invalid Votes	—	—
Valid Votes	652,073	—
Fernando Romeo Lucas García (PID/PR/CAO)	262,960	40.3
Enrique Peralta Azurdia (MLN)	221,223	33.9
Ricardo Peralta Méndez (DCG/PRA)	167,890	25.7

[a] Massive electoral fraud; the results are not trustworthy.

1982[a]	Total number	%
Registered Voters	2,355,064	–
Votes cast	1,079,392	45.8
Invalid Votes	103,997	9.6
Valid Votes	975,395	90.4
Aníbal Guevara Rodríguez (PID/PR/FUN)	379,051	38.9
Mario Sandoval Alarcón (MLN)	275,487	28.2
Alejandro Maldonado Aguirre (UNO (1))[b]	221,810	22.7
Gustavo Anzuento Vielman (CAN)	99,047	10.2

[a] Massive electoral fraud. The elections were nullified after the *coup d'état* of 23 March 1982.
[b] Electoral alliance, comprised of DCG and PNR.

1985 (1st round)	Total number	%
Registered Voters	2,753,572	—
Votes cast	1,907,771	69.2
Invalid Votes	228,771	12.0
Valid Votes	1,679,000	88.0
Vinicio Cerezo Arévalo (DCG)	648,803	38.6
Jorge Carpio Nicolle (UCN)	339,695	20.2
Jorge Serrano Elías (PDCN/PR)	231,423	13.8
Mario Sandoval Alarcón (MLN/PID)	210,966	12.6
Mario David García (CAN)	105,540	6.3
Mario Solórzano Martínez (PSD)	57,368	3.4
Alejandro Maldonado Aguirre (PNR)	52,949	3.2
Lionel Sisniega Otero Barrios (PUA/MEC/FUN)	32,256	1.9

1985 (2nd round)	Total number	%
Registered Voters	—	–
Votes cast	—	—
Invalid Votes	—	—
Valid Votes	1,657,823	—
Vinicio Cerezo Arévalo (DCG)	1,133,517	68.4
Jorge Carpio Nicolle (UCN)	524,306	31.6

1990/91 (1st round)	Total number	%
Registered Voters	3,204,955	–
Votes cast	1,808,801	56.4
Blank Votes	90,221	5.0
Invalid Votes	164,267	9.1
Valid Votes	1,554,313	85.9
Jorge Carpio Nicolle (UCN)	399,777	25.7
Jorge Serrano Elías (MAS)	375,165	24.1
Alfonso Cabrera Hidalgo (DCG)	271,933	17.5
Alvaro Arzú Irigoyen (PAN)	268,796	17.3
Luis Ernesto Sosa Avila (MLN/FAN)	74,825	4.8
René de León Schlotter (PSD/AP5)	55,819	3.6
José Angel Lee Duarte (PR)	33,429	2.2
José Fernández González (PDCN)	32,325	2.1
Benedicto Lucas García (MEC)	16,894	1.1
Fernando Leal Estévez (PNR)	11,052	0.7
Leonel Hernández Cardona (FUR)	7,957	0.5
Jorge Reyna Castillo (PD)	6,341	0.4

1990/91 (2nd round)	Total number	%
Registered voters	—	–
Votes cast	1,449,489	45.2
Blank Votes	5,093	0.3
Invalid Votes	69,017	4.8
Valid Votes	1,375,379	94.9
Jorge Carpio Nicolle (UCN)	438,990	31.9
Jorge Serrano Elías (MAS)	936,389	68.1

1995/96 (1st round)	Total number	%
Registered Voters	3,711,589	–
Votes cast	1,737,033	46.8
Blank Votes	77,095	4.4
Invalid Votes	111,074	6.4
Valid Votes	1,548,864	89.2
Álvaro Enrique Arzú Irigoyen (PAN)	565,393	36.5
Alfonso Portillo Cabrera (FRG)	341,364	22.0
Fernando Andrade Díaz-Duran (AN[a])	200,393	12.9
Jorge Luis González del Valle (FDNG)	119,305	7.7
Acisclo Valladares Molina (PLP)	80,761	5.6
José Luis Chea Urruela (UD)	56,191	3.6
Rolando Torres Casanova (DIA)	39,425	2.6
Héctor Mario López Fuentes (MLN)	35,675	2.3
Others[b]	110,357	7.1

[a] Alliance composed of UCN, DCG and PSD.
[b] Another eleven candidates from the following parties or alliances: AP-5, CAMHINA, CAN, FDP, FUN/PID, MD, MPL/PCN, PDG, PDP, PP, and PREG.

1995/96 (2nd round)	Total number	%
Registered voters	—	–
Votes cast	—	—
Blank Votes	—	—
Invalid Votes	—	—
Valid Votes	1,310,758	—
Álvaro Enrique Arzú Irigoyen (PAN)	671,354	51.2
Alfonso Portillo Cabrera (FRG)	639,404	48.8

1999 (1st round)	Total number	%
Registered Voters	4,458,744	–
Votes cast	2,397,212	53.8
Blank Votes	85,912	3.6
Invalid Votes	119,788	5.0
Valid Votes	2,191,512	91.4
Alfonso Antonio Portillo Cabrera (FRG)	1,045,820	47.7
Óscar Berger Perdomo (PAN)	664,417	30.3
Álvaro Colom Caballeros (DIA/URNG)	270,891	12.4
Acisclo Valladares Molína (PLP)	67,924	3.1
Juan Francisco Bianchi Castillo (ARDE)	45,470	2.1
Ana Catalina Soberanis Reyes (FDNG)	28,108	1.3
José Enrique Asturias Rudeke (LOV/UD)	25,236	1.2
Danilo Julián Roca Barillas (UCN)	22,939	1.1
Carlos Humberto Pérez Rodríguez (MLN)	13,080	0.6
Others[a]	7,627	0.3

[a] Others include: Emilio Eva Saldívar (AD): 4,929 votes (0.2%) and Flor de María Alvarado Suárez de Solís (ARENA): 2,698 (0.1%).

1999 (2nd round)	Total number	%
Registered Voters	4,458,744	–
Votes cast	1,799,928	40.4
Blank Votes	9,841	0.5
Invalid Votes	55,747	3.1
Valid Votes	1,734,340	96.4
Alfonso Antonio Portillo Cabrera (FRG)	1,184,932	68.3
Óscar Berger Perdomo (PAN)	549,408	31.7

2003 (1st round)	Total number	%
Registered Voters	5,073,282	–
Votes cast	2,937,169	57.9
Blank Votes	114,004	3.9
Invalid Votes	139,386	4.7
Valid Votes	2,683,779	91.4
Óscar Berger Perdomo (GANA)	921,233	34.3
Álvaro Colom Caballeros (UNE (2))	707,578	26.4
José Efraín Ríos Montt (FRG)	518,328	19.3
Leonel Eliseo Lopez Rodas (PAN)	224,127	8.4
Friederich García-Galont Bischof (PU)	80,943	3.0
Rodrigo Asturias Amado (URNG)	69,297	2.6
José Eduardo Suger Cofiño (DIA)	59,774	2.2
Jacobo Arbenz Villanova (DCG)	42,186	1.6
José Angel Lee Duarte (DSP)	37,505	1.4
Others[a]	22,808	0.8

[a] Others include: Francisco Arredondo (UN): 11,979 votes (0.4%) and Manuel Eduardo Conde Orellana (MSPCN): 10,829 (0.4%).

2003 (2nd round)	Total number	%
Registered Voters	5,073,282	–
Votes cast	2,373,469	46.8
Blank Votes	24,192	1.0
Invalid Votes	67,106	2.8
Valid Votes	2,282,171	96.2
Óscar Berger Perdomo (GANA)	1,235,303	54.1
Álvaro Colom Caballeros (UNE (2))	1,046,868	45.9

2.10 List of Power Holders 1898–2004

Head of State	Years	Remarks
Manuel Estrada Cabrera	1898–1920	Took presidency as the first delegate on 09/02/1898. He was elected in 1904 and re-elected in a plebiscite in 1910 and again in 1916. On 08/02/1920, he was declared mentally incompetent by the national assembly.
Carlos Herrera y Luna	1920–1921	Nominated president by the national assembly; elected in 1920. Resigned due to military pressure on 05/12/1921.
José María Orellano	1921–1926	Member of the military; took over the government after Herrera had resigned. Constitutionally elected president. Died on 26/09/1926.
Lázaro T. Chacón	1926–1930	Member of the military, he assumed the presidency as a delegate. Elected on 15/03/1927. Resigned due illness on 14/12/1930.
Baudillo Palma	1930	Interim president. *Coup d'état* on 16/12/1930.
Manuel María Orellano	1930–1931	Interim president. Resigned on 02/01/1931 due to lack of support from the USA.
José María Reyna Andrade	1931	Interim president; until 15/02/1931.
Jorge Ubico Castañeda	1931–1944	Member of the military; elected in 1931. Prolonged his term after a plebiscite (1935) and a constitutional reform (1941). Resigned due to popular pressure on 01/07/1944.
Triunvirato	1944	Member of the military, led by Frederico Ponce Vaides. Resigned on 20/10/1944 after a *coup d'état*.
Junta de Gobierno	1944–1945	Military-civil junta; end of the provisional term on 15/03/1945.
Juan José Arévalo Bermejo	1945–1951	Constitutionally elected president. End of office on 15/03/1951.
Jacobo Arbenz Guzmán	1951–1954	Member of the military; constitutionally elected president. *Coup d'état* on 27–28/06/1954.
Carlos Enrique Díaz	1954	Member of the military; resigned due to US-pressure on 29/06/1954.
Junta de Gobierno	1954	Members of the military, headed by Elfego H. Monzón. Substituted on 02/09/1954 by a *Jefe de Estado*.
Carlos Castillo Armas	1954–1957	Member of the military; nominated president by military chiefs. Confirmed in plebiscite on 10/10/1954. Assassinated on 26/07/1957.

Guatemala

Head of State (cont.)	Years	Remarks
Luis Arturo González López	1957	Interim president; was vice president during the Castillo Armas-regime. *Coup d'état* on 24/10/1957.
Oscar Mendoza Azurdia	1957	Member of the military; in office only for two days.
Guillermo Flores Avendaño	1957–1958	Member of the military; Interim president. End of office on 02/03/1958.
Miguel Ydígoras Fuentes	1958–1963	Member of the military; constitutionally elected president. *Coup d'état* on 30/03/1963.
Alfredo Enrique Peralta Azurdia	1963–1966	Member of the military; interim president.
Julio César Méndez Montenegro	1966–1970	Constitutionally elected president. Began the presidency on 01/07/1966.
Carlos Arana Osorio	1970–1974	Member of the military; constitutionally elected president. Assumed office on 01/07/1970.
Eugenio Kjell Laugerud García	1974–1978	Member of the military; constitutionally elected president. Assumed office on 01/07/1974.
Romeo Lucas García	1978–1982	Member of the military; constitutionally elected president. Assumed office on 01/07/1978. *Coup d'état* on 23/03/1982.
Junta militar	1982	Composed of José Efraín Ríos Montt, Horacio Egberto Maldonado Schaad y Francisco Luis Gordillo Martínez. The latter two resigned on 08/06/1982.
José Efraín Ríos Montt	1982–1983	Member of the military; designated president on 09/06/1982. *Coup d'état* on 08/08/1983.
Oscar Humberto Mejía Víctores	1983–1986	Member of the military; was designated president by the military.
Vinicio Cerezo Arévalo	1986–1991	Constitutionally elected president, assumed presidency on 14/01/1986.
Jorge Antonio Serrano Elías	1991–1993	Constitutionally elected president, assumed presidency on 14/01/1991; failed *coup d'état* on 25/03/1993.
Ramiro de León Carpio	1993–1996	Interim president, ex-*Procurador de Derechos Humanos*, assumed office on 05/06/1993.
Alvaro Arzú Irigoyen	1996–2000	Constitutionally elected president; assumed office on 14/01/1996.
Alfonso Portillo	2000–2004	Constitutionally elected president, assumed office on 14/01/2000.
Óscar Berger Perdomo	2004–	Constitutionally elected president, assumed office on 14/01/2004.

3. Bibliography

3.1 Official Sources

Legislación Revolucionaria, Decretos emitidos por la Junta Revolucionaria de Gobierno, dated 20 October 1944. Guatemala: Unión Tipográfica.

'Ley Electoral de 1879', in *Recopilación de las Leyes emitidas por el gobierno democrático de la República de Guatemala, desde el 3 de junio de 1871, hasta el 30 de junio de 1881*. Guatemala 1881.

'Ley Electoral de 1887', in R. P. Méndez (ed.) (1927), *Leyes Vigentes, recopiladas por la Secretaría de Gobernación y Justicia*. Guatemala.

'Ley Electoral de 1937', in R. P. Méndez (ed.) (1937), *Leyes Vigentes de Gobernación y Justicia*. Guatemala.

'Ley Electoral de 1946, Decreto No. 255, modificada por los Decretos del Congreso Nos. 255, 286, 313, 324, 538 y 552', in Ministerio de Gobernación (ed.) (1948). *Recopilación de Leyes*. Guatemala.

Ley Electoral y de Partidos Políticos de 1985, Decreto no. 1–85 de la Asamblea Nacional Constituyente reformado por los Decretos Nos. 51–87 y 74–87 del Congreso de la República. Guatemala.

Secretaría de Gobernación y Justicia and Méndez, R. P. (eds.) (1927). *Leyes Vigentes*. Guatemala.

Tribunal Supremo Electoral (1984). *Memoria de la elección de Asamblea Nacional Constituyente*. Guatemala: TSE.

Tribunal Supremo Electoral (1985). *Memoria de las elecciones generales celebradas en los meses de noviembre y diciembre de 1985*. Guatemala: TSE.

Tribunal Supremo Electoral (1991). *Memoria Elecciones 90/91*. Guatemala.

Tribunal Supremo Electoral (1995). *Ley Electoral y de Partidos Políticos y su regolamento. Elecciones '95*. Guatemala: TSE.

Tribunal Supremo Electoral (1999). *Elecciones 99, 13/12/1999*. <Tse.org.gt> (as of 06 June 2003).

Tribunal Supremo Electoral (2000). *Memoria de Elecciones Generales 1999*. Guatemala.

3.2 Books, Articles, and Electoral Reports

Aguilera Peralta, G. (1985). 'Notas sobre elecciones y transición en Guatemala'. *Estudios Centroamericanos* (San Salvador), 40/446: 898–907.

Anderson, T. (1982). *Politics in Central America*. New York: Praeger.

Archiv der Gegenwart. various years.

Asociación de Investigación y Estudios Sociales (ed.) (1991). *VII Seminario sobre el rol de los partidos políticos en el proceso de elecciones 1990–91*. Guatemala: ASIES.

Azpuru, D. et al. (1999). *La Consulta Popular y el Futuro del Proceso de Paz en Guatemala (Documento de Trabajo No. 243)*. Washington, D.C.: Woodrow Wilson International Center for Scholars, Latin American Program.

Bendel, P. (1994). 'Partidos políticos y democratización en América Central. Un intento de romper una lanza a favor de los partidos – a pesar de los pesares'. *Anuario de Estudios Centroamericanos* (Universidad de Costa Rica), 20/2: 27–39.

— (1995). *Partidos políticos y sistema de partidos en Centroamérica* (working paper). San Salvador, El Salvador: Fundación Dr. Guillermo Manuel Ungo.

— (1996). *Parteiensysteme in Zentralamerika*. Opladen: Leske + Budrich.

Booth, J. A. et al. (1985). *The 1985 Guatemalan Elections. Will the Military Relinquish Power? Report of the Delegation sponsored by the Washington Office on Latin America and the International Human Rights Law Group*. Washington, D.C.

Borneo, H. and Torres-Rivas, E. (2000). *Por qué no votan los guatemaltecos? Estudio de participación y abstención electoral*. Guatemala: International IDEA/TSE/PNUD.

Bowdler, G. A. and Cotter, P. (1982). *Voter Participation in Central America, 1954–1981*. Washington, D.C.: University Press of America.

Calvert, P. (1985). *Guatemala. A Nation in Turmoil*. Boulder, Col./ London: Westview Press.

Cano del Cid, E. (1994). 'Consulta Popular. Guatemala, 30 de enero de 1994'. *Boletín Electoral Latinoamericana* (San José), XI: 29–42.

Castañeda Sandoval, G. (1990). 'Elecciones y democracia en Guatemala'. *Secuencia* (México, D.F.), nueva época, 17: 93–110.

Castillo Peralta, R. (1972). *Geografía electoral de Guatemala*. Guatemala: INCEP.

Castillo, R. (1990). 'De la revolución a la restauración. Elecciones en Centroamérica'. *Africa – América Latina* (Madrid), 2: 7–13.

CEDAL (1974). *La situación política en Guatemala*. Costa Rica.

Cehelsky, M. (1966). *Guatemalan Election Fact Book*. Washington, D.C.: ICOPS.

Dombrowski, J. et al. (1970). *Area Handbook for Guatemala*. Washington, D.C.: U.S. Government Printing Office.

Erbsen de Maldonado, K. and Schmid, G. (1996). 'Die allgemeinen Wahlen in Guatemala am 12.11.1995 und 7.1.1996'. *KAS Auslandsinformationen*, 12/2: 94–132.

Escobar Armas, C. (1987). *La Ley Electoral y de Partidos Políticos de Guatemala 1985 (sufragio y democracia)*. San José (Costa Rica).

Facts on File (New York). various years.

Figueroa Ibarra, C. (1978). 'Elecciones en Guatemala'. *Comercio Exterior* (Mexico), 28/3: 291–297.

Fischer-Bollin, P. (2000). 'Der Populismus siegt auch in Guatemala. Die allgemeinen Wahlen vom 7. November und 26. Dezember 1999'. *KAS Auslandsinformationen*, 16/1: 61–75.

Gálvez Borrell, V. (1991). 'Transición y régimen político en Guatemala 1982–1988'. *Cuadernos de Ciencias Sociales* (San José), 44.

García Laguardia, J. M. (1983). *La defensa de la Constitución*. Guatemala: Universidad de San Carlos de Guatemala.

— (1989). 'Evolución político-constitucional de la República de Guatemala en el siglo XX: 1920–1986', in *El constitucionalismo en las postrimerías del siglo XX: Constitucionalismo, colaboraciones extranjeras y nacionales*. Mexico City: UNAM, 569–608.

— (1999). *Constitución y Partidos Políticos en Guatemala*. Temas Electorales, Guatemala.

García Laguardia, J. M. and Vásquez Martínez, E. (1984). *Constitución y orden democrático*. Guatemala: Editorial Universitaria.

Georgetown University and Organización de Estados Americanos (2003). 'Guatemala. Elección al Congreso de 1995', in *Base de Datos de las Américas*. <http://www.georgetown.edu/pdba/Elecdata/Guate/leg95.html> (as of 20 August 2003).

González Davison, F. (1987). *El regimen liberal en Guatemala (1871–1944)*. Guatemala: Editorial Universitaria.

Grieb, K. J. (1979). *Guatemalan Caudillo. The Regime of Jorge Ubico, Guatemala 1931–1944*. Ohio.

Guerra Roldán, M. R. (1988). 'El Registro Electoral en Guatemala', in *Memoria de la Segunda Conferencia de la Asociación de Organismos Electorales de Centroamérica y el Caribe: El Registro Electoral en América Latina*. San José: IIDH–CAPEL, 75–107.

— (2000). 'La reforma electoral en Guatemala'. *Boletín Electoral Latinoamericano* (San José), XXIII: 101–112.

Handy, J. (1985). 'The Guatemalan Revolution and Civil Rights: Presidential Elections and the Judicial Process under Juan José Arévalo and Jacobo Arbenz Guzmán'. *Canadian Journal of Latin American and Caribbean Studies*, 19: 3–21.

Hauessler Yela, C. C. (1983). *Diccionario General de Guatemala*. Guatemala.

Herrera, T. (1986). *Guatemala: Revolución de octubre*. San José (Costa Rica): EDUCA.

Inforpress Centroamericana (1985). *Guatemala. Elecciones de 1985*. Guatemala.

Inforpress Centroamericana and Fundación Friedrich Ebert (1995). *Guatemala, elecciones '95*. Guatemala: Inforpress Centroamericana.

International IDEA (1998). *Democracia en Guatemala. La Misión de un Pueblo Entero*. Stockholm: International IDEA.

Instituto Centroamericano de Estudios Políticos (INCEP) (1990). 'Guatemala: Elecciones generales 1990'. *Panorama Centroamericano, Reporte Político* (Guatemala), 21, special issue, Guatemala: INCEP.

— (1995). 'Guatemala: Elecciones Generales'. *Panorama Centroamericano, Reporte Político*, 108, Guatemala: INCEP.

Instituto de Investigaciones Políticas y Sociales (IIPS) (1978). 'Los partidos políticos y el estado guatemalteco desde 1944 hasta nuestros días'. *Estudios Centroamericanos* (San Salvador), 33/356–357: 418–428.

Instituto Interamericano de Derechos Humanos/Centro de Asesoría y Promoción Electoral (1995). *Boletín electoral latinoamericano*, XIV, July–December, San José (Costa Rica).

International Human Rights Law Group and Washington Office on Latin America (1988*). Political Transition and the Rule of Law*. Washington, D.C.

Johnson, K. F. (1967). *The Guatemalan Presidential Election of March 6, 1966. An Analysis*. Washington, D.C.: ICOPS.

Krennerich, M. (1996). *Wahlen und Antiregimekriege in Zentralamerika. Eine vergleichende Studie*. Opladen: Leske + Budrich.

Kress, B. and Schmid, G. (1994). 'Die Wahlen zum Guatemaltekischen Kongreß am 14. August 1994'. *KAS Auslandsinformationen*, 10/10: 26–47.

Mariñas Otero, L. (1958). *Las Constituciones de Guatemala*. Madrid: Ediciones Cultura Hispánica.

Montenegro Ríos, C. R. (1980). *El Partido Demócrata Cristiano Guatemalteco y su desarrollo político e ideológico*. San José (Costa Rica): Universidad de Costa Rica.

— (1983). *El Partido Movimiento de Liberación Nacional*. San José (Costa Rica): Universidad de Costa Rica.

National Democratic Institute for International Affairs (1991). *The 1990 National Elections in Guatemala*. Washington, D.C.: International Delegation Report.

Nohlen, D., Picado, S., and Zovatto, D. (eds.) (1998). *Tratado de derecho electoral comparado de América Latina*. Mexico City: Fondo de Cultura Económica.

Nyrop, R. F. (ed.) (1983). *Guatemala: A Country Study*. Washington, D.C.: The American University.

Paiz Andrade, R. (1997). 'Guatemala 1978–1993. The Incomplete Process of the Transition to Democracy', in J. I. Domínguez and M. Lindenberg (eds.), *Democratic Transitions in Central America*. Gainesville, Fla.: University Press of Florida, 139–164.

Política y Sociedad (Guatemala) (1978). Special issue, April 1978.

Reyes, M. A. (1984). 'Guatemala. Elementos para comprender la jornada electoral'. *Polémica* (San José), 14/15: 34–55.

Rivas, J. M. (1978). 'Elecciones presidenciales en Guatemala: 1966–78. Ilegitimidad progresiva del gobierno'. *Estudios Centroamericanos* (San Salvador), 33/356–357: 429–436.

Rosada Granados, H. (1984). *Análisis de la conducta electoral en Guatemala (1944–1984)*. Guatemala: ASIES.

— (1985). *Guatemala 1984. Elecciones para Asamblea Nacional Constituyente*. San José (Costa Rica): CAPEL.

— (1987). Sociología política de Guatemala (1944–1985). Guatemala: ASIES.

— (1990). 'Guatemala 1990. Elecciones generales. Guatemala, 11 de noviembre 1990 y 6 de enero 1991'. *Boletín Electoral Latinoamericano* (San José: IIDH–CAPEL), 4: 36–49.

— (1992). 'Elecciones y democracia en America Latina. Guatemala 1990–1991', in R. Cerdas-Cruz et al. (eds.), *Una tarea in conclusa: Elecciones y democracia en America Latina: 1988-1991*, San José (Costa Rica): IIDH/CAPEL, 67–94.

Rosenberg, M. B. (1985). *Democracia en Centroamérica?*. San José (Costa Rica): CAPEL.

Ruddle, K. and Gillette, P. (eds.) (1972*). Latin American Political Statistics. Supplement to the Statistical Abstract of Latin America*. Los Angeles, Calif.: University of California.

Schneider, R. M. (1958). *Communism in Guatemala, 1944–1954*. New York: Praeger.

Seligson, M. A. and Booth, J. A. (1995*). Elections and Democracy in Central America, Revisited*. Chapel Hill, N.C./ London.

Silvert, K. H. (1954). *A Study in Government. Guatemala*. New Orleans: Tulane University.

Sloan, J. W. (1968). 'The 1966 Presidential Election in Guatemala. Can a Radical Party Desiring Fundamental Social Change Win an Election in Guatemala'. *Inter–American Economic Affairs*, 22/2: 15–32.

Solórzano Martínez, M. (1986). 'Centroamérica. Democracias de fachada'. *Polémica* (San José), 12, 41–55.

— (1987). *Guatemala. Autoritarismo y democracia*. San José (Costa Rica): EDUCA-FLACSO.

Torres-Rivas, E. (1984). 'Problems of Democracy and Counterrevolution in Guatemala', in W. Grabendorff, H.-W. Krumwiede, and J. Todt (eds.), *Political Change in Central America. Internal and External Dimensions*. Boulder, Colo./ London: Westview Press, 114–126.

— (1991). 'Imágenes, siluetas, formas en las elecciones centroamericanas. Las elecciones de la década', *Polémica* (San José), 14–15: 2–21.

Troussanit Ribot, M. (1988). *Guatemala.* Mexico City: Alianza Editorial Mexicana.

Trudeau, R. H. (1989). 'The Guatemalan Election of 1985. Prospects for Democracy', in J. A. Booth and M. A. Seligson (eds.), *Elections and Democracy in Central America.* Chapel Hill, N.C./ London, 93–125.

Villacorta, M. R. (1995). 'Guatemala. Elecciones Generales 12 de noviembre de 1995. *Boletín Electoral Latinoamericano* (San José), XIV: 17–30.

— (1998). 'Los processo electorales en Guatemala. 1992–1996', in Instituto Interamericano de Derechos Humanos (ed.), *Urnas y desencanto político. Elecciones y democracia en América Latina 1992–1996.* San José (Costa Rica): IIDH, 99–122.

Weiss, H.-J. (2004). 'Die allgemeinen Wahlen vom 9. November und 28. Dezember 2003 in Guatemala'. *KAS Auslandsinformationen*, 2/04: 98–112.

GUYANA
by Matthias Trefs[*]

1. Introduction

1.1 Historical Overview

Guyana, the only Anglophone country on the South American continent and one of the poorest states in the Western Hemisphere, gained independence from Britain in 1966. However, it was not until 1992 that international observers could classify elections as generally free and fair. Entirely peaceful and efficient elections are still prevented by party politics based on ethnic cleavages. As long as none of the ethnic groups are willing to accept their adversaries in government, they simply aggravate racial hostilities. Moreover, they maintain allegations of fraud in order to undermine the legitimacy of elections. Despite several attempts to solve the racial conflict, the political parties continue to exploit the deep-rooted ethnic divide. Unbalanced and biased reports in the media fuel the aggression.

East Indian Guyanese account for over 50% of the population, Afro-Guyanese constitute just over 40%, if citizens of mixed but predominantly black ancestry are included. Between 4 and 5% are indigenous Amerindians, and only about 3% are of Chinese and European origin. These structures are reflected in the party system, which is characterized by the antagonism between the Indo-Guyanese and the Afro-Guyanese parties. Hence, Guyanese society is often seen as ethnically bipolar. However, there is also the neglected minority of Amerindians who continue to protest against their oppression. This internal predisposition for conflict is exacerbated by external pressure in the form of boundary disputes with the neighboring countries of Suriname and Venezuela.

Compared to the rest of the countries in this region, the process of decolonization in British Guiana was difficult: in the context of the Cold War, both the British colonial power and the US wanted to prevent the establishment of a Marxist system. At first, the national elite in Guyana

---

[*] I would like to thank the Guyana Elections Commission for their valuable and friendly help.

was united in a widespread, predominantly anti-colonialist movement. However, in the mid-1950s the central political cleavage began to emerge. It developed from the ethnic divide between East Indians and Blacks. In the beginning, ideological differences and ethnic divides coincided, but soon the latter started to dominate politics.

Parliamentary tradition in Guyana goes back to 1928, when the British established a legislative council. Internal self-governance and universal suffrage, however, were not granted until 1953, when a new constitution was enacted, shortly before the first free elections in April. The elections were won clearly by the Peoples Progressive Party (PPP), which had arisen from the trade union movement. Founded in 1950, the PPP was the first modern mass party of British Guiana, supported by workers and intellectuals regardless of race. In the beginning, the multi-ethnic PPP was seen as a move towards social and political integration. Following trade unionist traditions, its main focus was the fight for the end of imperialism and its concern was to protect the workers' interests. However, ideological differences began to reflect the ethnic cleavage within the party. The radical leftist faction, defining itself as Marxist, was led by the East Indian Guyanese Cheddi Jagan. This group was opposed by the rather moderate socialist wing, centered around the Afro-Guyanese Forbes Burnham. Geographic and social contrasts only served to enhance these differences: whereas the Indian population was composed of land workers and small farmers, the blacks made up the proletariat and the urban middle class.

In 1953, Jagan defeated Burnham's wing and became prime minister. At this point, he was still able to keep the support of Burnham and his supporters by allocating them ministerial posts. Jagan's government sought to implement a policy of radical social reform directed against the colonial oligarchy. This alarmed the British government and troops were sent in response to the alleged threat of a Marxist revolution. The British governor general suspended the constitution in October 1953, only 133 days after it had been enacted, and set up a transitional government that consisted of conservative politicians, businessmen, and civil servants.

Before the 1957 elections, the gap between Burnham's increasingly moderate wing and Jagan's faction widened. Not surprisingly, after Jagan was again victorious in free and fair elections, the PPP finally broke apart along the ethnic divide. Burnham's group joined the United Democratic Party (UDP), which was based mainly on the Afro-Guyanese urban middle class. Together they formed the People's National Congress (PNC). From then on, Burnham gradually became the leader of all

Afro-Guyanese, skillfully bridging the ideological schism between the classes. Jagan also strengthened this development by vetoing Guyana's participation in the West Indies Federation. He feared the influence of the Caribbean nations, which were overwhelmingly of African descent. Thus, the population's political preferences and the conflict between the PPP and the PNC grew to be determined more and more by the ethnic cleavage.

Nevertheless, both parties worked towards independence, but were opposed by Great Britain and the United States, in particular, who did not want the country to become independent under Jagan's clearly Marxist government. In the 1961 elections, the PPP was again victorious. With only 1.6% more votes than the PNC, it received nearly twice as many seats. In an already tense atmosphere, these distorted results gave rise to mass demonstrations led by the PNC. With financial support from the US, the trade unions supporting the PNC initiated a general strike, which was accompanied by severe interracial violence. After several weeks, the British administration intervened: troops were sent in and the governor declared a state of emergency. Eventually, in an effort to quell the turmoil, Jagan gave in and it was decided to alter the electoral system. The British, the United States, and the Guyanese opposition hoped this reform would lead to a change of government. Thus, proportional representation was introduced in 1964—a unique case among the Commonwealth countries in this region. The new system was applied in the subsequent elections, and resulted in 24 seats for the PPP and only 22 seats for the PNC. However, together with the seven seats won by the United Front (UF), a right-wing party supported by business interests, Burnham was able to form an anti-Indian coalition government. Despite this clear result, Jagan refused to resign and had to be removed by the governor.

Once in power, Burnham secured the PNC's ascendancy by taking control of the electoral system. The PNC-dominated national assembly transferred the authority of the elections commission to a government department. This department was headed by a deputy loyal to the PNC and was therefore in Burnham's power. The colony began to stabilize, and broke with its brief Communist past. Great Britain and the US acknowledged these changes and now approved Guyana's request to become a fully sovereign state. This request had been continually opposed since 1963. Thus, the colony became independent on 26 May 1966 and took on the name of 'Guyana'.

1968 was the starting point for a series of fraudulent elections. The cases of manipulation were also confirmed by foreign observers. They always resulted in an overwhelming majority for Burnham's PNC. This manufactured concentration of power enabled Burnham to break from the pro-Western UF. He began to intensify the promotion of his cooperative socialism, a third way between US capitalism and Soviet socialism. On 23 February 1970, Burnham declared Guyana a 'Cooperative Republic'. The governor general, as the representative of the British Crown, was replaced by a ceremonial president as head of state. This was the final break with the British monarchy. Furthermore, Guyana joined the movement of non-aligned countries. In the 1973 elections the PNC obtained a two-thirds majority, which gave the party the power to amend the constitution. From then on, based on a new amendment, Guyanese citizens could no longer appeal to the British Privy Council as the highest court of appeal. In 1974, Burnham announced the 'Party Paramountcy' doctrine, which effectively reinstated the PNC's supremacy over state and society. Constitutional regulations envisaged the next elections to be held in 1978. However. they were suspended by the counterfeit referendum of 10 July 1978. Moreover, by means of this referendum the parliament elected in 1973 was declared the constituent assembly.

Although the opposition parties called for political reform, they failed to unite against the PNC. Some parties repeatedly boycotted elections, namely the UF and the multi-ethnic leftist Working People's Alliance (WPA). The latter was founded in 1979 and its leader, Walter Rodney, a prominent Caribbean historian, was assassinated in June 1980. The PPP, on the other hand, contested all the elections but boycotted parliament from 1973 to 1975. After this time the party moved to a policy of critical support of the government's non-aligned socialism. Burnham, however, did not depart from his policy of keeping the opposition from power.

On 6 October 1980, a new constitution was passed proclaiming Guyana a democratic state in transition from capitalism to socialism. The office of an executive president was created. As head of state and chief of the executive, this office was endowed with considerable veto power against the parliament. With a term of office of five years, presidency was linked to the legislative period of parliament. The leader of the political party with the highest percentage of votes was automatically elected president. This included the right to name the prime minister, who was granted only limited powers. Extensive nationalization of the economy—nearly the only lasting achievement of cooperative socialism—the formation of a large military apparatus, and the expansion of state bureaucracy allowed the PNC and Burnham in particular to secure power by means of clientelism.

After Burnham's unexpected death in August 1985, first vice president and prime minister Desmond Hoyte came to power. He acceded to some demands of the opposition by abolishing postal voting and restricting overseas voting, i.e. some of the instruments that enabled election fraud. Nevertheless, in December 1985, Hoyte's presidency was confirmed in manipulated elections. This experience finally prompted the opposition parties—PPP, WPA, and the reconstituted UF—to form the Patriotic Coalition for Democracy (PCD) in 1986. The PCD's main demand was for electoral reform. Faced with the country's disastrous economic situation and pressure from the USA, Hoyte shifted to a neoliberal policy of denationalization and support of private investment in 1988, thereby abandoning non-aligned socialism and thus alienating Burnham's old supporters. With this new policy, Hoyte sought to reestablish a positive relationship with the IMF and hoped for Western assistance and trading partners. However, with the declining conflict between East and West, anti-communism was no longer a sufficient condition for a developing country seeking Western assistance. Western states and international organizations began to make democratic reform a prerequisite for economic aid. Thus, Hoyte was forced to make concessions. He invited electoral observation missions from the British Commonwealth and the US American Carter Center, reinstalled an independent elections commission, ordered a complete revision of voter registration rolls, and introduced vote counting at polling stations. The fact that ballot papers were removed from the polls in order to count them, had made the electoral process particularly vulnerable to fraud.

The elections scheduled for 1990 were postponed several times. With the consent of the international observers, they were finally cancelled when the election authorities failed to present new (up-to-date) electoral rolls in time. The elections were eventually held on 5 October 1992. They were internationally monitored and, despite certain irregularities, they were considered free and fair—for the first time since 1964. They resulted in a peaceful transfer of power. Cheddi Jagan, who had given up his Marxist ideas, won with 54% of the vote and Hoyte (41%) gave into pressure from the international observers and accepted his electoral defeat. Jagan appointed Samuel Hinds as prime minister. Hinds was the head of the Civic Group (CIVIC) that formed a coalition with the PPP. In 1995, with international assistance, the new government initiated the creation of a comprehensive strategy for social and economic development, the so-called National Development Strategy. When Jagan died in

March 1997, Samuel Hinds became president and appointed Janet Jagan as prime minister. She was the US-born widow of Cheddi Jagan and a member of the PPP's central and executive committees. The following elections in December of that year were again won by the PPP/CIVIC coalition and Janet Jagan became president. The PNC, however, questioned the legality of these results and encouraged its supporters to protest. The discontent resulted in violent outbreaks in the capital. Since the social unrest would not cease, CARICOM mediators helped the PPP/CIVIC and the PNC to come to an agreement, the so-called Herdmanston Accord, signed in January 1998. The two parties committed themselves to political dialog and set up a reform agenda that was to have been implemented by a constitutional reform commission before the next elections in January 2001. However, by the end of 2000, it became clear that this date could not be kept and elections had to be postponed for organizational reasons. This, in turn, led to the question of who was to govern, because the mandate of President Jagdeo's government—Jagan had stepped down in 1999 because of ill health—would expire on 15 January. Although the supreme court subsequently declared the 1997 elections null and void, it ordered the incumbent government to stay in power until the next elections. Thus, the elections were held on 19 March 2001, in an atmosphere of social strife and amounting tension between the major political parties. These protests continued after the elections had been won by Jagdeo and the PPP/CIVIC, even though international observers concluded that the electoral process had been free and fair. The breakdown of an interparty dialog in March 2002 and the opposition's subsequent boycott of parliament are the most recent proof of the politicians' continued inability to overcome their fundamental racial bias.

1.2 Evolution of Electoral Provisions

Before Guyana's independence, its parliamentary history was varied. For over a decade, British and US American fears of a Marxist takeover led to several setbacks on the way to independence. Thus, the first constitution of April 1953, which granted internal self-governance, was suspended in October of the same year. As a consequence, the bicameral parliament with the elected legislative council was substituted by an entirely appointed unicameral assembly under British control. As tensions between Britain and British Guiana decreased, a large number of the parliamentarians were elected from 1957 on. In 1961, a bicameral parliament was reinstalled. It comprised a senate appointed by the governor and an elected legislative assembly. However, in 1964, two years prior to independence, the unicameral system with elected deputies (national assembly) was reintroduced by the British administration.

The next important break after the foundation of the Republic in 1970 was the 1980 Constitution. It established the position of an executive president with a term of office of five years. Formally, the system of government can be described as semi-presidential. Although the government is based on parliamentary support, the president has a superior position since the constitution endows him with many powers and veto rights.

De jure, universal, equal, direct, and secret suffrage has been in force since the 1953 elections. However, between 1968 und 1992, results were constantly manipulated in favor of the governing PNC. Prior to the 1973 elections, voting age was lowered from 21 to 18 years for active as well as passive suffrage.

With regard to the possibility of electoral fraud, the 'proxy voting' was a vulnerable point in the system. At first, this provision enabled each voter to cast up to two additional votes to represent other voters. In 1968, the allowed maximum of proxy votes rose to three. From 1964 to 1968, the share of proxy votes grew from 2.5 to 7.0% of cast votes. Citizens of Guyana residing outside the country could also vote from abroad, using the process of overseas voting. These provisions and the system of postal voting were open to abuse from a government-controlled apparatus: in 1964, a large amount of the elections commission's power was transferred to the commissioner of national registration. The commissioner was subject to the authority of the Ministry of Home Affairs. Thus, the government could, in fact, control the voter's list and the appointment of electoral officials. The fact that the transportation and counting of ballots on election day were also in the hands of the government added to the system's vulnerability. It is, therefore, not surprising that these provisions played a considerable role in subsequent PNC election victories.

In accordance with Westminster tradition, the first electoral system in British Guiana was the plurality system in SMCs. In 1964, it was replaced by proportional representation in one nation wide constituency. Seats were distributed to parties using the Droop quota (later the Hare quota) and the method of the largest remainder. The number of directly elected members in the 65-seat national assembly increased from 35 to 53. The remaining twelve deputies were indirectly elected local and regional representatives, one from each of the ten Regional Democratic

Councils and two from the National Congress of Local Democratic Organs. National closed and—from the voters' point of view—blocked party lists were introduced. Since the 1968 elections, parties had to list their candidates in alphabetical order and not according to a previously-determined ranking. It was only after elections that the party chairman determined which candidates from the list would get one of the party's seats in parliament. This system was thought to motivate all candidates regardless of list positions. Only the names and symbols of the parties' lists appeared on the ballot paper. The names of the candidates were made public prior to the elections and were also available at the polling stations on election day.

The 2001 elections were the first to be held under a new modified electoral system. It is still based on proportional representation but also provides for geographical representatives elected in the ten regions of Guyana. However, the Guyana Elections Commission (GECOM), political parties, and foreign observers agree that there is need for further evaluation and reform of the new electoral rules, since they are complex and hard to understand for both the electorate and officials. Thus, despite the great improvements of the last decade, the electoral process is still tainted by organizational problems.

1.3 Current Electoral Provisions

Sources: The 1980 Constitution laid down the basic electoral principles. The more detailed provisions were worked out in the following documents: the Representation of the People's Act (1964), the National Assembly (Validity of Elections) Act (1964), the National Registration Act (1967), the Local Democratic Organs Act (1980), and the Elections (Amendment) Act (2000).

Suffrage: The constitution guarantees direct, universal, equal, and secret suffrage in the elections to the national assembly. Every citizen over 18 years as well as Commonwealth citizens over 18 who are residents of Guyana are entitled to vote. Voting is not compulsory.

The right to be elected is granted to all citizens of Guyana over 18 with a sufficient command of the English language (both spoken and written). Mentally ill people, convicts, certain public officials, and members of the armed forces and the police force are excluded. Party membership is necessary in order to be nominated as a candidate on a list. National lists require the support of 300 registered voters, regional lists need at least 200 supporters.

Elected national institutions: Guyana's unicameral parliament, the national assembly, comprises 65 directly elected deputies. Forty of these represent the nation as a whole. The remaining 25 are representatives of the ten regions of Guyana.

The executive president is elected indirectly. As head of state and chief of the executive he nevertheless enjoys almost unlimited power. He can dissolve parliament and call elections at any time. The term of office for both parliamentarians and the executive president is five years according to constitutional regulations.

Nomination of candidates
- *presidential elections*: Each party's presidential candidate has to be clearly identified on the party's national top-up list and is not allowed to contest any of the geographical constituency seats.
- *parliamentary elections:* Candidates stand for election exclusively on party lists. The law requires national top-up and geographical lists of a particular party to be separate and distinct. However, double candidacy is allowed as long as the respective candidate only runs for one party, contests only one geographical constituency, and only assumes one seat if he or she is successful, no matter from which list. Each list has to contain two more names than there are seats contested; this means that geographical constituency lists feature between three and nine candidates and national top-up lists must consist of 42 candidates. The order of names on a list depends on the party and need not follow specific rules. However, there is a strict quota for the number of female candidates. One-third of the candidates on a party's national list and one-third on all of its regional lists taken together have to be women.

Electoral system
- *presidential elections*: Indirect election following plurality rules. The previously nominated chairman of the party with the highest share of votes is automatically elected president.
- *parliamentary elections*: Proportional representation according to the method of the largest remainder using the Hare quota in two separate tiers. The overall share of the 65 seats for each party is calculated by applying the Hare formula in one nation wide constituency. However, 25 out of the 65 deputies are elected separately in ten geographical constituencies that coincide with the ten regions of Guyana. These ten

MMCs differ in magnitude: one district of seven seats, two districts of three, five of two, and two of one. The seats that a party wins in any of these geographical constituencies are subtracted from its overall share of seats. This means that parties have to present two different sorts of lists: geographical constituency lists, one for each constituency contested, and a so-called national top-up list to fill their shares of the remaining 40 seats. Furthermore, each party is required to contest at least 13 seats in a minimum of six geographical constituencies. Despite the two kinds of lists, voters only have a single vote. This vote is cast for a party's regional list. Simultaneously, it is taken into account for the respective party's national list.

Organizational context of elections: On the basis of the electoral law, the GECOM is in charge of the policy for voter registration, the maintenance of voters' lists, and the administration of elections. The chairman of the commission is chosen by the president from a list of six candidates that is presented to him by the opposition. Furthermore, there are six commissioners, three of which are appointed by the president alone. The other three are chosen in agreement with the leader of the opposition. In practice, this means that the posts are divided between the two major parties. Currently, the commission serves a five-year term. International observers have suggested changing the composition of the commission in order to give the other ethnic groups equal access to the administration of elections.

1.4 Commentary on the Electoral Statistics

Most of the electoral data presented in the following tables have been provided by GECOM. These official figures do not always correspond to other sources. Additional information about seat shares, for instance, has been taken from secondary sources. Elections between 1968 and 1992 have to be regarded as fraudulent. As reported by international observers and national civic groups, elections in the nineties were free and fair, regardless of the fact that the loosing party kept claiming that they were fraudulent. The percentages have been calculated by the author. Where no other source is specified the demographic data corresponds to the United Nations midyear-estimates. However, it should be emphasized that estimates vary considerably (some sources indicate less then 700,000 citizens for recent years), even among different UN publications.

2. Tables

2.1 Dates of National Elections, Referendums, and Coups d'Etat

Year	Presidential elections[a]	Parliamentary elections		Elections for Constit. Assembly	Referen- dums	Coups d'état
		Lower Chamber	Upper Chamber			
1964		07/12				
1968		16/12				
1973		17/07				
1978					10/07	
1980		15/12				
1985		09/12				
1992		05/10				
1997		15/12				
2001		19/03				

[a] The presidential office was only introduced prior to the 1980 elections. The previously nominated chairman of the party with the highest share of votes becomes president automatically.

2.2 Electoral Body 1964–2001

Year	Type of election[a]	Population	Registered voters		Votes cast		
			Total number	% pop.	Total number	% reg. voters	% pop.
1964[b]	Pa	629,000	247,604	39.4	240,120	97.0	38.2
1968	Pa	719,000	369,088	51.3	314,246	85.1	43.7
1973	Pa	758,000	431,575	56.9	349,590	81.0	46.1
1978	Ref	820,000	—	—	—	97.7[c]	—
1980	Pa	865,000	493,550	57.1	406,265	82.3	47.0
1985	Pa	790,000	399,304	50.5	294,801	73.8	37.3
1992	Pa	805,000	384,195	47.7	308,852	80.4	38.4
1997	Pa	847,000	461,481	54.5	408,057	88.4	48.2
2001	Pa	856,000	440,185	51.4	403,734	91.7	47.2

[a] Pa = Parliament; Ref = Referendum.
[b] The collecting of electoral data began with the last pre-independence elections (26/05/1966).
[c] Figure provided by the government and heavily disputed by the opposition.

2.3 Abbreviations

AFG[a]	Alliance for Guyana
DLM	Democratic Labour Movement
GAP[b]	Guyana Action Party
GBG	God Bless Guyana
GDP	Guyana Democratic Party
GGG	Good and Green Guyana
GLP	Guyana Labour Party
GUMP	Guiana United Muslim Party
JFAP	Justice For All Party
JP	Justice Party
LP	Liberator Party
NDF	National Democratic Front
NFA	National Front Party
NIP	National Independent Party
NLF	National Labour Front
NRP	National Republican Party
PEPP	Peace Equality & Prosperity Party
PDM	People's Democratic Movement
PNC	People's National Congress
PPP[c]	People's Progressive Party
ROAR	Rise, Organize and Rebuild
UF/TUF	United Force/The United Force
UGI	Union of Guyanese International
URP	United Republican Party
UWP	United Workers Party
WPA	Working People's Alliance

[a] Coalition of WPA and GLP for 1997 elections.

[b] In 2001, the WPA decided to join the GAP in order to secure its own survival as a parliamentary party.

[c] Since the 1990s in coalition with the Civic Group, thus PPP/C.

2.4 Electoral Participation of Parties and Alliances 1964–2001

Party/Alliance	Years	Elections contested[a]
GUMP	1964–1968	2
JP	1964	1
NLF	1964	1
PEPP	1964	1
PNC	1964–2001	8
PPP	1964–2001	8
UF/TUF	1964–1968; 1980–2001	7
LP	1973	1
PDM	1973; 1985; 1992	3
DLM	1985–1992	2
NDF	1985–1997	3
WPA/AFG	1985–2001	4
GBG	1997	1
GDP	1997–2001	2
GGG	1997	1
JFAP	1997–2001	2
NIP	1997	1
NFA	2001	1
ROAR	2001	1

[a] Since 1980, parliamentary elections have also been indirect presidential elections.

2.5 Referendums

Only one referendum has been held in 1978, which was, however, subject to fraud by the government. Official sources claimed that 97.7% of the registered voters had cast their votes. 71.5% allegedly voted 'yes'. Other figures are unknown. The opposition, which abstained from the ballot, stated that in fact only between 10 and 14% of the registered voters took part.

2.6. Elections for Constitutional Assembly

Elections for constitutional assembly have not been held.

2.7 Parliamentary Elections 1964–2001

Year	1964		1968[a]	
	Total number	%	Total number	%
Registered voters	247,604	–	369,088	–
Votes cast	240,120	97.0	314,246	85.1
Invalid votes	1,590	0.7	1,855	0.6
Valid votes	238,530	99.3	312,391	99.4
PPP	109,332	45.8	113,991	36.5
PNC	96,657	40.5	174,339	55.8
UF	29,612	12.4	23,162	7.4
JP	1,334	0.6	–	–
GUMP	1,194	0.5	899	0.3
Others[b]	401	0.2	–	–

[a] Unfair elections.
[b] In 1964, others include: PEPP (224 votes) and NLF (177).

Year	1973[a]		1980[b]	
	Total number	%	Total number	%
Registered voters	431,575	–	493,550	–
Votes cast	349,590	81.0	406,265	82.3
Invalid votes	1,780	0.5	3,251	0.8
Valid votes	347,810	99.5	403,014	99.2
PPP	92,374	26.6	78,414	19.5
PNC	243,803	70.1	312,988	77.7
UF[c]	–	–	11,612	2.9
LP	9,580	2.8	–	–
PDM	2,053	0.6	–	–

[a] Unfair elections.
[b] Unfair elections. The only opposition parties which took part in the elections were the PPP and the UF.
[c] The UF formed an alliance with the LP.

Year	1985[a]		1992	
	Total number	%	Total number	%
Registered voters	399,304	–	348,195	–
Votes cast	294,801	73.8	308,852	88.7
Invalid votes	3,606	1.2	5,666	1.8
Valid votes	291,195	98.8	303,186[b]	98.2
PNC	228,718	78.5	128,286	42.3
PPP	45,926	15.8	162,058	53.5
UF	9,820	3.4	3,183	1.0
WPA	4,176	1.4	6,086	2.0
DLM	2,167	0.7	1,557	0.5
Others[c]	388	0.1	2,006	0.7

[a] Unfair elections. The PPP and the WPA withdrew from the contest on the election day. Later, however, they accepted the seats alloted to them.
[b] The parties' individual shares only add up to 303,176 votes.
[c] In 1985, others include: PDP (232 votes) and NDF (156). In 1992: URP (1,343), PDM (270), UGI (134), NRP (114), UWP (77), NDF (68).

Year	1997		2001	
	Total number	%	Total number	%
Registered voters	461,481	–	440,185	–
Votes cast	408,057	88.4	403,734	91.7
Invalid votes	8,747	2.1	7,218	1.8
Valid votes	399,310	97.9	396,516	98.2
PPP/C	220,667	55.3	210,013	53.0
PNC	161,901	40.5	165,866	41.8
UF/TUF	5,937	1.5	2,904	0.7
AFG/WPA	4,783	1.2	9,451	2.4
GDP	2,528	0.6	1,345	0.3
JFAP	1,265	0.3	2,825	0.7
ROAR	–	–	3,695	0.9
Others[a]	3,494	0.9	417	0.1

[a] In 1997, others include: GGG (1,552 votes), JFAP (1,265), GBG (314), NIP (258) and NDF (105). In 2001: NFA (417).

2.8 Composition of Parliament 1964–2001

Year	1964 Seats 53[a]	% 100.0	1968 Seats 53	% 100.0	1973 Seats 53	% 100.0	1980 Seats 53	% 100.0
PPP	24	45.3	19	35.8	14[b]	26.4	10	18.9
PNC	22	41.5	30	56.6	37	69.8	41	77.4
UF	7	13.2	4	7.5	2[c]	3.8	2	3.8

[a] The number of seats refers to the members of parliament who were directly elected.
[b] Because of fraudulent elections, the PPP boycotted parliament (until April 1975).
[c] Before the 1973 elections, the UF and the LP formed an electoral alliance. However, the LP boycotted parliament bcause of electoral fraud. Hence, the UF received both seats.

Year	1985 Seats 53[a]	% 100.0	1992 Seats 53	% 100.0	1997 Seats 53	% 100.0	2001 Seats 65	% 100.0
PNC	42	79.2	23	43.4	22	41.5	27	41.5
PPP	8	15.1	28	52.8	29	54.7	34	52.3
TUF	2	3.8	1	1.9	1	1.9	1	1.5
WPA[b]	1	1.9	1	1.9	–	–	–	–
AFG	–	–	–	–	1	1.9	–	–
GAP	–	–	–	–	–	–	2	3.1
ROAR	–	–	–	–	–	–	1	1.5

[a] The number of seats refers to the members of parliament who were directly elected.
[b] In 1997, the WPA merged with the GLP and they formed the AFG. In 2001, it joined the GAP.

2.9 Presidential Elections

Direct presidential elections have not been held. The executive president is elected indirectly.

2.10 List of Power Holders 1966–2004

Head of State	Years	Remarks
Queen Elisabeth II.	1966–1970	Represented by the following governors general: Sir Richard Edmonds Luyt (1966), Sir David James Gardiner Rose (1966–1969), Sir Edward Victor Luckhoo (1969–1970).
Sir Edward Victor Luckhoo	1970	First president of the newly founded Republic from 23/02/1970 to 17/03/1970.
Arthur Chung	1970–1980	From 17/03/1970 to 06/10/1980.

Head of State (cont.)	Years	Remarks
Forbes Burnham	1980–1985	First executive president according to the new constitution from 06/10/1980 to his death on 06/08/1985.
Desmond Hoyte	1985–1992	Former vice president, who stayed in power by means of counterfeited elections from 06/08/1985 to 09/10/1992.
Cheddi Jagan	1992–1997	Leader of the former opposition coalition, who acted from 09/10/1992 to his death on 06/03/1997.
Samuel Hinds	1997	As former prime minister, he succeeded Jagan on 06/03/1997. He stayed in office until the next elections on 19/12/1997.
Janet Jagan	1997–1999	The widow of Cheddi Jagan took office after the elections on 19/12/1997. Stepped back because of health problems on 11/08/1999.
Bharrat Jagdeo	1999–	As prime minister, he took office after the resignation of Jagan on 11/08/1999. From 15/01/2001 on, he governed by order of the supreme court, but was re-elected on 19/03/2001.

Head of Government	Years	Remarks
Forbes Burnham	1966–1980	Prime minister, from 26/05/1966 to 06/10/1980, when he became the first executive president.
Ptolemy Reid	1980–1984	From 06/10/1980 to 16/08/1984.
Desmond Hoyte	1984–1985	From 16/08/1984 to his inauguration as president on 06/08/1985.
Hamilton Green	1985–1992	From 06/08/1985 to 09/10/1992.
Samuel Hinds	1992–1997	Leader of the PNC's coalition partner CIVIC. Prime minister from 09/10/1992 until C. Jagan's death on 17/03/1997.
Janet Jagan	1997	From 17/03/1997 on, prime minister under Hinds until the elections on 22/12/1997, when she became president.
Samuel Hinds	1997–1999	Again prime minister from 22/12/1997 to 09/08/1999.
Bharrat Jagdeo	1999	In office from 09/08/1999 to 11/08/1999, when he succeeded J. Jagan as president.
Samuel Hinds	1999–	He became prime minister again on 11/08/1999.

3. Bibliography

3.1 Official Sources

Guyana Elections Commission (GECOM) (2003). *Comparative Analysis of Election Results during the Period 1964 to 1997*. Georgetown (Guyana).

Constitution of the Co-operative Republic of Guyana (1980). Georgetown (Guyana).

Guyana Elections Commission (GECOM) (2003). *Final Results of the 2001 National Assembly Elections*. Georgetown (Guyana).

Government of Guyana (2000). *The Official Gazette. Legal Supplement A of 24th November 2000*. Georgetown (Guyana).

Chief Elections Officer (1965). *Report on the House of Assembly. General Election 1964*. Georgetown (Guyana).

Chief Elections Officer. *Report on the National Assembly. General Election 1968*. Georgetown (Guyana).

Ministry of Legal Affairs (2002). *The Substantive Laws of Guyana*. Georgetown (Guyana).

3.2 Books, Articles, and Electoral Reports

Alexis F. R. (1984). *Changing Caribbean Constitutions*. Bridgetown (Barbados): Antilles Publications.

Americas Watch and Parliamentary Human Rights Group (1985). *Political Freedom in Guyana*. New York/London.

British Parliamentary Human Rights Group (1980). *Something to Remember. The Report of the International Team of Observers at the Elections in Guyana in December 1980*. London: House of Commons.

Carter Center (2001). *Carter Center's Final Statement of its Observation of the 2001 Guyana Elections*. <http://www.cartercenter.org/printdoc.asp?docID=644&submenu=news> (as of 04/03/03).

Chase, A. (1964). *A History of Trade Unionism in Guyana 1900 to 1961*. Demerara (Guyana): New Guyana Company.

Commonwealth Team of Observers (1965). *British Guiana: Report by the Commonwealth Team of Observers on the Election in December 1964*. London.

Council of Free Elected Heads of Governments, The (1992). *Observing Guyana's Electoral Process, 1990–1992*. Atlanta, Ga.: The Carter Center of Emory University.

Danns, G. K. (1982). *Domination and Power in Guyana. A Study of the Police in a Third World Context*. New Brunswick, N.J./London: Transaction Books.

Despres, L. A. (1967). *Cultural Pluralism and Nationalist Politics in British Guiana*. Chicago, Ill.: Rand McNally and Company.

Edie, C. J. (ed.) (1994). *Democracy in the Caribbean. Myths and Realities*. London: Praeger.

Electoral Asistance Bureau Guyana (1998). *General and Regional Elections Guyana 1997*. Guyana.

Greene, J. E. (1974). *Race vs. Politics in Guyana. Political Cleavages and Political Mobilisation in the 1968 General Election*. Mona/Kingstown (Jamaica): University of the West Indies.

— (1982). 'Cooperativism. Militarism. Party Politics. and Democracy in Guyana', in P. Henry and C. Stone (eds.), *The Newer Caribbean Decolonization, Democracy, and Development*. Philadelphia: Institute for the Study of Human Issues.

Henn, H. (1995). 'Guyana', in D. Nohlen and F. Nuscheler (eds.), *Handbuch der Dritten Welt, Vol. 3: Mittelamerika und Karibik*. Bonn: Dietz, 423–436.

Hillebrands, B. (1993). 'Guyana', in D. Nohlen (ed.), *Handbuch der Wahldaten Lateinamerikas und der Karibik*. Opladen: Leske + Budrich, 389–399.

Hintzen, P. C. (1989). *The Costs of Regime Survival, Racial Mobilization, Elite Domination and Control of the State in Guyana and Trinidad*. Cambridge: Cambridge University Press.

Hope, K. R. (1985). 'Electoral Politics and Political Development in Post-independence Guyana'. *Electoral Studies*, 4/3: 57–68.

— (1985). *Guyana: Politics and Development in an Emergent Socialist State*. Oakville/New York/London: Mosaic Press.

International IDEA (2001) (ed.). *Report of the Audit and Systems Review of the 2001 Elections Process in Guyana*. <http://www.idea.int/press/inside/Guyana_election_audit.pdf> (as of 05/03/03).

Inter-Parliamentary Union (ed.). *Chronicle of Parliamentary Elections and Development*. Geneva: International Centre for Parliamentary Documentation, various years.

Jagan C. (1989). *Forbidden Freedom. The Story of British Guiana*. London: Hansib Publishing.

James, R. W. and Lutchman, H. A. (1984). *Law and Political Environment in Guyana*. Georgetown (Guyana): University of Guyana.

Jeffrey, H. and Baber, C. (1986). *Guyana: Politics, Economics and Society. Beyond the Burnham Era*. London: Frances Pinter.

Keesing's Contemporary Archives Nr. 31059-31065. 04.09.1981.

Latin America Bureau (1984). *Guyana: Fraudulent Revolution*. London: Latin America Bureau.

Library of Congress (1992). *Guyana – a Country Study*. <http://lcweb2.loc.gov/frd/cs/gytoc.html> (as of 05/03/03).

Milne, R. S. (1981). *Politics in Ethnically Bipolar States: Guyana, Malaysia, Fiji*. Vancouver/London.

Nath, Dwarka (1982). *Guyana of the Guyanese, Part I-II*. London: Edición Propia.

Nohlen, D. (1978). *Wahlsysteme der Welt*. München: Piper.

Payne, D. W. (1998). 'The 1997 Guyana Elections. Post-election Report', in *Western Hemisphere Election Study Series*, 16/2, Washington, D.C.

Premdas, R. R. (1971). *Political Parties in a Bifurcated State: The Case of Guyana*. Ph.D. thesis, Illinois: University of Illinois.

— (1994). 'Guyana: Ethnic Politics and the Erosion of Human Rights and Democratic Governance', in C. J. Edie (ed.), *Democracy in the Caribbean: Myths and Realities*. Westport, Conn.: Praeger, 43–58.

Singh, C. (1988). *Guyana: Politics in a Plantation Society*. New York/Westport, Conn./London: Praeger.

Spackman, A. (1975). *Constitutional Development of the West Indies 1922–1968. A Selection from the Major Documents*. St. Lauwrence (Barbados): Caribbean University Press.

Sturm, R. and Clemente-Kersten, A. C. (2002). 'Guyana', in D. Nohlen (ed.), *Lexikon Dritte Welt* (12th edn.). Reinbek bei Hamburg: Rowolth, 357–360.

Thomas, C. Y. (1984). 'Guyana: the Rise and Fall of Co-operative Socialism', in A. Payne and P. Sutton (eds.), *Dependency Under Challenge. The Political Economy of the Commonwealth Caribbean*. Manchester: University Press, 77–104.

United Nations Department of International Economic and Social Affairs (various years). *United Nations Population and Vital Statistics Report. Statistical Papers, Series A*. New York.

Walker, W. (2001). 'TUF gets Parliament seat after results error found PPP/Civic to lose one', in *Stabroek News*, 29/03/01.

HAITI
by Felix Ulloa

1. Introduction

1.1 Historical Overview

Having once been France's richest colony, Haiti became an independent nation in 1804 when it was burned to the ground in the only successful slave revolution history has ever known. Half a million illiterate slaves, led by former slaves and mulattos educated in France, took on the French, British, and Spanish armies and won. However, Haiti has never really recovered from the devastation wrought by the revolution. This is due to a number of reasons: First, the newly-formed republic was viewed as a pariah on the international scene and put into diplomatic quarantine. France refused to recognize Haiti's independence until 1838 and the United States only recognized the nation after the end of the US civil war in 1865.

Haiti also had to deal with severe internal problems. More than ten years of war had created a huge military machine. The military leaders established large plantations and tried to coerce the workers into making money for them. However, the newly-liberated slaves preferred subsistence agriculture over the return to hard plantation work. This conflict resulted in a chronic state of insurgency that prevailed well into the beginning of the 20th century in rural areas.

Furthermore, there were pressing social issues left over from before the revolution. The pre-revolutionary regime was based on a hierarchy of skin colors: At the top were 35,000 white colonist, large plantation owners called *grands blancs*; next came the *petits blancs*, who were small plantation owners, colonial administrators, clergymen, the military and merchants. The *mulatres* or *affranchise* were a group of 30,000 free colored people, who had no civic and political rights despite their often wealthy economic position. At the bottom were almost half a million black slaves, whose status was similar to that of animals or commodities (*êtres meubles*).

Since the revolution, with the whites gone, the top of the pyramid was occupied by two antagonistic groups: former *mulatres* and *affranchise* competed for domination against black military commanders. At the bottom, the masses of former slaves turned laborers or peasants had no real chance of participating in the construction of a new state.

The mulattos were generally well educated. Although they made up less than 10% of the population, they were able to use the advantages of education and color to establish themselves as the ruling elite. They opted for a republican benevolent, elitist style of government and maintained a façade of modernity and openness.

The post revolutionary black military elite resented their exclusion from the mulattos' circles and often resorted to racial solidarity to mobilize the black masses in order to win power. More oriented toward the interior, their vision of a strong black feudal state led to the creation of three different monarchies in Haiti, that of Emperor Jean-Jacques Dessalines (1805–1806), King Henry I (1811–1816) and Emperor Faustin Soulouques I. (1849–1859).

The cleavages often resulted in the territory being divided into warring republics or kingdoms, which fueled insurrections, mass revolts and instability, aggravated by international pressure and foreign intervention.

Over time, the dichotomy widened along the urban-rural cleavage as the bourgeoisie moved into the cities. Black rural cultivators articulated demands for land reforms and took up arms. They expressed their discontent with the mulatto hegemony and demanded the election of a black president, whom they expected to be more sensitive to their plight. One way to appease these demands during the 19th century was the so-called *politique de doublure:* the mulatto elite installed a black puppet president, sometimes an illiterate. Between 1847 and 1915, most presidents were dark-skinned. In 1844 the Dominican Republic seceded from Haiti.

During the second decade of the 20th century, two rival political parties emerged. The National Party, dominated by black politicians, and the Liberal Party, dominated by mulatto intellectuals. Both parties were financed by foreign arms dealers and merchants and were engaged in an endless violent struggle that devastated the country.

In 1915 the US intervened militarily in Haiti, claiming its citizens were endangered by political anarchy. Apparently, however, it was the German influence in Haiti at the beginning of the World War I that bothered the US administration. The first political act of the US was to install a new president, Philippe-Sudre Dartiguenave.

With political stability came financial stability and control of corruption but also growing economic problems and increasing fiscal injustices. The Guard of Haiti was created as an army and fought together with US Marines against nationalist peasants who took up arms under the leadership of Haitian army officer Charlemagne Peralte and the rural school teacher Benoit Batraville.

The end of the 'mulatocratia era' came with the fall of President Elie Lescot, who resigned in early 1946 after a series of strikes and riots and the rebellion of a group of army officers led by Paul E. Magloire. The revolution had its ideological base in the *indegenisme*, the *noirisme* and the *négritude*, which were intellectual movements calling for empowerment of the black majority through a black political hegemony.

An alliance of black urban middle-class groups and rural feudal landlords took over the leadership of the movement and began a march toward power in the name of the exploited black masses and the *classe moyenne opprimée* (oppressed middle class). The military junta led by Magloire organized legislative elections. The new legislature elected Dumarsais Estimé, a black notable from the rural area of Fond-Verrettes as president. The 'black power' regimes continued until the fall of Jean Claude Duvalier in 1986.

From 1804, the year of independence, to 1987 Haiti passed 22 constitutions and 14 constitutional amendments. In general terms, the most relevant constitutional reforms introduced in the 20th century concerned the transfer of power. Reforms were often introduced to prolong the incumbent president's time in office or to enable a second term. That was the case of the presidents Sténio Vincent in 1935, Elie Lescot in 1944, Paul E. Magloire in 1956, and the two Duvaliers (Francois 'Papa Doc' and Jean-Claude 'Baby Doc') in 1964, 1971, and 1985. Eight alibi referendums were called (1918, 1928, 1935, 1939, 1964, 1971, 1985, 1987) to legitimize the reforms.

The only fair presidential elections were those of 1930, when Sténio Vincent was president; 1957, when François Duvalier, a black middle class physician presented himself as the heir of the middle-class *noirist* movement and finally in 1990, when the former catholic priest Jean Bertrand Aristide, close to the Theology of Liberation, and his popular movement LAVALAS won the elections.

Nevertheless, the 1950 presidential election was not competitive as Paul E. Magloire was the only candidate. The victory of François Duvalier in 1957 was the victory of those most willing to use violence: the army. The commander of the army General Antonio 'Thomson' Kebreau and his officers had taken charge of the ballot boxes and even though Louis Dejoie received more votes than Duvalier, the results were manipulated to have Duvalier elected.

The numerous changes of power and *coups d'état* before the establishment of the Duvalier regime illustrate the precarious equilibrium within society, where the transfer of political power from one group to another was most often achieved by violence. Elections really questioned the existing power structure on a few occasions only; more often they merely acted as instruments to consolidate the status quo.

During the 29 years of domination by the Duvalier group from 1957 to 1986, middle class and lower middle class blacks were favored with government patronage. But even though members of the traditional mulatto elite were oppressed, Duvalier gave privileges to loyal mulattos and gained support of an important segment of the mercantile bourgeoisie: immigrants of Arab, Syrian, Lebanese and Levantine origin who were traditionally despised as *bwatnando* (recently arrived immigrants).

'Papa Doc' Duvalier also manipulated institutions. He centralized universities in 1960 and prohibited unions in 1963. In 1961 he dissolved both chambers of parliament and established a new unicameral parliament. Many Haitians went into exile; a great number of them were middle class professionals and their departure had severe economic consequences for the country.

But even during Duvalier's rule a weak democratic façade upheld. The fraudulent elections of 1961, initially parliamentary, were later officially interpreted as presidential elections. The objective was to legitimize the president's re-election for a new six-year term.

The central government delegated almost all government functions to political friends around the country, who ran their regions almost independently and in accordance with their own interests. The only conditions they were required to fulfill were to ensure a minimum level of security and opress political opponents in their areas while regularly sending money to central government. Only these 'Duvalierists' had access to important posts in national politics.

In the new constitution of 1964, Duvalier declared himself president for life. He died in 1971 and his son Jean-Claude Duvalier was named his successor.

In the 1980s, confronted with strong opposition by the Church, Duvlier announced a new economic era, the 'Claudist revolution', and introduced democratic reforms. The strategy applied was a mixture of liberalism and repression. Duvalier invited Haitian exiles to take part in talks and he organized legislative elections for February 1985. A new constitutional amendment was passed in 1985. This amendment split the executive power into the presidency and a government.

When Jean Claude Duvalier was removed from power in 1986, some changes took place: The referendum, which overwhelmingly approved a new constitution in 1987, was the first free election in 30 years. The new constitution introduced an independent electoral commission, which, however, has never been established.

Further problems were the partly restricted and arbitrary registration of voters and candidates, long-term boycotts by opposition parties, difficulties in guaranteeing the functioning of the electoral process— especially at communal level— and irregularities regarding the security of ballots and the vote counting. From the mid 1980s to the mid 1990s, Haitian democracy was characterized by a high frequency of elections and military coups.

The first free and fair presidential elections in decades were held in 1990. Jean-Bertrand Aristide won, supported by a popular movement, intellectuals and religious sectors, who were united in an umbrella movement called *Front National de Concertation Démocratique* (FNCD; National Front for Change and Democracy). However, only seven months after assuming the presidency Aristide was deposed by a *coup d'état*. During the military regime that followed, human rights were violated and drug trafficking was supported. In 1994, US soldiers landed in Haiti and enabled Aristide to return to Haiti and to serve for the remainder of his term.

René Préval, elected in 1995, assumed the presidency. The 1997 parliamentary elections were marred by controversy after the first round and eventually canceled altogether. A new political crisis had begun: Prime Minister Rodney Smarth resigned in 1997 and the crisis continued throughout the year and into 1998. The distribution of power in parliament meant that the members were unable to set up a strong government, despite several attempts to do so. The term of this parliament ended at the beginning of 1999, but new elections were not held until May 2000.

The observation mission of the Organization of American States (OAS) questioned the tabulation method in several senate elections and the opposition contested the entire election, refusing to participate in the runoff and in the presidential elections held in November. Jean Bertrand Aristide won the presidential elections and assumed office in February 2001. In response, the opposition proclaimed its own president, Gérard Gourgue.

Negotiations between the government and the opposition were postponed on several occasions, but in September 2002 both sides finally reached an agreement, mediated by the OAS, to hold new parliamentary and municipal elections in 2003. However, this agreement does not seem to have helped the situation as the stalemate seems only to have led to greater political confrontation. Aristide's term of office was plagued by stiff raises in the price of gasoline together with student and labor unrest, demonstrations, general strikes and attempted *coups d'état*.

1.2 Evolution of Electoral Provisions

Haiti has had three fundamental acts, 22 constitutions, 14 amendments and one accord between 1801 and 1987. Furthermore, 25 Electoral Acts (1834, 1843, 1844, 1849, 1867, 1872, 1888, 1889, 1902, 1916, 1917, 1919, 1927, 1936, 1946, 1949, 1950, 1954, 1957, 1966, 1972, 1987, 1990, 1995, 1999) have been enacted. Originally, the president and the two chambers of parliament (chamber of deputies and senate) were elected. The 1957 Constitution introduced a unicameral system and the chamber of deputies became the only chamber to be elected; the number of its members increased in equal number to that of the former senators.

Until 1950, the president was elected indirectly by parliament. The presidential term of office has varied over the years: four years between 1806 and 1816, 1843 and 1846, 1867 and 1879, 1918 and 1928; five years between 1935 and 1944; six years between 1928 and 1935, 1946 and 1964; seven years between 1879 and 1918, 1944 and 1946; eight years between 1874 and 1879; for life between 1816 and 1843, 1846 and 1867, 1964 and 1986.

The provisions regarding presidential re-election have also changed. Sometimes re-election was permitted (1806–1816, 1972–1964), at other times prohibited (1843–1846, 1874–1918, 1844–1957) or restricted (1867–1874, 1918–1944). From 1867 to 1950, the president was elected indirectly via absolute majority by a joint session of both chambers of parliament. After the introduction of the direct presidential elections, the plurality system was established for the 1950 and 1957 elections.

The chamber of deputies had a two-year term from 1918 to 1932; a three-year term from 1843 to 1846 and 1867 to 1879; a four-year term from 1932 to 1957; a five-year term from 1816 to 1843, from 1846 to 1867 and from 1879 to 1918; and a six-year term in 1957.

As for the senate, the term varied as follows: four years from 1928 to 1932; six years from 1843 to 1846 and from 1867 to 1961; nine years from 1806 to 1843 and 1846 to 1867. Between 1806 and 1928, one third of the senate was renewed every two or three years, for six- or nine-year terms. Between 1928 and 1961 the renewal of the senate was total.

Between 1816 and 1918 the chamber of deputies elected the senate indirectly by a two-round system. From 1918, until the dissolution of the senate in 1961, the senators were directly elected, with the exception of the period 1932 to 1935, when the indirect system was reinstalled. Until 1950, suffrage was limited to men and restricted by certain property and income criteria.

1.3 Current Electoral Provisions

Sources: Constitution of 1987, Electoral Law of 1999, Electoral Acts of 1990 and 1995.

Suffrage: Suffrage is universal, equal, direct, and secret. All citizens over the age of 18 can vote. Voting is not compulsory.

Elected national institutions: The president is directly elected for a five-year term. The deputies are elected for a four-year term and the senators for a six-year term. One third of the senate is renewed every two years. Presidential re-election is permitted once, but not immediately after the first term; parliamentarians can be re-elected indefinitely. A partial renewal of one-third of the senate takes place every two years.

Nomination of candidates
- *presidential elections*: Candidates must be Haitians by birth, over 35 years old, live in Haiti and have never renounced their nationality. Candidates must also own real estate. Independent candidatures are possible.
- *parliamentary elections*: There are no limits for candidatures.

Electoral system
- *presidential elections*: The president is elected via absolute majority. If no candidate receives an absolute majority, a runoff is held between the two candidates with the most votes.
- *parliamentary elections*: Deputies are elected via plurality in SMCs. Senators are elected via absolute majority in MMCs which correspond

to the departments. Each MMC has three seats. Due to the partial renewal of the senate every two years the constituencies are, however, in fact, SMCs. If no candidate receives an absolute majority of votes, a runoff is held between the top two candidates.

Organizational context of elections: In principle, Haiti has an independent electoral authority, the Permanent Electoral Council, as provided for in the constitution. The council should consist of nine members representing different sectors of society. Elected assemblies in the departments would propose candidates. The government, parliament and the judiciary would then appoint three members each. However, the council has not yet been established. Only various provisional commissions have existed.

1.4 Commentary on the Electoral Statistics

Elections in Haiti have almost always been fraudulent and their organization has lacked professionalism. Therefore it is difficult to gather reliable data on Haitian elections.

2. Tables

2.1 Dates of National Elections, Referendums, and Coups d'Etat

Year	Presidential Elections	Parliamentary elections Lower Chamber	Upper Chamber	Elections. for Constit. Assembly	Referen-dums	Coups d'état
1915						28/07
1918					12/06	
1922					xx/xx	
1928					10–11/01	
1930		14/10	14/10			
1932		10/01	10/01			
1935					10/02	
1935					02/06	
1936		06/09	06/09			
1939					23/07	
1940		15/12	15/12			
1946		12/05[a]	12/05[a]	12/05		11/01
1950	08/10	08/10	08/10	08/10		10/05
1955		09/01	09/01			
1956						xx/xx
1957	22/09	22/09	22/09			
1961		30/04	30/04			
1964	14/06	14/06	14/06			
1967		22/01	22/01			
1971					30/01	
1973		11/02	11/02			
1979		xx/02	xx/02			
1983						27/08
1984		12/02	12/02			
1985					22/07	
1986				19/10		07/02
1987	29/11	29/11[b]	29/11[b]		29/03	
1988	17/01	17/01	17/01			19/06
1988						17/09
1990	16/12					10/03
1991		20/01	20/01			
1993		18/01	18/01			
1995	17/12					
1997		04/04	04/04			
2000		21/05 (I)	21/05 (I)			
2000		09/07 (II)	09/07 (II)			
2000	26/11					

[a] Simultaneously elections to the constitutional assembly.
[b] The elections were suspended after violence from paramilitary groups.

2.2 Electoral Body 1918–2000

Year	Type of election[a]	Population[b]	Registered voters Total number	% pop.	Votes cast Total number	% reg. voters	% pop.
1918	Ref	2,040,000	—	—	99,063	—	4.9
1922	Ref	2,040,000	—	—	—	—	—
1928	Ref	2,360,000	—	—	178,419	—	7.6
1930	Pa	2,450,000	—	—	—	—	—
1932	Pa	2,500,000	—	—	—	—	—
1935	Ref	2,610,000	—	—	455,529	—	17.5
1935	Ref	2,610,000	—	—	614,514	—	23.5
1936	Pa	3,000,000	—	—	—	—	—
1939	Pa	3,100,000	—	—	—	—	—
1940	Pa	3,100,000	—	—	—	—	—
1946	CA	3,291,000	—	—	—	—	—
1946	Pa	3,291,000	—	—	—	—	—
1950	CA	3,390,000	—	—	—	—	—
1950	Pr	3,390,000	—	—	527,625	—	15.6
1950	Pa	3,390,000	—	—	—	—	—
1955	Pa	3,305,000	—	—	—	—	—
1957	Pr	3,750,000	—	—	940,445	—	25.1
1957	Pa	3,750,000	—	—	—	—	—
1961	Pa	4,233,000	—	—	—	—	—
1964	Pa	3,850,000	—	—	—	—	—
1964	Ref	3,850,000	—	—	2,803,325	—	72.8
1967	Pa	4,581,000	—	—	—	—	—
1971	Ref	4,310,000	—	—	2,239,917	—	52.0
1973	Pa	5,200,000	—	—	—	—	—
1979	Pa	4,919,000	—	—	—	—	—
1984	Pa	5,185,000	—	—	—	—	—
1985	Ref	5,273,000	—	—	—	—	—
1986	CA	5,358,000	—	—	—	—	—
1987	Ref	5,440,000	—	—	—	—	—
1987	Pr	5,440,000	2,200,806	40.5	—	—	—
1987	Pa	5,440,000	2,200,806	40.5	—	—	—
1988	Pr	5,520,000	—	—	—	—	—
1988	Pa	5,520,000	—	—	—	—	—
1990	Pr	6,486,000	3,271,155	50.4	—	—	—
1991	Pa	6,625,000	—	—	—	—	—
1993	Pa	6,903,000	—	—	—	—	—
1995	Pr	7,180,000	3,578,155	49.8	—	—	—
1997	Pa	7,492,000	—	—	—	—	—
2000	Pa (I)	7,959,000	—	—	—	—	—

Year (cont.)	Type of election[a]	Population[b]	Registered voters Total number	% pop.	Votes cast Total number	% reg. voters	% pop.
2000	Pa (II)	7,959,000	—	—	—	—	—
2000	Pr	7,959,000	—	—	—	—	—

[a] CA = Constitutional Assembly, Pa = Parliamant, Pr = President, Ref = Referendum.
[b] The population data are mid-year estimates taken from various editions of the UN *Statistical Yearbook*, UN *Population and Vital Statistics Report*, *The Statesman's Yearbook*, and other sources.

2.3 Abbreviations

ALAH[a]	*Alliance pour la Libération et l'Avancement d'Haïti* (Alliance for the Liberation and Progress of Haiti)
ANDP	*Alliance Nationale pour la Démocratie et le Progrès* (National Alliance for Democracy and Progress)
APPA	*Afe Peyizan ak Pep Asysyen* (Peasant's and Haitian People's Affairs)
ARH	*Alliance pour la Renaissance Haïti* (Alliance for the Renaissance of Haiti)
BIP[b]	*Bloc Unitaire Patriotique* (United Patriotic Bloc)
CDSH	*Centre Démocratique Social Haïtien* (Haitian Social Democratic Center)
CED[c]	*Comité d'Entente Démocratique* (Democratic Accord Comity)
CFD[d]	*Coalition des Forces Démocratiques* (Coalition of Democratic Forces)
CREDO	(Full name unknown)
ESKANP[e]	*Espas Solidarite Kan Popilè* (Solidarity Space of the People's Camp)
ESPACE[f]	*Espace de Concertacion* (Space of Concertation)
FL	*Fanmi Lavalas* (Lavalas' Family)
FMR	*Force Militaire Révolutionnaire* (Military Revolutionary Force)
FNC[g]	*Front National de Concertation* (National Concertation Front)
FNCD[h]	*Front National pour le Changement et la Démocratie* (National Front for Change and Democracy)
FRONTCIPH[i]	*Front Civico-Politique Haïtien* (Haitian Political-Civilian Front)
FULNH	*Front Unifié de Libération Nationale d'Haïti* (Unified Front for the National Liberation of Haiti)
GIKAP	*Group Initiativ Pou Unité Kan Pep La* (Initiative Group for the Unity of the People's Camp)
GMRN	*Groupement du Mouvement de reconstruction nationale* (Faction of the National Reconstruction Movement)
KLE	*Konbit Liberasyon Ekonomik* (Union for Economic Liberation)
KNDA	*Konbit Nasyonal pou Develpman Ayiti* (National Union for Haitian Development)

KONAKOM	*Congrès National des Forces Démocratiques* (National Congress of Democratic Forces)
KOREGA	*Kowodisyon Resistans Grandans* (Coordination of Resistance of *Grandanse*)
MDN	*Mouvement pour le Développement National* (Movement for National Development)
MIDH	*Mouvement pour l'Instauration de la Démocratie en Haïti* (Movement for the Foundation of Democracy in Haiti)
MKN	*Mouvement cobite nationale* (National *cobite* Movement)
MNP-28[j]	*Mouvement National Patriotique du 28 Novembre* (November 28 National Patriotic Movement)
MOCHRENA	*Mouvement Chrétien pour une Nouvelle Haïti* (Movement Christians for a New Haiti)
MODEJHA	*Mouvement Démocratique de la Jeunesse Haïtienne* (Democratic Movement of the Haitian Youth)
MODELH[k]	*Mouvement Démocratique de Libération d'Haïti* (Democratic Movement for the Liberation of Haiti)
MOP (1)	*Mouvement Ouvrier Paysan* (Worker's and Peasant's Movement)
MOP (2)	*Mouvement pour l'Organisation du Pays* (Movement for the Country's Organization)
MPSN[l]	*Mouvement Patriotique pour le Sauvetage National* (Patriotic National Movement for National Salvation)
MRN	*Mouvement pour la Reconstruction Nationale* (Movement for the National Reconstruction)
MUR	*Mouvement d'Union Révolutionnaire* (Movement of the Revolutionary Union)
OPL[m]	Organisation du Peuple en Lutte (Organization of the Fighting People)
PACAPALHA	*Camp Patriotique de l'Alliance Haïtienne* (Patriotic Camp of the Haitian Alliance)
PADEMH	*Parti Democrate Haïtien* (Haitian Democratic Party)
PADH	*Parti Alternative pour le Développement d'Haïti* (Alternative Party for the Development of Haiti)
PAIN[n]	*Parti Agricole et Industriel National* (Agricultural and Industrial National Party)
PAIPH	(Full name unknown)
PAPP	*Parti des Associations Populaires et Politiques* (Party of Popular and Political Associations)
PANPRA	*Parti Nationaliste Progressiste Révolutionnaire Haïtien* (National Progressive Revolutionary Party)
PARADIS	*Parti Paradis* (Paradise Party)
PARAN	*Parti du Ralliement National* (Party of National Unity)
PCH	*Parti Communiste Haïtien* (Communist Party of Haiti)
PDCH	*Parti Démocrate-Chrétien d'Haïti* (Christian-Democratic Party of Haiti)
PDI	*Parti Démocrate Institutionaliste* (Democratic Institutionalist Party)

PDN-TJS	*Parti Démocratique National Travail Justice Sociale* (National Democratic Party for Work and Social Justice)
PDPJH	*Parti Démocratique Populaire de la Jeunesse Haïtienne* (Popular Democratic Party of the Haitian Youth)
PDRH	*Parti de la Défense et de la Reconstruction d'Haïti* (Party of the Defense and Reconstruction of Haiti)
PENH	*Parti pour l'Evolution National Haïtienne* (Party for the Haitian National Evolution)
PEP	*Parti d'Entente Populaire* (Popular Accord Party)
PITACH	(Full name unkown)
PL	*Parti Libéral* (Liberal Party)
PLB	*Parti Louvri Barye* (Open Gate Party)
PLR-BC	*Parti Liberal Républicain Bloc-Centriste* (Liberal Republican Party Centrist Block)
PMDN	*Parti pour la Mobilisation et le Développement National* (Mobilization and National Development Party)
PN	*Parti National* (National Party)
PNDPH	*Parti National Démocratique Progressiste d'Haïti* (National Progressive Democratic Party of Haiti)
PNH	*Parti Nationaliste Haïtien* (Haitian Nationalist Party)
PNL-APOPEA	*Parti National Libéral* (National Liberal Party)
PNP	*Parti National Progressiste* (National Progressive Party)
PNR	*Party National Republicain* (National Republican Party)
PNT	*Parti National du Travail* (National Labor Party)
PP	*Parti Progressiste* (Progressive Party)
PPH	*Parti des Patriotes Haïtiens* (Party of Haitian Patriots)
PPLN	*Parti Populaire de Libération Nationale* (Popular Party for National Liberation)
PPN°	*Parti Populaire National* (National Popular Party)
PPSC	*Parti Populaire Social Chrétien* (Social Christian Popular Party)
PPVM	*Parti Politique de la Vièrge Marie* (Political Party of the Virgin Maria)
PRD	*Parti de la Réaction Démocratique* (Democratic Reaction Party)
PRDH	*Parti Revolutionnaire Democrate Haïtien* (Haitian Democratic Revolutionary Party)
PRF	*Parti Reformiste Haïtien* (Haitian Reformist Party)
PROP	*Pouvoir Rassemblement des Organisations Populaires* (Power Association of Popular Organizations)
PSCH	*Parti Social-Chrétien d'Haïti* (Social Christian Party)
PSDH	*Parti Social Haïtien* (Haitian Social Party)
PSH	*Parti Socialiste Haïtien* (Socialist Haitian Party)
PSP	*Parti Socialiste Populaire* (Socialist Popular Party)
PSR	*Parti Social Renové* (Renewed Social Party)
PTH	*Parti des Travailleurs Haïtiens* (Haitian Workers' Party)
PUCH	*Parti Unifié Communiste d'Haïti* (Unified Communist Party of Haiti)

PUDH	*Parti Unité Démocratique Haïtienne* (Haitian United Democratic Party)
PUDN	*Union des Démocrates Nationaux* (Union of National Democrats)
PUN	*Parti de l'Unité Nationale* (National Unity Party)
RANFO	*Rassemblement National des Forces Démocratiques* (National Association of Democratic Forces)
RDC	*Rassemblement Démocrate Chrétien* (Christian Democratic Association)
RDF	*Ralliement des Démocrates Fignolistes* (*Fignolistes* Democratic Union)
RDNP	*Rassemblement des Démocrates Nationaux Progressistes* (Association of Nationalist and Progressive Democrats)
RDR	*Rassemblement des Démocrates pour la Republique* (Association of Democrats for the Republic)
RPH	*Rassemblement du Peuple Haïtien (Association of the Haitian People)*
RNFD	*Rassemblement National des Forces Démocratiques* (Association of National Democratic Forces)
UNDF	*Union Nationale de Forces Démocrates* (National Union of Democratic Forces)
UNDH	*Union Nationale des Démocrates Haïtiens* (National Union of Haitian Democrats)
UPAN	*Union des Patriotes pour l'Avancement National* (Union of the Patriots for National Progress)
UPH	*Union Patriotique Haïtien* (Patriotic Haitian Union)
URH	*Union Pour le Renouveau Haïtien* (Union for the Renewal of Haiti)
URN	*Union pour la Reconciliation Nationale* (Union for National Reconciliation)

[a] Small party affiliated to the MPSN.
[b] Coalition composed of MNR-28, PANPRA, and PNDPH for the 1987 elections.
[c] Coalition of four major opposition parties aimed to boycott the 1988 elections.
[d] The coalition was formed in 2000 of *Pouvwa Rasanbleman óganizasyon popilè* (PROP) and former FNCD.
[e] Alliance of KOREGA and the former anti-neoliberal parliamentary block.
[f] Alliance formed in 1999 of *Konfederasyon lnite Demokratik* (KID), Generation 2004, PANPRA, KONAKOM and *Ayiti Kapab*.
[g] Alliance of KONAKOM, BIP, and several other minor parties for the 1988/89 elections.
[h] Originally formed in the late 1980s as an alliance of *Konfederasyon lnite Demokratik* (KID), PNDPH, and KONAKOM. In 2000 it formed an electoral alliance with PROP, called CFD.
[i] Alliance of FRONTCIPH, PDCH, PNT, PAIN, the *Union des Patriotes Démocrates* (UPD), the *Union Patriotique des Démocrates Chrétiens* (UPDC), the mouvement *Kombite National* (MKN, formerly allied to MPSN), and MODELH-PRDH. Formed in 1999.
[j] Allied with MIDH and PANPRA in the 1990s. Not allied with MPSN.
[k] Part of the alliance FRONTCIPH.
[l] Alliance of MDN, MKN, MNP-28, and PDRN.
[m] Part of the alliance PAIN.
[n] Allied with PLB in the *Plateforme Politique Lavalas* in the 1995 elections.
[o] Former *Assemblée Populaire Nationale*.

2.4 Electoral Participation of Parties and Alliances

Data on the electoral participation of parties were not available.

2.5 Referendums

Year	1918[a]		1922	
	Total number	%	Total number	%
Registered voters	—	–	—	–
Votes cast	—	—	—	—
Invalid votes	—	—	—	—
Valid votes	99,063	100.0	—	—
Yes	98,294	99.2	—	—
No	769	0.8	—	—

[a] Plebiscite for the approval of the new constitution.

Year	1928[a]			
	Total number	%	Total number	%
Registered voters	—	–	—	–
Votes cast	—	—	—	—
	Question I		Question II	
Invalid votes	—	—	—	—
Valid votes	181,011	—	180,485	—
Yes	177,642	98.1	176,642	97.9
No	3,369	1.9	3,843	2.1
	Question III		Question IV	
Invalid votes	—	—	—	—
Valid votes	181,930	—	181,657	—
Yes	178,133	97.9	178,370	98.2
No	3,797	2.1	3,287	1.8
	Question V		Question VI	
Invalid votes	—	—	—	—
Valid votes	180,617	—	181,795	—
Yes	177,879	98.5	178,295	98.1
No	2,738	1.5	3,500	1.9
	Question VII		Question VIII	
Invalid votes	—	—	—	—
Valid votes	184,287	—	181,740	—
Yes	181,488	98.5	178,419	98.2
No	2,799	1.5	3,321	1.8

Year (continued)	1928[a]			
	Total number Question IX	%	Total number Question X	%
Invalid votes	—	—	—	—
Valid votes	179,430	—	181,940	—
Yes	175,179	97.6	177,919	97.8
No	4,251	2.4	4,021	2.2
	Question XI		Question XII	
Invalid votes	—	—	—	—
Valid votes	181,606	—	181,690	—
Yes	177,534	97.8	176,683	97.2
No	4,072	2.2	5,007	2.8
	Question XIII			
Invalid votes	—	—		
Valid votes	180,991	—		
Yes	175,613	97.0		
No	5,387	3.0		

[a] Referendum on 13 amendments to the constitution. Each of these amendments was voted separately.

Year	1935[a]		1935[b]	
	Total number	%	Total number	%
Registered voters	—	–	—	–
Votes cast	—	—	—	—
Invalid votes	—	—	—	—
Valid votes	455,529	100.0	614,514	100.0
Yes	454,357	99.7	614,217	100.0
No	1,172	0.3	297	0.0

[a] Referendum on a number of proposals made by the president. The measures should liberate the country from foreign financial control to improve the economic situation.
[b] Referendum on an amendment to the constitution proposed by the constitutional assembly to extend the tenure of President Stenio Vincent.

There is no information available on the referendum held in 1939.

Year	1964[a]		1971[b]	
	Total number	%	Total number	%
Registered voters	—	–	—	–
Votes cast	—	—	—	—
Invalid votes	—	—	—	—
Valid votes	2,803,235	100.0	2,239,917	—
Yes	2,800,000	99.9	2,239,917	100.0
No	3,235	0.1	–	–

[a] Referendum on the question whether the minimum age for becoming president should be lowered to 18 years.
[b] Referendum on a change of the constitution to appoint François Duvalier as president for life.

There is no information available on the referendum held in 1985.

Year	1987[a]	
	Total number	%
Registered voters	—	–
Votes cast	1,261,334	—
Invalid votes	187	0.0
Valid votes	1,261,147	100.0
Yes	1,258,980	99.8
No	2,167	0.2

[a] Referendum on the new constitution.

2.6 Elections for Constitutional Assembly

Constitutional assemblies were elected in 1946, 1950, and 1986. No results were available.

2.7 Parliamentary Elections

Before 1987, elections were autonomously carried out by local authorities on the constituency level. Therefore, no information is available on these results.

2.8 Composition of Parliament

2.8.1 House of Representatives 1957–2000

Year	1957		1961		1964		1967	
	Seats	%	Seats	%	Seats	%	Seats	%
	37	100.0	67	100.0	—	100.0	—	100.0
Duvalierists	35	94.6	–	–	—	—	—	—
Déjoieists	2	5.4	–	–	—	—	—	—
PUN	–	–	67	100.0	—	—	—	—

Year	1973		1979		1984		1988	
	Seats	%	Seats	%	Seats	%	Seats	%
	—	100.0	—	100.0	59	100.0	—	100.0
PUN	—	100.0	—	100.0	59	100.0	—	—

Year	1990 Seats 81	% 100.0	1995 Seats 83	% 100.0	2000[a] Seats 83	% 100.0
FNCD	27	33.3	–	–	–	–
ANDP	17	21.0	–	–	–	–
PDCH	7	8.6	–	–	–	–
PAIN	6	7.4	–	–	–	–
RNDP	6	7.4	–	–	–	–
MDN	5	6.2	–	–	–	–
MKN	5	6.2	–	–	–	–
PNT	3	3.7	–	–	–	–
FL	–	–	67	80.7	–	–
FNCD	–	–	2	2.4	–	–
GMRN	–	–	1	1.2	–	–
KONAKOM	–	–	1	1.2	–	–
PANPRA	–	–	1	1.2	–	–
PROP	–	–	1	1.2	–	–
MKN	–	–	1	1.2	–	–
RCD	–	–	1	1.2	–	–
MOCHRENA	–	–	–	–	3	3.6
PLB	–	–	–	–	2	2.4
ESPACE	–	–	–	–	2	1.2
OPL	–	–	–	–	1	1.2
ESCANP	–	–	–	–	1	1.2
Others	–	–	3	3.6	1	1.2
Independents	5	6.2	5	6.0	73	88.0

[a] The elections of 6 April 1997 were cancelled after violent outbursts.

2.8.2 Senate 1991–2000

Year	1991 Seats 26	% 100.0	1995 Seats 27	% 100.0	2000[a] Seats 19	% 100.0
FNCD	13	50.0	17	63.0	–	–
ANDP	6	23.1	–	–	–	–
MRN	2	7.7	–	–	–	–
PAIN	2	7.7	–	–	–	–
PDCH	1	3.8	–	–	–	–
PNT	1	3.8	–	–	–	–
FL	–	–	–	–	19	100.0
Others	–	–	10	37.0	–	–
Independents	1	3.8	–	–	–	–

[a] Partial renovation only. Two senators were elected in each of the nine constituencies, except in the central department, where three senators were elected due of the death of an incumbent.

2.9 Presidential Elections 1950–2000

1950	Total number	%
Registered voters	—	–
Votes cast	—	—
Invalid votes	—	—
Valid votes	527,625	—
Paul E. Magloire	527,625	100.0

1957	Total number	%
Registered voters	—	–
Votes cast	—	—
Invalid votes	—	—
Valid votes	940,445	—
François Duvalier	680,509	72.4
Louis Déjoie	249,956	26.6
Clement Jumelleb	9,980	1.1

1988	Total number	%
Registered voters	—	–
Votes cast	—	—
Invalid votes	—	—
Valid votes	1,063,537	100.0
Leslie F. Manigat (RDNP)	534,110	50.2
Hubert de Ronceray (MDN)	209,526	19.7
Gérard Philippe Auguste	151,391	14.2
Grégoire Eugène (PSCH)	97,556	9.2
Alphonse Lahèns	34,371	3.2
Michel Lamartinière Honorat	16,550	1.6
Jean L. Théagène	15,113	1.4
Others[a]	4,920	0.5

[a] Others include Hugo Noël: 2,892 votes (0.3%); Arnold J. Dumas: 1,264 (0.1%); Hector Estimé: 471 (0.0%); Dieuveuil Joseph: 149 (0.0%); Lysias C. Verret: 77 (0.0%); Edouard Francisque: 59 (0.0%) and Raphaël E. François: 8 (0.0%).

1990	Total number	%
Registered voters	3,271,155	–
Votes cast	—	—
Invalid votes	—	—
Valid votes	1,640,729	–
Jean Bertrand Aristide (FNCD)	1,107,125	67.5
Marc Louis Bazin (ANOP)	233,277	14.2
Louis Déjoie (PAIN)	80,057	4.9
Hubert de Ronceray (MDN)	54,871	3.3
Sylvio Claude (PDCH)	49,149	3.0
René Théodore (PUCH)	30,064	1.8
Thomas Désulmé (PNT)	27,362	1.7
Volvick Rémy Joseph (MKN)	21,351	1.3
François Latortue (MODELH)	15,060	0.9
Richard Vladimir Jeanty (PARADIS)	12,296	0.8
Fritz Simon (independent)	10,117	0.6

1995	Total number	%
Registered voters	3,578,155	–
Votes cast	994,599	27.8
Invalid votes	—	—
Valid votes	—	—
René Préval (LAVALAS)	818,014	—
Léon Jeune (independent)	23,188	—
Victor Benoît (CONACOM)	21,513	—
Rene Julien	12,960	—
Jean Jacques Clarck Parent	12,842	—
Others[a]	—	—

[a] Others include: Edy Volel, Richard Vladimir Jeanty, Francis Jean, Jean Arnold Dumas, Julio Larosiliere, Dieuveuil Joseph, Gerard Dalvius, Rockefeller Guerre and Fermin Jean-Louis.

2000	Total number	%
Registered voters	—	–
Votes cast	—	—
Invalid votes	—	—
Valid votes	2,871,602	—
Jean Bertrand Aristide (FL)	2,632,534	91.7
Arnold Dumas (indep.)	56,678	2.0
Evan Nicolas (URN)	45,441	1.6
Serge Sylvain (indep.)	37,371	1.3
Calixte Dorisca (indep.)	36,233	1.3
Jacques P. Dorce (indep.)	32,245	1.2
Paul A. Fleurival (indep.)	31,100	1.1

2.10 List of Power Holders 1804–2004

Head of State	Years	Remarks
Jean-Jacques Dessalines	1804–1806	Designated head of state on 01/01/1804. Crowned as emperor on 09/09/1804, killed on 17/10/1806.
Henri Christophe	1807–1820	Elected president on 28/12/1806 by a constitutional assembly. Crowned as King Henri I on 09/03/1811. Ruled over the northern part of the country. Commited suicide on 08/10/1820.
Alexandre Petion	1807–1818	President from 09/03/1807 to 29/03/1818. Re-elected in 1881 and 1815. Ruled over the southern and central part of the country.
Jean-Pierre Boyer	1818–1843	President from 13/03/1818 to 30/03/1843. Reunified the the country. Negotiated official recognition of Haiti by France.
Rivière Herard	1843–1844	President from 31/12/1843 to May 1844.
Philippe Guerrier	1844–1845	President from 03/05/1844 to 15/04/1845. Appointed by the Port-au-Prince bourgeoisie.
Louis Pierrot	1845–1846	President from 16/04/1845 to 01/03/1846.
Jean Philippe Riche	1846–1847	President from 01/03/1846 to 27/02/1847.
Faustin Soulouque	1847–1859	Elected president on 01/03/1847. Crowned as emperor on 20/09/1849. Overthrown by an insurrection on 13/02/1859.
Nicolas E. Geffrard	1859–1867	President from 20/01/1859 to 13/03/1867.
Sylvain Salnave	1867–1869	President from 14/06/1867 to 19/12/1860. Killed in office.
Nissage Saget	1870–1874	President from 11/03/1870 to 12/05/1874.
Michel Domingue	1874–1876	President from 11/06/1874 to 15/04/1876.
Boisrond Canal	1876–1879	President from 17/07/1876 to 17/07/1979.
Lysius Salomon	1879–1888	President from 23/10/1879 to 08/1888.
François Denis Legitime	1888–1889	President from 16/12/1888 to 22/08/1889.
Florvil Hyppolite	1889–1896	President from 09/10/1889 to 24/03/1896.
Tirésias Simon Sam	1896–1902	President from 31/03/1896 to 12/05/1902. Resigned.
Boisrond Canal	1902	Provisional president from 13/05 to 21/12.
Nord Alexis	1902–1908	President from 21/12/1902 to 02/12/1908. Overthrown by a rebellion.
Antoine Simon	1908–1911	President from 17/12/1908 to 02/08/1911. Forced in to exile.
Cincinnatus Leconte	1911–1912	President from 14/08/1911 to 08/08/1912. Died in the explosion of the presidential palace.

394   *Haiti*

Head of State (cont.)	Years	Remarks
Tancrède Auguste	1912–1913	President from 08/08/1912 to 04/05/1913. Died in office.
Michel Oreste	1913–1914	President from 04/05/1913 to 27/01/1914.
Oreste Zamor	1914	President from 08/02/1914 to 29/10/1914.
Davilmar Theodore	1914–1915	President from 11/1914 to 02/1915.
Vilbrun Guillaume Sam	1915	Assumed office on 07/03. He was killed by a mob.
Sudre Dartiguenave	1915–1922	President from 12/08/1915 to 15/05/1922.
Louis Borno	1922–1930	President; elected on 10/04/1922 by the State Council *(Conseil d'État)*. Re-elected on 12/04/1926, resigned on 15/05/1930.
Louis Eugène Roy	1930	Provisional president from 15/05 to 18/11.
Sténio Vincent	1930–1941	President; elected on 18/11/1930 by a national assembly. He was granted a second term through a referendum and resigned on 15/05/1941.
Élie Lescot	1941–1946	President, indirectly elected on 14/04/1941. Obtained a second seven years mandate through a constitutional reform on 19/04/1944, but resigned after popular pressure.
Military Executive Comittee	1946	Formed by Franck Lavaud, Antoine Levelt and Paul E. Magloire. Governed from 11/01/1946 to 16/08/1946.
Dumarsais Estime	1946–1950	President from 16/08/1945 to 10/05/1950. Forced into exile.
Military Government Junta	1950	Formed by Franck Lavaud, Antoine Levelt and Paul E. Magloire. Governed from 10/05/1950 to 06/12/1950.
Paul E. Magloire	1950–1956	President from 06/12/1950 to 06/12/1956.
Joseph Nemours Pierre Louis	1956–1957	President from 12/12/1956 to 03/02/1957. Elected by the national assembly.
Franck Sylvain	1957	Provisional president from 07/02 to 02/04. Elected by the national assembly.
Léon Cantave	1957	Self-proclaimed provisional president from 06/04 to 25/05.
Daniel Fignole	1957	Provisional president from 25/05/1957–14/06/1957.
Antonio T. Kebreau	1957	Provisional president from 14/06 to 22/10.
François Duvalier	1957–1971	Elected president; assumed office on 22/10/1957. Declared himself president for life in 1964. Transferred power to his son in 1971.
Jean-Claude Duvalier	1971–1986	President from 22/04/1971 until he was exiled on 07/02/1986.
Henry Namphy	1986–1988	Provisional president from 07/02/1986 to 07/02/1988.

Head of State (cont.)	Years	Remarks
Leslie Manigat	1988	President from 07/02 until he was forced into exile by a *coup d'état* on 19/06.
Henry Namphy	1988	Provisional president from 19/06 until he was deposed by a *coup d'état* on 17/09.
Prosper Avril	1988–1990	Provisional president from 17/09/1988 to 10/03/1990.
Hérard Abraham	1990	Provisional president from 10/03 to 13/03.
Ertha Pascal Trouillot	1990–1991	Provisional president from 13/03/1990 to 07/02/1991.
Jean-Bertrand Aristide	1991	President from 07/02 to 30/09. Deposed by a *coup d'état* and forced into exile.
Emmanuel Negrette	1991–1992	President from 08/10/1991 to 17/06/1992.
Marc Bazin	1991–1992	Prime Minister. There was no president during his time in office.
Emile Jonassaint	1994	President from 11/05/1994 to September 1994.
Robert Malval	1994	Interim prime minister.
Jean-Bertrand Aristide	1994–1996	Returned to Haiti after the US military intervention and terminated his tenure, which ended on 07/02/1996.
René Préval	1996–2001	President from 07/02/1996 to 06/02/2001.
Jean-Bertrand Aristide	2001–2004	Assumed office for the fourth time on 07/02/2001, although there were charges of fraud. A major rebellion in 2004 forced him to resign and go into exile again.
Boniface Alexandre	2004–	Provisional president since 29/02/2004. As Chief Justice of the Supreme Court he was next in the presidential line of succession.

3. Bibliography

3.1 Official Sources

'Amendements à la Constitution adoptés par le pouvoir législatif et devant etre soumis à la ratification populaire 10 janvier 1928', in *Bulletin de lois et actes 1928*. Port-au-Prince: Imprimerie Nationale, 4–7.

Bulletin des lois et actes, années 1916–1932. Port-au-Prince: Imprimerie Nationale.

Bulletin des décrets et actes du Comité Exécutif Militaire, 11 janvier 1946– 16 août 1946. Port-au-Prince: Imprimerie de l'État.

Bulletin des lois et actes (1941–1945). (Various volumes). Port-au-Prince: Imprimerie de l'État.

(2001). *La Constitution de 1801*. Collection Patrimoire.

Constitution de 1888. Port-au-Prince.

Constitution de la République d'Haïti de 1889. Port-au-Prince.

Constitution de 1918 de la République d'Haïti. Amendée par le plébiscite des 10 et 11 janvier 1928. Port-au-Prince: Imprimerie du Service Technique.

Constitution de la République d'Haïti 1932. Port-au-Prince: Imprimerie Nationale.

'Constitution du 15 juillet 1932', in *Bulletin des lois et actes 1932*. Port-au-Prince: Imprimerie Nationale, 141–163.

'Constitution de la République d'Haïti, ratifiée par le plébiscite du 2 juin 1935', in *Bulletin des lois et actes 1935*. Port-au-Prince: Imprimerie Nationale, 233–247.

'Constitution de la République d'Haïti ratifiée par le plébiscite du 2 juin 1935, révisée par le referendum populaire du 23 juillet 1939, et amendée par l'Assemblée Nationale le 19 avril 1944', in *Bulletin des lois et actes 5 septembre 1943 – 15 septembre 1944*. Port-au-Prince: Imprimerie de l'État, 493–508.

'Constitution de la République d'Haïti de 1932 remise en vigueur avec modification, par le décret de l'Assemblée Nationale Constituante en date du 12 août 1946', in *Bulletin des lois et actes 1946*. Port-au-Prince: Imprimerie de l'État, 49–74.

Constitution de la République d'Haïti du 22 novembre 1946. Port-au-Prince: Imprimerie de l'État.

'Constitution du 25 novembre 1950'. *Le Moniteur* 137/105.

Constitution du 19 décembre 1957. Port-au-Prince: Henri Deschamps.

'Constitution 1987'. *Le Moniteur* 28/04/1987: 561–609.

Décret du Comité Exécutif Militaire du 12 février 1946, modifiant la loi électorale de 1930. Port-au-Prince.

Décret du 3 août 1950, convoquant les assemblées primaires et décret électoral du 4 août 1950. Port-au-Prince.

Décret électorale du 1er mars 1957, suivie du décret modificatif de 12 mars 1957. Port-au-Prince: Imprimerie de l'État.

Décret électoral du 28 août 1957. Port-au-Prince: Imprimerie de l'État.

Décret électoral du 22 octobre 1966. Port-au-Prince: Presses Nationales d'Haïti.

Décret électoral du 27 novembre 1972. Port-au-Prince: Presses Nationales d'Haïti.

Décret-loi du 15 juillet 1936, modifiant la loi électorale du 4 juillet 1930. Port-au-Prince: Imprimerie de l'État.

'Décret-loi du 15 juillet 1936, modifiant la loi électorale du 4 juillet 1930', in *Bulletin des lois et actes 1936.* Port-au-Prince: Imprimerie de l'État, 296–314.

Décret réglementant le mode des élections pour le 15 janvier 1917 etc (1916). Port-au-Prince.

Janvier, L. J. (1886). *Les Constitutions d'Haïti (1801–1885).* Paris: Marpon & Flammarion.

Las Constituciones de Haití. Madrid: Cultura Hispánica.

Loi du 28 mars 1996 portant organisation de la collectivité territoriale de section communale

'Loi électorale du 4 août 1919', in *Bulletin des lois et actes 1919.* Port-au-Prince: Imprimerie Nationale, 251–265.

'Loi électorale du 29 septembre 1927, modifiant les articles 18, 25, 51 et 62 de la loi électorale du 4 août 1919', in *Bulletin des lois et actes 1927.* Port-au-Prince: Imprimerie Nationale, 227–229.

'Loi électorale du 7 septembre 1949', in *Bulletin des lois et actes 1949.* Port-au-Prince: Imprimerie de l'État, 563–581.

Loi électorale du 21 juillet 1954, suivie de la Loi modificative du 8 octobre 1954. Port-au-Prince: Imprimerie de l'État.

Loi Electorale 18 septembre 1978, sur délimitations territoriales.

Loi électorale du 29 juillet 1987. Port-au-Prince: Conseil Electoral Provisoire.

Loi électorale du 16 décembre 1987. Port-au-Prince.

'Loi Electorale du 20 août 1987'. *Le Moniteur.*

Loi Electorale du 9 juillet 1990.

Loi Electorale du 14 février 1995.

'Loi Electorale 22 juillet 1999'. *Le Moniteur.*

Nau, M. and Telhomme, N. (eds.) (1930). *Législation électorale. Recueil contenant les lois et actes relatifs aux assemblées électorales 1817–1930.* Port-au-Prince: Nemours Telhomme.

Projet de Constitution de la République d'Haïti, soumis à la ratification populaire 1935. Port-au-Prince: Imprimerie de l'État.

'Révision partielle de la Constitution de 1983, le 6 juin 1985. Articles Amendés' (1985). *Le Petit Samedi Soir* 14/598: 163–166.

3.2 Books, Articles, and Electoral Reports

Agence Haïtienne de Presse (2001). *Haïti 2000 au Quotidien.* Port-au-Prince: AHP.

Comité de Presse pour l'Action Civique (2001). *Haïti. Les Elections de l'An 2000.* Port-au-Prince.

De Cauna, J. (1997). *Haïti. L'Eternelle Révolution.* Port-au-Prince: Henri Deschamps.

Edie, C. J. (ed.) (1994). *Democracy in the Caribbean. Myths and Realities.* London: Praeger.

Gallé, F. (1992). 'Haiti', in D. Nohlen (ed.), *Handbuch der Wahldaten Lateinamerikas und der Karibik.* Opladen: Leske + Budrich, 401–421.

James, C. L. R. (1989). *The Black Jacobins. Toussaint l'Overture and the San Domingo Revolution* (2nd edn.). New York: Vintage Books.

Jean, J.-C. and Maesschalk, M. (1999). *Transition Politique en Haïti. Radiographie du pouvoir Lavalas.* Paris: L'Harmattan.

— (2000). 'Jonction Bulletin d'Information d'Initiatives Démocratiques'. *Numéro Spécial* 2/1.

Ledan Fils, J. (1996). *A propos de l'Histoire d'Haïti. Saviez-vous que....* (Various volumes). Port-au-Prince: Henri Deschamps.

Madiou, T. (1988). Histoire d'Haïti. (various volumes). Port-au-Prince.

Manigat, L. (2002). *Eventail d'Histoire Vivante d'Haïti. Un prélude à la Révolution de Saint Domingue jusqu'a nos jours (1789–1999).* Port au Prince: CHUDAC.

Manigat, M. (2000). *Traité de Droit Constitutionnel Haïtien.* (Two volumes.) Port-au-Prince: Université Quisqueya.

Moise, C. (1997). *Constitutions et luttes de pouvoir en Haïti.* Port-au-Prince: CIDHCA.

Nelson, S. (1998). 'Haitian Elections and the Aftermath', in K. Kumar (ed.), *Postconflict elections, Democratization and International Assistance.* Boulder, Colo.: Lynne Riener.

Oriol, M. (2002). *Histoire et Dictionnaire de la révolution et de l'indépendance d'Haïti.* Port-au-Prince: Fondation pour la Recherche Iconographique et Documentaire.

— (2002). *Histoire et Education Civique.* Port-au-Prince: Fondation pour la Recherche Iconographique et Documentaire.

Trouillot, M.-R. (1990). 'Haiti, State Against Nation. Origins and Legacy of Duvalierism'. *Monthly Review Press.*

HONDURAS

by Alexander Somoza[*]

1. Introduction

1.1 Historical Overview

After briefly being independent from Spanish colonial rule up to 1821, Honduras then became part of the Mexican Empire (1821–1823) before joining the Central American Federation in 1824. In 1838, the country left the Federation and declared independence again, by enacting its own constitution in 1839. For decades afterwards, Honduras' political history was characterized by numerous border clashes, frequent and often violent changes of government, military dictatorships, and, mainly in the first half of the 20th century, US-American military and economic intervention. However, since 1980 the country has managed to achieve a considerable degree of political stability, with constitutional governments and regular changes of power. In addition to the military domination, political life has also been dominated by two major parties in the 20th century: the *Partido Liberal* (PL; Liberal Party) and the *Partido Nacional* (PN; National Party).

The 1839 Constitution established a presidential form of government. Except for the period between 1848 and 1865, when parliament was bicameral, the legislature has always consisted of a unicameral national congress (*Congreso Nacional*). The constitution of 1924 briefly enabled parliament to designate ministers by a vote of censure. However, this right was abolished in 1936.

Despite, or maybe as a consequence of, the numerous constitutions between 1839 and the mid-20th century, Honduras' political reality was dominated by de facto powers and developed contrary to the constitutions. Between 1838 and 1878, politics was characterized by commonly violent personal conflicts between various regional leaders *(caudillos)*. Electoral processes remained noticeably irregular during this period, and

---

[*] Parts of this contribution are based on an article previously published by Petra Bendel. The author wishes to thank her.

it was not until the years 1876 to 1878 that several reform measures were finally implemented. They came to be known as the 'Liberal Reform' and were promoted by Marco Aurelio Soto. These measures were devised to curtail the traditional oligarchic dominance formed by the landholders, the clergy, and the military. In particular, the separation of the State and the Church, established in the 1879 Constitution, was now actually implemented.

It was in this context that two political forces started to emerge, namely, the reforming Liberals and the Conservatives. Both groups founded political parties: The *Partido Liberal*, formed in 1891, and the *Partido Nacional*, which only became a formal party in 1923.

Political evolution in the 20th century was largely linked to the country's economic development. In 1899, foreign capital was allowed to enter the country, which led to major US-American banana companies (i.e. United Fruit Company, Cayamel Fruit Company) developing extensive economic activities in Honduras. Due to the significant concessions received by the Honduran government, these companies grew and built up the country's infrastructure and labor force. Yet in doing so, they created a typical *enclave* economy that based all investments on producing, processing, and marketing bananas. The fruit companies had tremendous influence over the political decision-making process, an effect that increased due to the absence and/or weakness of the national oligarchy and the population's exclusion from political and economic participation. Likewise, the conflicts between the parties and their internal divisions were affected by the interests of the fruit companies. Whereas the United Fruit Company allied with the National Party, the Cayamel Fruit Company allied with the Liberal Party.

The political instability of the country, expressed in the violent alternation of power and internal division of parties, led to frequent civil wars during the 1910s and 1920s. Only the elections of 1924, 1928, and 1932 can be considered as having been relatively fair. During these years, the military of the United States intervened on several occasions, with the objective of protecting the economic interests and the properties of US companies. Only when the Cayamel Fruit Company was bought by the United Fruit Company in 1929 did the conflict between the companies end and the Liberal Party started to loose ground to the National Party. This new dominance was represented by the presidency of Tiburcio Carías Andino between 1933 and 1949, whose rule gradually became a dictatorship from 1936 on. Backed by the military, he managed to prolong his presidency by implementing numerous constitutional reforms.

As the military became more and more professional during the 1940s, they reinforced their role as 'independent arbiters' of national politics and started to intervene frequently in the country's political development and to overthrow civil governments. Attempts to liberalize politics and to pave the way for the emergence of new political parties, under the presidency of Juan Manuel Gálvez (1949–1954), and the attempt to implement agrarian reforms, under the presidency of José Ramón Villeda Morales (1957–1963), were all interrupted by military coups. By the mid-1960s the military had become the most important political factor, thus marginalizing political parties. This was the beginning of a period marked by various military governments and it lasted until 1982. During this authoritarian, military-controlled period elections were suspended and political parties lost their relevance. The only exception to the military rule during this time was the short-lived civil government between 1971 and 1972.

The worsening of the economic situation, and the internal pressure from the employers' groups and political parties, together with the mobilization of guerrilla groups forced the military into a process of transition. In 1980, elections to a constituent assembly were held, followed by presidential and parliamentary elections in 1981. The old political parties re-emerged, with the PL and PN becoming the strongest political forces in the elections. The promulgation of a new constitution in 1985 completed the transition to democracy. However, the constant military presence and the continuing violations of human rights cast a shadow over the process of democratization. These violations only ended once the Central American conflict was solved and the region became generally pacified in the late 1980s. Since then, the political development has been characterized by relatively fair elections and constitutional governments. In 1990, for the first time in Honduran history, power was transferred peacefully from the Liberal Party to the National Party. Alternations in power were repeated in 1994 and 2002. Although new parties were founded during the transition process of the 1980s, the classic Honduran two-party system remains relatively unchallenged.

1.2 Evolution of Electoral Provisions

Since independence in 1838, elections in Honduras have been held under twelve different constitutions (1839, 1848, 1865, 1873, 1880, 1894, 1906, 1924, 1936, 1957, 1965, and 1982) and the corresponding electoral laws. The laws of 1895, 1906, 1936, 1957, 1960, 1966, 1977, and 1981 are the most important. The 1894 Constitution introduced equal, secret, and direct suffrage, although it was limited to the male population. Suffrage became universal when women gained the right to vote in 1954. Voting has always been compulsory for the male population, whereas for the female population it only became compulsory in 1981. Voting age alternated between 18 and 21 years, finally becoming 18 years in 1981. Those active in military service have been disenfranchised since 1895. Regulations for external voting had already been laid down in the 1981 Electoral Law, but were only put into practice in 2001.

Honduras has always had a unicameral parliament with the exception of the period from 1848 to 1865, when a two-chamber parliament existed. Elections have been held since independence in 1839, although they were rather irregular during the 19th century. The terms of office varied in accordance with the different constitutions: from 1839 to 1848 the term was two years, from 1848 to 1936 it was four years without re-election of the president, from 1936 to 1965 six years, and since 1965 four years, again, without presidential re-election. Parliamentary size was fixed at 128 seats in 1988 (first applied in 1989). Before 1988 it had depended on the size of the population. The 1839 Constitution specified one seat for every 20,000 inhabitants, which was changed in 1849 to one seat for every 15,000; in 1865 to one seat for every 10,000; in 1924 to one seat for every 15,000; in 1936 to one seat for every 25,000; in 1957 to one seat for every 30,000; and in 1977 to one seat for every 40,000. Unfortunately, it is no longer possible, to establish the exact total size of all parliaments. Presidential and parliamentary elections have traditionally been held on the same day. Until 1989, both institutions were simultaneously elected on one ballot paper with a single vote. Since 1993, president and parliament are elected with different votes on the same ballot paper.

The 1966 Electoral Law stipulated that parties could only participate in the elections if they had been registered. To do so, they had to prove a minimum of 15,000 members. This figure was lowered to 10,000 in 1977 (for the 1980 elections), raised to 30,000 in 1981, and lowered to 20,000 in 1986. Since 1997, any party that wins less than 10,000 votes in an election looses its official party status. Independent candidature was introduced for the 1980 elections; candidates required the signatures of 1% (2% since 1986) of the registered voters in his or her respective constituency to be able to stand for election.

Until 1966, the president was elected by absolute majority. If no candidate reached 50% of the valid votes, congress chose the president from the two (sometimes the three) best-placed candidates. Since 1966, the system of plurality has been applied. The Electoral Law was changed temporarily for the 1985 elections, and stipulated that general and internal party elections were to be held simultaneously. Every internal group of a party could, therefore, present its own candidate for the presidency. The best-placed candidate from the party with the highest number of votes was elected president. In the following elections this system was abandoned.

Until 1957, parliamentary elections had to be won by an absolute majority in single-member constituencies with no run off. If no candidate achieved the required 50%, the Electoral Commission (*Junta Electoral*) had to decide between the two best-placed candidates. The 1957 Electoral Law introduced a system of proportional representation in single-member, two-member, and multi-member constituencies using the Hare quota and highest remainder. Between 1936 and 1957 an additional system of minority representation was applied: ten additional seats were distributed among those candidates who had achieved at least 1,300 valid votes but had not won their respective constituency. The Electoral Law of 1977 set up the *Tribunal Nacional de Elecciones* (National Election Court) as an independent body to organize and supervise all elections.

1.3 Current Electoral Provisions

Sources: Constitution of the Republic of Honduras (1982) with an amendment concerning the 1999 elections; Electoral Law (*Ley Electoral y de las Organizaciones Políticas*, 1981) with amendments in 1982, 1984, 1986, 1989, 1991, and 1992; Special Law for the Voting Rights of Hondurans Living Abroad (*Ley Especial para el Ejercicio del Sufragio de los Hondureños en el Exterior*, 2001).

Suffrage: The principles of universal, equal, secret, and direct suffrage are applied. Every Honduran citizen who has reached the age of 18 is entitled to vote. Voting is compulsory. If citizens do not vote, they are fined 20 *Lempiras*. Voting rights are suspended for people serving a prison sentence, the armed forces, and the police. Hondurans living abroad only have the right to vote for the presidential elections. Before each election, the *Tribunal Nacional de Elecciones* (TNE; National Election Court) determines the Honduran consulates in which external voting is possible. For the 2001 elections the consulates in the US-American cities of New Orleans, Miami, Washington, New York, and Los Angeles were designated polling stations. These consulates were also responsible for updating the voter registration of Hondurans living within their jurisdiction. This meant that Hondurans living within the jurisdiction of other consulates were not entitled to an external vote.

Elected national institutions: The president and the unicameral 128-seat national congress are both directly elected for a regular term of four years. Re-election of the president is not allowed. The elections to president and the national congress are held on the same day and on a single ballot paper, but with separate votes. Regular voting day is the last Sunday in November.

Nomination of candidates
- *presidential elections*: In order to be eligible for presidency, candidates must by Honduran citizens by birth, at least 30 years old, and in possession of their full civil rights. High-ranking public officials, active military personnel, representatives of state-concessionary firms and close relatives of these groups are not allowed to run for presidency. Candidates may either run on a party ticket or as independents. An independent candidate must show the support of 2% of the registered voters nationwide.
- *parliamentary elections*: Candidates running for parliament must be Honduran by birth, at least 21 years of age, and in possession of their full civil rights. They must be born in the constituency for which they want to stand or have resided there for the last five years preceding the election. Exclusion from voting is similar to those excluded from voting in the presidential elections. In addition, the current president and the judges of the supreme court are not allowed to run for the national congress. Candidates can stand for a party or as an independent candidate. Independent candidates need the signatures of at least 2% of the registered voters in the constituency they wish to run for.

Only registered parties may compete in the elections. In order to be registered by the TNE, parties need to present a political action program, a basic organizational structure, and the signatures of at least 20,000 registered voters. No party can be registered within the six months prior to the elections. If a party gains less than 10,000 valid votes in a nation-wide election its registration is cancelled by the TNE.

Electoral system
- *presidential elections*: Plurality system.
- *parliamentary elections*: Plurality system in two SMCs and proportional representation in 16 MMCs from closed and blocked party lists, ranging in size from 2 to 23 seats (six constituencies with two to five seats; eight constituencies with six to ten seats, one constituency with 20 seats and one constituency with 23 seats; average size 7.9). The constituencies correspond to the country's departments; their magnitude depends on a population criterion. Seats are allocated at constituency level according to the Hare quota and the largest remainder.

Organizational context of elections: The *Tribunal Nacional de Elecciones* (TNE) is responsible for organizing, holding, and supervising the elections. Members are appointed to the TNE by the supreme court, which can appoint one member, and the political parties (each registered party can appoint one member) for a four-year term. If the total number of members is even, the president of the Republic assigns an additional member, in order to reach an odd number. The presidency of the TNE changes on a yearly rotary basis among its members. The TNE is an independent and autonomous body with an own jurisdiction. It has the initiative on all electoral law material. The TNE sets up a special body (*Registro Nacional de la Personas*) that continuously updates voter registration.

In order to organize the elections, the TNE establishes regional (*Tribulanes Departamentales de Elecciones*) and local (*Tribunales Locales de Elecciones*) electoral courts and nominates the members according to propositions of the registered parties. Each registered party is entitled to have one representative in every court. The local electoral courts set up the polling stations, with one polling station for 300 registered voters.

1.4 Commentary on the Electoral Statistics

Official electoral data from 1980 onwards can easily be accessed through TNE's website (http://www.tne.hn). However, it was difficult to find official sources for the elections before this date, and any data that existed were often incomplete and inconsistent. Secondary sources often contained contradictory data. This is especially true of parliamentary elections and the elections before 1956. Where sources differed, the author tried to rely on official sources or on secondary sources that were based on official data.

The population data are mid-year estimates taken from the UN *Statistical Yearbooks* and *Population and Vital Statistic Reports*, as well as *The Statesman's Yearbooks*.

2. Tables

2.1 Dates of National Elections, Referendums, and Coups d'Etat

Year	Presidential elections	Parliamentary elections	Elections for Constitutional Assembly	Referendums	Coups d'état
1902	xx/10	xx/10			
1907					25/03
1911	29–31/10				
1916	xx/10				
1919	26–28/10				
1923	27–29/10				
1924	28–30/12				31/07
1928	28/10				
1932	28/10				
1936			xx/01		08/03
1948	10/10	10/10			
1954	10/10	10/10			
1956			07/10		21/10
1957			22/09		22/09
1963					03/10
1965			12/02		
1971	28/03	28/03			
1972					04/12
1975					23/04
1978					07/08
1980			20/04		
1981	29/11	29/11			
1985	24/11	24/11			
1989	26/11	26/11			
1993	27/11	27/11			
1997	30/11	30/11			
2001	25/11	25/11			

2.2 Electoral Body 1902–2001

Year	Type of election[a]	Population	Registered voters Total number	% pop.	Votes cast Total number	% reg. voters	% pop.
1902	Pr/Pa	380,000	—	—	58,653	—	15.4
1911	Pr	560,000	—	—	—	—	—
1916	Pr	606,000	—	—	77,832[b]	—	12.8
1919	Pr	630,000	—	—	97,650[b]	—	15.5
1923	Pr	773,000	—	—	105,125[b]	—	13.6
1924	Pr	785,000	—	—	—	—	—
1928	Pr	846,000	—	—	110,064[b]	—	13.0
1932	Pr	958,000	—	—	—	—	—
1936	CA	1,030,000	—	—	134,994[b]	—	13.1
1948	Pr/Pa	1,326,000	300,496	22.7	258,345	86.0	19.5
1954	Pr/Pa	1,608,000	411,354	25.6	252,624	61.4	15.7
1956	CA	1,711,000	—	—	512,694	—	30.0
1957	CA	1,769,000	522,359	29.5	331,660[b]	63.5	18.7
1965	CA	2,284,000	815,261	35.7	613,888	75.3	26.9
1971	Pr/Pa	2,635,000	900,658	34.2	608,342	67.5	23.1
1980	CA	3,691,000	1,233,756	33.4	1,003,470	81.3	27.2
1981	Pr/Pa	3,821,000	1,546,797	40.5	1,214,779	78.5	31.8
1985	Pr/Pa	4,372,000	1,901,757	43.5	1,598,247	84.0	36.6
1989	Pr/Pa	4,951,000	2,363,448	47.7	1,799,146	76.1	36.3
1993	Pr/Pa	5,595,000	2,734,116	48.9	1,771,825	64.8	31.7
1997	Pr	6,338,000	2,883,919	45.5	2,096,646	72.7	33.1
1997	Pa	6,338,000	2,883,919	45.5	2,062,379	71.5	32.5
2001	Pr	6,577,000	3,448,280	52.4	2,285,067	66.3	34.7
2001	Pa	6,577,000	3,437,454	52.3	2,279,366	66.3	34.7

[a] Pr = President, Pa = Parliament, CA = Constitutional Assembly.
[b] Figures refer to valid votes. The total number of registered voters was not available.

2.3 Abbreviations

FPH	*Frente Patriotico Hondurño* (Honduran Patriotic Front)
MNR	*Movimiento Nacional Reformista* (National Reformist Movement)
PASO	*Partido Socialista de Honduras* (Socialist Party of Honduras)
PCH	*Partido Comunista de Honduras* (Communist Party of Honduras)
PCH-ML	*Partido Comunista de Honduras–Marxista-Leninista* (Communist Party of Honduras–Marxist-Leninist)
PDC	*Partido Demócrata Cristiano de Honduras* (Christian Democratic Party of Honduras)
PINU-SD	*Partido de Innovación y Unidad–Social Demócrata* (Party of Innovation and Unity–Social Democratic)
PL	*Partido Liberal de Honduras* (Liberal Party of Honduras)
PLC	*Partido Liberal Constitucionalista* (Constitutionalist Liberal Party)
PN	*Partido Nacional de Honduras* (National Party of Honduras)
PND	*Partido Nacional Democrático* (Democratic National Party)
PUD	*Partido Unificación Democrática* (Democratic Unification Party)
PUN[a]	*Partido de Unidad Nacional* (Party of National Unity)

[a] Appears in some sources as *Coalición Unión Nacional* (National Unity Coalition); in others as *Instituto Cívico de la Unión Nacional* (Civic Institution of National Unity, ICUN).

2.4 Electoral Participation of Parties and Alliances 1902–2001

Party / Alliance	Years	Elections contested[a]	
		Presidential	Parliamentary
Club Unión Patriótico	1902	1	1
La Democracia	1902	1	1
PL	1902, 1919–1923, 1928–2001	14	15
Nacionalista	1916	1	0
PND	1919	1	0
PLC	1923	1	0
PN	1923–2001	13	14
Bloque de Obreros y Campesinos	1932	1	0
MNR	1954, 1957	1	2
PUN	1956	0	1
PINU-SD	1980–2001	6	7
PDC	1981–2001	6	6
PUD	1997–2001	2	2

[a] Total number of presidential elections: 17; total number of parliamentary elections (including CA elections): 15.

2.5 Referendums

Referendums have not been held.

2.6 Elections for Constitutional Assembly

1936	Total number	%	Seats	%
Registered voters	—	–		
Votes cast	—	—		
Invalid votes	—	—		
Valid votes	134,994	—		
			—	—
PN	132,948	100.0	—	—
PL	46	0.0	—	—

1956[a]	Total number	%	Seats	%
Registered voters	—	–		
Votes cast	512,694	—		
Invalid votes	—	—		
Valid votes	414,045	80.8		
			58	100.0
PUN	370,318	89.4	58	100.0
PL	41,724	10.1	0	0.0
PN	2,003	0.5	0	0.0

[a] During Lozano Díaz's dictatorship elections were extremely fraudulent. Lozano broke with both PL and PN and founded his own party, PUN. The PL abstained, and its leader, Villeda Morales, was exiled.

1957	Total number	%	Seats	%
Registered voters	522,359	–		
Votes cast	—	—		
Invalid votes	—	—		
Valid votes	331,660	—		
			58	100.0
PL	205,135	61.9	36	62.1
PN	98,088	29.6	18	31.0
MNR	28,437	8.6	4	6.9

1965	Total number	%	Seats	%
Registered voters	815,261	–		
Votes cast	613,888	75.3		
Blank votes	4,644	0.8		
Invalid votes	2,400	0.4		
Valid votes	606,844	98.9		
			64	100.0
PN	334,646	55.1	35	54.7
PL	272,198	44.9	29	45.3

1980[a]	Total number	%	Seats	%
Registered voters	1,233,756	–		
Votes cast	1,003,470	81.3		
Blank votes	19,847	2.0		
Invalid votes	24,221	2.4		
Valid votes	959,402	95.6		
			71	100.0
PL	495,779	51.7	35	49.3
PN	423,623	44.2	33	46.5
PINU-SD	35,052	3.7	3	4.2
Independents	4,948[b]	0.5	0	0.0

[a] The PDC and other leftist parties were excluded from the elections. On 20 February, PDC, PCH, PCH–ML, PASO and 40 social organizations joined forces under the label FPH and called for electoral abstention.
[b] Three independent candidates ran in the department of Cortés, gaining 2,214 (0.2%), 2,076 (0.2%), and 658 (0.1%) votes, respectively.

2.7 Parliamentary Elections 1971–2001

Year	1971		1981	
	Total number	%	Total number	%
Registered voters	900,658	–	1,546,797	–
Votes cast	608,342	67.5	1,214,779	78.5
Blank votes	—	—	17,430	1.4
Invalid votes	—	—	17,244	1.4
Valid votes	569,796	93.7	1,180,105	97.1
PN	299,807	52.6	491,089	41.6
PL	269,989	47.4	636,437	53.9
PINU-SD	–	–	29,419	2.5
PDC	–	–	19,163	1.6
Independents	–	–	3,997[a]	0.3

[a] Three independent candidates ran: Delgado Pérez (Department of Cortés): 2,572 votes; Mayorga Madrid (Department of Yoro): 911 votes; López López (Department of Copán): 514 votes.

412   *Honduras*

Year	1985		1989	
	Total number	%	Total number	%
Registered voters	1,901,757	–	2,363,448	–
Votes cast	1,598,247	84.0	1,799,146	76.1
Blank votes	28,247	1.8	18,483	1.0
Invalid votes	27,713	1.7	27,107	1.5
Valid votes	1,542,287	96.5	1,753,556	97.5
PL	786,771	51.0	776,983	44.3
PN	701,492	45.5	917,168	52.3
PDC	30,303	2.0	25,453	1.5
PINU-SD	23,721	1.5	33,952	1.9

Year	1993		1997	
	Total number	%	Total number	%
Registered voters	2,734,116	–	2,883,919	–
Votes cast	1,771,825	64.8	2,062,379	71.5
Blank votes	17,907	1.0	99,810	4.8
Invalid votes	43,181	2.4	64,176	3.1
Valid votes	1,710,737	96.6	1,898,393	92.0
PL	906,793	53.0	940,575	49.5
PN	735,123	43.0	789,015	41.6
PINU-SD	48,471	2.8	78,495	4.1
PDC	20,350	1.2	49,650	2.6
PUD	–	–	40,658	2.1

Year	2001	
	Total number	%
Registered voters	3,437,454	–
Votes cast	2,279,366	66.3
Blank votes	132,065	5.8
Invalid votes	64,515	2.8
Valid votes	2,082,786	91.4
PN	967,733	46.5
PL	850,290	40.8
PINU-SD	95,059	4.6
PUD	92,818	4.5
PDC	76,886	3.7

2.8 Composition of Parliament 1971–2001

Year	1971[a]		1981		1985		1989	
	Seats	%	Seats	%	Seats	%	Seats	%
	64	100.0	82	100.0	134	100.0	128	100.0
PL	32	50.0	44	53.7	67	50.0	56	43.8
PN	32	50.0	34	41.5	63	47.0	71	55.5
PINU-SD	–	–	3	3.7	2	1.5	0	0.0
PDC	–	–	1	1.2	2	1.5	1	0.8

[a] Following a political agreement between the PN and the PL on 17 January 1971, the seats were allocated equally to both parties, disregarding the electoral results.

Year	1993		1997		2001	
	Seats	%	Seats	%	Seats	%
	128	100.0	133	100.0	128	100.0
PL	71	55.5	72	54.1	55	43.0
PN	55	43.0	55	41.4	61	47.7
PDC	0	0.0	2	1.5	4	3.1
PINU-SD	2	1.6	3	2.3	3	2.3
PUD	–	–	1	0.8	5	3.9

2.9 Presidential Elections 1902–2001

1902[a]	Total number	%
Registered voters	—	–
Votes cast	58,653	—
Invalid votes	64	0.1
Valid votes	58,589[b]	99.9
Manuel Bonilla (La Democracia)	28,550	48.7
Juan Angel Arias (PL)	25,118	42.9
Mario Aurelio Soto (Club Unión Patriótica)	4,857	8.3
Others	14	0.0

[a] Official data, probably fraudulent.
[b] The votes sum up to 58,539.

1916	Total number	%
Registered voters	—	–
Votes cast	—	—
Invalid votes	—	—
Valid votes	77,832	—
Francisco Bertrand Barahona (Nacionalista)	77,832	100.0

1919	Total number	%
Registered voters	—	–
Votes cast	—	—
Invalid votes	—	—
Valid votes	97,650	—
Rafael López Gutiérrez (PL)	79,068	81.0
Manuel Membreño (Partido Nacional Democrático)	18,582	19.0

1923	Total number	%
Registered voters	—	–
Votes cast	—	—
Invalid votes	—	—
Valid votes	105,125	—
Tiburcio Carías Andino (PN)	49,541	47.1
Policarpio Bonilla (Partido Liberal Constitucionalista)	35,160	33.4
Juan Angel Arias (PL)	20,424	19.4

1924[a]	Total number	%
Registered voters	—	–
Votes cast	—	—
Invalid votes	—	—
Valid votes	—	—
Miguel Paz Barahona (PN)	72,021	—

[a] The PL refused to nominate a candidate for president.

1928	Total number	%
Registered voters	—	–
Votes cast	—	—
Invalid votes	—	—
Valid votes	110,064	—
Vicente Mejía Colindres (PL)	62,319	56.6
Tiburcio Carías Andino (PN)	47,745	42.4

1932	Total number	%
Registered voters	—	–
Votes cast	—	—
Invalid votes	—	—
Valid votes	—	—
Tiburcio Carías Andino (PN)	81,211	—
Angel Zúñiga Huete (PL)	61,643	—
Manuel Herrera Cálix (Bloque de Obreros y Campesinos)	—	—

1948	Total number	%
Registered voters	300,496	–
Votes cast	258,345	86.0
Blank votes	1,036	0.4
Invalid votes	2,119	0.8
Valid votes	255,190	98.8
Juan Manuel Gálvez (PN)	254,802	99.8
Angel Zúñiga Huete (PL)[a]	210	0.1
Others	178	0.1

[a] The PL did not contest the elections due to the fact that their electoral campaign was restricted. Their candidate Ángel Zúñiga Huete was in exile and called for electoral abstention.

1954	Total number	%
Registered voters	411,354	–
Votes cast	252,624	61.4
Invalid votes	644[a]	0.3[a]
Valid votes	251,980	99.7
Ramón Villeda Morales (PL)	121,213	48.1
Tiburcio Carías Andino (PN)	77,726	30.8
Abraham Williams Calderón (MNR)	53,041	21.1

[a] Figures calculated by the author.

1971[a]	Total number	%
Registered voters	900,658	–
Votes cast	608,342	67.5
Invalid votes	38,546[b]	6.3
Valid votes	569,796	93.7
Ramón Cruz (PN)	299,807	52.6
Jorge Bueso (PL)	269,989	47.4

[a] Only PL and the PN were allowed to register for the elections. PINU-SD and other parties such as PDC and PCH called for a boycott. Therefore, they rejected the so-called '*Pacto Político de Unidad Nacional*' (Political Pact of National Unity).
[b] Figure calculated by the author.

1981	Total number	%
Registered voters	1,546,797	–
Votes cast	1,214,779	78.0
Blank votes	17,430	1.4
Invalid votes	17,244	1.4
Valid votes	1,180,105	97.1
Roberto Suazo Córdova (PL)	636,437	53.9
Ricardo Zúñiga Augustinus (PN)	491,089	41.6
PINU-SD[a]	29,419	2.5
PDC[a]	19,163	1.6
Independents[b]	3,997	0.3

[a] INU-SD and PDC participated in the elections without a presidential candidate.
[b] The political left (organized in the FPH) was banned from the elections but presented independent candidates in the departments of Copán, Cortés and Yoro.

1985[a]	Total number	%
Registered voters	1,901,757	–
Votes cast	1,598,247	84.0
Blank votes	28,247	1.8
Invalid votes	27,713	1.7
Valid votes	1,542,287	96.5
PL	786,771	51.0
PN	701,492	45.5
PDC	30,303	2.0
PINU-SD	23,721	1.5

[a] The data are presented following the electoral system valid only for the elections of 1985. Under this system, intra-party elections were held simultaneously with the presidential elections (1985 *'Acta de Compromiso'*).

1989	Total number	%
Registered voters	2,363,448	–
Votes cast	1,799,146	76.0
Blank votes	18,483	1.0
Invalid votes	27,107	1.5
Valid votes	1,753,556	97.5
Rafael Callejas Romero (PN)	917,168	52.3
Carlos Flores Facussé (PL)	776,983	44.3
Antonio Aguilar Cerrato (PINU-SD)	33,952	1.9
Efraín Díaz Arrivillaga (PDC)	25,453	1.5

1993	Total number	%
Registered voters	2,734,116	–
Votes cast	1,771,825	64.8
Blank votes	17,907	1.2
Invalid votes	43,181	2.5
Valid votes	1,710,737	96.3
Carlos Roberto Reina (PL)	906,793	53.0
José Oswaldo Ramos Soto (PN)	735,123	43.0
Olban Valladares Ordóñez (PINU-SD)	48,471	2.8
Marco Orlando Iriate (PDC)	20,350	1.2

1997	Total number	%
Registered voters	2,883,919	–
Votes cast	2,096,646	72.7
Blank votes	34,056	1.6
Invalid votes	86,617	4.1
Valid votes	1,975,973	94.2
Carlos Flores Facussé (PL)	1,040,403	52.7
Nora Gúnera de Melger (PN)	844,985	42.8
Olban Valladares Ordóñez (PINU-SD)	41,605	2.1
Arturo Corrales Álvarez (PDC)	24,737	1.3
Matías Funes Valladares (PUD)	24,243	1.2

2001	Total number	%
Registered voters	3,448,280	–
Votes cast	2,285,067	66.3
Blank votes	23,927	1.0
Invalid votes	81,959	3.6
Valid votes	2,179,181	95.4
Ricardo Maduro Joest (PN)	1,137,734	52.2
Rafael Pineda Ponce (PL)	964,590	44.3
Olban Valladares Ordóñez (PINU-SD)	31,666	1.5
Matías Funes Valladares (PUD)	24,102	1.1
Marco Orlando Iriarte (PDC)	21,089	1.0

2.10 List of Power Holders 1899–2004

Head of State	Years	Remarks
Terencio Sierra	1899–1903	Constitutional president, elected by the national assembly. Assumed office on 01/02/1899.
Cabinet (*Consejo de Ministros*)	1903	Composed of: Juan A. Arias, Máximo B. Rosales, Daniel Fortín H., Manuel Sabino López, Rafael Alvarado Guerrero, and Francisco Artschul. Held power from 01/02/1903 to 18/02/1903, while Sierra fought against an uprising led by Manuel Bonilla.
Juan Angel Arias	1903	Assumed office on 18/02/1903; appointed by congress, even though Manuel Bonilla had won the 1902 elections.
Manuel Bonilla Chirinos	1903–1907	Assumed office by proclamation after the uprising against Arias. Was declared constitutionally elected on 12/05/1903.
Cabinet (*Consejo de Ministros*)	1907	Comprised of: Miguel Oquelí Bustillo, Máximo B. Rosales and J. Ignacio Castro. Assumed office after *coup d'état* against Bonilla on 25/03/1907.
Miguel R. Dávila	1907–1911	Provisional president appointed by the government junta on 18/04/1907. Declared constitutional president on 01/01/1908 after being elected by the constitutional assembly; resigned on 28/03/1911.
Francisco Bertrand Barahona	1911–1912	Provisional president between 28/03/1911 and 21/01/1912.
Manuel Bonilla Chirinos	1912–1913	Elected president in 1911 (he was the only candidate). Assumed office on 01/02/1912. Died in 1913.
Francisco Bertrand Barahona	1913–1915	Provisional president. Being the vice president, he automatically assumed office as president after Bonilla's death on 20/03/1913. Resigned on 28/07/1915 to run for president.
Alberto Membreño Márquez	1915–1916	Provisional president. Assumed office due to his function as vice president on 28/07/1915.
Francisco Bertrand Barahona	1916–1919	Elected president (only candidate in the elections). Took over office on 01/02/1916. Left the country on 09/09/1919 amidst struggles for his succession.

Head of State (cont.)	Years	Remarks
Francisco Bográn Barahona	1919–1920	Provisional president in his capacity as second designated successor. Assumed office on 05/10/1919.
Rafael López Gutiérrez	1920–1924	Elected president. Assumed presidency on 01/02/1920. Carried out a 'self-*coup d'état*' and declared himself de facto president on 01/02/1924 during the civil war which had started after the 1923 elections. He died on 10/03/1924.
Cabinet (Consejo de Ministros)	1924	Provisional government. Headed by Ángel Zúñiga Huete. Assumed office on 10/03/1924.
Vicente Tosta Carrasco	1924–1925	Provisional president. Assumed office on 30/04/1924 after a political arrangement with the US.
Miguel Paz Barahona	1925–1929	Elected president. Assumed office on 01/02/1925.
Vicente Mejía Colindres	1929–1933	Elected president. In office until 01/02/1933.
Tiburcio Carías Andino	1933–1949	Elected president. Assumed office on 01/02/1933. Arranged an unconstitutional re-election by the newly installed national constitutional assembly for the period 1936–1942 and by congress for the period 1942–1949.
Juan Manuel Gálvez Durón	1949–1954	Elected president (only candidate). Assumed office on 01/01/1949.
Julio Lozano Díaz	1954–1956	Provisional president. Assumed office on 16/11/1954 in his capacity as vice president, due to Gálvez's absence. Declared himself de facto president on 05/12/1954. Deposed on 21/10/1956.
Military junta	1956–1957	Composed of: Héctor Caraccioli, Roque J. Rodríguez, and Roberto Gálvez Barnes. Assumed power after the *coup d'état* on 21/10/1956.
Military junta	1957	Composed of Oswaldo López Arellano and Héctor Caraccioli. Took over power on 17/11/1957.
Ramón Villeda Morales	1957–1963	Elected president by the national constitutional assembly. Assumed office on 21/12/1957. Deposed by a *coup d'état* on 03/10/1963.

Head of State (cont.)	Years	Remarks
Oswaldo López Arellano	1963–1971	Military. Assumed power after a *coup d'état* on 03/10/1963. Elected president by the constitutional assembly; assumed presidency on 06/06/1965.
Ramón Ernesto Cruz Uclés	1971–1972	Elected president. Assumed office on 06/06/1971. Deposed by a *coup d'état* on 04/12/1972.
Oswaldo López Arellano	1972–1975	Military. Assumed power after a *coup d'état* on 04/12/1972.
Juan Alberto Melgar Castro	1975–1978	Military. Assumed power and became de facto president after a *coup d'état* on 22/04/1975.
Military junta	1978–1980	Composed of: Policarpio Paz García, Domingo Alvarez, and Amílcar Zelaya R. Assumed power after a *coup d'état* on 07/08/1978.
Policarpio Paz García	1980–1982	Provisional president. Assumed power on 25/07/1980. Remained in government after the 1980 elections because no candidate received the absolute majority.
Roberto Suazo Córdova	1982–1986	Elected president. Assumed office on 27/01/1982.
José Azcona del Hoyo	1986–1990	Elected president. Assumed office on 27/01/1986.
Rafael Callejas Romero	1990–1994	Elected president. Assumed office on 27/01/1990.
Carlos Roberto Reina	1994–1998	Elected president. Assumed office on 27/01/1994.
Carlos Flores Facussé	1998–2002	Elected president. Assumed office on 27/01/1998.
Ricardo Maduro Joest	2002–	Elected president. Assumed office on 27/01/2002.

3. Bibliography

3.1 Official Sources

Constitución de la República de Honduras (1982).
Ley Electoral y de las Organizaciones Políticas (1981).

3.2 Books, Articles, and Electoral Reports

Centro de Investigación y Promoción de los Derechos Humanos (ed.) (1997). *Análisis de la participación política en Honduras.* Tegucigalpa: CIPRODEH.
García Laguardia, J. M. (1999). *Honduras: evolución político constitucional 1824–1936.* Mexico: UNAM.
González de Oliva, A. A. (1996). *Gobernantes Hondureños. Siglos XIX y XX.* 2 vols. Tegucigalpa: Editorial Universitaria.
Izaguirre, R. (2000). 'Análisis del caso Honduras', in Instituto Interamericano de Derechos Humanos (ed.), *Sistema de elecciones parlamentarias y su relación con la gobernabilidad democrática.* San José (Costa Rica): IIDH, 203–246.
Nohlen, D., Picado, S., and Zovatto, D., (ed.) (1998). *Tratado de derecho electoral comparado de América Latina.* México: Fondo de Cultura Económica.
Rosenberg, M. B. (1995). 'Democracy in Honduras. The Electoral and Political Reality', in M. A. Seligson and J. A. Booth (eds.), *Elections and Democracy in Central America, revisited.* Chapel Hill, N.C./London: The University of North Carolina Press, 66–83.
Salomón, L. (ed.) (1994). *Los retos de la democrácia.* Tegucigalpa: Centro de Documentacíon de Honduras.
Sieder, R. (1998). *Elecciones y democratización en Honduras desde 1980.* Tegucigalpa: Editorial Universitaria.

JAMAICA

by Andreas M. Wüst[*]

1. Introduction

1.1 Historical Overview

Since 1944, there has been a run of uninterrupted parliamentary elections in Jamaica, and the competitive character of elections has led to regular changes in government. As a result of both political tradition and the electoral system, power has always been shared between two parties: the Jamaica Labour Party (JLP), which was originally based on the support of the unions, and the People's National Party (PNP), which originally centered around the middle classes. Elections have often been disturbed by violent riots, culminating in approximately 800 people being killed in 1980.

In the elections held before independence (1944–1962) the most notable feature of the political and electoral processes was personalism, with political competition centering on the charismatic party leaders Alexander Bustamante (JLP) and Norman Manley (PNP).

After the British granted Jamaica internal self-governance in 1959, Manley became the first prime minister. His plans to extend the island's autonomy to foreign affairs, by joining the West Indies Federation, were rejected by the electorate in a referendum held in 1961. The position the parties took with regards to the island's autonomy turned out to be a decisive factor in the following elections (1962), which were won by Bustamante. On 6 August 1962, Jamaica was declared an independent state incorporating a Westminster-style parliamentary system.

Until 1972 the two parties favored the so-called 'Industrialization by invitation', with regards to the national development policy. The revenue of the bauxite industry in particular contributed to the success of

[*] A significantly shorter version of this article has been published earlier in German (Sturm 1993). Roland Sturm's consent to integrate parts of the German version into the completely revised English version is gratefully acknowledged. The author would also like to thank Dean M. Smith of the Electoral Office of Jamaica for his research assistance.

these policies and the resulting improvements in social standards. However, these efforts were soon undermined by the beginning of the world energy crisis in 1973. Already by the late 1960s, increasing party competition led to the emergence of a polarized party system, following a left-right pattern. Along with a significant urban migration and subsequently housing shortages, so-called 'garrison communities' developed. These garrisons have been created along party lines and have ever since been party fortresses and critical areas of political conflict, election fraud and intimidation.

Concerning economic policy, the left-wing PNP, led by Michael Manley, who succeeded his father as PNP party chairman after his death in 1969, proclaimed a greater national share in the bauxite revenues (the country's most important resource), the creation of a raw materials cartel, and the extension of state-subsided social benefits. The official introduction of 'Democratic Socialism' in 1974 marked a paradigmatic change, which caused tensions between the government and the small but powerful elite of the island, and with foreign investors. Jamaica came into conflict with the USA, not only because of its economic policies, but also because of some of the political alignments Jamaica entered into with other countries (among others, Jamaica established friendly relations with Cuba 1972 and with the Soviet Union 1976). Due to economic and political problems, social and political tensions increased.

The rapid failure of the socialist experiment was partly due to the loss of national capital and partly due to the decrease in exports and the lack of revenue from the tourist industry. This failure forced Manley to negotiate with the International Monetary Fund (IMF) shortly after his re-election in 1976. To avoid bankruptcy, Manley decided to accept the conditions set by the IMF. However, this did not lead to a lasting upturn in the economy. When Manley broke with the IMF and called for early elections in 1980, he had already lost popularity because of the drastic reduction in social benefits towards the end of the 1970s. On the eve of the election, the major concern of most Jamaicans was the country's economic misery. The most promising way out of this seemed to be to vote for the US-supported JLP candidate, Edward Seaga, who celebrated a landslide victory in 1980 after an aggressive election campaign. The people placed their hopes on the North American 'Caribbean Basin Initiative', and on a reorientation of the economic policy toward 'Reaganomics'. Jamaica also entered into closer political relations with the USA, but again, no lasting economic progress was achieved.

The PNP boycotted the 1983 elections after the JLP had refused to update the electoral roll, although it had previously been agreed that they would do so in 1980. As a result of the absence of the PNP, less than 3% of the citizens entitled to vote went to the polls. However, the PNP was able to return to power in 1989. Major reasons for this change in government were the lasting economic problems, the deficient social policy of the JLP, and the authoritarian rule of Seaga.

The election of 1989 was accompanied by widespread public protest, mainly due to the fact that the major political opposition had been missing in parliament. Meanwhile, however, the main parties had given up the polarized political positions they had held in the late 1970s and early 1980s and they eventually agreed on several economic issues. Manley, who had by now abandoned the idea of a socialist experiment, started to emphasize the need for greater social equality to mitigate the consequences (primarily inflation, increases of taxes, and high unemployment rates) of Jamaica's entrance into world trade.

A period in Jamaican history came to an end in March 1992, when Michael Manley had to resign as prime minister and party chairman due to health problems. Percival James Patterson, previously deputy prime minister and minister of finance, called the 'black prince', succeeded him as party chairman and prime minister. Despite falling net national income, a widening trade deficit, high inflation, and high unemployment, the PNP was able to win 52 of the 60 constituencies in the 1993 election. The election was marred by fraud, police intimidation, and several killings. Together with the 1980 election, this election was the most violent in the country's history.

The PNP's landslide victory in 1997 was partly due to a neo-liberal program that effectively took the wind out of the opposition's sails, but mainly due to the ongoing internal rivalry within the JLP. In October 1995 Bruce Golding, former party chairman of the JLP, left the party and formed the neo-liberal National Democratic Movement (NDM). In spite of a good showing in early polls, the NDM was not able to win a single seat in the 1997 election, which was also due to the ambitious attempt of running in 58 out of 60 constituencies. The 1997 election was again dominated by Patterson's PNP, although the economic strategy of the Patterson administration—lowering tariffs and privatizing state-owned companies—did not turn out to improve the economic situation. In 1995, the rate of inflation increased to 25.5% and the national debt grew tremendously, and a year later the banking system collapsed.

As a result of the violent riots and the election fraud during the 1993 elections, an international team of observers from the Carter Center was asked to monitor the poll. This invitation to the observers was initiated by the Citizens' Action for Free and Fair Elections (CAFFE). In cooperation with 2,000 volunteers, who had been trained by CAFFE, the 58 observers facilitated reasonably free and fair elections. In 2002 the international observers, who had returned to the country, witnessed an even more satisfying accomplishment. The 'culmination of procedural improvements and the inception of innovative conflict prevention and resolution mechanisms' (Neuman 2003: 19) the Carter Center was able to assess for the 2002 election, was however not reflected throughout the preceding electoral campaign. The assassination of a West Kingston PNP community leader once more led to violent conflicts. Not at least due to the fact that West Kingston was Edward Seaga's constituency, and that the JLP was accused of being responsible for the assassination, violence accompanied the electoral campaign in 2001 and 2002.

Throughout the spring of 2002, polls have indicated an extremely close race, and a number of PNP party scandals including allegations of corruption as well as rumors that Prime Minister Patterson was about to retire, helped the JLP's electoral campaign. Further, Bruce Golding's (NDM) return to the JLP following a defeat in a 2001 by-election, was expected to be beneficial for Seaga. Yet, despite losses and the lowest margin since 1955, the PNP also managed to win the 2002 election. The outcome was about as close as polls had indicated. Nevertheless the JLP managed to catch up, and received the highest vote share in a regular election (leaving aside the 1983 election) since 1980.

1.2 Evolution of Electoral Provisions

When Jamaica gained independence a bicameral system was established. The house of representatives is directly elected and the senate is formed by 21 members appointed by the governor general. There has been universal, equal, secret, and direct suffrage since the 1944 elections to the house of representatives. Every citizen of Jamaica and of the Commonwealth, residing in the country for at least twelve months before the elections, is entitled to vote. Before the 1976 poll, the minimum age required for the elections to the house of representatives was reduced from 21 to 18.

Plurality system in single-member constituencies (SMCs) has always been applied. The number of constituencies was initially 35 and rose to 60 by 1976 (1959: 45; 1967: 53).

Until 1979, a parliamentarian commission (Delimitations Committee) was in charge of dividing the electoral territory. From then on it was the responsibility of the Electoral Advisory Committee (EAC). When the EAC was first formed, the opposition was excluded from the decision-making process regarding the territorial division in constituencies. It was not until after the 1983 elections (boycotted by the PNP) that the opposition came to be represented in the EAC.

1.3 Current Electoral Provisions

Sources: The Jamaican (Constitution) Order in Council 1962 (enacted 6 August 1962, last modified through Amendment Act 18 of 1999). The Representation of the People Act (enacted 20 November 1944, last modified through Amendment Act 16 of 1997).

Suffrage: Suffrage is universal, equal, direct, and secret. Every Jamaican citizen of at least 18 years of age, who is resident in Jamaica on the day of registration, is eligible to vote. Any Commonwealth citizen who has been a permanent resident in the country for twelve months prior to the completion of the register of electors is entitled to vote. The mentally infirm, people sentenced to death or imprisoned for more than six months, people convicted of electoral fraud, and persons holding core offices connected to the elections are disqualified from voting. Although registration is compulsory, voting is not. Members of the police force or the armed forces are deleted from the voter list of each precinct, but are listed on separate constituency lists. Members of the armed forces and the police force are able to cast their votes at special voting centers on a fixed day up to three days before election day. In 2002, EOJ staff and election day workers were also allowed to vote along with the security forces. Jamaican electoral law does not provide for postal or external voting.

Elected national institutions: The house of representatives is directly elected, while the 21 senators are appointed by the governor general, 13 on the advice of the prime minister and eight on the advice of the opposition leader.

The session of the house of representatives automatically ends five years after its first sitting. The governor general may dissolve parliament at any time on the advice of the prime minister or on a vote of no confidence by an absolute majority of MPs. Elections have to be held within a period of three months after dissolution. The period between the last sitting of one session and the first sitting of a following session must be less than six months. In case of war, parliament may extend the term of office up to twelve months.

Nomination of candidates: Every Jamaican citizen over 21 years of age can be elected. The support of at least ten voters of the constituency is required in order to run as a candidate. One further prerequisite is a monetary deposit of 3,000 $Jam (equal to approximately 63 US$) which is not returned unless the candidate obtains one-eighth of the votes cast in his or her constituency. Certain civil servants and judges (Supreme Court, Court of Appeal) cannot stand for election, and members of the armed forces need a special authorization to run as candidates.

Electoral system: Plurality system in SMCs is applied in the election to the house of representatives. In the 2002 elections there were 60 constituencies. According to the Second Schedule of the constitution, the limits of the electoral constituencies must remain within the limits of the administrative divisions (counties and parishes). Each parish has to be divided into at least two constituencies. The number of electors per constituency cannot be lower than two thirds or higher than one and a half of the average figure obtained by dividing the total amount of electors by the total amount of constituencies. Within each constituency, electoral precincts ('polling divisions') of approximately 250 voters are to be created.

If vacancies arise, the corresponding seats are filled *via* by-elections which have to be held within three months.

Organizational context of elections: There are two electoral institutions in Jamaica: the Electoral Office of Jamaica (EOJ) and the Electoral Advisory Committee (EAC). While the EOJ is responsible for planning and organizing elections, the EAC, created by parliament in 1979, controls the EOJ's work and advises the Director of Elections, the head of the EOJ. The EAC consists of six members. Three members are appointed by the governor general in consultation with the prime minister and with the leader of the opposition, one member is appointed according to nominations of the prime minister and another according to the leader of the opposition. The sixth member becomes the director of elections and is appointed by the five other EAC members. The director has no voting rights within the EAC. Members of the EAC are appointed for a period of 18 months (party nominees), four years (independent members), and seven years (director of elections) by the governor general, but are eligible for reappointment.

The EAC is an influential institution whose advice and recommendations must be followed by the EOJ. If the director of elections refuses to follow any advice or recommendation, he or she must report the matter to parliament within 14 days. The major issue of Jamaican electoral reform in the 1990s has been voter enumeration and registration to guarantee voting rights by providing an accurate voter's list for each election. In 2002, an internet query system allowed the entries to be checked and verified.

1.4 Commentary on the Electoral Statistics

The electoral data presented in the following tables have been taken primarily from the official reports of the supervisor/director of elections for the years 1962–1997 (the 2002 data have been provided by the EOJ directly). While these data are considered reliable, results for candidates from small parties are usually not specified individually, but grouped together as 'independents'. In this case and particularly for the period 1944–1961, secondary sources including the Electoral Office's website have been consulted for a detailed tabulation. In case of inconsistencies, detailed data for other parties are not provided. These facts might also result in an incomplete party list for some elections (Table 2.4), but any missing entries are considered negligible.

Percentages have been calculated by the author, but do usually not deviate from the data in the electoral reports. Where no other source is specified, the demographic data correspond to the evaluations of the United Nations or of the Statistical Institute of Jamaica.

2. Tables

2.1 Dates of National Elections, Referendums, and Coups d'Etat

Year	Presidential elections	Parliamentary elections	Elections for Constitutional Assembly	Referendums	Coups d'état
1944		12/12			
1949		20/12			
1955		12/01			
1959		28/07			
1961				19/09	
1962		10/04			
1967		21/02			
1972		29/02			
1976		15/12			
1980		30/10			
1983		15/12			
1989		09/02			
1993		03/30			
1997		18/12			
2002		16/10			

2.2 Electoral Body 1944–2002

Year	Type of election[a]	Population[b]	Registered voters Total number	% pop.	Votes cast Total number	% reg. voters	% pop.
1944[c]	Pa	1,265,221	663,069	52.4	389,109	58.7	30.8
1949	Pa	1,350,100	732,217	54.2	477,107	65.2	35.3
1955	Pa	1,541,700	761,238	49.4	495,682	65.1	32.2
1959	Pa	1,598,776	853,539	53.4	563,974	66.1	35.3
1961	Ref	1,652,000	779,965	47.1	479,220	61.5	29.0
1962	Pa	1,675,681	796,540	47.5	580,517	72.9	34.6
1967	Pa	1,836,700	543,307	29.6	446,815	82.2	24.3
1972	Pa	1,932,400	605,662	31.3	477,771	78.9	24.7
1976	Pa	2,072,300	870,972	42.0	742,149	85.2	35.8
1980	Pa	2,172,900	990,417	45.6	860,746	86.1	39.6
1983	Pa	2,240,800	990,019	44.2	27,043	2.7	1.2
1989	Pa	2,392,000	1,078,760	45.1	845,485	78.4	35.4
1993	Pa	2,434,800	1,002,599	41.2	675,296	60.3	27.7
1997	Pa	2,540,300	1,182,294	46.5	771,068	65.2	30.4
2002	Pa	2,618,600	1,301,638	49.7	768,758	59.1	29.4

[a] Pa = Parliament; Ref = Referendum.
[b] Results of the pop. censuses: 1911: 831,383; 1921: 858,118; 1943: 1,237,063; 1953: 1,486,723; 1960: 1,609,814; 1970: 1,848,512; 1982: 2,205,507; 1991: 2,380,667; 2001: 2,599,334.
[c] The electoral data has been collected from the introduction of universal suffrage onward.

2.3 Abbreviations

CCM	Christian Conscience Movement
CDP	Christian Democratic Party
CIP	Convention Independent Party
FP	Farmer's Party
IEWFPP	Imperial Ethiopian World Federation Incorporated Political Party
ILP	Independent Labour Party
JDP	Jamaica Democratic Party
JIM	Jamaica Independent Movement
JLP	Jamaica Labour Party
JUF	Jamaica United Front
JUP	Jamaica United Party
JWP	Jamaica We Party
NDM	National Democratic Movement
NJA	Jamaica National Alliance for Unity
NLP	National Labour Party
PFM	People's Freedom Movement
PNP	People's National Party
PPP	People's Political Party
RP	Republican Party
UPJ	United Party of Jamaica
UPP	United People's Party

2.4 Electoral Participation of Parties and Alliances 1944–2002

Party / Alliance	Years	Elections contested[a]
JDP	1944	1
JLP	1944–2002	14
PNP	1944–1980; 1989–2002	13
AIP	1949	1
UPJ	1949	1
FP	1955	1
NLP	1955	1
PFM	1955	1
RP	1955; 1967; 1983	3
TRP	1955	1
CIP	1959	1
ILP	1959	1
JIM	1959	1
PPP	1962	1
JUP	1967	1
JWP	1967	1
CDP	1972	1
CCM	1983	1
JUF	1983	1
NDM	1997–2002	2
IEWFIPP	2002	1
NJA	2002	1
UPP	2002	1

[a] Election total: 14.

2.5 Referendums

Year	1961[a]	
	Total number	%
Registered voters	777,965	–
Votes cast	479,220	61.5
Invalid votes	5,640	1.2
Valid votes	473,580	98.8
Yes	217,319	45.9
No	256,261	54.1

[a] The question was: 'Should Jamaica remain in the Federation of the West Indies?' Jamaica subsequently left the Federation, and the Federation dissolved in 1962.

2.6. Elections for Constitutional Assembly

Elections for constitutional assembly have not been held.

2.7 Parliamentary Elections 1944–2002

Year	1944		1949	
	Total number	%	Total number	%
Registered voters	663,069	–	732,217	–
Votes cast	389,109	58.7	477,107	65.2
Invalid votes	39,982	10.3	9,928	2.1
Valid votes	349,127	89.7	467,179	97.9
JLP	144,661	41.4	199,538	42.7
PNP	82,029	23.5	203,048	43.5
JDP	14,123	4.0	–	–
Others	3,500	1.0	5,803[a]	1.2
Independents	104,814	30.0	58,790	12.6

[a] Includes UPJ: 1,110.

Year	1955		1959	
	Total number	%	Total number	%
Registered voters	761,238	–	853,539	–
Votes cast	495,680	65.1	563,974	66.1
Invalid votes	9,036	1.8	6,277	1.1
Valid votes	486,644	98.2	557,794	98.9
JLP	189,929	39.0	247,149	44.3
PNP	245,750	50.5	305,642	54.8
FP	13,258	2.7	–	–
NLP	6,004	1.2	–	–
ILP	–	–	4,697	0.8
Independents	31,703[a]	6.5	304[b]	0.1

[a] Others and independents; includes PFM: 647; RP: 108.
[b] Others and independents.

Year	1962		1967	
	Total number	%	Total number	%
Registered voters	796,540	–	543,307	–
Votes cast	580,517	72.9	446,815	82.2
Invalid votes	4,738	0.8	4,243	0.9
Valid votes	575,779	99.2	442,572	99.1
JLP	288,130	50.0	224,180	50.7
PNP	279,771	48.6	217,207	49.1
PPP	4,955	0.9	–	–
Others	–	–	341[a]	0.1
Independents	2,923	0.5	844	0.2

[a] JUP: 163; JWP: 133; RP: 45.

Year	1972		1976	
	Total number	%	Total number	%
Registered voters	605,662	–	870,972	–
Votes cast	477,771	78.9	742,149	85.2
Invalid votes	4,120	0.9	6,201	0.8
Valid votes	473,651	99.1	735,948	99.2
PNP	266,927	56.4	417,768	56.8
JLP	205,587	43.4	318,180	43.2
Others	109[a]	0.0	–	–
Independents	1,028	0.2	–	–

[a] CDP: 109.

Year	1980		1983[a]	
	Total number	%	Total number	%
Registered voters	990,417	–	990,586	–
Votes cast	860,746	86.9	26,543	2.7
Invalid votes	8,040	0.9	488	1.8
Valid votes	852,706	99.1	26,055	98.2
JLP	502,115	58.9	23,363	89.7
PNP	350,064	41.1	–	–
CCM	–	–	704	2.7
RP	–	–	257	1.0
JUF	–	–	144	0.6
Independents	527	0.1	1,587	6.1

[a] The PNP appealed for electoral abstention.

Year	1989			1993	
	Total number	%		Total number	%
Registered voters	1,078,760	–		1,002,599	–
Votes cast	845,485	78.4		675,296	67.4
Invalid votes	8,514	1.0		6,479	1.0
Valid votes	836,971	99.0		668,817	99.0
JLP	362,589	43.3		263,711	39.4
PNP	473,754	56.6		401,131	60.0
Independents	628	0.1		3,975	0.6

Year	1997			2002	
	Total number	%		Total number	%
Registered voters	1,182,294	–		1,301,638	–
Votes cast	771,068	65.2		768,758	59.1
Invalid votes	6,284	0.8		7,393	1.0
Valid votes	764,784	99.2		761,365	99.0
PNP	429,805	56.2		396,590	52.1
JLP	297,387	38.9		360,718	47.4
NDM[a]	36,707	4.8		2,895	0.4
Others	–	–		710[b]	0.1
Independents	885	0.1		452	0.1

[a] 2002: NDM/NJA.
[b] Others are UPP: 548; IEWFIPP: 162.

2.8 Composition of Parliament 1944–2002

Year	1944		1949		1955		1959	
	Seats	%	Seats	%	Seats	%	Seats	%
	32	100.0	32	100.0	32	100.0	45	100.0
JLP	22	68.8	17	53.1	14	43.8	16	35.6
PNP	5	15.6	13	40.6	18	56.3	29	64.4
Independents	5	15.6	2	6.3	–	–	–	–

Year	1962		1967		1972		1976	
	Seats	%	Seats	%	Seats	%	Seats	%
	45	100.0	53	100.0	53	100.0	60	100.0
JLP	26	57.8	33	62.3	16	30.2	13	21.7
PNP	19	42.2	20	37.7	37	69.8	47	78.3

Year	1980		1983		1989		1993	
	Seats	%	Seats	%	Seats	%	Seats	%
	60	100.0	60	100.0	60	100.0	60	100.0
JLP	51	85.0	60	100.0	15	25.0	8	13.3
PNP	9	15.0	0	0.0	45	75.0	52	86.6

Year	1997		2002	
	Seats	%	Seats	%
	60	100.0	60	100.0
PNP	50	83.3	34	56.6
JLP	10	16.7	26	43.3

2.9 Presidential Elections

Presidential elections have not been held.

2.10 List of Power Holders 1944–2004

Head of State	Years	Remarks
King George IV	(1936)–1952	Governors: Sir John Huggins (1943–1951), Sir Hugh Mackintosh Foot (1951–1957).
Queen Elizabeth II	1952–	Governor: Sir Kenneth Blackburne (1957–1962); governor generals nominated by the prime minister: Sir Kenneth Blackburne (1962) Sir Clifford Campbell (1962–1973), Sir Herbert Duffus (acting 1973), (Sir) Florizel Glasspole (1973–1991), Edward Zacca (interim, 1991), Sir Howard Cooke (1991–).

Head of Government	Years	Remarks
Alexander Bustamante	1953–1955	Founder of the JLP (1943), first chief minister, appointed 05/05/1953.
Norman Washington Manley	1955–1962	Founder of the PNP (1938), chief minister 1955–1959, appointed 02/02/1955, first prime minister 1959–1962, appointed 04/07/1959.
Sir Alexander Bustamante	1962–1967	Second prime minister (JLP); appointed 29/04/1962; Jamaica became independent during his term (06/08/1962).
(Sir) Donald Burns Sangster	1967	JLP prime minister; appointed 23/02/1967; died in office 11/04/1967.
Hugh Lawson Shearer	1967–1972	JLP prime minister; appointed 11/04/1967.
Michael Manley	1972–1980	PNP prime minister; appointed 02/03/1972; son of Norman Manley.
Edward Seaga	1980–1989	JLP prime minister; appointed 01/11/1980.
Michael Manley	1989–1992	Appointed 10/02/1989; resigned 30/03/1992.
Percival J. Patterson	1992–	Appointed 30/03/1992; PNP chairman; deputy prime minister 1989–1992; re-elected in 1993, 1997, and 2002.

3. Bibliography

3.1 Official Sources

General Election 1962, Report of the Chief Electoral Officer Jamaica. Kingston.
General Election 1967, Report of the Chief Electoral Officer Jamaica. Kingston.
General Election 1972, Report of the Chief Electoral Officer Jamaica. Kingston.
General Election 1976, Report of the Chief Electoral Officer Jamaica. Kingston.
General Election 1980, Report of the Director of Elections Jamaica. Kingston.
General Election 1983, Report of the Director of Elections Jamaica. Kingston.
General Election 1989, Report of the Director of Elections Jamaica. Kingston.
General Election 1993, Report of the Director of Elections Jamaica. Kingston.
General Election 1997, Report of the Director of Elections Jamaica. Kingston.

3.2 Books, Articles, and Electoral Reports

Carter Center (2002). *Fourth Statement by The Carter Center on the Jamaican Electoral Process, 2002.* <http://www.cartercenter.org>.

Eaton, G. E. (1975). *Alexander Bustamante and Modern Jamaica.* Kingston: Kingston Publishers.

Edie, C. J. (ed.) (1994). *Democracy in the Caribbean. Myths and Realities.* London: Praeger.

Hurwitz, S. and Hurwitz, E. F. (1971). *Jamaica. A Historical Portrait.* New York/ Washington, D.C./ London: Praeger.

Kaufman, M. (1985). *Jamaica under Manley.* London: Zed Books.

Lacey, T. (1977). *Violence and Politics in Jamaica 1960–70. Internal Security in a Developing Country.* Manchester: Manchester University Press.

Lee, N. B. (1988). 'El sistema de empadronamiento y Registro de Electores en Jamaica', in *Memoria de la Segunda Conferencia de la Asociación de Organismos Electorales de Centroamérica y el Caribe. El Registro Electoral en América Latina.* San José, Costa Rica: IIDH-CAPEL, 277–313.

Leuteritz, K. (1996). 'Die Verfassungen karibischer Commonwealth-Staaten'. *Verfassung und Recht in Übersee*, 29/1: 139–162.

Manley, M. (1982). *Jamaica. Struggle in the Periphery.* London: The Third World Media Limited.

Mills, G. E. (1981). 'Electoral Reform in Jamaica'. *The Parliamentarian*, April 1981: 97–104.

Munroe, T. (1972). *The Politics of Constitutional Decolonization. Jamaica 1944–1962.* Kingston, Jamaica: Institute of Social and Economic Studies, University of the West Indies.

Payne, A. J. (1995). *Politics in Jamaica.* New York: St. Martin's Press.

Philips, F. (1985). *West Indian Constitutions. Post-Independence Reform.* New York/ London/ Roma: Oceana Publishers.

Robertson, P. D. (1972). 'Party "Organization" in Jamaica'. *Social and Economic Studies* (Kingston), 21/1: 30–43.

Senior, O. (1972). *The Message is Change. A Perspective of the 1972 General Elections.* Kingston, Jamaica: Kingston Publishers.

Spackman, A. (1975). *Constitutional Development of the West Indies 1922–1968. A Selection from the Mayor Documents.* St. Lauwrence (Barbados): Caribbean University Press.

Stephens, E. H. and Stephens, J. D. (1986). *Democratic Socialism in Jamaica. The Political Movement and Social Transformation in Dependent Capitalism.* London: Macmillan Education.

Stone, C. (1977). 'The 1976 Parliamentary Election in Jamaica'. *Journal of Commonwealth and Comparative Politics*, 15: 251–265.

— (1980). *Democracy and Clientelism in Jamaica.* New Brunswick, N.J./ London: Transaction Books.

— (1986). *Class, State, and Democracy in Jamaica.* New York: Praeger.

— (1989). *Politics versus Economics. The 1989 Elections in Jamaica.* Kingston, Jamaica: Heinemann Publishers.

Sturm, R. (1984). 'Wahlen und gesellschaftlicher Wandel. Der Fall Jamaika', in D. Nohlen (ed.), *Wahlen und Wahlpolitik in Lateinamerika.* Heidelberg: Esprint, 85–108.

— (1993). 'Jamaika', in D. Nohlen (ed.), *Handbuch der Wahldaten Lateinamerikas und der Karibik.* Opladen: Leske + Budrich, 447–456.

Wheeler, J. P. (ed.) (1967). *Jamaica. Election Factbook, 21 February 1967.* Washington, D.C.: Institute for the Comparative Study of Political Systems.

MEXICO
by Dieter Nohlen[*]

1. Introduction

1.1 Historical Overview

The first norms of the Mexican electoral system appeared in the first national constitution of 1824. However, the continuous political instability, reflected in numerous *coups d'état* and armed conflicts among the different political factions (especially between conservatives and liberals) prevented the elections from being consolidated and used as an instrument for changes in power. During the regime of General Porfirio Díaz (1876–1910), the 1857 liberal constitution, which specifically established universal and secret suffrage, was systematically violated.

The abolishment of several articles contained in the 1857 Constitution, in particular the prohibition of the presidential re-election, was one of the factors that motivated the movement which, under the slogan 'effective suffrage–no re-election', contested the 1910 presidential elections with the purpose of re-establishing liberal democracy. The repression of this movement unleashed an open rebellion against Díaz. It succeeded in forcing his resignation on 25 May 1911, and culminated in a battle among several political factions during the Mexican Revolution (1910–1917). The complex objectives of the different revolutionary sectors, which combined both social demands—particularly agrarian reform—with political ones—mainly the re-establishment of a constitutional system—was reflected in the constitution passed on 5 February 1917. This constitution, which is still valid today, represents the legacy of the revolution. Particularly important are the regulations on land ownership, working rights, the definition of the state's responsibility to provide free and compulsory education and the nationalization of natural resources.

[*] The author would like to thank Manuel Carrillo and José de Jesús Orozco Henríquez for providing important information on electoral results.

The 1917 Constitution established the political organization of the Mexican State as a representative, democratic and federal republic. It also provided for the division of power among the executive, legislative and judicial powers. An executive with wide-ranging powers strengthened the presidential system established by the constitution. Nevertheless, re-election was prohibited. This was one of principles that had precipitated the revolution and it acted as a counterweight to the presidential authority. The first post-revolutionary electoral law, passed on 6 February 1917, established the bases of the electoral system, which remained practically unaltered until 1946.

Even though the 1917 Constitution created the institutional framework of the Mexican political system political stability was first established with President Plutarco Elías Calles' government (1924–1928). In this context, a basic factor was the foundation of the *Partido Nacional Revolucionario* (PNR; National Revolutionary Party) in 1929 as a confederation of national and regional parties, incorporating every group and political force of the 'revolutionary family'. The political system that originated in the revolution finally consolidated under Lázaro Cárdenas' government (1934–1938). From then on it remained in close contact with the domination of the ruling party. During Cárdenas' tenure, the PNR, whose name was changed to *Partido de la Revolución Mexicana* (PRM; Mexican Revolution Party) in 1938, ceased being a coalition among the various revolutionary factions with a high degree of autonomy for local governors, to become a four-sector structure: rural, working, popular and military sectors (the latter disappeared in 1940). This also included the peasant and labor organizations: the *Confederación Nacional Campesina* (CNC; National Peasant Federation) and the *Confederación de Trabajadores Mexicanos* (CTM; Mexican Labor Federation). The most remarkable achievements of Cárdenas' government were a substantial agrarian reform and the nationalization of the oil industry. His government highlighted the social and economic aspects of the legacy of the Revolution, and gave the political system a certain corporate character, which was strengthened by the virtually absolute domination of the regime's party since 1930.

A period of political stability almost unique in Latin America began with Lázaro Cárdenas' government. Since 1920 (and without interruption from then on), both presidential elections and the elections to federal congress have been held regularly. Every president since 1934 has also been constitutionally elected and has served out his presidential term. Due in part to the domination of the government party, whose name changed again in 1946 to the *Partido Revolucionario Institucional*

(PRI, Institutional Revolutionary Party), and to its virtual monopoly of the presidential elections, the chamber of congress and the local governments since 1930, however, the electoral competition ceased to express the political and social conflicts of the Mexican society.

Thus, in the presidential elections held between 1940 and 1982, the PRI's candidates obtained between 74% and 94% of the vote. In 1976, the only candidate was José López Portillo of the PRI. During this period, the party maintained a minimum of 80% of the seats in the chamber of deputies and all the seats in the senate. Until 1989, every state governor was a member of the PRI, which was also pre-eminent in state congresses and municipalities.

Both the electoral and the party systems were relatively exclusive in the decades following the Revolution; however, with the consolidation of the Mexican political system and the PRI, they evolved towards greater political liberalization and pluralism. Likewise, the continuous reforms of the electoral legislation modified the conditions of parliamentary representation for the different political forces, and therefore affected the evolution of the party system. Thus, other parties appeared in the opposition, dominated up to now by the *Partido de Acción Nacional* (PAN; National Action Party), created in 1939. Some of these, such as the *Partido Comunista Mexicano* (PCM; Mexican Communist Party) and the *Partido Popular Socialista* (PPS; Popular Socialist Party), registered in the 1940s, and others did so in the 1950s, namely the *Partido Auténtico de la Revolución Mexicana* (PARM; Authentic Party of the Mexican Revolution).

In 1963, when the presidential term of office was extended from four to six years, the constitutional reform modified the majority representation system applied so far in the chamber of deputies, and introduced the so-called 'party deputies', which actually acted as an instrument for the representation of minorities. Parties receiving less than 20 seats in majority representation constituencies (actually every party except the PRI) were assigned five seats if they obtained more than 2.5% of the national vote and one seat more for every 0.5% beyond this threshold. Under this system, the opposition increased its representation in the lower chamber from 6 to 35 deputies in 1964 (out of a total of 210). The PAN increased its representation from 5 to 20 deputies. In 1972, the threshold for 'party deputies' was lowered to 1.5%, and the maximum of seats to be allocated through this procedure rose to 25. As a result, in the 1973 elections, the representation of the opposition increased from 35 to 42 seats, out of a total of 231.

The following decades were marked by a general tendency to extend political pluralism by electoral reform. The electoral law was changed before every election. As a result of these very controversial changes, the PRI slowly lost its dominant position. Two reforms were crucial: first the extension of minority representation to proportional representation within a segmented electoral system; second the establishment of an increasingly independent electoral authority, which finally reached full autonomy in the mid-nineties. These developments can be seen as the Mexican model of transition to democracy.

In 1977, the number of seats in the chamber of deputies was established at 400, and the proportional representation principle was introduced for the election of one part of the deputies. This meant the introduction of a segmented system with 300 deputies elected in SMCs using plurality and 100 deputies elected in five MMCs using the proportional representation system reserved exclusively for minority parties. In the 1979 elections, the opposition attained what was then the largest representation, with 104 seats. Along with the PAN (43 seats), the PARM (12) and the PPS (11), other parties gained representation for the first time: the PCM (18), the *Partido Demócrata Mexicano* (PDM; Democratic Mexican Party) (10) and the *Partido Socialista de los Trabajadores* (PST; Socialist Workers' Party) (10).

Although this composition of Parliament basically remained the same after the 1982 elections, this election marked the beginning of a gradual decline in the PRI's electoral domination; this reflected the transformation in Mexican society during the previous decades. In particular, demographic growth, industrialization, the process of urbanization and the improvement of education, fostered demands for wider political liberalization and pluralism. After 1982, the debt crisis helped erode the support for the PRI and the government among the organized popular sectors. Thus, the number of votes won by the PRI's presidential candidate in 1982, Miguel de la Madrid, was the lowest since 1952 (74.3%). As a result, during the 1980s, the PRI ceased to be the dominant party, although it maintained a clear majority in parliament.

The 1986 constitutional reform and the 1987 reform of the Electoral Law increased the number of deputies elected through proportional representation from 100 to 200, and the total number of seats from 400 to 500. However, the majority party could still take part in the allocation of proportional representation seats, provided its total number of seats remained under 350. Furthermore, the so-called 'governability clause' was introduced, according to which the party that obtained the relative majority of deputies and at least 35% of the national vote would be assigned the number of seats needed to attain the absolute majority in the Chamber. Hence, the reform increased the chances of minority parties to participate, at the same time as securing the PRI's absolute majority. In the 1988 elections, the PRI's majority in the chamber of deputies was reduced to 260 out of 500 seats, the lowest figure recorded so far in modern Mexican history. Thus, the PRI failed to keep the two-thirds of seats needed to pass constitutional reforms. The representation of the PAN increased considerably, along with that of the PPS, the PARM and the PTS, now called *Partido Frente Cardenista de Reconstrucción Nacional* (PFCRN; Cardenista Front for National Reconstruction Party). Apart from these forces, the *Partido Mexicano Socialista* (Mexican Socialist Party), founded in 1987, also won representation.

In these elections, the PRI's candidate—Carlos Salinas de Gortari—was elected president with only 50.4% of the vote, the lowest percentage obtained so far by the party. The second-ranking candidate, Cuauthémoc Cárdenas from the *Frente Democrático Nacional* (FDN; National Democratic Front) received 31.1% of the vote. The contested character of these elections and the numerous accusations of fraud, which was evidence of the irregularity of the electoral process, forced President Salinas's government into liberalizing both the political and electoral systems. When assuming office, Salinas pledged to clear up the political scene, consolidate democracy, legitimize the electoral process and modernize the party system.

In order to carry out these objectives, new electoral reforms were implemented. Supported by the PRI and the PAN in 1989 and in 1990, congress agreed on several amendments to the constitution and on a new *Código Federal de Instituciones y Procedimientos Electorales* (COFIPE, Federal Law of Political Organizations and Electoral Processes). Some of the most significant innovations brought about by this law were the creation of the *Instituto Federal Electoral* (IFE; Federal Electoral Institute), to organize and supervise elections; the elaboration of a new electoral roll and new voting cards for the electorate; and the establishment of the *Tribunal Federal Electoral* (TRIFE; Federal Electoral Court), whose tasks were to regulate imputations and to penalize violations of the electoral law. In 1989, the majority that a party could hold was limited to 70% of the seats. In 1990, any party receiving 35% of single member districts deputies and 35% of the national vote was guaranteed an absolute majority in the chamber (governability clause). At the same time, the absolute majority was limited to 60% of the seats or up to 315 seats if a party obtained more than 60% of the popular vote.

The 1991 elections witnessed a recovery of the PRI, which received 61.4 % of the vote and gained an overwhelming majority in the chamber of deputies (320 seats). During the first years of President Salinas' tenure, the two main opposition parties consolidated: the PAN and the *Partido de la Revolución Democrática* (PRD; Democratic Revolutionary Party), which split from the PRI in 1989 with the aim of grouping the leftist opposition that had supported Cuauhtémoc Cárdenas in 1988. The PAN in particular secured its position as the second most important Mexican party: in 1989, as the first opposition party, it had won the gubernatorial elections in the state of Baja California, and the following years saw its victory in three other states as well as in some important mayoralties. The charges against the PRI relating to irregularities and electoral fraud continued, and turned the question of credibility and legitimacy of the electoral processes into a constant source of trouble between the Government and the PRI, on the one hand, and the opposition, on the other hand.

In 1993, a new electoral reform supported by the PRI and the PAN abolished the 'governability clause' and limited the maximum number of seats for the parties to 65% of the total, independent of the percentage of their vote. This measure introduced a principle by which no party could approve reforms or amendments to the constitution alone. The number of senators increased from 64 to 128, four per state. Allocating the fourth senator to the first minority party was intended to increase the representation of the opposition in the senate. However, the reform also tried to provide fairer conditions for competition among parties, and introduced campaign spending limits and restrictions on the financial, individual or institutional support given to the parties; finally, it also regulated the parties' access to the media.

The political instability that preceded the 1994 general elections (the uprising of the *Ejército Zapatista de Liberación Nacional* (EZLN; Zapatista Army of National Liberation) in Chiapas, in January 1994, and the assassination of the PRI's presidential candidate Luis Donaldo Colosio in March, contributed to a consensus among the political forces to introduce new reforms. A *Pacto para la Paz, la Democracia y la Justicia* (Pact for Peace, Justice, and Democracy) was signed by all the relevant parties except the PPC. The most significant results of this pact were the strengthening of the autonomy of the electoral organs and the establishment of a majority of independents in the IFE. Afterwards, congress introduced some reforms into the COFIPE which, among other things, defined the functions of the electoral observers and for the first time allowed international observers to be present at elections. Several of these reforms responded to the demands of the opposition, and enjoyed unprecedented political support.

In the 1994 elections, the PRI's presidential candidate, Ernesto Zedillo Ponce de León, received 50.2% of the valid vote. The electoral turnout was recorded at 77.7%, much greater than the 51.9% registered in the 1988 elections, and Zedillo gained more than seven million more votes than Carlos Salinas de Gortari. In the chamber of deputies, the PRI renewed its absolute majority with 298 seats; yet, in relation to 1991, this can be seen as a considerable loss. The PAN, whose presidential candidate, Diego Fernández de Cavallo, received 26.7% of the vote and gained 122 deputies, confirmed its position as the second strongest party.

From the beginning of his tenure, President Zedillo undertook to end the cycle of 'reform, election, reform' which had been the norm during the past decades; yet, his 'definitive electoral reform' could not fully eradicate the doubts and suspicions about the impartiality and transparency of the electoral process. This intention led to an agreement known as *Compromiso para un Acuerdo Político Nacional* (Commitment to a National Political Agreement), signed on 17 January 1995 by President Zedillo and the four parties represented in congress: the PRI, the PAN, the PRD and the *Partido del Trabajo* (PT; Labor Party), which obtained representation for the first time in 1994. The signatories agreed to establish the conditions that would allow electoral issues to be solved democratically, as well as to secure the legality, equity and transparency of the electoral processes.

However, it was only in July 1996, after 19 months of negotiations, that the four parties reached an agreement to reform 19 articles of the constitution, only after they were approved by both chambers of congress. One of the most significant reforms concerned the composition of the IFE: the executive ceased to be represented. This measure is considered as the final consolidation of the autonomy and impartiality of the IFE. It was also decided to incorporate the TRIFE within the judicial power, so that a special organ of the Supreme Court would act as the highest authority to resolve disputes about electoral issues. Other modifications were introduced to create fairer conditions in the political-electoral competition: first, a new system of public funding for political parties (campaign spending limits, control mechanisms) and second, the improvement of the parties' access to the mass media.

However, the agreement among the parties now reduced the number of seats allocated to each party to 300. Likewise, the difference between the percentage of seats allocated to one party in the chamber and the percentage of the vote obtained by this party in the national vote could not be higher than 8 %. If this only happens in SMCs by plurality, the rule does not apply. The legal threshold was raised from 1.5% to 2.0%. At the same time, the national constituency for proportional representation was replaced by five MMCs. As regards the senate, the agreement introduced a segmented system so that three-quarters of the members of the upper chamber were elected by plurality with representation of minorities and one-quarter by proportional representation. The number of senators for each state was reduced from four to three and one single nationwide MMC created for the election of 32 senators by proportional representation. Furthermore, the agreement established the direct election of the mayor of Mexico City for the first time in 1997, who had previously been appointed by the president. Nonetheless, the opposition disagreed with the PRI in relation to the financing of political parties, and refused to support the passage of the Electoral Law, which was finally put into effect thanks only to the vote of the PRI parliamentary majority.

The mid-term elections held in June 1997 were a benchmark in Mexican electoral history. The PRI lost its absolute majority in the chamber of deputies with 39.1% of the vote. It had to cede 136 uninominal seats to the opposition parties: 70 to the PRD, 65 to the PAN and 1 to the PT. As the renewal of the senate was only partial, the PRI managed to maintain its absolute majority. The most important result in the medium term was the victory of Cuauhtémoc Cárdenas (PRD), with 41% of the vote, in the elections to mayor of Mexico City.

Three years later, the presidential elections of 2000 provoked a fundamental change in Mexican political history as well as the confirmation of the transition to democracy in the form of the substantial electoral reform of 1996. For the first time in 71 years, the revolutionary party lost a presidential election. Vicente Fox Quesada from PAN obtained 44.2% of the valid votes, while the PRI candidate, Francisco Labastida Ochoa, won only 37.5%. In the parliamentary elections, the victory of PAN was smaller, 39% against 37.8%, and as PRD obtained 19.1% of the votes, the structure of power relations in congress was also changed. No party had an absolute majority. In the 2003 mid-term elections, this general tendency of tripartism in Mexico was confirmed. While PRI maintained its position, PAN lost votes and PRD was able to narrow the gap between itself and the top two parties.

1.2 Evolution of Electoral Provisions

The main sources of electoral provisions are the constitutions of 1824, 1857 and 1917 with their many amendments and the electoral laws *(Códigos Electorales)*, the first one of 1857. The most important constitutional reforms concerning electoral provisions date from 1946, 1963, 1977, 1987, 1989, 1990, 1993, 1994, and 1996.

The constitution of 1857 established universal male suffrage. Female suffrage was first introduced in 1954. In 1973, the minimum age for active suffrage was reduced from 21 to 18 years. Originally, elections were indirect for both the president and parliament. It was only in 1912 that a presidential decree *(Decreto Presidencial)* abolished indirect elections.

Until 1928, the term of office for the president was four years, later on six. As of the constitution of 1917, re-election was completely prohibited. The term of office for deputies was initially two years, increased by the constitutional reform of 1933 to three years. Senators were elected for a term of six years. In 1933, the term was reduced to four years, half of the members being renewed every two years. Since 1986, the senate is renewed every three years. Re-election of deputies and senators is only permitted after a full intermediate term has passed.

According to all constitutions, a candidate has to win elections by an absolute majority to become president. Originally, the candidate with the second highest number of votes was declared vice president. In 1836, the office of vice president was abolished, and the constitution prescribed that if the president had to step down within the first two years of his term of office, the congress would elect an interim president by absolute majority who would prepare new elections.

The plurality system was applied for parliamentary elections. With the reform of 1963, minority representation was established for the chamber of deputies. Proportional elements were introduced in 1977, and were increased by the following reforms so that the electoral system became segmented. In detail: Until 1963, elections were only held in SMCs. In 1917, a population of 60,000 or a minimum of 20,000 inhabitants served as the basis for forming districts. Later on, this number was continuously increased. Since 1963, the national territory with regard to electoral districting consisted of 178 SMCs *(candidaturas mayoritarias)* and one MMC for minority representation *(candidaturas minoritarias)*. Ten years later, the number of SMCs was increased to 194. In 1977, 100 seats were added to the now 200 SMCs. They were initially distributed in three MMCs, since 1982 in four MMCs. These seats were increased in 1986 to 200, distributed since 1985 in five MMCs of 40 members each.

Special arrangements had been prescribed in order to limit the majority one party could have: in 1986 and 1990, the electoral provisions limited the number of seats a party could obtain to 70% of the total; that percentage was reduced in 1993 to 65% and in 1996 to 60%. On the other hand, in 1990 the *cuota de gobernabilidad* was introduced. The party obtaining more than 35% of the valid votes was entitled to receive an absolute majority of seats. This quota was abolished in 1996, and a further limit to disproportionality introduced. The maximum difference between the share of votes and the share of seats was limited to eight percentage points, except when the winning party gained as many members in the SMCs as to pass the share of votes plus 8% of the total vote. The threshold was increased in 1996 from 1.5 to 2%.

Until 1963, candidatures were individual. Since then, SMCs continued to exist, but at national level closed and blocked lists were introduced. Despite the two forms of candidature, voters had only one vote. Since 1977, voters had two votes, one for a candidate in a SMC, and one for a party list in one of the MMCs. In 1987, the number of votes was again restricted to one, and in 1989 extended again to two. Currently, the voter has one vote. Until 1963, plurality was the only method used to distribute seats. Once the rule of minority representation had been introduced, other rules were added. In 1963, minority seats were distributed as follows: in order to take part in the distribution, parties had to obtain at least 2.5% of the valid votes cast. Party lists that passed this barrier got five seats. For each additional 0.5% of the votes, parties obtained one more seat. In total, a minority party was entitled to obtain 20 seats. If a minority party won 20 seats in SMCs, it was excluded from the minority seats distribution. The distribution of minority seats within a party between candidates was governed by the individual votes obtained by minority candidates, comparing electoral results in SMCs, and not by the national closed and blocked list. In 1973, the legal threshold was reduced to 1.5% and the number of minority seats for one party was increased to 25. In 1996, however, the legal threshold was increased to 2%.

The type of electoral system was changed in 1977 when a segmented system was introduced. The plurality rule was maintained in 300 SMCs. For the additional 100 seats (since 1985, 200 seats), proportional representation was introduced, based on a modified Hare quota. The quota was calculated by dividing the 'effective votes', that is the sum of the valid votes minus the sum of the votes that did not pass the legal threshold, by the number of seats to be distributed plus two. Parties that had obtained more than 60 (since 1985, 70) seats in SMCs, were excluded from participating in the distribution of proportional seats. Electoral alliances were prohibited in 1989 and permitted again in 1996 under certain circumstances.

1.3 Current Electoral Provisions

Sources: Constitution of 1917 (*Constitución Política de los Estados Unidos Méxicanos*), Electoral Law (*Código Federal de Instituciones y Procedimientos Electorales*).

Suffrage: The principles of universal, equal, direct and secret suffrage are applied. To acquire the right to active suffrage a person needs to have the Mexican citizenship. All Mexican citizens over the age of 18 may vote. In order to be a citizen, one has to have an honest way of living. In practice, this requirement often functions as a means for withdrawing a citizen's rights. In order to exercise active suffrage, citizens must be entered in the electorate registry and have a photo voting card, which can be issued by the Federal Electoral Institute (IFE).

Elected national institutions: President of the United Mexican States (term of office of six years, no re-election); Congress of the Union, made up of two branches, chamber of deputies and senate. The chamber of deputies has 500 representatives, elected for a three-year term and may only be re-elected after an intermediate period. The senate consists of 128 members, elected for a six-years term. They may only be re-elected after an intermediate period.

Nomination of Candidates: In order to have the right to be elected, the requisites are basically the same as the ones stipulated for active suffrage plus additional requirements.
- *presidential elections*: The constitution prohibits a citizen who has already held this post whether by popular election or on an interim, provisional, or substitute basis, to hold this office again under any condition. According to the constitution, in order to be elected president a person must (a) be a citizen and Mexican by birth, child of a Mexican and have resided in the country for at least twenty years; (b) be at least 35 years old on the day of the election; (c) have resided within the

country for a full year prior to the day of the election; (d) not be a minister of any church.

The constitution establishes two additional criteria that excludes a person from voting: (a) a person in active military service, or any person who was a member of the armed forces six months prior to the election; (b) a person who is secretary or vice secretary of state, chief of staff or secretary general of administration, attorney general of the republic, or governor of any federal entity, unless the person resigns from the post at least six months prior to election day.

- *parliamentary elections*: Deputies and senators cannot be re-elected for the next consecutive period. Another temporal impediment exists for persons who serve in public office, unless they resign their post one year prior to the date of initiation of an electoral process, that is to say 21 months before the date of the election.

For the chamber of deputies, the constitution and federal legislation establish the following requirements: a person must be Mexican by birth, with full enjoyment of her/his rights; at least 21 years old on the day of the election; born in the federal entity that he/she wishes to represent, that is a SMC (first case) or a regional MMC (second case), or be a resident there for at least six months prior to election day (in both cases); be registered in the Federal Electoral Registry and have a photo voting card. For the senate the same requirements apply, except for the age limitation: candidates must be 28 years old on the day of the election. Up to 60 candidates of the same party can be registered both in individual form in SMCs and in the regional list within MMCs.

Electoral system
- *presidential elections*: the candidate who obtains a relative majority of the votes is elected president.
- *parliamentary elections*: Chamber of deputies is elected through a segmented system. Each voter has one vote, which counts for both the SMC and the MMC. Out of the 500 members, 300 are elected by plurality in SMCs. The distribution of the 300 uninominal constituencies among the 32 federal entities is determined according to the percentage of the population residing in each, compared with the national total (a population census is carried out in Mexico every ten years). No federal entity may have less than two seats. The remaining 200 members are elected by proportional representation in five regional MMCs, each of which has 40 members. The regional lists are blocked and closed. Political parties are assigned a number of proportional seats in each MMC according to the percentage of national votes they obtain.

Two further conditions may determine the distribution of seats: (a) no political party can hold more than 300 seats by adding those received by relative majority and those of proportional representation (so that no party can hold two-thirds of the total number of seats required to approve initiatives on constitutional reform alone); and (b) a party's share of seats may not exceed by more than eight percentage points its share of votes.

To participate in the distribution of seats through proportional representation parties must meet two conditions: (a) have registered candidates in at least 200 of the 300 SMCs; and (b) have achieved at least 2% of the votes cast for the regional lists in the MMCs.

Senate: In each of the 32 federal entities there are three senators, two are assigned to the party that has obtained the highest number of votes and the third for the first minority. The 32 remaining senators are elected by proportional representation in one national MMC. The formula used is the Hare quota and greatest remainder.

Organizational context of elections: There are two main institutions, separating the administrative function from the judicial one. The Federal Electoral Institute (IFE; *Instituto Federal Electoral*), a public organization with its own patrimony, is responsible for organizing the federal elections. It was founded in 1990 as a result of a series of reforms of the constitution approved in 1989. It underwent significant change and was finally established as a permanent autonomous institution in 1996.

The IFE is in charge of vote counting, taking into account the resolutions of the Electoral Tribunal of the Supreme Court of Justice of the Federation, and publishing the results, except the official results of the presidential elections, for which the Electoral Tribunal is responsible.

The Electoral Tribunal of the Supreme Court of Justice of the Federation (*Tribunal Electoral del Poder Judicial de la Federación*), a branch of the Supreme Court, is responsible for the judicial review of the electoral process. It assigns the seats to members of both chambers, elected by proportional representation. It is entitled to grant the validity of the elections and to announce the president. It has the power to resolve the legal challenges made by political parties against the results of the elections or against decisions taken by the IFE.

1.4 Commentary on the Electoral Statistics

Since the establishment of the IFE and the Electroal Tribunal the electoral results have been fully reliable. Results from earlier elections might be manipulated, although this cannot be proven with certainty.

2. Tables

2.1 Dates of National Elections, Referendums, and Coups d'Etat

Year	Presidential Elections	Parliamentary Elections	Elections for Constitutional Assembly	Referendums	Coups d'Etat
1917	11/03				
1920	xx/xx				
1924	xx/xx				
1928	xx/xx				
1929	xx/xx				
1934	01/07				
1940	07/07				
1943		15/08			
1946	07/07	07/07			
1949		03/07			
1952	07/07	07/07			
1955		04/07			
1958	06/07	06/07			
1961		02/07			
1964	05/07	05/07			
1967		02/07			
1970	05/07	05/07			
1973		01/07			
1976	04/07	04/07			
1979		01/07			
1982	04/07	04/07			
1985		07/07			
1988	06/07	06/07			
1991		18/08			
1994	21/08	21/08			
1997		06/06			
2000	06/07	06/07			
2003		06/07			

2.2 Electoral Body 1917–2003

Year	Type of election[a]	Population[b]	Registered voters Total number	% pop.	Votes cast Total number	% reg. voters	% pop.
1917	Pr	13,417,751	—	—	812,928	—	6.1
1920	Pr	13,965,933	—	—	—	—	—
1924	Pr	14,853,238	—	—	—	—	—
1928	Pr	16,021,000	—	—	—	—	—
1929	Pr	16,302,000	—	—	—	—	—
1934	Pr	17,773,000	—	—	—	—	—
1940	Pr	19,815,000	—	—	—	—	—
1943[c]	Pa	21,417,000	2,124,549	9.9	—	—	—
1946	Pr	23,183,000	2,556,949	11.0	—	—	—
1946	Pa	23,183,000	2,556,949	11.0	—	—	—
1949	Pa	25,826,000	2,992,084	11.6	—	—	—
1952	Pr	27,415,000	4,924,293	18.0	—	—	—
1952	Pa	27,415,000	4,924,293	18.0	—	—	—
1955[d]	Pa	30,015,000	8,941,020	29.8	—	—	—
1958	Pr	32,895,000	10,443,465	31.8	—	—	—
1958	Pa	32,895,000	10,443,465	31.8	—	—	—
1961	Pa	36,091,000	10,004,696	27.7	—	—	—
1964	Pr	39,422,000	13,589,594	34.5	—	—	—
1964	Pa	39,422,000	13,589,594	34.5	—	—	—
1964[e]	S	39,422,000	13,589,594	34.5	—	—	—
1967	Pa	45,671,000	15,821,075	34.6	9,938,814	62.8	21.8
1970	Pa	50,670,000	21,654,217	42.7	13,940,862	64.4	27.5
1970	S	50,670,000	21,654,217	42.7	13,940,862	64.4	27.5
1970	Pr	50,670,000	21,654,217	42.7	—	—	—
1973	Pa	54,303,000	24,890,261	45.8	15,009,984	60.3	27.6
1976	Pr	62,329,000	25,913,066	45.8	—	—	—
1976	S	62,329,000	25,913,066	41.6	16,727,993	64.6	26.8
1976	Pa	62,329,000	25,913,066	41.6	16,068,911	62.0	25.8
1979	Pa[f]	69,381,000	27,912,053	40.2	13,796,410	49.4	19.9
1979	Pa[g]	69,381,000	27,912,053	40.2	13,772,729	49.3	19.9
1982	Pr	73,011,000	31,526,386	43.2	23,592,888	74.8	32.2
1982	Pa[f]	73,011,000	31,520,884	43.2	20,919,880	66.4	28.7
1982	Pa[g]	73,011,000	31,516,370	43.2	22,866,719	72.6	31.3
1982	S	73,011,000	31,520,884	43.2	—	—	—
1985	Pa[f]	78,524,000	35,278,369	44.9	17,879,924	50.7	22.8
1985	Pa[g]	78,524,000	35,278,369	44.9	18,281,851	51.8	23.3
1988	Pr	82,734,000	38,074,926	46.0	19,640,722	51.6	23.7
1988	Pa	82,734,000	38,074,926	46.0	18,820,415	49.4	22.8
1988	S	82,734,000	38,074,926	46.0	18,915,722	49.7	22.9
1991	Pa[f]	82,737,000	39,517,979	47.8	24,032,482	60.8	29.0

Year (cont.)	Type of election[a]	Population[b]	Registered voters Total number	% pop.	Votes cast Total number	% reg. voters	% pop.
1991	Pa[g]	82,737,000	39,517,979	47.8	24,194,239	61.2	29.2
1991	S	82,737,000	39,517,979	47.8	24,302,640	61.5	29.4
1994	Pr	87,362,000	45,729,053	52.3	35,285,291	77.2	40.4
1994	Pa[h]	87,362,000	45,729,053	52.3	34,686,916	75.9	39.7
1994	Pa[i]	87,362,000	45,729,053	52.3	35,406,684	77.4	40.5
1994	S	87,362,000	45,729,053	52.3	35,302,831	77.2	40.4
1997	Pa[h]	92,247,000	52,208,966	56.6	29,771,671	57.0	32.3
1997	Pa[i]	92,247,000	52,208,966	56.6	30,119,853	57.7	32.7
1997	S[i]	92,247,000	52,208,966	56.6	30,153,712	57.8	32.7
2000	Pr	97,362,000	58,782,737	60.4	37,601,618	64.0	38.6
2000	Pa[h]	97,362,000	58,782,737	60.4	37,174,460	63.2	38.2
2000	Pa[i]	97,362,000	58,782,737	60.4	37,421,025	63.7	38.4
2000	S[h]	97,362,000	58,782,737	60.4	37,285,855	63.4	38.3
2000	S[i]	97,362,000	58,782,737	60.4	37,534,641	63.9	38.6
2003	Pa[h]	102,806,000	64,710,596	62.9	26,579,616	41.1	25.9
2003	Pa[i]	102,806,000	64,710,596	62.9	26,738,924	41.3	26.0

[a] CA = Constitutional Assembly; Pa = Parliament; Pr = President; S = Senate.
[b] Population data based on census information.
[c] Data on parliamentary elections prior to 1943 were not available.
[d] Women suffrage was introduced in 1955.
[e] Data on senate elections prior to 1964 were not available.
[f] Results for the *'diputados de mayoría'*.
[g] Results for the *'diputados de partido'*.
[h] By plurality.
[i] By proportional representation.

2.3 Abbreviations

BOC	*Bloque Obrero Campesino* (Workers' and Farmers' Block)
CD	*Convergencia para la Democracia* (Convergence for Democracy)
CDO	*Centro Director Obregón* (Director Obregón Center)
CRPI	*Confederación Revolucionaria de Partidos Independientes* (Revolutionary Confederation of Independent Parties)
DSPPN	*Democracia Social Partido Político Nacional* (Social Democracy National Political Party)
FDN[a]	*Frente Democrático Nacional* (National Democratic Front)
FPPM	*Federación de Partidos del Pueblo Mexicano* (Federation of the Mexican People's Parties)
LLD	*La Liga Democrática* (The Democratic League)
LPN	*Liga Política Nacional* (National Political League)
MAUS	*Movimiento de Acción y Unidad Socialista* (Action and Socialist Unity Movement)

PAM	*Partido Antireeleccionista Mexicano* (Mexican Anti Re-election Party)
PAN	*Partido Acción Nacional* (National Action Party)
PARM	*Partido Auténtico de la Revolución Mexicana* (Authentic Party of the Mexican Revolution)
PCD	*Partido Central Democrático* (Democratic Central Party)
PCM	*Partido Comunista Mexicano* (Mexican Communist Party)
PDM (1)	*Partido Democrático Mexicano* (Mexican Democractic Party)
PDM (2)	*Partido Demócrata Mexicano* (Mexican Democratic Party)
PEM	*Partido Ecologista de México* (Ecologist Party of Mexico)
PFCRN	*Partido del Frente Cardenista de Reconstrucción Nacional* (Party of the *Cardenista* Front of National Reconstruction)
PLC	*Partido Liberal Constitucionalista* (Liberal Constitutionalist Party)
PLM	*Partido Laborista Mexicano* (Mexican Labor Party)
PMS	*Partido Mexicano Socialista* (Mexican Socialist Party)
PMT	*Partido Mexicano de los Trabajadores* (Mexican Workers' Party)
PNC	*Partido Nacional Constitucionalista* (National Constitutionalist Party)
PNM	*Partido Nacional Mexicano* (Mexican National Party)
PNR[b]	*Partido Nacional Revolucionario* (National Revolutionary Party)
PNRPR	*Partido Nacional Reivindicador Popular Revolucionario* (Revolutionary, National, Claim-Laying, Popular Party)
PP[c]	*Partido Popular* (Popular Party)
PPM	*Partido del Pueblo Mexicano* (Mexican Party of the People)
PPS[c]	*Partido Popular Socialista* (Socialist Popular Party)
PRD	*Partido de la Revolución Democrática* (Party of the Democratic Revolution)
PRI[b]	*Partido Revolucionario Institucional* (Institutional Revolutionary Party)
PRM[b]	*Partido de la Revolución Mexicana* (Party of the Mexican Revolution)
PRN	*Partido Republicano Nacionalista* (Nationalist Republican Party)
PRT	*Partido Revolucionario de los Trabajadores* (Revolutionary Workers' Party)
PRUN	*Partido Revolucionario de la Unificación Nacional* (Revolutionary Party of National Unification)
PSD	*Partido Social Demócrata* (Social Democratic Party)
PAS	*Partido Alianza Social* (Social Alliance Party)
PSI	*Partido Socialista de las Izquierdas* (Socialist Parties of the Lefts)
PSN	*Partido de la Sociedad Nacionalista* (Party of the Nationalist Society)
PSR	*Partido Socialista Revolucionario* (Revolutionary Socialist Party)
PST	*Partido Socialista de los Trabajadores* (Socialist Party of the Workers)
PSUM[d]	*Partido Socialista Unificado de México* (Unified Socialist Party of Mexico)
PT	*Partido de Trabajo* (Labor Party)

[a] Electoral alliance in 1988 between PFCRN, PPS and PARM.
[b] The *Partido Revolucionario* was founded in 1929. Until 1938 it was called PNR, then renamed to PRM. Since 1946 it carries the name PRI.
[c] PP was renamed to PPS.
[d] Electoral alliance between PCM, PMT, PPM, PSR and MAUS.

2.4 Electoral Participation of Parties and Alliances 1917–2000

Party / Alliance	Years	Elections contested[a]
LLD	1917	1
PLC	1917	1
CDO	1920; 1928	2
PRN	1920	1
LPN	1924	1
PLM	1924	1
BOC	1929	1
PAM	1929	1
PNR/PRM/PRI	1929–1988	13
CRPI	1934	1
PCM	1934	1
PSI	1934	1
PRM	1940	1
PRUN	1940	1
PDM (1)	1946	1
PNC	1946	1
PNRPR	1946	1
FPPM	1952	1
PAN	1952–1970; 1982–2000	8
PP	1952	1
PDM (2)	1982–1994	3
PRT	1982–1988	2
PSD	1982	1
PST	1982	1
PSUM	1982	1
FDN	1988	1
PRD	1994–2000	2
PT	1994	1
PVCRN	1994	1
PVEM	1994	1
PARM	1994–2000	2
PPS	1994	1
PCD	2000	1
DSPPN	2000	1

[a] Only presidential elections. Total number: 17.

2.5. Referendums

Referendums have not been held.

2.6. *Elections for Constitutional Assembly*

Elections for constitutional assembly have not been held.

2.7 *Parliamentary Elections*

2.7.1 Lower Chamber (House of Representatives) 1943–2003

Year	1943[a]		1946	
	Total number	%	Total number	%
Registered voters	2,124,549	–	2,556,949	–
Votes cast	—	—	—	—
Invalid votes	—	—	—	—
Valid votes	408,101	—	2,294,928	—
PRI	376,000	92.1	1,687,284	73.5
PAN	21,749	5.3	51,312	2.2
PCM	–	–	10,542	0.5
Others	–	–	545,790	23.8
Non-registered candidates	10,352	2.5	–	–

[a] No data were available for parliamentary elections prior to 1943.

Year	1949		1952	
	Total number	%	Total number	%
Registered voters	2,992,084	–	4,924,293	–
Votes cast	—	—	—	—
Invalid votes	—	—	—	—
Valid votes	2,163,582	—	3,651,483	—
PRI	2,031,783	93.9	2,713,419	74.3
PAN	121,061	5.6	301,986	8.3
PPS	10,738	0.5	32,194	0.9
FPPM	–	–	579,745	–
PNM	–	–	24,139	–
Others	–	–	–	16.5

Year	1955		1958	
	Total number	%	Total number	%
Registered voters	8,941,020	–	10,443,465	–
Votes cast	—	—	—	—
Invalid votes	—	—	—	—
Valid votes	6,190,376	—	7,332,429	—
PRI	5,562,761	89.9	6,467,493	88.2
PAN	567,678	9.2	749,519	10.2
PPS	42,621	0.7	50,145	0.7
Others	17,316[a]	0.3	65,272[b]	0.9

[a] PNM

[b] Others include: PARM: 32,464 votes (0.4%); PNM: 22,499 (0.3%) and non-registered candidates: 10,309 (0.1%).

Year	1961		1964	
	Total number	%	Total number	%
Registered voters	10,004,696	–	13,589,594	–
Votes cast	—	—	—	—
Invalid votes	—	—	—	—
Valid votes	6,845,826	—	9,051,524	—
PRI	6,178,434	90.3	7,807,912	86.3
PAN	518,652	7.6	1,042,396	11.5
PPS	65,143	1.0	123,837	1.4
PARM	33,671	0.5	64,409	0.7
PNM	19,082	0.3	–	–
Non-registered candidates	30,844	0.5	12,970	0.1

Year	1967		1970	
	Total number	%	Total number	%
Registered voters	15,821,075	–	21,654,217	–
Votes cast	—	—	13,940,862	64.4
Invalid votes	—	—	585,874	4.2
Valid votes	9,938,814	—	13,354,988	95.8
PRI	8,342,114	83.9	11,125,770	83.3
PAN	1,223,926	12.3	1,893,289	14.2
PPS	215,087	2.3	188,854	1.4
PARM	138,799	1.4	111,883	0.8
Non-registered candidates	18,888	0.2	35,192	0.3

Year	1973		1976	
	Total number	%	Total number	%
Registered voters	24,890,261	–	25,913,066	–
Votes cast	15,009,984	60.3	16,068,911	62.0
Invalid votes	1,493,267	10.0	910,431	5.7
Valid votes	13,516,717	90.1	15,158,480	94.3
PRI	10,458,618	77.4	12,868,104	85.0
PAN	2,207,069	16.3	1,358,403	9.0
PPS	541,833	4.0	479,228	3.2
PARM	272,339	2.0	403,274	2.7
Non-registered candidates	36,858	0.3	49,471	0.3

Year	1979[a]		1979[b]	
	Total number	%	Total number	%
Registered voters	27,912,053	–	27,912,053	–
Votes cast	13,796,410	49.4	13,772,729	49.3
Invalid votes	683,728	5.0	833,146	6.1
Valid votes	13,112,682	95.0	12,939,583	94.0
PRI	9,714,151	74.1	9,418,178	72.8
PAN	1,485,593	11.3	1,525,111	11.8
PCM	691,229	5.3	703,068	5.4
PPS	380,719	2.9	389,590	3.0
PDM	296,623	2.3	293,540	2.3
PST	294,727	2.3	311,913	2.4
PARM	238,892	1.8	298,183	2.3
Non-registered candidates	10,748	0.1	–	–

[a] Votes for the *'diputados de mayoría'*.
[b] Votes for the *'diputados de partido'*.

Year	1982[a]		1982[b]	
	Total number	%	Total number	%
Registered voters	31,520,884[c]	–	31,516,370[c]	–
Votes cast	20,919,880	66.4	22,866,719	72.6
Invalid votes	10,192	0.1	1,121,378	4.9
Valid votes	20,909,688	100	21,745,341	95.1
PRI	14,501,988	69.4	14,289,793	65.7
PAN	3,663,846	17.5	3,786,348	17.4
PPS	395,006	1.9	459,303	2.1
PDM	475,099	2.3	534,122	2.1
PST	372,679	1.8	428,153	2.0
PARM	282,971	1.4	282,004	1.3
PSUM	914,365	4.4	932,214	4.3
PRT	264,632	1.3	308,099	1.4
PSD	38,994	0.2	53,306	0.3
Non-registered candidates	108	0.0	671,999	3.1

[a] Votes for the *'diputados de mayoría'*.
[b] Votes for the *'diputados de partido'*.
[c] The number of registered voters differs due to a later special election in the 24th district.

Year	1985[a]		1985[b]	
	Total number	%	Total number	%
Registered voters	35,278,369	–	35,278,369	–
Votes cast	17,879,924	50.7	18,281,851	51.8
Invalid votes	840,195	4.7	930,348	5.1
Valid votes	17,039,729	95.3	17,351,503	94.9
PRI	11,588,230	68.0	10,981,938	63.3
PAN	2,787,218	16.4	2,831,248	16.3
PSUM	575,121	3.4	602,530	3.5
PDM	489,025	2.9	507,710	2.9
PPS	349,680	2.1	441,567	2.6
PST	440,751	2.6	593,022	3.4
PRT	225,636	1.3	289,626	1.7
PARM	295,434	1.7	416,780	2.4
PMT	276,712	1.6	291,127	1.7
Others	11,922	0.1	395,955	2.3

[a] Votes for the *'diputados de mayoría'*.
[b] Votes for the *'diputados de partido'*.

Year	1988[a]	
	Total number	%
Registered voters	38,074,926	–
Votes cast	18,820,415	49.4
Invalid votes	620,220	3.3
Valid votes	18,200,195	96.7
PRI	9,276,934	51.0
PAN	3,276,824	18.0
PFCRN	1,704,532	9.4
PPS	1,673,863	9.2
PARM	1,124,575	6.2
PMS	810,372	4.5
PDM	244,458	1.3
PRT	88,637	0.5

[a] For this election, the number of votes was reduced to one.

Year	1991[a]		1991[b]	
	Total number	%	Total number	%
Registered voters	39,517,979	–	39,517,979	–
Votes cast	24,032,482	60.8	24,194,239	61.2
Invalid votes	1,160,050	4.8	1,168,631	4.8
Valid votes	22,872,432	95.2	23,025,608	95.2
PRI	14,051,349	61.4	14,145,234	61.4
PAN	4,042,316	17.7	4,068,712	17.7
PRD	1,900,750	8.3	1,913,174	8.3
PFCRN	990,440	4.3	998,158	4.3
PARM	489,732	2.1	492,514	2.1
PPS	411,848	1.8	414,780	1.8
PEM	329,714	1.4	332,603	1.4
PT	258,595	1.1	260,266	1.1
PDM	248,431	1.1	249,915	1.1
PRT	135,360	0.6	136,341	0.6
Non-registered candidates	13,897	0.1	13,911	0.1

[a] Votes for *'diputados de mayoría'*.
[b] Votes for *'diputados de partido'*.

Year	1994			
	By plurality		By proportional representation	
	Total number	%	Total number	%
Registered voters	45,729,053	–	45,729,053	–
Votes cast	34,686,916	75.9	35,406,684	77.4
Invalid votes	1,121,006	3.2	1,126,381	3.2
Valid votes	33,565,910	96.8	34,280,303	96.8
PRI	16,851,082	50.2	17,236,836	50.3
PAN	8,664,384	25.8	8,833,468	25.8
PRD	5,590,391	16.7	5,728,733	16.7
PT	896,426	2.7	909,251	2.7
PVEM	470,951	1.4	479,594	1.4
PFCRN	379,960	1.1	390,402	1.1
PARM	285,526	0.9	290,489	0.9
PPS	231,162	0.7	239,371	0.7
Others	196,028[a]	0.6	172,159[b]	0.5

[a] Others include PDM: 148,279 votes (0.4%) and independents: 47,749 (0.1%).
[b] Others include PDM: 151,100 votes (0.4%) and independents: 21,059 (0.1%).

Year	1997			
	By plurality		By proportional representation	
	Total number	%	Total number	%
Registered voters	52,208,966	–	52,208,966	–
Votes cast	29,771,671	57.0	30,119,853	57.7
Invalid votes	845,803	2.8	856,732	2.8
Valid votes	28,925,868	97.2	29,263,121	97.2
PRI	11,305,957	39.1	11,438,719	39.1
PAN	7,698,840	26.6	7,795,538	26.6
PRD	7,435,456	25.7	7,518,903	25.7
PVEM	1,105,688	3.8	1,116,137	3.8
PT	748,869	2.6	756,125	2.6
PC	325,465	1.1	328,872	1.1
PDM	191,779	0.7	193,903	0.7
PPS	98,176	0.3	99,109	0.3
Independents	15,638	0.5	15,815	0.5

| Year | 2000 | | | |
| | By plurality | | By proportional representation | |
	Total number	%	Total number	%
Registered voters	58,782,737	–	58,782,737	–
Votes cast	37,174,460	63.2	37,421,025	63.7
Invalid votes	863,262	2.3	868,516	2.3
Valid votes	36,311,198	97.7	36,552,509	97.7
Alliance for Change (PAN)	14,212,476	38.2	14,323,649	38.2
PRI	13,720,453	36.9	13,800,306	36.9
Alliance for Mexico (PRD)	6,948,204	18.7	6,990,143	18.7
DS	698,683	1.9	703,532	1.9
PCD	428,577	1.2	430,812	1.2
PARM	272,425	0.7	273,615	0.7
Others	30,380	0.1	30,452	0.1

| Year | 2003 | | | |
| | By plurality | | By proportional representation | |
	Total number	%	Total number	%
Registered voters	64,710,596	–	64,710,596	–
Votes cast	26,579,616[a]	41.1	26,738,924	41.3
Invalid votes	896,649	3.4	899,227	3.4
Valid votes	25,682,967	96.6	25,839,697	96.6
PRI	9,804,043	38.2	9,833,856	38.1
PAN	8,189,699	31.9	8,219,649	31.8
PRD	4,694,365	18.3	4,707,009	18.2
Alianza para Todos				
PVEM	1,063,741	4.1	1,068,721	4.1
PT	640,724	2.5	642,290	2.5
Convergencia	602,392	2.3	605,156	2.3
México Posible	242,280	0.9	243,361	0.9
PAS	197,488	0.8	198,075	0.8
Fuerza Ciudadania	123,499	0.5	124,022	0.5
Others	124,736[b]	0.5	197,558[c]	0.8

[a] Official results state 26,651,645 votes cast.

[b] Others include PLM: 108,377 votes (0.4%) and non-registered candidates: 16,359 (0.1%).

[c] Others include PLM: 108,844 votes (0.4%); PSN: 72,267 (0.3%) and non-registered candidates: 16,447 (0.1%).

2.7.2 Upper Chamber (Senate) 1964–2000

Year[a]	1964		1970	
	Total number	%	Total number	%
Registered voters	13,589,594	–	21,654,217	–
Votes cast	—	—	13,940,862	64.4
Invalid votes	—	—	717,010	5.1
Valid votes	8,923,001	—	13,223,852	94.9
PRI	7,837,364	87.8	11,154,003	84.4
PAN	1,001,045	11.2	1,889,157	14.3
PPS	57,617	0.7	143,648	1.1
PARM	13,007	0.2	3,476	0.0
Non-registered candidates	13,968	0.2	33,568	0.3

[a] There were no data available for the senate elections prior to 1964.

Year	1976		1982	
	Total number	%	Total number	%
Registered voters	25,913,066	–	31,520,884	–
Votes cast	16,727,993	64.6	—	—
Invalid votes	1,407,472	8.4	—	—
Valid votes	15,320,521	91.6	—	—
PRI	13,406,825	87.5	—	—
PAN	1,245,406	8.1	—	—
PPS	438,850	2.9	—	—
PARM	188,788	1.2	—	—
PFCRN	–	–	—	—
PMS	–	–	—	—
PDM	–	–	—	—
PRT	–	–	—	—
Non-registered candidates	40,662	0.3	—	—

Year	1988		1991	
	Total number	%	Total number	%
Registered voters	38,074,926	–	39,517,979	–
Votes cast	18,915,722	49.7	24,302,640	61.5
Invalid votes	689,542	3.6	1,138,260	4.7
Valid votes	18,226,180[a]	96.4	23,164,380[b]	95.3
PRI	9,263,810	50.8	14,256,447	61.5
PAN	3,293,460	18.1	4,100,287	17.7
PFCRN	1,727,376	9.5	1,202,425	5.2
PPS	1,702,203	9.3	97,780	0.4
PARM	1,154,811	6.3	487,258	2.1
PMS	770,659	4.2	–	–
PDM	223,631	1.2	276,661	1.2
PRT	76,135	0.4	156,918	0.7
PRD	–	–	878,115	3.8
PVEM	–	–	326,251	1.4
PT	–	–	258,510	1.1
Non-registered candidates	13,222	0.1	14,284	0.1

[a] The official *'Informe Oficial'* states 18,240,767 valid votes.
[b] There is a difference of 13,496 votes between the official total stated here and the sum of all party's votes.

Year	1994	
	Total number	%
Registered voters	45,729,053	–
Votes cast	35,302,831	77.2
Invalid votes	1,078,198	3.1
Valid votes	34,224,633	96.9
PRI	17,195,536	50.2
PRD	5,759,949	16.8
PAN	8,805,038	25.7
PFCRN	400,019	1.2
PPS	215,673	0.6
PARM	269,735	0.8
PDM	120,419	0.4
PT	977,072	2.9
PVEM	438,941	1.3
Independents	42,251	0.1

Year	1997 By proportional representation[a]		
	Total number	%	
Registered voters	52,208,966	–	
Votes cast	30,153,712	57.8	
Invalid votes	872,421	2.9	
Valid votes	29,281,291	97.1	
PRI	11,266,155	38.5	
PRD	7,564,656	25.8	
PAN	7,881,121	26.9	
PC	337,328	1.2	
PT	745,881	2.6	
PVEM	1,180,004	4.0	
PPS	96,500	0.3	
PDM	193,509	0.7	
Non-registered candidates	16,137	0.1	

[a] This election was the first after the constitutional reform of 1996, which introduced a segmented system for the senate. Only the 32 senators through the proportional formula were elected to serve for three years together with the other senators still in office. The first total renovation under the new system was scheduled for 2000.

Year	2000 By plurality		By proportional representation	
	Total number	%	Total number	%
Registered voters	58,782,737	–	58,782,737	–
Votes cast	37,285,855	63.4	37,534,641	63.9
Invalid votes	852,106	2.3	854,459	2.3
Valid votes	36,433,749	97.7	36,680,182	97.7
PRI	13,699,799	36.7	13,755,787	36.7
Alliance for Mexico (PRD)	7,027,944	18.9	7,072,994	18.8
Alliance for Change (PAN)	14,208,973	38.1	14,339,963	38.2
PCD	521,178	1.4	523,569	1.4
PARM	275,051	0.7	276,109	0.7
DS	669,725	1.8	676,388	1.8
Non-registered candidates	31,079	0.1	30,892	0.1

2.8 Composition of Parliament

2.8.1 Lower Chamber (House of Representatives) 1940–2003

Year	1940 Seats 173	% 100.0	1943 Seats 147	% 100.0	1946 Seats 147	% 100.0	1949 Seats 147	% 100.0
PRM[a]	172	99.4	147	100.0	141	95.9	—	—
PAN	–	–	–	–	4	2.7	4	2.7
PPS	–	–	–	–	–	–	1	0.7
PRI[a]	–	–	–	–	–	–	142	96.2
Others	1	0.6	–	–	2	1.4	–	–

[a] Seats for PRM and PRI given here were determined by subtracting the number of other parties' seats from the total. PRM and PRI did not always occupy all of those seats, however, there is no precise information available.

Year	1952 Seats 161	% 100.0	1955 Seats 162	% 100.0	1958 Seats 162	% 100.0	1961 Seats 178	% 100.0
PRI[a]	151	93.8	153	94.5	153	94.5	172	96.6
PAN	5	3.1	6	3.7	6	3.7	5	2.8
PPS	2	1.2	2	1.2	1	0.6	1	0.6
PARM	–	–	–	–	1	0.6	–	–
Otros	3	1.9	1	0.6	1	0.6	–	–

[a] Seats for PRI given here were determined by subtracting the number of other parties' seats from the total. The party did not always occupy all of those seats, however, there is no precise information available.

Year	1964 Seats 210	% 100.0	1967 Seats 212	% 100.0	1970 Seats 213	% 100.0	1973 Seats 231	% 100.0
PRI[a]	175	83.3	177	83.5	178	83.6	189	81.8
PAN	20	9.5	20	9.4	20	9.4	25	10.8
PPS	10	4.8	10	4.7	10	4.7	10	4.3
PARM	5	2.4	5	2.4	5	2.4	7	3.0

[a] Seats for PRI given here were determined by subtracting the number of other parties' seats from the total. The party did not always occupy all of those seats, however, there is no precise information available.

Year	1976 Seats 237	% 100.0	1979 Seats 400	% 100.0	1982 Seats 372	% 100.0	1985 Seats 400	% 100.0
PRI[a]	195	82.3	296	74.0	299	80.4	292	73.0
PAN	20	8.4	43	10.8	51	13.7	38	9.5
PPS	12	5.1	11	2.8	10	2.7	11	2.8
PARM	10	4.2	12	3.0	–	–	11	2.8
PCM	–	–	18	4.5	–	–	–	–
PST	–	–	10	2.5	–	–	–	–
PDM	–	–	10	2.5	12	3.2	12	3.0
PMS	–	–	–	–	–	–	18[b]	4.5
PFCRN	–	–	–	–	–	–	12[c]	3.0
PRT	–	–	–	–	–	–	6	1.5

[a] Seats for PRI given here were determined by subtracting the number of other parties' seats from the total. The party did not always occupy all of those seats, however, there is no precise information available.
[b] Seats won by the PMS' two predecessors, the PSUM and the PTM.
[c] Seats won by the PST, the PFCRN's predecessor.

Year	1988 Seats 500	% 100.0	1991 Seats 500	% 100.0	1994 Seats 500	% 100.0	1997 Seats 500	% 100.0
PRI	260[a]	52.0	320[a]	64.0	300	60.0	239	47.8
PAN	101	20.4	89	17.8	119	23.8	121	24.2
PFCRN	38[b]	7.6	23	4.6	0	0.0	0	0.0
PPS	37[b]	7.4	12	2.4	0	0.0	0	0.0
PARM	30[b]	6.0	15	3.0	–	–	–	–
PMS	18[b]	3.6	–	–	–	–	–	–
Coalición FDN	15[b]	3.0	–	–	–	–	–	–
PRD	–	–	41	8.2	71	14.2	125	25.0
PT	–	–	–	–	10	2.0	7	1.4
PVEM	–	–	–	–	–	–	8	1.6

[a] Seats for PRI given here were determined by subtracting the number of other parties' seats from the total. The party did not always occupy all of those seats, however, there is no precise information available.
[b] For the 1988 elections, PPS, PFCRN, PARM and PMS built an alliance called FDN. Some candidates ran separately under the label *'Coalición'*.

Year	2000		2003	
	Seats	%	Seats	%
	500	100.0	500	100.0
PRI	208	42.2	224	44.8
PAN	207	41.2	151	30.2
PRD	53	10.0	97	19.4
PVEM	17	3.4	17	3.4
PT	7	1.4	6	1.2
PCD	4	0.8	–	–
PSN	3	0.6	0	0.0
PAS	2	0.4	0	0.0
Convergencia	–	–	5	1.0

2.8.2 a) Upper Chamber (Senate) 1982–2000

Year	1982[a]		1988		1991		1994	
	Seats	%	Seats	%	Seats	%	Seats	%
	64	100.0	64	100.0	64	100.0	128	100.0
PRI	63	98.4	60	93.8	61	95.3	95	74.2
PPS	1	1.6	–	–	–	–	0	0.0
Alianzas	–	–	4	6.3	–	–	0	0.0
PRD	–	–	–	–	2	3.1	8	6.3
PAN	–	–	–	–	1	1.6	25	19.6

[a] Before 1982, PRI held all senate seats.

Year	1997		2000	
	Seats	%	Seats	%
	128	100.0	128	100.0
PRI	77	60.2	60[a]	46.9
PRD	16	12.5	15[b]	11.7
PAN	33	25.8	46	35.9
PT	1	0.8	1[b]	0.8
PVEM	1	0.8	5[a]	3.9
PCD	–	–	1	0.8

[a] PAN and PVEM formed an alliance called *Alianza por el Cambio*.
[b] PRD, PT, PSN and PAS formed an alliance called *Alianza por México*.

2.8.2 b) Upper Chamber (Senate): Distribution of Seats According to the Parts of the Segmented Electoral System, 1994–2000

Year	1994		1997[b]			2000		
	Plur.[a]	Min.	Plur.	Min.	Prop.	Plur.	Min.	Prop.
	96	32	–	–	32	64	32	32
PRI	64	–	–	–	13	32	15	13
PRD	–	8	–	–	8	4	7	4
PAN	–	24	–	–	9	27	10	9
PT	–	–	–	–	1	–	–	1
PVEM	–	–	–	–	1	1	–	4
PCD	–	–	–	–	–	–	–	1

[a] Plur. = plurality, min. = first minority, prop. = proportional representation.
[b] Only senators by proportional representation were elected in 1997.

2.9 Presidential Elections 1917–2000

1917[a]	Total number	%
Registered voters	—	–
Votes cast	812,928	—
Invalid votes	70,000	8.6
Valid votes	742,928	91.4
Venustiano Carranza (PLC)	727,305	97.9
Pablo González (LLD)	11,615	1.7
Alvaro Obregón	4,008	0.5

[a] Before 1917 presidents were elected indirectly.

1920	Total number	%
Registered voters	—	–
Votes cast	—	—
Invalid votes	—	—
Valid votes	1,181,550	—
Alvaro Obregón (CDO)	1,131,751	95.8
Alfredo Robles Domínguez (PRN)	47,442	4.0
Others	2,357	0.2

1924	Total number	%
Registered voters	—	–
Votes cast	—	—
Invalid votes	—	—
Valid votes	1,593,257	—
Plutarco Elías Calles (PLM and others)	1,340,634	84.1
Angel Flores (LPN and others)	252,599	15.9
Others	24	0.0

1928	Total number	%
Registered voters	—	–
Votes cast	—	—
Invalid votes	—	—
Valid votes	1,670,453	—
Alvaro Obregón (CDO)	1,670,453	100.0

1929	Total number	%
Registered voters	—	–
Votes cast	—	—
Invalid votes	—	—
Valid votes	2,082,106	—
Pascual Ortiz Rubio (PNR)	1,947,848	93.6
José Vasconcelos (PAM)	110,979	5.3
Pedro V. Rodríguez Triana (BOC)	23,279	1.1

1934	Total number	%
Registered voters	—	–
Votes cast	—	—
Invalid votes	—	—
Valid votes	2,265,971	—
Lázaro Cárdenas del Río (PNR)	2,225,000	98.2
Antonio I. Villareal (CRPI)	24,395	1.1
Adalberto Tejeda (PSI)	16,037	0.7
Hernán Laborde (PCM)	539	0.0

1940	Total number	%
Registered voters	—	–
Votes cast	—	—
Invalid votes	—	—
Valid votes	2,637,222	—
Manuel Avila Camacho (PRM)	2,476,641	93.9
Juan Andrew Almazán (PRUN)	151,101	5.7
Rafael Sánchez Tapía	9,840	0.4

1946	Total number	%
Registered voters	2,556,949	–
Votes cast	—	—
Invalid votes	—	—
Valid votes	2,294,728	—
Miguel Alemán (PRI)	1,786,901	77.9
Ezequiel Padilla (PDM)	443,357	19.3
Carlos I. Calderón (PNRPR)	33,952	1.5
J. Agustín Castro (PNC)	29,337	1.3
Others	1,181	0.1

1952	Total number	%
Registered voters	4,924,293	–
Votes cast	—	—
Invalid votes	—	—
Valid votes	3,651,483	—
Adolfo Ruiz Cortines (PRI)	2,713,419	74.3
Miguel Henríquez Guzmán (FPPM)	579,745	15.9
Efraín González Luna (PAN)	285,555	7.8
Vicente Lombardo Toledano (PP)	72,482	2.0
Others	282	0.0

1958	Total number	%
Registered voters	10,443,465	–
Votes cast	—	—
Invalid votes	—	—
Valid votes	7,463,403	—
Adolfo López Mateos (PRI)	6,747,754	90.4
Luis H. Alvarez (PAN)	705,303	9.4
Others	10,346	0.1

1964	Total number	%
Registered voters	13,589,594	–
Votes cast	—	—
Invalid votes	—	—
Valid votes	9,422,185	—
Gustavo Díaz Ordaz (PRI)	8,368,446	88.8
José Gonzáles Torres (PAN)	1,034,337	11.0
Others	19,402	0.2

1970	Total number	%
Registered voters	21,654,217	–
Votes cast	—	—
Invalid votes	—	—
Valid votes	13,915,963	—
Luis Echeverría Alvarez (PRI)	11,970,893	86.0
Efraín Gonzáles Morfín (PAN)	1,945,070	14.0

1976	Total number	%
Registered voters	25,913,066	–
Votes cast	—	—
Invalid votes	—	—
Valid votes	16,727,993	—
José López Portillo (PRI)	16,727,993	100.0

1982	Total number	%
Registered voters	31,526,386	–
Votes cast	23,592,888	74.8
Invalid votes	1,053,616	4.5
Valid votes	22,539,272	95.5
Miguel de la Madrid Hurtado (PRI)	16,748,006	74.3
Pablo Emilio Madero (PAN)	3,700,045	16.4
Arnoldo Martínez Verdugo (PSUM)	821,995	3.7
Ignacio González Gollaz (PDM)	433,886	1.9
Rosario Ibarra de Piedra (PRT)	416,448	1.9
Cándido Díaz Cerecedo (PST)	342,005	1.5
Manuel Moreno Sánchez (PSD)	48,413	0.2
Non-registered candidates	28,474	0.1

1988	Total number	%
Registered voters	38,074,926	–
Votes cast	19,640,722	51.6
Invalid votes	548,879	2.8
Valid votes	19,091,843	97.2
Carlos Salinas de Gortari (PRI)	9,687,926	50.7
Cuauhtémoc Cárdenas Solórzano (FDN)	5,929,585	31.1
Manuel J. Clouthier del Rincón (PAN)	3,208,584	16.8
Gumersindo Magaña Negrete (PDM)	190,891	1.0
Rosario Ibarra de Piedra (PRT)	74,857	0.4

1994	Total number	%
Registered voters	45,729,053	–
Votes cast	35,281,291	77.2
Invalid votes	1,008,291	2.9
Valid votes	34,277,000	97.1
Ernesto Zedillo (PRI)	17,181,651	50.1
Cuauhtémoc Cárdenas Solórzano (PRD)	5,852,134	17.1
Diego Fernández de Cevallos (PAN)	9,146,841	26.7
Cecilia Soto (PT)	970,121	2.8
Rafael Aguilar (PFCRN)	297,901	0.9
Jorge González (PVEM)	327,313	0.9
Alvaro Pérez T. (PARM)	192,795	0.6
Marcelo Lombardo (PPS)	166,594	0.5
Pablo E. Madero (PDM)	97,935	0.3

2000	Total number	%
Registered voters	58,782,737	–
Votes cast	37,601,618	64.0
Invalid votes	788,157	2.1
Valid votes	36,812,461	97.9
Vicente Fox Quesada *(Alianza por el Cambio)*	15,989,636	43.4
Francisco Labastida Ochoa (PRI)	13,579,718	36.9
Cuauthémoc Cárdenas Solórzano *(Alianza por México)*	6,256,780	17.0
DSPPN	592,381	1.6
Manuel Camacho Solís (PCD)	206,589	0.6
Porfirio Muñoz Ledo (PARM)	156,896	0.4
Others	30,461	0.1

2.10 List of Power Holders 1900–2004

Head of State	Years	Remarks
Porfirio Díaz	1900–1911	President from 01/12/1900–25/05/1904, deposed.
Francisco León de la Barra	1911	Provisional president from 26/05–05/11.
Francisco Indalecio Madero	1911–1913	President from 06/11/1911–19/02/1913; deposed and assassinated.
Pedro Lascurain	1913	Provisional president on 20/02.
Victoriano Huerta	1913–1914	Provisional president from 20/02/1913–14/07/1914.
Francisco Carbajal	1914	15/07–12/08/1914; Presidente substituto.
Alvaro Obregón	1914	Military officer; president from 14/08–19/08.
Venustiano Carranza	1914	Military officer; supreme commander of the army, president from 20/08–24/11.
Eulalio Gutiérrez	1914–1915	Military officer; in charge of the executive from 13/12/1914–20/01/1915.
Roque González Garza	1915	In charge of the executive from 30/01–11/03.
Francisco Lagos Chazaro	1915	President from 30/06–30/11.
Venustiano Carranza	1915–1920	President from 01/12/1915–21/05/1920.
Adolfo de la Huerta	1920	Provisional president elected by congress from 01/06–30/11.
Alvaro Obregón	1920–1924	01/12/1920–30/11/1924; Presidente constitucional.
Plutarco Elías Calles	1924–1928	Military officer; president from 01/12/1924–30/11/1928.
Alvaro Obregón	1928	Assassinated before assuming the post.

Head of State (cont.)	Years	Remarks
Emilio Portes Gil	1928–1930	Provisional president from 01/12/1928–05/02/1930; elected by congress after Alvaro Obregón, the designated president, was assassinated before he could take over power.
Pascual Ortiz Rubio	1930–1932	President from 05/02/1930–03/09/1932.
Abelardo L. Rodríguez	1932–1934	Provisional president from 04/09/1932–30/11/1934.
Lázaro Cárdenas del Río	1934–1940	President from 10/12/1934–30/11/1940.
Manuel Avila Camacho	1940–1946	President from 01/12/1940–30/11/1946.
Miguel Alemán Valdés	1946–1952	President from 01/12/1946–30/11/1952.
Adolfo Ruiz Cortines	1952–1958	President from 01/12/1952–30/11/1958.
Adolfo López Mateos	1958–1964	President from 01/12/1958–30/11/1964.
Gustavo Díaz Ordaz	1964–1970	President from 01/12/1964–30/11/1970.
Luis Echeverría Alvarez	1970–1976	President from 01/12/1970–30/11/1976.
José López Portillo	1976–1982	President from 01/12/1976–30/11/1982.
Miguel de la Madrid Hurtado	1982–1988	President from 01/12/1982–30/11/1988.
Carlos Salinas de Gortari	1988–1994	President from 01/12/1988–30/11/1994.
Ernesto Zedillo Ponce de León	1994–2000	President from 01/12/1994–30/11/2000.
Vicente Fox Quesada	2000–	President since 01/12/2000.

3. Bibliography

3.1 Official Sources

Código Federal de Instituciones y Procedimientos Electorales (1996). Mexico City: Instituto Federal Electoral.

Comisión Federal Electoral (1988). *Resultados electorales presidenciales 1988*. Mexico City.

— (1988). *Resultados electorales parlamentarias 1988 (por el princípio de representación proporcional)*. Mexico City.

— (1991). *Resultados electorales parlamentarias 1991 (por el principio de representación proporcional)*. Mexico City.

Diario Oficial de la Federación (various years). Mexico City.

Instituto Federal Electoral (various years). *Foro electoral*. Mexico City.

— (various years). *Gaceta electoral*. Mexico City.

— (1991). *El sistema electoral mexicano*. Mexico City.

— (1991). *Legislación electoral mexicana. 1946–1990*. Mexico City.

— (1991). *Presencia electoral de la oposición en elecciones presidenciales. México 1982–1988*. Mexico City.

— (2000). *The Mexican Electoral Regime and the Federal Elections of the Year 2000*. Mexico City.

García Orozco, Antonio (ed.) (1989). *Legislación electoral mexicana. 1946–1990*. Mexico City: Adeo.

Tribunal Electoral del Poder Judicial de la Federación (2000) *Declaratoria de validez de la elección presidencial 2000*. Mexico City: TRIFE.

3.2 Books, Articles, and Electoral Reports

Acosta Romero, M. (1989). *Reflexiones sobre el tribunal de lo contencioso electoral federal de México*. San José/Costa Rica: IIDH-CAPEL.

Alcocer V. J. (ed.) (1994). *Elecciones, diálogo y reforma*. Mexico City: Nuevo Horizonte.

Anguiano, A. (ed.) (1988). *La transición democrática*. Mexico City: Universidad Autónoma Metropolitana.

Anlén, J. (1973). *Origen y evolución de los partidos políticos en México*. Mexico City: Porrua.

Barquín, M. (1987). *La reforma electoral de 1986–1987 en México. Retrospectiva y análisis*. (Cuadernos CAPEL 22). San José: CAPEL.

Berlin Valenzuela, F. (1990). 'Ventajas y desventajas de los sistemas "Organismos del Proceso Electoral"'. *Excelsior* (Mexico City), 06./07.06.1990.

Brambila, A. (1976). 'Evolución del sistema electoral mexicano'. *Línea* (Mexico City) 20: 37–48.

Cline, H. F. (1953). The United States and Mexico. Cambridge: Harvard University Press.

— (1963). *Mexico. Revolution to Evolution 1940–1960*. London: Oxford University Press.

Cosio Villegas, D. (1973). *El sistema político mexicano. Las posibilidades de cambio*. Mexico City: Joaquín Mortiz.

Crespo, J. A. (1999). *Fronteras democráticas en México*. Mexico City: Oceano.

Ezcurdia, M. (1968). *Análisis teórico del Partido Revolucionario Institucional*. Mexico City: Costa-Amic.

Franco, J. F. (1991). 'La reforma electoral en México', in H. de la Calle Lombana et al, *La reforma electoral en Latinoamérica. Memorias IV Curso Anual Interamericano de Elecciones*. Vol. 3. San José: IIDH-CAPEL, 193–214.

Galeana, P. (ed.) (1998). *El camino de la democracia en México*. Mexico City: UNAM.

Gomboa Villafranca, X. (1987). *La lucha electoral en México 1985*. Mexico City: UNAM.

González Casanova, P. and Cadena Roa, J. (eds.) (1989). *Primer informe sobre la democracia. México 1988*. Mexico City: Siglo Veintiuno.

Gonzalez Roura, F., Nohlen, D., and Zovatto, D. (1997). *Análisis del sistema electoral méxicano. Informe de un Grupo de Expertos.* Mexico City: IFE et al.

Hernández Molina, M. (1970). *Los partidos políticos en México 1892–1913.* Puebla: José M. Cajía.

Lehr, V. G. (1980). 'La problemática de la estadística electoral mexicana. Participación y legitimidad', in H.-A. Steger and J. Schneider (eds.), *Wirtschaft und gesellschaftliches Bewußtsein in Mexiko seit der Kolonialzeit.* (Lateinamerika–Studien 6). Munich: Fink, 499–520.

— (1981). *Der mexikanische Autoritarismus. Parteien, Wahlen, Herrschaftssicherung und Krisenpotential.* Munich: Wilhelm Fink.

— (1984). 'Wahlen und Herrschaftssicherung im mexikanischen Autoritarismus', in D. Nohlen (ed.), *Wahlen und Wahlpolitik in Lateinamerika.* Heidelberg: Esprint, 133–174.

— (1985). 'Modernización y movilización electoral 1964–1976. Un estudio ecológico'. *Estudios Políticos* (Mexico City) 4/1: 54–61.

Lomnitz Adler, L. et al. (1992). 'El fondo de la forma. Actos públicos de la campaña presidencial del Partido Revolucionario Institucional. México 1988', in D. Nohlen (ed.), *Elecciones y sistemas de partidos en América Latina.* San José/Costa Rica: IIDH, 223–266.

McDonald, R. and Ruhl, M. J. (1989). *Party Politics and Elections in Latin America.* Boulder, Colo.: Westview.

Michaels, A. L. (1972). 'Las elecciones de 1940'. *Historia Mexicana* (Mexico City) 21/81: 80–134.

Molina Piñeiro, L. J. (1988). *Aportes para una teoría del gobierno mexicano.* Mexico City: UNAM.

Molinar Horcasitas, J. (1991). *El tiempo de la legitimidad. Elecciones, autoritarismo y democracia en México.* Mexico City: Aguilar.

Moya Palencia, M. (1964). *La reforma electoral.* Mexico City: Plataforma.

Nohlen, D. (2004). *Sistemas electorales y partidos políticos* (3rd edn.). Mexico City: FCE.

Nohlen, D., Picado, S., and Zovatto, D. (eds.) (1998). *Tratado de Derecho Electoral Comparado de América Latina.* Mexico City: FCE.

Núñez Jiménez, A. (1991). *El nuevo sistema electoral mexicano.* Mexico City: FCE.

Orozco Henríquez, J. J. (ed.) (1999). *Memoria del III Congreso Internacional de Derecho Electoral.* 4 vols. Mexico City: IFE et al.

Patino Camarena, J. (1994). *Derecho electoral mexicano.* Mexico City: UNAM.

Rancaño Ramírez, M. (1977). 'Estadísticas electorales presidenciales'. *Revista Mexicana de Sociología* (Mexico City) 39/1: 271–302.

Valadés, D. (1986). *El desarrollo municipal como supuesto de la democracia y del federalismo mexicano.* San José/Costa Rica: IIDH-CAPEL.

Woldenberg, J. (2002). *La construcción de la democracia.* Mexico City: Plaza y Janés.

NICARAGUA

by Michael Krennerich

1. Introduction

1.1 Historical Overview

Nicaragua enacted its first national constitution in 1826. It was inspired by liberal ideas and established a presidential system with a relatively weak executive. In 1838, the country left the Central-American Federation and drew up a new constitution that introduced a two-chamber system. However, Nicaragua's political life contravened the constitutional rules until the 1850s. It was characterized by violent conflicts among the liberal and conservative caudillos, whose strongholds were in León and Granada, respectively.

Since the late 1840s, the USA and Great Britain clashed in their interests over Nicaragua (Great Britain had hitherto enjoyed a dominant position in the region, with its own protectorate on the Atlantic coast) and began to have an effect on the Nicaraguan political process. In the following decade, the North American mercenary William Walker intervened in the civil war on the side of the liberals and was elected president in 1856, even though the constitution only authorized Nicaraguan citizens to hold this office. Walker's defeat in 1857 started a new period, known as the 'Thirty Years of Conservative Government'. A new constitution was drawn up in 1858, which maintained the system of government but reinforced the power of the executive. The title 'President of the Republic' replaced that of 'Supreme Director', and the number of fundamental rights contained in the 1838 Constitution was reduced. The period was characterized by relative political stability. The elections were generally indirect and scarcely competitive, and the constitutional prohibition of presidential re-election was not always observed (1863, 1891).

In 1893, the so-called Liberal Revolution ended when José Santos Zelaya assumed presidential office, a position he then held until 1909. The liberal-inspired constitution of 1893 introduced direct elections and extended fundamental rights, including voting rights. The president's authority was reduced in favor of a one-chamber legislative and judicial power. The subsequent constitutions of 1896 and 1905 departed from the liberal spirit of 1893. However, the political reality had never really adjusted to the constitutional regulations, and Zelaya governed in a dictatorial manner. During his tenure, the country continued to modernize, based on coffee exports. The State separated from the Church and became stronger and more centralized.

Zelaya finally fell under US pressure. The United States intervened directly in Nicaragua's domestic policy, establishing a semi-protectorate with military presence and domination over the country's economy. During this period, the conservative presidents were elected in direct but scarcely competitive elections that needed the approval of the North American government. In 1925, the US troops left Nicaragua temporarily, only to intervene once again when a new civil war broke out. The 1928, 1930, and 1932 elections were held under the guidance of the United States and developed in a democratic way. To a great extent, this development was a result of the foreign supervision, since the civil war still being fought in the country meant that the situation in some departments was not conducive to celebrating free elections.

The North American troops began to withdraw again in 1932. In 1933 the civil war led by Augusto C. Sandino came to an end, and he was assassinated in 1934. The new strongman, Anastasio Somoza García, head of the US-created National Guard of Nicaragua, assumed presidency in 1937 and established a dictatorship based mainly on the control of the military and the state apparatus, as well as on the support of the United States. The dictatorship of Anastasio Somoza García (assassinated in 1956) and his two sons, Luis and Anastasio Somoza Debayle, lasted for about forty years. The Somoza family achieved economic power through systematic corruption. In order to secure power and gain recognition from foreign governments, the Somozas enacted four constitutions (1939, 1948, 1950, 1974) with their corresponding reforms (1955, 1959, 1962, 1966). The formal separation of an executive in the hands of the president and a two-chamber legislative remained. However, neither Somoza's nor any of his allies' presidencies were ever at a risk in any of the seven presidential elections, characterized by the lack of competition and electoral fraud, and actually destined to maintain Somoza's family in power. The—somewhat artificial—two-party system was made up of the hegemonic party *Partido Liberal Nacionalista* (PLN; National Liberal Party) controlled by the Somozas, and the opposition party *Partido Conservador de Nicaragua* (PCN; National Conservative Party), controlled by the conservative oligarchies. When the latter boycotted the elections, the splitter party *Partido Conservador Nica-ragüense* replaced them. Apart from these parties, only the *Partido Liberal Independiente* (PLI; Independent Liberal Party) and the *Partido Social Cristiano* (PSC; Social Christian Party) enjoyed a brief period of parliamentary representation before 1979. However, in order to do so, they had to build informal (1947) or formal (1967) alliances with the PCN. Other opposition parties—especially the more left wing—were not allowed to participate in elections.

During Somoza's dictatorship, Nicaragua's social and economic structures underwent a profound transformation, which was, however, not reflected at the political level. In the 1970s, this process led to a crisis in the regime, which had already lost its prestige due to the massive electoral fraud, the blatant corruption following the earthquake of 1972, and the increasing repression. Thus, the relations between Somoza and the traditional elites deteriorated, at the same time as a growing sector of the population became more radical. Towards the end of the 1970s, Somoza's repressive and corrupt regime was nationally and internationally isolated.

The revolution triumphed in 1979 and brought about a radical restructuring of the State. At the institutional level, the political power was concentrated in a *Junta Provisional de Reconstrucción Nacional* (Provisional Junta of National Reconstruction); a newly created council of State was given some legislative power. In 1984, during a brief relaxation of the emergency state (re-established from 1985 to 1988) a president and a national assembly were elected; their duties were formally defined in the 1987 Constitution. This constitution established a presidential system with a one-chamber congress and a president with broad authority. In fact, from 1979 to 1990, both the political institutions and the party system were controlled by the *Frente Sandinista de Liberación Nacional* (FSLN; *Sandinista* National Liberation Front), who had led the revolution against Somoza. The *Sandinista* policies and politics, however, led to an open conflict not only with the political opposition but also with the counterrevolutionary forces known as the *Contra*. These forces enjoyed considerable financial and logistic support from the United States, and in the early 1980s they embarked on a destructive war against the government. It was not until the end of the decade that a political solution to the armed conflict seemed tangible.

In a climate of political opportunity, 1990 witnessed the fairest elections in Nicaragua's history to that date. The outgoing *Sandinista* President Daniel Ortega (1984–1990) fared strikingly badly against Violeta Barrios de Chamorro, who led the large anti-*Sandinista* coalition *Unión*

Nacional Opositora (UNO; National Opposition Union). The *Sandinista* electoral defeat meant the end of the *Contra* war, yet not of the climate of violence. In 1992, during a parliamentary crisis, the government of Barrios de Chamorro lost the UNO's support and had to rely on the backing of very unstable majorities. Intra-party conflicts resulted in a rupture of the party system. The most extreme sectors of the anti-*Sandinistas* and the FSLN had now gained control over the political arena, and hampered any attempt to arrive at agreements or compromises.

In the 1996 elections, Arnoldo Alemán, the markedly anti-*Sandinista* ex-governor of Managua, competed at the head of the *Alianza Liberal* (Liberal Alliance), led by the *Partido Liberal Constitucionalista* (PLC; Liberal Constitutional Party), against Daniel Ortega. The international observers revealed several irregularities and problems in the organization of the elections, but agreed to qualify them as correct. The electoral results were only accepted by the *Sandinistas* after heated complaints, due essentially to the *Alianza Liberal*'s clear advantage in the vote.

Despite the long political enmity between the two strongest parties, PLC and FSLN, before the 2001 elections their leaders agreed to a controversial political pact intended to defend the interests of the party elites and to foster the bipartisan structure of political life. The constitutional reforms and the new electoral law passed in 2000 politicized the judiciary and the supreme electoral council and granted membership in parliament to the outgoing (corrupt) president and to Ortega, which provided them with immunity from prosecution. In the 2001 elections, Daniel Ortega (FSLN) was defeated by Enrique Bolaños (PLC), former vice president of the Alemán administration. Despite some minor problems, international observers qualified the elections as free and fair. The new president launched an anti-corruption campaign against Alemán that resulted in a split of the PLC, a severe parliamentary crisis and the sentencing of the ex-president.

1.2 Evolution of Electoral Provisions

Nicaragua has been under authoritarian rule for a long time. Nevertheless, in the 20th century the country has held elections to constitutional assemblies, as well as several presidential and parliamentary polls. These, though, have often fallen short of the standards of free and fair elections.

Before the 1979 revolution, the electoral law was basically laid down in the constitutions of 1893, 1905, 1911, 1939, 1948, 1950, and 1974, and their respective reforms, as well as in some decrees and agreements relating to the elections. The legal framework for the first elections held after the revolution (in 1984) was mainly established by the party law of 1983 and the electoral law of 1984. The following elections were held under the 1987 Constitution (together with the 1995 and 2000 reforms) and the corresponding electoral laws (1988, 1995, 2000).

Nicaraguan citizens have enjoyed direct vote since 1893. Yet, the exercising of this right has often been temporarily suspended, especially during Somoza's dictatorship. Secret ballots were also introduced in 1893, only to be abolished by the 1910 electoral law, and to become constitutional again only in 1962. The year 1893 also brought about the introduction of universal male suffrage. For most of the time, the voting age was between 21 years and, provided that certain prerequisites regarding family status and/or education were fulfilled, 18 years. After the 1979 revolution, the voting age was lowered to 16 years for the whole electorate.

Female suffrage was first applied in the 1957 elections, after the constitutions of 1939, 1948, and 1950 had made its introduction subject to the attainment of a qualified parliamentary majority in its favor.

The compulsory vote, included in the constitutions of 1893, 1939, 1948, 1950, and 1974, was abolished after the revolution, but the compulsory electoral registration, in force since 1939, remained.

For the elections held under the Somoza dictatorship (1936–1979), the presidential term varied between four and six years, although the temporary provisions of the 1939 Constitution granted the president an eight-year term on one occasion. Before the 1979 Revolution, the president could not be immediately re-elected, except for the period between 1955 and 1959.

If the presidential and parliamentary elections coincided during the Somoza dictatorship, the president, deputies, and senators were elected through the same vote. From 1947 onwards the president was elected by plurality of votes (until then he had needed an absolute majority. If this majority was not achieved, the two-chamber parliament chose the president from the top two candidates).

Regarding the two-chamber parliament, deputies and senators were elected by plurality up to 1950. That year, the so-called *representación de minorías* was introduced, which allocated the major party and the minor party a fixed number of seats in both chambers. Initially, this essentially meant that only two parties competed in the electoral competition. In the elections to the constitutional assembly in 1950, the legislative decree of 15 April allocated 40 of the elected seats to the major party and 17 to the minor party. The 1950 Constitution ensured that the minor party had one-third of the seats in both parliamentary chambers.

Elements of proportional representation were introduced in 1962, which, together with the *representación de minorías*, made it possible for other parties to contest elections. The simple quota system and the method of the largest remainder were introduced, respecting the minority guarantee. The opposition parties were allotted a total of one-third of the parliamentary seats, even if they had not attained this share in the election according to the simple quota. If there were several minor parties, the simple quota (plus largest remainder) was applied again to allocate the seats among them (excluding the votes for the major party). In the elections to the constitutional assembly of 1972 and 1974 the simple quota system was maintained (Hare quota), and the minority guarantee increased to two fifths of the seats.

After the revolution, presidential and parliamentary elections were held every six years since 1984, and every five years since 1996. Though elections were held at the same time, voters used separate electoral ballots. The prohibition of the immediate re-election of the president was lifted, but reintroduced in 1995.

The plurality system was initially maintained for presidential elections, but in 1995 a threshold of 45% of the valid votes was introduced. If no candidate reached this amount, a runoff election had to be held between the top two candidates.

In parliamentary elections, proportional representation has been applied since 1984. The 1984 and 1990 elections followed a PR system in multi-member constituencies (MMCs). In 1984 there were ten constituencies of different sizes (1, 2, 3, 9, 10, 11, 12, 13, 14, and 15 seats). Candidates were presented in closed lists, and each voter was entitled to one vote. The Hare quota was applied. The remaining seats were allocated by calculating a new Hare quota with the remaining votes and seats. If there were still vacant seats after the second round, these were distributed according to the method of the largest remainder.

In 1990 the PR-system in MMCs was also used, but this time the size of the constituencies was different (nine constituencies of 1, 2, 3, 9, 10, 11, 14, 15, and 25 seats), as was the mode of seat allocation, since different quotas were applied in the constituencies. In the six large constituencies, the Hare quota was applied together with the method of the largest remainder. For the two- and three-member constituencies, however, the electoral law provided for the use of the Hagenbach-Bischoff quota system (Droop quota). In the case of the single-member constituency, the divisor was the number of seats ascribed to the constituency plus two. There, plurality was the de facto method of decision. In addition, the presidential candidates who had not been elected were allotted one parliamentary seat, provided they had achieved a number of votes equal to or higher than the average number needed in the constituencies to gain a parliamentary seat (the mean of the electoral quotas of all the constituencies).

Voters were entitled to two different votes for the first time in the 1996 parliamentary elections—one for a national party list, and the other for a departmental party list. There were 20 deputies 'of a national character', arranged in closed lists at the national level and elected using the Hare quota. For the remaining seats (at the national level), the method of the largest remainder was applied.

70 seats were distributed at departmental or regional constituency level. The country was divided into twelve small constituencies (from one to three seats), one of four, two of six, and one of 19 seats. The lists were closed. The conversion of votes into seats followed different distribution procedures. In the first allocation the Hare quota was applied. In order to distribute the remaining seats, the remaining votes from the departmental or regional constituencies, where not all the seats had been allocated, were added up. The simple quota formula of the remaining vote was intended to allocate the so-called 'additional seats', which were actually remaining seats. If there were still some seats to be allocated, the method of the largest remainder was applied. Then, the remaining seats were distributed among the lists and candidates in the following manner: First, a given seat percentage was allocated to each constituency according to a decreasing order of valid votes obtained by each party; next, in each constituency the seats were distributed among the parties in a decreasing order of the votes obtained by each constituency in the previous stage. The number of remaining seats allotted to one constituency could never surpass the number of deputies to be elected in it. The redundant seats were transferred to the next constituencies in decreasing order of the vote. This process was repeated until all the remaining seats were distributed among the constituencies. Additionally, all (unsuccessful) presidential candidates who had obtained more than 1% of the vote received a parliamentary seat, which made a total of 93 members of parliament in 1996.

1.3. Current Electoral Provisions

Sources: The basic principles of the electoral legislature are written into the 1987 Constitution and its reforms of 1995 and 2000, as well as in the 2000 Electoral Law.

Suffrage: The principles of universal, equal, direct, and secret suffrage are applied. All Nicaraguan citizens over 16 who are registered in the roll are eligible to vote. Registration in the roll is compulsory, but voting is not.

Elected national institutions: The president (together with the vice president) as well as the one-chamber parliament (*Asamblea Nacional*) are elected for a five-year term. The immediate re-election of the president is forbidden. The presidential and parliamentary elections are held simultaneously on the same date with separate electoral ballots.

Nomination of candidates
- *presidential elections*: Every citizen 28 years of age or older, who is in full possession of his/her civil and political rights and has resided continuously in Nicaragua for at least five years before the elections, is eligible to run for the presidency. Relatives of the out-going president are excluded from candidature. Several persons (vice president, president of the national assembly, secretaries of states etc.) are only qualified to stand for presidential elections if they have left their position at least twelve months before the elections.
- *parliamentary elections*: Every citizen 21 years of age or older, who is in full possession of his/her civil and political rights and has resided continuously for at least two years in Nicaragua before the elections, is qualified to stand as a candidate for parliament.

Electoral system
- *presidential elections*: The president and the vice president are elected together through plurality. However, a threshold of 40% of the valid votes is required (unless a candidate obtains more than 35% of the valid votes and, at the same time, has at least a five percentage points lead over the second candidate). If no candidate attains this percentage, a runoff election is held between the top two candidates.
- *parliamentary elections*: Proportional representation in MMCs with an additional national list. Each voter is entitled to two votes—one for a national list and the other for a departmental list. There are 20 deputies

'of a national character', presented in closed lists. The voter is entitled to one single vote to elect the deputies at the national level. Seats are distributed using the Hare quota. For the remaining seats (at the national level), the highest average method is applied. 70 parliamentary seats are distributed at departmental or regional constituency level. The country is divided into constituencies of the following size: one of one seat, five of two, six of three, one of four, three of six, and one of 19 seats. The lists are closed. Each voter is entitled to one single vote to elect the deputies at the constituency level. The Hare quota is applied in the seat alloca-tion. In order to distribute the remaining seats at constituency level, the highest average method is used. Finally, parliamentary seats are pro-vided for both the outgoing president (if he or she had been elected by popular vote for the outgoing presidential term) and the candidate who ranks the second in the presidential elections. There are 92 members of parliament.

Organizational context of elections: The *Consejo Supremo Electoral* (CSE; Central Electoral Commission) is responsible for organizing and supervising the elections. It is a permanent body made up of seven members (and three supplementary members). Each member of the CSE is elected separately with a qualified majority (60%) by parliament. In practice, the CSE is highly influenced by political interests and con-flicts. The elections in Nicaragua have been closely monitored by inter-national and national observers since 1990.

1.4 Commentary on the Electoral Statistics

The following tables are based partly on official sources (1924, 1928, 1932, 1947, 1950, 1984, 1990, and 2001). Where official data were not available, the author resorted to a wide variety of historiographical and sociological sources.

It is worth mentioning that a (relatively) accurate vote count and documentation only took place between 1928 and 1932 (under US su-pervision) and after the revolution of 1979. The, still controversial, 1984 elections were, in a purely technical sense, fairly correct, but the politi-cal context in which they evolved was still unfavorable to competitive elections. The elections of 1990, 1996, and 2001, some minor technical problems apart, have been qualified as free and fair by international ob-servers.

The elections held since the 1980s are well documented. For the 1996 polls, however, no official report was available, so we resorted to the data presented by Núñez Vargas (1996), who referred to information from the Nicaraguan Supreme Electoral Council. Differing data on the 1996 elections are provided by the *Political Database of the Americas* (www.georgetown.edu/pdba). This latter source, however, does not provide consistent presidential results, and only documents the votes for the national (not the departmental) lists for parliamentary elections.

In contrast to recent polls, all the elections held during the Somoza dictatorship (1936–1979) can be considered rigged. Due to their limited political importance, they have rarely been documented. Information about these elections is extremely difficult to obtain and should be regarded cautiously. Finally, the author has calculated the percentages recorded in the following tables.

2. Tables

2.1 Dates of National Elections, Referendums, and Coups d'Etat

Year	Presidential elections	Parliamentary elections	Elections for Constitutional Assembly	Referendums	Coups d'état
1912	02/11		02/11		
1914	06/12	06/12[a]			
1916	06/10	06/10[b, c]			
1920	03/10	03/10[b, c]			
1924	05/10	05/10[b, c]			
1926					16/02
1926					30/10
1928	04/11	04/11[b, c]			
1930		02/11[b, c]			
1932	06/11	06/11[b, c]			
1934		07/10[b, c]			
1936	08/12	08/12[b, c]			02/06
1947	02/02	02/02[b]			26/05
1950	21/05		21/05		
1957	03/02	03/02[b]			
1963	03/02	03/02[b]			
1967	05/02	05/02[b]			
1972			06/02		
1974	01/09	01/09[b]			
1979					19/07[d]
1984	04/11		04/11[e]		
1990	25/02	25/02			
1996	20/10	20/10			
2001	04/11	04/11			

[a] Only elections to the senate.
[b] Elections to the chamber of deputies and to the senate.
[c] Mid-term elections.
[d] *Sandinista* Revolution.
[e] The national assembly acted both as constitutional assembly and as legislative assembly.

2.2 Electoral Body 1924–2001

Year	Type of election[a]	Population[b]	Registered voters Total number	% pop.	Votes cast Total number	% reg. voters	% pop.
1924	Pr	660,000	120,490	18.3	84,096[c]	69.8	12.7
1928	Pr	670,000	148,831	22.2	133,663[c]	89.8	19.9
1932	Pr	690,000	154,720	22.4	130,114[c]	84.1	18.6
1936	Pr	750,000	—	—	80,663[c]	—	10.8
1947	G	980,000	—	—	169,708[c]	—	17.3
1950	CA	1,057,023	—	—	202,698[c]	—	19.2
1957	G	1,290,000	—	—	355,178[c]	—	27.5
1963	G	1,535,588	570,000	37.1	451,064[c]	79.1	29.4
1967	G	1,700,000	—	—	540,714[c]	—	31.8
1972	CA	1,950,000	970,792	49.8	709,068[c]	73.0	36.4
1974	G	2,080,000	1,152,260	55.4	799,982[c]	69.4	38.5
1984	Pr	3,165,000	1,551,597	49.0	1,170,142	75.4	37.0
1984	CA	3,165,000	1,551,597	49.0	1,170,102	75.4	37.0
1990	Pr	3,800,000	1,752,088	46.1	1,510,838	86.2	39.8
1990	Pa	3,800,000	1,752,088	46.1	1,512,107	86.3	39.8
1996	Pr	4,706,000	2,421,067	51.4	1,849,362	76.4	39.3
1996	Pa	4,706,000	2,421,067	51.4	1,830,807[d]	75.6	38.9
2001	Pr	4,918,000	—	—	2,162,213[c]	—	44.0
2001	Pa	4,918,000	—	—	2,149,444[c, d]	—	43.7

[a] CA = Constitutional Assembly, Pa = Parliament, Pr = President, G = General Elections (president, chamber of deputies, senate).

[b] The data for 1950 and 1963 are based on the official population censuses of 31/05/1950 and 25/04/1963. Other population censuses: 01/06/1906: 505,377; 01/01/1920: 638,119; 23/05/1940: 835,686; 1971: 1,894,690 (provisional).

[c] Only valid votes.

[d] Only votes for the national lists. Regarding the departmental lists for parliament, the voter turnout was slightly higher (see Table 2.7).

2.3 Abbreviations

AL	*Alianza Liberal* (Liberal Alliance)
ANC	*Acción Nacional Conservadora* (Conservative National Action)
APC	*Partido Alianza Popular Conservadora* (Conservative Popular Alliance Party)
CCN	*Partido Camino Cristiano Nicaragüense* (Nicaraguan Christian Way Party)
EL MAR	*Movimiento de Acción Renovadora* (Movement of Renewal Action Party)
FSLN	*Frente Sandinista de Liberación Nacional* (*Sandinista* National Liberation Front)
MAC	*Movimiento Acción Conservadora* (Conservative Action Movement)
MAP-ML	*Movimiento de Acción Popular – Marxista Leninista* (Popular Action Movement – Marxist Leninist)
MDN	*Movimiento Democrático Nicaragüense* (Nicaraguan Democratic Movement)
MORENA	*Movimiento Renovación Nacional* (National Renewal Movement)
MRS	*Movimiento Renovador Sandinista* (Sandinista Renewal Movement)
MUR	*Movimiento de Unidad Revolucionaria* (Revolutionary Unity Movement)
PAD	*Partido Acción Democrática* (Democratic Action Party)
PADENIC	*Alianza Democrática Nicaragüense* (Nicaraguan Democratic Alliance)
PALI	*Partido Neo-Liberal* (Neoliberal Party)
PAN	*Partido de Acción Nacional* (National Action Party)
PC[a]	*Partido Conservador* (Conservative Party)
PCDN	*Partido Conservador Demócrata de Nicaragua* (Democratic Conservative Party of Nicaragua)
PC de N	*Partido Comunista de Nicaragua* (Communist Party of Nicaragua)
PCN[b]	*Partido Conservador de Nicaragua* (Conservative Party of Nicaragua)
PDCN	*Partido Democrático de Confianza Nacional* (Democratic Party of National Confidence)
PIAC	*Partido Integracionista de América Central* (Integrating Party of Central America)
PJN	*Partido de Justicia Nacional* (National Justice Party)
PLC	*Partido Liberal Constitucionalista* (Constitutional Liberal Party)
PLI	*Partido Liberal Independiente* (Independent Liberal Party)
PLIUN	*Partido Liberal de Unidad Nacional* (Liberal Party of National Unity)
PLN	*Partido Liberal Nacionalista* (Nationalist Liberal Party)
PNC	*Partido Nacional Conservador* (Conservative National Party)
PND	*Partido Nacional Demócrata* (Democratic National Party)

PPSC	*Partido Popular Social Cristiano* (Christian Social Popular Party)
PRONAL	*Projecto Nacional* (National Project)
PRN	*Partido Resistencia Nicaragüense* (Nicaraguan Resistance Party)
PRT	*Partido Revolucionario de los Trabajadores* (Revolutionary Worker's Party)
PSC	*Partido Social Cristiano* (Social Christian Party)
PSD	*Partido Social Demócrata* (Social Democratic Party)
PSN	*Partido Socialista Nicaragüense* (Nicaraguan Socialist Party)
PSOC	*Partido Social Conservatismo* (Social Party of Conservatism)
PUCA	*Partido Unionista Centroamericano* (Central American Unionist Party)
PUL	*Partido de Unidad Liberal* (Liberal Unity Party)
PUNOCP	*Partido Unidad Nicaragüense Obreros, Campesinos y Profesionales* (Nicaraguan Unity Party Workers, Farmers, and Professionals)
U	*Alianza Unidad* (Unity Alliance)
UNO^c	*Unión Nacional Opositora* (National Opposition Union)
UNO 96	*Unión Nacional Opositora 96* (National Opposition Union 96)

[a] Nicaragua's traditional conservative party bore first the label *Partido Conservador* (PC) and afterwards *Partido Conservador de Nicaragua* (PCN).

[b] The abbreviation PCN has stood for three different Nicaraguan parties: The first one was the *Partido Conservador de Nicaragua*, the traditional conservative party (also *Partido Conservador Tradicionalista*, PCT). The second and third parties were 'artificial' opposition parties, founded on Somoza's initiative: the *Partido Conservador Nacionalista* and the *Partido Conservador Nicaragüense*. For the sake of clarity, in this handbook PCN does not refer to these two parties. In 1996 one section of the conservatives contested as *Partido Conservador Nicaragüense*. In 2001 the conservatives ran again under the label *Partido Conservador de Nicaragua*.

[c] Three different alliances have used the name *Unión Nacional Opositora* (UNO) (1959, 1966/67 and 1990). These should not be mistaken with the *Unidad Nicaragüense Opositora*, which garnered *Contras* in the 1980s.

2.4 Electoral Participation of Parties and Alliances 1912–2001

Party / Alliance[a]	Years	Elections contested	
		Presidential	Parliamentary
PC(N)[b]	1912–1950; 1967; 1974; 1996–2001	13	—
PLN[c]	1920–1974	11	—
Partido Conservador Progresista	1924	1	—
Partido Conservador Republicano	1924	1	—
Partido Liberal Republicano	1924	1	—
Partido Conservador Nacionalista	1936	1	—
Partido Liberal Constitucionalista	1936	1	—
PLI[d]	1947; 1967; 1984–1996	5	5
Partido Conservador Nicaragüense	1957–1967	3	3
UNO[e]	1967	1	1
PSC[f]	1967; 1984–1990	3	3
FSLN	1984–2001	4	4
MAP-ML	1984–1996	2	3
PCDN	1984–1990	2	2
PC de N[g]	1984–1996	3	3
PPSC	1984–1990	2	2
PSN[g]	1984–1996	3	3
APC[g]	1990–1996	2	2
MUR	1990	1	1
PLC[h]	1990–2001	3	3
PLIUN[i]	1990–1996	2	2
PRT	1990	1	1
PSD[g]	1990–1996	2	0
PSOC	1990	1	1
PUCA	1990	1	1
UNO[j]	1990	2	2
AL[k]	1996	1	1
ANC	1996	1	1
CCN	1996	1	1
EL MAR	1996	1	1
MORENA	1996	1	1
MRS	1996	1	1
PAD	1996	1	1
PADENIC	1996	1	1

Party / Alliance (continued)	Years	Elections contested Presidential	Parliamentary
Pan y Fuerza	1996	1	1
PIAC[l]	1996	1	1
PJN	1996	1	1
PRN	1996	1	1
PRONAL	1996	1	1
PUL	1996	1	1
PUNOCP	1996	1	1
U	1996	1	1
UNO 96[m]	1996	1	1
PAMUC	2001	0	1
YATAMA	2001	0	1

[a] General note: Only those parties are included in the table that have independently contested elections at least once.

[b] In Nicaragua's electoral history, the Conservative Party was often split. Included are all the elections where a party with the label PC(N) has participated. Split parties which bore a different name have been specified.

[c] We have not considered the smaller party, which in 1996 contested as PLN as part of AL.

[d] In 1947 the PLI used the label PCN. In 1967 and 1990, the PLI became part of the UNO alliance.

[e] In 1967, alliance comprised of the PCN, PLI and PSC.

[f] In 1967, the PSC was a member of the UNO

[g] The party contested within the UNO alliance.

[h] In 1990 the PLC was part of the UNO and in 1996 of the AL.

[i] In 1996 the PLIUN was part of AL.

[j] In 1990, the electoral alliance comprised the following parties (in alphabetical order): APC, MDN, PALI, PAN, PC de N, PDCN, PLC, PLI, PNC, PSD, PSN, as well as the groups ANC and PIAC, which had not been legally recognized as political parties before.

[k] In 1996, alliance comprised of the PLC, PLIUN, PALI and PLN. After its foundation and in the period previous to the electoral campaign, factions and persons of other parties—such as the PLI, the PLN and the PRN—have joined the AL, often after having been defeated in their own intra-party elections.

[l] In the 1990 elections, the PIAC was still not legally recognized as a party, but it supported the UNO.

[m] Alliance comprising PND, MDN, and MAC.

2.5 Referendums

Referendums have not been held.

2.6 Elections for Constitutional Assembly

1950[a]	Total number	%	Seats	%
Registered voters	—	–		
Votes cast	—	—		
Invalid votes	—	—		
Valid votes	202,698	—		
			57	100.0
PLN	153,297	75.6	40	70.2
PCN	49,401	24.4	17	29.8

[a] '*Elecciones pactistas*'. Before the elections the so-called *Pacto de los Generales* was signed.

1972[a]	Total number	%	Seats	%
Registered voters	970,792	–		
Votes cast	—	—		
Invalid votes	—	—		
Valid votes	709,068	—		
			100	100.0
PLN	534,171	75.3	60	60.0
PCN	174,897	24.7	40	40.0

[a] '*Elecciones pactistas*'. Before the elections the Somoza-Agüero pact ('*Kupia Kumi*') was signed.

1984	Total number	%	Seats	%
Registered voters	1,551,597	–		
Votes cast	1,170,102	75.4		
Invalid votes	78,224	6.7		
Valid votes	1,091,878	93.3		
			96	100.0
FSLN	729,159	66.8	61	63.5
PCDN	152,883	14.0	14	14.6
PLI	105,497	9.7	9	9.4
PPSC	61,525	5.6	6	6.3
PC de N	16,165	1.5	2	2.1
PSN	15,306	1.4	2	2.1
MAP-ML	11,343	1.0	2	2.1

2.7 Parliamentary Elections 1947–2001

Year	1947[a, b]		1957[a]	
	Total number	%	Total number	%
Registered voters	—	–	—	–
Votes cast	—	—	—	—
Invalid votes	—	—	—	—
Valid votes	169,708	—	355,178	—
PLN	96,731	57.0	316,998	89.3
PCN	64,904	38.2	–	–
Nacionalista	8,073	4.8	–	–
Nicaragüense	–	–	38,180	10.8

[a] Deputies and senators were elected by the same vote.
[b] Blatant electoral fraud.

Year	1963[a]		1967[a, b]	
	Total number	%	Total number	%
Registered voters	570,000	–	—	–
Votes cast	—	—	—	—
Invalid votes	—	—	—	—
Valid votes	451,064	—	540,714	—
PLN	408,131	90.5	380,162	70.3
Nicaragüense	42,933	9.5	3,120	0.6
UNO[c]	–	–	157,432	29.1

[a] Deputies and senators were elected by the same vote.
[b] Blatant electoral fraud.
[c] Electoral alliance comprised of the PCN, PLI and PSC.

Year	1974[a]		1990	
	Total number	%	Total number	%
Registered voters	1,152,260	–	1,752,088	–
Votes cast	—	–	1,512,107	86.3
Invalid votes	—	—	92,723	6.1
Valid votes	799,982	—	1,419,384	93.9
PLN	733,662	91.7	–	–
PCN	66,320	8.3	–	–
UNO[b]	–	–	764,748	53.9
FSLN	–	–	579,723	40.8
PSC/PPSC	–	–	22,218	1.6
MUR	–	–	13,995	1.0
PRT	–	–	10,586	0.7
MAP-ML	–	–	7,643	0.5
Others	–	–	20,471[c]	1.4

[a] Deputies and senators were elected by the same vote.
[b] Alliance composed of the following political parties (in alphabetical order): APC, MDN, PALI, PAN, PC de N, PDCN, PLC, PLI, PNC, PSD, PSN, as well as ACN and PIAC, which had not been legally recognized as political parties before.

[c] Including: PSOC: 6,308 votes (0.4%); PUCA: 5,565 (0.4%); PCDN: 5,083 (0.4%); PLIUN: 3,515 (0.2%).

Year	1996[a]		1996[b]	
	Total number	%	Total number	%
Registered voters	2,421,067	–	2,421,067	–
Votes cast	1,830,807	75.6	1,839,312	76.0
Invalid votes	113,391	6.2	113,169	6.2
Valid votes	1,717,416	93.8	1,726,143	93.8
AL	789,533	46.0	781,068	45.2
FSLN	626,178	36.6	629,939	36.5
CCN	63,867	3.7	63,986	3.7
PRONAL	40,656	2.4	36,417	2.1
PCN	36,543	2.1	39,153	2.3
MRS	22,789	1.3	23,554	1.4
PRN	21,068	1.2	27,970	1.6
U	14,001	0.8	13,848	0.8
PLI	12,459	0.7	13,697	0.8
UNO 96	10,706	0.6	12,720	0.7
ANC	9,811	0.6	13,011	0.8
Pan y Fuerza	9,724	0.6	12,016	0.7
PJN	8,155	0.5	8,527	0.5
PUL	7,531	0.4	9,893	0.6
Others	41,395[c]	2.4	40,344[d]	2.3

[a] Votes for the National Lists.
[b] Votes for the Departmental Lists.
[c] Including: APC: 6,726 votes (0.4%); PC de N: 6,360 (0.4%); PUNOCP: 5,641 (0.3%); PAD: 5,272 (0.3%); MORENO: 4,988 (0.3%); PSN: 2,980 (0.2%); PIAC: 2,834 (0.2%); MAP-LN: 2,446 (0.1%); El MAR: 2,418 (0.1%); PADENIC: 1,730 (0.1%).
[d] Including: PC de N: 6,970 (0.4%); APC: 6,335 votes (0.4%); PAD: 6,254 (0.4%); PUNOCP: 5,067 (0.3%); MORENO: 3,788 (0.2%); PSN: 3,228 (0.2%); El MAR: 2,992 (2.0%); PIAC: 2,406 (0.1%); PADENIC: 2,060 (0.1%); PSD: 724 (0.0%); MAP-LN: 520 (0.0%).

Year	2001[a]		2001[b]	
	Total number	%	Total number	%
Registered voters	—	–	—	–
Votes cast	—	—	—	—
Invalid votes	—	—	—	—
Valid votes	2,149,444	—	2,153,919	—
PLC	1,144,182	53.2	1,132,876	52.6
FSLN	905,589	42.1	901,254	41.8
PCN	99,673	4.6	105,130	4.9
YATAMA	–	–	11,139	0.5
PAMUC	–	–	3,520	0.2

[a] Votes for the National Lists.
[b] Votes for the Departmental Lists.

2.8 Composition of Parliament 1990–2001

In the years before 1950 only the names of the elected deputies are
available, not the parties they belonged to. From 1950 onwards, the seat
distribution was carried out in compliance with the *representación de
minorías* (minority representation) regulations. There is no reliable information on the actual composition of parliament.

Year	1990		1996		2001		
	Seats	%	Seats	%	Seats	%	
	92[a]	100.0	93[c]	100.0	92[d]	100.0	
UNO[b]	51	55.4	–	–	–	–	
FSLN	39	42.4	36	38.7	38	41.3	
MUR	1	1.1	–	–	–	–	
PSC	1	1.1	–	–	–	–	
AL	–	–	42	45.2	–	–	
CCN	–	–	4	4.3	–	–	
PCN	–	–	3	3.2	2	2.2	
PRONAL	–	–	2	2.2	–	–	
MRS	–	–	1	1.1	–	–	
ANC	–	–	1	1.1	–	–	
PRN	–	–	1	1.1	–	–	
PLI	–	–	1	1.1	–	–	
U	–	–	1	1.1	–	–	
PLC	–	–	–	–	52	56.5	

[a] Including two seats for unsuccessful presidential candidates.
[b] Alliance comprised of the following parties (in alphabetical order): APC, MDN, PALI, PAN,
PC de N, PDCN, PLC, PLI, PNC, PSD, PSN, as well as the groups ANC y PIAC, both without
legal recognition as political parties.
[c] 20 seats by national lists, 70 seats by departmental lists and three seats for unsuccessful presidential candidates.
[d] 20 seats by national lists, 70 seats by departmental lists, one seat for the unsuccessful presidential candidate and one seat for the outgoing president. The distribution of the seats by the CSE
was contested by the FSLN that claimed to have won a few more seats. Due to parliamentary
crisis in 2002, party composition of parliament has changed significantly.

2.9 Presidential Elections 1912–2001

1912	Total number	%
Registered voters	—	–
Votes cast	—	—
Invalid votes	—	—
Valid votes	25,739	—
Adolfo Díaz (PC)	23,467	91.2
Emiliano Chamorro (PC)[a]	2,229	8.6
Francisco Baca (PL)[a]	43	0.2

[a] Neither Emiliano Chamorro nor Francisco Baca were official candidates. The PL did not contest the elections due to US pressure.

1916	Total number	%
Registered voters	—	–
Votes cast	—	—
Invalid votes	—	—
Valid votes	58,810	—
Emiliano Chamorro (PC)[a]	58,810	100.0

[a] The PL could not participate.

1920[a]	Total number	%
Registered voters	—	–
Votes cast	—	—
Invalid votes	—	—
Valid votes	90,428	—
Diego Manuel Chamorro (PC)	66,974	—
José Esteban González (PL/Partido Conservador Progresista)	22,519	—
José Andrés Urtecho (PC fraction)	940	—

[a] Alleged electoral fraud.

1924[a]	Total number	%
Registered voters	121,490	–
Votes cast	—	—
Invalid votes	—	—
Valid votes	84,096	—
Carlos Solórzano/ Juan Bautista Sacasa (PLN)	48,072	57.2
Emiliano Chamorro (PC)	28,760	34.2
Luis Felipe Corea (Partido Liberal Republicano)	7,264	8.6

[a] Serious irregularities during the electoral process.

1928[a]	Total number	%
Registered voters	148,831	–
Votes cast	—	—
Invalid votes	—	—
Valid votes	133,663	—
José María Moncada (PLN)	76,676	57.4
Martín Benárd (PC)	56,987	42.6

[a] Elections held under US supervision.

1932[a]	Total number	%
Registered voters	154,720	–
Votes cast	—	—
Invalid votes	—	—
Valid votes	130,114	—
Juan Bautista Sacasa (PLN)	76,269	58.6
Adolfo Díaz (PC)	53,845	41.4

[a] Elections held under US supervision.

1936[a]	Total number	%
Registered voters	—	–
Votes cast	—	—
Invalid votes	—	—
Valid votes	80,663	—
Anastasio Somoza García (PLN/ Partido Conservador Nacionalista)	64,000	79.3
Leonardo Agüello (PC/Partido Liberal Constitucionalista)	16,663	20.7

[a] Alleged electoral fraud.

1947[a]	Total number	%
Registered voters	—	–
Votes cast	—	—
Invalid votes	—	—
Valid votes	169,708	—
Leonardo Argüello (PLN/ Partido Conservador Nacionalista)[b]	104,804	61.8
Enoc Aguado (PCN)[c]	64,904	38.2

[a] Blatant electoral fraud.
[b] The PLN and the *Partido Conservador Nacionalista* supported the same candidate; the former received 96,731 votes and the latter 8,073 votes.
[c] The PLI was not legally recognized. Due to this reason, its candidate Enoc Aguado appeared officially as candidate of the PCN.

1950[a]	Total number	%
Registered voters	—	–
Votes cast	—	—
Invalid votes	—	—
Valid votes	202,698	—
Anastasio Somoza García (PLN)	153,297	75.6
Emilio Chamorro Benard (PCN)	49,401	24.4

[a] *Elecciones pactistas*: Before the elections, the so-called *Pacto de los Generales* was signed.

1957	Total number	%
Registered voters	—	–
Votes cast	—	—
Invalid votes	—	—
Valid votes	355,178	—
Luis Somoza Debayle (PLN)	316,998	89.3
Edmundo Amador Pineda (Partido Conservador Nicaragüense)	38,180	10.8

1963	Total number	%
Registered voters	570,000	–
Votes cast	—	—
Invalid votes	—	—
Valid votes	451,064	—
René Schick Gutiérrez (PLN)	408,131	90.5
Diego Manuel Chamorro Jr. (Partido Conservador Nicaragüense)	42,933	9.5

1967[a]	Total number	%
Registered voters	—	–
Votes cast	—	—
Invalid votes	—	—
Valid votes	540,714	—
Anastasio Somoza Debayle (PLN)	380,162	70.3
Fernando Agüero Rocha (UNO)[b]	157,432	29.1
Alejandro Abaúnza Marenco (Partido Conservador Nicaragüense)	3,120	0.6

[a] Blatant electoral fraud.
[b] Alliance comprised of the PCN, PLI and PSC.

1974	Total number	%
Registered voters	1,152,260	–
Votes cast	—	—
Invalid votes	—	—
Valid votes	799,982	—
Anastasio Somoza Debayle (PLN)	733,662	91.7
Edmundo Papuagua Irías (PCN)	66,320	8.3

1984	Total number	%
Registered voters	1,551,597	–
Votes cast	1,170,142	75.4
Invalid votes	71,209	6.1
Valid votes	1,098,933	93.9
Daniel Ortega Saavedra (FSLN)	735,967	67.0
Clemente Guido (PCDN)	154,327	14.0
Virgilio Godoy Reyes (PLI)	105,560	9.6
Mauricio Díaz Davila (PPSC)	61,199	5.6
Alán Zambrana Salmeron (PC de N)	16,034	1.5
Domingo Antonio Sánchez Salgado (PSN)	14,494	1.3
Isidro Téllez Toruño (MAP-ML)	11,352	1.0

1990	Total number	%
Registered voters	1,752,088	–
Votes cast	1,510,838	86.2
Invalid votes	90,249	6.0
Valid votes	1,420,544	94.0
Violeta Barrios de Chamorro (UNO[a])	777,552	54.8
Daniel Ortega Saavedra (FSLN)	579,886	40.8
Moisses Hassan (MUR)	16,751	1.2
Eric Ramírez (PSC/PPSC)	11,136	0.8
Bonifacio Miranda (PRT)	8,590	0.6
Isidora Téllez (MAP-ML)	8,115	0.6
Others[b]	18,514	1.3

[a] Alliance comprising the following parties (in alphabetical order): APC, MDN, PALI, PAN, PC de N, PDCN, PLC, PLI, PNC, PSD, PSN, as well as the groups ANC y PIAC, which were not legally recognized as political parties.

[b] Others include: Fernando Agüero (PSOC): 5,798 votes (0.4%); Blanca Rojas (PUCA): 5,065 (0.4%); Eduardo Molina (PCDN): 4,500 (0.3%); Rodolfo Robelo (PLIUN): 3,151 (0.2%).

1996	Total number	%
Registered voters	2,421,067	–
Votes cast	1,849,362	76.4
Invalid votes	91,587	5.0
Valid votes	1,757,775	95.0
José Arnoldo Alemán Lacayo (AL)	896,207	51.0
Daniel Ortega Saavedra (FSLN)	664,909	37.8
Guillermo Antonio Osorno Molina (CCN)	71,908	4.1
Noel José Vidaurre Argüello (PCN)	39,983	2.3
Benjamín Ramón Lanzas Selva (PRONAL)	9,265	0.5
Others[a]	75,503	4.4

[a] Others include: Sergio Ramírez Mercado (MRS): 7,665 votes (0.4%); Francisco José Mayorga Balladares (Pan y Fuerza): 7,102 (0.4%); Francisco José Duarte Tapia (ANC): 6,178 (0.4%); Edgar Enrique Quiñónes Tuckler (PRN): 5,813 (0.3%); Andrés Abelino Robles Pérez (PUNOCP): 5,789 (0.3%); Virgilio Abelardo Godoy Reyes (PLI): 5,692 (0.3%); Jorge Alberto Díaz Cruz (PJN): 5,582 (0.3%); Alejandro Serrano Caldera (U): 4,873 (0.3%); Elí Altamirano Pérez (PC de N): 4,802 (0.3%); Miriam Auxiliadora Argüello Morales (APC): 4,632 (0.3%); Ausberto Narváez Argüello (Unidad Liberal): 3,887 (0.2%); Alfredo César Aguirre (UNO 96): 3,664 (0.2%); Allan Antonio Tefel Alba (MORENA): 2,641 (0.2%); James Odnith Webster Pitts (PAD): 1,895 (0.1%); Sergio Abilio Mendieta Castillo (PIAC): 1,653 (0.1%); Issa Moises Hassán Morales (EL MAR): 1,393 (0.1%); Gustavo Ernesto Tablada Zelaya (PSN): 1,352 (0.1%); Roberto Urcuyo Muñoz (PADENIC): 890 (0.1%).

2001	Total number	%
Registered voters	—	–
Votes cast	—	—
Invalid votes	—	—
Valid votes	2,162,213	—
Enrique Bolaños Geyer (PLC)	1,216,863	56.3
Daniel Ortega Saavedra (FSLN)	915,417	42.3
Alberto Saborio (PC)	29,933	1.4

2.10 List of Power Holders 1893–2004

Head of State	Years	Remarks
José Santos Zelaya	1893–1909	Assumed the head of the provisional government after the resignation of the government junta; confirmed by the new constitutional assembly; re-elected in 1905. Resigned in December 1909 due to uprisings.
José Madriz	1909–1910	Nominated by the legislative assembly in December 1909. Forced to resign by uprisings in August 1910.
José Dolores Estrada	1910	Provisional president, nominated by congress
Juan José Estrada	1910–1911	Provisional president, nominated by congress in September 1990. Resigned on 09/05/1911 due to uprisings.
Adolfo Díaz	1911–1917	Assumed power in his capacity as vice president. Elected president in 1912.
Emiliano Chamorro Vargas	1917–1920	Elected in 1916. Assumed presidency in January 1917.
Diego Manuel Chamorro	1921–1923	Elected in 1920. Assumed presidency on 01/01/1921. Died on 12/10/1923.
Bartolomé Martínez	1923–1924	Assumed office in his capacity as vice president.
Carlos Solórzano	1925–1926	Elected in 1924; assumed presidency on 01/01/1925; resigned due to uprisings on 16/02/1926.
Emiliano Chamorro	1926	Took hold of the government after Solórzano's resignation and the vice president's forced exile. Resigned on 30/10/1926 due to US pressure.
Sebastián Uriza	1926	Elected provisional president by the national assembly, in his capacity as senator. Forced to resign in November 1926.
Adolfo Díaz	1926–1928	Provisional president.
José María Moncado	1929–1932	Elected in 1928. Assumed presidency on 01/01/1929.
Juan Bautista Sacasa	1933–1936	Elected in 1932. Assumed presidency on 01/01/1933. Resigned on 02/06/1936 due to uprisings.
Carlos Brenes Jarquín	1936	Provisional president until 31/12/1936.
Anastasio Somoza García	1937–1947	Elected in 1936. Assumed presidency on 01/01/1937. Appointed president in 1939 by the national assembly until 01/05/1947.
Leonardo Argüello	1947	Elected in 1947. After 25 days in office congress declared him mentally incompetent due to Somoza's pressure.

Head of State (cont.)	Years	Remarks
Benjamín Lacayo Sacasa	1947	Interim president (26/5–14/8/1947) appointed by Somoza.
Víctor Manuel Román y Reyes	1947–1950	Elected president by congress. Died in 1950.
Anastasio Somoza García	1950–1956	Elected by congress; re-elected in 1951. Assassinated on 21/09/1956.
Luis A. Somoza Debayle	1956–1963	Assumed office in his capacity as chairman of congress. Elected in 1957. Assumed presidency constitutionally on 01/05/1957.
René Schick Gutiérrez	1963–1966	Elected in 1963. Assumed presidency on 01/05/1963. Died on 03/08/1966.
Lorenzo Guerrero Gutiérrez	1966–1967	Interim president.
Anastasio Somoza Debayle	1967–1972	Elected in 1967. Presidential tenure from 01/05/1967 to 30/04/1972.
Triunvirato	1972–1974	Comprised of Roberto Martínez Lacayo, Alfonso López Cordero and Fernando Agüero Rocha (Edmundo Papuaga Irías since 1973). Appointed by the national assembly following a pact established between Somoza and Agüero. End of tenure on 01/12/1974.
Anastasio Somoza Debayle	1974–1979	Elected in 1974. Ousted by the revolution on 19/07/1979.
Junta de Gobierno de Reconstrucción Nacional	1979–1980	Comprised of Daniel Ortega Saavedra, Sergio Ramírez Mercado, Moisses Hassan, Violeta Barrios de Chamorro, Alfonso Robelo. Founded in exile on 16/06/1979. Chamorro resigned on 18/04/1980 and Robelo on 22/04/1980.
Junta de Gobierno de Reconstrucción Nacional	1980–1981	Comprised of Daniel Ortega Saavedra, Sergio Ramírez Mercado, Moisses Hassan, Rafael Córdova Rivas, Arturo Cruz. The head of the FSLN designated Rafael Córdova Rivas and Arturo Cruz to take part in the junta. The size of the junta was reduced on 03/04/1981.
Junta de Gobierno de Reconstrucción Nacional	1981–1985	Comprised of Daniel Ortega Saavedra, Sergio Ramírez Mercado, Rafael Córdova Rivas. Transfer of government to the elected president on 10/01/1985.
Daniel Ortega Saavedra	1985–1990	Elected in 1984. End of presidential tenure on 25/04/1990.
Violeta Barrios de Chamorro	1990–1997	Elected in 1990. Assumed office on 25/04/1990.
Arnoldo Alemán	1997–2002	Elected in 1996. Assumed office on 10/01/1997.
Enrique Bolaños Geyer	2002–	Elected in 2001. Assumed office on 10/01/2002.

3. Bibliography

3.1.Official sources

Constitución Política, in *La Gaceta – Diario Oficial* (Managua), 5, 09/01/1987.
Consejo Nacional de Elecciones (1924). *Nicaragua 1924 – Informe al Congreso Nacional.* Managua.
Consejo Nacional de Elecciones (1928). *Informe al Congreso Nacional.* Managua.
Consejo Nacional de Elecciones (1933). *El proceso electoral en 1932.* Managua.
Consejo Nacional de Elecciones (1956). *El Juicio Electoral en 1950.* Managua.
Consejo Supremo Electoral (1989). *Elecciones 1984.* Managua.
Consejo Supremo Electoral (1990). *Elecciones 1990.* Managua.
Consejo Supremo Electoral (1995). *Las Leyes Electorales en la historia de Nicaragua,* vol. I–III. Managua.
Decreto Legislativo de 15/04/1950, in *La Gaceta – Diario Oficial* (Managua), 75, 15/04/1950.
Elecciones de Autoridades Supremas de Nicaragua, in *La Gaceta – Diario Oficial,* 270, 09/12/1936.
La Gaceta – Diario Oficial (Managua), 49, 05/03/1947.
Ley de Reforma Parcial a la Constitución Política de Nicaragua (1995). <http:www.asamblea.gob.nic>.
Ley de Reforma Parcial a la Constitución de la República de Nicaragua (2000). <http://www.asamblea.gob.nic>.
Ley Electoral (1996), in *La Gaceta – Diario Oficial,* 6, 09/01/1996.
Ley Electoral (2000), in *La Gaceta – Diario Oficial,* 16, 19/01/2000.
Resultado de las elecciones del 5 de octubre de 1924, para Autoridades Supremas de la República, Manifiesto Presidencial, in *La Gaceta – Diario Oficial* (Managua), 272, 01/12/1924.

3.2. Books, Articles, and Electoral Reports

Alvarez Lejarua, E. (1958). *Las Constituciones de Nicaragua.* Madrid: Ediciones Cultura Hispánica.
Arendaña Sandino, R. (1966). *Proceso electoral en Nicaragua.* Ph.D. thesis, León: Universidad Nacional de Nicaragua.
Avendaño Rojas, X. (1996). 'El pactismo. El mecanismo de ascenso de los notables, 1858-1893'. *Revista de Historia* (Managua), 7: 26–41.

Avendaño Rojas, X. and Peña, L. M. (1996). 'Cronología de la historia electoral nicaragüense'. *Revista de Historia* (Managua), 7: 68–78.

Barquero, S. (1945). *Gobernantes de Nicaragua*. Managua: Talleres Nacionales.

Booth, J. A. (1986). 'Election Amid War and Revolution. Toward Evaluating the 1984 Nicaraguan National Elections', in P. W. Drake and E. Silva (eds.), *Elections And Democratization in Latin America, 1980–85*. La Jolla: University of California at San Diego, 37–60.

— (1990). 'Elecciones y democracia en Nicaragua. Una evaluación de las elecciones de febrero de 1990'. *Polémica* (San José), segunda época, 11: 29–43.

— and Richard, P. B (1997). 'The Nicaraguan Elections of October 1996'. *Electoral Studies*, 16/3: 386–393.

Bowdler, G. A. and Cotter, P. (1982). *Voter Participation in Central America, 1954–1981*. Washington D.C.: University Press of America.

Burín des Roziers, P. (1985). 'Les élections au Nicaragua (4 Novembre 1984)'. *Problèmes d'Amerique Latine*, 76: 41–73.

Chamorro, A. (1967). *145 años de historia política - Nicaragua*. Managua.

Chamorro Mora, R. (1987). 'Las constituciones políticas de Nicaragua'. *Encuentro* (Managua), 21: 31–59.

Close, D. (1984). 'The Nicaraguan Elections of 1984'. *Electoral Studies*, 4: 152–158.

— (1998). *Nicaragua. The Chamorro Years*. Boulder, Colo./ London: Lynne Rienner.

Collado Herrera, C. (1988). *Nicaragua*. Mexico City: Alianza Editorial Mexicana.

Cortés Domínguez, G. (1990). *La lucha por el poder*. Managua: Vanguardia.

Council of Freely-Elected Heads of Government, The (1990). *Observing Nicaragua's Elections*, 1989–1990. Atlanta: The Carter Center.

Dodd, T. J. (1975). 'Los Estados Unidos en la política nicaragüense. Elecciones supervisadas 1928–1932'. *Revista de Pensamiento Centroamericano* (Managua), 30/148: 28–92.

— (1992). Managing Democracy in Central America. A Case Study: United States Election Supervision in Nicaragua, 1927–1933. Boulder, Colo.: Lynne Rienner Publishers.

English, B. H. (1967). *Nicaragua Election Fact Book, February 5, 1967*. Washington D.C.: Institute for the Comparative Study of Political Systems.

Esgueva Gómez, A. (1996). 'El marco jurídico electoral en Nicaragua: 1812–1990. Cambios y continuidades'. *Revista de Historia* (Managua), 7: 6–25.

Fiallos Oyanguren, M. (1992). 'Nicaragua. Las elecciones de 1990', in R. Cerdas Cruz, J. Rial, and D. Zovatto (eds.), *Una tarea inconclusa: Elecciones y democracia en América Latina. 1988-1991*. San José: IIDH-CAPEL, 135–150.

Fuchs, J. (1988). 'Die Verfassungsentwicklung in Nicaragua'. *Jahrbuch des öffentlichen Rechts*, 37: 621–719.
— (2004). *Nicaragua. Demokratischer Anspruch und gesellschaftliche Realität*. Frankfurt a. M. et al: Peter Lang.
Galindo Velez, F. H. (1977). 'Nicaragua', in A. P. Blaustein and G. H. Flanz (eds.), *Constitutions of the Countries of the World*. New York.
García, S. (1990). *Nicaragua. Informe al Consejo Supremo Electoral sobre el proceso electoral*. Caracas: República de Venezuela.
Geer, V. L. (1985). 'State Department Policy in Regard to the Nicaraguan Election of 1924'. *Hispanic American Historical Review*, 34.
Godoy Reyes, V. (1990). 'Nicaragua 1944–1984. Political Parties and Electoral Processes', in L. Goodman, W. LeoGrande, and J. Mendelson (eds.), *Political Parties and Democracy in Central America*. Boulder, Colo./ San Franciso/ Oxford: Westview Press, 175–185.
González-Roura, F. (1990). 'Elecciones generales. Nicaragua, 25 de febrero de 1990'. *Boletín Electoral Latinoamericano* (San José), 3: 17–31.
Hemisphere Initiatives (1989). *Establishing the Ground Rules. A Report on the Nicaraguan Electoral Process*. Boston, Mass.
Instituto Centroamericano de Estudios Políticos (INCEP) (1996). *Nicaragua: Elecciones generales 1996*. Guatemala: INCEP.
Kamman, W. (1968). *A Search for Stability. United States Diplomacy Toward Nicaragua 1925–1933*. Notre Dame, Ind.: University of Notre Dame.
Krennerich, M. (1993). 'Competitividad de las elecciones en Nicaragua, El Salvador y Guatemala en una perspectiva histórica comparada', in D. Nohlen (ed.), *Elecciones y sistemas de partidos en América Latina*. San José: IIDH/CAPEL, 169–203.
— (1996). *Wahlen und Antiregimekriege in Zentralamerika. Eine vergleichende Studie*. Opladen: Leske + Budrich.
— (1996a). 'Esbozo de la historia electoral nicaragüense, 1950–1990'. *Revista de Historia* (Managua), 7: 42–67.
Latin American Studies Association (LASA) (1985). *Report of the Latin American Studies Association Delegation to Observe the Nicaragua General Election of November 4, 1984*. Washington, D.C.
Latin American Studies Association (LASA) (1990). *Electoral Democracy under International Pressure. The Report of the Latin American Studies Association Commission to Observe the 1990 Nicaraguan Election*. Pittsburgh, Pa.
López Mejía, N. (1963). *Historia constitucional de Nicaragua*. Ph.D. thesis, León: Universidad Nacional de Nicaragua.
López Pintor, R. and Nohlen, D. (1991). 'Elecciones de apertura. El caso de Nicaragua de 1990', in R. Espinal et al. (eds.), *Análisis de los procesos electorales en América Latina. Memorias IV Curso Anual Interamericano de Elecciones*. San José: IIDH-CAPEL, 323–344.

McDonald, R. H. (1971). *Party Systems and Elections in Latin America.* Chicago, Ill.: Markham.

Millet, R. (1977). *Guardians of the Dynasty. A History of the U.S. Created Guardia Nacional de Nicaragua and the Somoza Family.* Maryknoll, New York: Orbis Books.

United Nations (1989). *Informe de una Misión de Asistencia Técnica. Análisis de las leyes electorales de Nicaragua.* Managua.

United Nations, ONUVEN (1989/1990). *Primer–cuarto informe al Secretario General de la Misión de Observadores de las Naciones Unidas encargada de verificar el proceso electoral en Nicaragua.* Managua.

Nohlen, D. (1984). *Un análisis del sistema electoral nicaragüense.* Managua: Fundación Manolo Morales.

Núñez Vargas, E. (1996). 'Elecciones Generales, Nicaragua, 20 de octubre de 1996'. *Boletín Electoral Latinoamericano* (San José), 16, 37–68.

Organization of American States (OAS) (1989/1990). *Primer-cuarto informe sobre la observación del proceso electoral de Nicaragua.* Washington, D.C.

Patterson, H. (1997). 'The 1996 Elections and Nicaragua's Fragile Transition'. *Government and Opposition*, 32/3: 380–398.

República de Venezuela, Consejo Supremo Electoral (1989). *Informe de la Misión Electoral a Nicaragua.* Caracas.

Richard, P. B. and Booth, J. A. (1995). 'Election Observation and Democratization: Reflections on the Nicaraguan Case', in M. A. Seligson and J. Booth (eds.), *Elections and Democracy in Central America Revisited.* Chapel Hill, N.C./ London: The University of North Carolina Press, 202–223.

Robinson, W. I. (1992). *A Faustian Bargain. U.S. Intervention in the Nicaraguan Elections and American Foreign Policiy in the Post-Cold-War-Era.* Boulder, Colo./ London: Westview Press.

Ruddle, K. and Gillette, P. (eds.) (1972). *Latin American Political Statistics. Supplement to the Statistical Abstract of Latin America.* Los Angeles, Calif.: University of California.

Ryan, J.M. et al. (1970). *Area Handbook on Nicaragua.* Washington, D.C.: U.S. Government Printing Office.

Saballos, A. (without year). *Elecciones '90.* Managua: CIRA.

Solórzano, M. (1986). 'Centroamérica. Democracias de fachada'. *Polémica* (San José), segunda época, 12: 40–55.

Torres-Rivas, E. (1984). 'Nicaragua. Sufragio y guerra'. *Polémica* (San José), 14–15, 66–76.

Vanhanen, T. (1975*). Political and Social Structures, Part 1: American Countries 1850–1973.* Tampere: University of Tampere.

Vargas, O.-R. (1990). *Elecciones presidenciales en Nicaragua, 1912–1932 (Análisis sociopolítico).* Managua: Fundación Manolo Morales.

— (1990a). *Partidos políticos y la búsqueda de un nuevo modelo*. Managua: Centro de Investigación y Desarrollo ECOTEXTURA/Comunicaciones Nicaragüenses.

Vilas, C. M. (1990). 'Especulaciones sobre una sorpresa: las elecciones en Nicaragua'. *Secuencia* (Mexico City), 17: 119–148.

Walker, T. W. (ed.) (1997): *Nicaragua without Illusions. Regime Transition and Structural Adjustment in the 1990s*. Wilmington, Del.: SR Books.

Washington Office on Latin America/ International Human Rights Law Group (1984). *A Political Opening in Nicaragua. Report on the Nicaraguan Elections of November 4, 1984*. Washington, D.C.

Wilkie, J. W. et al. (eds.) (1990*). Statistical Abstract of Latin America*, 28, Los Angeles, Calif.: University of California.

Zelaya Velásquez, R. M. (1988). 'El registro electoral en Nicaragua', in *Memoria de la Segunda Conferencia de la Asociación de Organismos Electorales de Centroamérica y el Caribe*. San José (Costa Rica): IIDH/CAPEL.

PANAMA

by Petra Bendel, Michael Krennerich, and Claudia Zilla

1. Introduction

1.1 Historical Overview

The history of the Republic of Panama has been shaped considerably by its peculiar geography: The isthmus form of the country represented a structural precondition for the construction of the Panama Canal, the use and control of which have closely linked Panama's national politics with North American interests.

After independence from Spain on 28 November 1821, Panama gained sovereignty as a result of its gradual detachment from Great Colombia. This process was concluded on 3 November 1903 after the liberal battles against centralism—the so-called 'Thousand Year War'—and the US armed invasion of 1903. The latter was a reaction to the refusal of the Colombian parliament to ratify the Canal Construction Treaty, which both the Colombian and North American governments had signed. A few days later, the representatives of the new State of Panama and the Roosevelt Administration signed the Hay-Buneau Varilla Treaty. This treaty granted the United States indeterminate sovereignty over the Panama Canal (a ten-mile zone) and the right to military intervention beyond the Canal zone with the aim of reestablishing public peace and constitutional order. The USA would also have the right to supervise the electoral process at the government's or the opposition's request. Such intervention and supervision was frequently requested up to the 1930s. Several disputes between Panama and Washington led to several new developments in the country: In 1936 the treaty was reviewed and the USA's right to intervention was abolished; in 1960 Panama's sovereignty over the canal zone was formally recognized; in 1963 diplomatic relations between Panama and the USA were disrupted (Flag Struggle), and in 1979 a new treaty was ratified. This new treaty set the course for the sovereignty rights to the canal and the canal zone to be transferred to Panama by 2000. This took place on 1 January.

The 1904 Constitution, which remained in force, with modifications, until 1941, established a unitarian, republican, and presidential government, as well as a unicameral parliament (*Asamblea Legislativa*). Currently, Panama's constitution is based on the 1972 Constitution, with reforms from 1978, 1983, and 1984. This constitution established the democratic and representative character of the government. Panama remained a centralist state organized politically and administratively into 9 provinces, 74 districts, 4 indian comarcs, and 597 *corregimientos*.

Although elections were held regularly until 1968—interrupted only by two *coups d'état* in 1931 and 1941—their results were usually questioned and labeled fraudulent. During this period, the party system was controlled by the Liberals and Conservatives. However, these groups were based around personalities and lacked a serious program. The *Partido Conservador* (PC; Conservative Party) quickly lost relevance, and as of 1908 all the elected presidents came from the *Partido Liberal* (PL; Liberal Party). The 1930s saw the formation of the *Partido Comunista* (Communist Party) and the *Partido Socialista* (PS; Socialist Party), and the latter received a high percentage of votes. The nationalist *Asociación Acción Comunal* (Communal Action Association), under the direction of the Arias brothers, managed to mobilize the urban middle class. It was, in fact, this group that carried out the first *coup d'état* in the history of Panama, in 1931. In 1940, one of the leading figures of this party, the populist Arnulfo Arias, was elected president amidst great controversy, but was overthrown by a military coup in 1941. In 1946 a new constitution was passed, which abolished the race-based prohibitions of the 1941 Constitution and reestablished the rule of law of the 1904 Constitution, together with the regulations on voting rights, which were now also extended to women. Under this constitution only the political parties were allowed to present candidates. Despite the constitutional regulations, the elections during the following two decades could still not be described as free or competitive. Only the results of the 1964 elections were accepted by all the contestants, most of whom belonged to the different liberal currents.

The dispute caused by Arnulfo Arias' triumph culminated in a *coup d'état* of the National Guard (Officers' Corps) in 1968. The de facto government of General Omar Torrijos dissolved parliament and proscribed political parties (until 1978). In 1972, a constitution was drafted to replace the *Estatuto Provisional de Gobierno* and granted Torrijos extraordinary personal powers for six years. The result was an authoritarian regime completely opposed to the principles of democracy. From 1977, the pressure exerted by Jimmy Carter's US government and domestic opposition compelled Torrijos' government to tackle the democratization of the political system. In 1978 and 1983 constitutional reforms were implemented that reintroduced the separation of powers and the direct election of the president and the deputies. The opposition parties, among them the *Partido Panamenista Auténtico* (PPA; Authentic Panamenista Party) and the *Partido Demócrata Chrstiano* (PDC; Christian Democratic Party), recovered their legal status. In addition, the *Partido Revolucionario Democrático* (PRD; Democratic Revolutionary Party), a pro-government party, was founded. With Torrijos' death in 1981, the armed forces were realigned and General Antonio Noriega gained control of power.

The 1984 elections were based on the 1983 Constitutional Act and were direct, universal, free, and secret. The contest was, however, blemished by electoral offences, and its winner was the pro-government candidate Nicolás Ardito Barletto. The next elections, held in 1989, were annulled by the government when it became clear that the opposition candidate would win. There were even personal attacks on the opposition candidates. This conflict prompted another US invasion in December of the same year. After this invasion, Guillermo Endara Galimany, the opposition leader who had originally won the elections that were later annulled by the international observers, was appointed president. As a consequence of the US invasion, the army was dissolved and the security system reorganized. The fragility of the ruling coalition became obvious a few months after its acquisition of power. President Endara's lack of charisma and the general questions regarding his situation aggravated the government's problems, especially as it had become difficult to reach pragmatic compromises. The population's general disappointment in the government increased after the 1992 referendum concerning a package of constitutional reforms, which included the suppression of the armed forces. The turnout was very low (40% of the electorate) and the proposals were eventually rejected.

The PRD's rapid political recovery (they now represented the cause of social democrats) would not have been possible without the poor performance of Endara's government. In the 1994 elections, Pérez Balladares was elected president at the head of a three-party alliance called *Pueblo Unido* (United People). This alliance obtained 33.3% of the vote, 30.5% of which was won by the PRD. The second political force was the *Partido Arnulfista* (Arnulfista Party) with 19.9% of the vote. The third-ranking force was the *Movimiento Papa Egoró* (Papa Egoro Movement), with 17.1%. The poor result of the Christian Democrats

(2.4% of the vote, that is, one deputy) was striking, considering that it was the most well-organized party.

Five years later, and for the first time in Panama's history, a woman became president. Mireya Moscoso, the widow of Arnulfo Arias Madrid and head of the Arnulfista Party, won the 1999 presidential election with the support of the opposition electoral alliance *Unión por Panamá* (Union for Panama), which became the second political force (33.8% of the seats) in the legislative power. The electoral alliance *Nueva Nación* (New Nation) obtained the absolute majority (57.7%) of the seats in the *Asamblea Legislativa*. However, at the beginning of her presidency Moscoso was able to form an alliance that gave her control of the assembly. After the first year, the PRD and the PDC—now joined in opposition—controlled the legislative power.

Comparing the legislative election results on the levels of votes and seats shows a concentration effect. The legislative assembly is elected through a system that is considered to be proportional representation, yet, due to the small size of the constituencies, real proportional representation is hardly ever attained.

1.2 Evolution of Electoral Provisions

On 12 December 1903 the provisional government set the date for the elections to the *Convención Nacional Constituyente* for January 1904. This was the first electoral activity in Panama, and was followed by the enactment of the first political constitution. Limited female suffrage was first introduced in the 1941 Constitution for women older than 21. Law No. 98 (enacted on 5 July 1941) regulated and limited this right to vote (only valid for elections at the local level) to women with university, normal (tertiary), or secondary education. In 1945 (election of the second constitutional assembly), women voted for the first time. The 1946 Political Constitution provided women with political rights identical to those of men. Until 1972, only persons older than 21 had the right to vote. The 1972 Constitution reduced the minimum age to 18.

In Panama, the head of government and chief of state has not always been elected directly by the people. In 1904, the *Asamblea Nacional Constituyente* elected the president according to an absolute majority system. Between 1908 and 1916 the presidential elections were indirect. At province level, the population voted for *electores* (electoral representatives) whose sole function was to elect the president from candidates put forward using the plurality system. From 1920 to 1968, elections were direct. In accordance with the 1972 Constitution, the 1972 and the 1978 elections were again indirect. On those occasions, the (directly elected) *Asamblea Nacional de Representantes de Corregimientos* was responsible for electing the president and vice presidents. After the 1983 reforms, the president was elected directly once more.

In Panama's history, there have been three (1903, 1945, and 1972) elected national constitutional assemblies (*Asamblea Nacional Constituyente*; ANC) that acted as the legislative assembly. The ANC of 1945 functioned as a parliament until 1948, when new deputies were elected. The ANC of 1972 approved a new constitution and then became the *Asamblea Nacional de Representantes de Corregimientos* (ANRC). In accordance with the 1972 Constitution, the ANRC and the *Consejo Nacional de Legislación* (CNL)—mainly composed of members of the executive—shared the legislative functions. In 1980, one third of the CNL was elected directly. The other two thirds of this legislative body were elected from the members of the ANRC. Since 1984, all members of the legislative assembly are elected directly.

1.3. Current Electoral Provision

Sources: The current electoral law is governed by the 1972 Constitution, the 1983 Constitutional Act, and the 1983 Electoral Code and their respective reforms.

Suffrage: The principles of universal, secret, and direct adult suffrage apply. Voters have to be 18 years old, in possession of an identity card, and registered in the *Registro Electoral*. Voting is compulsory.

Elected national institutions: The president and two vice presidents as well as the legislative assembly, the sole chamber of parliament, are directly elected for five-year terms on the same day. The legislative assembly is made up of 71 deputies. The president and the vice presidents are elected together. Re-election of the president is only allowed after two periods of government have passed.

Nomination of candidates: Only the parties can propose presidential, vice presidential, and legislative candidates. A candidate can be proposed by several parties at the same time.
The constitution recognizes the role of parties for political pluralism and participation, and the formation of the people's will. However, it regu-

lates their existence, which depends on the electoral results. Those parties that do not reach 5% of the valid votes are dissolved.

Electoral System
- *presidential elections*: Plurality system.
- *parliamentary elections*: Proportional representation in small constituencies. The provinces of Panama and the region of San Blas are subdivided into 40 constituencies (*circuitos electorales*) of different sizes. 26 are SMCs and 14 are MMCs: seven of 2 deputies, one of 3, three of 4, two of 5, and one of 6 deputies.

In the SMCs the voter is entitled to one vote; plurality decides. In MMCs there are closed and non-blocked lists; the voter is entitled to several votes and can vote for as many candidates as there are seats to be allocated (preferential and selective vote). The allocation of seats follows three stages: in the first stage, seats are allocated on the basis of the votes received by the lists, using the simple electoral quota. In the second stage, only the parties that did not receive any seats in the first stage take part, and the half quota method is applied. The procedure followed in the third stage is considered as the largest remainder, but the votes are ordered considering the candidates (and not the lists, which means that several parties may present the same candidate). The remaining seats are distributed in the constituencies among the candidates with the highest percentage of the vote, in decreasing order. The constitution provides for the allocation of additional seats to those parties that, having competed in the elections (more than 5% of the valid votes), did not get any seats. In this case, the additional seats are assigned to the candidate in the party who received the most votes.

In the 1999 elections, of the 45 multi-member seats, eleven were allocated in the first stage (quota), 18 (1994: 20) in the second (half quota) and 16 (1994: 19) in the third stage (remainder).

Organizational context of elections: In 1904, Law No. 89 (07/07) created electoral institutions at the national, regional, and local level responsible for organizing elections. The name and functions of these institutions have since been changed many times. The second political constitution (1941) recognized these electoral institutions.

The *Tribunal Electoral* and the *Fiscalía Electoral* together form the Electoral Jurisdiction, based on articles 136 and 138 of the constitution and on the Organic Law No. 4 (10/02/1976–1978), which regulate the functioning of both institutions, and on decrees No. 76 (05/04/1979) and No. 107 (26/10/1990). Three magistrates, chosen by the executive, legislative, and judicial powers (Supreme Court of Justice) respectively, are appointed to the *Tribunal Electoral* for a ten-year period. The *Tribunal Electoral* is responsible for the electoral registration of citizens and parties, for the organization of elections and referendums, and the administration of electoral justice. This last function is carried out by the *Tribunal Electoral* and the *Fiscalía Electoral*, an independent institution headed by a public prosecutor, who is appointed by the executive and approved by the legislative assembly.

1.4 Commentary on the Electoral Statistics

The main source of the electoral data included in this article is the *Tribunal Electoral,* which publishes the official results of Panama's elections. These statistics are relatively accurate but not complete. This is partly due to the fact that Panama's electoral history has been characterized by fraud, alterations in procedure, electoral annulments, and problems of legitimacy. Therefore, the following tables do not contain figures for all the election years. The scrutiny of the blank votes has not always been uniform: sometimes they were counted separately from, and sometimes together with, the invalid votes.

Data from the *Tribunal Electoral* concerning the number of registered voters and electoral participation has only been available since 1948. The population statistics are taken from official censuses.

2. Tables

2.1 Dates of National Elections, Referendums, and Coups d'Etat

Year	Presidential elections	Parliamentary elections	Elections for Constitutional Assembly	Referendums	Coups d'état
1904	xx/xx	xx/xx			
1908	xx/xx				
1910		xx/xx			
1912	xx/xx				
1914		xx/xx			
1916	xx/xx				
1918		xx/xx			
1920	xx/xx				
1924	xx/xx	xx/xx			
1928	xx/xx	xx/xx			
1931					02/01
1932	xx/xx	xx/xx			
1936	xx/xx	xx/xx			
1940	xx/xx	xx/xx		15/12[a]	
1941					09/10
1945		xx/xx	05/05		
1948	xx/xx	xx/xx			
1949					20/11
1952	11/05	11/05			
1956	13/05	13/05			
1960	08/05	08/05			
1964	10/05	10/05			
1968	12/05	12/05			11/10
1972	xx/xx	xx/xx	06/08[b]		
1977				xx/xx[c]	23/10
1978	xx/xx	xx/xx			
1980		xx/xx			
1983				xx/xx[d]	24/04
1984	06/05	xx/xx			
1989	07/05[e]	xx/xx			20/12[f]
1991		xx/01			
1992				xx/11[d]	
1994	08/05	08/05			
1998				30/08[d]	
1999	02/05	02/05			
2004	02/05	02/05			

[a] National referendum to decide on the enactment of the constitution of 1941.
[b] Elections to the first *Asamblea Nacional de los Representantes de Corregimientos,* which functioned as a constitutional assembly.

^c National referendum to approve the Panama Canal Treaties.
^d National referendums to decide on reforms for the political constitution. The population only approved the 1983 reforms package.
^e Electoral manipulation.
^f US military invasion.

2.2 Electoral Body 1932–2004

Year	Type of election[a]	Population[b]	Registered voters Total number	% pop.	Votes cast Total number	% reg. Voters	% pop.
1932	Pr	500,000	—	—	—	—	—
1936	Pr	560,000	—	—	—	—	—
1940	Pr	622,576	—	—	—	—	—
1940	Pa	622,576	—	—	146,689	—	23.6
1945	CA	700,000	—	—	106,276^c	—	15.2
1948	Pr	760,000	305,123	40.1	216,214	70.9	28.4
1952	Pr	840,000	343,353	40.9	231,848	67.5	27.6
1956	Pr	950,000	386,672	40.7	306,770	79.3	32.3
1960	Pr	1,075,541	435,454	40.5	258,039	59.3	24.0
1964	Pr	1,200,000	486,420	40.5	326,401	67.1	27.2
1968	Pr	1,350,000	544,135	40.3	327,048	60.1	24.2
1972	ANRC^d	1,520,000	629,630	41.4	531,362	84.4	35.0
1977	Pa	1,770,000	787,251	44.5	766,232	97.3	43.3
1978	ANRC^d	1,810,000	787,251	43.5	658,421	83.6	36.4
1983	Pa	2,090,000	834,409	39.9	556,969	66.8	26.6
1984	Pr	2,130,000	917,677	43.1	674,075	73.5	31.6
1984	Pa^e	2,130,000	917,677	43.1	631,908	68.9	29.7
1989	Pr	2,329,329	1,184,320	51.0	757,797^f	64.0	32.5
1989	Pa	2,329,329	1,184,320	51.0	—	—	—
1994	Pr	2,609,000	1,499,451	57.5	1,104,578	73.7	42.3
1994	Pa	2,609,000	1,499,451	57.5	1,091,756	72.8	41.8
1999	Pr	2,839,177	1,746,989	61.3	1,330,730	76.2	46.9
1999	Pa	2,839,177	1,746,989	61.3	1,306,911	74.8	46.0
2004	Pr	2,940,000	1,999,553	68.0	1,537,342	76.9	52.3
2004	Pa	2,940,000	1,999,553	68.0	1,524,976	76.3	51.9

^a Pr = President, CA = Constitutional Assembly, Pa = Parliament, ANRC = elections for the *Asamblea Nacional de los Representantes de Corregimientos*.
^b Population data for 1940, 1960, 1989, and 1999 are based on censuses. The other figures are estimated by the author. Other censuses were held in: 1930: 467,459; 1950: 805,285; 1970: 1,428,082; 1980: 1,830,175.
^c Valid votes.
^d The 1972 ANRC acted formally as the constitutional assembly.
^e Elections to the *Consejo Nacional de Legislación* functioning as parliament.

[f] Decree No. 58, (10/5/1989) annulled the elections before all the votes had been counted. On 26/12/1989 Decree No. 127 declared the annulment to be valid. The result corresponds to a new official counting based on existing electoral documents.

2.3 Abbreviations

AAO	*Alianza Acción Opositora* (Opposition Action Alliance)
AC	*Alianza Civilista* (Civic Alliance)
AD	*Alianza Democrática* (Democratic Alliance)
ADO	*Alianza Democrática de Oposición* (Opposition Democratic Alliance)
ADOC	*Alianza Democrática de Oposición Civilista* (Democratic Alliance of Civic Opposition)
ANN	*Alianza Nueva Nación* (New Nation Alliance)
ANO	*Alianza Nacional de Oposición* (National Opposition Alliance)
AP	*Alianza del Pueblo* (People's Alliance)
APU	*Alianza Pueblo Unido* (United People Alliance)
ARN	*Partido Arnulfista* (*Arnulfista* Party)
AUPP	*Alianza Unión por Panamá* (Union for Panama Alliance)
C94	*Cambio 94* (Change 94)
CN	*Concertación Nacional* (National Concertation)
COLINA	*Coalición de Liberación Nacional* (National Liberation Coalition)
CPN	*Coalición Patriótica Nacional* (National Patriotic Coalition)
FP	*Frente Patriótico* (Patriotic Front)
FPo	*Frente Popular* (Popular Front)
FRAMPO	*Frente Amplio Popular* (Popular Broad Front)
MLN	*Movimiento de Liberación Nacional* (National Liberation Movement)
MOLIRENA	*Movimiento Liberal Republicano Nacionalista* (Nationalist Republican Liberal Movement)
MORENA	*Movimiento de Renovación Nacional* (Movement of National Renewal)
MPE	*Movimiento Papa Egoró* (Papa Egoró Movement)
MUN	*Misión de Unión Nacional* (National Union Mission)
PAD	*Partido Acción Democrática* (Democratic Action Party)
PALA	*Partido Laborista* (Labor Party)
PAN	*Partido Acción Nacional* (National Action Party)
PAPO	*Partido Acción Popular* (Popular Action Party)
PAR	*Partido Acción Radical* (Radical Action Party)
PC	*Partido Conservador* (Conservative Party)
PCD	*Partido Cambio Democrático* (Democratic Change Party)
PCN	*Partido Cívico Nacional* (National Civic Party)
PD	*Partido Dipa* (Dipa Party)

PDC[a]	*Partido Demócrata Cristiano* (Christian Democratic Party)
PDT	*Partido Democrático de los Trabajadores* (Democratic Worker's Party)
PIR	*Partido Istmeño Revolucionario* (Revolutionary Party of the Isthmus)
PL	*Partido Liberal* (Liberal Party)
P Lab	*Partido Laborista* (Labor Party)
PL-Ch	*Partido Liberal Chiarista* (*Chiarista* Liberal Party)
PLA	*Partido Laborista Agrario* (Agrarian Labor Party)
PL-Aut	*Partido Liberal Auténtico* (Authentic Liberal Party)
PLD	*Partido Liberal Demócrata* (Democratic Liberal Party)
PLDo	*Partido Liberal Doctrinario* (Doctrinaire Liberal Party)
PLN	*Partido Liberal Nacional* (National Liberal Party)
PLR	*Partido Liberal Renovador* (Liberal Renewal Party)
PLRep	*Partido Liberal Republicano (*Republican Liberal Party)
PLU	*Partido Liberal Unido* (United Liberal Party)
PN	*Partido Nacionalista* (Nationalist Party)
PNP	*Partido Nacionalista Popular* (Popular Nationalist Party)
PNR	*Partido Nacional Revolucionario* (Revolutionary National Party)
POPULAR[a]	*Partido Popular* (Popular Party)
PP	*Partido Panameñista* (Panamanian Party)
PPA	*Partido Panameñista Auténtico* (Authentic Panamanian Party)
PPD	*Partido Panameñista Doctrinario (Doctrinary Panamenist Party*
PPN	*Partido Progresista Nacional* (National Progressive Party)
PPP	*Partido del Pueblo Panameño* (Panamanian People's Party)
PR	*Partido Republicano* (Republican Party)
PRA	*Partido Revolucionario Auténtico* (Authentic Revolutionary Party)
PRC	*Partido Renovación Civilista* (Civic Renewal Party)
PRCL	*Partido Resistencia Civil Liberal* (Liberal Civic Resistance Party)
PRD	*Partido Revolucionario Democrático* (Democratic Revolutionary Party)
PREN	*Partido Renovador* (Renewal Party)
PRI	*Partido Revolucionario Institucional* (Institutional Revolutionary Party)
PRN	*Partido Reformista Nacional* (National Reformist Party)
PRT	*Partido Revolucionario de los Trabajadores* (Worker's Revolutionary Party)
PS	*Partido Socialista* (Socialist Party)
PST	*Partido Socialista de los Trabajadores* (Worker's Socialist Party)
PUP	*Partido Unión Popular* (Popular Union Party)
RC	*Resistencia Civil* (Civic Resistance)
SOLID	*Solidaridad* (Solidarity)

TPN	*Tercer Partido Nacionalista* (Third Nationalist Party)
UDI	*Unión Democrática Independiente* (Independent Democratic Union)
UN	*Unión Nacional* (National Union)
UNADE	*Unión Nacional Democrática* (National Democratic Union)
UNO	*Unión Nacional de Oposición* (National Opposition Union)

[a] In 2004, the PDC was renamed POPULAR.

2.4 Electoral Participation of Parties and Alliances 1932–1999

Party / Alliance	Years	Elections contested[a]
PLDo	1932; 1936; 1940; 1948	4
PLR	1932; 1936; 1940; 1948	4
FPo[b]	1936	1
PC	1936; 1940; 1952	3
PL–Ch	1936; 1940	2
PLD	1936; 1940; 1948; 1952	4
PLU	1936; 1940; 1948	3
PNR	1936; 1940; 1948; 1952	4
PS	1936; 1940; 1948; 1964	4
FP	1948; 1952	2
PARA	1948; 1952	2
PL	1948[c]; 1952; 1984; 1989; 1994; 1999	6
PREN	1948; 1952; 1960; 1964	4
PUP	1948; 1952	2
AC	1952[d]	1
CPN	1952[e]; 1956; 1960; 1964; 1968	5
PLN	1952; 1956; 1960; 1964; 1968; 1999; 2004	7
PRI	1952	1
MLN	1960; 1964; 1968	3
PD	1960; 1964	2
PPN	1960; 1964; 1968	3
PR	1960; 1964; 1968; 1989	4
PRCL	1960[f]; 1964	2
TPN	1960; 1964; 1968	3
UNO	1960[g]; 1964[h]	2
ANO	1964[i]	1
PAD	1964; 1968	2
PAR	1964	1
PCN	1964	2
PDC	1964; 1968; 1984; 1989; 1994; 1999	6

Party / Alliance (continued)	Years	Elections contested[a]
PIR	1964	1
PLA	1964; 1968; 1994	3
PN	1964	1
PP(A)[j]	1964; 1968	2
PRN	1964	1
AP	1968[k]	1
UN	1968[l]	1
ADO	1984[m]	1
FRAMPO	1984	1
MOLIRENA	1984; 1989; 1994; 1999; 2004	5
PALA	1984, 1989; 1994	3
PAN	1984; 1989	2
PAPO	1984	1
PNP	1984, 1999	2
PPA	1984; 1989	2
PPP	1984; 1989	2
PRD	1984; 1989; 1994; 1999; 2004	5
PRT	1984	1
PST	1984	1
REP	1984	1
UNADE	1984[n]	1
ADOC	1989[o]	1
COLINA	1989[p]	1
PDT	1989	1
PL-Aut	1989	1
PP	1989	1
AD	1994[q]	1
APU	1994[r]	1
ARN	1994; 1999; 2004	3
C94	1994[s]	1
CN	1994[t]	1
MORENA	1994; 1999	2
MPE	1994; 1999	2
MUN	1994	1
PPD	1994	1
PRC	1994; 1999	2
SOLID	1994; 1999 ; 2004	3
UDI	1994	1
AAO	1999[u]	1
ANN	1999[v]	1
AUPP	1999[w]	1
PCD	1999; 2004	2
POPULAR	2004	1

[a] Given the large number of political parties that contested elections exclusively as members of an electoral alliance and the lack of complete information about the parliamentary elections, this table includes only parties and alliances that contested presidential elections. Total number: 15.

[b] The FPO comprised the PLD, PLDo, PLR, and PS.

[c] Liberal union among the PL, PLD, PLDo, PLR, and PLU.

[d] The electoral alliance ACF comprised the FP, PLD, PLN, and PRI.

[e] The electoral alliance CPN comprised PL, PNR, PARA, PREN, and PUP.

[f] The electoral alliance PRCL comprised the PRCL, the PREN, the PPN, and PD.

[g] The electoral alliance UNO comprised the PLN, PR, TPN, and MLN.

[h] The electoral alliance UNO comprised the PLN, PR, MLN, PLA,PAD, PPN, PN, and PIR.

[i] The electoral alliance ANO comprised the CPN, TPN, PREN; PRCL, PD, and PCN.

[j] In 1968 the PP contested as member of the UN. In the 1980s it took the name *Partido Panameñista Auténtico* (PPA), in order to be distinguished from a minor splinter group of the same name.

[k] The AP comprised the PLN, PLA, MLN, PPN.

[l] The electoral alliance UN comprised the CPN, PP, PR, TPN, and PAD.

[m] The electoral alliance ADO comprised the PDC, MOLIRENA, and PPA.

[n] The electoral alliance UNADE comprised the PRD, PL, FRAMPO, PALA, REP, and PAN.

[o] The electoral alliance ADOC comprised the PPA, PDC, MOLIRENA, and PL-Aut.

[p] The electoral alliance COLINA comprised the PRD, PALA, PDT, PPP; PL, PR, PAN, and PP.

[q] The electoral alliance AD comprised the ARN, PLA, PL, and UDI.

[r] The electoral alliance APU comprised the PRD, and PALA.

[s] The electoral alliance C94 comprised the MOLIRENA; PRC, and MORENA.

[t] The electoral alliance CN comprised the SOLID, and MUN.

[u] The electoral alliance AAO comprised the PDC, PRC, PNP, and PL.

[v] The electoral alliance ANN comprised the PRD, MPE, SOLID, and PLN.

[w] The electoral alliance AUPP comprised the MOLIRENA, ARN, MORENA, and PCD.

2.5 Referendums

Year	1940[a]		1977[b]	
	Total number	%	Total number	%
Registered voters	—	–	787,251	–
Votes cast	146,689	—	766,232	97.3
Blank votes	5,124	0.3	—	—
Invalid votes	—	—	14,310[c]	1.9
Valid votes	146,177	99.7	751,922	98.1
Yes	144,312	98.7	506,805	67.4
No	1,865	1.3	245,117	32.6

[a] National referendum to decide on the enactment of the Constitution.

[b] National referendum for the appraisal of the Torrijos-Carter Treaties on the Panama Canal.

[c] Blank and invalid votes.

Year	1983[a]		1992[b]	
	Total number	%	Total number	%
Registered voters	834,409	–	—	–
Votes cast	556,969	66.8	—	40.0
Blank votes	6,590	1.2	—	—
Invalid votes	7,216	1.3	—	—
Valid votes	543,163	97.5	—	—
Yes	476,716	87.8	—	33.3
No	66,447	12.2	—	66.6

[a] Referendum to decide on the reforms to the political constitution of 1972.
[b] Referendum concerning a package of constitutional reforms, including the suppression of the armed forces.

Year	1998[a]	
	Total number	%
Registered voters	1,718,602	–
Votes cast	1,124,112	—
Blank votes	11,708	1.0
Invalid votes	10,119	1.0
Valid votes	1,102,286	98.0
Yes	385,885	34.3
No	716,401	63.7

[a] Referendum to decide on the reforms to the political constitution, which would allow the re-election of the president.

2.6 Elections for Constitutional Assembly

1945	Total number	%	Seats	%
Registered voters	—	–	–	–
Votes cast	—	—	–	–
Blank votes	—	—	–	–
Invalid votes	—	—	–	–
Valid votes	106,276	—	–	–
			Total seats	100.0
PLR	34,147	32.1	12	25.0
PNR	20,833	19.6	10	20.8
PLD	15,399	14.5	7	14.6
PLDo	13,545	12.7	7	14.6
PL	13,244	12.5	8	16.7
PS	5,997	5.6	2	4.2
PC	3,111	2.9	2	4.6

1972[a]	Total number	%	Seats	%
Registered voters	629,630	–	–	–
Votes cast	531,362	84.4	–	–
Blank votes	9,739	1.8	–	–
Invalid votes	8,600	1.6	–	–
Valid votes	513,023	96.5	–	–

[a] Elections to the *Asamblea Nacional de los Representantes de Corregimientos*, which acted formally as constitutional assembly. The candidates to the 505 *Representantes de Corregimientos* were not presented by political parties, as these were banned.

2.7 Parliamentary Elections 1960–2004

Year	1960[a]		1978[b]	
	Total number	%	Total number	%
Registered voters	—	–	787,251	–
Votes cast	—	—	658,421	83.6
Blank votes	—	—	11,274	1.7
Invalid votes	—	—	13,546	2.1
Valid votes	124,924	—	633,601	96.2
CPN	46,962	37.6	–	–
PR	21,243	17.0	–	–
PLN	18,306	14.7	–	–
MLN	11,350	9.1	–	–
TPN	10,589	8.5	–	–
PREN	5,605	4.5	–	–
PRCL	5,198	4.2	–	–
PD	2,980	2.4	–	–
PPN	2,691	2.2	–	–

[a] Preliminary vote counting, excluding the provinces of Chiriquí and Panamá.

[b] Elections to the *Asamblea Nacional de los Representantes de Corregimientos*. The candidates to the 505 *Representantes de Corregimientos* were not presented by political parties, as these were outlawed.

Year	1984[a] Total number	%	1989[b] Total number	%
Registered voters	917,677	–	—	–
Votes cast	631,908	68.9	—	—
Invalid votes[c]	22,571	3.6	—	—
Valid votes	609,337	96.4	609,231	—
PRD	153,182[d]	25.1	114,741[e]	18.8
PPA	124,562[f]	20.4	–	–
PALA	74,430[d]	12.2	47,775[e]	7.8
PDC	69,998[f]	11.5	219,944[g]	36.1
PR	51,103[d]	8.4	8,602[e]	1.4
MOLIRENA	50,936[f]	8.4	122,974[g]	20.2
PL	36,040[d]	5.9	17,712[e]	2.9
PNP	12,596	2.1	–	–
PAPO	8,471	1.4	–	–
PP	8,063[d]	1.3	2,917[e]	0.5
FRAMPO	7,813[d]	1.3	–	–
PPP	7,315	1.2	4,988[e]	0.8
PRT	3,545	0.6	–	–
PST	1,283	0.2	–	–
PDT	–	–	1,075[e]	0.2
PPR	–	–	3,572[e]	0.6
PLA	–	–	61,916[g]	10.2
PPA	–	–	3,015	0.5

[a] Blatant electoral fraud.

[b] The 1989 elections were annulled on 10 May, before all the votes were counted.

[c] Blank and invalid votes.

[d] These parties contested under their own names, but were part of the UNADE, an import electoral alliance, especially at the level of presidential elections (total vote: 330,631).

[e] These parties contested under their own names, but were part of the electoral alliance COLINA (total vote: 201,382).

[f] These parties contested under their own names, but participated in ADO, an electoral alliance which became important especially at the level of presidential elections (total vote: 245,496).

[g] These parties contested under their own names, but were part of the part in the electoral alliance ADOC (total vote: 404,834).

Year	1994[a]		1999[b]	
	Total number	%	Total number	%
Registered voters	1,499,451	–	1,746,989	–
Votes cast	1,091,756	72.8	1,306,911	74.8
Invalid votes	58,184	5.3	33,427	2.6
Blank votes	—	—	43,484	3.3
Valid votes	1,033,572	94.7	1,230,000	94.1
PRD	236,319	22.9	393,356	32.0
ARN	150,217	14.5	266,030	21.6
MOLIRENA	116,833	11.3	92,972	7.5
MPE	99,760	9.65	21,841	1.8
MORENA	68,581	6.6	42,996	3.5
SOLID	67,306	6.5	71,860	5.8
PDC	66,411	6.4	107,179	8.7
PRC	57,590	5.6	37,705	3.1
PL	35,516	3.4	41,848	3.4
PLA	31,045	3.0	–	–
PALA	28,172	2.7	–	–
MUN	27,017	2.6		–
LIBRE	24,979	2.4	–	–
UDI	13,106	1.3	–	–
PPD	10,720	1.0	–	–
PNP	–	–	11,506	0.9
PLN	–	–	75,866	6.2
PCD	–	–	66,841	5.5

[a] Data based on 99.7% of the total votes.
[b] Data based on 99.2% of the total votes.

Year	2004			
	Total number	%		
Registered voters	1,999,553	–		
Votes cast	1,524,976	76.3		
Invalid votes	30,253	2.0		
Blank votes	41,635	2.7		
Valid votes	1,453,088	95.3		
PRD	549,948	37.8		
ARN	279,560	19.2		
SOLID	227,604	15.7		
MOLIRENA	125,547	8.6		
PCD	107,511	7.4		
POPULAR	86,727	6.0		
PLN	76,191	5.2		

2.8 Composition of Parliament 1956–1964 and 1984–2004

Year	1956 Seats 53	% 100.0	1960 Seats 53	% 100.0	1964 Seats 42	% 100.0	1984 Seats 67	% 100.0
CPN	42	79.2	18	34.0	3	7.1	–	–
PLN	11	20.8	8	15.1	8	19.0	–	–
PR	–	–	9	17.0	4	9.5	3	4.5
TPN	–	–	7	13.2	4	9.5	–	–
MLN	–	–	4	7.5	2	4.8	–	–
PRCL	–	–	3	5.7	0	0.0	–	–
PPN	–	–	2	3.8	2	4.8	–	–
PREN	–	–	1	1.9	1	2.4	–	–
PD	–	–	1	1.9	0	0.0	–	–
PP	–	–	–	–	12	28.6	–	–
PAD	–	–	–	–	1	2.4	–	–
PAR	–	–	–	–	1	2.4	–	–
PDC	–	–	–	–	1	2.4	6	9.0
PLA	–	–	–	–	1	2.4	–	–
PRN	–	–	–	–	1	2.4	–	–
PS	–	–	–	–	1	2.4	–	–
PRD	–	–	–	–	–	–	34	50.7
PPA	–	–	–	–	–	–	13	19.4
PALA	–	–	–	–	–	–	7	10.4
MOLIRENA	–	–	–	–	–	–	3	4.5
PL	–	–	–	–	–	–	1	1.5

Year	1994[a]		1999		2004	
	Seats	%	Seats	%	Seats	%
	72	100.0	71	100.0	73	100.0
PRD	30[b]	41.7	34[c]	47.9	40	54.8
ARN	14[d]	19.4	18[e]	25.4	17	23.3
MPE	6	8.3	0[c]	0.0	–	–
MOLIRENA	5[e]	6.9	3[f]	4.2	3	4.1
SOLID	4[g]	5.6	4[c]	5.6	8	11.0
PRC	3[e]	4.2	1[f]	1.4	–	–
PL	2[d]	2.8	0[f]	0.0	–	–
PL-Aut.	2[d]	2.8	–	–	–	–
PLRep	2[b]	2.8	–	–	–	–
UDI	1[d]	1.4	–	–	–	–
MORENA	1[e]	1.4	1[h]	1.4	–	–
P Lab	1[b]	1.4	–	–	–	–
PDC	1	1.4	5[f]	7.0	–	–
MUN	0[g]	0.0	–	–	–	–
PPD	0	0.0	–	–	–	–
PLN	–	–	3[c]	4.2	1	1.4
PCD	–	–	2[f]	2.8	2	2.7
PNP	–	–	0[g]	0.0	–	–
POPULAR					2	2.7

[a] The 1989 elections were annulled on 10 May, before all the votes could be counted. Seats were not allocated.

[b] These parties contested under their own names, but were part of the *Alianza Pueblo Unido* (total seats 33; 45.8%).

[c] These parties contested under their own names, but were part of the *Alianza Nueva Nación* (total seats: 41; 57.7%).

[d] These parties contested under their own names, but were part of the *Alianza Democrática* (total seats: 19; 26.4%).

[e] These parties contested under their own names, but were part of the alliance *Cambio 94* (total seats: 9; 12.5%).

[f] These parties contested under their own names, but were part of the *Alianza Opositora* (total seats: 6; 8.5%).

[g] These parties contested under their own names, but were part of the alliance CN (total seats: 4; 5.6%).

[h] These parties contested under their own names, but were part of the *Alianza Unión por Panamá* (total seats: 24, 33.8%).

2.9 Presidential Elections 1932–2004

1932	Total number	%
Registered voters	—	–
Votes cast	—	—
Invalid votes	—	—
Valid votes	—	—
Harmodio Arias Madrid (PLDo)	39,533	—
Francisco Arias Paredes (PLR)	29,282	—

1936	Total number	%
Registered voters	—	–
Votes cast	—	—
Invalid votes	—	—
Valid votes	—	—
Juan Demóstenes Arosemena Díaz (PNR/PL-Ch/PC)	41,835	—
Domingo Díaz Arosemena (Fpo)[a]	39,830	—
Belisario Porras (PLU)	—	—

[a] Comprised the PLD, PLDo, PLR and PS.

1940	Total number	%
Registered voters	—	–
Votes cast	—	—
Invalid votes	—	—
Valid votes	—	—
Arnulfo Arias Madrid (PNR/ PL-Ch/PLD/PLU/PC)[a]	—	—

[a] Ricardo J. Alfaro, who ran for *Alianza Civil* (PLDo, PLR and PS), withdrew his candidacy due to political repression.

1948[a]	Total number	%
Registered voters	305,123	–
Votes cast	216,214	70.9
Invalid votes	17,853	8.3
Valid votes	198,361	91.7
Domingo Díaz Arosemena (PL[b]/PS)	76,459	38.5
Arnulfo Arias Madrid (PRA)	71,897	36.2
José Isaac Fábrega (PREN/PNR)	41,296	20.8
Sergio González Ruiz (PUP/FP)	5,634	2.8
Porras	3,075	1.6

[a] Only the number of registered voters and of votes cast are reliable.
[b] Liberal union among the PL, PLD, PLDo, PLR and PLU.

1952	Total number	%
Registered voters	343,353	–
Votes cast	231,848	67.5
Invalid votes	18,572	8.0
Valid votes	213,276	92.0
José Antonio Remón Cantera (CPN[a])	133,215	62.5
Roberto Francisco Chiari Remón (AC[b])	78,094	36.6
Pedro Moreno Correa (PC)	1,967	0.9

[a] Electoral alliance formed by PL, PNR, PRA, PREN and PUP.
[b] Formed by FP, PLD, PLN and PRI.

1956	Total number	%
Registered voters	386,672	–
Votes cast	306,770	79.3
Invalid votes	47,400	15.5
Valid votes	259,370	84.5
Ernesto de la Guardia (CPN)	177,633	68.5
Víctor Florencio Goytía (PLN)	81,737	31.5

1960	Total number	%
Registered voters	435,454	–
Votes cast	258,039	59.3
Invalid votes	16,561	6.4
Valid votes	241,478	93.6
Roberto Francisco Chiari Remón (UNO)	100,042[a]	41.4
Ricardo Manuel Arias Espinosa (CPN)	85,981	35.6
Víctor Florencio Goytía (PRCL)	55,455[b]	23.0

[a] The votes received by the electoral alliance UNO were distributed as follows: PLN: 42,394; PR: 26,073; TPN: 16,068; MLN: 15,507.
[b] The votes received by this electoral alliance were distributed as follows: PRCL: 29,031; PREN: 9,785; PPN: 8,635; PD: 8,004.

1964	Total number	%
Registered voters	486,420	–
Votes cast	326,401	67.1
Invalid votes	9,230	2.8
Valid votes	317,171	97.2
Marco Aurelio Robles (UNO)	129,933[a]	41.0
Arnulfo Arias Madrid (PP)	119,201	37.6
Juan de Arco Galindo (ANO)	47,753[b]	15.1
José Antonio Molino (PDC)	9,681	3.1
Florencio Harris (PS)	4,374	1.4
Norberto Navarro (PAR)	3,708	1.2
José de la Rosa Castillo (PRN)	2,521	0.8

[a] The votes received by the electoral alliance UNO were distributed as follows: PLN: 48,574; PR: 32,445; MLN: 12,920; PLA: 11,483; PAD: 10,975; PPN: 9,800; PN: 2,803; PIR: 933.
[b] The votes received by the electoral alliance ANO were distributed as follows: CPN: 23,872; TPN: 11,442; PREN: 4,218; PRCL: 4,096; PD: 3,046; PCN: 1,079.

1968	Total number	%
Registered voters	544,135	–
Votes cast	327,048	60.1
Invalid votes	6,358	1.9
Valid votes	320,690	98.1
Arnulfo Arias Madrid (UN)	175,432[a]	54.7
David Samudio Avila (AP)	133,887[b]	41.8
Antonio González Revilla (PDC)	11,371	3.6

[a] The votes received by the *Unión Nacional* were distributed as follows: CPN: 19,072; PP: 99.076; PR: 35,739; TPN: 10,475; PAD: 11,070.
[b] The votes received by the *Alianza del Pueblo* were distributed as follows: PLN: 66,515; PLA: 31,151; MLN: 20,987; PPN: 15,234.

1984[a]	Total number	%
Registered voters	917,677	–
Votes cast	671,090	73.1
Invalid votes	30,897	4.6
Valid votes	640,193	95.4
Nicolás Ardito Barletto (UNADE)	300,748[b]	45.6
Arnulfo Arias Madrid (ADO)	299,035[c]	46.7
Rubén Darío Paredes (PNP)	15,976	2.5
Carlos Iván Zúñiga (PAPO)	13,782	2.2
Carlos del Cid (PPP)	4.598	0.7
José Renán Esquivel (PRT)	3,969	0.6
Ricardo Barría (PST)	2,085	0.3

[a] Blatant electoral fraud.
[b] The votes received by the electoral alliance UNADE were distributed as follows: PRD: 175,722; PL: 28.568; FRAMPO: 5,280; PALA: 45,384; REP: 34, 215; PAN: 11,579.
[c] The votes received by the electoral alliance ADO were officially distributed as follows: PDC: 46,963; MOLIRENA: 30,737; PPA: 221,335.

1989[a]	Total number	%
Registered voters	1,184,320	–
Votes cast	757,797	64.0
Invalid votes	92,223	12.2
Valid votes	665,574	87.8
Carlos Duque (COLINA)[b]	473,838	71.2
Guillermo Endara (ADOC)[c]	188,914	28.4
(PP)	2,822	0.4

[a] The elections were annulled on 10 May 1989, before all the votes could be counted, in order to avoid the defeat of the government's candidate. On 26 December 1989, the annulment was declared invalid. The result corresponds to a new official counting based on 83.1% of the total polls.
[b] Pro-Government alliance made up of PRD, PALA, PDT, PPP, PL, PR, PAN and PP.
[c] Opposition alliance formed by PPA, PDC, MOLIRENA and PL-*Auténtico*.

1994[a]	Total number	%
Registered voters	1,499,451	–
Votes cast	1,104,578	73.7
Invalid votes	37,734	3.4
Valid votes	1,066,844	96.6
Ernesto Pérez Balladares (APU)[b]	355,307	33.3[c]
Mireya Moscoso de Gruber (AD)[d]	310,372	29.1
Rubén Blades (MPE)	182,405	17.1
Rubén Carles (C94)[e]	171,192	16.1
Eduardo Vallarino (PDC)	25,476	2.4
Samuel Lewis Galindo (CN)[f]	18,424	1.7
José Salvador Muñoz (PPD)	3,668	0.3

[a] The results correspond to a counting based on 99.9% of the total votes.
[b] The votes received by the *Alianza Pueblo Unido* were officially distributed as follows: PRD: 326,095; PALA: 17,046; Free: 12,166.
[c] 91.8% of the alliance votes were PRD votes.
[d] The votes received by the *Alianza Democrática* were officially distributed as follows: ARN: 211,780; PLA: 43,797; PL: 46,775; UDI: 8,020.
[e] The votes received by the electoral alliance *Cambio 94* were officially distributed as follows: MOLIRENA: 115,478; PRC: 23,592; MORENA: 32,122.
[f] The votes received by the electoral alliance *Concertación Nacional* were officially distributed as follows: SOLID: 9,120; MUN: 9,304.

1999	Total number	%
Registered voters	1,746,989	–
Votes cast	1,330,730	76.2
Blank votes[a]	16,574	1.2
Invalid votes	35,688	2.7
Valid votes	1,278,468	96.1
Mireya Moscos (AUPP)[b]	572,717	44.8
Martín Torrijos (ANN)[c]	483,501	37.8
Alberto Vallarino (AAO)[d]	222,250	17.4

[a] At the 1999 election, blank votes were counted separately.
[b] The votes received by the electoral alliance *Unión por Panamá* were officially distributed as follows: MOLIRENA: 140,240; ARN: 367,865; MORENA: 28,544; PCD: 36,068.
[c] The votes received by the *Alianza Nueva Nación* were officially distributed as follows: PRD: 403,649; MPE: 20,217; SOLID: 23,524; PLN: 36,111.
[d] The votes received by the *Alianza Acción Opositora* were officially distributed as follows: PDC: 141,283; PRC: 45,192; PNP: 10,196; PL: 25,579.

2004	Total number	%
Registered voters	1,999,553	–
Votes cast	1,537,342	76.9
Blank votes	17,145	1.1
Invalid votes	21,150	1.4
Valid votes	1,499,047	
Martín Torrijos (PRD)[a]	711,447	47.4
Guillermo Endara (SOLID)	462,824	30.9
José Miguel Alemán (ARN)[b]	245,568	16.4
Ricardo Martinelli (PCD)	79,491	5.3

[a] The votes received by the electoral alliance *Patria Nueva* were officially distributed as follows: PRD: 649,157; POPULAR: 62,007.
[b] The votes received by the *Visión de País* were officially distributed as follows: ARN: 162,830; MOLIRENA: 60,106; PLN: 22,632.

2.10 List of Power Holders 1904–2004

Head of State	Years	Remarks
Manuel Amador Guerrero	1904–1908	First constitutional president, elected by the so-called *Convención Nacional Constituyente* (20/02/1904–30/09/1908).
José Domingo de Obaldía	1908–1910	Elected constitutional president. Assumed presidency on 01/10/1908. Died on 01/03/1910.
Carlos Antonio Mendoza	1910	Interim president (01/03/1910–30/09/1910).
Federico Boyd	1910	Provisional president from 01/10/1910 to 04/10/1910 as second designate.
Pablo Arosemena	1910–1912	Provisional president (05/10/1910–01/02/1912).
Rodolfo Chiari	1912	Provisional president (02/02/1912–06/03/1912).
Pablo Arosemena	1910–1912	Designated president; assumed office after returning from Chile (06/03/1912–30/09/1912).
Belisario Porras	1912–1916	Elected constitutional president (01/10/1912–30/09/1916).
Ramón Maximiliano Valdés	1916–1918	Elected constitutional president. Assumed presidency on 01/10/1916. Died on 03/06/1918.
Ciro Luis Urriola	1918	Provisional president (03/06/1918–30/09/1918).
Pedro Antonio Díaz	1918	Provisional president (01/10/1918–11/10/1918).
Belisario Porras	1918–1920	Elected first designate by the national assembly on 12/10/1918, to finish Valdés' presidential term. Resigned on 29/01/1920 in order to participate in the elections.
Ernesto Fido Tisdel Lefevre	1920	Provisional president elected by the national assembly (31/01/1920–30/09/1920).
Belisario Porras	1920–1924	Elected constitutional president (01/10/1920–30/09/1924).

Head of State (continued)	Years	Remarks
Rodolfo F. Chiari	1924–1928	Elected constitutional president (01/10/1924–30/09/1928).
Florencio Harmodio Arosemena	1928–1931	Elected constitutional president. Assumed presidency on 01/10/1928. Resigned on 02/01/1931.
Harmodio Arias Madrid	1931	Appointed provisional president on 02/01/1931. End of provisional tenure on 15/01/1931.
Ricardo Joaquín Alfaro	1931–1932	Assumed office as first designate (16/01/1931–30/09/1932).
Harmodio Arias Madrid	1932–1936	Elected constitutional president (01/10/1932–30/09/1936).
Juan Demóstenes Arosemena Díaz	1936–1939	Elected constitutional president. Assumed presidency on 01/10/1936. Died on 16/07/1939.
Ezequiel Fernández Jaén	1939	Provisional president; held office as second designate (16/12/1939–18/07/1939).
Augusto Samuel Boyd	1939–1940	Provisional president; held office as first designate (18/12/1939–30/09/1940).
Arnulfo Arias Madrid	1940–1941	Elected constitutional president (single candidate) Assumed presidency on 01/10/1940. Deposed formally for leaving his office on 09/10/1941; at the time, he was in Cuba without the relevant authorization.
Ernesto Jaén Guardia	1941	Provisional president; held office as second designate. Resigned on the same day under pressure after appointing a new cabinet (09/10/1941).
Ricardo Adolfo De La Guardia	1941–1945	Provisional president; held office as the eldest minister of the cabinet. Assumed presidency 09/10/1941. Resigned on 15/06/1945.
Enrique Adolfo Jiménez	1945–1948	Provisional president; elected first designate by the Convención Constituyente (15/06/1945–30/09/1948).
Domingo Díaz Arosemena	1948–1949	Elected constitutional president. Assumed presidency on 01/10/1948. Resigned due to health problems on 27/07/1949 and died in August 1949.
Daniel Chanis (Junior)	1949	Provisional president; held office in his capacity as first designate since 28/07/1949. Coup d'état on 20/11/1949.
Roberto Francisco Chiari Remón	1949	Held office as second vice president (20/11/1949–24/11/1949). The Supreme Court of Justice declared Chanis president.

Head of State (continued)	Years	Remarks
Arnulfo Arias Madrid	1949–1951	Appointed president after 'votes were recounted' and verified his victory in the 1948 elections. Assumed presidency on 24/11/1949). Forced to resign by the *coup d'état* of 10/05/1951.
Alcibíades Arosemena	1951–1952	Provisional president; held office as first vice president (10/05/1951–30/09/1952).
José Antonio Remón Cantera	1952–1955	Army officer; elected constitutional president. Assumed presidency on 01/10/1952. Assassinated on 02/01/1955.
José Ramón Guizado	1955	Provisional president; held office as vice president since 03/01/1955. Deposed by the national assembly on charges of complicity in the assassination of Remón Cantera on 14/01/1955.
Ricardo Manuel Arias Espinoza	1955–1956	Provisional president; held office in his capacity as vice president (15/01/1955–30/09/1956).
Ernesto De la Guardia (Junior)	1956–1960	Elected constitutional president (01/10/1956–30/09/1964).
Roberto Francisco Chiari Remón	1960–1964	Elected constitutional president (01/10/1960–30/09/1964).
Marco Aurelio Robles	1964–1968	Elected constitutional president (01/10/1964–30/09/1968).
Arnulfo Arias Madrid	1968	Elected constitutional president. Assumed presidency on 01/10/1968. *Coup d'état* on 11/10/1968 headed by Omar Torrijos Herrera.
José M. Pinilla	1968–1969	Army officer; appointed president by the *coup* leaders on 13/10/1968. Resigned due to health problems 09/06/1969.
Bolívar Urrutia	1969	Army officer; provisional president until the *coup* attempt of 15/12/1969.
Omar Torrijos Herrera	1969	Army officer; governed from 15/12/1969 to 27/12/1969.
Demetrio Lakas Bahas	1969–1978	Appointed president by Torrijos on 19/12/1969. Elected constitutional president by the ANRC in 1972 till 11/10/1978. Torrijos Herrera was constitutionally recognized as the 'supreme leader of the Panamanian revolution' and governed for six years.
Arístides Royo Sánchez	1978–1982	Elected by the ARNC on 11/10/1978. Resigned in July 1982 under pressure from the military.
Ricardo de la Espriella	1982–1984	Provisional president; held office in his capacity as vice president since 30/07/1982. Resigned 13/02/1984.

538   *Panama*

Head of State (continued)	Years	Remarks
Jorge Illueca	1984	Provisional president (13/02/1984–10/10/1984).
Nicolás Ardito Barleta	1984–1985	Elected constitutional president in fraudulent elections. Assumed presidency on 11/10/1984. Resigned due to military pressure on 27/09/1985.
Eric Arturo Del Valle	1985–1988	Assumed presidential office as vice president on 28/09/1985. Deposed on 25/02/1988 after trying to overthrow General Noriega as head of the armed forces.
Manuel Solís Palma	1988–1989	Appointed minister in charge of the presidency by the legislative assembly, the cabinet council and the Supreme Court of Justice (25/02/1988–30/08/1989).
Francisco Rodríguez	1989	Appointed provisional president after the invalid elections (07/05) on 01/09/1989. The US military invasion of 20/12/1989 brought about a change of government.
Guillermo Endara Galimany	1989–1994	Appointed president as the alleged winner of the invalid elections of May 1989 within the context of the US military invasion. Confirmed in his office after the votes from the 1989 elections were counted a second time (19/12/1989–01/09/1994).
Ernesto Pérez Balladares	1994–1999	Elected constitutional president in fair elections (01/09/1994–31/08/1999).
Mireya Elisa Moscoso Rodríguez	1999–2004	Elected constitutional president in fair elections. Assumed presidency on 01/08/1999.
Martín Torrijos Espino	2004–	Assumed office on 01/09/2004.

3. Bibliography

3.1. Official sources

Boletín Tribunal Electoral (Edición Oficial) (various years).
Compendio Electoral de la República de Panamá, 1 de mayo de 2001.
'Constitución Política de la República de Panamá de 1972, reformada por los Actos reformatorios de 1978 y por el Acto Constitucional de 1983', in *Gaceta Oficial* (Panama), 80/19.826, 06/06/1983.
Constituciones de la República de Panamá de 1904, 1941, 1946, edición preparada por Ramón E. Fábrega F. 1969. Panama.
Dirección de Estadística y Censo (1958). *Estadística Electoral: Elecciones populares de 1952 y 1956*. Panama.

Dirección de Estadística y Censo (1962). *Estadística Electoral: Elecciones de 1960*. Panama.
Dirección de Estadística y Censo (1965). *Estadística Electoral: Elecciones de 1964*. Panama.
Tribunal Electoral. *Leyes Fundamentales del Tribunal Electoral 1979*. Panama.
Tribunal Electoral (1972). *Legislación Electoral. Elecciones populares para escoger representantes de corregimientos 6 de agosto de 1972*. Panama.
Tribunal Electoral (1978). *Resumen de trabajo 1968–1978*. Panama.
Tribunal Electoral (1983). *Memoria 1982–1983*. Panama.
Tribunal Electoral (1983). *Código Electoral de la República de Panamá y normas complementarias 1983*. Panama.
Tribunal Electoral (1984). *Memoria 1984*. Panama.
Tribunal Electoral (1986). *Memoria 1985–1986*. Panama.
Tribunal Electoral. *Elecciones de 1984, 1989, 1994, 1999 y 2004*. Panama.

3.2. Books, Articles, and Electoral Reports

Archiv der Gegenwart (various years). Sankt Augustin.
Arias de Para, R. (1984). *Así fue el fraude. Las elecciones presidenciales de Panamá 1984*. Panama.
Basil, C. and Hedrick, A. K. (1970). *Historical Dictionary of Panama*. Metuchen, NJ.
Calvert, P. and Calvert, S. (1990). *Latin America in the Twentieth Century*. Houndmills/ London: MacMillan.
Close, D. (1991). 'Central American Elections 1989–90. Costa Rica, El Salvador, Honduras, Nicaragua, Panama'. *Electoral Studies*, 10/1: 60–76.
Espino, R. and Martínez, R. (1988). *Panamá*. Mexico City: Alianza Editorial Mexicana.
Gandásegui, M. A. (1988). 'La democracia en Panamá'. *Estudios Sociales Centroamericanos* (San José), 47: 113–132.
González H. S. (1985). *La crisis del torrijismo y las elecciones de 1984*. Panama: Ediciones Horizonte.
Goytía, V. F. (1954). *Las Constituciones de Panamá*. Madrid: Ediciones Cultura Hispánica.
Hoffmann, K.-D. (1990). 'Panama I. Das Wahldesaster vom 7. Mai 1989'. *Lateinamerika. Analysen, Daten, Dokumentation*, 13: 77–82.
— (1992). 'Panama', in P. Waldmann and H.-W. Krumwiede (eds.), *Politisches Lexikon Lateinamerika*. Munich: Beck, 241–253.
— (1995). 'Panama', in D. Nohlen and F. Nuscheler (eds.), *Handbuch der Dritten Welt, Mittelamerika und der Karibik*. Bonn: Dietz, 234–276.
Institute for the Comparative Study of Political Systems (ICOPS) (1968). *Panama Election Factbook*. Washington, D.C.: ICOPS.

Krennerich, M. (2002). 'Panama', in D. Nohlen (ed.), *Lexikon Dritte Welt* (12th edn.). Reinbek: Rowohlt, 650–653.

Leis, R. (1984). *Radiografía de los partidos*. Panama: Centro de Capacitación Social.

McDonald, R. H. and Ruhl, J. M. (1989). *Party Politics and Elections in Latin America*. Boulder, Colo.: Westview Press.

Martínez H. M. (1990). *Panamá 1978–1990. Una crisis sin fin*. Panama: CEASPA.

Modglin, T. W. (1984). *The Panamanian Presidential and Legislative Elections*. Washington, D.C.: Center for Strategic & International Studies.

Nyrop, R. F. (ed.) (1981). *Panama. A Country Study*. Washington, D.C.: US Government Printing Office.

Priestley, G. (1986). *Military Goverment and Popular Participation in Panama*. Boulder, Colo.: Westview Press.

Pulice de Rodríguez, Y. (1988). 'El Registro Electoral panameño', in *Memoria de la Segunda Conferencia de la Asociación de Organismos Electorales de Centroamérica y el Caribe*, San José: IIDH–CAPEL, 135–199.

— (1989). 'Sistema electoral panameño', in Friedrich Ebert Foundation/ Centro de Estudios Democráticos de América (CEDAL) (eds.), *Análisis comparativo de los sistemas electorales de los países del istmo centroamericano*, San José.

Quintero, C. (1988). *Evolución constitucional de Panamá*. Bogotá: Universidad Externado de Colombia.

Ricord, H. E. (1987). *Las constituciones panameñas del siglo XX*. Editora Pérez y Pérez.

Rodríguez E. M. (1989). 'Elecciones anuladas. Panamá, 7 de mayo de 1989'. *Boletín Electoral Latinoamericano* (San José: IIDH-CAPEL), 1: 30–35.

Ropp, S. C. (1982). *Panamanian Politics. From Guarded Nation to National Guard*. New York: Praeger.

Ruddle, K. and P. Gillette (eds.) (1972). *Latin American Political Statistics. Supplement to the Statistical Abstract of Latin America*, Los Angeles: University of California.

Sarti Castañeda, C. (1984). 'Panamá. Transicionales versus oligarquía'. *Polémica* (San José), 14–15: 56–65.

Selser, G. (1985). 'Panamá. Las exequias del torrijismo'. *Nueva Sociedad* (Caracas), 75: 4–7.

Smith Wilshire, D. A. (1986). 'El sistema de partidos, los partidos políticos y los procesos electorales en Panamá', in Asociación de Investigación y Estudios Sociales (ASIES) (ed.), *Los sistemas de partidos políticos en Centro América y las perspectivas de los procesos de democratización*, Guatemala: ASIES, 116–127.

— (1986). 'La democracia representativa en Panamá. Elementos para un debate', in Friedrich Ebert Foundation (ed.), *Sistemas electorales y representación política latinoamericana*, Madrid.

— (1991). 'El proceso político: las elecciones parciales. Panamá, 27 de enero de 1991'. *Boletín Electoral Latinoamericano* (San José: IIDH/CAPEL), 5: 11–17.

The Carter Center of Emory University (1989). *The May 7, 1989 Panamanian Elections. Pre-election Report Based on the Findings of an International Delegation*. Atlanta.

Vásquez, G. R. (1967). 'El sistema de elección de los diputados a la Asamblea Nacional y la estructura de este órgano estatal', in *Cuaderno de la Facultad de Derecho y Ciencias Políticas* (Panama), 5: 89–119.

Wilkie, J. W. et al. (eds.) (1990). *Statistical Abstract of Latin America*, Vol. 28, Los Angeles: University of California.

PUERTO RICO
by Dieter Nohlen

1. Introduction

1.1 Historical Overview

Puerto Rico, an island located in the eastern Caribbean Sea, is not an independent state, but a self-governing Commonwealth in association with the United States (in Spanish *Estado Libre Asociado*: Free Associated State). Ethnically, the population is a mixture of mestizos and mulatoes, with whites constituting a minority. The island's inhabitants possess all the rights and obligations of United States citizens such as paying social security, receiving federal welfare and serving in the armed forces. However, they are not allowed to vote in presidential elections and do not have to pay federal taxes. The head of state is the president of the United States of America.

The island of Puerto Rico was colonized by the Spanish Crown 15 years after it had been discovered by Christopher Columbus in 1508. A sugar industry developed under the colonial regime, which was crucial for relations with the governing country for several centuries. As on neighboring islands, the indigenous population was wiped out by wars and slavery in the plantations. The need for workforce was compensated by importing African slaves (15,000 in 1560).

Ramon Emeterio Betances first declared national independence in 1868, five years after the abolition of slavery. This became the point of reference for all future independence movements. Yet, the revolt was suppressed by the Spanish. Due to its defeat in the Spanish-American war, Spain lost its last Caribbean territories (possessions) in the Treaty of Paris in 1898, ceding Puerto Rico to the United States. Despite the Puerto Rican expectation that they would be granted autonomy, in 1900, the US Congress passed the Foraker Act (enacted 12 April), which conceded only a minimum of self-governance. From then on, the political status of Puerto Rico became to be the main political issue of the 20th century. In the following years, political parties were founded, mainly demanding autonomy or independence for the island. In 1917, political agitation led the US Congress to pass the Jones Act (enacted 2 March), which granted Puerto Ricans US citizenship, a Bill of Rights, and a legislature consisting of two chambers, the lower one elected by popular vote. The governor continued to be appointed by the US president.

In the following decades a process of 'Americanization' took place. This process was initiated by the new colonial administration, and led to political, administrative, and economic dependence on the United States and to an internalized heteronomy (patterns of consumption, values) still evident today. The introduction of English language in the schools, the diffusion of the concepts of Common Law, the assumption of the most important offices by US citizens, and the decision to declare Puerto Ricans US citizens and to integrate the country into the US tariff system and the US Constitution, were the most salient measures of integration.

During this process of Americanization, the widespread claims for independence slowly diminished as its social basis disappeared. This is especially true of the working class. The union movement can be traced back to 1890, when artisans, typographers, and farm laborers organized the first labor unions. The Labor Federation, founded in 1899 to represent the interests of artisans and farmers, was based on concepts of industrial conflict similar to those of the industrialized world: Not only collective action, but also alternative draft laws to improve working conditions. Consequently, the working class took part in politics and integrated into the US American labor movement. Yet, the industrial conflicts showed antagonisms: On the one hand, the activities of the major enterprises on the island were criticized, on the other hand the leaders of the movement called for the total integration of Puerto Rico into the US society as a guarantee for more rights and liberties. As early as 1924, the working class Socialist Party formed a pro-statehood alliance with the upper class capitalist Republican Party. Later on, at the end of the thirties, the young political leader Luis Muñoz Marín became convinced of the major importance of social and economic issues over that of political status. He founded the *Partido Popular Demócratico* (PPD; Democratic Popular Party) that won the elections in 1940 and ruled for the next 28 years. Under his leadership, the island underwent fundamental economic and social changes based on state interventionism. While social welfare increased and a new and growing middle class was created, the question of political status reemerged. In 1947, the United States amended the Jones Act to allow Puerto Ricans to elect their own governor, then on 3 July 1950, the US Congress approved Law 600, granting Puerto Ricans the right to draft their own constitution, although this was subject to review by the US Congress. The US initiative was welcomed by the

Puerto Rican voters in a referendum on 4 June 1951 by a majority of 76% of the valid votes. The Constituent Convention, elected on 27 August 1951, made up of 70 members from the PDP, 15 from the *Partido Estadista* and seven from the Socialist Party, began its deliberations the following September. On 3 March 1952 the electorate approved the new constitution, President Harry S. Truman signed it on 3 July, and on 25 July Governor Muñoz Marín proclaimed the Commonwealth of Puerto Rico, by which the island was associated to the United States as a self-governing polity. The USA retained full sovereignty over the island and most federal laws continue to apply to Puerto Rico.

Puerto Rican institutions control internal affairs unless US law is involved, as in matters of public health and pollution. The major differences between Puerto Rico and the 50 states are its local taxation system and exemption from the Internal Revenue Code, its lack of voting representation in both houses of the US Congress, the ineligibility of Puerto Ricans to vote in presidential elections, and its ineligibility for some revenues reserved for the states. Puerto Rico is permanently represented in Washington by a Resident Commissioner (with a voice, but no vote) in the Congress of United States.

The political system of Puerto Rico is presidential. The executive branch is formed by the governor, elected in direct elections by the electorate for a four-year term. He serves as Commander-in-Chief and has the right to proclaim martial law. The parliament consists of two chambers: a senate (with between 27 and 36 members) and a house of representatives (with between 51 and 54 members). With the exception of budget laws, the initiation of which is limited to the house of representatives, both chambers have the right of initiative. The governor proclaims the draft laws ratified by parliament or sends them, with his comment or veto, back to the legislature within ten days. If a two-thirds majority is achieved, the governor has to proclaim the law immediately.

The Puerto Rican party system has developed according to the disputed issue of the island's political status. A further dimension was the affirmation or rejection of capitalist development, a dimension that independentists rightly consider dependent from the question of the political status. The PPD, the dominating party until 1968, still advocates the maintenance of the political status quo (Commonwealth), reasoning that this would be the best way to preserve the cultural identity of Puerto Rico. This position is reconcilable with the claim for more competencies, in order, for example, to impose restrictions on industry or on control investments more efficiently. On the other hand, the *Partido Nuevo Progressista* (PNP; New Progressive Party) that emerged from the

United Statehood Movement in 1967, a split from the Statehood Republican Party (SRP), advocates total integration into the United States (Statehood), an alternative favored especially by the lower classes that expect the transfer of more social aid from the United States. After having obtained 39% in the referendum of 1967, PNP took advantage of some internal divisions of the PPD to win the elections of 1968. Since then, the Puerto Rican party system can be said to be bipolar, especially since the option for independence lost internal electoral support (exactly at the moment when external political support from Fidel Castro, the Movement of Non-Aligned Nations and the Decolonization Committee of the United Nations was at its highest).

The independentists, represented by three different groups, originally combined the claim for independence with socialist aims. Yet, both the contents and the political strategies followed differ considerably. The *Partido Independentista Puertoriqueño* (PIP; Puerto Rican Party for Independence), led by Berrios Martínez, promoted a moderately socialist independent republic. The self-image of the *Partido Socialista Puertoriqueño* (PSP; Puerto Rican Socialist Party), led by the left wing extremist lawyer Juan Mari Bras, who was also leader of the Castrist independence movement, was that of a Marxist-Leninist party campaigning for an independent socialist republic modeled on Cuba. The *Fuerzas Armadas de Liberación Nacional* (FALN; Armed Forces for National Liberation) was a militant underground movement fighting for independence. The FALN used bomb attacks and assassinations to try to attract the world's attention to their claim for independence. Two other movements shared the FALN's method of political action: *Los Macheteros* and Boricua People's Army. Since 1974 the activities of these movements have been aimed at US major enterprises and military facilities on the island and in the United States.

Three referendums were held on the question of political status. In 1967, 60.4% of the population opted for the Commonwealth status. In 1993 and 1998, the majority decreased, but nevertheless, these referendums confirmed the political status quo. Furthermore, the referendum held in 1991 resulted in 55% of the vote going against more political and cultural independence as advocated by Rafael Hernández Colón and the governing PPD. In the following year Pedro Rosello (PNP) was elected Governor and tried to implement total integration of the island into the United States by the referendum of 1993. However, only 46.2% voted for Statehood, while the majority (48%) opted for Commonwealth, and 4.4% for independence. In 1998, voters had to decide between different alternatives, changing the actual status quo, and none of them. This last option, favored by the PPD in protest against the 'territorial' definition of the actual Commonwealth Status on the ballot, obtained an absolute majority of 50.5%, while the Statehood option, launched by the governing PNP, gained 46.6%.

The advantages and disadvantages of the chosen political status of Puerto Rico have to be considered with regard to their economic consequences. Those who are most affected by differing states of development and crises of the prevailing growth model, the marginalized, opt for Statehood. The proponents of the status quo fear that Puerto Rico would be subjected to the US federal tax system, and would, therefore, be less interesting for US American and foreign investors. It seems paradoxical, but given the options of Commonwealth or Statehood, the status quo is the more attractive solution for capital. In view of the total political dependence of the island on the United States, the Puerto Rican model of industrial and economic growth, under the keyword 'Puertoricanization', was often associated with the idea of extremely dependent development at the expense of wage workers and national self-determination concerning the basic socio-economic and political issues.

In addition to the three referendums on the political status, other issues, mainly projects concerning constitutional reform, were also decided by popular vote and created a Puerto Rican tradition of direct democracy.

1.2 Evolution of Electoral Provisions

In 1898, the US military government passed a provisional electoral law granting suffrage to literate and custom paying male citizens over 21 years. In 1900, the Foraker Act established a Commissioner (*Comisionado*), the official representative of Puerto Rico for all the departments of the Federal Government. In 1904, this Commissioner (since 1917: Resident Commissioner) got a seat in the US House of Representatives, but without voice. Furthermore, the Foraker Act established a chamber of delegates of 35 members with a two-year term of office as a lower house, while the executive council, nominated by the US president, functioned as the upper house. In 1917, the US Congress approved the Jones Act, which increased the number of representatives by four to 39 members and established a popularly-elected upper house with 19 members. A further step towards greater internal autonomy was the introduction of popular direct election for the governor in 1948.

The Commonwealth Constitution of 1952 extended membership of the house of representatives to a minimum of 51 members and a maximum of 68, that of the senate from a minimum of 27 members to a maximum of 36. The number of SMCs was increased from 35 to 40, that of bi-nominal constituencies from seven to eight.

Suffrage was granted to literate women in 1929. In 1936, another amendment of the Jones Act led to the introduction of universal suffrage without any restriction except that of voter registration. Furthermore, the *colegio cerrado* was introduced to overcome the widespread clientelism and corruption. Electors had to assemble at a certain hour in a public place, the doors were closed and voting began. For the elections of 1980 the electoral identity card (*cedula*) was introduced, and in 1984, the *colegio abierto* was abolished. Voting has never been compulsory, but absentees loose their registration as voter and have to be re-registered in order to be entitled to vote. Since 1984, people can register at any time during the year; the process of registration is permanent.

The traditional electoral system has been based on plurality, but in different types of constituencies: The Jones act of 1917 established 35 SMCs for the house of representatives and seven binominal constituencies for the senate. Furthermore, four representatives and five senators were elected on a nationwide list (*acumulación*). When the dominant party practically monopolized political representation in both houses in the elections of 1944 and 1948, a need was felt to guarantee the adequate representation of minorities. Indeed, the constitution of 1952 introduced a mechanism to avoid extreme majorities: No party was allowed to obtain more then two-thirds of the seats in either house. In order to strengthen minority representation, the number of members elected on a nationwide list was increased to eleven seats in both chambers, by individual vote for candidates nominated on nationwide party lists. Furthermore, if the victorious party obtains more than two-thirds of the seats while its candidate for governor does not obtain this majority, the opposition party or parties will obtain as many minority seats for a maximum of 17 seats in the house of representatives and nine in the senate. This mechanism is called the Law of Minorities (*Ley de Minorías*). This law was applied in the elections of 1952, 1956, 1960, 1964, 1972 1988, 1992, 1996, and 2000. In order to facilitate even more political pluralism in 1964, the number of votes required to keep the status of a political party was reduced from 10% to 5% of the votes. Later on, it was lowered to 3%.

Originally, voters only had one ballot to fill all the different offices at national and municipal level, which meant they could only vote for one party ('straight ticket'). From 1984 onwards, the municipal elections were separated from the national ones, and in 1996, different ballots were introduced for executive (governor, Commissioner) and legislative offices.

1.3 Current Electoral Provisions

Sources: Constitution of the Commonwealth of Puerto Rico from 25 July 1952; Electoral Law, Law No. 4, called *Ley Electoral de Puerto Rico*, from 20 December 1977, with several amendments, the last revision was made in 2000.

Suffrage: Universal, equal, direct, and secret suffrage is applied. Those entitled to vote are citizens of Puerto Rico and the United States resident in Puerto Rico, who are 18 years old und have been entered in the Register of the Electorate (*Registro del Cuerpo Electoral*). Citizens can loose their status by not voting. If they do so, they have to register to be able to vote in further elections. Indigenous inhabitants are US citizens but do not vote in US presidential elections.

Elected national institutions: The governor is elected by popular vote for a four-year term. The resident commissioner is directly elected for a four-year term. Legislative assembly (*Asamblea Legislativa*), bicameral, senate (*Senado*) and chamber of representatives (*Cámara de Representations*), both houses directly elected. The number of members can vary between 28 and 40 senators and between 54 and 68 representatives. Each house is elected for a four-year term.

Nominations of candidates: All citizens who are entered in the Register of the Electorate and are over 35 years old in the case of presidential elections, and 25 years old in the case of parliamentary elections, may run as candidates. Candidates have to deliver a report on their financial situation to the Office of Governmental Ethics (*Oficina de Etica Gobernamental*). All victorious candidates have to pass a course on administration of public fonds, offered by the office of Controller before the certification of the electoral results by the State Commission of Elections. With regard to the party lists, political parties can determine the ranking of candidates on the ballot. With regard to one-member or two-member constituencies, all political parties are allowed to nominate only one candidate for one seat to be filled.

Electoral system: Chamber of Representatives: 40 members are elected in SMCs, eleven in a nationwide multi-member constituency (MMC) and three to allow the opposition to have one-third of the seats. At SMC level, the voter has one vote, and another one in the nationwide constituency.

Senate: 16 members are elected in two-member constituencies and eleven in a nationwide constituency, one to allow the opposition to have one-third of the seats. At two-member constituency level, the voter has two votes, including the vote in a nationwide constituency, for the senate three votes in total.

In general, a voter can vote for a party and a candidate. If he or she votes for a party (placing a mark under the party symbol), he or she votes for all the candidates nominated by that party competing individually for the offices to be filled (*voto íntegro*). In this case, the party lists for the eleven seats are blocked and closed. If the voter votes for candidates separately, the party lists are open, which means that he or she can vote, at MMC level, for a candidate from party lists different from the one he or she voted for at SMC level. This is called mixed voting (*voto mixto*).

No party can attain more than two-thirds of the seats. If a party receives more than two-thirds of the seats, but wins less than two-thirds of the vote in the election for governor, the number of members of the house of representatives will be increased by a maximum of 17 members and that of the senate by nine members. In order to distribute these seats, first the votes are totaled for those parties that obtained at least 3% of the votes. Then, the number of votes obtained by each party entitled to participate in this distribution of seats is divided by the total number of votes of these parties and then multiplied by the number of seats to be allocated. The remaining number corresponds to the number of seats that will be assigned to that party. Within a party list, the number of individual votes obtained by candidates is decisive.

Organizational context of elections: The State Commission of Elections is made up of a president and one commissioner to represent each political party entered in the Register of Political Parties. The president of the electoral commission is appointed by the governor in accordance with the majority of each house of the legislative assembly. The commissioners are appointed by the governor on the petition of the Central Directive Committee of the political parties. The political party loses its status if it fails to obtain three percent of the vote in general elections.

1.4 Commentary on the Electoral Statistics

The *Comisión Estatal de Elecciones de Puerto Rico* publishes the results of elections and referendums (see www.ceepur.net/cgi-bin/eventos.pl). Although the data are very detailed, much of the data at the national level are not aggregated, especially for legislative elections, partially due to the complex electoral system. A lot of attention is paid to the results of the election for governor and the nationwide elections of the legislative assembly. Furthermore, before the establishment of the Commonwealth of Puerto Rico, at a time when election practices were partly corrupt, the historical data is deficient. As of 1952, results are certainly reliable.

2. Tables

2.1 Dates of National Elections, Referendums, and Coups d'Etat

Year	Presidential Elections	Parliamentary elections		Elections for Constit. Assembly	Referendums	Coups d'état
		Lower Chamber	Upper Chamber			
1932		08/11				
1936		03/11				
1940		05/11				
1944		07/11				
1948	02/11	02/11	02/11			
1951					04/06	
1952	04/11	04/11	04/11		03/03	
					04/11	
1956	06/11	06/11	06/11			
1960	08/11	08/11	08/11		08/11	
1961					10/12	
1964	03/11	03/11	03/11		03/11	
1967					23/07	
1968	05/11	05/11	05/11			
1970					01/11	
1972	07/11	07/11	07/11			
1976	02/11	02/11	02/11			
1980	04/11	04/11	04/11			
1984	06/11	06/11	06/11			
1988	08/11	08/11	08/11			
1991					08/12	
1992	03/11	03/11	03/11			
1993					14/11	
1994					06/11	
1996	05/11	05/11	05/11			
1998					13/12	
2000	07/11	07/11	07/11			

2.2 Electoral Body 1932–2000

Year	Type of election[a]	Population[b]	Registered voters Total number	% pop.	Votes cast Total number	% reg. voters	% pop.
1932	R	1,600,000	452,738	28.3	383,722	84.8	24.0
1936	R	1,743,000	764,602	43.9	549,500	71.9	31.5
1940	R	1,869,255	714,960	38.2	568,851	79.6	30.4
1944	R	2,062,000	719,759	34.9	591,978	82.2	28.7
1948	Gov	2,187,000	873,085	39.9	640,714[c]	73.4	29.3
1951	Ref	2,211,000	781,914	35.4	506,185[c]	64.7	22.9
1952	Ref	2,227,000	883,219	39.7	457,572[c]	58.5	20.5
1952	Gov	2,227,000	883,219	39.7	664,947[c]	75.3	29.9
1952	Ref	2,227,000	883,219	39.7	477,719[c]	54.1	21.4
1956	Gov	2,249,000	873,085	38.8	701,738	80.4	31.2
1960	Ref	2,349,544	941,034	40.1	485,271[c]	51.6	20.7
1960	Gov	2,349,544	941,034	40.1	796,429	84.6	33.9
1961	Ref	2,402,000	802,032	33.4	465,593[c]	58.1	19.4
1964	Ref	2,550,000	1,002,000	39.3	400,332[c]	40.0	15.7
1964	Gov	2,550,000	1,002,000	39.3	839,678	83.8	32.9
1967	Ref	2,645,000	1,067,349	40.4	708,692	66.4	26.8
1968	Gov	2,669,000	1,176,895	44.1	922,822	78.4	34.6
1970	Ref	2,712,033	1,043,733	38.5	362,696	34.7	13.4
1972	Gov	2,868,000	1,555,504	54.2	1,250,978	80.4	43.6
1976	Gov	3,214,000	1,701,217	52.9	1,464,600	86.1	45.6
1980	Gov	3,196,520	2,071,777	64.8	1,619,790	78.2	50.7
1984	Gov	3,349,000	1,959,877	58.5	1,741,638	88.9	52.0
1988	Gov	3,461,000	2,144,583	62.0	1,812,357	84.5	52.4
1991	Ref	3,523,000	2,052,690	58.3	1,246,663	60.7	35.4
1992	Gov	3,573,000	2,242,381	62.8	1,881,872	84.8	52.7
1992	R	3,573,000	2,242,381	62.8	1,854,314	82.7	51.9
1992	S	3,573,000	2,242,381	62.8	1,846,571	82.3	51.7
1993	Ref	3,608,000	2,312,912	64.1	1,700,990	73.5	47.1
1994	Ref	3,645,000	2,126,248	58.3	1,330,055	62.6	36.5
1996	Gov	3,733,000	2,380,676	63.8	1,967,705	82.8	52.7
1996	R	3,733,000	2,380,676	63.8	1,911,776	80.3	51.2
1996	S	3,733,000	2,380,676	63.8	1,910,529	80.3	51.2
1998	Ref	3,860,000	2,197,824	56.9	1,566,270	71.3	40.6
2000	Gov	3,808,610	2,447,032	64.3	2,012,135	82.2	52.8
2000	R	3,808,610	2,447,032	64.3	1,953,121	79.8	51.3
2000	S	3,808,610	2,447,032	64.3	1,948,393	79.6	51.2

[a] Gov = Governor, R = House of Representatives (Lower Chamber), Ref = Referendum, S = Senate (upper chamber).
[b] During the 20th century, censuses were held every ten years (1910, 1920 etc.). The other data are estimates.
[c] Valid votes.

2.3 Abbreviations

PAC	*Partido Acción Cristiana* (Christian Action Party)
PAS	*Partido Auténtico Soberanista* (Authentic Party for Sovereignty)
PIP	*Partido Independista Puertorriqueño* (Puerto Rican Party for Independence)
PNP	*Partido Nuevo Progresista* (New Progressive Party)
PP	*Partido del Pueblo* (People's Party)
PPD	*Partido Popular Demócratico* (Democratic Popular Party)
PRP	*Partido Renovación Puertoriquena* (Puerto Rican Renewal Party)
PS	*Partido Socialista* (Socialist Party)
PSP	*Partido Socialista Puertorriqueño* (Puerto Rican Socialist Party)
UR	*Unión Republicana* (Republican Union)

2.4 Electoral Participation of Parties and Alliances 1952–2000

Party / Alliance	Years	Elections contested	
		Parliamentary[a]	Governor[b]
PIP	1952–2000	13	13
PPD	1952–2000	13	13
PS	1952	1	1
UR	1952–1964	4	0
PAC	1960–1964	2	2
PNP	1968–2000	9	9
PP	1968–1972	2	2
PAS	1972	1	0
PSP	1976–1980	2	2
PRP	1984; 1988	1	1

[a] Only elections to the house of representatives under the Commonwealth constitution (1952) are taken into account. Total number: 13.
[b] Total number: 13.

2.5 Referendums

2.5 a) Referendums on the political status of Puerto Rico

Year	1967[a]		1993[b]	
	Total number	%	Total number	%
Registered voters	1,067,349	–	2,312,912	–
Votes cast	703,692	65.9	1,700,990	73.5
Invalid votes	3,601	0.5	10,748[c]	0.6
Valid votes	700,091[d]	99.5	1,690,242[e]	99.4
Commonwealth	425,132	60.4	826,326	48.6
Statehood	274,312	39.0	788,296	46.3
Independence	4,248	0.6	75,620	4.4

[a] *Estado libre* (Free State).
[b] *Estado Libre Asociado* (Free Associated State).
[c] Including 4,199 blank votes.
[d] Official data are inconsistent. The sum of votes in favor of the alternatives (703,692) exceeds the reported number of valid votes.
[e] Calculated by the author.

Year	1998	
	Total number	%
Registered voters	2,197,824	–
Votes cast	1,566,270	71.3
Blank votes	1,890	0.1
Invalid votes	2,956	0.2
Valid votes	1,561,424	99.7
Statehood	728,157	46.6
Independence.	39,838	2.6
Free Association	4,536	0.3
'Territorial Common-wealth'	993	0.0
None of the above	787,900	50.5

2.5 b) Referendums on other issues

Year	1951[a]		1952[b]	
	Total number	%	Total number	%
Registered voters	781,914	–	781,914	–
Votes cast	—	—	—	—
Invalid votes	—	—	—	—
Valid votes	506,185	—	457,572	—
Si	387,016	76.5	374,649	81.9
No	119,169	23.5	82,923	18.1

[a] On Law Nr. 600.
[b] On the Constitution of a Free Associated State (Commonwealth).

Year	1952[a]		1952[b]	
	Total number	%	Total number	%
Registered voters	883,219	–	883,219	–
Votes cast	—	—	—	—
Invalid votes	—	—	—	—
Valid votes	478,520	—	477,719	—
Yes	420,036	87.8	419,515	87.8
No	58,484	12.2	58,204	12.2

[a] On amendments of the Constitution with regard to the federal order.
[b] On some educational issue regarding the financing of private schools by public fonds.

Year	1960[a]		1961[b]	
	Total number	%	Total number	%
Registered voters	941,034	–	802,032	–
Votes cast	—	—	—	—
Blank votes	—	—	—	—
Invalid votes	—	—	—	—
Valid votes	485,271	—	465,593	—
Yes	380,523	78.4	385,369	82.8
No	104,748	21.6	80,224	17.2

[a] On judicial reform.
[b] On financial issue.

Year	1964[a]		1970[b]	
	Total number	%	Total number	%
Registered voters	1,002,000	–	1,043,733	–
Votes cast	—	—	362,696	34.7
Blank votes	—	—	—	—
Invalid votes	—	—	—	—
Valid votes	400,332	—	360,819	99.5
Yes	310,431	77.5	213,782	59.2
No	89,901	22.5	147,037	40.8

[a] Elimination of special elections to fill vacant legislative parliamentary seats.
[b] Active suffrage for citizens of an age of 18 years.

Year	1991		1994[a]	
	Total number	%	Total number	%
Registered voters	2,052,690	–	2,126,248	–
Votes cast	1,246,663	60.7	1,330,055	62.6
Blank votes	2,538	0.2	6,828	0.5
Invalid votes	24,702	2.0	5,079	0.4
Valid votes	1,219,423	97.8	1,318,157	99.1
Yes	559,159	45.9	605,866	45.6
No	660,264	54.1	712,291	53.6

[a] Constitutional Amendment to eliminate the absolute right to bail.

Year	1994[a]	
	Total number	%
Registered voters	2,126,248	–
Votes cast	1,330,055	62.6
Blank votes	11,159	0.8
Invalid votes	5,098	0.4
Valid votes	1,313,798	98.8
Yes	595,425	44.8
No	718,373	54.0

[a] Constitutional Amendment to increase the number of Supreme Court judges.

2.6 Elections for Constitutional Assembly

Results of the election to the Constitutional Convention on 27 August 1951 have not been available.

2.7 Parliamentary Elections

2.7.1 House of Representatives 1952–2000

Year	1952		1956	
	Total number	%	Total number	%
Registered voters	883,219	–	873,842	–
Votes cast	640,714	72.5	701,738	80.3
Blank votes	—	—	—	—
Invalid votes	—	—	—	—
Valid votes	—	—	—	—
PPD	—	64.8	—	62.5
UR	—	12.9	—	25.0
PIP	—	19.0	—	3.3
PS	—	3.3	–	–
Others	–	–	—	9.2

Year	1960		1964	
	Total number	%	Total number	%
Registered voters	941,034	–	1,002,000	–
Votes cast	796,429	84.6	839,678	83.8
Blank votes	—	—	—	—
Invalid votes	—	—	—	—
Valid votes	—	—	—	—
PPD	—	62.4	—	59.4
UR	—	34.3	—	34.6
PIP	—	2.7	—	2.7
AC	—	0.6	—	3.3

Year	1968		1972	
	Total number	%	Total number	%
Registered voters	1,176,895	–	1,555,504	–
Votes cast	922,822	78.4	1,250,978	80.4
Blank votes	—	—	—	—
Invalid votes	—	—	—	—
Valid votes	—	—	—	—
PNP	—	42.3	—	41.1
PPD	—	40.0	—	48.7
Others	—	17.7[a]	—	10.2[b]

[a] *Partido Estadista Republicano*, PIP, and PP. The individual shares have not been available.
[b] PAS, PIP, PP, and *Unión Puertorriqueña*. The individual shares have not been available.

Year	1976		1980	
	Total number	%	Total number	%
Registered voters	1,701,217	–	2,071,777	–
Votes cast	1,464,600	86.1	1,619,790	78.2
Blank votes	—	—	2,664	0.2
Invalid votes	—	—	5,461	0.3
Valid votes	—	—	1,611,665	99.5
PNP	—	48.3	—	47.2
PPD	—	45.3	—	47.0
Others[a]	—	6.4	—	5.8

[a] PIP and PSP. The individual shares have not been available.

Year	1984			1988	
	Total number	%		Total number	%
Registered voters	1,959,877	–		—	–
Votes cast	1,741,638	88.9		—	—
Blank votes	5,707	0.3		—	—
Invalid votes	6,823	0.4		—	—
Valid votes	1,729,108	99.3		—	—
PPD	—	47.8		—	48.7
PNP	—	44.6		—	45.8
PIP	—	7.6[a]		—	5.5

[a] PIP and PRP. The individual shares have not been available.

Year	1992			1996	
	Total number	%		Total number	%
Registered voters	2,242,381	–		2,380,676	–
Votes cast	1,866,513	83.2		1,911,776	80.3
Blank votes	7,526	0.4		17,705	0.9
Invalid votes	4,673	0.3		5,396	0.3
Valid votes	1,854,314	99.3		1,888,675	98.8
PNP	860,843	46.4		906,693	48.0
PPD	728,919	39.3		814,952	43.1
PIP	262,235	14.1		140,964	7.5
Others	2,317	0.1		346	0.0
Independents	–	–		25,720	1.4

Year	2000[a]			2000[b]	
	Total number	%		Total number	%
Registered voters	2,447,032	–		2,447,032	–
Votes cast	1,970,287	79.8		1,053,121	43.0
Blank votes	14,162	0.7		14,162	1.3
Invalid votes	4,800	0.2		4,800	0.5
Valid votes	1,951,321[c]	99.0		–	–
PPD	934,611	47.9		857,614	–
PNP	902,708	46.3		851,506	–
PIP	112,592	5.8		224,765	–
Others	1,410	0.0		274	–

[a] First votes in SMCs.

[b] Second votes for national list ('*acumulación*').

[c] Calculated by the author. Data are slightly inconsistent. The sum of blank votes, invalid votes, and party votes (1,970,283) is lower than the reported number of votes cast (1,970,287).

2.7.2 Senate 1992–2000

For the senate elections of 1984 and 1988 no detailed data have been available.

Year	1992[a]		1996[a]	
	Total number	%	Total number	%
Registered voters	2,242,381	–	2,380,676	–
Votes cast	1,858,770	82.9	1,910,529	80.3
Blank votes	7,526	0.4	17,705	0.9
Invalid votes	4,673	0.3	5,396	0.3
Valid votes	1,846,571	99.3	1,887,428	98.8
PNP	848,576	46.0	886,455	47.0
PPD	717,041	38.8	772,044	40.9
PIP	209,009	11.3	160,005	8.5
Others	1,756	0.1	458	0.2
Independents	70,189	3.8	68,466	3.6

[a] Votes for the national list ('*acumulación*').

Year	2000[a]		2000[b]	
	Total number	%	Total number	%
Registered voters	2,447,032	–	2,447,032	–
Votes cast	—	—	1,948,393	79.6
Blank votes	14,162	—	14,162	0.7
Invalid votes	4,800	—	4,800	0.2
Valid votes	3,850,375	—	1,929,431	99.0
PPD	1,850,091	48.0	855,013	44.3
PNP	1,778,197	46.2	856,886	44.4
PIP	221,411	5.8	217,390	11.3
Others	676	0.0	142	0.0

[a] First votes in two-seats constituencies. Voters have two votes at this level. The given numbers of blank and invalid votes refer to the numbers of blank and invalid ballots.
[b] Votes in the national constituency by '*acumulación*'.

2.8 Composition of Parliament

2.8.1 House of Representatives 1968–2000

For the elections held between 1952 and 1964, no reliable information on the distribution of seats was available.

Year	1968		1972		1976		1980	
	Seats	%	Seats	%	Seats	%	Seats	%
	51	100.0	54	100.0	51	100.0	51	100.0
PPD	26	51.0	37	68.5	18	35.3	26	51.0
PNP	25	49.0	15	27.8	33	64.7	25	49.0
PIP	–	–	2	3.7	0	0.0	0	0.0

Year	1984		1988		1992		1996	
	Seats	%	Seats	%	Seats	%	Seats	%
	51	100.0	53	100.0	53	100.0	54	100.0
PPD	34	66.7	36	67.9	16	30.2	16	29.6
PNP	16	31.4	15	28.3	36	67.9	37	68.5
PIP	1	1.9	2	3.8	1	1.9	1	1.9

Year	2000	
	Seats	%
	51	100.0
PPD	30	58.8
PNP	20	39.2
PIP	1	2.0

2.8.2 Senate 1968–2000

For the elections held between 1952 and 1964, no reliable information on the distribution of seats was available.

Year	1968		1972		1976		1980	
	Seats	%	Seats	%	Seats	%	Seats	%
	27	100.0	29	100.0	27	100.0	27	100.0
PPD	15	55.6	20	69.0	13	48.1	15	55.6
PNP	12	44.4	8	27.6	14	51.9	12	44.4
PIP	0	0.0	1	3.4	0	0.0	0	0.0

Year	1984		1988		1992		1996	
	Seats	%	Seats	%	Seats	%	Seats	%
	27	100.0	27	100.0	29	100.0	28	100.0
PPD	18	66.7	18	66.7	8	27.6	8	28.6
PNP	8	29.6	8	29.6	20	69.0	19	67.9
PIP	1	3.7	1	3.7	1	3.4	1	3.6

Year	2000 Const.	Nat.	Add.	Total	%
	16	11	1	28	100.0
PPD	14	5	0	19	67.9
PNP	2	5	1	8	28.6
PIP	0	1	0	1	3.6

2.9 Elections for Executive Offices

2.9.1 Presidential Elections

The president of the United States of America is head of state. Puerto Ricans are not entitled to vote in US presidential elections.

2.9.2 Elections for Governor 1948–2000

1948	Total number	%
Registered voters	873,085	–
Votes cast	—	—
Invalid votes	—	—
Valid votes	640,714	—
Luis Muñoz Marín (PPD)	392,386	61.2
Martín Travieso (PEP, PS, PRP)	182,977	28.6
Francisco M. Susoni (PIP)	65,351	4.5

1952	Total number	%
Registered voters	883,219	–
Votes cast	—	—
Invalid votes	—	—
Valid votes	664,947	—
Luis Muñoz Marín (PPD)	431,409	64.9
Fernando Milán, Hijo (PIP)	126,228	19.0
Francisco López Domínguez (PER)	85,591	12.9
Luis R. Moczó (PS)	21,719	3.3

1956	Total number	%
Registered voters	873,085	–
Votes cast	701,738	80.4
Invalid votes[a]	5,164	0.7
Valid votes	696,574	99.3
Luis Muñoz Marín (PPD)	435,255	62.5
Luis A. Ferré (PER)	174,683	25.1
Francisco M. Susoni, Hijo (PIP)	86,636	12.4

[a] Calculated by the author.

1960	Total number	%
Registered voters	941,034	–
Votes cast	796,429	84.6
Invalid votes[a]	6,942	0.9
Valid votes	789,487	99.1
Luis Muñoz Marín (PPD)	459,759	58.2
Luis A. Ferré (PER)	253,242	32.1
Salvador Perea Roselló (PAC)	52,275	6.6
Julio García Diaz (PIP)	24,211	3.1

[a] Calculated by the author.

1964	Total number	%
Registered voters	1,002,000	–
Votes cast	839,678	83,8
Invalid votes[a]	8,227	1.0
Valid votes	831,451	99.0
Roberto Sánchez Vilella (PPD)	492,531	59.2
Luis A. Ferré (PER)	288,504	34.7
Francisco González Baena (PAC)	27,076	3.3
Gilberto Concepción de Gracia (PIP)	23,340	2.8

[a] Calculated by the author.

1968	Total number	%
Registered voters	1,176,895	–
Votes cast	922,822	74.4
Invalid votes	3,993	0.4
Valid votes	918,829	99.6
Luis Ferré (PNP)	400,815	43.6
Luis Negrón López (PPD)	374,040	40.7
Roberto Sánchez Vilella (PP)	107,359	11.7
Antonio J. González (PIP)	32,166	3.5
Others	4,449	0.5

1972	Total number	%
Registered voters	1,555,504	–
Votes cast	1,250,978[a]	80.4
Invalid votes	—	—
Valid votes	1,299,884[a]	—
Luis A. Ferré (PNP)	563,609	43.4
Rafael Hernández Colón (PPD)	658,856	50.7
Noel Colón Martínez (PIP)	69,654	5.4
Others	7,765	0.6

[a] According to the inconsistent official data, the sum of valid votes exceeds the votes cast.

1976	Total number	%
Registered voters	1,701,217	–
Votes cast	1,464,600	86.1
Invalid votes	6,466	0.4
Valid votes	1,458,034	99.6
Carlos Romero Barceló (PNP)	703,968	48.3
Rafael Hernández Colón (PPD)	660,301	45.3
Rubén Berríos Martínez (PIP)	83,037	5.7
Juan Mari Bras (PSP)	10,728	0.7

1980	Total number	%
Registered voters	1,835,160	–
Votes cast	1,619,790	88.3
Invalid votes	10,479	0.6
Valid votes	1,609,311	99.4
Carlos Romero Barceló (PNP)	759,926	47.2
Rafael Hernández Colón (PPD)	756,889	47.0
Rubén Berríos Martinez (PIP)	87,272	5.4
Luis Lausell Hernández (PSP)	5,224	0.3

1984	Total number	%
Registered voters	1,959,877	–
Votes cast	1,741,638	88.9
Invalid votes	18,851	1.1
Valid votes	1,722,787	98.9
Rafael Hernández Colón (PPD)	822,709	47.8
Carlos Romero Barceló (PNP)	768,959	44.6
Fernando Martín García (PIP)	61,312	3.6
Hernan Padilla Ramírez (PRP)	69,807	4.1

1988	Total number	%
Registered voters	2,144,583	–
Votes cast	1,812,862	84.5
Blank votes	—	—
Invalid votes	—	—
Valid votes	1,791,406	—
Rafael Hernández Colón (PPD)	871,858	48.7
Baltazar Corrada del Río (PNP)	820,342	45.8
Rubén Berríos Martínez (PIP)	99,206	5.5

1992	Total number	%
Registered voters	2,242,381	–
Votes cast	1,881,872	83.9
Blank votes	—	—
Invalid votes	—	—
Valid votes	—	—
Pedro Rosselló (PNP)	938,969	—
Victoria Muñoz Mendoza (PPD)	862,989	—
Fernando Martín (PIP)	79,219	—
Others	695	—

1996	Total number	%
Registered voters	2,380,676	–
Votes cast	1,967,705	82.7
Blank votes	4,887	0.3
Invalid votes	4,522	0.2
Valid votes	1,958,296	99.5
Pedro Rosselló (PNP)	1,006,331	51.4
Héctor Luis Acevedo (PPD)	875,852	44.7
David Noriega Rodríguez (PIP)	75,305	3.8
Others	808	0.0

2000	Total number	%
Registered voters	2,447,032	–
Votes cast	2,012,135	82.2
Blank votes	4,103	0.2
Invalid votes	4,564	0.2
Valid votes	2,003,468	99.6
Sila María Calderón (PPD)	978,860	48.9
Carlos I. Pesquera (PNP)	919,194	45.9
Ruben Berríos Martínez (PIP)	104,705	5.2
Others	709	0.0

2.9.3 Elections for Resident Commissioner 1980–2000

1980	Total number	%
Registered voters	2,071,777	–
Votes cast	—	—
Invalid votes	—	—
Valid votes	1,594,471	—
Baltazar Corrada del Rio (PNP)	760,580	47.7
José Arsenio Torres (PPD)	749,983	47.0
Marta Font de Calero (PIP)	83,908	5.3

1984	Total number	%
Registered voters	1,959,877	–
Votes cast	—	—
Invalid votes	—	—
Valid votes	1,700,651	—
Jaime B. Fuster Berlingeri (PPD)	827,380	48.7
Nelson Famadas (PNP)	769,951	45.3
Francisco A. Catalá Oliveras (PIP)	64,001	3.8
Angel Viera Martínez (PRP)	39,319	2.3

1988	Total number	%
Registered voters	2,144,583	–
Votes cast	—	—
Invalid votes	—	—
Valid votes	1,771,968	—
Jaime B. Fuster Berlingeri (PPD)	867,532	49.0
Pedro J. Rosselló (PNP)	824,879	46.6
Luis Pío Sánchez Longo (PIP)	79,557	4.5

1992	Total number	%
Registered voters	2,242,381	–
Votes cast	—	—
Invalid votes	—	—
Valid votes	1,860,263	—
Carlos Romero Barceló (PNP)	908,067	48.6
Antonio J. Colorado (PPD)	891,176	47.9
Victor García San Inocencio (PIP)	63,472	3.4
Others	1,548	0.1

1996	Total number	%
Registered voters	2,380,676	–
Votes cast	1,956,379	82.2
Blank votes	4,887	0.2
Invalid votes	4,522	0.2
Valid votes	1,946,970	99.5
Carlos Romero Barceló (PNP)	973,654	50.0
Celeste Benítez (PPD)	904,048	46.4
Manuel Rodríguez Orellana (PIP)	68,828	3.5
Others	440	0.0

2000	Total number	%
Registered voters	2,447,032	–
Votes cast	1,993,483	81.5
Blank votes	4,103	0.2
Invalid votes	4,564	0.2
Valid votes	1,984,816	99.6
Anibal Acevedo Vilá (PPD)	983,488	49.6
Carlos Romero Barceló (PNP)	905,690	45.6
Manuel Rodríguez Orellana (PIP)	95,067	4.8
Others	571	0.0

2.10 List of Power Holders 1946–2004

The president of the United States of America is head of state of Puerto Rico. For the list of heads of state see the chapter on the United States.

Head of Government[a]	Years	Remarks
Jesús Toribio Piñero	1946–1949	In office from 03/09/1946 to 02/01/1949.
Luis Muñoz Marín	1949–1965	In office from 02/01/1949 to 02/01/1965.
Roberto Sánchez Vilella	1965–1969	In office from 02/01/1965 to 02/01/1969.
Luis Alberto Ferré	1969–1973	In office from 02/01/1969 to 02/01/1973.
Rafael Hernández Colón	1973–1977	In office from 02/01/1973 to 02/01/1977.
Carlos Romero Barceló	1977–1985	In office from 02/01/1977 to 02/01/1985.
Rafael Hernández Colón	1985–1993	Second term. In office from 02/01/1985 to 02/01/1993.
Pedro Rosselló	1993–2001	In office from 02/01/1993 to 02/01/2001.
Sila M. Calderón	2001–	Holds office since 02/01/2001.

[a] Directly elected.

3. Bibliography

3.1 Official Sources

Comision Estatal de Elecciones (1980). *Elecciones generales de 1980. Informe Estadistico*. San Juan.
Comision Estatal de Elecciones (1984). *Elecciones generales 1984. Informe Estadistico*. San Juan

3.2 Books, Articles, and Electoral Reports

Alexander, R. J. (ed.) (1982). *Political Parties of the Americas*. Westport, Conn.: Greenwood Press.
Anderson, R. W. (1965). *Party Politics in Puerto Rico*. Stanford, Calif.: Stanford University Press.
— (ed.) (1998). *Política electoral en Puerto Rico*. Plaza Mayor.
Bayrón Toro, F. (2000). *Elecciones y partidos politicos de Puerto Rico 1809–2000* (5th edn.). Mayagüez: Editorial Isla.
Edie, C. J. (ed.) (1994). *Democracy in the Caribbean. Myths and Realities*. London: Praeger.
Espinal, R. (2000). 'La relación entre sistemas electorales y sistemas de partidos políticos en el Caribe'. *Justicia Electoral*, 14: 39–62.
Farr, K. (1973). *Personalism and Party Politics in Puerto Rico: The Institutionalization of the Popular Democratic Party*. San Juan: Inter-American University Press.
Fernández, R., Méndez Méndez, S., and Cueto, G. (1998). *Puerto Rico Past and Present: An Encyclopedia*. Westport, Conn.: Greenwood Press.
García-Passalacqua, J. M. and Heine, J. (1991). 'Society and Voting Behaviour in Puerto Rico', in C. Clarke (ed.), *Society and Politics in the Caribbean*. Oxford: McMillan, 245–276.
Nohlen, D. (1995). 'Puerto Rico', in D. Nohlen and F. Nuscheler (eds.), *Handbuch der Dritten Welt, Vol. 3: Mittelamerika und Karibik*. Bonn: Dietz, 646–663.
Wells, H. (1969). *The Modernization of Puerto Rico*. Cambridge, Mass.: Harvard University Press.

SAINT KITTS AND NEVIS

by Bernd Hillebrands and Johannes Schwehm

1. Introduction

1.1 Historical Overview

From 1956, the three islands Saint Christopher (also referred to as St. Kitts), Nevis, and Anguilla were administered as one single colony by the British governor of the Leeward Islands Federation. In 1958, however, they entered the West Indies Federation, founded by ten British insular colonies as a territorial union to achieve economic and political independence from Britain. This union, however, was disbanded as early as 1962. After the granting of internal self-governance in 1967, and the secession of Anguilla (remaining a British dependency) in 1980, St. Kitts and Nevis declared independence on 19 September 1983. Elections in St. Kitts and Nevis have always been considered free and fair. The organization of the electoral process satisfies international standards.

The existence of a political workers' movement meant that a broad cross-section of the population was encouraged to participate in national politics. In 1932, the St. Kitts Workers League (WL) was founded, and this union was the core from which the St. Kitts-Nevis Trades and Labour Union (SKNTLU) emerged in 1940. The SKNTLU became the country's most important union, and its basis was formed by the sugar plantation workers. Members of this union created the St. Kitts-Nevis-Anguilla Labour Party (SKNALP)—after the secession of Anguilla in 1980, it was renamed St. Kitts-Nevis-Labour Party (SKNLP)—and the two maintained close connections. Robert L. Bradshaw led both the SKNTLU and the SKNALP from 1946 to 1978, combining these two leadership responsibilities in his position as head of government, an office he held almost without interruption during these years.

From the 1952 elections, when universal suffrage was introduced, up to 1966, no opposition party threatened the SKNALP's political hegemony. The electoral results of this period showed a trend in the voters' behavior, which was to support a particular party in each island. In St.

Kitts, the SKNALP obtained all the seats; in Nevis and Anguilla on the other hand, the seats were shared between independent candidates and representatives of a local party. The only major competitor of the SKNALP in all three islands was the People's Action Movement (PAM), a party with bourgeois tendencies founded before the 1966 elections, and the party was only able to maintain this success during its initial years.

In 1967, Saint Christopher, Nevis, and Anguilla were awarded the Associated Statehood, and were granted internal self-government. In the same year, Bradshaw's government was the target of a failed coup, which is alleged to have been carried out by secessionist groups from Anguilla.

At the same time as the secessionist struggles in Anguilla began, the Nevis Reformation Party (NRP) was formed in Nevis, before the 1971 elections, as an attempt to defend the island's autonomy. From 1971 onwards, Anguilla no longer took part in parliamentary elections. However, the SKNALP's government insisted on maintaining the territorial limits of the colonial period, which entailed the political-administrative unity of the three islands. The distribution of the constituencies also remained, even in the 1980 elections (Saint Christopher: seven; Nevis: two; Anguilla: one) though Anguilla's parliamentary seat was left vacant.

The 1980 elections brought about the first change in government since 1952. The death of the long-time SKNALP leader Bradshaw in 1978, and the weakness of his successors Southwell and Lee Moore, were considered to be possible reasons for the party's loss of influence. However, the main cause was that the party was no longer seen as being important. This was due to the decline in the sugar industry, which was triggered by the falling world market prices. Moreover, the sugar nationalisation in 1975 only worsened the grave problems of this industrial sector, and contributed to an even greater decline in the government's popularity.

On 19 December 1980, during Prime Minister Kennedy Simmonds' coalition government (PAM-NRP), Anguilla's secession from Saint Kitts and Nevis (which had existed de facto since 1971) was officially recognized. On 19 September 1983 Saint Christopher and Nevis was granted national independence by the British government. A constitutional monarchy with Westminster-style parliament was established. The Queen of England continued as the head of state and the governor general was her representative in the country.

Having ruled the country for almost 15 years, the coalition of the PAM and the NRP was defeated in the premature elections of 1995, which had become necessary after the regular elections in 1993 had produced a political stalemate situation, leaving no party with a majority, in a country where conditions were becoming increasingly unstable. Civil unrest rose and a three-week state of emergency was declared, after the governor general had asked PAM leader Simmonds to form a minority government (together with the NRP, the coalition won five out of eleven seats).

The SKNLP was returned to power in the 1995 elections, winning seven out of eight constituencies in St. Christopher. Denzil Douglas, leader of the party, became the new prime minister. The clear defeat of Simmonds, who even lost his seat in parliament, was due less to the country's economic difficulties and more to the fact that the opposition revealed the government's links to drug traffickers.

A year after the five deputies in the local assembly of Nevis had voted unanimously for secession from St. Christopher on 10 August 1998, a referendum to secede the federation from St. Christopher was held in Nevis. The twin-island federation barely survived, as the two-thirds majority, required by the constitution for secession, was only missed by a small margin (votes for secession: 61.7%, required: 66.7%).

The premature elections in 2000 confirmed Mr. Douglas' position in office. While the SKNLP was able to win all eight constituencies in St. Christopher, PAM, the party that had previously served for fifteen years, was not able to win even one constituency in the first past the post system, even though it won almost one-third of the votes. Consequently, PAM was not represented in the parliament for the first time since national independence.

The fact that the PAM and the SKNLP still did not contest any constituencies in Nevis and the NRP and the Concerned Citizen Movement (CCM) did not contest any constituencies in St. Christopher, meant that the exclusive regional character of the parties was maintained up to the most recent elections.

1.2 Evolution of Electoral Provisions

The constitution of 1967 introduced reforms that replaced the legislative council with a one-chamber national assembly. It was made up of directly elected representatives and senators who were appointed by the governor general.

There has been universal, equal, secret, and direct suffrage since the 1952 legislative elections. In the run up to the 1984 elections the minimum age for active suffrage in parliamentary elections was reduced from 21 to 18 years. A few years later, in 1989, the minimum age for passive suffrage was reduced from 25 to 21 years.

As to the electoral system, the plurality system in single-member constituencies was applied in 1952. Before the 1985 elections the number of constituencies was raised from ten (Saint Christopher: seven; Nevis: two; Anguilla: one) to eleven (Saint Christopher: eight; Nevis: three).

1.3 Current Electoral Provisions

Sources: The 1984 Constitution contains the fundamental electoral principles. The individual provisions are recorded in detail in the Electoral Act.

Suffrage: The principles of universal, equal, secret, and direct suffrage are applied. Every citizen of St. Christopher and Nevis, who has lived in the country for at least one year, and who is at least 18 years old, is entitled to vote. Voting is not compulsory. Voters can register throughout the year.

Elected national institutions: There is a one-chamber legislature (the national assembly) made up of eleven representatives, who are directly elected, and three senators appointed by the British governor general (two on the advice of the prime minister and one on the advice of the opposition leader).

The term of office is five years. The prime minister can set an earlier date for the elections by dissolving parliament. In case of vacant parliamentary seats, by-elections are held within 90 days.

Nomination of candidates: Every citizen of Saint Kitts-Nevis of at least 21 years of age, with civil rights in the country and residing there at the time of the candidates' nomination can be elected. The candidates need the support of at least two voters in their constituency to be able to stand. They also have to make a deposit of a sum equivalent to 55 US$, which is paid back if the candidate is able to obtain one-eighth of the votes cast in the constituency concerned. Among others members of the clergy and persons with an allegiance to a foreign state cannot be elected.

Electoral system: Plurality system in eleven single-member constituencies (Saint Christopher: eight; Nevis: three).

Organizational context of elections: The supervisor of elections and the electoral commission are responsible for managing the electoral process. The supervisor, who is appointed by the governor general, directs the administrative process of the elections and publicizes dates and information to the participating parties and the electors. In his ex officio function as chief registration officer he is responsible for registering eligible voters, and appointing assistant registration officers. The electoral commission consists of three members all appointed by the governor general. The chairman is appointed at the governor general's own discretion, one member is appointed on the advice of the prime minister and the other on the advice of the leader of the opposition. The main function of the electoral commission is to oversee the supervisor of elections.

1.4 Commentary on the Electoral Statistics

The electoral data presented in the following tables were obtained from P. A. M. Emmanuel (1992) and, for the elections since 1980, from the official reports of the supervisor of elections. These data are considered reliable. The percentages have been calculated by the authors. Where no other source is indicated, the demographic data correspond to the evaluations—halfway through the year—of the United Nations Organisation. Any electoral provisions that are not stated in the constitution were taken from secondary sources.

2. Tables

2.1 Dates of National Elections, Referendums, and Coups d'Etat

Year[a]	Presidential elections	Parliamentary elections	Elections for Constitutional Assembly	Referendums	Coups d'état
1952		06/10			
1957		06/11			
1961		16/11			
1966		25/07			
1971		10/05			
1975		01/12			
1980		18/02			
1984		25/07			
1989		21/03			
1993		29/11			
1995		03/07			
2000		06/03			

[a] Data collection starts with the introduction of universal suffrage.

2.2 Electoral Body 1952–2000

Year	Type of election[a]	Population[b]	Registered voters Total number	% pop.	Votes cast Total number	% reg. voters	% pop.
1952	Pa	47,000	—	—	13,267	—	28.2
1957	Pa	51,000	—	—	—	—	—
1961	Pa	51,000	18,310	35.9	—	—	—
1966	Pa	48,000	20,121	41.9	14,135	70.2	29.4
1971	Pa	46,000	17,202	37.4	15,113	87.9	32.9
1975	Pa	48,000	17,685	36.8	12,740	72.0	26.5
1980	Pa	44,404	19,921	44.7	14,850	74.5	33.4
1984	Pa	46,000	23,328	50.7	18,135	77.7	39.4
1989	Pa	44,000	26,481	60.2	17,682	66.8	40.2
1993	Pa	42,000	28,987	69.0	19,256	66.4	45.8
1995	Pa	41,000	31,726	77.4	21,690	68.4	52.9
2000	Pa	41,000	34,166	83.3	21,949	64.2	53.5

[a] Pa = Parliament.
[b] Population data are based on UN estimates. Censuses were held in 1980: 44,404 and 1991: 40,618.

2.3 Abbreviations

CCM	Concerned Citizens' Movement
KWMB	Kelsick and Wilkin Monopoly Breakers
NRP	Nevis Reformation Party
PAM	People's Action Movement
PDM	People's Democratic Movement
PLP	Progressive Liberal Party
PPM	People's Political Movement
SKDP	St. Kitts Democratic Party
SKNLP	St. Kitts and Nevis Labour Party
UNM	United National Movement
UPP	United People's Party

2.4 Electoral Participation of Parties and Alliances 1952–2000

Party / Alliance	Years	Elections contested[a]
SKNLP	1952–2000	12
SKDP	1957	1
PPM	1961	1
UNM	1961–1971	3
PAM	1966–2000	9
NRP	1971–2000	2
KWMB	1984–1989	2
CCM	1989–2000	4
PDM	1989	1
PLP	1989	1
UPP	1993–1995	3

[a] Total number: 12.

2.5 Referendums

Referendums have not been held.

2.6. Elections for Constitutional Assembly

Elections for constitutional assembly have not been held.

2.7 Parliamentary Elections 1952–2000

Year	1952 Total number	%	1957 Total number	%[a]
Registered voters	—	–	—	–
Votes cast	13,267	—	—	—
Invalid votes	261	2.0	—	—
Valid votes	13,006	98.0	9,833[a]	—
SKNLP	11,016	84.7	5,270	53.6
SKDP	–	–	905	9.2
Independents	1,990	15.3	3,658	37.2

[a] Calculated by the author.

Year	1961 Total number	%	1966 Total number	%
Registered voters	18,310	–	20,121	–
Votes cast	—	—	14,135	70.2
Invalid votes	—	—	30	0.2
Valid votes	12,109	—	14,105	99.8
SKNLP	7,808	64.5	6,249	44.3
PPM	1,346	11.1	–	–
UNM	876	7.3	834	5.9
PAM	–	–	4,936	35.0
Independents	2,079	17.2	2,086	14.8

Year	1971 Total number	%	1975 Total number	%
Registered voters	17,202	–	17,685	–
Votes cast	15,113	87.9	12,740	72.0
Invalid votes	526	3.5	502	3.9
Valid votes	14,587	96.5	12,238	96.1
SKNLP	7,416	50.8	7,363	60.2
PAM	5,397	37.0	2,859	23.4
NRP	1,127	7.7	1,987	16.2
UNM	647	4.4	–	–
Independents	–	–	29	0.2

Year	1980			1984		
	Total number	%		Total number	%	
Registered voters	19,921	–		23,328	–	
Votes cast	14,850	74.6		18,135	77.7	
Invalid votes	143	1.0		70	0.4	
Valid votes	14,707	99.0		18,065	99.6	
SKNLP	7,355	50.0		7,463	41.3	
PAM	4,990	33.9		8,596	47.6	
NRP	2,356	16.0		1,830	10.1	
PLP	–	–		144	0.8	
Others[a]	–	–		32	0.2	
Independents	6	0.0		–	–	

[a] Others include for 1984: KWMB.

Year	1989			1993		
	Total number	%		Total number	%	
Registered voters	26,481	–		28,987	–	
Votes cast	–[a]	–		19,256	64.4	
Invalid votes	—	—		55	0.3	
Valid votes	17,831	—		19,201	99.7	
SKNLP	6,642	37.3		8,405	43.8	
PAM	8,090	45.4		6,449	33.6	
NRP	1,948	10.9		1,641	8.5	
CCM	1,135	6.4		2,100	10.9	
UPP	–	–		605	3.1	
Others[b]	16	0.1		–	–	
Independent	–	–		1	0.0	

[a] IDEA estimate: 17,682.
[b] Others include for 1989: PLP: 12 votes (0.1%); KWMB: 4 (0.0%).

Year	1995			2000		
	Total number	%		Total number	%	
Registered voters	31,726	–		34,166	–	
Votes cast	21,690	68.4		21,949	64.2	
Invalid votes[a]	126	0.6		108	0.5	
Valid votes	21,564	99.4		21,841	99.5	
SKNLP	10,662	49.2		11,762	53.6	
PAM	7,530	34.7		6,462	29.6	
CCM	1,777	8.2		1,901	8.7	
NRP	1,521	7.0		1,710	7.8	
Others[b]	71	0.3		–	–	
Independent	3	0.0		–	–	

[a] Number of invalid votes was calculated by the authors.
[b] Others include for the 1995 election: UPP.

2.8 Composition of Parliament 1952–2000

Year	1952		1957		1961		1966	
	Seats	%	Seats	%	Seats	%	Seats	%
	8	100.0	8	100.0	10	100.0	10	100.0
SKNLP	8	100.0	5	62.5	7	70.0	7	70.0
UNM	–	–	–	–	2	20.0	1	10.0
PAM	–	–	–	–	–	–	2	20.0
Independents	0	0.0	3	37.5	1	10.0	0	0.0

Year	1971		1975		1980		1984	
	Seats[a]		Seats		Seats	%	Seats	%
	9	100.0	9	100.0	9	100.0	11	100.0
SKNLP	7	77.8	7	77.8	4	44.4	2	18.2
NRP	1	11.1	–	–	2	22.2	3	27.3
PAM	1	11.1	2	22.2	3	33.3	6	54.6
CCM	–	–	–	–	–	–	–	–

[a] The number of seats refers to the elected members of Parliament; the others are designated.

Year	1989		1993		1995		2000	
	Seats[a]	%	Seats	%	Seats	%	Seats	%
	11	100.0	11	100.0	11	100.0	11	100.0
PAM	6	54.6	4	36.4	1	9.1	0	0.0
NRP	2	18.2	1	9.1	1	9.1	1	7.7
SKNLP	2	18.2	4	36.4	7	63.6	8	61.5
CCM	1	9.1	2	18.2	2	18.2	2	15.4

[a] The number of seats refers to the elected members of Parliament; the others are designated.

2.10 List of Power Holders 1980–2004

Head of State	Years	Remarks
Queen Elizabeth II	1983–	Represented by governors general: Sir Clement Arrindell (19/09/1983–31/12/1995) and Sir Cuthbert Montroville Sebastian (01/01/1996–).

Head of Government	Years	Remarks
Kennedy Simmonds	1983–1995	Simmonds won the 1980 election and assumed office on 21/02/1980; he became first prime minister of St. Christopher and Nevis after the country reached independence on 19/09/1983. He was re-elected in 1984. 1989, and 1993. Electoral defeat in 1995.
Denzil Douglas	1995–	Douglas had won the premature elections in 1995 and assumed office on 04/07/1995. He was re-elected in 2000.

3. Bibliography

3.1 Official Sources

Supervisor of Elections (1980). *Report on the General Elections 1980*. Basseterre (St. Christopher and Nevis).
— (1984). *Report on the General Elections 1984*. Basseterre (St. Christopher and Nevis).
— (1989). *Report on the General Elections 1989*. Basseterre (St. Christopher and Nevis).
— (1993). *Report on the General Elections 1993*. Basseterre (St. Christopher and Nevis).
— (1995). *Report on the General Elections 1995*. Basseterre (St. Christopher and Nevis).
— (2000). *Report on the General Elections 2000*. Basseterre (St. Christopher and Nevis).

3.2 Books, Articles, and Electoral Reports

Alexis, F. R. (1984). *Changing Caribbean Constitutions*. Bridgetown (Barbados): Antilles Publications.

Bai, D. (1981). 'Nationalization of the St. Kitts Sugar Industry and the Demise of the Labour Party'. *Canadian Journal of Anthropology* (Edmonton/Alberta), 2: 55–60.

Buchanan, I. and Tapley Seaton, J. W. (2001). 'A historical Analysis of the Union of St. Kitts and Nevis'. *The Parliamentarian*, 82: 379–384.

Emmanuel, P. A. M. (1979). *General Elections in the Eastern Caribbean. A Handbook*. Cave Hill (Barbados): University of the West Indies.

Hillebrands, B. (1993). 'Probleme bei der Bewältigung eines schwierigen Ergebnisses. Die Parlamentswahlen in St. Kitts (Christopher) and Nevis vom 29.11.1993'. *Lateinamerika. Analysen-Daten-Dokumentation*, 25/26: 151–153.

IDEA (ed.) (2002). *Voter Turnout Since 1945. A Global Report*. Stockholm.

Inter-Parliamentary Union (various years). *Chronicle of Parliamentary Elections and Developments*. Geneva: IPU.

Kunsman Jr., C. H. (1963). *The Origins and Development of Political Parties in the British West Indies*. Ph.D. thesis, Berkeley, Calif.: University of California.

Midgett, D. (1983). 'Eastern Caribbean Elections, 1950–1982: Antigua, Dominica, Grenada, St. Kitts–Nevis, St. Lucia, and St. Vincent'. *Development Series* (Iowa-City), 13.

SAINT LUCIA
by Bernd Hillebrands and Dieter Nohlen

1. Introduction

1.1 Historical Overview

Saint Lucia, a former British Crown Colony (since 1814), became independent on 22 February 1979. The road to representative government began in 1924, when the British colonial authorities conceded the election of three elected members (out of 13) to the legislative council, which had been established as early as 1832. To vote or to be elected depended on strict property or income qualifications, which were reduced somewhat in 1936, when the number of elected members rose to five (out of twelve). The number of voters was extremely low, both in relation to the total population and in comparison with the other countries in the region. The majority of the population was excluded from political participation due to their insufficient command of English (the official language). This was due to the fact that under the long period of French occupation (1651 to 1814) the language spoken in the island was patois, a Creole French. During the following decades, popular pressure for wider participation grew continually, particularly since the labor movement provided by middle-class people succeeded in establishing labor unions—the Saint Lucia Workers Union (SLWU) in particular. This union, formed in 1939 and legally recognized in 1940, raised the civic awareness of the workers and their desire for full political rights. During the 1940s several union leaders were elected as independent candidates to the legislative council.

The influence of independent politicians decreased throughout the 1950s. They were replaced by the St. Lucia Labour Party (SLP), founded in 1949, and the People's Progressive Party (PPP), founded in 1950. The former enjoyed the backing of the St. Lucia Workers Cooperative Union (SLWCU), the fundamental trade union of the urban elites. The importance of political parties increased even further when universal suffrage was introduced in 1951 and the number of elected members in the legislative council was first increased to a majority and, at the end of the decade, extended to all but three of its members. At this time, the cabinet form of government was established. Members of the legislative council could exercise executive functions. The chief minister was chosen by the British Administrator of the island taking into account the minister's ability to achieve a majority in the legislative council. This body had the function of a speaker, a function previously exercized by the British Administrator.

In 1958, Saint Lucia joined the British West Indies Federation as it was founded. Previously, it had been administered by the governor of the Leeward Islands Federation. The British West Indies Federation was intended to be a territorial for economic and political affairs, with a joint government, legislature and supreme court, independent of Great Britain. However, it failed and the British government formally dissolved it in May 1962. When a smaller federation, known as the Little Eight, also collapsed in March 1967, Saint Lucia became one of the West Indies Associated States (until 1979) with full internal self-government, while external affairs and defense responsibilities were left to the United Kingdom. The legislative council was replaced by a house of assembly, the administrator became the governor and the chief minister became prime minister.

In the 1957 elections, the SLP defeated the PPP for the first time, by seven seats to one. The SLWCU made this victory possible by mobilizing the population in favor of the SLP through its fight for the improvement of the salaries of sugar plantation workers. At the end of 1961 a group split from the SLP as a result of internal personalist power conflicts, and founded the National Labour Movement (NLM). In the elections held in April 1961, the SLP gained a majority of nine seats. The remaining seat went to the PPP. The victory was divided between the SLP and the NLM, with six and three seats, respectively.

The SLP's attempt to bring the banana production (which had, in the meantime, generally substituted sugar production) under state control contributed to its losing the majority in parliament. Shortly before the early elections of June 1964, the PPP and the NLP allied under the United Workers Party (UWP). The UWP achieved a landslide victory and remained in power until the elections of December 1979. Its leader was John Compton, whose electoral campaign of 1974 was based on his policy of independence for the island. He became the first prime minister after independence, on 22 February 1979, when the new constitution of 20 December 1978 came into effect.

This new constitution established a political system resembling the the Westminster Model: a governor general, a citizen appointed by the

British monarch as his or her representative in Saint Lucia, and a bicameral parliament, consisting of His or Her Majesty, a senate and a house of assembly (cf. Art. 23). The governor general is expected to be politically neutral. He or she appoints the prime minister, but must appoint a member of the house of assembly who appears to him or her likely to command the support of the majority of the members of the house (cf. Art. 60 (2)). He or she can remove the prime minister from office if a resolution of no-confidence is passed by the house and the prime minister does not either resign from his office or advise the governor general to dissolve parliament within three days (cf. Art. 60 (6)).

In 1979, a few months after Saint Lucia declared independence, new elections were held. For this occasion, a new electoral roll was drawn up and the number of voters rose by approximately 70% compared to the 1975 elections. Although the UWP gained 46.5% of the vote, it only won five of the 17 seats in the house of assembly. The SLP won the election, but its government, under Prime Minister Allan Louisly, was marked by political instability. Causes of this instability were the internal power struggles for the party's leadership and the ideological differences between its right and left sections. After two years, the party removed the moderate Allan Louisly from office when a vote of no-confidence was passed against him in June 1981. George Odlum, the leader of the radical faction, separated from the SLP and founded the Progressive Labour Party (PLP). Louisly was replaced by Winston Cenac, but his government collapsed in January 1982. Michael Pilgrim, deputy leader of the PLP, succeeded him as interim prime minister for the next five months in order to bring about general elections, which were held in May 1982. The differences among the various wings of the SLP persisted even after the party lost power in 1982.

Compton's UWP won the elections in 1982 with 56.2% of the vote, gaining 14 out of 17 seats. Taking into account the context of socialist trends in the English-speaking region of the Caribbean, this victory was considered a triumph for the conservative forces. However, the stance of the UWP, also backed by the unions, did not differ significantly in its economic and political aspects from that of the SLP. In regard to foreign and defence policies, however, the differences were indeed marked. Thus, Prime Minister Compton, in contrast to the SLP, approved the 1983 North-American invasion of Grenada, and in 1985 allowed US troops together with those of other Caribbean states to conduct joint military manoeuvres in Saint Lucia.

In the elections held on 6 April 1987, the UWP only achieved a majority of one vote over the SLP: Prime Minister Compton's immediate reaction was to dissolve parliament and to call for new elections with the aim of achieving a larger majority, but the result was confirmed in the next poll, on 30 April 1987. Finally, in June 1987 Compton's government saw its situation improve, when the former SLP leader and prime minister Cenac decided to co-operate with the government, being appointed foreign minister. The UWP majority rose to three seats. In the 1992 elections, Compton's party gained an overwhelming majority of seats.

In the elections of 23 May 1997, the balance of power altered dramatically, attributed mainly to the new political leadership in both parties and the SLP's strategy, designed by its new leader Kenny Anthony, to unite all opposition parties—particularly the Citizens' Democratic Party (CDP)—and opposition leaders—George Odlum in particular—against the traditionally dominating UWP, which had won all the elections over the past 30 years. As the former government party failed to gain more than one seat, the most striking result was the transformation of the house of assembly into basically a one-party parliament. In the elections of 3 December 2001, the SLP was able to defend its leading position.

Saint Lucia has an almost perfect two-party system. It came into existence before the introduction of universal suffrage. Since then, in 14 elections, the UWP and the SLP have won seven elections each. The winning party always obtained a share of more than half of the votes, so that all absolute parliamentary majorities were earned majorities. Usually, disproportionality between the shares of votes and seats was high, except for the results in 1987, when there was an exact correspondence of percentages of votes and seats in both elections held in that year. On two occasions the opposition party was reduced to only one seat. Three-party elections are rare. Since 1951, there has only been one election (1982) in which a third party (PLP) obtained a seat. Furthermore, in the elections of 1997 the SLP alliance was an important factor in the strategy of the winning party. Another remarkable electoral feature is the fact that the leadership of the opposition depends on the capability of that person to win a constituency. In 2001, the leader of the UWP, Morella Joseph, failed to win a seat, so that Marius Wilson became the leader of the parliamentary opposition.

1.2 Evolution of Electoral Provisions

The electoral provisions are marked by an extraordinary stability in the context of an emerging parliamentary democracy. This process of democratization was concluded with the constitution of 1978. It provided for a bicameral parliament, made up of the house of assembly, directly elected for a five-year term, and an eleven-member senate (two members appointed by the governor general on his or her own judgement, six in accordance with the advice from the prime minister and three in accordance with the advice of the opposition leader). The salient features of this process are detailed in section 1.1.

Universal, equal, secret, and direct suffrage was introduced for the 1951 elections. The constitution of 1978 established the minimum age for voting at 21 years but opened the way for parliament to lower this required age, although to no lower than 18 years (cf. Art. 33 (2c)). Before the 1984 elections to the house of assembly, the voting age was reduced to 18 years. Every citizen, in accordance with some qualifications relating to residence or domicile in Saint Lucia, is entitled to be registered as a voter. The constitution of 1978 listed the following qualifications to be elected: a candidate must be a citizen 21 years or older, born in Saint Lucia and resident there at the date of his or her nomination or, having been born elsewhere, to have been resident there for a period of twelve months immediately before the date; and able to speak the English language with a degree of proficiency sufficient to be able to take an active part in the proceedings in the house.

Parliamentary elections were based on the plurality system in single member constituencies. The number of constituencies was originally eight, before being raised to ten in 1961, and to 17 in 1974. No major changes have been made to St. Lucia's Electoral Law since 1978.

1.3 Current Electoral Provisions

Sources: The 1979 Constitution contains the fundamental electoral principles. The Electoral Act details the specific provisions.

Suffrage: The principles of universal, equal, secret, and direct suffrage are applied. Every Commonwealth member over 18 who is a citizen of Saint Lucia is entitled to vote. Voting is not compulsory. Voters can register throughout the year. Police officers vote separately, a few days before the elections are held.

Every Saint Lucian citizen over 21, born in the country and resident there when candidates are nominated, is entitled to be elected.

Elected national institutions: There is a two-chamber legislature, consisting of the house of assembly and the senate, but only the house of assembly with 17 members is directly elected. The senate comprises eleven members appointed by the British governor general: six are appointed on the advice of the prime minister, three on the advice of the opposition leader, and two in consultation with civic and religious organizations. The parliamentary term of office is five years. The prime minister can bring forward the date established for the elections by dissolving parliament. By-elections are held to fill any vacant parliamentary seats.

Nomination of candidates: An adequate command of the English language and the support of six voters are essential prerequisites in order to stand as a candidate. A monetary deposit is also compulsory, and this is retained unless the candidate wins one-eighth of the votes cast in one constituency. The clergy, among other groups, are not entitled to passive suffrage.

Electoral system: Plurality system in single-member constituencies. There are 17 constituencies. All constituencies must contain an approximately equal number of inhabitants subject to the Constituency Bounderies Commission judgement in as far as practicability allow. The commission may depart from this principle as it considers expedient in order to take into account the following facts: a) the density of population, and in particular the need to ensure the adequate representation of sparsely-populated rural areas; b) the means of communication; c) geographical features; and d) the boundaries of administrative areas.

Organizational context of elections: The Supervisor of Elections and the Electoral Commission are responsible for managing the electoral process. The Supervisor, who is appointed by the governor general, organizes the administrative processes of the elections and publishes dates and information to the competing parties and the electors. In his or her ex officio function as chief registration officer he or she is responsible for registering eligible voters, and appointing assistant registration officers. The Electoral Commission consists of three members appointed by the governor general. The chairman is appointed at the governor general's own discretion, one member is appointed on the advice of the prime minister and the other on the advice of the leader of the opposition. The main function of the Electoral Commission is to oversee the Supervisor of Elections.

1.4 Commentary on the Electoral Statistics

The electoral data presented in the following tables were taken from the official reports of the Supervisor of Elections for the years 1979–2001. These data are considered reliable. For the parliamentary elections from 1951 to 1974, secondary sources were consulted. The percentages have been calculated by the author. Where no other source is specified, the demographic data correspond to the mid-year evaluations of the United Nations Organisation. The electoral provisions that do not appear in the constitution were taken from secondary sources.

588 *Saint Lucia*

2. Tables

2.1 Dates of National Elections, Referendums, and Coups d'Etat

Year[a]	Presidential elections	Parliamentary elections Lower Chamber	Upper Chamber	Elections. for Constit. Assembly	Referen- dums	Coups d'état
1951		12/10				
1954		23/09				
1957		18/09				
1961		14/04				
1964		25/06				
1969		25/04				
1974		07/05				
1979		02/07				
1982		03/05				
1987		06/04				
1987		30/04				
1992		27/04				
1997		23/05				
2001		03/12				

[a] Data collection starts with the introduction of universal suffrage.

2.2 Electoral Body 1951–2001

Year	Type of election[a]	Population[b]	Registered voters Total number	% pop.	Votes cast Total number	% reg. voters	% pop.
1951	Pa	71,000	28,398	40.0	16,786	59.1	23.6
1954	Pa	75,000	34,452	45.9	17,006	49.4	22.7
1957	Pa	80,000	39,147	48.9	22,244	56.8	27.8
1961	Pa	86,500	—	—	19,362	—	22.4
1964	Pa	92,000	37,748	41.0	19,601	51.9	21.3
1969	Pa	100,000	44,868	44.9	23,892	53.3	23.9
1974	Pa	107,000	39,815[c]	37.2[c]	33,498[c]	84.1[c]	31.3[c]
1979	Pa	115,153	67,917	59.0	46,191	68.0	40.1
1982	Pa	123,000	75,343	61.3	50,384	66.9	40.3
1987	Pa	131,000	83,153	63.5	50,511	60.8	38.6
1987	Pa	131,000	83,257	63.6	53,883	64.7	41.1
1992	Pa	151,000[d]	97,403	64.5	61,154	62.8	39.2
1997	Pa	151,700	111,330	73.4	73,535	66.7	48.5
2001	Pa	163,300	119,844	73.4	62,655	52.3	38.4

[a] Pa=Parliament.
[b] In 1980, a population census took place.
[c] Preliminary electoral results.
[d] 1990.

2.3 Abbreviations

CDP	Citizens' Democratic Party
NA	National Alliance
NFP	National Freedom Party
NLM	National Labour Movement
PLP	Progressive Labour Party
PPP	People's Progressive Party
SLAM	Saint Lucia Labour Action Movement
SLP	St. Lucia Labour Party
UWP	United Workers Party

2.4 Electoral Participation of Parties and Alliances 1951–2001

Party / Alliance	Years[a]	Elections contested
PPP	1951–1961; 1992	5
SLP	1951–2001	14
UWP	1964–2001	10
PLP	1982–1987	3
NA	2001	1
NFP	2001	1

[a] Beginning with the first election after the introduction of universal suffrage. From 1951 to 1974, elections before independence (22/02/1979).

2.5 Referendums

Referendums have not been held.

2.6 Elections for Constitutional Assemblies

Elections for constitutional assemblies have not been held.

2.7 Parliamentary Elections 1951–2001

Year	1951		1954	
	Total number	%	Total number	%
Registered voters	28,398	–	34,452	–
Votes cast	16,786	59.1	17,006	49.4
Invalid votes	1,360	8.1	1,275	7.5
Valid votes	15,426	91.9	15,731	92.5
SLP	7,648	49.6	7,462	47.4
Others[a]	7,778	50.4	8,269	52.6

[a] PPP and Independents.

Year	1957		1961	
	Total number	%	Total number	%
Registered voters	39,147	–	—	–
Votes cast	22,244	56.8	19,362	—
Invalid votes	662	3.0	—	—
Valid votes	21,582	97.0	19,362	100.0
SLP	14,345	66.5	11,898	61.5
Others[a]	7,237	33.5	7,464	38.5

[a] PPP and Independents.

Year	1964		1969	
	Total number	%	Total number	%
Registered voters	37,748	–	44,868	–
Votes cast	19,601	51.9	23,892	53.2
Invalid votes	933	4.8	950	4.0
Valid votes	18,668	95.2	22,942	96.0
UWP	9,615	51.5	13,328	58.1
SLP	5,617	30.1	8,271	36.1
Others	3,436	18.4	1,343	5.9

Year	1974[a]		1979	
	Total number	%	Total number	%
Registered voters	39,815	–	67,917	–
Votes cast	33,498	84.1	46,191	68.0
Invalid votes	1,081	3.2	1,191	2.6
Valid votes	32,417	96.8	45,000	97.4
UWP	17,300	53.4	19,706	43.8
SLP	14,554	44.5	25,294	56.2
Independents	650	2.0	–	–

[a] Preliminary results. Source: Chief Elections Officer, 2002.

Year	1982			1987	
	Total number	%		Total number	%
Registered voters	75,343	–		83,153	–
Votes cast	50,384	66.9		50,511	60.8
Invalid votes	1,083	2.2		1,158	2.3
Valid votes	48,507	97.8		49,353	97.7
UWP	27,252	56.2		25,892	52.5
SLP	8,122	16.7		18,889	38.3
PLP	13,133	27.1		4,572	9.3

Year	1987			1992	
	Total number	%		Total number	%
Registered Voters	83,257	–		97,403	–
Votes cast	53,883	64.7		61,155	—
Invalid votes	1,146	2.1		1,931	—
Valid votes	52,737	97.9		59,224	—
UWP	28,046	53.2		33,562	56.7
SLP	21,515	40.8		25,565	43.2
PLP	3,176	6.0		–	–
PPP	–	–		97	0.2

Year	1997			2001	
	Total number	%		Total number	%
Registered Voters	111,330	–		119,844	–
Votes cast	73,535	66.1		62,655	52.3
Invalid votes	1,563	2.1		1,650	2.6
Valid votes	71,972	97.9		61,005	97.4
UWP	26,325	36.6		23,095	37.9
SLP	44,153	61.3		34,142	56.0
NA	–	–		2,240	3.7
Others[a]	1,494	2.1		1,528	2.5

[a] Includes NFP and others.

2.8 Composition of Parliament

Lower Chamber (House of Assembly) 1974–2001

Year	1951		1954		1957		1961	
	Seats	%	Seats	%	Seats	%	Seats	%
	8	100.0	8	100.0	8	100.0	10	100.0
SLP	5	62.5	5	62.5	7	87.5	9	90.0
Others[a]	3	37.5	3	37.5	1	12.5	1	10.0

[a] PPP and Independents.

Year	1964		1969		1974		1979	
	Seats	%	Seats	%	Seats	%	Seats	%
	10	100.0	10	100.0	17	100.0	17	100.0
UWP	6	60.0	6	60.0	10	58.8	5	29.4
SLP	2	20.0	3	30.0	7	41.2	12	70.6
Others	2	20.0	1	10.0	–	–	–	–

Year	1982		1987		1992		1997	
	Seats	%	Seats	%	Seats	%	Seats	%
	17	100.0	17	100.0	17	100.0	17	100.0
UWP	14	82.4	9	52.9	11	64.7	3	17.6
SLP	2	11.8	8	47.1	6	35.3	14	82.4
PLP	1	5.9	–	–	–	–	–	–

Year	2001	
	Seats	%
	17	100.0
UWP	3	17.6
SLP	14	82.4

2.9 Presidential Elections

Presidential elections have not been held.

2.10 List of Power Holders 1974–2004

Head of State	Years	Remarks
Queen Elizabeth II	1979–	Represented by governors general: Sir Allen Montgomery Lewis (from 22/02/1979 to 19/06/1980, first time); Boswell Williams (from 19/06/1980 to 13/12/1982, acting to 1981); Sir Allen Montgomery Lewis (from 13/12/1982 to 30/04/1987, second time); Vincent Floissac (from 30/04/1987 to 10/10/1988); Sir Stanislaus A. James (from 10/10/1988 to 01/06/1996); Sir George Mallet (from 01/06/1996 to 17/09/1997); Dame Pearlette Louisy (from 17/09/1997, acting).

Head of Government	Years	Remarks
John George Melvin Compton	1974–1979	UWP; held office from 06/05/1974 to 02/07/1979 (first time).
Allan Louisy	1979–1981	UWP; held office from 02/07/1979 to 30/04/1981.
Winston Cenac	1981–1982	UWP; replaced the elected prime minister on 30/04/1981. Stayed in office until 16/01/1982.
Michael Pilgrim	1982	PLP; interim prime minister from 16/01 to 03/05.
John George Melvin Compton	1982–1996	UWP; assumed office on 03/05/1982. He was re-elected three times and stayed in office until 02/04/1996 (second time).
Vaughan Lewis	1996–1997	UWP; replaced elected prime minister on 02/04/1996 and stayed in office until 23/05/1997.
Kenny Davis Anthony	1997–	SLP; assumed office on 23/05/1997. Re-elected on 03/12/2001.

3. Bibliography

3.1 Official Sources

Chief Elections Officer (1982). *Report on Proceedings leading to and after the General Elections, 1982*. Castries (St. Lucia).

Chief Elections Officer (1987). *Report of the Chief Elections Officer on the General Elections of April 6, 1987*. Castries (St. Lucia).

Chief Elections Officer (1987). *Report of the Chief Elections Officer on the General Elections of April, 30, 1987*. Castries (St. Lucia).

Chief Elections Officer (1992). *The Saint Lucia Report on the General Elections of 27 April 1992*. Castries (St. Lucia).

Chief Elections Officer (1997). *The Saint Lucia Report on the General Elections of 23 May 1997*. Castries (St. Lucia).

Government of Saint Lucia, Electoral Department (2002). *Report on Electoral Results 1979–2001*. Castries (St. Lucia).

Her Majesty's Stationary Office (1978). *The Saint Lucia Constitution Order 1978*. London.

House of Assembly (Elections) *Act, 1979*, No. 8. Laws of St. Lucia.

Office of the Supervisor of Elections (1979). *Report on the General Elections, 1979*. Castries (St. Lucia).

Supervisor of Elections (1954). *Report on the General Election Results, 1954*. Castries (St. Lucia).

Supervisor of Elections (1957). *Report on the Legislative Council General Elections, 1957*. Castries (St. Lucia).
Supervisor of Elections (1964). *Report on the Legislative Council General Elections, 1964*. Castries (St. Lucia).
Supervisor of Elections (1969). *Report on the House of Assembly General Elections, 1969*. Castries (St. Lucia).

3.2 Books, Articles, and Electoral Reports

Alexis, F. R. (1984). *Changing Caribbean Constitutions*. Bridgetown (Barbados): Antilles Publications.
Barrow-Giles, C. (1998). 'The 1997 Vote in St. Lucia: The Beginning of a New Era'. *The Journal of Caribbean History*, 32/1–2: 145–160.
Emmanuel, P. A. M. (1979). *General Elections in the Eastern Caribbean. A Handbook*. Cave Hill (Barbados): University of the West Indies.
— (1992). *Elections and Party Systems in the Commonwealth Caribbean 1944–1991*. Bridgetown: Caribbean Development Services.
— (1994). 'Parties and Electoral Competition in the Anglophone Caribbean, 1944–1991: Challenges to Democratic Theory', in C. J. Edie (ed.), *Democracy in the Caribbean: Myths and Realities*. Westport, Conn.: Praeger, 251–264.
Inter-Parliamentary Union (ed.) (various years). *Chronicle of Parliamentary Elections and Developments*. Geneva: International Centre for Parliamentary Documentation.
Kunsman Jr., C. H. (1963). *The Origins and Development of Political Parties in the British West Indies*. Ph.D. thesis, Berkeley, Calif.: University of California.
Midgett, D. (1983). *Eastern Caribbean Elections, 1950-1982: Antigua, Dominica, Grenada, St. Kitts-Nevis, St. Lucia, and St. Vincent*. Development Series no. 13, Iowa-City, Iowa: University of Iowa.
Ryan, S. (1994). 'Problems and Prospects for the Survival of Liberal Democracy in the Anglophone Caribbean', in C. J. Edie (ed.), *Democracy in the Caribbean: Myths and Realities*. Westport, Conn.: Praeger, 233–250.
Thorndike, T. (1991). 'Politics and Society in the South-Eastern Caribbean', in C. Clarke (ed.), *Society and Politics in the Caribbean*. Oxford: MacMillan, 110–144.
United Nations Population and Vital Statistics Report (various years). *Department of International Economic and Social Affairs*. Statistical Papers, Series A, New York: United Nations.

SAINT VINCENT AND THE GRENADINES

by Bernd Hillebrands and Matthias Trefs

1. Introduction

1.1 Historical Overview

The British colony of St. Vincent and the Grenadines remained under the administration of the governor of the Windward Islands Federation until 1958, when it joined the British West Indies Federation. The latter was founded by ten British insular colonies in order to form a territorial union that was economically and politically independent from Great Britain. However, this federation only lasted until 1962. From 1974 onwards, elections have been held regularly. Since then, independent candidates have not played a significant role. The system has been characterised by a two-party competition with few exceptions. However, only one party has managed to constantly gain seats since 1979.

Following the characteristic constitutional development of the British West Indies in the post-war period, Great Britain allowed the gradual establishment of an autonomous local government in the colony. The 1951 constitutional reform introduced universal suffrage and direct election of the majority of the legislative council members, a measure that restricted the political power of the white planter oligarchy. In 1957, several ministries were created and vested with limited government functions.

From the mid 1930s to the 1950s, the independent candidates, supported by the workers' movement, dominated parliamentary elections. Before the 1951 election, the candidates of the United Workers, Peasants and Ratepayers Union (UWPRU), a trade union founded in 1950, formed an alliance called the Eighth Army of Liberation, that won all eight parliamentary seats. Internal conflicts between the various factions of the Eighth Army led to the creation of the People's Political Party (PPP) in 1952. The PPP was the first lasting nationwide party and maintained close links with the workers' movement.

In 1955, the social democratic St. Vincent Labour Party (SVLP) was created. In the wake of the 1961 election, the SVLP began to take on the role of the opposition party against the PPP that stayed in government from 1957 to 1967 and from 1972 to 1974. The political competition between the PPP and the SVLP determined the country's two-party system from 1961 to 1974. It focused more on their respective leaders than on their ideological differences.

In 1969, the country gained Associated Statehood status, which entitled it to internal self-governance. The state comprised the main island, Saint Vincent, and the seven smaller Grenadine islands (Bequia, Canouan, Mayreau, Mustique, Prune Island, Petit St. Vincent and Union Island). Ten years later, on 27 October 1979, it was recognized as a fully sovereign state and member of the Commonwealth.

In the 1979 election, the SVLP maintained the majority it already had won in 1974. The PPP had stood against the country's independence and, as a consequence, suffered a devastating defeat, resulting in a loss of its political relevance. In 1974, several of its leading members formed an electoral group with Mitchell, which became known as the Mitchell/Sylvester Faction (M/SF) or Junta. The PPP dissolved itself in 1984. The New Democratic Party (NDP), founded in 1975, became the most important opposition party. During the government of Prime Minister R. Milton Cato, the population rose against the government's ineffective and inefficient social and economic policies as well as against the increasing repression of the trade unions and opposition groups that formed the National Committee in Defence of Democracy in 1981.

Shortly before the 1984 elections, the Movement for National Unity (MNU) split from the marxist United People's Movement (UPM), because a majority in the latter refused to depart from Fidel Castro's political guidelines.

After the 1984 parliamentary elections, the NDP led by James F. Mitchell came to power and ended the ten years of the SVLP government under Milton Cato. The SVLP's electoral defeat was attributed both to the corruption scandals that the government was involved in and to the deteriorating national economic situation.

The new Prime Minister Mitchell, who had stood as an independent parliamentarian in 1972 and had then become prime minister of the PPP's government, had distinguished himself as a relevant political figure thanks to his ideas on foreign policy. Mitchell advocated the development of the Organisation of Eastern Caribbean States (OECS), in order to strengthen this union. However, he opposed the militarization of the Caribbean region, the Regional Security Systems (RSS) under the auspices of the USA in particular. His attitude was reinforced by the US intervention in Grenada in 1983.

In the 1989 elections, Mitchell's NDP won all 15 parliamentary seats in an unprecedented landslide victory, while the opposition saw its representation reduced to the two SVLP-appointed senators. Weakened and fragmented, the opposition formed a coalition called the Unity Labour Party (ULP) and was able to gain three seats in the elections of 1994. The next elections in 1998 brought seven seats for the ULP, but the NDP still remained in power.

However, in May 2000, an outbreak of protests against NDP policies led to an agreement brokered by the OECS to call early elections in March 2001. The continued success of the coalition showed in the 12 seats it won in these elections, reducing the number of NDP seats to three. The 2001 elections were the first to be monitored by international observers.

1.2 Evolution of Electoral Provisions

The foundations of a unicameral system were established in Saint Vincent and the Grenadines under British rule. The legislative council, which later became the house of assembly, comprised eight members who were elected directly and six senators who were appointed by the governor general, the national representative of the British monarch. The maximum term of office was five years.

From 1951, elections to the house of assembly were held under universal, equal, secret, and direct suffrage. In 1979, the minimum age for active suffrage was reduced from 21 to 18 years.

Representatives are elected in SMCs according to plurality system. The number of constituencies was increased before each of the following elections: in 1961 it was raised from 8 to 9; in 1972 from 9 to 13 (in both elections the Grenadines consisted of one constituency), and in 1989 to 15 (the Grenadines consisted of two constituencies).

1.3 Current Electoral Provisions

Sources: The 1979 Constitution contains the fundamental electoral principles. The detailed provisions are found in the Representation of the People Act of 1982, No. 7.

Suffrage: Elections to the house of assembly are held under universal, equal, secret, and direct suffrage. Every member of the British Commonwealth, over 18, who has been a resident of Saint Vincent and the Grenadines for the last twelve months prior to the respective elections is entitled to vote. Voting is not compulsory.

Elected national institutions: Saint Vincent and the Grenadines has a unicameral parliament: the house of assembly is composed of 15 directly elected representatives and six senators appointed by the governor general (four on the advice of the prime minister and two on the advice of the opposition leader). The parliamentarian term of office is five years, although the prime minister is entitled to call early elections before the established date by dissolving parliament. However, the dissolution of the parliament can be refused by the governor general.

Nomination of candidates: Every voter over 21 can stand as a candidate. The prerequisites are: a sufficient command of the English language and the support of six voters of his or her constituency. Furthermore, a monetary deposit is required, which will not be returned if the candidate gains less than one-eighth of the total amount of votes cast in his or her constituency. Members of the clergy, the police and the armed forces, among other groups, are not entitled to passive suffrage.

Electoral system: Seats in the house of assembly are allocated according to plurality system in single-member constituencies. In the 2001 elections, there were 15 constituencies (13 in Saint Vincent and two in the Grenadines). By-elections are held to fill any vacant parliamentary seats.

Organizational context of elections: The constitution provides for an independent supervisor of the elections who has to report to the house of representatives. This official is selected and dismissed by the public service commission if the person is a civil servant. Otherwise, the commission has to consult the prime minister beforehand. The supervisor is responsible for administering the elections and fixing the constituency boundaries. The constituencies are reviewed regularly by a commission chaired by the governor general. Of the two remaining members, one is appointed by the prime minister and the other by the leader of the opposition.

1.4 Commentary on the Electoral Statistics

The electoral data presented in the following tables was taken from the official reports of the supervisor of elections for the years 1979–2001. This data is considered reliable. Secondary sources were consulted for parliamentary elections before independence. The percentages have been calculated by the authors. The electoral provisions that do not appear in the constitution were taken from secondary sources.

2. Tables

2.1 Dates of National Elections, Referendums, and Coups d'Etat

Year	Presidential elections	Parliamentary elections	Elections for Constitutional Assembly	Referendums	Coups d'état
1951		xx/xx			
1954		xx/xx			
1957		12/09			
1961		20/04			
1966		22/08			
1967		19/05			
1972		07/04			
1974		09/12			
1979		05/12			
1984		25/07			
1989		16/05			
1994		21/02			
1998		15/06			
2001		28/03			

2.2 Electoral Body 1951–2001

Year	Type of election[a]	Population[b]	Registered voters Total number	% pop.	Votes cast Total number	% reg. voters	% pop.
1951	Pa	69,000	27,409	39.7	19,110	69.2	27.7
1954	Pa	72,000	29,188	40.5	17,465	59.8	24.3
1957	Pa	82,000	30,960	37.8	21,943	70.9	26.8
1961	Pa	82,000	31,086	37.9	23,976	77.1	29.2
1966	Pa	90,000	33,044	36.7	27,787	84.1	30.9
1967	Pa	90,000	33,044	36.7	27,278	82.6	30.3
1972	Pa	100,000	42,707	42.7	32,289	75.6	32.3
1974	Pa	87,305	45,181	51.8	28,574	63.2	32.7
1979	Pa	97,845	52,073	53.2	33,276	63.9	34.0
1984	Pa	101,000	47,863	47.4	42,507	88.8	42.1
1989	Pa	105,000	61,091	58.2	44,218	72.4	42.1
1994	Pa	110,000	71,954	65.4	47,212	65.6	43.0
1998	Pa	111,000	76,469	68.9	51,513	67.4	46.4
2001	Pa	112,000	84,536	75.5	58,498	69.2	52.2

[a] Pa = Parliament.
[b] Censuses were held in 1974 and 1979. The other numbers are based on UN estimates.

2.3 Abbreviations

DFM	Democratic Freedom Movement
M/SF	Mitchell/Sylvester Faction
MNU	Movement for National Unity
NDP	New Democratic Party
PDP	People's Democratic Party
PLM	People's Liberation Movement
PPM	People's Progressive Party
PPP	People's Political Party
PWP	People's Working Party
SVLP	St. Vincent Labour Party
UPM	United People's Movement
WINP	West Indian National Party
ULP	Unity Labour Party

2.4 Electoral Participation of Parties and Alliances 1951–2001

Party / Alliance	Years	Elections contested[a]
Eighth Army	1951	1
PLM	1957	1
DFM	1974	1
M/SF	1974	1
PPP	1954–1979	8
SVLP	1957–1994	10
WINP	1974	1
NDP	1979–2001	6
UPM	1979–1989	3
MNU	1984–1994	3
PDP	1984	1
PWP	1998	1
ULP	1998–2001	2
PPM	2001	1

Total number: 14.

2.5 Referendums

Referendums have not been held.

2.6 Elections for Constitutional Assembly

Elections for a constitutional assembly have not been held.

2.7 Parliamentary Elections 1951–2001

Year	1951		1954	
	Total number	%	Total number	%
Registered voters	27,409	–	29,188	–
Votes cast	19,110	69.7	17,465	59.8
Invalid votes	1,298	6.8	1,825	10.4
Valid votes	17,812	93.2	15,640	89.6
Eighth Army	12,544	70.4	–	–
PPP	–	–	6,301	49.4
Independents	5,268	29.6	9,399	59.7

Year	1957		1961	
	Total number	%	Total number	%
Registered voters	30,960	–	31,086	–
Votes cast	21,943	70.9	23,976	77.1
Invalid votes	2,285	10.4	658	2.7
Valid votes	19,658	89.6	23,318	97.3
PPP	9,702	49.4	11,500	49.2
SVLP	3,741	19.0	11,164	47.9
PLM	2,981	15.2	–	–
Independents	3,324	16.4	654	2.8

Year	1966		1967	
	Total number	%	Total number	%
Registered voters	33,044	–	33,044	–
Votes cast	27,787	84.1	27,278	82.6
Invalid votes	552	2.0	312	1.1
Valid votes	27,235	98.0	26,966	98.9
PPP	13,427	49.0	12,465	46.2
SVLP	13,930	50.9	14,501	53.8
Independents	28	0.1	–	–

Year	1972		1974	
	Total number	%	Total number	%
Registered Voters	42,707	–	45,181	–
Votes cast	32,289	75.6	28,574	63.2
Invalid Votes	344	1.1	215	0.8
Valid Votes	31,945	98.9	28,359	99.2
SVLP	16,108	50.4	19,579	69.0
PPP	14,507	45.4	3,806	13.4
M/SF	–	–	4,641	16.4
DFM	–	–	217	0.8
Others[a]	–	–	116	0.4
Independents	1,330	4.2	–	–

[a] Others include: WINP (116 votes).

Year	1979		1984	
	Total number	%	Total number	%
Registered Voters	52,073	–	47,863	–
Votes cast	33,276	63.9	42,507	88.8
Invalid Votes	321	1.0	299	0.7
Valid Votes	32,955	99.0	42,208	99.3
SVLP	17,876	54.2	17,493	41.5
NDP	9,022	27.4	21,700	51.4
PPP	1,492	4.5	–	–
UPM	4,467	13.6	1,350	3.2
MNU	–	–	855	2.0
PDP	–	–	810	1.9
Independents	98	0.3	–	–

Year	1989		1994	
	Total number	%	Total number	%
Registered Voters	61,091	–	71,954	–
Votes cast	44,218	72.4	47,212	65.6
Invalid Votes	351	0.8	278	0.6
Valid Votes	43,867	99.2	46,934	99.4
NDP	29,079	66.3	25,789	54.9
SVLP	13,290	30.3	12,455	26.5
MNU	1,030	2.4	8,178	17.4
UPM	468	1.1	–	–

Year	1998 Total number	%	2001 Total number	%
Registered voters	76,469	–	84,536	–
Votes cast	51,513	67.4	58,498	69.2
Invalid votes	185	0.4	214	0.4
Valid votes	51,328	99.6	58,284	99.6
ULP	28,025	54.6	32,925	56.5
NDP	23,258	45.3	23,844	40.9
PMP	–	–	1,515	2.6
Others[a]	45	0.1	–	–

[a] Others include: PWP (45 votes).

2.8 Composition of Parliament 1951–2001

Year	1951 Seats 8[a]	% 100.0	1954 Seats 8	% 100.0	1957 Seats 8	% 100.0	1961 Seats 9	% 100.0
Eighth Army	8	100.0	–	–	–	–	–	–
PPP	–	–	3	37.5	5	62.5	6	66.7
SVLP	–	–	–	–	0	0.0	3	33.3
PLM	–	–	–	–	1	12.5	–	–
Independents	0	0.0	5	62.5	2	25.0	0	0.0

[a] The number of seats corresponds to the number of elected members; the other members are nominated.

Year	1966 Seats 9	% 100.0	1967 Seats 9	% 100.0	1972 Seats 13	% 100.0	1974 Seats 13	% 100.0
PPP	5	55.6	3	33.3	6	46.2	2	15.4
SVLP	4	44.4	6	66.7	6	46.2	10	76.9
M/SF	–	–	–	–	–	–	1	7.7
DFM	–	–	–	–	–	–	0	0.0
WINP	–	–	–	–	–	–	0	0.0
Independents	0	0.0	–	–	1	7.7	–	–

Year	1979 Seats 13	% 100.0	1984 Seats 13	% 100.0	1989 Seats 15	% 100.0	1994 Seats 15	% 100.0
SVLP	11	84.6	4	30.8	0	0.0	2	13.3
NDP	2	15.4	9	69.2	15	100.0	12	80.0
PPP	0	0.0	–	–	–	–	–	–
UPM	0	0.0	0	0.0	0	0.0	–	–
MNU	–	–	0	0.0	0	0.0	1	6.7
PDP	–	–	0	0.0	–	–	–	–
Independents	0	0.0	–	–	–	–	–	–

Year	1998		2001	
	Seats	%	Seats	%
	15	100.0	15	100.0
NDP	8	53.3	3	20.0
ULP	7	46.7	12	80.0
PWP	0	0.0	0	0.0
PMP	–	–	0	0.0

2.9 Presidential Elections

Presidential elections have not been held.

2.10 List of Power Holders 1979–2004

Head of State	Years	Remarks
Queen Elizabeth II	1979–	Represented by governors general: Sir Sidney Gun-Munro (1979–1985), Joseph Lambert Eustace (1985–1988), Henry Harvey Williams (1988–1989), Sir David Jack (1989–1996), Sir Charles Antrobus (1996–2002) and Monica Dacon (2002–).

Head of Government	Years	Remarks
Milton Cato	1969–1972	From 27/10/1969 to April 1972.
James Fitz-Allen Mitchell	1972–1974	From April 1972 to 08/12/1974. As an independent candidate, he formed a coalition with the PPP (M/SF) against his old party, the SVLP.
Milton Cato	1974–1984	Second time. From 08/12/1974 to 30/07/1984.
James Fitz-Allen Mitchell	1984–2000	Second time. From 30/07/1984 to 27/10/2000. He relinquished his posts as head of government and party leader to Arnhim Eustace.
Arnhim Eustace	2000–2001	From 27/10/2000 to 29/03/2001. The NDP was defeated in early elections after public protests.
Ralph Gonsalves	2001–	Assumed office on 29/03/2001. After accusations of corruption and cronyism towards Mitchell and his party, the ULP was finally able to end 17 years of NDP government.

3. Bibliography

3.1 Official Sources

The Supervisor of Elections (1980). *Report on the General Elections Held on 5th December, 1979*. Kingstown (St. Vincent & the Grenadines).
The Supervisor of Elections (1986). *Information on the Last General Election – 1984*. Kingstown (St. Vincent & the Grenadines).

3.2 Books, Articles, and Electoral Reports

Alexis, F. R. (1984). *Changing Caribbean Constitutions*. Bridgetown (Barbados): Antilles Publications.
Emmanuel, P. A. M. (1979). *General Elections in the Eastern Caribbean. A Handbook*. Cave Hill (Barbados): University of the West Indies.
— (1992). *Elections and Party Systems in the Commonwealth Caribbean, 1944–1991*. Bridgetown (Barbados): CADRES.
— (1993). *Governance and Democracy in the Commonwealth Caribbean: An Introduction*. Cave Hill (Barbados): ISER.
— (1994). 'Parties and Electoral Competition in the Anglophone Caribbean, 1944–1991: Challenges to Democratic Theory', in Edie, C. J. (ed.), *Democracy in the Caribbean: Myths and Realities*. Westport, Conn.: Praeger, 251–264.
Inter-Parliamentary Union (ed.) (various years). *Chronicle of Parliamentary Elections and Developments*. Geneva: International Centre for Parliamentary Documentation.
Kunsman Jr., C. H. (1963). *The Origins and Development of Political Parties in the British West Indies*. Ph.D. thesis, Berkeley, Calif.: University of California.
Midgett, D. (1983). 'Eastern Caribbean Elections, 1950–1982: Antigua, Dominica, Grenada, St. Kitts–Nevis, St. Lucia, and St. Vincent'. *Development Series* 13, Iowa City: University of Iowa.
Nuscheler, F. (1995). 'St. Vincent und die Grenadinen', in Nohlen, D. and Nuscheler, F. (eds.), *Handbuch der Dritten Welt, Vol. 3: Mittelamerika und Karibik*. Bonn: Dietz, 537–549.
Ryan, S. (1994). 'Problems and Prospects for the Survival of Liberal Democracy in the Anglophone Caribbean', in Edie, C. J. (ed.), *Democracy in the Caribbean: Myths and Realities*. Westport, Conn.: Praeger, 233–250.
The Vincentian, 26 May 1989.
United Nations (various years). 'United Nations Population and Vital Statistics Report: Department of International Economic and Social Affairs', *Statistical Papers, Series A*, New York: United Nations.
United States Department of State (2002). *Background Note on St. Vincent and the Grenadines*. <http://www.state.gov/r/pa/ei/bgn/2345.htm> (as of 07/05/03).

SURINAME

by Philip Stöver[*]

1. Introduction

1.1 Historical Overview

Suriname, the small state lying to the north of Brazil, was colonized by the British in 1652, ceded to the Netherlands 15 years later, and finally became independent in 1975. Since the colony, formerly known as Dutch Guyana, was granted autonomy in internal affairs, the prominent feature of the national politics was ethnicity. To date, internal conflicts between rival groups and continuing economic dependence on foreign aid, prevent political stabilization and development.

The fact that economic activity has traditionally focused on only a few sectors, thus preventing diversification, is one of the main causes of the economic difficulties of Suriname. Under early colonial rule, sugar and tobacco production was predominant. It was only from the Second World War onwards, due to the continuing crisis in the sugar sector, that the main economic activity was reoriented towards the mining, refining, and exportation of bauxite, the basic material for aluminium, to the United States. Agriculture has always been an important contributing factor to the national income, but Suriname has never overcome the dependence on Dutch aid.

The colonial and industrial history of Suriname has resulted in an ethnically-diverse society. According to a population census conducted by the Central Bureau of Statistics in 1993, the population is made up of 34% Creoles, principally descending from African slaves, 33% Hindus, 19% Indonesians, 9% Maroons (the so-called 'Bush Negros'), 3% Amerindian, as well as Chinese, and Europeans. The Maroons are descendants of African slaves who fled from the plantations before the abolition of slavery (1863) in order to establish independent communities in the country's interior. The ancestors of the people of Indian, In-

---

[*] The description of the evolution of electoral provisions and the tables section of this article are based on a contribution by Felix Gallé.

donesian, and Chinese origin largely came to Suriname as indentured laborers replacing African slaves. Immigrants came from Europe and Aisa.

The prospect of autonomy in internal affairs—promised in the early 1940s and fulfilled in 1954 when Suriname was granted internal self-government—incited considerable political activity. Parties and labor organizations were established and most of the parties were organized along ethnic lines. Apart from a few exceptions, such as the Communist Party, parties did not organize along class lines and could not generally be identifed with the organized labor movement, with the exception of the *Nationale Partij Suriname* (NPS; Suriname National Party) or the *Partij Nationalistischhe Republiek* (PNR; Nationalist Republic Party).

Until the late 1960s, the predominant ethnic parties established a system combining ethnic partisanship with a strategy of *verbroedering* (fraternization) among the largest ethnic parties. The coalition between the Creole NPS and the Indian *Verenigde Hindostaanse Partij* (VHP; Progressive Reform Party) marked the longest period of political stability under autonomy. VHP-NPS rule only came to an end when Prime Minister J. Pengel resigned in 1969 due to social unrest. Another Creole party, the *Progressieve Nationale Partij* (PNP; Progressive National Party), formed the new government, and PNP leader J. Sedney became prime minister.

While the system of 'ethnic consociationalism' was in existence, conflicts between and within the hierarchically-organized ethnic parties intensified from the late 1960s, when the reduction of Dutch aid diminished the ressources to be allocated. Patronage and fragmentation became main features of intra and inter-party dynamics. Politically, the issue of independence became more important and played a predominant role in the 1973 general elections. A new NPS-led alliance, the *Nationale Partji Kombinatie* (NPK; Combined National Party), which advocated full national sovereignty, won 22 of 39 seats in the *Staten* (assembly). The VHP had been reluctant to introduce independence, fearing discrimination of the East Indians minority, but finally consented, and an independence constitution was drafted to establish a republican system of parliamentary democracy. Under the NPS leader and Prime Minister H. Arron, Suriname became independent on 25 November 1975.

In the 1970s, however, Suriname was heavily affected by the international oil crisis. Even before the proclamation of independence, thousands of Surinamers migrated to the Netherlands. Unemployment and inflation challenged the consolidation of the new democracy, and the government was beset with charges of corruption. In this context, army officers and liberal and leftist politicians overthrew the Government on 25 February 1980. A state of emergency was declared and the constitution was suspended. A mixed civilian-military government exerted power for two years before the authoritarian regime, led by D. Bouterse, reinforced its repression both against guerrilla resistance (especially the Maroons) and other oppositional forces, and imposed martial law. Consequently, the US and the Netherlands suspended their financial aid to Suriname.

From 1984 onwards, the old ethnic parties—NPS, VHP, and the Indonesian *Kerukanan Tulodo Pranatan Ingil* (KTPI; Party for National Unity and Solidarity)—benefited politically from the enduring economic difficulties, which the internationally isolated regime was unable to overcome. The parties were consulted and this led to an opening of the political scene. In 1985, VHP and KTPI members joined the government supreme council. A nominated national assembly, representing the political organization of the regime, and social and economic interests, drafted a constitution that was adopted by referendum in 1987. According to the new constitution, a president, elected by parliament is head of state, and the vice president serves as prime minister. Both are responsible to parliament. As a result of the negotiated regime change, the military could maintain a strong position and was represented, beside the social partners and the parties, in the governmental advisory council of state.

In November 1987, the first national elections for ten years were held. VHP, NPS, and KTPI allied as the *Front voor Democratie en Ontwikkeling* (FDO; Front for Democracy and Development) and came back to power. The party of the military regime *Nationaal Democratische Partij* (NDP; National Democratic Party) under former dictator Bouterse formed the opposition. Arron became head of the government again. In light of the continuing political instability, the government could neither ensure peace nor enhance the economic situation, the military took power again in December 1990. A general election, called for in May 1991, supervised by the OAS (Organization of American States), was won by the *Nieuw Front* (NF; New Front), including the FDO members and the *Surinaamse Partij van de Arbeid* (SPA; Surinamese Labor Party). However, with only 30 seats from a possible 51, they did not win the two-thirds majority necessary for the election of the president. In this case, the constituion provides for a United People's Assembly (*Vereinigde Volksvergardering*), a body consisting of the members of parliament, 106 district representatives, and 712 local officials. On 6 September 1991, the people's assembly elected R. Venetiaan president.

The re-election of the civil forces allowed them to amend the 1987 Constitution in order to prevent further military interference. Political stability, however, was hard to guarantee. The economic decline and hyperinflation, which were largely due to the authoritarian rule of the 1980s, could only be stopped by implementing the IMF's structural adjustment programs. This, however, led to public discontent and massive protests against the government.

Despite these circumstances, the incumbent NF won the 1996 elections. However, the ethnic-based coalition not only lost six seats, but also broke up, which resulted in a new coalition, led by Bouterse's NDP, holding a majority of 29 seats. As in 1991, a people's assembly had to be convened in order to elect the president. On 5 September, J. Wijdenbosch, the NDP candidate, prevailed over incumbent President Venetiaan.

During Wijdenbosch's term, as in the past, opposition organized in the light of the continuing disastrous economic situation and rampant inflation. The protest from the opposition parties, unions, and civic organizations culminated on the occasion of the allegedly unconstitutional nomination of judges. After a general strike had paralyzed the capital for several days and Bouterse's call for his party colleague Wijdenbosch's resignation, the national assembly passed a motion of no confidence against Wijdenbosch by 27 votes to 14. Even though they failed to gain the required two-thirds majority, President Wijdenbosch was committed to call a general election for May 2000. The opposition was able to benefit from the situation; the NF secured 33 of the 51 seats. For a second time after 1991, R. Venetiaan was elected president.

The electoral system of proportional representation in small, medium, and large multi-member constituencies, applied since 1987, has played a limited role in structuring the political process and the party system in Suriname. On the one hand, despite their rivalry the ethnic-based parties were quick to adopt the tactics of electoral alliances, thus assuring (coalition) majorities before the polls. On the other hand, the ethnic dimension has traditionally structured the Surinamese party system, which has been dominated by a handful of ethnic-based parties. The number of Surinamese parties and their ethnic variety should be considered more a 'cause' of the electoral provisions, which allow for the representation of smaller parties, rather than a result of them. Another non-institutional variable is the tendency to fragmentation, resulting from splits due to internal conflicts, and the example most often cited is the disintegration of the NF in 1996.

The outcome of the electoral system as regards proportionality, however, is not evident: passable proportionality could be observed in 1991, when the NF won 58.8% of the seats with 54.3% of the votes and the PND won 23.2% of the seats with 21.7% of the votes, while in 2000, when an importantly larger number of parties contested, a manufactured majority in favor of the NF was produced (64.7% of the seats for 47.5% of the votes).

1.2 Evolution of Electoral Provisions

Electoral provisions were provided for by the autonomy statutes (*Statsregelingen*) of 1948 and 1955, the 1975 Constitution, and the corresponding electoral laws.

The colony of Dutch Guyana was administered by a governor assisted by a political council, the members of which were nominated by the colonial planter class and appointed by the governor. Since 1866, the members of the Colonial Assembly (*Koloniale Staten*), the principal representative body until independence, were elected from a small group of colonial planters, who were extended the franchise on the basis of a poll tax.

Before the introduction of universal male and female suffrage in 1948, a large part of the indigenous population was not entitled to vote due the prerequisite of minimum possession. From 1949 onwards, all 21 members of the *Koloniale Staten* were directly elected. Citizens of the Netherlands were entitled to vote. The minimum age for voting and standing for elections was lowered in 1973 from 23 to 21 years. An electoral system combining proportional and majority elements was applied, with one ten-member constituency, three two-member constituencies, and five SMCs. This system was re-introduced in 1958, after the apportionment had been changed to one ten-member constituency, one four-member constituency and three SMCs for the 155 elections. With the reform of 1963, three more SMCs and a nationwide twelve-member constituency were introduced, raising the number of deputies to 36. For the elections of 1967 and 1973, a six-member constituency was introduced, and the number of SMCs was lowered to three.

The independence constitution of 1975 also provided for the large constituencies, without determining the electoral formula. The other mandates were distributed in SMCs and two-member constituencies, where a system of plurality was applied.

1.3 Current Electoral Provisions

Sources: Constitution; Electoral Law (as amended in October 1987).

Suffrage: Universal, equal, direct, and secret suffrage is applied. Voters have to be Surinamese Citizens and at least 18 years of age. Those prohibited from voting include persons who have judically been denied the right to vote, persons who are serving a prison sentence, or persons who have lost the right to dispose of their property by a judicial decision due to insanity or mental deficiency. Voting is not compulsory.

Elected national institutions: The 51 members of the national assembly (NA) are elected for a five-year term. According to the 1987 Constitution, the president and the vice president are elected by the NA for five-year terms through a two-thirds majority of the members of the NA. The NA also decides on their premature resignation. The vote for vice president is taken at the same time as the vote for the prime minister.

Nomination of candidates: Those qualified to be elected as a member of the NA are all citizens of 21 years of age or older, who are qualified electors. A candidate must be a Surinamese citizen who has lived in the constituency for two years prior to the elections, and he or she must be a member of an officially-registered political party. Parties may place as many candidates on their lists as there are seats available in the district (and another ten extra candidates, if they wish). Vacancies arising during the parliamentary term are filled by succession according to the order of names of each party list.

Electoral system: PR in ten multi-member constituencies of different size, ranging from two to 17 seats (one constituency with two seats, four with three seats, two with four seats, one with five, one with seven, and one with 17 seats; average size: 5.1), is applied. The deputies are elected through party lists with the highest average (d'Hondt) and preferential votes. After the total number of seats has been awarded to a political organization, the number of votes on that list is divided by the number of seats awarded. The candidates who have gained more votes than this amount, have been chosen by preference. For the rest, and if candidates have gained an equal amount of preferential votes, the seats are awarded in accordance with the sequence on the lists of candidates submitted by the political organization.

Organizational context of elections: The Ministry of Home Affairs and the Central Bureau for Population Affairs, which prepares the voter lists, are responsible for the organization of elections at the national level. The electoral process is organized, at the district level, by appointed local government officials, the District Commissioners. Electoral results for each district are compiled in the respective Main Polling Station, which is the office of the District Commissioners. The nationwide results are compiled by the *Centraal Hoofd Stembureau* (Central Polling Authority) in the capital.

The independent electoral council (*Onafhankelijk Kiesbureau*, OKB) monitors and supervises the electoral process. The OKB plays does not prepare or administer the elections, but performs an audit on the basis of information gathered by its election observers. If there are any irregularities in the electoral process, the OKB is entitled to intervene and request remedial action. Electoral results only become official when they are announced by the OKB.

1.4 Commentary on the Electoral Statistics

Electoral data for elections held before 1975 were taken from secondary sources. The other data were drawn from official publications and United Nations reports. The unofficial and official data provided are consistent. The assumption that at least the newer electoral statistics are reliable is backed by the fact that the OAS has observed all phases of the electoral process since 1991, stating that electoral proceedings were conducted in a satisfactory manner.

2. Tables

2.1 Dates of National Elections, Referendums and Coups d'Etat

Year	Presidential Elections	Parliamentary elections	Elections for Constit. Assembly	Referen-dums	Coups d'état
1949		30/05			
1951		14/03			
1955		29/03			
1958		25/06			
1958		xx/03			
1963		xx/03			
1967		xx/03			
1969		xx/11			
1973		19/11			
1977		31/10[a]			
1980					25/02
1987		25/11		30/09[b]	
1990					25/12[c]
1991		25/05			
1996		23/05			
2000[c]		25/05			

[a] First general elections after independence.
[b] Passing of the 1987 Constitution.
[c] After premature dissolution.

2.2 Electoral Body 1949–2000

Year	Type of election[a]	Population[b]	Registered voters Total number	% pop.	Votes cast Total number	% reg. voters	% pop.
1949[c]	Pa	173,300	96,466	55.7	—	47.5	—
1951	Pa	183,800	—	—	—	38.4	—
1955	Pa	211,700	—	—	—	—	—
1958	Pa	237,300	—	—	—	—	—
1963	Pa	289,300	—	—	—	—	—
1967	Pa	329,800	—	—	—	—	—
1969	Pa	344,700	—	—	—	—	—
1973	Pa	384,175	161,400[d]	42.0	122,771[e]	76.1	32.0
1977	Pa	365,787	159,082[d]	43.5	123,713[e]	77.8	33.8
1987	Ref	394,750	208,356	52.8	122,335	58.7	31.0
1987	Pa	394,750	208,356	52.8	181,921	87.3	46.1
1991	Pa	397,000	246,926	62.2	158,809[e]	64.3	40.0
1996	Pa	423,000	269,165	63.6	179,416	66.7	42.4
2000	Pa	429,000	264,942	61.8	190,841	72.0	44.5

[a] Pa = Parliament; Ref = Referendum.
[b] Population censuses: 1971: 379,607; 1980: 355,240. Population data are estimated by the author or taken from secondary sources. UN estimate at mid-1997: 437,000.
[c] The collecting of electoral data began with the first elections after the acquisition of internal self-government in 1948.
[d] Official estimate.
[e] Valid votes. The number of voters is not available.

2.3 Abbreviations

ABOP	*Algemene Bevrijdings- en Ontwikkelings Partij* (General Liberation and Development Party)
AF	*Actie Front* (Action Front)
AG	*Actie Groep* (Action Group)
AFDihaat	(full name not known)
Alliantie[a]	*Progressieve Ontwikkelings Alliantie* (Progressive Development Alliance)
AP	*Agrarische Partij* (Agrarian Party)
APS (I)	*Arbeider Partij Suriname* (Suriname Labor Party)
APS (II)	*Amazone Partij Suriname* (Amazon Party of Suriname)
BEP	*Bosnegers Eenheid Partij* (Bush Negro Unity Party)
BVD	*Basispartij voor Vernieuwing en Democratie* (Basic Party for Renewal and Democracy)
CP	*Congres Partij* (Congress Party)
CSP	*Cristelijke Sociale Partij* (Christian-Social Party)
D-21	*Democraten van de 21ste eeuw* (Democrats of the 21st Century)
DA '91[b]	*Democratische Alternatief '91* (Democratic Alternative '91)

DC	*Dames Comité*
DNP 2000	*Democratisch Nationaal Platform 2000* (Democratic National Platform 2000)
DOE	*Partij voor Democratie en Ontwikkeling in Eenheid* (Party for Development in Unity)
DUS	*Democratische Unie Suriname* (Democratic Union of Suriname)
DVF	*Democratische Volksfront* (Democratic People's Front)
EF	*Eenheidsfront* (Unity Front)
FDO[c]	*Front voor Democratie en* Ontwikkeling (Front for Democracy and Development).
H–JPP	*Hindostanse–Javaans Politieke Partij* (East Indian-Javanese Political Party)
HPP	*Hernieuwde Progressieve Partij* (Renewed Progressive Party)
HPS	*Hindoe Partij Suriname* (Surinamese Hindu Party)
IWU	*Internationale Werklozen Unie* (International Unemployeds' Union)
KG	*Kerngroep*
KPS	*Kommunistische Partij van Suriname* (Communist Party of Suriname)
KTPI[d]	*Kerukanan Tulodo Pranatan Ingil* (Party for National Unity and Solidarity)
MC[e]	*Millennium Combinatie* (Millennium Combination)
MP	*Moeslim Partij* (Muslim Party)
NDP	*Nationaal Democratische Partij* (National Democratic Party)
NF[f]	*Nieuw Front* (New Front)
NHP	*Nationale Hervormings Partij* (National Reformation Party)
NK	*Naya Kadam* (New Choice)
NPK	*Nationale Partij Kombinatie* (National Party Combination)
NPLO	*Nationale Partij voor Leiderschap en Ontwikkeling* (National Party for Leadership and Development)
NPP	*Neger Politieke Partij* (Negro Political Party)
NPS	*Nationale Partij Suriname* (Suriname National Party)
PALU	*Progressieve Arbeiders en Landbouwers Unie* (Progressive Worker's and Farm Labourer's Union)
PBIS	*Pergerakan Bangsa Indonesia Suriname* (Union of Indonesians in Suriname)
PBP	*Progressive Bosneger Partij* (Progressive Bush Negro Party)
PL	*Pendawa Lima*
PLP	*Progressieve Landbouwers Partij* (Progressive Farm Laborer's Party)
PNP	*Progressieve Nationale Partij* (Progressive National Party)
PNR	*Partij Nationalistische Republiek* (Nationalist Republic Party)
PPRS	*Partij Perbangunan Rakjat Suriname*
PS	*Partij Suriname* (Party of Suriname)
PSP	*Progressieve Socialistische Partij* (Progessive Socialist Party)
PSV	*Progressieve Surinaamse Volkspartij* (Suriname Progressive People's Party)
PVDL	*Partij van de Landbouw* (Farming Party)
PVF	*Politieke Vleugel van de Federatie van Agrariers en Landbouwers* (Political Wing of Federation of Farmers and Laborers – FAL)

SDP	*Surinaamse Democratische Partij* (Surinamese Democratic Party)
SHP	*Surinaamse Hindoe Partij* (Surinamese Hindu Party)
SLO	*Surinaamse Landbouwers Organisatie* (Surinamese Farm Laborer's Organization)
SPA	*Surinaamse Partij van de Arbeid* (Surinamese Labor Party)
SPS	*Socialistische Partij Suriname* (Socialist Party of Suriname)
SRI	*Sarikat Rakyat Indonesia* (Indonesian People's Party)
SSP	*Surinaamse Socialistische Partij* (Surinamese Socialist Party)
SVP	*Surinaamse Volks Partij* (Surinamese People's Party)
VDP	*Verenigde Democratische Partijen* (United Democratic Party)
VIP	*Verenigde Indiaanse Partij* (United Indian Party)
VHP[g]	*Vooruitstrevende Hervormings Partij* (Progressive Reform Party)
VMP	*Vooruitstrevende Moslim Partij* (Progressive Muslim Party)
VP	*Volks Partij* (People's Party)
VVP/SVF	*Verenigde Volks Partij/Surinaamse Vrouwen Front* (United People's Party/Surinamese Women Front)

[a] Electoral alliance including HPP, PVF, and PSV.
[b] Social-Democratic electoral alliance comprising *Alternatief Forum* (Alternative Forum), *Onafhankelijk Progressief Demokratisch Alternatief* (OPDA; Independent Progressive Democratic Alternative), and *Vereniging Broedershap en Eenheid in Politiek* (BEP; Brotherhood and Unity in Politics). Subsequent to the 1996 elections, the *Alternatief Forum* and BEP left the alliance, while the OPDA continued to be known as the DA'91.
[c] Electoral alliance among NPS, VHP, and KTPI.
[d] Founded in 1947 as *Kaum-Tani Persuatan Indonesia*.
[e] Alliance comprising Democratisch Alternatief, KTPI, and NDP.
[f] Coalition formed by KTPI, NPS, SPA, Pertjajah Luhur, and VHP.
[g] VHP meant initially: *Verenigde Hindostaanse Partij*. In 1967, it kept the same abbreviation but changed its name into *Vatan Hitkari Partij* (Party for the Advancement of the National Well-being) and finally in 1973, it became *Vooruitstrevende Hervormings Partij* (VHP).

2.4 Electoral Participation of Parties and Alliances 1949–2000

Party / Alliance	Years	Elections contested[a]
CSP	1949–1955	3
DC	1949	1
H–JPP	1949	1
IWU	1949	1
KTPI	1949–1973; 1987–1991	10
NPP	1949	1
NPS	1949–1973; 1987–1991	10
PBIS	1949	1
PSV	1949; 1955–1977; 1991; 2000	11
VHP	1949–1991	12
AP	1951	1
CP	1951–1955	2
APS (I)	1955	1

Party / Alliance (continued)	Years	Elections contested[a]
EF	1955–1963	3
SDP	1955–1969	5
SVP	1958	1
AF	1963–1967	2
AG	1963–1973	4
KG	1963	1
PNR	1963–1977	5
PVDL	1963	1
VIP	1963	1
SRI	1967–1973	3
PNP	1967–1977	4
AFDihaat	1967	1
PBP	1969–1973	2
PNP–bloc	1969	1
VHP–bloc	1969–1977	3
BEP	1973	1
DUS	1973	1
DVF	1973–1977	2
HPP	1973–1977; 2000	3
NPK	1973–1987	3
VVP/SVF	1973	1
PALU	1977–1991; 2000	4
VDP	1977	1
VMP	1977	1
VP	1977; 1991	2
FDO	1987	1
NDP	1987–1996	3
PL	1987–1991	2
PPRS	1987–1991	2
SPA	1987	1
ABOP	1991–2000	3
DA '91	1991–2000	3
NF	1991–2000	4
Alliantie	1996	1
APS (II)	2000	1
D-21	2000	1
DNP 2000	2000	1
DOE	2000	1
MC	2000	1
NHP	2000	1
NK	2000	1
NPLO	2000	1
PVF	2000	1

[a] Only the number of parliamentary elections is indicated. Total number of elections: 13.

2.5 Referendums

Year	1987[a]	
	Total number	%
Registered Voters	195,099	–
Votes cast	122,335	62.7
Invalid Votes	3,999	3.3
Valid Votes	118,336	96.7
Yes	114,719	96.9
No	3,617	3.1

[a] Referendum to subject the new constitution to approval or repeal.

2.6. Elections for Constitutional Assembly

Elections for constitutional assembly have not been held.

2.7 Parliamentary Elections 1967–2000

Year	1967[a]		1969	
	Total number	%	Total number	%
Registered Voters	—	–	—	–
Votes cast	—	—	—	—
Invalid Votes	—	—	—	—
Valid Votes	207,119	—	204,041	—
NPS	61,085	29.5	55,482[c]	27.2
VHP	47,708	23.0	–[d]	–
AG	28,010	13.5	–[d]	–
PNP	19,930	9.6	–[c]	–
SDP	12,075	5.8	3,152	1.5
KTPI	11,705	5.7	–[c]	–
PSV	9,223	4.5	–[c]	–
SRI	8,183[b]	4.0	–[d]	–
PNR	5,378	2.6	15,943	7.8
AFDihaat	2,012	1.0	–	–
VHP–bloc	–	–	75,963[d]	37.2
PNP–bloc	–	–	47,690	23.4
HPS	–	–	2,154	1.1
Others	–	–	3,657	1.8
Independents	1,810	1.0	–	–

[a] Data for the elections held in the period 1949–1963 are not available.
[b] Joint list with the VHP in two constituencies.
[c] The NPS competed in 1969 as an electoral alliance among PNP, PSV, PBP and KTPI.
[d] The VHP-bloc competed in 1969 as an electoral alliance among VHP, SRI and AG.

Year	1973 Total number	%	1977 Total number	%
Registered Voters	161,400	–	159,082	–
Votes cast	—	—	—	—
Invalid Votes	—	—	—	—
Valid Votes	122,711	—	123,720	—
NPK	61,700[a]	50.3	56,176[c]	45.4
VHP	47,931[b]	39.1	–[d]	–
PNP	3,908	3.2	225	0.2
BEP	3,198	2.6	–[e]	–
HPP	3,121	2.5	–[c]	–
VVP/SVF	1,215	1.0	–	–
DVF	676	0.6	964[e]	0.8
AG	628	0.5	–	–
DUS	334	0.3	–	–
VDP	–	–	54,583[d]	44.1
PNR	–[a]	–	5,871	4.7
VP	–	–	4,534	3.7
PALU	–	–	1,006	0.8
VMP	–	–	361	0.3

[a] The NPK competed in 1973 as an electoral alliance among NPS, PNR, PSV and KTPI.
[b] Electoral alliance formed by VHP, SRI and PBP.
[c] The NPK competed in 1977 as an electoral alliance among NPS, KTPI, PSV and HPP.
[d] The VDP competed in 1977 as an electoral alliance among VHP, VVP, NPD, SPS and PL.
[e] The DVF competed in 1977 as an electoral alliance among DVF, VIP, PLP, BEP and PBP.

Year	1987 Total number	%	1991 Total number	%
Registered Voters	208,356	–	246,926	–
Votes cast	177,025	85.0	—	—
Invalid Votes	4,895	2.0	—	—
Valid Votes	172,130[a]	97.2	158,809	—
FDO[b]	147,196	85.5	–	–
NDP	16,000	9.3	34,429	21.7
PALU	2,910	1.7	4,807	3.0
SPA	2,704	1.6	–	–
PL	2,676	1.6	–	–
PPRS	664	0.4	4,463	2.8
NF[c]	–	–	86,217	54.3
DA '91	–	–	26,446	16.7
VP	–	–	1,232	0.8
ABOP	–	–	616	0.4
PSV	–	–	599	0.4

[a] According to official data, the sum total corresponding to the parties' votes differs in 20 votes from the total of valid votes.
[b] Electoral alliance formed by NPS, VHP, KTPI.
[c] Electoral alliance among NPS, VHP, KTPI and SPA.

Year	1996 Total number	%	2000 Total number	%
Registered Voters	269,165	–	264,942	–
Votes cast	179,416	66.7	190,841	72.0
Invalid Votes	5,944	3.3	8,068[a]	4.2
Valid Votes	173,472	96.7	182,773	95.8
NF[b]	72,480	41.8	86,803	47.5
NDP	45,466	26.2	–	–
DA '91	22,548	13.0	11,183	6.1
PL	16,040	9.2	1,432	0.8
Alliantie	14,578	8.4	–	–
ABOP	2,360	1.4	3,160	1.7
PALU	–	–	1,290	0.7
MC	–	–	27,481	15.0
DNP 2000	–	–	18,154	9.9
PVF	–	–	8,173	4.5
BVD	–	–	5,865	3.2
DOE	–	–	4,561	2.5
HPP	–	–	4,510	2.5
NK	–	–	4,361	2.4
D-21	–	–	2,323	1.3
NPLO	–	–	1,893	1.0
Others	–	–	1,584[c]	0.8

[a] Calculated by the author.
[b] Electoral alliance comprising NPS, VHP, KTPI, and SPA.
[c] Including: NHP: 790 votes (0.4%), APS: 608 (0.3%), PSV: 186 (0.1%).

2.8 Composition of Parliament 1949–2000

Year	1949 Seats 21	% 100.0	1951 Seats 21	% 100.0	1955 Seats 21	% 100.0	1958 Seats 21	% 100.0
NPS	13	61.9	13	61.9	2	9.5	9	42.9
VHP	6	28.6	6	28.6	6	28.6	4	19.0
KTPI	2	9.5	2	9.5	2	9.5	2	9.5
PSV	0	0.0	–	–	–	–	4	19.0
EF	–	–	–	–	11	52.4	2	9.5

Year	1963		1967		1969		1973	
	Seats	%	Seats	%	Seats	%	Seats	%
	36	100.0	39	100.0	39	100.0	39	100.0
NPS	14	38.9	17	43.6	11	28.2	13[a]	33.3
VHP	8	22.2	11	28.2	–	–	–	–
AF	6	43.1	0	0.0	–	–	–	–
KTPI	4	11.1	0	0.0	0	0.0	2	5.1
PSV	4	11.1	0	0.0	–	–	3	7.7
PNR	0	0.0	0	0.0	1	2.6	4	10.3
AG	0	0.0	4	10.1	0	0.0	0	0.0
PNP	–	–	3	7.7	–	–	0	0.0
SDP	–	–	2	5.1	0	0.0	–	–
SRI	–	–	2	5.1	0	0.0	1	2.6
VHP–bloc	–	–	–	–	19	48.7	16	41.0
PNP–bloc	–	–	–	–	8	20.5	–	–

[a] Competed in the NPK-alliance with PSV, KTPI and HPP.

Year	1977		1987		1991		1996	
	Seats	%	Seats	%	Seats	%	Seats	%
	39	100.0	51	100.0	51	100.0	51	100.0
VHP–bloc	17[a]	43.6	–	–	–	–	–	–
NPS	22	56.4[b]	14[c]	27.5	–	–	–	–
VHP	0	0.0	16[c]	31.4	–	–	–	–
KTPI	–	–	10[c]	19.6	–	–	–	–
PL	–	–	4	7.8	–	–	4	7.8
PALU	0	0.0	4	7.8	0	0.0	–	–
NDP	–	–	3	5.9	12	23.5	16	31.4
NF[d]	–	–	–	–	30	58.8	24	48.1
DA '91	–	–	–	–	9[e]	17.7	4	7.8
Alliantie	–	–	–	–	–	–	3	4.9

[a] Electoral alliance consisting of VHP, PL, PSP, and PALU.
[b] Electoral alliance consisting of HPP, NPS, PSV and KTPI.
[c] VHP, NPS, and KTPI contested in 1987 as FDO.
[d] VHP, NPS, KTPI, and SPA have contested since 1991 as NF.
[e] In 1991 DA '91 was a coalition including PL, whose two seats were thus part of the nine seats for DA '91.

Year	2000	
	Seats	%
	51	100.0
NF	33	64.7
MC	10	19.6
DNP 2000	3	5.9
DA '91	2	3.9
PVF	2	3.9
PALU	1	2.0

2.9 Presidential Elections

Direct presidential elections have not been held. The president is elected by the national assembly.

2.10 List of Power Holders 1975–2004

Head of State	Years	Remarks
Johan Ferrier	1975–1980	Assumed office on 25/11/1975.
Dési Bouterse	1980	Assumed office on 13/08/1980; first term; national army commander.
Hendrick R. Chin A Sen	1980–1982	Assumed office on 15/08/1980.
Dési Bouterse	1982	Second term. Assumed office on 04/02/1982.
L.F. Ramdat Misier	1982–1988	Assumed office on 08/02/1982.
Ramsewak Shankar	1988–1990	Assumed office on 25/01/1988.
Ivan Graanoogst	1990	Assumed office on 24/12/1990; national army commander
Johan Kraag	1990–1991	Assumed office on 29/12/1990.
Ronald Venetiaan	1991–1996	Assumed office on 16/09/1991.
Jules Wijdenbosch	1996–2000	Elected by a people's assembly convened on 05/09/1996. Assumed office on 15/09/1996.
Ronald Venetiaan	2000–	Second term. Assumed office on 12/08/2000.

Head of Government	Years	Remarks
Henck Arron	1975–1980	Assumed office on 24/12/1973.
Hendrick R. Chin A Sen	1980–1982	In office from 15/03/1980 to 04/02/1982.
Henry Neyhorst	1982	In office from 31/03/1982 to 09/12/1982.
Errol Alibux	1983–1984	In office from 26/02/1983 to 08/01/1984.
Wim Udenhout	1984–1986	In office from 03/02/1984 to 17/07/1986.
Pretaapnarian Radhakishun	1986–1987	In office from 17/07/1986 to 07/04/1987.
Jules Wijdenbosch	1987–1988	In office from 07/04/1987 to 26/01/1988.
Henck Arron	1988–1990	Second term. In office from 26/01//1988 to 24/12/1990.
Jules Wijdenbosch	1991	Second term. Assumed office on 07/01/1991.
Jules Ajodhia	1991–1996	Assumed office on 16/09/1991.
Pretaapnarian Radhakishun	1996–2000	Second term; from 15/09/1996 to 12/08/2000.
Jules Ajodhia	2000–	Second term. In office since 12/08/2000.

3. Bibliography

3.1 Official Sources

'The Constitution of the Republic of Suriname', in Pool. M. S. and Tjon Sie Fat, A. (eds.) (1996), *Surinamese Legislation in English Translation*. Paramaribo: The Waterfront Press [with the amendments according to Bulletin of Acts and Decreees 1992 no. 38].

Algemeen Bureau voor de Statistiek (1967). *Derde Algemene Volkstelling van maart 1964*. Paramaribo.

Algemeen Bureau voor de Statistiek (1972). *Voorlopige resultaten van de Vierde Algemene Volkstelling van December 1971*. Paramaribo.

Centraal Bureau van Burgerlijke Stand en Bevolkingsregister (1921). *Erste Algemeene Volkstelling van juli 1921*. Paramaribo.

Ministerie van Onderwijs en Volksontwikkeling (1987). 'Electoral Law'. *Offizial Gazette*, 73.

Welfaartsfonds (1954). *Tweede Algemene Volkstelling van 31 october 1950*. Paramaribo.

3.2 Books, Articles, and Electoral Reports

Alexander, R. J. (1982). 'Surinam', in Alexander, R. J. (ed.), *Political Parties of the Americas, Vol. 2*. Westport, Conn.: Greenwood Press, 645–655.

Amnesty International (1987). *Suriname. Violations of Human Rights*. London: Amnesty International Publications.

Brana-Shute, G. (1986). 'Back to the Barracks? Five Years "Revo"' in Suriname'. *Journal of Interamerican Studies and World Affairs* 28/1: 93–121.

Chin, H. E. and Budding, H. (1987). *Suriname. Politics, Economics, and Society*. London: Continuum International Publishing.

Derveld, R. (1999). 'Veranderingen in de Surinaamse politiek 1975–1998'. *Tijdschrift voor Surinaamse taalkunde, letterkunde, cultuur en geschiedenis* 18/1: 5–21.

DeSales Affigne, A. (1997). *Racial Politics in the Postcolonial Americas. Lessons from Suriname*. Paper prepared for presentation at the 1997 Annual Meeting of the Southern Political Science Association, Norfolk, Virginia, November 1997.

Dew, E. (1974). 'Testing Elite Perceptions of Deprivation and Satisfaction in a Culturally Plural Society'. *Comparative Politics* 6/2: 271–285.

— (1976). 'Anti-consociationalism and Independence in Suriname'. *Boletín de Estudios Latinoamericanos y del Caribe* (Netherlands) 21: 3–15.

— (1996). *The Difficult Flowering of Suriname. Ethnicity and Politics in a Plural Society*. Paramaribo: Vaco.

Dodge, P. (1966). 'Ethnic Fragmentation and Politics: The Case of Surinam'. *Political Science Quaterly*. 81: 593–601.

Duncan, N. C. (1991). 'Elecciones generales: Suriname, 25 de mayo de 1991'. *Boletín Electoral Latinoamericano* (San José: IIDH–CAPEL) 5: 34–41.

Edie, C. J. (ed.) (1994). *Democracy in the Caribbean. Myths and Realities.* London: Praeger.

van Eeuwen, Y. (1989). 'Suriname de la révolution des sergeants au retour à la démocratie'. *Problèmes d'Amérique Latine* (Paris) 91: 25–46.

Fernandes Mendes, H. (1987). 'De Nieuwe (Ontwerp) Grondwet van Suriname'. *Nederlans Juristenbled* 62/3: 1096–1099.

Gastmann, A. (1964). *The Place of Suriname and the Netherlands Antilles in the Political and Constitutional Structure of the Kingdom of the Netherlands*. PhD thesis, New York: Columbia University.

General Secretariat of the Organization of American States, Unit for the Promotion of Democracy (2002). 'Electoral Observation in Suriname 2000'. *Electoral Observation in the Americas Series* 32.

Goslinga, C. C. (1979). *A Short History of the Netherlands Antilles and Surinam*. Den Haag: Martinus Nijhoff.

Helsdingen, W. H. van (1957). *De Staatsregeling van Suriname van 1955*. Den Haag: Staatsdrukkerij.

Hira, S. (1983). 'Class Formation and Class Struggle in Suriname: The Background and Development of the Coup d'Etat', in Fitzroy, A., Ambursley, and Cohen, R. (eds.), *Crisis in the Caribbean*. London: Heinemann.

Hoppe, R. (1976). 'Het Politiek system van Suriname: Elite-Kartel-Demokratie'. *Acta Politica* (Netherlands) 11/2: 145–177.

Inter-Parliamentary Union (1997). 'Suriname', in *Chronicle of Parliamentary Elections July 1, 1995–December 31, 1996*. Geneva: IPU, 265–267.

International Commission of Jurists (1981). *Suriname. Recent Developments Relating to Human Rights. Report by a Mission to Suriname in February 1981 by Prof. J. Griffiths*. Ginebra.

Lampe, A. (1982). 'Nuevos acontecimientos en Surinam'. *El Caribe Contemporáneo* (México) 6: 67–69.

Lier, R. A. M. van (1971). *Frontier Society: A Social Analysis of the History of Surinam*. Den Haag: Martinus Nijhoff.

McDonough, J (1999). 'Suriname', in *South America, Central America and the Caribbean 2000*. London: Europa Publications, 637–650.

Ooft, C. D. (1973). *Ontwikkeling van het Constitutionele Recht van Suriname*. Assen: Van Gorcum.

Payne, D. W. (1996). 'The 1996 Suriname Elections. Post-Election Report'. *Western Hemisphere Election Study Series* 14/4.

Sedoc-Dahlberg, B. (1994). 'The Politics of Transition from Authoritarianism to Democrarcy, 1988–1992', in Edie, C. J. (ed.), *Democracy in the Caribbean. Myths and Realities.* London: Praeger, 131–146.

Thomas-Hope, E. (1987). 'Suriname', in *South America, Central America and the Caribbean 1988.* London: Europa Publications, 610–620.

TRINIDAD AND TOBAGO

by Matthias Catón[*]

1. Introduction

1.1. Historical Overview

The island of Trinidad and its smaller neighbor Tobago belong to the Caribbean Lesser Antilles and lie northeast of Venezuela. When Columbus discovered Trinidad in 1498 it was inhabited by native Arawaks and Caribs. The Spaniards colonized it in 1532 and it remained in their possession until 1797, when it was conquered by the British. Spain officially ceded it to Britain in 1802 under the Treaty of Amiens. Tobago, originally inhabited by Caribs, was settled by Europeans only from the 17th century on. Until 1814—when it was finally granted to Britain in the Treaty of Paris—it was disputed between French, British and Dutch settlers. In 1889 the two islands were merged into one colony. Today, Trinidad and Tobago is the second largest English-speaking country in the Caribbean after Jamaica.

Many Blacks were brought to the islands as slaves until slavery was abolished in 1834. In the following decades—roughly until 1917—nearly 150,000 workers from India were brought to Trinidad and Tobago as so-called indentured laborers to serve on the islands' sugarcane plantations. These people of Indian descent are locally referred to as East Indians.

The struggle for parliamentary representation began in 1846 when a petition was sent to the Colonial Office asking for a representative assembly. A council had been established in 1831, but it consisted of appointed members only. It took another eight decades until the first elected members entered the legislative council.

From the mid-1800s on the Black population increasingly urbanized and the emerging Afro-Creole middle class started to demand political rights. After World War I this trend increased, especially when Trinidad

---

[*] Parts of the electoral data listed in this chapter have been collected by Bernd Hillebrands.

began to industrialize. Oil exploitation boomed since the beginning of
the 20th century.

In 1922, a commission from Britain led by Major Wood recommended the establishment of an assembly with 26 members, consisting
of seven elected and 19 nominated representatives. Three years later
suffrage rights were granted to literate, English speaking men over 21
and women over 30—roughly 6% of the population. Candidates had to
possess a certain amount of real estate; furthermore, work in the legislative assembly was unpaid and hence only possible for people with an
independent income.

The first elections under the new regulation were held in 1925, when
partial self-determination was introduced. One of the newly-elected
council members was Arthur Cipriani, the leader of the trade union
Trinidad Workingmen's Association (TWA). The TWA's importance
rose and it was renamed Trinidad Labour Party (TLP) in 1934, becoming the island's first political party. Cipriani and the TWA wanted to reform the system from within by gradually achieving improvements for
the workers.

Worldwide economic depression in the 1930s made it difficult for the
party to show its supporters that real progress was being achieved and
soon more radical voices were heard. One of them belonged to Tubal
Uriah Butler, a charismatic Black who founded the British Empire
Workers and Citizens House Rule Party, normally referred to as the Butler Party (BP). He organized the oil workers and replaced the TLP as the
major political voice of the workers. The BP supported several strikes
and riots in the 1930s, among them the riots of 1936/37, while the TLP
opposed them.

As a consequence of the uprisings, the Crown decided to grant several privileges to workers during the 1940s, such as the right to strike, in
order to stimulate the foundation of more moderate unions. This did in
fact happen and several new parties also developed. They were usually
close to one of the unions and their respective leaders and usually only
existed for a brief period.

In 1946 universal suffrage was introduced. The same year, a new legislative council was set up with half of its members being elected. Although the lower classes now constituted a majority among the voters,
its representatives—above all the union leaders—were unable to agree
on a joint platform and the resulting fragmentation both on the ballot
and in the council greatly reduced their influence, especially after some
of the representatives entered the executive council, an organ assessing
the governor in running the colony.

The number of members in the legislative council was increased in 1950 to 27, of whom 18 were to be elected. In the following elections moderate and conservative forces managed to gain sufficient seats to assure a majority for the governor in the council together with the nominated members. In the following years, politics was mainly dominated by independent politicians from small minorities, such as those of Portuguese and Syrian descent. In 1956 the number of seats in the legislative council was again increased, this time to 31; 24 members were to be elected. Also, the office of a chief minister was introduced.

In the 1950s a structured party system began to evolve. From the beginning it clearly split along ethnic lines and this cleavage remains the decisive factor in the country's politics to date. Each of the two main ethnic groups—Blacks and East Indians—today accounts for roughly 40% of the population.

The People's National Movement (PNM) was founded by Eric Williams (also called the 'Father of the Nation') in 1956. He won the elections the same year and governed from 1956 until his death in 1981. The PNM has its base among Afro-Creole voters, both workers and middle class. It also courts non-Hindu East Indians, mainly Muslims and Christians. The PNM's East Indian counterpart was at first the People's Democratic Party (PDP), founded in 1953, which was replaced by the Democratic Labour Party (DLP) after 1956.

Britain granted full internal self-determination in 1961 and Trinidad and Tobago got a two-chamber parliament and a prime minister with a proper cabinet.

After being a member of the West Indies Federation, Trinidad and Tobago decided against this federation and unilaterally declared independence on 31 August 1962. At first it remained a monarchy with the Queen as head of state but on 1 August 1976 it became a republic within the Commonwealth and since then has a president.

After an initial period of enthusiasm directly after independence, the country's economy worsened and unemployment rose. However, as the opposition was divided—externally and also internally within the DLP—it was unable to unseat the PNM in the 1966 elections.

By the end of the 1960s Black Power movements reached Trinidad and Tobago and protests became more and more violent. After several people had died in riots, Prime Minister Williams declared a state of emergency in April 1970 and arrested the leaders of the radical Black movement. This led to a coup attempt by the armed forces, which was defeated after a few days.

Violence continued during the following years. All major opposition parties boycotted the 1971 elections after a frustrated attempt to unify against the PNM and because of alleged fraud with the voting machinery at the previous elections. Subsequently, the PNM won all seats in the house of representatives.

By the end of the year the government imposed another state of emergency. Williams now relied on commissions and directorates composed of technocrats to run the government rather than on his party or parliament.

The economic situation improved after 1973, when the Arabian oil embargo made oil prices skyrocket. Increasingly, the state intervened in the economy; key sectors (such as the oil industry) where partly nationalized.

In 1975 union leaders made an attempt to unify the mainly Afro-Creole oil industry workers and the predominantly East Indian sugar plantation workers. They founded the United Labour Front (ULF) which participated in the 1976 elections. However, the attempt to create a multiracial worker party failed. The party was labeled communist by its opponents and this alienated decisive voter groups. In the end, the ULF won a quarter of the votes; it did particularly well among East Indian voters and thus emerged—contrary to its initial intentions as a multiracial force—as the DLP's successor. The DLP did not win a single seat in this election.

The following years were marked by an economic boom thanks to high oil prices. While large parts of the population benefited from it, at same time, though, bureaucracy was rampant and the public sector inflated excessively.

After William's death George Chambers became prime minister. He won the 1981 elections but declining oil prices considerably harmed the country's economy and unemployment rose again.

In 1986 the newly founded NAR won the elections. This alliance had been formed by former PNM heavyweights and opposition parties, among them the ULF led by Basdeo Panday. The NAR wanted to be a multi-racial alliance to overcome the ethnical gap that divided the country.

Arthur N. R. Robinson became prime minister and pledged to liberalize the economy by selling most public companies and to lower the country's dependency on oil by diversifying economic activity. The NAR also wanted to reform the civil service. However, the coalition soon disintegrated after disputes over government posts and economic policies. After one year in government some ministers defected. Foreign

Minister Panday was expelled in 1988 and subsequently founded a new East Indian party called United National Congress (UNC). The idea of multi-racial politics had failed.

In 1990 the radical muslim group *Jamaat al Muslimeem* tried to overthrow the government. The prime minister and other government officials were held hostage for almost a week, there was extensive looting and several dozens of people were killed, but finally the insurrection failed. The armed forces remained loyal to the government during the clashes.

One year later, the government was democratically defeated in elections and the PNM returned to power under Prime Minster Patrick Manning. The NAR had mainly been criticized for its economic liberalization policy and could only retain the two seats from Tobago, the home of NAR leader Robinson. The PNM won almost two-thirds of the seats and the UNC one-third, hence the country was again politically divided at its racial cleavage.

The new government was unable to significantly improve the country's economic situation and was also confronted with rising crime, mainly related to drug trafficking and money laundering.

Prime Minister Manning had to call new elections prematurely in 1995 after the PNM majority had fallen to only one seat due to one defection and a lost by-election. The electoral decision was clearly between the PNM and the UNC and concentrated on five swing constituencies in which the population was ethnically balanced.

In the end, both the PNM and the UNC won 17 votes. The UNC formed a coalition with the NAR, and UNC leader Basdeo Panday became Trinidad and Tobago's first prime minister of Indian descent.

The government was re-elected in 2000 but lost its majority in parliament after four representatives defected.

The 2001 elections resulted in a stalemate with both the UNC and the PNM winning 18 seats. President Robinson nominated PNM's Patrick Manning as prime minister but Manning was unable to secure a majority in the house of representatives and had to call new elections for 2002.

This time, his party won. The 2002 electoral campaign saw a significant rising in racial appeals of both PNM and UNC. The PNM was also supported by the Muslim group *Jamaat al Muslimeen* which had tried to overthrow the government ten years earlier. Nevertheless, beside racial differences both parties essentially promoted the same policies: strengthening market economy, reducing crime and improving social services.

As many of the Caribbean states, Trinidad and Tobago inherited Britain's electoral system. The origins of the party system lie in the union movements of the 1930s and 40s. At that time, parties were small and usually short-lived factions attached to individual union leaders. The PNM was the first major stable party and is the only one that participated in all elections since 1956. It governed constantly with interruptions only from 1986 to 1991 and from 1995 to 2001.

There are two reasons for the PNM's dominant position: first, the party took full advantage of the racial divisions in Trinidad and Tobago. It secured the support of the Afro-Creole population and additionally appealed to non-Hindu East Indians. Second, the opposition was, almost without exception, divided. The first successful attempt of the opposition to unify in a multi-racial alliance against the PNM was the creation of the NAR. However, as the alliance disintegrated shortly afterwards, the PNM was able to win the next elections and the NAR was cut back to a mere representation of Tobago.

Only recently, the UNC emerged as a serious rival and subsequently the country experienced a political stalemate between PNM and UNC after the 2001 elections.

Today, the political landscape of Trinidad and Tobago continues to be organized along the country's only significant cleavage: ethnicity. Election campaigns concentrate on a handful of swing constituencies, in which the ethnic population mix is balanced and which either of the big parties could win over.

The electoral system has obviously supported the alignment along this cleavage. It has impeded the creation of smaller parties which might be able to break up the political landscape. Those parties could have represented the country's different minorities or could have focused on issues other than ethnicity.

In the last decade volatility has sharply decreased and proportionality has risen. However, these figures hide the problems of Trinidad and Tobago's political system, which have rather increased then decreased in recent times.

1.2 Evolution of Electoral Provisions

In 1921 the Wood Commission recommended establishing an assembly with 26 members, consisting of 7 elected and 19 nominated representatives plus the governor. In 1925 a new council was installed with 18 of its 27 members being elected. In 1950 the number of elected members was increased to 18, plus six nominated and three ex officio members. Six years later another reform followed and the total number of council members was elevated to 31, with 24 elected, 5 nominated and 2 ex officio members.

The next major reform occurred in 1961: full internal self-determination was introduced. The legislative council was replaced by a two-chamber parliament, consisting of a house of representatives with 30 members and a senate with 21 members. All representatives were elected, while the senators were appointed by the governor: twelve on the advice of the prime minister, two on advice of the leader of the opposition and seven at the governor's discretion. After independence the number of representatives was increased to 36.

Suffrage was granted to men over 21 and women over 30 in 1924. Universal suffrage was introduced in 1946. The voting age was lowered from 21 to 18 years in 1976.

1.3 Current Electoral Provisions

Sources: Constitution of the Republic of Trinidad and Tobago, Representation of the People Act, Elections and Boundaries Commission Act No. 18 of 1967, Tobago House of Assembly Act No. 37 of 1980.

Suffrage: Suffrage is universal, equal, direct, and secret for all Trinidad and Tobago citizens aged 18 or over who resided for at least one year in the country and for at least two months in their constituency prior to election day. Insane people and those serving a prison sentence of more then 12 months are excluded from voting.

Elected national institutions: Trinidad and Tobago has a bicameral parliamentary system with a senate and a house of representatives. The 31 senators are appointed by the president for a five-year term. The prime minister chooses 16 senators, the leader of the opposition six and the remaining nine are chosen by the president at his discretion. The senators can be revoked at any time by the official who nominated them.

The 36 representatives (34 from Trinidad and 2 from Tobago) are elected for five-year terms.

The president is indirectly elected by an electoral college consisting of both chambers of the parliament. He also serves a five-year term.

Nomination of candidates
- *presidential elections*: Presidential candidates must be citizens of Trinidad and Tobago and at least 35 years old. When assuming office, the elected candidate must have resided in the country for at least ten years immediately preceding his election. To get on the ballot candidates need the signatures of at least twelve members of the house of representatives.
- *parliamentary elections*: Candidates for parliament must be citizens of Trinidad and Tobago in possession of active voting rights, be at least 25 years old and have been resident in Trinidad and Tobago for at least two years prior to the election. To be entered on the ballot they need the support of at least six registered voters in their constituency and have to make a deposit of TT$ 250. The amount is only reimbursed if the candidate achieves more then 1/8 of the votes in his constituency.

Electoral system: The representatives are elected by plurality in SMCs. Vacancies are filled through by-elections.

Organizational context of elections: The Elections and Boundaries Commission is responsible for running the elections, for voter registration, and for drawing up constituencies. It consists of a chairman and two to four other members, all chosen by the president for five years after consultations with the prime minister and the leader of the opposition.

Recently, the Elections and Boundaries Commission has been criticized for irregularities with voter lists and has been subject to an investigation by a special commission appointed by the president.

1.4 Commentary on the Electoral Statistics

The electoral data were drawn from the official 'Reports on the General Elections' and 'Reports on the Parliamentary Elections' published by the Elections and Boundaries Commission. These reports are reliable. The results for the 1961–1986 elections had been previously collected by Bernd Hillebrands (1993). Data for the 1946–1956 elections were taken from Emmanuel (1992). Percentages and totals were calculated by the author. Population data are mid-year estimates of the United Nations, if not otherwise stated.

2. Tables

2.1 Dates of National Elections, Referendums, and Coups d'Etat

Year	Presidential elections	Parliamentary elections	Elections for Constitutional Assembly	Referendums	Coups d'état
1946		28/10			
1950		18/09			
1956		24/09			
1961		04/12			
1966		07/11			
1971		24/05			
1976		13/09			
1981		09/11			
1986		15/12			
1991		16/12			
1995		06/11			
2000		11/12			
2001		10/12			
2002		07/10			

2.2 Electoral Body 1946–2002

Year	Type of election[a]	Population[b]	Registered voters Total number	% pop.	Votes cast Total number	% reg. voters	% pop.
1946	Pa	557,970[c]	259,512	46.5	137,281	52.9	24.6
1950	Pa	627,000	283,050	45.1	198,458	70.1	31.7
1956	Pa	743,000	339,030	45.6	271,534	80.1	36.5
1961	Pa	859,000	378,511	44.1	333,512	88.1	38.8
1966	Pa	1,000,000	459,839	46.0	302,548	65.8	30.3
1971	Pa	1,030,000	357,568	34.7	118,597	33.2	11.5
1976	Pa	1,098,000	565,646	51.5	315,809	55.8	28.8
1981	Pa	1,095,000	736,104	67.2	415,416	56.4	37.9
1986	Pa	1,178,000	882,029	74.9	577,300	65.5	49.0
1991	Pa	1,253,000	794,486	63.4	520,049	65.5	41.5
1995	Pa	1,283,000	837,741	65.3	530,311	63.3	41.3
2000	Pa	1,294,000[d]	875,260	67.6	608,830	69.6	47.1
2001	Pa	1,300,000[d]	849,874	65.3	561,993	66.1	43.2
2002	Pa	1,306,000[e]	875,260	67.0	609,571	69.6	46.7

[a] Pa = House of Representatives (Lower Chamber).
[b] Estimates are taken from the UN Statistical Yearbooks, if not otherwise stated.
[c] Census of 09/04/1946.

^d Estimates taken from the UN Population and Vital Statistics Reports.
^e Calculation based on UN data.

2.3 Abbreviations

ANC	African National Congress
BP	Butler Party (British Empire Workers and Citizens House Rule Party)
CA	Citizens Alliance
CNLP	Caribbean National Labour Party
CPDP	Caribbean People's Democratic Party
CSP	Caribbean Socialist Party
DAC	Democratic Action Congress
DLP	Democratic Labour Party
DPTT	Democratic Party of Trinidad and Tobago
FHM	Fargo House Movement
LAP	Liberation Action Party
LP	Liberal Party
MUP	Movement for Unity and Progress
NAR	National Alliance for Reconstruction
NDO	National Democratic Organization
NDP	National Development Party
NFP	National Freedom Party
NJAC	National Joint Action Committee
NLP	Natural Law Party
NTM	National Transformation Party
NTTP	National Trinidad and Tobago Party
ONR	Organization for National Reconstruction
PDP	People's Democratic Party
PEP	People's Empowerment Party
PNM	People's National Movement
POPPG	Party of Political Progress Groups
PPM	People's Popular Movement
PrDP	Progressive Democratic Party
PRP	People's Republican Party
PVP	People's Voice Party
SDLP	Social Democratic Labour Party
SIP	Seukeran Independent Party
Tapia	Tapia House Movement
TLP	Trinidad Labour Party
TMS	The Mercy Society
TUC	Trade Union Council
TUCSP	Trades Union Congress and Socialist Party
TUN	Team Unity
UF	United Front

UFP	United Freedom Party
ULF	United Labour Front
UNC	United National Congress
WFP	Workers and Farmers Party
WIIP	West Indian Independence Party
WINP	West Indian National Party
WIPCM	West Indian Political Congress Movement
YPNP	Young People's National Party

2.4 Electoral Participation of Parties and Alliances 1946–2002

Party / Alliance	Years	Elections contested
UF	1946	1
BP	1946–1966	5
TUCSP	1946; 1950	2
TLP	1946; 1950	2
PrDP	1946; 1956	2
TUC	1950	1
POPPG	1950; 1956	2
CSP	1950	1
PNM	1956–2002	12
PDP	1956; 1966	2
CNLP	1956	1
TLP	1956; 1981	2
WIIP	1956	1
CPDP	1956	1
DLP	1961–1976	4
ANC	1961; 1971	2
LP	1966	1
WFP	1966	1
SIP	1966	1
ULF	1976; 1981	2
DAC	1976; 1981	2
Tapia	1976; 1981	2
SDLP	1976	1
WINP	1976	1
UFP	1976	1
LAP	1976	1
NTTP	1976	1
YPNP	1976	1
ONR	1981	1

Party / Alliance (continued)	Years	Elections contested
NJAC	1981–1991	3
NFP	1981	1
FHM	1981	1
WIPCM	1981	1
PRP	1981	1
NAR	1986–2002	6
PPM	1986	1
UNC	1991–2002	5
MUP	1995	1
NLP	1995	1
NTM	1995	1
PVP	1995	1
PEP	2000	1
TMS	2000	1
NDO	2001–2002	2
TUN	2001	1
CA	2002	1
DPTT	2002	1

2.5 Referendums

Referendums have not been held.

2.6 Elections for Constitutional Assembly

Elections for constitutional assemblies have not been held.

2.7 Parliamentary Elections 1946–2002

Year	1946 Total number	%	1950 Total number	%
Registered voters	259,512	–	283,050	–
Votes cast	137,281	52.9	198,458	70.1
Invalid votes	8,408	6.1	8,492	3.0
Valid votes	128,873[a]	83.9	189,998[b]	97.0
UF	37,891	29.4	–	–
BP	28,767	22.3	41,928	22.1
TUCSP	22,191	17.2	19,917	10.5
TLP	1,356	1.1	14,992	7.9
PrDP	515	0.4	–	–
TUC	–	–	9,025	4.8
POPPG	–	–	6,507	3.4
CSP/BP	–	–	4,529	2.4
Independents	38,198	29.6	93,100	49.0

[a] There is a difference of 45 votes between the total stated here and the sum of all votes below.
[b] There is a difference of 32 votes between the total stated here and the sum of all votes below.

Year	1956 Total number	%	1961 Total number	%
Registered voters	339,030	–	378,511	–
Votes cast	271,534	80.1	333,512	88.1
Invalid votes	6,991	2.6	149	0.0
Valid votes	264,903[a]	97.4	333,363	100.0
PNM	105,513	39.8	190,003	57.0
PDP	55,148	20.8	–	–
DLP	–	–	138,910	41.7
ANC	–	–	1,634	0.5
Others	104,242[b]	39.4	2,816[c]	0.8

[a] There is a difference of 360 votes between the total stated here and the sum of all votes below.
[b] Includes POPPG, CNLP, BP, TLP, PrDP, WIIP, CPDP and independents.
[c] Others includes BP: 1,314 votes (0.4%) and other unknown parties.

Year	1966		1971	
	Total number	%	Total number	%
Registered voters	459,839	–	357,568	–
Votes cast	302,548	65.8	118,597	33.2
Invalid votes	146	0.0	73	0.1
Valid votes	302,402	100.0	118,524	99.9
PNM	158,573	52.4	99,723	84.1
DLP	102,792	34.0	14,940	12.6
LP	26,870	8.9	–	–
WFP	10,484	3.5	–	–
ANC	–	–	2,864	2.4
Others	2,216[a]	0.7	–	–
Independents	1,467	0.5	997	0.8

[a] Others include PDP: 943 votes (0.3%); BP: 704 (0.2%); and SIP: 569 (0.2%).

Year	1976		1981	
	Total number	%	Total number	%
Registered voters	565,646	–	736,104	–
Votes cast	315,809	55.8	415,416	56.4
Invalid votes	3,824	1.2	2,638	0.6
Valid votes	311,985	98.8	412,778	99.4
PNM	169,194	54.2	218,557	52.9
ULF	84,780	27.2	62,781[b]	15.2
DAC	25,586	8.2	15,390[b]	3.7
Tapia	12,021	3.9	9,401[b]	2.3
DLP	9,404	3.0	–	–
SDLP	5,928	1.9	–	–
ONR	–	–	91,704	22.2
NJAC	–	–	13,710	3.3
Others	3,380[a]	1.1	1,196[c]	0.3
Independents	1,692	0.5	39	0.0

[a] Others include WINP: 1,242 votes (0.4%); UFP: 1,047 (0.3%); LAP: 872 (0.3%); NTTP: 115 (0.0%); and YPNP: 104 (0.0%).
[b] ULF, DAC and Tapia formed an electoral alliance called 'Trinidad and Tobago National Alliance'. Both votes and seats were counted separately, though.
[c] Others include NFP: 864 votes (0.2%); FHM: 143 (0.0%); WIPCM: 130 (0.0%); TLP: 34 (0.0%); and PRP: 25 (0.0%).

Year	1986		1991	
	Total number	%	Total number	%
Registered voters	882,029	–	794,486	–
Votes cast	577,300	65.5	520,049	65.5
Invalid votes	4,037	0.7	2,775	0.5
Valid votes	573,263	99.3	517,274	99.5
NAR	380,029	66.3	127,335	24.6
PNM	183,635	32.0	233,150	45.1
NJAC	8,592	1.5	5,743	1.1
PPM	796	0.1	–	–
UNC	–	–	151,046	29.2
Independents	211	0.0	–	–

Year	1995		2000	
	Total number	%	Total number	%
Registered voters	837,741	–	947,689	–
Votes cast	530,311	63.3	597,525	63.1
Invalid votes	4,985	0.9	2,650	0.4
Valid votes	525,326	99.1	594,875	99.6
PNM	256,159	48.8	276,334	46.5
UNC	240,372	45.8	307,791	51.7
NAR	24,983	4.8	7,409	1.2
Others	3812[a]	0.7	2,213[b]	0.4
Independents	–	–	1,128	0.2

[a] Others include MUP: 2,123 votes (0.4%); NLP: 1,590 (0.3%); NTM: 83 (0.0%); and PVP: 16 (0.0%).
[b] Others include PEP: 2,071 votes (0.3%) and TMS: 142 (0.0%).

Year	2001		2002	
	Total number	%	Total number	%
Registered voters	849,874	–	875,260	–
Votes cast	561,993	66.1	609,571	69.6
Invalid votes	2,818	0.5	2,804	0.5
Valid votes	559,175	99.5	606,767	99.5
UNC	279,002	49.9	284,391	46.9
PNM	260,075	46.5	308,762	50.9
TUN	14,207	2.5	–	–
NAR	5,841	1.0	6,776	1.1
CA	–	–	5,983	1.0
Others	50[a]	0.0	855[b]	0.1

[a] = NDO.
[b] Others include DPTT: 662 votes (0.1%) and independents: 193 (0.0%).

2.8 Composition of Parliament 1946–2002

Year	1946		1950		1956		1961	
	Seats	%	Seats	%	Seats	%	Seats	%
	9[a]	100.0	18[a]	100.0	24[a]	100.0	30	100.0
UF	3	33.3	–	–	–	–	–	–
BP	3	33.3	6	33.3	2	8.3	0	0.0
TUCSP	2	22.2	1	5.6	–	–	–	–
TLP	0	0.0	2	11.1	2[b]	8.3	–	–
POPPG	–	–	2	11.1	0	0.0	–	–
CSP/BP	–	–	1	5.6	–	–	–	–
PNM	–	–	–	–	13	54.2	20	66.7
PDP	–	–	–	–	5	20.8	–	–
DLP	–	–	–	–	–	–	10	33.3
Independents	1	11.1	6	33.3	2	8.3	0	0.0

[a] The numbers refer to the elected seats. Percentages have also been calculated on this basis. The total number of seats in the legislative council was 18 in 1946; 27 in 1950 and 31 in 1956. In 1961 the council was replaced by the house of representatives, which was entirely elected.
[b] Participated as TLP-NDP.

Year	1966		1971		1976		1981	
	Seats	%	Seats	%	Seats	%	Seats	%
	36	100.0	36	100.0	36	100.0	36	100.0
PNM	24	66.7	36	100.0	24	66.7	26	72.2
DLP	12	33.3	0	0.0	0	0.0	–	–
ULF	–	–	–	–	10	27.8	8	22.2
DAC	–	–	–	–	2	5.6	2	5.6

Year	1986		1991		1995		2000	
	Seats	%	Seats	%	Seats	%	Seats	%
	36	100.0	36	100.0	36	100.0	36	100.0
NAR	33	91.7	2	5.6	2	5.6	1	2.8
PNM	3	8.3	21	58.3	17	47.2	16	44.4
UNC	–	–	13	36.1	17	47.2	19	52.8

Year	2001		2002	
	Seats	%	Seats	%
	36	100.0	36	100.0
PNM	18	50.0	20	55.6
UNC	18	50.0	16	44.4

2.9 Presidential Elections

Presidential elections have not been held.

2.10 List of Power Holders 1952–2004

Head of State	Years	Remarks
Queen Elizabeth II	1952–1976	Represented by governors Sir Hubert E. Rance (–1955), Sir Edward Beetham (1955–1960), Sir Solomon Hochoy (1960–1972, governor general since 1962) and Governor-General Sir Ellis E. I. Clarke (1973–1976).
Sir Ellis E. I. Clarke	1976–1987	President from 01/03/1976–13/03/1987, acting president until 28/01/1977.
Michael Williams	1987	Acting president from 13/03–18/03.
Noor M. Hassanali	1987–1997	President from 18/03/1987–18/03/1997.
Arthur N. R. Robinson	1997–2003	President from 18/03/1997–17/03/2003.
George Maxwell Richards	2003–	President since 17/03/2003.

Head of Government	Years	Remarks
Eric E. Williams	1956–1981	Chief minister until 1961, then prime minister. Head of government of an independent country since 31/08/1962. Died in office on 29/03/1981.
George M. Chambers	1981–1986	Prime minister from 30/03/1981 to 18/12/1986.
Arthur N. R. Robinson	1986–1991	Prime minister from 18/12/1986 to 17/12/1991.
Patrick A. M. Manning	1991–1995	Prime minister from 17/12/1991 to 09/11/1995.
Basdeo Panday	1995–2001	Prime minister from 09/11/1995 to 24/12/2001.
Patrick A. M. Manning	2001–	Prime minister since 24/12/2001.

3. Bibliography

3.1 Official Sources

Elections and Boundaries Commission (1961). *Report on the General Elections 1961*. Port of Spain.
— (1966). *Report on the General Elections 1966*. Port of Spain.
— (1971). *Report on the General Elections 1971*. Port of Spain.
— (1976). *Report on the General Elections 1976*. Port of Spain.
— (1981). *Report on the General Elections 1981*. Port of Spain.
— (1986). *Report on the General Elections 1986*. Port of Spain.
— (1991). *Report on the General Elections 1991*. Port of Spain.
— (1993). *The Exercise of the Franchise in Trinidad and Tobago 1946 to Present*. Port of Spain.
— (1995). *Report on the Parliamentary Elections 1995*. Port of Spain.
— (2000). *Report on the Parliamentary Elections 2000*. Port of Spain.
— (2001). *Report on the Parliamentary Elections 2001*. Port of Spain.
— (2002). *Report on the Parliamentary Elections 2002*. Port of Spain.
(2002). Report of the Commission of Inquiry into the Functioning of the Elections and Boundaries Commission of Trinidad and Tobago. Port of Spain. <http://www.nalis.gov.tt/ebc2/ebc2.htm> (as of 04/07/03).

3.2 Books, Articles, and Electoral Reports

Alexis, F. (1983). *Changing Caribbean Constitutions*. Bridgetown, Barbados: Antilles.
Braveboy-Wagner, J. A. (1989). 'The Regional Foreign Policy of Trinidad and Tobago. Historical and Contemporary Aspects'. *Journal of Interamerican Studies and World Affairs* 31/3: 37–61.
Collihan, K. M. and Danopoulos, C. P. (1993). 'Coup d'État attempt in Trinidad. Its Causes and Failure'. *Armed Forces and Society* 19/3: 435–450.
DeMerieux, M. (1992). *Fundamental Rights in Commonwealth Caribbean Constitutions*. Bridgetown, Barbados: Faculty of Law Library, University of the West Indies.
Edie, C. J. (ed.) (1994). *Democracy in the Caribbean. Myths and Realities*. London: Praeger.
Emmanuel, P. A. M. (1992). *Elections and Party Systems in the Commonwealth Caribbean, 1944–1991*. St. Michael, Barbados: CADRES.
Ghany, H. (1997). 'Eric Williams. The Constitutional Scholar and the Introduction of Bicameralism in Trinidad and Tobago'. *Journal of Legislative Studies* 3/4: 92–114.

— (1998). 'Parliamentary Crisis and the Removal of the Speaker. The Case of Trinidad and Tobago'. *Journal of Legislative Studies* 3/2: 112–138.

Hackshaw, J. M. (1997). *Party Politics and Public Policy. A New Political Culture Needed for Trinidad and Tobago.* Trinidad: Diego Martin.

Henry, A.-V. (1994). 'Multi-Ethnicity and National Identity. The Case of Trinidad and Tobago'. *Ethnic Studies Report* 12/2: 136–153.

Hillebrands, B. (1993). 'Trinidad and Tobago', in D. Nohlen (ed.), *Handbuch der Wahldaten Lateinamerikas und der Karibik.* Opladen: Leske + Budrich, 719–729.

Inamete, U. (1992). 'Politics and Governance in Trinidad and Tobago. Major Issues and Developments'. *Caribbean Studies* (Río Piedra) 25/3–4: 305–324.

LaGuerre, J. G. (1983). 'The General Elections of 1981 in Trinidad and Tobago'. *Journal of Commonwealth and Comparative Politics* 21/2: 133–157.

— (ed.) (1997). *The General Elections of 1995 in Trinidad and Tobago.* St. Augustin: University of the West Indies Press.

Ledgister, F. S. J. (1998). *Class Alliances and the Liberal Authoritarian State. The Roots of Post-Colonial Democracy in Jamaica, Trinidad and Tobago, and Surinam.* Trenton, N.J./ Asmara, Eritrea: Africa World Press.

Ling, M. (1997). 'Trinidad und Tobago. Ende der afrotrinidadischen Dominanz?', in K. Gabbert et al. (eds.), *Land und Freiheit.* Bad Honnef: Horlemann, 280–287.

MacDonald, S. B. (1986). *Trinidad and Tobago. Democracy and Development in the Caribbean.* New York: Praeger.

Maingot, A. P. (2001). 'Global Economics and Local Politics in Trinidad's Divestment Program', in J. Stark (ed.), *The Challenge of Change in Latin America and the Caribbean.* Miami: University of Miami, 111–157.

Millette, J. (1985). *Society and Politics in Colonial Trinidad.* Trinidad: Omega.

Naipaul, V. S. (1958). *The Suffrage of Elvira.* London: Deutsch.

Nuscheler, F. and Schultze, R.-O. (1995). 'Trinidad und Tobago', in D. Nohlen and F. Nuscheler (eds.), *Handbuch der Dritten Welt Vol. 3. Mittelamerika und Karibik.* Bonn: Dietz, 569–586.

Parris, C. D. (1990). 'Trinidad and Tobago 1956–86. Has the Political Elite Changed?'. *The Round Table* 314: 147–156.

Payne, D. W. (1995a). *Democracy in the Caribbean. A Cause for Concern.* (Policy Papers on the Americas VI, 3). Washington, D.C.: Center for Strategic and International Studies.

— (1995b). *The Trinidad and Tobago Elections. Post-Election Report.* (Western Hemisphere Elections Study Series XIII 7): CSIS.

Phillips, F. (1985). *West Indian Constitutions. Post-Independence Reform.* New York/ London/ Rom: Oceana.

Premdas, R. R. and Ragoonath, B. (1998). 'Ethnicity, Elections and Democracy in Trinidad and Tobago. Analysing the 1995 and 1996 Elections'. *Journal of Commonwealth and Comparative Politics* 36/3: 30–53.

Premdas, R. R. and Williams, H. (1992). 'Tobago. The Quest for Self-Determination in the Caribbean'. *Canadian Review of Studies in Nationalism* 19/1–2: 117–127.

Ragoonath, B. (1993). 'The Failure of the Abu Bakr Coup. The Plural Society, Cultural Traditions and Political Development in Trinidad'. *Journal of Commonwealth and Comparative Politics* 31/2: 158–182.

Regis, L. (1998). *The Political Calypso. The Opposition in Trinidad and Tobago 1962–1987.* Kingston, Jamaica: University of the West Indies Press.

Ryan, S. D. (1972). *Race and Nationalism in Trinidad and Tobago. A Study of Decolonization in a Multiracial Society.* Toronto/ Buffalo, N.Y.: University of Toronto Press.

— (1979). 'Trinidad and Tobago. The General Elections of 1976'. *Caribbean Studies* (Río Piedra) 19/1–2: 5–36.

— (ed.) (1988). *Trinidad and Tobago. The Independence Experience 1962–1987.* St. Augustin, Trinidad and Tobago: University of the West Indies.

Spackman, A. (1967). 'The Senate of Trinidad and Tobago'. *Social and Economic Studies* (Kingston, Jamaica) 16: 77–100.

— (ed.) (1975). *Constitutional Development of the West Indies 1922–1968. A Selection from the Major Documents.* St. Lawrence, Barbados: Caribbean University Press.

Stark, J. (ed.) (2001). *The Challenge of Change in Latin America and the Caribbean.* Miami: University of Miami.

Sutton, P. (1983). 'Black Power in Trinidad and Tobago. The "Crisis" of 1970'. *Journal of Commonwealth and Comparative Politics* 21/2: 115–132.

Taboada, H. G. H. (1994). 'El golpe de estado islámico en Trinidad'. *Cuadernos americanos* 47: 205–216.

Will, W. M. (1991). 'A Nation Divided. The Quest for Caribbean Integration'. *Latin American Research Review* 26/2: 3–37.

Williams, E. (1964). *History of the People of Trinidad and Tobago.* London: Deutsch.

Yelvington, K. A. (1987). 'Vote Dem Out. The Demise of the PNM in Trinidad and Tobago'. *Caribbean Review* (Miami) 15/4: 8–12, 29–33.

UNITED STATES OF AMERICA

by Ralf Lindner and Rainer-Olaf Schultze

1. Introduction

1.1 Historical Overview

Since the creation of the United States of America in the late 18th century, the central institutions of the republic—congress, presidency, federalism, the first-past-the-post electoral system—have remained principally unaltered in spite of the fact that the Union of initially 13 states with approximately 2.5 million settlers was gradually expanded to 50 states with a population of currently more than 280 million. The constitution, which was ratified in 1789 after a lengthy process of constitutional debate and which continues to be a chief foundation of authority in the United States' political system, lays down the principles of representative democracy and a complex system of vertical and horizontal separation and interweavement of powers. At the outset, only the lower chamber of congress, the house of representatives, was directly elected by popular vote. The election of the members of the upper chamber, the senate, was gradually democratized, and since 1913 all senators are required to be directly elected. The president continues to be elected by the electoral college, the members of which were initially appointed by the state legislatures. Since 1828, the presidential electors are designated by popular vote.

The nascence of the new nation is deeply intertwined with the colonies' liberation from the British Empire, and fundamental political traditions, which are still pivotal to the understanding of US American politics today, can be traced back to the colonial period. The United States were not only the first nation state to emerge from a European colonial empire, but also created a stable and enduring political order in the aftermath of a violent struggle for independence from the British. The successful transition from colonial rule to an independent nation without falling into a phase of anarchy and terror can be ascribed to the fact that several generations of colonists had established functioning institutions of self-governance under the colonial administration. Due to the general availability of land and property, it was not feasible to impose a system on the American colonies that was based on hereditary aristocracy and land ownership and which determined the status of a privileged ruling class in rural England of the time. Instead of upholding artificial privileges, the settlers were able to establish structures of representative government already in the course of the 17th century, which were open to and accepted by the emerging middle class of farmers, craftsmen and merchants. From the beginning, the American colonial society had displayed an extraordinary level of self-sufficiency and independence. At first, the local community was the most important level of government for the settlers. Later, the colonies expressed their relative autonomy through colonial assemblies, the activities of which were mostly accepted by Crown appointed governors.

Until the 1760s, the British rule was indeed relatively benevolent. Under King George III, however, London changed its colonial policy and began to exercise much greater control over the colonies and imposed numerous, mainly economic, restrictions and new taxes on the settlers. The colonial elites and most of the citizens viewed these measures as unacceptable violations of their fundamental rights as 'true born Englishmen'. In this context it has to be noted that European Enlightenment and its idea that men possessed certain inalienable rights were particularly popular in colonial America. The public outrage over the arrogant British rule intensified over the next years, resulting in ever more protests, riots and violence. In 1774, twelve of the 13 colonial assemblies sent delegates to the first Continental Congress—the colonists' first formal statement of national self-determination—as a reaction to the harsh sanctions that had been imposed on the colony of Massachusetts after the 'Boston Tea Party' in 1773. By 1775 hostilities had started in Massachusetts and in 1776 the congress embraced the Declaration of Independence ('Life, Liberty and the pursuit of Happiness'), symbolizing the birth of the United States of America. During the next five years the 'rebels' fought the revolutionary war, and in 1781 the British army was forced to surrender.

Strictly speaking, the liberation from colonial rule did not fully qualify as a revolution. Unlike most revolutionary wars, the War of Independence and the ensuing construction of a new constitutional system had few direct effects for the fabric of society, as the political transformation rather reinforced the existing distribution of wealth and power. Nonetheless, an integral element of the former colonists' self-conception was their belief to represent a genuinely new type of society, to be 'God's chosen people'. The strong quasi-religious elements inherent in

America's exceptionalism explain to a great extent the recurrent periods of intensified moral-idealistic rhetoric—in both foreign and domestic affairs—in US American politics. The essential values of the 'American Creed'—the abstract ideals of liberty, equality of opportunity, radical economic individualism, and anti-statism—were already deeply entrenched in the new society and still effectively outweigh other systems of beliefs today. The unchallenged dominance of liberal values creates the impression of the United States as a 'one ideology-society'. Due to the absence of a feudal-aristocratic tradition and the successive democratization of the electoral system, ideological currents of European-style conservatism and socialism remained at the margins throughout most of the country's history. The liberal public philosophy has doubtlessly facilitated the integration of and the identification with a society marked by pronounced ethno-cultural diversities, regional differences, and socio-economic disparities.

During the War of Independence, the Continental Congress designed and passed the first American constitution, representing the continuation of the constitutional revolution on the level of the Union. However, the new system of government under the Articles of Confederation (1781–1789), which was marked by radical anti-centralism and profound distrust in political authority, proved to be ill-suited to address the growing centrifugal tendencies within the Confederation in the immediate post-colonial period. By the mid-1780s, the escalating political and economic crisis had convinced the elites in most of the states of the necessity for fundamental institutional reforms. After several attempts to strengthen congress, a national constitutional convention was agreed upon. In 1787, 55 delegates, who had been appointed by the state legislatures, assembled in Philadelphia in order to design new constitutional arrangements. The debates within the convention were dominated by four central areas of disagreement, all of which were eventually settled by compromise: (1) The separation of powers within the federal government, (2) the relationship between the federal government and the states, (3) the distribution of power between small and large states, and (4) the economic conflicts between Northern and Southern states. After the convention had brought forward the proposal for the new political system, passionate public debates accompanied the two-year ratification process that ultimately legitimized the new constitution. The proponents of the constitution relied heavily on the sophisticated arguments that Alexander Hamilton, James Madison, and John Jay published in a series of 85 newspaper articles that were later collected as the Federalist Papers. The opponents, labeled Anti-Federalists, concentrated their attacks on the presidency as a 'disguised monarchy'. In the end, the Federalists prevailed and the constitution came into force in 1788. 'The genius of the constitution was that, although it was the first written constitution ever to be adopted by a country, and although it propounded the virtues of a republican form of government, it remained intrinsically conservative in content and implication' (McKay 1993: 47).

The constitution established a presidential system and generally declared a republican regime. In response to what the settlers in the British-American colonies viewed as unjust and despotic interference in their business by the British, the Founding Fathers carefully crafted a constitution aiming to prevent the concentration and abuse of political authority. Consequently, the exercise of power by the major federal institutions is guarded by a system of checks and balances and by the principle of limited government. Executive and legislative branches of government are generally separated but concurrently interwoven in selected points. In order to establish law, both chambers of congress in Washington D.C. are required to approve a bill; the president, however, is entitled to exercise a veto on legislative motions. Yet, the house of representatives and the senate may override a presidential veto by a two-thirds majority. The system of checks and balances does not insinuate equality of power, as the framers of the constitution designated congress—here mainly the house—to be the chief authority regarding policy. The lower chamber, which initially was to be the only directly-elected federal institution, was assigned with distinctive responsibility for revenue bills, thus responding to the popular demand of the revolutionary years for 'no taxation without representation'.

At first glance, the constitution provides for the concentration of crucial executive functions in the institution of the presidency, assigning to the president the roles of the head of state, chief executive, commander in chief of the armed forces, chief diplomat, chief recruiting officer and legislator. Despite these impressive formal powers, the president's autonomy to exercise them is restricted in several ways: international treaties require the authorization of two-thirds of the senate; federal public servants, diplomats, and federal judges may only be appointed upon approval of the majority of the senate. The principle of executive accountability is most firmly expressed by congress' power to remove the president, any member of the executive and the judges of the supreme court from office by the means of impeachment, which has to be brought into action by a majority of the house. Any indictment, however, has to be based on sufficient allegations of treason, bribery, or other high crimes and misdemeanours. The trial is conducted by the senate; a conviction requires the support of two-thirds of the senators.

The most controversial debates within the constitutional convention were fought on the issue of federalism and the delineation of power between the states and the federal institutions. Eventually, the constitution was defined as the 'supreme law of the land', ensuring its supremacy over the states' constitutional and legal arrangements. Political authority between the central government and the states is divided along the lines of interstate federalism. The primary powers at the federal level, such as the treaty making power, are explicitly enumerated in the constitution, whereas—according to the 10th Amendment—the residual powers rest with the individual states. The question of the states' representation at the federal level was dominated by the conflict between large and small states. The disagreement was solved by applying two different principles of representation with regard to the composition of congress: the allocation of seats in the house of representatives was to be based on the respective size of state populations, whereas each state, regardless of its size, was granted two seats in the senate. The clash of interests between the North and the slave-based economy of the South was potentially an even greater threat to the success of the convention. The conflict was solved by the 'great compromise', in which slaves were counted as three-fifths of a free person for the purpose of representation in the house and in distributing federal taxes. This provision was superseded by the 14th Amendment in 1868.

The supreme court is the only federal court mentioned in the constitution. At the outset, the court was designed to function as the court of ultimate resort in the Union, and as a court of first instance in cases involving the states and certain diplomats. With the seminal ruling Marbury v. Madison of 1803 however, the supreme court claimed the authority of judicial review, thus emerging as the final arbiter of the constitution. The power to declare any act of congress, action of the executive branch, and even certain operations of a state as incompatible with the constitution has been utilized with increasing frequency, bringing about profound consequences for the workings of the political system.

The constitutional amendment procedure necessitates the participation of the states. An amendment may be proposed either by a two-thirds majority of both chambers of congress or by a constitutional convention which has to be summoned by two-thirds of the states. The ratification of an amendment requires the support of at least three-quarters of the states.

If the first ten Amendments (The Bill of Rights of 1791), which were a crucial ingredient in the initial ratification process, are excluded, the US Constitution has only been amended 17 times since its inception. Thus, virtually the same document applies today as it applied over two centuries ago. The constitution's success is partly based on its overall vagueness, as it says remarkably little about the precise powers of the central institutions or how authority ought to be divided between the federal and the state governments. The workings of US American federalism, for instance, proved to be highly flexible, and the political system was able to respond to new political imperatives such as the growing role of central governments in social and economic policy during the 20th century. Hence, constitutional change by judicial interpretation owes much more to the evolution of US American politics than the wording of the constitution as such.

Although the framers of the constitution viewed parties or factions principally as detrimental to a sound development of the new political community, a two-party system emerged during the formative years of the republic, which has been dominated by the democratic and republican parties for nearly 150 years. In contrast to European party systems, which had been structured by the macro-historical processes of nation-building and industrialization, US American parties did not evolve along the lines of durable class, regional, or religious-cultural cleavages. Instead, the parties' electoral support was, and still is, based on heterogeneous and fluid coalitions of ethnic, religious, and socio-economic groups. Accordingly, US American party history is defined by consecutive electoral coalitions. During phases of relative political stability, the majority party is able to combine the most significant socio-economic interests of the time and consequently dominates the political process. Each of the party systems has been demarcated by critical elections in which significant segments of the electorate durably changed allegiance or newly enfranchised groups entered the electoral arena and thus may have been mobilized to support the emerging majority party. The appearance of third parties at the national level, particularly during phases of shifting party alignments, has been a regular phenomenon, but none of these contenders—with the exception of the replacement of the Whigs by the Republicans in 1856—was ever able to establish a sustainable performance. Realignments have usually been precipitated by profound social and/or economic crises such as the Civil War or the Great Depression and entailed significant policy change. The theory of realignment, which was developed by the political scientists Vladimer O. Key (1955) and Walter D. Burnham (1970), remains valuable as an interpretative tool for understanding past processes of periodic change in US American politics. This macro-sociological concept however, cannot be applied ahistorically in order to predict time and circumstances of future party changes. Despite the ongoing debates regarding the exact starting points of the realignments, there is broad agreement among political historians that at least five party systems can be distinguished:

Party Systems in US American History[a]

Period	Majority party	Minority party
1788–1800	Federalist: Coalition of urban commercial interests and Northern landowners.	Anti-Federalist until 1796, then Democratic-Republican (1790s–1832): Primarily rural, agrarian interests in Central and Southern states favouring states' rights and individual freedom; initially opposed to ratification of the constitution.
1800–1856	Democratic-Republican: Party broadened mass appeal, extended suffrage and popular control of government. After 1824 the party splintered into two factions. The group led by Jackson retained the name Democratic-Republican, which was shortened to Democratic in 1832. The other faction, headed by President Adams, assumed the name National-Republican (1828–1832).	Federalist (until 1816): Party was perceived as a party of the aristocracy. Virtually no opposition 1816–1824 until emergence of the National-Republicans (1828–1832). After the party went out of existence, their members provided the base for a new anti-Jackson party, the Whigs. Whig Party (1834–1856): Amalgam of forces opposed to Jackson, mainly Southerners and later businessmen. Party disintegrated over slavery issue.
1856–1896	Republican: Initially coalition of anti-slavery forces, former Whigs, Free Soil and dissident Democrats, later the party of business interests, Northern and Western farmers.	Democratic: Party strength rooted in the South. Coalition of both poor whites and larger landowners, but pockets of support among Northern and Western farmers and workers who felt threatened by rapid industrialization.

Period (cont.)	Majority party	Minority party
1896–1932	Republican: Party became associated with Northern industrial interests.	Democratic: Stronghold of the South was elevated; supporters of the Populist Party have been absorbed.
1932–1968	Democratic: Era of the New Deal coalition (Southern voters, blacks, Jews, academics, organized labour, urban ethnic voters).	Republican: Main electoral support from rural areas, big business, the West and New England.
1968–	Controversial interpretation of party system development: some political scientists consider current period as a continuation of dealignment as split-ticket voting and the number of independents are increasing. Others argue that the 1970s have been a phase of transition and identified the 1980s as a period of a Republican majority, the 1990s as a period of a Democratic majority.	

[a] For similar historical party system classifications with deviating time periods at certain points see Burnham (1970, 1982), Chambers and Burnham (1975), McKay (1993).

(1) During the first decade of the Republic, the two parties competing for power were the Federalists, the first majority party, and the Jefferson-Republicans or Democratic-Republicans (until 1796 Anti-Federalists), who can be seen as the precursors of the contemporary Democratic Party. The Federalists, among them such prominent figures as Alexander Hamilton, John Adams, and George Washington, primarily represented a coalition of tradesmen and landowners of the New England states and were in favour of a strong federal government. The opposition, led by Thomas Jefferson, had its base of support mainly among farmers and Southern planters, and emphasized the constitutional rights of the individual states.

(2) After the turn of the century the opposition improved organizationally and was able to attract broad electoral support. Led by James Madison and later by Andrew Jackson and Martin Van Buren, the Democratic-Republicans (since 1832 Democratic Party) replaced the Federalists (from the 1830s–1850s Whigs) as the majority party by successfully appealing to egalitarian attitudes of the farmers and the urban middle-classes. Particularly during Andrew Jackson's presidency, important reforms were introduced with regard to the electoral process, which enhanced popular participation in government ('Jacksonian Democracy').

(3) Triggered off by the bitter conflict over the issue of slavery and the subsequent Civil War between the Northern and Southern states (1861–1865), the party system was subject to the next major realign-

ment. The political vacuum caused by the decline of the Whig Party and the failure of third parties such as Know-Nothing and Free Soil created space for a new political movement. The Republicans, founded in 1854, successfully gathered antislavery forces and, under John C. Fremont's and Abraham Lincoln's leadership, quickly became the majority party. The Republican coalition consisted of members of the new industrial and financial business class, some industrial workers, and farmers in the North and the West. The Democrats were mainly the party of poor white men and Southern landowners. The black population broadly supported the Republicans as they had officially abolished slavery in 1860, but most former slave states circumvented the relevant anti-discrimination provisions of the constitution and effectively disenfranchised this group. The Democratic coalition was not confined to the Southern states as it included larger cities in the North-East as well as farmers in the Mid-West who felt threatened by the process of rapid industrialization and the growing influence of the financial sector.

(4) Another significant electoral realignment began with the watershed election of the Republican William McKinley in 1896 following the depression of 1893. The animosities of the Civil War had been largely replaced by more urgent economic concerns. The tensions stirred by the rapid process of industrialization led to the foundation of the Populist Party, which was eventually absorbed by the Democrats. The conflicting economic and regional interests of this period increased the Democrats' stronghold over the agrarian South, while the Republicans became the party of the industrialized North. The decades towards the turn of the century were also the era of the so-called party machines. Particularly in large cities such as Chicago or Albany, the parties developed strong organizations that had the power to determine who gained access to local public offices, and strongly influenced the process of presidential nomination. While the machines often applied corrupt and illegal practices, they also fulfilled important societal functions, such as integrating the growing immigrant workforce into the political system and providing basic welfare benefits. Around the turn of the century, the middle-class-based Progressive Movement condemned the undemocratic practices of the machines and was eventually able to instigate reforms such as the direct primaries, which effectively weakened the link between parties and their voters.

(5) To date, the last outstanding and undisputed realignment of the party system occurred during the Great Depression of the 1930s. The Democrats gained the position of majority party by responding to the economic crisis with Keynesian policies of increased state intervention

and thus attracted large segments of the electorate that suffered the most because of the economic and social circumstances. The New Deal coalition, closely associated with President Franklin D. Roosevelt's policies, brought together a disparate group of interests, adding to the Democratic Party's traditional base of support from unionized workers, blacks, Jews, intellectuals, and various ethnic minorities. The Republicans primarily represented the interests of businesses and banks, middle-class suburbanites, and rural areas.

(6) Since the late 1960s, the support for the two main parties has generally become more volatile and unpredictable. The New Deal coalition lost its earlier electoral strength as the former 'Solid Democratic South'—partly as a reaction to the Democrats' proximity to the civil rights movement—and large parts of the Rocky Mountain States are now strongly leaning towards the Republican Party. Yet, former Democratic dominance broke down without having been replaced by a clear-cut shift in political alignments. Judging from election results of the past 25 years, none of the parties can convincingly claim to be in the position of the undisputed majority party. Political observers have repeatedly highlighted the contradictory developments within the US American party system since the 1970s. Several indicators, such as the continuing low turnout rates, rarely exceeding 55%, decreasing party identification, and increasing ticket splitting, support the notion of declining parties. On the other hand, developments are underway that seem to imply the opposite. At the party level, organizational revitalization and growing vertical integration can be observed, entailing a somewhat stronger position of the parties during election campaigns and in the processes of candidate selection. In addition, party unity in congress has increased due to the general resurgence of ideological differences between the parties. Taken together, these developments increased the likelihood of 'divided government' and thus added to the difficulties of governing a highly fragmented polity.

1.2 Evolution of Electoral Provisions

No other nation selects as many public officials through elections as the United States. All levels of government combined, US American citizens may regularly elect approximately 525,000 public officials, from local school board members, attorneys, state governors and legislators to the members of congress, vice president, and president. The prominence of elections in the political process is rooted in long-standing republican and populist traditions. Yet, this egalitarian brand of democracy only slowly gained ascendancy and suffered severe setbacks during the 19th and 20th centuries over the more elitist views of the Founding Fathers. At the beginning, the framers of the constitution set rigorous limitations to democracy—at least by contemporary standards. These restrictions, manifested, for example, in the indirect system of election for the chief executive, reflected their fear of unrestricted majority rule and elective despotism. Another crucial factor in the evolution of US American electoral provisions is the decentralized nature of the relevant legal-institutional core, causing a highly fragmented patchwork of divergent regulations between, but also within, the states.

According to Article 2, section 1 of the constitution, the appointment of the members of the electoral college falls under state jurisdiction, thus giving the legislators the discretion to determine the method of choosing electors. In the early years of the republic, the states applied nine different approaches to select presidential electors, ranging from selection by legislature to state-wide, direct, popular elections. By 1820, 15 of the 24 states had adopted the state wide winner-take-all method, and by 1836 all states but South Carolina, which followed suit in 1868, used the same method. The rapid democratization of the presidential vote is due to the legislatures' responsiveness to the strong demands for public input on choosing the president. Nevertheless, the indirect method of electing the president is still applied today, violating the 'one-person, one vote' principle and thus, at times, causing decisive disproportions between popular and electoral vote. In the presidential election of 2000, for example, an elector in South Dakota represented 230,000 people while an elector in New York represented 550,000. In three instances—in 1876, 1888, and 2000—a candidate received a majority in the electoral college but fewer popular votes than the opposing contender. After the tie of the electoral college vote between Thomas Jefferson and Aaron Burr in 1800 (see Table 2.9.2), the 12th Amendment of 1804 ensured that any election in which a candidate received less than a majority of the college would then be decided in a runoff election in the house, and the votes for president and vice president were combined. The original constitution provided that each elector had two votes and was required to cast these votes for different persons. The candidate with the largest majority would become president and the runner-up would become vice president. As a result, the electoral votes of each state were often scattered among several candidates because the electors did not designate which of their votes was for president and which for vice president. Another cause of occasional splits in a state's electoral vote is the so-called 'faithless elector'. Although the electors in 24 states are not obliged to vote for any particular candidate by state law, in reality they are almost always faithful to the candidate of the party with which they are affiliated. However, on rare occasions, electors have broken ranks to vote for candidates not supported by their parties (see Table 2.9.2). In comparison with the evolution of the presidential elections, the electoral procedures concerning the house of representatives—at the outset the only direct link between the people and the government—were subject to changes of technicalities rather than of principle. Until 1880, when most of the states had changed to even-numbered year elections, a two-year election cycle was in effect. In addition, states varied in terms of how they allocated their seats, using a range of district, district-state, and state-only combinations. As a first substantial step towards reducing the deviations between the states, congress prohibited all MMC voting schemes in 1842. However, it was not until 1968 that all 50 states had adopted the SMC system for house elections. The appointment of the senators, who were initially selected by the state legislatures, experienced a similar progression towards democracy as the presidential elections. Partly due to increasing instances of partisan deadlock in the selection of senators in the state legislatures around the turn of the century and partly due to mounting demands from the Progressive Movement for popular election of the senate, the house passed several resolutions for a constitutional amendment for the direct election. After continued political pressure, the senate finally approved the wording of the amendment and in 1913 the 17th Amendment, stipulating that the senate was to be elected by popular vote, was ratified.

The most important aspect for the evolution of US American suffrage was that the constitution (Article 1, section 2) entitled the individual states to design their own election laws for the selection of their representatives in congress—regardless of the fact that the house is a national institution. Consequently, the states were allowed to define the eligible electorate and to set up the qualifications for individuals running for office. The logic of the states' crucial position with regard to the universality of the democratic process was maintained in principle even in the course of the gradual democratization of both presidential and senatorial elections. However, as many states denied universality by discriminating against distinct groups, national intervention occurred repeatedly, at times requiring dramatic measures. The history of the suffrage in the United States can be subdivided into three major periods (cf. Rusk 2001: 13–20):

(1) 1788–1850s: In spite of the democratic spirit of the American Revolution, the states' early voting rules tended to be inspired by colonial tradition. Consequently, suffrage was initially restricted to upper class white males. In most states, certain economic requirements, either in form of freehold, personal property, tax regulations, or a combination of these, had to be met in order to vote. With the gradual replacement of landownership qualifications by less stringent ones as in the case of personal property and taxpaying requirements, middle- and lower-class white males were increasingly given the opportunity to participate in elections. However, not all states followed the path towards a more inclusive suffrage. In some cases, taxpaying was introduced not as an alternate but as an additional requirement for voting. At the end of the 1850s, universal white male suffrage was widely achieved. While a few states still upheld taxpaying qualifications, these taxes were low and functioned more as a registry fee. Residency requirements were a second set of qualifications limiting the eligibility of the electorate. Upon entry into the Union, many states applied various combinations of residency required in different geographic entities, such as state, county, city, or precinct; in some states even multiple residency requirements were in effect. Over time, the length of residency required for voting tended to decline. A third set of suffrage qualifications related to citizenship. While most of the original states did not mention citizenship as a formal requirement in their early election laws, in practice the right to vote was restricted to citizens.

(2) 1860s–1920: this period was marked by cross-currents rather than consistent developments. During the years of reconstruction in the aftermath of the Civil War, the suffrage was formally extended to black males. Prior to the Reconstruction Acts of 1867 and the 15th Amendment of 1870, which sought to remove racial barriers to voting in the former Confederate states as a precondition to being readmitted to the Union, the majority of the states—including the non-Southern states—had actually excluded blacks from the vote. After a short period, in which blacks were allowed to exercise their right to vote in the South, the situation changed with the removal of federal troops from the region as part of the Compromise of 1877 (see Table 2.9.2, 1876). Subsequently, Southern Democrats systematically purged the black vote by imposing numerous obstacles for electoral participation. Part of this strategy was the introduction of poll tax requirements. While seemingly small, the amount of these taxes was particularly burdensome for blacks, but also for poor whites. Furthermore, seven of the former Confederate states and Oklahoma enacted literacy tests, thereby erecting an addi-

tional barrier to the vote. These tests usually required that a person be able to read and write English. So-called 'understanding clauses' were an alternative way of meeting the requirements, thus allowing illiterate whites to pass the tests. The decision as to whether a person gave a 'reasonable' interpretation of a text that was read aloud rested with the election registrar. However, it should be noted that non-Southern states passed literacy requirements as well. While some of the earlier actions were motivated by anti-immigrant attitudes that were articulated by groups such as the American Party ('Know-Nothings'), the literacy tests introduced around the turn of the century can be seen as a reaction to the Progressive Movement and its demands that voters be informed and responsible citizens. In the early 1900s, the Southern System was extended to the nomination process of the Democratic Party by introducing white primary laws. Taken together, the poll tax, literacy tests, and the white primaries effectively disenfranchised the black population in the South and contributed to the firm one-party dominance of the 'Solid South'. During the second suffrage period, many states passed new citizenship requirements and alien voting laws. The overall tendency in the second half of the 19th century was to weaken citizenship requirements. However, with regard to the enactment of alien voting laws, which allowed immigrants to vote even before actually attaining citizenship, pronounced regional differences emerged. The new states in the Mid-West and West needed to encourage people to move west, and offering immigrants the right to vote immediately upon arrival was seen as an additional incentive next to the promise of cheap land. The alien voting legislation in the South was motivated by the desire to build up a—preferably white—workforce after the tremendous casualties suffered by this region in the Civil War. In the New England states no alien voting laws were passed, reflecting the more elitist political philosophy of this part of the country. Once more, the Progressive Movement and its perception of immigrants as people that are ignorant and easy to manipulate created much of the momentum leading to the repeal of all alien voting laws by 1926. A clear exception to the rather restrictive election laws at the turn of the century was the movement towards women's suffrage. In 1889, Wyoming was the first state to experiment with legislation with regard to female suffrage, and soon other states in the West followed suit (Colorado 1893, Utah 1895, Idaho 1896). Prior to the ratification of the 19th Amendment in 1920, which formally established universal suffrage, 27 states had granted women the right to vote. A substantial advancement in the democratic quality of the voting process itself was achieved in the late 19th century. Before the official ballot was introduced in Massachusetts in 1888, the ballot papers were usually provided by the competing parties or candidates and voting was not effectively secret. By 1896, most of the states had adopted the official ballot.

(3) 1920–present: During the third suffrage period, the goal of achieving an essentially unrestricted national franchise was finally achieved—both legally and in practice. The racist restrictions that had been impeding the blacks from electoral participation were removed step by step. In some instances, the constitutional rights of blacks had to be enforced by federal authorities. In 1944, the supreme court declared the Southern all-white primary to be unconstitutional. The 24th Amendment of 1964 outlawed the poll tax, and the related Voting Rights Act of 1965 eliminated literacy tests in certain areas of the South. The 1970 Voting Rights Act went further and banned literacy tests for voting in those non-Southern states that were still operating these requirements. This act also reduced existing variations in residency restrictions to a minimum by imposing a 30-day residency requirement for voting in presidential elections, and a subsequent supreme court decision in 1972 recommended similar residency rules for other elections. The inclusiveness of the democratic process was finally enhanced by the 26th Amendment of 1971 that lowered voting age to 18 years.

Unlike the democratization of the elected national bodies and the development of the suffrage, the regulations for campaign finance were mostly driven by the federal level. Concerns about rising campaign costs in the late 1950s and early 1960s led congress to enact the Federal Election Campaign Act (FECA) in 1971. The law established contribution limits on the amount a candidate could give to his or her own campaign, set ceilings on the amount a campaign could spend in primaries and general elections, and imposed public disclosure procedures on federal candidates and political committees. Prior to the FECA, a series of supreme court decisions had dealt with matters of election financing and a few federal regulations in this area had been codified. In 1974, the FECA was thoroughly revised in response to the pressure for comprehensive reform in the wake of the Watergate scandal. The amended legislation established the Federal Election Commission (FEC) as an independent agency to regulate election financing. The 1974 reform also created an optional program for full public financing for presidential election campaigns. Before the new rules could take effect, the supreme court ruled against the spending limits established for house and senate candidates in 1976. The spending ceilings allowed to stand were those for publicly-funded presidential campaigns and the contribution ceilings with respect to individuals, party organizations, and political action committees (PACs). Changes in the financial regime in 1979 paved the way for the phenomenon known as 'soft money'; that is, the common name given to party funds that are not regulated by federal law but for which the FEC allows party committees to accept and spend on administrative expenses associated with party building and for certain grass roots expenditures. Soft monies held by national organizations could include funds donated by unions and corporations since such funds could be contributed for party building purposes. The rise of soft money meant that hard monies could be freed-up for massive political campaign advertisements. An explosion in funding occurred in the 1990s, as parties found a new way to spend soft money. These issue advocacy ads do not expressly advocate the election or defeat of a federal candidate and thus are not subject to federal regulation. As a reaction to the expansion of soft money, the FEC issued new disclosure regulations in 1991, requiring the parties to file regular reports of their contributions and disbursements with the FEC. In 1996, the supreme court struck down the longstanding rule against party organizations engaging in independent expenditures. In response to this ruling, the Republican and Democratic parties established political operations separate from their national committees in order to make independent expenditures on behalf of their senate committees. In effect, the parties now have an additional avenue to spend even more sums on federal campaigns.

The legacy of the states' power to determine the contours of the franchise continues to be most evident in the details of voting and election laws. Provided that the established key federal principles of voting are not violated, the states are free to govern the ground rules of the electoral process—such as the organizational context, the registration records, the ballot design, the addition of the vote, the rules concerning the determination of the intent of the voter, and dispute settlement procedures. In many states, decisions on certain aspects of the electoral process are passed down to jurisdictional subunits. The dubious stalemate of the presidential election of 2000 and the dramatic partisan disputes regarding the count of the vote in a number of Florida counties as well as in many other states were the upshot of a historically evolved, pieced together amalgam of state and federal laws. Nevertheless, despite the changes to the electoral laws that have been instigated by several states as well as by Congress (e.g. Help America Vote Act of 2002) in an effort to avoid future embarrassments such as those in Florida, major reforms of the US American electoral process are not to be expected.

1.3. Current Electoral Provisions

Sources: US Constitution (particularly Article 1, Section 2; Article 2, Sections 2 and 4); the 12th (1804), 14th (1868), 15th (1870), 17th (1913), 19th (1920), 20th (1932), 22nd (1951), 23rd (1961), 24th (1964), 25th (1965), and 26th (1971) Amendments to the US Constitution; Apportionment Act of 1929; Federal Elections Campaign Acts of 1971, 1974, 1976, 1977, 1979, 1981, 1983, 1984, 1989, 1990, 1991, 1992, 1993,1994, 1995, 1996, 1999, 2000, 2002 and 2004 (2 U.S.C. 431 through 442); Help America Vote Act of 2002 (42 USC 15301); National Voter Registration Act of 1993 (42 U.S.C. 1973gg and 11 CFR 8); Presidential Election Campaign Fund Act (26 U.S.C. 95); Uniformed and Overseas Citizen Absentee Voting Act of 1986 (42 U.S.C. 1973ff through 1973ff–6, 39 U.S.C. 3406, and 18 U.S.C. 608–609); Voting Accessibility for the Elderly and Handicapped Act of 1984 (42 U.S.C. 1973ee through 1973ee–6); Voting Rights Acts of 1965, 1970, 1975 and 1982 (42 U.S.C. 1971 through 1973 et seq.).

Suffrage: The principles of universal, equal, direct, and secret suffrage are applied. Every citizen of 18 years of age or older is entitled to vote in congressional and presidential elections. The right to vote is constitutionally guaranteed due to successive constitutional amendments aiming to eliminate the exclusion of voters based on race, gender, illiteracy, and property or income requirements. Regulations concerning compulsory voting are not in effect. Certain individuals such as inmates of correctional institutions are excluded from the franchise in most states.

Registration: No nationwide system of permanent voter registration is in force. In most states, persons legally qualified to participate in a general election are required to register individually prior to the election day in order to be entitled to vote. The statutory time periods for registration differ from state to state. The registration procedure may require that individuals take an oath or sign an affidavit stating, for example, that they are citizens of the United States, residents of the state, and 18 years or older. Under the National Voter Registration Act, which applies to all federal elections in all states except Idaho, Minnesota, New Hampshire, North Dakota, Wisconsin, and Wyoming, citizens must be given the opportunity to register to vote or to update their registration data when applying for or renewing a motor vehicle driver's license or other personal identification document issued by a state authority. In addition, registration opportunities must be available in any state office that provides public services and assistance. Most states require that citizens establish residency by living within a voting jurisdiction for a fixed period of time (usually 30 days) before they are entitled to vote. The degree to which the formal registration requirements are restricted varies strongly from state to state, accounting for some of the substantial differences of the turnout rates between states. The provisions for clearing names from the registration lists differ from state to state.

Provisional ballot: If a citizen does not appear on the official list of eligible voters for the polling place or his/her registration is otherwise invalid, the person is permitted to cast a provisional ballot on election day. The voter's eligibility is then verified after the election, and, if the person's right to vote is confirmed, the ballot is counted.

Absentee voting: Absentee ballot papers are available for registered voters who are not able to cast their vote on election day of a presidential election, provided that they have applied for an absentee ballot no later than seven days before the election (or a lesser period if state law permits). The ballots have to be returned to the appropriate election official no later than the close of the polls. Persons who move to a new state within 30 days prior to the election and who may therefore fail to qualify for registration in their new state are permitted to vote as an absentee in their state of former residence. For members of the armed services and merchant marines and their eligible family members, and civilian citizens residing outside the United States, absentee registration and voting is available in elections for federal office; special regulations apply.

Special voting regulations: Provisions for voters who require assistance to vote due to blindness, disability, or inability to read or write apply to all elections in all jurisdictions. Bilingual election requirements apply to certain jurisdictions, requiring them to provide registration and voting materials and oral assistance in the language of a qualified minority group as well as in English. Federal legislation requires that each political subdivision responsible for conducting elections within each state assure that polling places for federal elections are accessible to elderly and handicapped voters.

Election day: National general elections must be held on the first Tuesday after the first Monday in November of even-numbered years. Elections are held for all house seats, for one-third of the senate seats, and, in even-numbered years divisible by four, for the presidency. The electoral college gives its vote for president and vice president on the first Monday after the second Wednesday in December.

Ballots: State laws regulate access to the ballot and its design. In many states, modern voting techniques such as the voting machine or punch-card voting have replaced the paper ballot.

Addition of votes: Bipartisan Canvassing Boards at the local and state levels are responsible for the collection, tabulation and certification of election results.

Disenfranchisement: Most states prohibit criminals who are in prison from voting. Ex-felons are allowed to vote in most of the states. However, in some states special procedures for restoring a person's civil rights are in force. A few states refuse to restore the right to vote to certain ex-criminals. The regulations regarding the disenfranchisement of the mentally infirm vary from state to state. The courts have not yet developed any solid guidelines to determine when a person loses his or her mental capacity to vote.

Elected national institutions: Both chambers of the US Congress are directly elected. The lower chamber, the house of representatives, consists of 435 members, reflecting the principle of representation by population. The upper chamber (senate) is made up of 100 senators, two senators for each of the 50 states, reflecting equal representation by states. All members of the house of representatives are elected on a bi-annual basis; the senators are elected for a six-year term. One-third of the senate is up for election every two years. The president is elected by the electoral college. The presidential electors are elected by direct popular vote. The presidential term is four years; no person may be elected president more than twice.

Nomination of candidates: Formal requirements: in most states, candidates for public office must be qualified to vote in a general election and be formally nominated. The required period of time a candidate must have resided in the district or state varies, depending on the state and the office. The constitution stipulates that the president must be a natural born citizen. The following minimum age requirements for an individual to be a candidate for a federal elective office are established by the constitution: 35 years for the presidency, 30 years for a senator, and 25 years for a member of the house of representatives. Durational residency requirements in the United States for presidency are 14 years, for a senator nine years, and for a representative seven years. No maximum age requirements for vacating an elective federal office are in effect. Certain federal and public service employees are prohibited from actively participating in political campaigns and becoming a candidate for federal elected office in a partisan election. In the absence of constitutional or federal provisions, persons in prison and ex-criminals are not disqualified to run for office, unless state laws place restrictions on the right to be a candidate.

Procedure: Nominations may be submitted by citizens who are entitled to vote and by qualified political parties. The legal requirements vary from state to state, but in most cases candidates must file for election with the secretary of state. In some cases, formal notification of the appropriate official is sufficient, but the more common requirement is that the candidate provides the official with petitions signed by a percentage of registered voters from the jurisdiction in which she or he will run and/or provide a cash deposit that will be refunded if the candidate receives a sufficient number of votes.

Primary elections: Primaries are the method most often used to select party nominees. Two basic categories have to be distinguished: the open primary allows voters to participate regardless of their party affiliation. The closed primary is restricted to voters formally affiliated with a party. (The states have adopted different requirements with regard to the declaration of party affiliation.) In either case, the voter may participate in the nomination process of only one party. Some states, almost exclusively in the South, require that a candidate receives a majority of the votes before becoming the nominee, which means that run-off primaries between the two finishers may be necessary. To prevent individuals who lose a party's primary from running as an independent candidate in the following general election, most states have passed so-called 'sore loser statutes'. In lieu of these statutes, some states require independent candidates to file nomination papers to run in the general election at a specified day before the primary election and thus prohibit independent candidates from filing in a party's primary.

- *presidential elections*: Presidential nominations are formally made at each party's national convention, normally held in the summer of the election year. To receive a party's nomination, a candidate must gain the support of the majority of his or her party's delegates at the national convention. The delegates are selected at the state level on the basis of presidential primaries or by so-called 'caucuses' (a gathering of party members and/or legislators for the purpose of choosing party candidates). The presidential primaries are the most widely applied method of delegate selection. The decision whether primaries are held and how they are conducted lies with the individual states. In most states, presidential primaries elect delegates who are committed to vote for a particular candidate, whereas in some states, the primaries are not binding.

In some states, not all parties use the primary to select convention delegates. In other states, parties currently use the caucus to register preferences for those wanting to run for the position of president.

- *parliamentary elections*: The states overwhelmingly select their candidates for the senate and the house in primary elections. A few states allow either the convention or a combination of the primary and the convention methods. Minor parties are often required to obtain petitions so that their candidates can run in the primary or the general election.

Each state has developed its own approach to the problem of distinguishing major parties from minor parties and independent candidates. Most states require a certain percentage of the popular vote mostly in the last gubernatorial elections to officially approve a group as a major political party. Automatic access to the ballot is the main privilege given to major parties. The status as a qualified party is a prerequisite in the majority of the states in order to file candidates. Independent candidates and minor parties must submit a petition of supporters to the state officials in order to be allowed to participate in an election campaign. The quorum for the signatures varies from state to state. The Federal Election Campaign Act defines the party status for the purpose of public funding of presidential campaigns (see public financing).

Election financing: The Federal Election Campaign Act provides the legal framework within which campaign financing is orchestrated. The Federal Election Commission (FEC), which was established by the act, monitors the conduct of some aspects of the election campaigns and is partly responsible for implementing public financing of presidential candidates.

Contributions: Campaign contribution limits provide that individuals in any single election may not contribute more than US $ 2,000 to any candidate, US $ 25,000 to a national party committee, US $ 10,000 to a state party committee, and US $ 5,000 to other political committees in any single year. During the period which begins on January 1 of an odd-numbered year and ends on 31 December of the next even-numbered year, no individual may make contributions aggregating more than US $ 37,500, in the case of contributions to candidates and the authorized committees of candidates; US $ 57,500, in the case of any other contributions, of which not more than US $ 37,500 may be attributable to contributions to political committees which are not political committees of national political parties. Political Action Committees (PACs) may not contribute more than US $ 5,000 to any candidate with respect to a federal election, US $ 15,000 to a national party committee, and

US $ 5,000 to other political committees in any calendar year. The Federal Election Campaign Act requires candidate committees, party committees, and PACs to file periodic reports disclosing the money they raise and spend. Candidates must identify all PACs and party committees that make contributions, and they must identify contributions from individuals of US $ 200 or more per year. Provisions are also in force regarding so-called independent campaign committees, which may raise money in support of or in opposition to candidates as long as these activities are carried out independently and not coordinated with the campaign for any candidate. Such committees are required to report to the FEC as well. Contributions are prohibited from the following: the treasuries of corporations, labour organizations, national banks, federal government contractors (however, contributions from PACs are allowed), and foreign nationals who do not have permanent residence in the United States. Cash contributions which exceed US $ 100 in aggregate from one person, and anonymous contributions over US $ 50 are prohibited.

Expenses: National committees of both major and minor parties are allowed to spend up to US $ 0.02 (plus cost-of-living adjustments) per person of voting age on behalf of their presidential candidates. In the case of candidates for congressional office, the national or state party committees may not spend more than US $ 0.02 (plus cost-of-living adjustments) multiplied by the voting age population of the state. The Federal Election Campaign Act introduced ceilings on presidential campaign expenditure of publicly funded candidates (see public financing). All presidential candidates must disclose expenditures exceeding US $ 200 per year. Independent groups such as PACs may make unlimited expenditures advocating the election or defeat of a clearly identified candidate if the expenditure is made independently of a candidate's campaign. Persons making independent expenditures must report them to the FEC and disclose the sources of the funds.

Public financing: Under the Presidential Campaign Fund Act partial public funding for the presidential primary and election campaigns is available to qualified candidates who agree to accept limits of US $ 10 million to their total campaign expenditures prior to nomination (plus cost-of-living adjustments). Such candidates can qualify for matching funds during the primary process by raising at least US $ 5,000 in 20 different states (that is, over US $ 100,000) from contributions of US $ 250 or less. Once qualified, candidates receive matching funds on a dollar-for-dollar basis for every contribution of US $ 250 or less. Only contributions from individuals will be matched.

In presidential elections, each major party's candidate is eligible to receive a grant to cover all the expenses of their campaign. The basic fund is US $ 20 million; the amount is adjusted for inflation each presidential election year. Nominees who accept the funds may not raise private contributions (from individuals, PACs, or party committees) and must limit their campaign expenditures to the amount of public funds they receive. Candidates may spend up to US $ 50,000 from their own personal funds. Minor party candidates (a nominee of a party whose candidate received between 5 and 25% of the total popular vote in the preceding presidential election) may be eligible for partial public funding. The amount to which a minor candidate is entitled is based on the ratio of the party's popular vote in the preceding presidential election to the average popular vote of the two major party candidates in that election. A new party candidate is entitled to partial public funding after the election if he or she receives five percent or more of the vote. The amount is based on the ratio of the new party's candidate popular vote in the current election to the average popular vote of the two major party candidates in the election. Although minor and new party candidates may supplement public funds with private contributions, they are otherwise subject to the same spending limit and other requirements that apply to major party candidates.

Each major party may receive public funds for its national presidential nomination convention. The base amount for each party to finance its national presidential nomination convention is set at US $ 4 million (plus cost-of-living adjustments). Other parties may also be eligible for partial public financing of conventions provided that their nominees received at least five percent of the popular vote in the previous presidential election.

The public funds for presidential primaries, general elections, and national party conventions are exclusively financed by a voluntary tax check off. Individual taxpayers may check a box on their income tax returns indicating that they agree to direct US $ 3.00 of their tax to the presidential campaign fund.

Electoral system
- *presidential elections*: Single-member plurality system ('first-past-the-post'). The constitutional requirement to be elected president and vice president is that the candidates receive a majority of votes in the electoral college. Thus, in a presidential election the individual voter actually votes for a slate of electors committed to a particular presidential candidate and his running-mate. Each party in a state has a separate slate

of electors who virtually gain the right to cast a state's electoral votes if their party's candidate places first in the state's popular vote. Currently, the states Maine and Nebraska deviate from the statewide 'at-large' election system as two of the states' electors are selected within congressional districts and two are determined on the basis of a statewide vote. If no candidate receives a majority in the 538-member college, the election of the president is determined by the house of representatives on the basis of one vote per state delegation, the failure to select a vice president is resolved by the senate.

Electoral college: Each state has a number of electoral votes equal to the number of its representatives in congress; in addition, the District of Columbia (D.C.) has three electoral votes. Accordingly, candidates gain electoral votes in 51 separate races, one in each state and one in D.C. The electors do not assemble as a national body but cast their ballots from their respective states. The constitution allows each state to design the formal procedures for choosing the electors. Although electors are not legally bound to vote for any particular candidate in currently 24 states, they are almost always faithful to the candidate of the party with which they are affiliated. Since 1828, the states' electoral college votes have, with very rare exceptions, been cast as a block for the candidate with a plurality of the popular vote in the respective state.

- *parliamentary elections*: Single-member plurality system ('first-past-the-post').

House of representatives: Since 1911, the number of members of the house is limited to 435. In 1967, a statute formally established the single-member-district system of representation in the house requiring each state to contain as many congressional districts as it has members in the house.

Reapportionment: The distribution of the 435 seats among the states is based on the decennial population census, creating the possibility that some states lose seats if their proportion of the country's total population decreases. The method of equal proportion involves complicated calculations: each of the 50 states is initially assigned one seat to which it is entitled by the constitution. The remaining 385 seats are distributed by calculating so-called 'priority numbers' for the states to receive second seats, third seats, and so on, by dividing the state's population by the square root of $n(n-1)$, 'n' being the number of seats for that state. The priority numbers are then lined up in order and the seats are given to the states with priority numbers until all seats are awarded.

Redistricting: The constitution mandates reapportionment every ten years based upon the census. States gaining or losing representatives must draw new district lines. According to a series of supreme court rulings on the 'one person, one vote principle', the states must apportion congressional districts within a state to be roughly equal in population. In most states, the legislatures are responsible for drawing up and enacting the new district maps. An effective national ban on gerrymandering is currently not in effect.

Vacancies: In the case of a vacancy, the governor of the affected state usually calls a special election to fill the vacancy.

Senate: Since 1913 (17th Amendment) senators are directly elected by popular vote. Each senator represents an entire state. The single-member plurality system of representation is applied accordingly.

Classes: The senate is divided into three classes of members, depending on the year in which the member is elected. Class one senators began their regular terms in the years 1789, 1791, 1797 etc., class two in the years 1789, 1793, 1799 etc., and class three in the years 1789, 1795, 1801 etc.

Vacancies: Under the 17th Amendment, state legislatures are allowed to empower governors to make temporary appointments until the vacancy can be filled by a special election. Special elections—elections held to fill terms that have not expired—are usually held in November of an even-numbered year. In some states, however, special elections must be held within a few months after the vacancy occurs. Arizona does not allow for temporary appointments to fill vacancies.

Organizational context of elections: Generally, voting practices vary considerably from state to state, reflecting the extremely decentralized character of the voting process. The responsibility for administration and management of the general elections process rests with states and their subordinate jurisdictions. However, under the Voting Rights Act, federal officials—particularly the Attorney General and the District Court of D.C.—are allowed to review new election laws that certain jurisdictions might use to make voting and running for office more burdensome. The supreme court upheld the constitutionality of the Act and its amendments; the basic provisions of the Act will be in effect to the year 2007.

The Federal Election Commission (FEC), consisting of six members appointed by the president with approval of the senate, is an independent regulatory agency that enforces federal election campaign laws. All campaigns for federal office must submit regular reports to the FEC that indicate the nature of campaign expenditures and sources of campaign contributions. In addition, the FEC oversees the public funding of presidential elections.

The smallest district around which the election process is organized is the precinct, normally containing between 150 and 1,200 registered voters. Each precinct has a polling station where voters may cast their ballot at election time.

1.4 Commentary on the Electoral Statistics

The highly decentralized and fragmented character of the electoral process is echoed in the available electoral data. Due to the long history in which there was no central authority responsible for the administration, supervision, and certification of federal elections, no federal institution has published election results in a comprehensive and coherent manner. Even with regard to recent elections, the most respected data collections occasionally report different results. Significant discrepancies can be observed across the most commonly used sources, such as the publications of Congressional Quarterly, the Elections Research Center together with Richard Scammon's contributions, the Inter-university Consortium for Political and Social Research (ICPSR) at the University of Michigan, or the pioneering efforts of political scientists such as Walter D. Burnham, Svend Petersen, and Michael Dubin. However, substantial improvements have been achieved by Jerrold G. Rusk's (2001) reference work, which is the most comprehensive and accurate US electoral data collection available to date.

The difficulties are primarily caused by three common errors: (1) particularly in the late 18th and early 19th centuries, some electoral districts did not report their results, and certain results are considered to be inaccurate or are unavailable. Inconsistencies between various sources emerge when these missing or doubtful data sets are accounted for differently. In some collections, missing results have been estimated and included in the compilations. Moreover, vague documentation in regard to how the variables of interest are counted increases the frequency of discrepancies. (2) In many instances, the 'other' vote and the 'scatter' vote, such as those for marginal or write-in candidates, as well as the 'invalid' vote have not been reported. As a result, calculations regarding participation rates, the total vote, and certain percentages of the total vote, tend to be inconsistent. (3) The most frequent source of difficulties is the failure to report the party labels candidates used for the ballot. This is particularly the case for minority party candidates. In addition, party labels are often misinterpreted as it is difficult to verify under which label a candidate ran. In the 19th century, factional and fusion candidacies were quite common. Candidates labeled as independent, for instance, were often tied to a major or minor party, and candidates may also have received joint endorsements by two parties at the same time. The compilation of national totals is further complicated by the widespread use of different party labels by candidates representing the same party in different districts.

As the chief responsibility for the conduct of national elections rests with the states, the national aggregate, which is the central focus of this publication, is particularly incomplete and prone to inaccuracies. Of the three directly-elected federal institutions, the national election results for the electoral college are—albeit with certain drawbacks—the least disputed. Most problematic in terms of reliability and comprehensiveness is the data available for the house elections. The results of the house-election cycle 1788–89, for instance, are only available for seven of the 13 original states. In order to reduce the degree of confusion, existing partial-data of individual states for all reported federal elections are not included in the aggregation. Most data sources report elections since the 1820s or 1830s, the historical period which is broadly recognized as the beginning of mass electoral politics in the United States. Rusk (2001) was the first to provide popular election results for the period since 1788/89. Based on his collection, data for presidential and house races for the early electoral period has been included. It has to be noted though, that the election returns during the early period are subject to shortcomings due to missing data and the lack of official regulations. The popular election results are generally coded according to the conventional system that classifies the major-party candidates—distinct from 'others'—as those who appear on the ballots as Democrat or Republican or as their respective historical antecedents.

Population statistics and participation rates: A continuous source of inaccuracy throughout US American electoral history are the eligible voting population, the number of registered voters, and the total number of votes in any given election. The popular sources normally fail to report this data or, when reported, they hardly ever agree on the figures. Accurate records corresponding to the eligible electorate do not exist due to the aforementioned deviations between the states in terms of the legal requirements for the franchise throughout US American history. Consequently, the available information is usually based on estimates. As the total numbers of eligible voters—defined as residents legally allowed to participate in federal elections—presented by most sources are not reliable, the authors decided not to include these figures for the period between 1788 and 1928 (Table 2.2). The more recent data is taken from the Congressional Quarterly's collections (1994, 1997). The percentages of the total population that are eligible electors and the turnout data are based on Rusk (2001) and his estimates. Despite the precautions that were applied in the process of selecting the data, there should be no doubt that these statistics are nonetheless subject to severe shortcomings.

In the case of the aggregate participation data 'registered voters', 'votes cast', and 'invalid votes' (Tables 2.7.1, 2.7.2 and 2.9.1), the authors chose not to include these figures as they are either unavailable, incomplete, or inaccurate, and the relevant sources display a significant lack of consistency. In a few instances the data is included provided it is available and undisputed.

Congressional elections: Most sources on house and senate elections merely include district and state results. Data collections reporting the national aggregate are rare. The national election results for congress are taken from Rusk (2001) who partly eliminated the common errors of other sources. As noted in 1.2, until 1880 elections to the house were held within a two-year election cycle. The data reported in this volume combines results even when scattered over two calendar years. This has to be taken into account when attempting to interpret electoral behavior during this historical period. The data for the composition of congress is taken from several Congressional Quarterly publications, Dubin (1998), Scammon (1952–1998) and, for the early election period, Rusk (2001). More recent results have been retrieved from congressional internet sources. As the official results of the 2004 election were not available prior to the editorial deadline, only the information on the composition of parliament is listed.

Presidential elections: The popular election results reported are primarily based on Congressional Quarterly's data (1994, 1997). Election data prior to 1824, which has long been regarded as unavailable, is taken from Rusk (2001). The information on the votes in the electoral college is taken from Congressional Quarterly's Presidential Elections (1997). More recent results have been retrieved from FEC and National Archives & Records Administration online sources. All presidential candidates are normally listed with their respective electoral votes unless the vote is scattered among numerous nominees. In this case, the electoral vote is combined in 'others'.

2. Tables

2.1 Dates of National Elections, Referendums, and Coups d'Etat

Year	Presidential elections[a]	Parliamentary elections Lower Chamber[b]	Upper Chamber[c]	Elections. for Constit Assembly	Referendums	Coups d'état
1848	07/11					
1852	02/11					
1856	04/11					
1860	06/11					
1864	08/11					
1868	03/11					
1870		08/11				
1872	05/11	05/11				
1874		03/11				
1876	07/11	07/11				
1878		05/11				
1880	02/11	02/11				
1882		07/11				
1884	04/11	04/11				
1886		02/11				
1888	06/11	06/11				
1890		04/11				
1892	08/11	08/11				
1894		06/11				
1896	03/11	03/11				
1898		08/11				
1900	06/11	06/11				
1902		04/11				
1904	08/11	08/11				
1906		06/11				
1908	03/11	03/11				
1910		08/11				
1912	05/11	05/11	05/11			
1914		03/11	03/11			
1916	07/11	07/11	07/11			
1918		05/11	05/11			
1920	02/11	02/11	02/11			
1922		07/11	07/11			
1924	04/11	04/11	04/11			
1926		02/11	02/11			
1928	06/11	06/11	06/11			
1930		04/11	04/11			
1932	08/11	08/11	08/11			

Year (cont.)	Presidential elections[a]	Parliamentary elections		Elections. for Constit Assembly	Referendums	Coups d'état
		Lower Chamber[b]	Upper Chamber[c]			
1934		06/11	06/11			
1936	03/11	03/11	03/11			
1938		08/11	08/11			
1940	05/11	05/11	05/11			
1942		03/11	03/11			
1944	07/11	07/11	07/11			
1946		05/11	05/11			
1948	02/11	02/11	02/11			
1950		07/11	07/11			
1952	04/11	04/11	04/11			
1954		02/11	02/11			
1956	06/11	06/11	06/11			
1958		04/11	04/11			
1960	08/11	08/11	08/11			
1962		06/11	06/11			
1964	03/11	03/11	03/11			
1966		08/11	08/11			
1968	05/11	05/11	05/11			
1970		03/11	03/11			
1972	07/11	07/11	07/11			
1974		05/11	05/11			
1976	02/11	02/11	02/11			
1978		07/11	07/11			
1980	04/11	04/11	04/11			
1982		02/11	02/11			
1984	06/11	06/11	06/11			
1986		04/11	04/11			
1988	08/11	08/11	08/11			
1990		06/11	06/11			
1992	03/11	03/11	03/11			
1994		08/11	08/11			
1996	05/11	05/11	05/11			
1998		03/11	03/11			
2000	07/11	07/11	07/11			
2002		04/11	04/11			
2004	02/11	02/11	02/11			

[a] The dates refer to the election of presidential electors. Prior to 1848 presidential elections were held over a period of several weeks, generally from early October to mid-November. Since 1848, elections are held on the Tuesday following the first Monday in November.

[b] Until 1870, elections to the house were staggered over a thirteen month period. Since then they are held on the Tuesday following the first Monday in November in even-numbered years. A few states deviated from the common election day until the 1890s.

[c] The popular elections for the senate are held on the common election day as well.

2.2 Electoral Body 1789–2004

Year	Type[a]	Population[b]	Registered voters[c] Total number	% pop.	Votes cast[d] Total number	% reg. voters[e]	% pop.[f]
1788	Pr	3,929,000	—	42.5	30,522	17.2	0.8
1788–89	R	3,929,000	—	—	—	17.2	—
1790–91	R	3,929,000	—	—	—	16.4	—
1792	Pr	4,194,000	—	42.9	8,924	28.4	0.2
1792–93	R	4,262,000	—	—	—	26.2	—
1794–95	R	4,537,000	—	—	—	20.9	—
1796	Pr	4,745,000	—	43.1	71,926	23.1	1.5
1796–97	R	4,814,000	—	—	—	22.9	—
1798–99	R	5,228,000	—	—	—	30.8	—
1800	Pr	5,297,000	—	43.3	52,321	29.9	1.0
1800–01	R	5,393,000	—	—	—	35.5	—
1802–03	R	5,969,000	—	—	—	29.8	—
1804	Pr	6,065,000	—	44.0	136,054	23.8	2.2
1804–05	R	6,162,000	—	—	—	39.0	—
1806–07	R	6,742,000	—	—	—	35.0	—
1808	Pr	6,838,000	—	44.4	169,054	35.0	2.5
1808–09	R	6,946,000	—	—	—	55.8	—
1810–11	R	7,239,000	—	—	—	40.8	—
1812	Pr	7,700,000	—	44.0	250,327	39.7	3.2
1812–13	R	7,818,000	—	—	—	47.5	—
1814–15	R	8,537,000	—	—	—	48.1	—
1816	Pr	8,659,000	—	43.2	109,896	16.1	1.3
1816–17	R	8,779,000	—	—	—	42.3	—
1818–19	R	9,498,000	—	—	—	33.2	—
1820	Pr	9,618,000	—	42.8	102,318	10.2	1.1
1820–21	R	9,781,000	—	—	—	41.8	—
1822–23	R	10,761,000	—	—	—	42.0	—
1824	Pr	10,924,000	—	42.3	365,833	26.9	3.3
1824–25	R	11,088,000	—	—	—	42.1	—
1826–27	R	11,745,000	—	—	—	46.5	—
1828	Pr	12,237,000	—	42.3	1,148,018	55.2	9.4
1828–29	R	12,394,000	—	—	—	57.1	—
1830–31	R	12,866,000	—	—	—	54.4	—
1832	Pr	13,742,000	—	42.6	1,293,973	55.4	9.4
1832–33	R	13,952,000	—	—	—	59.1	—
1834–35	R	14,793,000	—	—	—	62.1	—
1836	Pr	15,423,000	—	43.1	1,503,534	54.4	9.7
1836–37	R	15,635,000	—	—	—	57.5	—
1838–39	R	16,484,000	—	—	—	69.9	—
1840	Pr	17,120,000		43.3	2,411,808	77.5	14.1
1840–41	R	17,426,000	—	—	—	69.9	—

Year (cont.)	Type[a]	Population[b]	Registered voters[c] Total number	% pop.	Votes cast[d] Total number	% reg. voters[e]	% pop.[f]
1842–43	R	18,651,000	—	—	—	62.1	—
1844	Pr	19,569,000	—	43.7	2,703,659	74.5	13.8
1844–45	R	19,875,000	—	—	—	71.8	—
1846–47	R	21,100,000	—	—	—	58.9	—
1848	Pr	22,018,000	—	44.2	2,879,184	67.3	13.1
1848–49	R	22,380,000	—	—	—	63.5	—
1850–51	R	23,191,000	—	—	—	56.6	—
1852	Pr	24,911,000	—	44.9	3,161,830	63.2	12.7
1852–53	R	25,324,000	—	—	—	62.0	—
1854–55	R	26,975,000	—	—	—	60.2	—
1856	Pr	28,212,000	—	45.1	4,054,647	70.9	14.4
1856–57	R	28,625,000	—	—	—	67.9	—
1858–59	R	30,276,000	—	—	—	62.1	—
1860	Pr	31,513,000	—	45.5	4,685,561	72.1	14.9
1860–61	R	31,932,000	—	—	—	70.4	—
1862–63	R	33,607,000	—	—	—	56.3	—
1864	Pr	34,863,000	—	45.9	4,031,887	66.2	11.6
1864–65	R	35,282,000	—	—	—	61.9	—
1866–67	R	36,957,000	—	—	—	62.4	—
1868	Pr	38,213,000	—	48.5	5,722,440	71.8	15.0
1868–69	R	38,683,000	—	—	—	69.6	—
1870–71	R	38,558,000	—	—	—	66.8	—
1872	Pr	41,972,000	—	45.8	6,467,679	72.2	15.4
1872–73	R	42,489,000	—	—	—	74.0	—
1874–75	R	44,557,000	—	—	—	65.0	—
1876	Pr	46,107,000	—	46.2	8,413,101	82.9	18.2
1876–77	R	46,627,000	—	—	—	81.3	—
1878–79	R	48,704,000	—	—	—	65.3	—
1880	Pr	50,262,000	—	46.5	9,210,420	80.5	18.3
1880	R	50,262,000	—	—	—	79.3	—
1882	R	52,821,000	—	—	—	66.1	—
1884	Pr	55,379,000	—	46.8	10,049,754	78.8	18.1
1884	R	55,379,000	—	—	—	77.6	—
1886	R	57,938,000	—	—	—	64.0	—
1888	Pr	60,496,000	—	47.0	11,383,320	80.9	18.8
1888–89	R	61,709,000	—	—	—	79.9	—
1890	R	62,979,000	—	—	—	64.9	—
1892	Pr	65,666,000	—	47.2	12,056,097	76.2	18.4
1892	R	65,666,000	—	—	—	74.9	—
1894–95	R	68,928,000	—	—	—	67.4	—
1896	Pr	70,885,000	—	47.5	13,935,738	79.7	19.7
1896	R	70,885,000	—	—	—	78.1	—
1898	R	73,490,000	—	—	—	60.0	—

Year (cont.)	Type[a]	Population[b]	Registered voters[c] Total number	% pop.	Votes cast[d] Total number	% reg. voters[e]	% pop.[f]
1900	Pr	76,094,000	—	47.4	13,970,470	73.6	18.4
1900	R	76,094,000	—	—	—	72.2	—
1902	R	79,130,000	—	—	—	55.4	—
1904	Pr	82,166,000	—	46.8	13,518,964	65.4	16.4
1904	R	82,166,000	—	—	—	63.7	—
1906–07	R	85,134,000	—	—	—	51.1	—
1908	Pr	88,710,000	—	46.4	14,882,734	65.5	16.8
1908	R	88,710,000	—	—	—	63.6	—
1910–11	R	92,228,000	—	—	—	51.3	—
1912	Pr	95,335,000	—	48.1	15,040,963	58.8	15.8
1912	C	95,335,000	—	—	—	55.7	—
1914	C	98,648,000	—	—	—	50.1	—
1916	Pr	101,961,000	—	52.6	18,535,022	61.9	18.2
1916	C	101,961,000	—	—	—	59.0	—
1918	C	104,211,000	—	—	—	40.0	—
1920	Pr	106,461,000	—	89.7	26,768,613	49.2	25.1
1920	C	106,461,000	—	—	—	47.0	—
1922	C	110,285,000	—	—	—	35.8	—
1924	Pr	114,109,000	—	91.2	29,095,023	48.8	25.5
1924	C	114,109,000	—	—	—	45.0	—
1926	C	117,309,000	—	—	—	32.8	—
1928	Pr	120,509,000	—	92.5	36,805,951	56.8	30.5
1928	C	120,509,000	—	—	—	52.7	—
1930	C	123,202,000	73,623,000	—	—	36.7	—
1932	Pr	124,949,000	75,768,000	93.6	39,758,759	56.8	31.8
1932	C	124,949,000	75,768,000	—	—	53.6	—
1934	C	126,565,000	77,997,000	—	—	44.6	—
1936	Pr	128,181,000	80,174,000	94.4	45,654,763	61.1	35.6
1936	C	128,181,000	80,174,000	—	—	57.6	—
1938	C	130,152,000	82,354,000	—	—	46.9	—
1940	Pr	132,122,000	84,728,000	95.1	49,900,418	62.9	37.8
1940	C	132,122,000	84,728,000	—	—	58.8	—
1942	C	135,256,000	86,465,000	—	—	34.0	—
1944	Pr	138,397,000	85,654,000	96.4	47,976,670	56.0	34.7
1944	C	138,397,000	85,654,000	—	—	52.6	—
1946	C	142,514,000	92,659,000	—	—	38.7	—
1948	Pr	146,631,000	95,573,000	97.6	48,793,826	53.1	33.3
1948	C	146,631,000	95,573,000	—	—	50.0	—
1950	C	151,325,000	98,134,000	—	—	42.5	—
1952	Pr	156,954,000	99,929,000	98.0	61,550,918	63.5	39.2
1952	C	156,954,000	99,929,000	—	—	59.6	—
1954	C	163,026,000	102,075,000	—	—	43.0	—
1956	Pr	168,221,000	104,515,000	97.9	62,026,908	61.4	36.9

Year (cont.)	Type[a]	Population[b]	Registered voters[c] Total number	% pop.	Votes cast[d] Total number	% reg. voters[e]	% pop.[f]
1956	C	168,221,000	104,515,000	—	—	57.5	—
1958–59	C	176,184,000	106,447,000	—	—	44.6	—
1960	Pr	180,671,000	109,672,000	97.8	68,838,219	65.2	38.1
1960	C	180,671,000	109,672,000	—	—	61.3	—
1962	C	186,538,000	112,952,000	—	—	47.6	—
1964	Pr	191,889,000	114,090,000	97.8	70,644,592	63.3	36.8
1964	C	191,889,000	114,090,000	—	—	59.5	—
1966	C	196,560,000	116,638,000	—	—	46.6	—
1968	Pr	200,706,000	120,285,000	97.7	73,211,875	62.5	36.5
1968	C	200,706,000	120,285,000	—	—	57.1	—
1970	C	203,302,000	124,498,000	—	—	46.3	—
1972	Pr	209,896,000	140,777,000	97.8	77,718,554	56.4	37.0
1972	C	209,896,000	140,777,000	—	—	52.9	—
1974	C	213,854,000	146,338,000	—	—	38.0	—
1976	Pr	218,035,000	152,308,000	97.1	81,555,889	55.3	37.4
1976	C	218,035,000	152,308,000	—	—	51.5	—
1978	C	222,585,000	158,369,000	—	—	37.3	—
1980	Pr	227,726,000	164,595,000	96.5	86,515,221	55.1	38.0
1980	C	227,726,000	164,595,000	—	—	50.8	—
1982	C	232,188,000	169,936,000	—	—	41.1	—
1984	Pr	236,348,000	174,468,000	95.7	92,652,842	56.4	39.2
1984	C	236,348,000	174,468,000	—	—	52.5	—
1986	C	240,651,000	178,566,000	—	—	36.5	—
1988	Pr	245,021,000	182,779,000	94.9	91,594,809	53.4	37.4
1988	C	245,021,000	182,779,000	—	—	49.3	—
1990	C	248,709,000	185,812,000	—	—	36.2	—
1992	Pr	255,410,000	189,524,000	94.3	104,425,014	58.6	40.9
1992	C	255,410,000	189,524,000	—	—	54.7	—
1994	C	260,637,000	193,650,000	—	—	39.8	—
1996	Pr	265,502,000	196,511,000	93.7	96,277,223	52.1	36.3
1996	C	265,502,000	196,511,000	—	—	49.4	—
1998	C	270,509,000	200,929,000	—	—	37.1	—
2000	Pr	281,421,000	205,815,000	—	105,405,100	51.2	37.4
2000	C	281,421,000	205,815,000	—	—	—	—
2002	C	288,369,000	210,421,000	—	88,903,000	42.2	30.8
2004[g]	Pr	294,920,000	—	—	119,073,000	—	40.4
2004[h]	C	294,920,000	—	—	—	—	—

[a] Type of election: Pr = President, R = House of Representatives, C = Congress.

[b] Based on decennial census data; population data between census years are based on estimates. Alaska and Hawaii are included from 1960 onwards. The figure for 1788 is based on the census of 1790.

[c] Due to insufficient data, these figures correspond to the respective total number of eligible electorate (see 1.4). However, as the total number of eligible electorate between 1788–1928 is largely inaccurate and disputed, the authors decided not to provide these data. The data 1930–

1992 were taken from Congressional Quarterly's Presidential Elections 1789–1996 (1997: 81); the most recent data are based on FEC and Census Bureau online sources. The percentages for eligibility are based on data from Rusk (2001: 50).
[d] Due to insufficient data, these figures correspond to valid votes (see 1.4).
[e] Votes cast by eligible electorate. Presidential turnout 1788–1998 is taken from Rusk (2001: 52); turnout of house elections 1788-1910 and combined turnout for both chambers of congress 1912–1998 are taken from Rusk (2001: 54).
[f] Valid votes by total population.
[g] Preliminary data.
[h] Complete data not available prior to editorial deadline.

2.3 Abbreviations

D	Democrat
D-R	Democratic-Republican
F	Federalist
N-R	National-Republican
R	Republican
W	Whig

2.4 Electoral Participation of Parties and Alliances 1788–2004

Party / Alliance	Years	Elections contested[a]
Federalist	1788–1816	8
D-R	1796–1828	9
N-R	1828–1832	2
Anti-Mason	1832–1836	2
D	1832–2004	43
W	1836–1856	6
Liberty	1840–1848	3
Free Soil	1848–1852	2
American ('Know-Nothing')	1856	1
R	1856–2004	37
Constitutional Union	1860	1
Southern Democrat	1860	1
Liberal Republican	1872	1
Prohibition	1872–2004	33
Straight Out Democrat	1872	1
Greenback	1876–1884	3
Union Labor	1888	1
Socialist Labor	1892–1976	21
Populist	1892–1908, 1984–1996	8
National Democrat	1896	1
Socialist	1900–1956, 1976–1988	17
Progressive ('Bull Moose')	1912	1

Party / Alliance (continued)	Years	Elections contested[a]
Farmer Labor	1920	1
Communist	1924–1940, 1968–1984	8
Progressive (La Follette)	1924	1
Union	1936	1
Socialist Workers	1940–2004	16
Progressive (Henry Wallace)	1948	1
States' Rights Democrat	1948	1
Constitution	1956	1
Workers World	1960–2004	12
American Independent (George Wallace)	1968	1
American	1972	1
Libertarian	1972–2004	8
People's	1972–1976	2
Independent	1976–1984, 1992	4
US Labor	1976–1996	5
Citizens Party	1980–1984	2
National Unity (Independent John B. Anderson)	1980–1988	3
New Alliance	1988–1992	2
United We Stand, America (Independent Ross Perot)	1992	1
Reform	1996–2004	3
Green	1996–2004	3

[a] Parliamentary elections have not been listed due to the following reasons: The number of groups contesting these elections exceeds the number of contestants in presidential elections by far. Furthermore, some of these groups did not contest elections nationwide. This problem is exacerbated by the fact that the names and labels of contesting groups were often inconsistent across counties and states. As a consequence, nationally aggregated data is insufficient in this regard.

2.5 Referendums

Nationwide referendums have not been held.

2.6 Elections for Constitutional Assembly

Elections for the federal constitutional convention of 1787 have not been held as the legislatures of the original states, except Rhode Island, appointed 74 delegates to the convention in Philadelphia. A number did not accept or could not attend. In all, 55 delegates attended the sessions. The proceedings were chaired by George Washington.

2.7 Parliamentary Elections

Since adequate data on the total numbers of registered voters, votes cast and invalid votes are either insufficient or not available, only the numbers of valid votes are listed (see 1.4). As to the 2004 congressional elections, only the data on the composition of both chambers is stated. Unfortunately, the popular results of the most recent elections were not available prior to the editorial deadline.

2.7.1 House of Representatives 1788–2002

Years	1788–1789		1790–1791	
	Total number	%	Total number	%
Valid votes	56,640	–[a]	57,036	–
Democratic	10,148	17.9	3,132	5.5
Republican	13,861	24.5	7,154	12.5
Others	32,631	57.6	46,750	82.0

[a] Percentage is not applicable because the number of votes cast is not available.

Years	1792–1793		1794–1795	
	Total number	%	Total number	%
Valid votes	103,742	–	91,360	–
Democratic	35,095	33.8	35,738	39.1
Republican	40,962	39.5	50,571	55.3
Others	27,685	26.7	5,051	5.5

Years	1796–1797		1798–1799	
	Total number	%	Total number	%
Valid votes	114,704	–	170,620	–
Democratic	40,721	35.5	67,405	39.5
Republican	69,688	60.7	99,433	58.3
Others	4,295	3.7	3,782	2.2

Years	1800–1801		1802–1803	
	Total number	%	Total number	%
Valid votes	198,295	–	167,568	–
Democratic	111,711	56.3	96,398	57.5
Republican	79,700	40.2	68,129	40.7
Others	6,884	3.5	3,041	1.8

684

United States of America

Years	1804–1805 Total number	%	1806–1807 Total number	%
Valid votes	241,377	–	202,782	–
Democratic	151,303	62.6	129,656	63.9
Republican	88,838	36.8	68,367	33.7
Others	1,336	0.5	4,756	2.3

Years	1808–1809 Total number	%	1810–1811 Total number	%
Valid votes	409,522	–	356,534	–
Democratic	219,879	53.7	217,878	61.1
Republican	182,100	44.5	128,523	36.0
Others	7,543	1.8	10,133	2.8

Years	1812–1813 Total number	%	1814–1815 Total number	%
Valid votes	447,762	–	298,341	–
Democratic	223,309	49.9	148,080	49.6
Republican	218,045	48.7	149,777	50.2
Others	6,408	1.4	484	0.2

Years	1816–1817 Total number	%	1818–1819 Total number	%
Valid votes	334,201	–	307,016	–
Democratic	180,570	54.0	211,070	68.7
Republican	122,330	36.6	61,836	20.1
Others	31,301	9.4	34,110	11.1

Years	1820–1821 Total number	%	1822–1823 Total number	%
Valid votes	447,659	–	430,683	–
Democratic	329,415	73.6	327,493	76.0
Republican	92,734	20.7	50,559	11.7
Others	25,510	5.7	52,631	12.2

Years	1824–1825 Total number	%	1826–1827 Total number	%
Valid votes	472,822	–	623,650	–
Democratic	317,841	67.2	233,119	37.4
Republican	39,812	8.4	255,025	40.9
Others	115,169	24.4	135,506	21.7

Years	1828–1829		1830–1831	
	Total number	%	Total number	%
Valid votes	616,239	–	983,495	–
Democratic	317,213	51.5	505,776	51.4
Republican	243,282	39.5	311,220	31.6
Others	55,744	9.0	166,499	16.9

Years	1832–1833		1834–1835	
	Total number	%	Total number	%
Valid votes	1,159,116	–	1,302,488	–
Democratic	595,771	51.4	650,139	49.9
Republican	297,246	25.6	561,802	43.1
Others	266,099	23.0	90,547	6.9

Years	1836–1837		1838–1839	
	Total number	%	Total number	%
Valid votes	1,352,045	–	1,746,481	–
Democratic	668,662	49.5	868,851	49.7
Republican	641,191	47.4	870,603	49.8
Others	42,192	3.1	7,027	0.4

Years	1840–1841		1842–1843	
	Total number	%	Total number	%
Valid votes	1,996,495	–	1,839,392	–
Democratic	957,480	48.0	940,561	51.1
Republican	1,029,612	51.6	824,387	44.8
Others	9,403	0.5	74,444	4.0

Years	1844–1845		1846–1847	
	Total number	%	Total number	%
Valid votes	2,491,200	–	2,235,263	–
Democratic	1,214,293	48.7	1,155,687	51.7
Republican	1,189,562	47.7	960,112	42.9
Others	87,345	3.5	119,464	5.3

Years	1848–1849		1850–1851	
	Total number	%	Total number	%
Valid votes	2,561,133	–	2,311,293	–
Democratic	1,137,376	44.4	1,082,727	46.8
Republican	1,183,768	46.2	996,046	43.1
Others	239,989	9.4	232,520	10.1

Years	1852–1853		1854–1855	
	Total number	%	Total number	%
Valid votes	2,765,468	–	3,072,810	–
Democratic	1,402,819	50.7	1,421,899	46.3
Republican	1,209,081	43.7	791,021	25.7
Others	153,568	5.5	859,890	28.0

Years	1856–1857		1858–1859	
	Total number	%	Total number	%
Valid votes	3,749,806	–	3,605,877	–
Democratic	1,771,273	47.2	1,818,744	50.4
Republican	1,421,301	37.9	1,267,464	35.1
Others	557,232	14.9	519,669	14.4

Years	1860–1861		1862–1863	
	Total number	%	Total number	%
Valid votes	3,820,790	–	3,213,797	–
Democratic	1,650,435	43.2	1,546,915	48.1
Republican	1,987,871	52.0	1,610,452	50.1
Others	182,484	4.8	56,430	1.8

Years	1864–1865		1866–1867	
	Total number	%	Total number	%
Valid votes	3,896,070	–	4,113,271	–
Democratic	1,645,716	42.2	1,809,747	44.0
Republican	2,096,655	53.8	2,265,155	55.1
Others	153,699	3.9	38,369	0.9

Years	1868–1869		1870–1871	
	Total number	%	Total number	%
Valid votes	5,884,620	–	5,151,030	–
Democratic	2,605,134	44.3	2,481,531	48.2
Republican	3,147,981	53.5	2,591,797	50.3
Others	131,505	2.2	77,702	1.5

Years	1872–1873		1874–1875	
	Total number	%	Total number	%
Valid votes	6,604,705	–	6,207,020	–
Democratic	2,927,921	44.3	3,099,918	49.9
Republican	3,491,873	52.9	2,817,263	45.4
Others	184,911	2.8	289,839	4.7

Years	1876–1877		1878–1879	
	Total number	%	Total number	%
Valid votes	8,317,582	–	7,062,827	–
Democratic	4,322,100	52.0	3,313,147	46.9
Republican	3,905,401	46.9	2,862,571	40.5
Others	90,081	1.1	887,109	12.6

Year	1880		1882	
	Total number	%	Total number	%
Valid votes	9,073,155	–	7,995,274	–
Democratic	4,440,239	48.9	4,062,716	50.8
Republican	4,220,865	46.5	3,336,406	41.7
Others	412,051	4.5	596,152	7.5

Year	1884		1886	
	Total number	%	Total number	%
Valid votes	9,891,709	–	8,578,047	–
Democratic	5,016,423	50.7	4,233,021	49.3
Republican	4,682,168	47.3	3,906,416	45.5
Others	193,118	1.9	438,610	5.1

Years	1888–1889		1890	
	Total number	%	Total number	%
Valid votes	11,461,731	–	9,782,378	–
Democratic	5,579,308	48.7	5,029,443	51.4
Republican	5,468,975	47.7	4,212,903	43.1
Others	413,448	3.6	540,032	5.5

Years	1892		1894–1895	
	Total number	%	Total number	%
Valid votes	11,848,009	–	11,263,855	–
Democratic	5,946,971	50.2	4,438,515	39.4
Republican	4,902,506	41.4	5,454,350	48.4
Others	998,532	8.4	1,370,990	12.2

Year	1896		1898	
	Total number	%	Total number	%
Valid votes	13,657,029	–	10,935,745	–
Democratic	6,218,664	45.5	5,149,719	47.0
Republican	6,893,934	50.5	5,380,574	49.1
Others	544,431	4.0	423,452	3.9

Year	1900		1902	
	Total number	%	Total number	%
Valid votes	13,709,295	–	10,987,921	–
Democratic	6,434,532	46.9	5,088,122	46.3
Republican	6,948,459	50.7	5,478,660	49.9
Others	326,304	2.4	421,139	3.8

Years	1904		1906–1907	
	Total number	%	Total number	%
Valid votes	13,163,037	–	11,179,089	–
Democratic	5,400,170	41.0	4,891,691	43.8
Republican	7,172,968	54.5	5,708,031	51.1
Others	589,899	4.5	579,367	5.2

Years	1908		1910–1911	
	Total number	%	Total number	%
Valid votes	14,445,524	–	12,210,784	–
Democratic	6,551,965	45.4	5,750,691	47,1
Republican	7,237,227	50.1	5,682,268	46.5
Others	656,332	4.5	777,825	6.4

Year	1912		1914	
	Total number	%	Total number	%
Valid votes	14,258,039	–	13,646,100	–
Democratic	6,233,325	43.7	5,806,505	42.5
Republican	5,012,648	35.2	5,832,617	42.7
Others	3,012,030	21.1	2,006,978	14.7

Year	1916		1918	
	Total number	%	Total number	%
Valid votes	16,732,791	–	12,768,082	–
Democratic	7,709,350	46.1	5,568,265	43.6
Republican	8,025,364	48.0	6,610,510	51.8
Others	998,077	6.0	589,307	4.6

Year	1920		1922	
	Total number	%	Total number	%
Valid votes	25,528,511	–	20,410,828	–
Democratic	9,150,957	35.8	9,062,740	44.4
Republican	14,847,251	58.3	10,633,303	52.1
Others	1,503,303	5.9	714,785	3.5

Year	1924		1926	
	Total number	%	Total number	%
Valid votes	26,854,166	–	20,398,829	–
Democratic	10,746,697	40.0	8,271,764	40.5
Republican	15,009,086	55.9	11,610,611	56.9
Others	1,098,383	4.1	516,454	2.5

Year	1928		1930	
	Total number	%	Total number	%
Valid votes	34,201,958	–	24,800,840	–
Democratic	14,216,500	41.6	11,087,763	44.7
Republican	19,369,186	56.6	13,051,778	52.6
Others	616,272	1.8	661,299	2.7

Year	1932		1934	
	Total number	%	Total number	%
Valid votes	37,526,062	–	32,279,984	–
Democratic	20,267,306	54.0	17,457,671	54.1
Republican	15,726,307	41.9	13,185,721	40.8
Others	1,532,449	4.1	1,636,592	5.1

Year	1936		1938	
	Total number	%	Total number	%
Valid votes	42,996,578	–	36,128,468	–
Democratic	24,196,344	56.3	17,927,403	49.6
Republican	17,025,266	39.6	16,972,061	47.0
Others	1,774,968	4.1	1,229,004	3.4

Year	1940		1942	
	Total number	%	Total number	%
Valid votes	46,659,159	–	28,077,247	–
Democratic	24,266,432	52.0	13,239,668	47.1
Republican	21,346,565	45.7	14,253,793	50.8
Others	1,046,162	2.2	583,786	2.1

Year	1944		1946	
	Total number	%	Total number	%
Valid votes	45,073,644	–	34,364,954	–
Democratic	23,458,538	52.0	15,496,218	45.1
Republican	21,183,304	47.0	18,409,852	53.6
Others	431,802	1.0	458,884	1.3

Year	1948		1950	
	Total number	%	Total number	%
Valid votes	45,899,302	–	40,311,778	–
Democratic	22,025,949	48.0	19,998,288	49.6
Republican	20,697,755	45.1	19,763,965	49.0
Others	3,175,598	6.9	549,525	1.4

Year	1952		1954	
	Total number	%	Total number	%
Valid votes	57,845,497	–	42,585,072	–
Democratic	28,994,253	50.1	22,490,589	52.8
Republican	28,320,766	49.0	19,895,605	46.7
Others	530,478	0.9	198,878	0.5

Years	1956		1958–1959	
	Total number	%	Total number	%
Valid votes	58,171,123	–	45,756,327	–
Democratic	29,956,895	51.5	25,727,794	56.2
Republican	28,074,609	48.3	19,875,549	43.4
Others	139,619	0.2	152,984	0.3

Year	1960		1962	
	Total number	%	Total number	%
Valid votes	64,058,173	–	51,082,893	–
Democratic	35,059,315	54.7	26,424,880	51.7
Republican	28,738,811	44.9	24,461,879	47.9
Others	260,047	0.4	196,134	0.4

Year	1964		1966	
	Total number	%	Total number	%
Valid votes	65,624,101	–	52,592,840	–
Democratic	37,633,283	57.3	26,742,798	50.8
Republican	27,665,266	42.1	25,394,956	48.3
Others	325,552	0.5	455,086	0.9

Year	1968		1970	
	Total number	%	Total number	%
Valid votes	65,963,280	–	52,860,151	–
Democratic	33,180,963	50.3	28,361,957	53.6
Republican	32,030,978	48.6	23,730,423	44.9
Others	751,339	1.1	767,771	1.4

Year	1972		1974	
	Total number	%	Total number	%
Valid votes	69,184,723	–	50,397,179	–
Democratic	36,084,414	52.2	29,050,981	57.6
Republican	32,146,173	46.5	20,408,393	40.5
Others	954,136	1.4	937,805	1.7

Year	1976		1978	
	Total number	%	Total number	%
Valid votes	71,846,829	–	52,552,878	–
Democratic	40,358,475	56.2	28,093,358	53.5
Republican	30,229,202	42.1	23,679,754	45.1
Others	1,259,152	1.7	779,766	1.5

Year	1980		1982	
	Total number	%	Total number	%
Valid votes	73,818,591	–	61,673,392	–
Democratic	36,934,769	50.0	33,954,496	55.1
Republican	35,623,558	48.3	26,739,456	43.4
Others	1,260,264	1.7	979,440	1.6

Year	1984		1986	
	Total number	%	Total number	%
Valid votes	79,528,202	–	56,959,811	–
Democratic	41,395,632	52.0	30,996,645	54.4
Republican	37,436,165	47.1	25,425,142	44.6
Others	696,405	0.9	538,024	0.9

Year	1988		1990	
	Total number	%	Total number	%
Valid votes	77,757,635	–	58,869,424	–
Democratic	41,668,053	53.6	31,148,060	52.9
Republican	35,167,206	45.2	26,442,421	44.9
Others	922,376	1.2	1,278,943	2.2

Year	1992		1994	
	Total number	%	Total number	%
Valid votes	90,445,379	–	66,928,613	–
Democratic	46,257,050	51.1	30,544,369	45.6
Republican	40,903,585	45.2	34,900,685	52.1
Others	3,284,744	3.6	1,483,559	2.2

Year	1996		1998	
	Total number	%	Total number	%
Valid votes	84,510,360	–	63,848,018	–
Democratic	41,327,666	48.9	30,519,753	47.8
Republican	40,864,430	48.4	31,279,825	49.0
Others	2,318,264	2.7	2,048,440	3.2

Year	2000		2002	
	Total number	%	Total number	%
Valid votes	98,799,963	–	74,707,574	–
Democratic	46,411,559	47.0	33,642,873	45.9
Republican	46,750,175	47.3	37,091,540	50.6
Others	5,638,229	5.7	2,505,373	3.4

2.7.2 Senate 1912–2002

Year	1912		1914	
	Total number	%	Total number	%
Valid votes	1,328,945	–	10,893,870	–
Democratic	588,552	44.3	4,369,156	40.1
Republican	532,021	40.0	4,456,558	40.9
Others	208,372	15.7	2,068,156	19.0

Year	1916		1918	
	Total number	%	Total number	%
Valid votes	12,025,049	–	6,272,003	–
Democratic	5,347,622	44.5	2,949,345	47.0
Republican	5,988,367	49.8	3,021,493	48.2
Others	689,060	5.7	301,165	4.8

Year	1920		1922	
	Total number	%	Total number	%
Valid votes	19,510,650	–	15,650,066	–
Democratic	7,375,577	37.8	7,114,494	45.5
Republican	10,577,309	54.2	7,504,600	47.9
Others	1,557,764	8.0	1,030,972	6.6

Year	1924		1926	
	Total number	%	Total number	%
Valid votes	14,529,122	–	16,170,192	–
Democratic	6,166,855	42.4	7,222,971	44.7
Republican	7,645,318	52.6	8,570,397	53.0
Others	716,949	4.9	376,824	2.3

Year	1928 Total number	%	1930 Total number	%
Valid votes	26,045,872	–	13,010,966	–
Democratic	10,646,998	40.9	6,750,996	51.9
Republican	14,347,353	55.1	5,783,617	44.4
Others	1,051,521	4.0	476,353	3.7

Year	1932 Total number	%	1934 Total number	%
Valid votes	28,522,233	–	25,145,034	–
Democratic	15,637,272	54.8	12,463,210	49.6
Republican	11,354,447	39.8	10,969,496	43.6
Others	1,530,514	5.4	1,712,328	6.8

Year	1936 Total number	%	1938 Total number	%
Valid votes	21,342,079	–	27,971,846	–
Democratic	11,796,556	55.3	14,424,247	51.6
Republican	8,048,762	37.7	12,932,410	46.2
Others	1,496,761	7.0	615,189	2.2

Year	1940 Total number	%	1942 Total number	%
Valid votes	35,802,741	–	13,551,167	–
Democratic	16,962,421	47.4	6,330,213	46.7
Republican	17,195,023	48.0	6,693,305	49.4
Others	1,646,297	4.6	527,649	3.9

Year	1944 Total number	%	1946 Total number	%
Valid votes	34,765,389	–	27,253,830?	–
Democratic	18,403,431	52.9	11,988,304	44.0
Republican	16,172,703	46.5	14,984,371	55.0
Others	189,255	0.5	281,155	1.0

Year	1948 Total number	%	1950 Total number	%
Valid votes	22,600,270	–	32,180,637	–
Democratic	12,750,654	56.4	15,610,698	48.5
Republican	9,663,279	42.8	16,166,666	50.2
Others	186,337	0.8	403,273	1.2

Year	1952		1954	
	Total number	%	Total number	%
Valid votes	44,802,307	–	20,549,952	–
Democratic	20,602,942	46.0	11,435,689	55.6
Republican	23,263,955	51.9	8,838,877	43.0
Others	935,410	2.1	275,386	1.3

Year	1956		1958	
	Total number	%	Total number	%
Valid votes	43,853,336	–	37,429,098	–
Democratic	22,499,347	51.3	20,854,861	55.7
Republican	21,259,021	48.5	16,171,640	43.2
Others	94,968	0.2	402,597	1.1

Year	1959		1960	
	Total number	%	Total number	%
Valid votes	164,808	–	31,783,629	–
Democratic	77,647	47.1	17,638,881	55.5
Republican	87,161	52.9	14,014,291	44.1
Others	—	—	130,457	0.4

Year	1962		1964	
	Total number	%	Total number	%
Valid votes	39,186,193	–	52,702,939	–
Democratic	19,673,520	50.2	30,034,984	57.0
Republican	19,318,958	49.3	22,209,269	42.1
Others	193,715	0.5	458,686	0.9

Year	1966		1968	
	Total number	%	Total number	%
Valid votes	25,797,971	–	50,827,171	–
Democratic	12,357,323	47.9	25,059,044	49.3
Republican	13,170,556	51.0	24,168,867	47.5
Others	270,092	1.0	1,599,260	3.1

Year	1970		1972	
	Total number	%	Total number	%
Valid votes	48,527,771	–	37,825,420	–
Democratic	25,371,421	52.3	17,235,409	45.6
Republican	19,509,090	40.2	19,831,998	52.4
Others	3,647,260	7.5	758,013	2.0

Year	1974		1976	
	Total number	%	Total number	%
Valid votes	40,938,099	–	58,862,476	–
Democratic	22,637,869	55.3	32,002,771	54.4
Republican	16,421,373	40.1	24,878,982	42.3
Others	1,878,857	4.6	1,980,723	3.4

Year	1978		1980	
	Total number	%	Total number	%
Valid votes	28,387,122	–	58,635,680	–
Democratic	14,333,525	50.5	29,890,042	51.0
Republican	13,548,511	47.7	27,002,551	46.0
Others	505,086	1.8	1,743,087	3.0

Year	1982		1984	
	Total number	%	Total number	%
Valid votes	51,595,585	–	45,464,125	–
Democratic	28,041,926	54.3	22,219,681	48.9
Republican	22,636,946	44.0	22,851,333	50.3
Others	859,713	1.7	393,111	0.9

Year	1986		1988	
	Total number	%	Total number	%
Valid votes	48,262,469	–	67,432,125	–
Democratic	24,290,210	50.3	35,279,275	52.3
Republican	23,487,987	48.7	31,341,091	46.5
Others	484,272	1.0	811,759	1.2

Year	1990		1992	
	Total number	%	Total number	%
Valid votes	33,067,132	–	69,983,414	–
Democratic	17,022,004	51.5	35,184,182	50.3
Republican	15,532,598	47.0	31,870,144	45.5
Others	512,530	1.5	2,929,088	4.2

Year	1994		1996	
	Total number	%	Total number	%
Valid votes	56,771,151	–	49,029,747	–
Democratic	25,633,008	45.1	23,501,140	47.9
Republican	28,889,442	50.9	24,211,723	49.4
Others	2,248,701	4.0	1,316,884	2.7

Year	1998		2000	
	Total number	%	Total number	%
Valid votes	53,798,771	–	78,191,797	–
Democratic	26,924,649	50.0	36,780,875	47.0
Republican	25,718,603	47.8	36,725,431	47.0
Others	1,155,519	2.1	4,685,491	6.0

Year	2002	
	Total number	%
Valid votes	41,689,666	–
Democratic	18,956,449	46.1
Republican	20,626,192	50.2
Others	1,508,796	3.7

2.8 Composition of Parliament

2.8.1 House of Representatives 1789–2005

Years	1789–1791		1791–1793		1793–1795		1796–1797	
	Seats	%	Seats	%	Seats	%	Seats	%
	65	100.0	69	100.0	105	100.0	105	100.0
Federalists	18	27.7	5	7.2	22	20.9	49	46.7
Democrats	6	9.2	1	1.5	18	17.1	56	53.3
Others	41	63.1	63	91.3	65	61.9	0	0.0

Years	1797–1799		1799–1801		1801–1803		1803–1805	
	Seats	%	Seats	%	Seats	%	Seats	%
	106	100.0	106	100.0	106	100.0	142	100.0
Federalists	58	54.7	64	60.4	43	40.7	41	28.9
Democrats	48	45.3	42	39.6	63	59.4	101	71.1

Years	1805–1807		1807–1809		1809–1811		1811–1813	
	Seats	%	Seats	%	Seats	%	Seats	%
	142	100.0	142	100.0	142	100.0	142	100.0
Federalists	30	21.1	26	18.3	55	38.7	41	28.9
Democrats	111	78.2	111	78.2	87	61.3	100	70.4
Others	1	0.7	5	35.2	0	0.0	1	0.7

Years	1813–1815		1815–1817		1817–1819		1819–1821	
	Seats	%	Seats	%	Seats	%	Seats	%
	182	100.0	182	100.0	184	100.0	186	100.0
Federalists	72	39.6	71	39.0	43	23.4	30	16.1
Democrats	110	60.4	111	61.0	141	76.6	156	83.9

Years	1821–1823		1823–1825		1825–1827		1827–1829	
	Seats	%	Seats	%	Seats	%	Seats	%
	187	100.0	213	100.0	213	100.0	213	100.0
Federalists	31	16.6	24	11.3	22	10.3	–	–
National-Republicans/ Whigs	–	–	–	–	–	–	80	37.6
Democrats	154	82.3	149	69.9	127	59.6	92	43.2
Others	2	1.1	40	18.8	64	30.0	41	19.2

Years	1829–1831		1831–1833		1833–1835		1835–1837	
	Seats	%	Seats	%	Seats	%	Seats	%
	213	100.0	213	100.0	240	100.0	241	100.0
National-Republicans/ Whigs	75	35.2	68	31.9	62	25.8	81	33.6
Democrats	132	62.0	120	56.3	144	60.0	145	60.2
Others	6	2.8	25	11.7	34	14.2	15	6.2

Years	1837–1839		1839–1841		1841–1843		1843–1845	
	Seats	%	Seats	%	Seats	%	Seats	%
	242	100.0	242	100.0	242	100.0	223	100.0
National-Republicans/ Whigs	104	43.0	118	48.8	142	58.7	70	31.4
Democrats	131	54.1	124	51.2	99	40.9	150	67.3
Others	7	2.9	0	0.0	1	0.4	3	1.3

Years	1845–1847		1847–1849		1849–1851		1851–1853	
	Seats	%	Seats	%	Seats	%	Seats	%
	223	100.0	228	100.0	232	100.0	233	100.0
National-Republicans/ Whigs	81	36.3	118	51.7	107	46.1	89	38.2
Democrats	136	61.0	108	47.4	117	50.4	129	55.4
Others	6	2.7	2	0.9	8	3.4	15	6.4

Years	1853–1855		1855–1857		1857–1859		1859–1861	
	Seats	%	Seats	%	Seats	%	Seats	%
	234	100.0	234	100.0	236	100.0	238	100.0
National-Republicans/ Whigs	72	30.8	58	24.8	–	–	–	–
Republicans	–	–	13	5.5	93	39.4	119	50.0
Democrats	158	67.5	84	35.9	130	55.1	99	41.6
Others	4	1.7	79	33.8	13	5.5	20	8.4

Years	1861–1863		1863–1865		1865–1867		1867–1869	
	Seats	%	Seats	%	Seats	%	Seats	%
	171	100.0	183	100.0	192	100.0	193	100.0
Republicans	114	66.7	108	59.0	145	75.5	143	74.1
Democrats	52	30.4	75	41.0	35	18.2	50	25.9
Others	5	2.9	0	0.0	12	6.2	0	0.0

Years	1869–1871		1871–1873		1873–1875		1875–1877	
	Seats	%	Seats	%	Seats	%	Seats	%
	244	100.0	244	100.0	292	100.0	292	100.0
Republicans	165	67.6	138	56.6	202	69.2	108	37.0
Democrats	72	29.5	95	38.9	86	29.4	179	61.3
Others	7	2.9	11	4.5	4	1.4	5	1.7

Years	1877–1879		1879–1881		1881–1883		1883–1885	
	Seats	%	Seats	%	Seats	%	Seats	%
	293	100.0	293	100.0	293	100.0	325	100.0
Republicans	141	48.1	136	46.4	152	51.9	120	36.9
Democrats	152	51.9	152	51.9	138	47.1	197	60.6
Others	0	0.0	5	1.7	3	1.0	8	2.5

Years	1885–1887		1887–1889		1889–1891		1891–1893	
	Seats	%	Seats	%	Seats	%	Seats	%
	325	100.0	325	100.0	326	100.0	332	100.0
Republicans	142	43.7	152	46.8	164	50.3	87	26.2
Democrats	183	56.3	170	52.3	162	49.7	238	71.7
Others	0	0.0	3	0.9	0	0.0	7	2.1

Years	1893–1895		1895–1897		1897–1899		1899–1901	
	Seats	%	Seats	%	Seats	%	Seats	%
	356	100.0	357	100.0	357	100.0	357	100.0
Republicans	130	36.5	245	68.6	211	59.1	184	51.5
Democrats	221	62.1	107	30.0	142	39.8	172	48.2
Others	5	1.4	5	1.4	4	1.1	1	0.3

Years	1901–1903		1903–1905		1905–1907		1907–1909	
	Seats	%	Seats	%	Seats	%	Seats	%
	357	100.0	386	100.0	386	100.0	391	100.0
Republicans	198	55.5	205	53.1	251	65.0	224	57.3
Democrats	159	44.5	180	46.6	135	35.0	167	42.7
Others	0	0.0	1	0.3	0	0.0	0	0.0

Years	1909–1911		1911–1913		1913–1915		1915–1917	
	Seats	%	Seats	%	Seats	%	Seats	%
	391	100.0	393	100.0	435	100.0	435	100.0
Republicans	219	56.0	167	42.5	145	33.3	191	43.9
Democrats	172	44.0	226	57.5	279	64.1	236	54.2
Others	0	0.0	0	0.0	11	2.5	8	1.8

Years	1917–1919		1919–1921		1921–1923		1923–1925	
	Seats	%	Seats	%	Seats	%	Seats	%
	435	100.0	435	100.0	435	100.0	435	100.0
Republicans	216	49.6	243	55.9	302	69.4	225	51.7
Democrats	215	49.4	190	43.7	131	30.1	207	47.6
Others	4	0.9	2	0.4	3	0.7	3	0.7

Years	1925–1927		1927–1929		1929–1931		1931–1933	
	Seats	%	Seats	%	Seats	%	Seats[a]	%
	435	100.0	435	100.0	435	100.0	435	100.0
Republicans	247	56.8	237	54.5	269	61.8	217	49.9
Democrats	183	42.1	195	44.8	165	37.9	216	49.6
Others	5	1.1	3	0.7	1	0.2	2	0.4

[a] Democrats organized the house of representatives after the 1930 election despite the vote result, since Republican seat vacancies occurred shortly after the election due to deaths and the contesting of one house election.

Years	1933–1935		1935–1937		1937–1939		1939–1941	
	Seats	%	Seats	%	Seats	%	Seats	%
	435	100.0	435	100.0	435	100.0	435	100.0
Republicans	117	26.9	103	23.7	89	20.5	170	39.1
Democrats	313	71.9	322	74.0	335	77.0	262	60.2
Others	5	1.1	10	2.3	11	2.5	3	0.7

Years	1941–1943		1943–1945		1945–1947		1947–1949	
	Seats	%	Seats	%	Seats	%	Seats	%
	435	100.0	435	100.0	435	100.0	435	100.0
Republicans	163	37.5	210	48.3	191	43.9	246	56.5
Democrats	267	61.4	222	51.0	242	55.6	188	43.2
Others	5	1.1	3	0.7	2	0.5	1	0.2

Years	1949–1951		1951–1953		1953–1955		1955–1957	
	Seats	%	Seats	%	Seats	%	Seats	%
	435	100.0	435	100.0	435	100.0	435	100.0
Republicans	171	39.3	199	45.7	221	50.8	203	46.7
Democrats	263	60.4	235	54.0	213	49.0	232	53.3
Others	1	0.2	1	0.2	1	0.2	0	0.0

Years	1957–1959		1959–1961		1961–1963		1963–1965	
	Seats	%	Seats	%	Seats	%	Seats	%
	435	100.0	436	100.0	437	100.0	435	100.0
Republicans	201	46.2	153	35.1	174	39.8	176	40.5
Democrats	234	53.8	283	64.9	263	60.2	259	59.5

Years	1965–1967		1967–1969		1969–1971		1971–1973	
	Seats	%	Seats	%	Seats	%	Seats	%
	435	100.0	435	100.0	435	100.0	435	100.0
Republicans	140	32.2	187	43.0	192	44.1	180	41.4
Democrats	295	67.8	248	57.0	243	55.9	255	58.6

Years	1973–1975		1975–1977		1977–1979		1979–1981	
	Seats	%	Seats	%	Seats	%	Seats	%
	435	100.0	435	100.0	435	100.0	435	100.0
Republicans	192	44.1	144	33.1	143	32.9	158	36.3
Democrats	243	55.9	291	66.9	292	67.1	277	63.7

Years	1981–1983		1983–1985		1985–1987		1987–1989	
	Seats	%	Seats	%	Seats	%	Seats	%
	435	100.0	435	100.0	435	100.0	435	100.0
Republicans	192	44.1	166	38.2	182	41.8	177	40.7
Democrats	243	55.8	269	61.8	253	58.2	258	59.3

Years	1989–1991		1991–1993		1993–1995		1995–1997	
	Seats	%	Seats	%	Seats	%	Seats	%
	435	100.0	435	100.0	435	100.0	435	100.0
Republicans	175	40.2	166	38.2	176	40.4	228	52.4
Democrats	260	59.8	268	61.6	258	59.3	206	47.3
Others	0	0.0	1	0.2	1	0.2	1	0.2

Years	1997–1999		1999–2001		2001–2003		2003–2005	
	Seats	%	Seats	%	Seats	%	Seats	%
	435	100.0	435	100.0	435	100.0	435	100.0
Republicans	226	51.9	223	52.3	221	50.8	229	52.6
Democrats	207	47.6	211	48.5	212	48.7	204	46.8
Others	2	0.5	1	0.2	2	0.5	2[a]	0.6

[a] One vacancy.

Years	2005–2007	
	Seats	%
	435	100.0
Republicans	232	53.3
Democrats	202	46.4
Others	1	0.2

2.8.2 Senate 1788–2005

Years	1788–1789		1790–1791		1792–1793		1794–1795	
	Seats	%	Seats	%	Seats	%	Seats	%
	26	100.0	29	100.0	30	100.0	32	100.0
Democrats	8	30.8	13	44.8	14	46.7	11	34.4
Republicans	18	69.2	16	55.2	16	53.3	21	65.6

Years	1796–1797		1798–1799		1800–1801		1802–1803	
	Seats	%	Seats	%	Seats	%	Seats	%
	32	100.0	32	100.0	32	100.0	34	100.0
Democrats	10	31.2	10	31.2	17	53.1	25	73.5
Republicans	22	68.7	22	68.7	15	46.9	9	26.5

Years	1804–1805		1806–1807		1808–1809		1810–1811	
	Seats	%	Seats	%	Seats	%	Seats	%
	34	100.0	34	100.0	34	100.0	36	100.0
Democrats	27	79.4	28	82.3	27	79.4	30	83.3
Republicans	7	20.5	6	17.6	7	20.5	6	16.7

Years	1812–1813		1814–1815		1816–1817		1818–1819	
	Seats	%	Seats	%	Seats	%	Seats	%
	36	100.0	38	100.0	42	100.0	46	100.0
Democrats	28	77.8	26	68.4	30	71.4	37	80.4
Republicans	8	22.2	12	31.6	12	28.6	9	19.6

Years	1820–1821		1822–1823		1824–1825		1826–1827	
	Seats	%	Seats	%	Seats	%	Seats	%
	48	100.0	48	100.0	48	100.0	48	100.0
Democrats	44	91.7	44	91.7	26	54.2	27	56.2
Republicans	4	8.3	4	8.3	22	45.8	21	43.7

Years	1828–1829		1830–1831		1832–1833		1834–1835	
	Seats	%	Seats	%	Seats	%	Seats	%
	48	100.0	48	100.0	48	100.0	52	100.0
Democrats	25	52.1	25	52.1	22	45.8	26	50.0
Republicans	23	47.9	23	47.9	26	54.2	24	46.1
Others	0	0.0	0	0.0	0	0.0	2	3.8

Years	1836–1837		1838–1839		1840–1841		1842–1843	
	Seats	%	Seats	%	Seats	%	Seats	%
	52	100.0	52	100.0	52	100.0	52	100.0
Democrats	35	67.3	30	57.7	22	43.1	23	44.2
Republicans	17	32.7	22	42.3	29	56.9	29	55.8

Years	1844–1845		1846–1847		1848–1849		1850–1851	
	Seats	%	Seats	%	Seats	%	Seats	%
	56	100.0	60	100.0	62	100.0	62	100.0
Democrats	34	60.7	38	63.3	35	56.4	36	58.1
Republicans	22	39.3	21	35.0	25	40.3	23	37.1
Others	0	0.0	1	1.7	2	3.2	3	4.8

Years	1852–1853		1854–1855		1856–1857		1858–1859	
	Seats	%	Seats	%	Seats	%	Seats	%
	62	100.0	62	100.0	66	100.0	66	100.0
Democrats	38	61.3	42	67.7	41	62.1	38	57.6
Republicans	22	35.5	15	24.2	20	30.3	26	39.4
Others	2	3.3	5	8.1	5	7.6	2	3.0

Years	1860–1861		1862–1863		1864–1865		1866–1867	
	Seats	%	Seats	%	Seats	%	Seats	%
	49	100.0	52	100.0	54	100.0	66	100.0
Democrats	15	30.6	10	19.2	11	20.4	9	13.6
Republicans	34	69.4	37	71.1	40	74.1	57	86.4
Others	0	0.0	5	9.6	3	5.5	0	0.0

Years	1868–1869		1870–1871		1872–1873		1874–1875	
	Seats	%	Seats	%	Seats	%	Seats	%
	74	100.0	74	100.0	73	100.0	75	100.0
Democrats	12	16.2	18	24.3	19	26.0	28	37.3
Republicans	62	83.8	56	75.7	47	64.4	46	61.3
Others	0	0.0	0	0.0	7	9.6	1	1.3

Years	1876–1877		1878–1879		1881		1883	
	Seats	%	Seats	%	Seats	%	Seats	%
	76	100.0	76	100.0	76	100.0	76	100.0
Democrats	35	46.0	42	55.3	37	48.7	36	47.4
Republicans	40	52.6	33	43.4	37	48.7	38	50.0
Others	1	1.3	1	1.3	2	2.6	2	2.6

Year	1885		1887		1889		1891	
	Seats	%	Seats	%	Seats	%	Seats	%
	76	100.0	76	100.0	88	100.0	88	100.0
Democrats	34	44.7	37	48.7	37	42.0	39	44.3
Republicans	42	55.3	39	51.2	51	57.9	47	53.4
Others	0	0.0	0	0.0	0	0.0	2	2.3

Year	1893		1895		1897		1899	
	Seats	%	Seats	%	Seats	%	Seats	%
	88	100.0	90	100.0	90	100.0	89	100.0
Democrats	44	50.0	40	44.4	34	37.8	26	29.2
Republicans	40	45.4	44	48.9	44	48.9	53	59.5
Others	4	4.5	6	6.7	12	13.3	10	11.2

Year	1901		1903		1905		1907	
	Seats	%	Seats	%	Seats	%	Seats	%
	90	100.0	90	100.0	90	100.0	92	100.0
Democrats	32	35.6	33	36.7	32	35.6	31	33.7
Republicans	56	62.2	57	63.3	58	64.4	61	66.3
Others	2	2.2	0	0.0	0	0.0	0	0.0

Year	1909		1911		1913		1915	
	Seats	%	Seats	%	Seats	%	Seats	%
	92	100.0	96	100.0	96	100.0	96	100.0
Democrats	32	34.8	44	45.8	51	53.1	56	58.3
Republicans	60	65.2	52	54.2	44	45.8	40	41.7
Others	0	0.0	0	0.0	1	1.0	0	0.0

Year	1917		1919		1921		1923	
	Seats	%	Seats	%	Seats	%	Seats	%
	96	100.0	96	100.0	96	100.0	96	100.0
Democrats	54	56.2	47	49.0	37	38.5	42	43.7
Republicans	42	43.7	49	51.0	59	61.5	53	55.2
Others	0	0.0	0	0.0	0	0.0	1	1.0

Year	1925		1927		1929		1931	
	Seats	%	Seats	%	Seats	%	Seats	%
	96	100.0	96	100.0	96	100.0	96	100.0
Democrats	41	42.7	47	49.0	39	40.6	47	49.0
Republicans	54	56.2	48	50.0	56	58.3	48	50.0
Others	1	1.0	1	1.0	1	1.0	1	1.0

Year	1933		1935		1937		1939	
	Seats	%	Seats	%	Seats	%	Seats	%
	96	100.0	96	100.0	96	100.0	96	100.0
Democrats	59	61.5	69	71.9	76	79.2	69	71.9
Republicans	36	37.5	25	26.0	16	16.7	23	24.0
Others	1	1.0	2	2.1	4	4.2	4	4.2

Year	1941		1943		1945		1947	
	Seats	%	Seats	%	Seats	%	Seats	%
	96	100.0	96	100.0	96	100.0	96	100.0
Democrats	66	68.7	57	59.4	57	59.4	45	46.9
Republicans	28	29.2	38	39.6	38	39.6	51	53.1
Others	2	2.1	1	1.0	1	1.0	0	0.0

Year	1949		1951		1953		1955	
	Seats	%	Seats	%	Seats	%	Seats	%
	96	100.0	96	100.0	96	100.0	96	100.0
Democrats	54	56.2	49	51.0	47	49.0	48	50.0
Republicans	42	43.8	47	49.0	49	51.0	47	49.0
Others	0	0.0	0	0.0	0	0.0	1	1.0

Year	1957		1959		1961		1963	
	Seats	%	Seats	%	Seats	%	Seats	%
	96	100.0	100	100.0	100	100.0	100	100.0
Democrats	49	51.0	65	65.0	64	64.0	66	66.0
Republicans	47	49.0	35	35.0	36	36.0	34	34.0

Year	1965		1967		1969		1971	
	Seats	%	Seats	%	Seats	%	Seats	%
	100	100.0	100	100.0	100	100.0	100	100.0
Democrats	68	68.0	64	64.0	57	57.0	54	54.0
Republicans	32	32.0	36	36.0	43	43.0	44	44.0
Others	0	0.0	0	0.0	0	0.0	2	2.0

Year	1973 Seats 100	% 100.0	1975 Seats 100	% 100.0	1977 Seats 100	% 100.0	1979 Seats 100	% 100.0
Democrats	56	56.0	60	60.0	61	61.0	58	58.0
Republicans	42	42.0	38	38.0	38	38.0	41	41.0
Others	2	2.0	2	2.0	1	1.0	1	1.0

Year	1981 Seats 100	% 100.0	1983 Seats 100	% 100.0	1985 Seats 100	% 100.0	1987 Seats 100	% 100.0
Democrats	46	46.0	46	46.0	47	47.0	55	55.0
Republicans	53	53.0	54	54.0	53	53.0	45	45.0
Others	1	1.0	0	0.0	0	0.0	0	0.0

Year	1989 Seats 100	% 100.0	1991 Seats 100	% 100.0	1993 Seats 100	% 100.0	1995 Seats 100	% 100.0
Democrats	55	55.0	56	56.0	57	57.0	48	48.0
Republicans	45	45.0	44	44.0	43	43.0	52	52.0

Year	1997 Seats 100	% 100.0	1999 Seats 100	% 100.0	2001 Seats 100	% 100.0	2003 Seats 100	% 100.0
Democrats	45	45.0	45	45.0	50	50.0	48	48.0
Republicans	55	55.0	55	55.0	50	50.0	51	51.0
Others	0	0.0	0	0.0	0	0.0	1	1.0

Year	2005 Seats 100	% 100.0
Democrats	44	44.0
Republicans	55	55.0
Others	1	1.0

2.9 Presidential Elections 1788–2004

2.9.1 Electoral College Popular Vote 1788–2004

Since adequate data on the total numbers of registered voters, votes cast and invalid votes are either insufficient or not available for most elections, with few exceptions only the numbers of valid votes are listed (see 1.4).

1788[a]	Total number	%
Valid votes	30,522	–
George Washington (F)	28,242	92.5
Others	2,280	7.5

[a] Popular elections were held in Delaware, Maryland, Massachusetts, New Hampshire, Pennsylvania and Virginia.

1792[a]	Total number	%
Valid votes	8,924	–
George Washington (F)	8,924	100.0
Others[b]	—	—

[a] Popular elections were held in Maryland, Massachusetts, New Hampshire, Pennsylvania, Virginia and Kentucky.
[b] Data on the vote shares of these candidates were not available. Only the votes for G. Washington were reported.

1796[a]	Total number	%
Valid votes	71,926	–
John Adams (F)	37,532	52.2
Thomas Jefferson (D-R)	18,956	26.3
Others	15,438	21.5

[a] Popular elections were held in Georgia, Maryland, Massachusetts, New Hampshire, Pennsylvania, Virginia, North Carolina and Kentucky.

1800[a]	Total number	%
Valid votes	52,321	–
Thomas Jefferson (D-R)	33,976	64.9
John Adams (F)	18,345	35.1

[a] Popular elections were held in Maryland, Virginia, North Carolina, Rhode Island and Kentucky.

1804[a]	Total number	%
Valid votes	136,054	–
Thomas Jefferson (D-R)	97,795	71.9
Charles Cotesworth Pinckney (F)	38,259	28.1

[a] Popular elections were held in Maryland, Massachusetts, New Hampshire, New Jersey, Pennsylvania, Virginia, North Carolina, Rhode Island, Kentucky, Tennessee and Ohio.

1808[a]	Total number	%
Valid votes	169,011	–
James Madison (D-R)	111,105	65.7
Charles Cotesworth Pinckney (F)	54,402	32.2
Others	3,504	2.1

[a] Popular elections were held in Maryland, New Hampshire, New Jersey, Pennsylvania, Virginia, New York, North Carolina, Rhode Island, Kentucky, Tennessee and Ohio.

1812[a]	Total number	%
Valid votes	250,327	–
James Madison (D-R)	129,996	51.9
George Clinton (F)	120,331	48.1

[a] Popular elections were held in Maryland, Massachusetts, New Hampshire, Pennsylvania, Virginia, Rhode Island, Kentucky, Tennessee and Ohio.

1816[a]	Total number	%
Valid votes	109,896	–
James Monroe (D-R)	74,696	68.0
Rufus King (F)	17,611	16.0
Others	17,589	16.0

[a] Popular elections were held in Maryland, New Hampshire, New Jersey, Pennsylvania, Virginia, North Carolina, Rhode Island, Kentucky, Tennessee and Ohio.

1820[a]	Total number	%
Valid votes	102,318	–
James Monroe (D-R)	82,444	80.6
John Q. Adams (D-R)	16,727	16.3
Others	3,147	3.1

[a] Popular elections were held in Connecticut, Maryland, Massachusetts, New Hampshire, New Jersey, Pennsylvania, Virginia, North Carolina, Rhode Island, Kentucky, Tennessee, Ohio, Illinois, Maine and Mississippi.

1824[a]	Total number	%
Valid votes	365,833	–
John Q. Adams (D-R)	113,122[b]	30.9
Andrew Jackson (D-R)	151,271	41.3
Henry Clay (D-R)	47,531	13.0
William H. Crawford (D-R)	40,856	12.2
Others	13,053	3.6

[a] Popular elections were held in Connecticut, Maryland, Massachusetts, New Hampshire, New Jersey, Pennsylvania, Virginia, North Carolina, Rhode Island, Kentucky, Tennessee, Ohio, Indiana, Alabama, Illinois, Maine, Mississippi and Missouri.
[b] Adams was elected president by the house after neither of the candidates had received a majority in the electoral college.

1828[a]	Total number	%
Valid votes	1,148,018	–
Andrew Jackson (D-R)	642,553	56.0
John Q. Adams (N-R)	500,897	43.6
Others	4,568	0.4

[a] Popular elections were held in Connecticut, Georgia, Maryland, Massachusetts, New Hampshire, New Jersey, Pennsylvania, Virginia, New York, North Carolina, Rhode Island, Vermont, Kentucky, Tennessee, Ohio, Louisiana, Indiana, Alabama, Illinois, Maine, Mississippi and Missouri.

1832[a]	Total number	%
Valid votes	1,293,973	–
Andrew Jackson (D)	701,780	54.2
Henry Clay (N-R)	484,205	37.4
William Wirt (Anti-Mason)	100,715	7.8
Others	7,273	0.6

[a] All states except South Carolina had adopted the popular vote for presidential electors.

1836	Total number	%
Valid votes	1,503,534	–
Martin Van Buren (D)	764,176	50.8
William H. Harrison (W)	550,816	36.6
Hugh L. White (W)	146,107	9.7
Daniel Webster (W)	41,201	2.7
Others	1,234	0.1

1840	Total number	%
Valid votes	2,411,808	–
William H. Harrison (W)	1,275,390	52.9
Martin Van Buren (D)	1,128,854	46.8
James G. Birney (Liberty)	6,797	0.3
Others	767	0.0

1844	Total number	%
Valid votes	2,703,659	–
James K. Polk (D)	1,339,494	49.5
Henry Clay (W)	1,300,004	48.1
James G. Birney (Liberty)	62,103	2.3
Others	2,058	0.1

1848	Total number	%
Valid votes	2,879,184	–
Zachary Taylor (W)	1,361,393	47.3
Lewis Cass (D)	1,223,460	42.5
Martin Van Buren (Free Soil)	291,501	10.1
Others	2,830	0.1

1852	Total number	%
Valid votes	3,161,830	–
Franklin Pierce (D)	1,607,510	50.8
Winfield Scott (W)	1,386,942	43.9
John P. Hale (Free Soil)	155,210	4.9
Others	12,168	0.4

1856	Total number	%
Valid votes	4,054,647	–
James Buchanan (D)	1,836,072	45.3
John C. Fremont (R)	1,342,345	33.1
Millard Fillmore (American)	873,053	21.5
Others	3,177	0.1

1860	Total number	%
Valid votes	4,685,561	–
Abraham Lincoln (R)	1,865,908	39.9
Stephen A. Douglas (D)	1,380,202	29.5
John C. Breckinridge (Southern Democrat)	848,019	18.1
John Bell (Constitutional Union)	590,901	12.6
Others	531	0.0

1864[a]	Total number	%
Valid votes	4,031,887	–
Abraham Lincoln (R)	2,218,388	55.0
George B. McClellan (D)	1,812,807	45.0
Others	692	0.0

[a] Eleven Confederate states did not participate in election because of the Civil War.

1868[a]	Total number	%
Valid votes	5,722,440	–
Ulysses S. Grant (R)	3,013,650	52.7
Horatio Seymour (D)	2,708,744	47.3
Others	46	0.0

[a] Mississippi, Texas and Virginia did not participate in the election due to Reconstruction. In Florida the state legislature cast the electoral vote. South Carolina adopted the popular vote for presidential electors.

1872	Total number	%
Valid votes	6,467,679	–
Ulysses S. Grant (R)	3,598,235	55.6
Horace Greeley (D, Liberal Republican)	2,834,761	43.8
Charles O'Connor (Straight Out Democrat)	18,602	0.3
Others	16,081	0.3

1876	Total number	%
Valid votes	8,413,101	–
Rutherford B. Hayes (R)	4,034,311[a]	48.0
Samuel J. Tilden (D)	4,288,546[a]	51.0
Peter Cooper (Greenback)	75,973	0.9
Others	14,271	0.2

[a] Hayes was elected president (see Table 2.9.2, 1876).

1880	Total number	%
Valid votes	9,210,420	–
James A. Garfield (R)	4,446,158	48.3
Winfield S. Hancock (D)	4,444,260	48.3
James B. Weaver (Greenback)	305,997	3.3
Others	14,005	0.2

1884	Total number	%
Valid votes	10,049,754	–
Grover Cleveland (D)	4,874,621	48.5
James G. Blaine (R)	4,848,936	48.2
Benjamin F. Butler (Greenback)	175,096	1.7
John P. St. John (Prohibition)	147,482	1.5
Others	3,619	0.1

1888	Total number	%
Valid votes	11,383,320	–
Benjamin Harrison (R)	5,443,892	47.8
Grover Cleveland (D)	5,534,488	48.6
Clinton B. Fisk (Prohibition)	249,819	2.2
Alson J. Streeter (Union Labor)	146,602	1.3
Others	8,519	0.1

1892	Total number	%
Valid votes	12,056,097	–
Grover Cleveland (D)	5,551,883	46.1
Benjamin Harrison (R)	5,179,244	43.0
James B. Weaver (Populist)	1,024,280	8.5
John Bidwell (Prohibition)	270,770	2.2
Others	29,920	0.2

1896	Total number	%
Valid votes	13,935,738	–
William McKinley (R)	7,108,480	51.0
William J. Bryan (Democrat, Populist)	6,511,495	46.7
John M. Palmer (National Democrat)	133,435	1.0
Joshua Levering (Prohibition)	125,072	0.9
Others	57,256	0.4

1900	Total number	%
Valid votes	13,970,470	–
William McKinley (R)	7,218,039	51.7
William J. Bryan (D)	6,358,345	45.5
John G. Wooley (Prohibition)	209,004	1.5
Eugene V. Debs (Socialist)	86,935	0.6
Others	98,147	0.7

1904	Total number	%
Valid votes	13,518,964	–
Theodore Roosevelt (R)	7,626,593	56.4
Alton B. Parker (D)	5,082,898	37.6
Eugene V. Debs (Socialist)	402,489	3.0
Silas C. Swallow (Prohibition)	258,596	1.9
Others	148,388	1.1

1908	Total number	%
Valid votes	14,882,734	–
William H. Taft (R)	7,676,258	51.6
William J. Bryan (D)	6,406,801	43.0
Eugene V. Debs (Socialist)	420,380	2.8
Eugene W. Chafin (Prohibition)	252,821	1.7
Others	126,474	0.8

1912	Total number	%
Valid votes	15,040,963	–
Woodrow Wilson (D)	6,293,152	41.8
Theodore Roosevelt (Progressive)	4,119,207	27.4
William H. Taft (R)	3,486,333	23.2
Eugene V. Debs (Socialist)	900,369	6.0
Others	241,902	1.6

1916	Total number	%
Valid votes	18,535,022	–
Woodrow Wilson (D)	9,126,300	49.2
Charles E. Hughes (R)	8,546,789	46.1
Allan L. Benson (Socialist)	589,924	3.2
J. Frank Hanly (Prohibition)	221,030	1.2
Others	50,979	0.3

1920	Total number	%
Valid votes	26,768,613	–
Warren G. Harding (R)	16,153,115	60.3
James M. Cox (D)	9,133,092	34.1
Eugene V. Debs (Socialist)	915,490	3.4
Parley P. Christensen (Farmer-Labor)	265,229	1.0
Others	301,687	1.1

1924	Total number	%
Valid votes	29,095,023	–
Calvin Coolidge (R)	15,719,921	54.0
John W. Davis (D)	8,386,704	28.8
Robert M. La Follette (Progressive)	4,832,532	16.6
Herman P. Faris (Prohibition)	56,292	0.2
Others	99,574	0.3

1928	Total number	%
Valid votes	36,805,951	–
Herbert C. Hoover (R)	21,437,277	58.2
Alfred E. Smith (D)	15,007,698	40.8
Norman M. Thomas (Socialist)	265,583	0.7
William Z. Foster (Communist)	46,896	0.1
Others	48,497	0.1

1932	Total number	%
Valid votes	39,758,759	–
Franklin D. Roosevelt (D)	22,829,501	57.4
Herbert C. Hoover (R)	15,760,684	39.6
Norman M. Thomas (Socialist)	884,649	2.2
William Z. Foster (Communist)	103,253	0.3
Others	180,672	0.5

1936	Total number	%
Valid votes	45,654,763	–
Franklin D. Roosevelt (D)	27,757,333	60.8
Alfred M. Landon (R)	16,684,231	36.5
William Lemke (Union)	892,267	2.0
Norman M. Thomas (Socialist)	187,833	0.4
Others	133,099	0.3

1940	Total number	%
Valid votes	49,900,418	–
Franklin D. Roosevelt (D)	27,313,041	54.7
Wendell Willkie (R)	22,348,480	44.8
Norman M. Thomas (Socialist)	116,410	0.2
Roger W. Babson (Prohibition)	58,708	0.1
Others	63,779	0.1

1944	Total number	%
Valid votes	47,976,670	–
Franklin D. Roosevelt (D)	25,612,610	53.4
Thomas E. Dewey (R)	22,017,617	45.9
Norman M. Thomas (Socialist)	79,003	0.2
Claude A. Watson (Prohibition)	74,779	0.2
Others	192,661	0.4

1948	Total number	%
Valid votes	48,793,826	–
Harry S Truman (D)	24,179,345	49.6
Thomas E. Dewey (R)	21,991,291	45.1
J. Strom Thurmond (States' Rights Democrat)	1,176,125	2.4
Henry A. Wallace (Progressive)	1,157,326	2.4
Others	289,739	0.6

1952	Total number	%
Valid votes	61,550,918	–
Dwight D. Eisenhower (R)	33,936,234	55.1
Adlai E. Stevenson (D)	27,314,992	44.4
Vincent Hallinan (Progressive)	140,023	0.2
Stuart Hamblen (Prohibition)	72,949	0.1
Others	86,720	0.1

1956	Total number	%
Valid votes	62,026,908	–
Dwight D. Eisenhower (R)	35,590,472	57.4
Adlai E. Stevenson (D)	26,022,752	42.0
T. Coleman Andrews (Constitution)	111,178	0.2
Eric Hass (Socialist Labor)	44,450	0.1
Others	258,056	0.4

1960	Total number	%
Valid votes	68,838,219	–
John F. Kennedy (D)	34,226,731	49.7
Richard M. Nixon (R)	34,108,157	49.5
Eric Hass (Socialist Labor)	47,522	0.1
Unpledged[a]	116,248	0.2
Others	339,561	0.5

[a] Votes from Mississippi for unpledged electors who carried the state and cast electoral votes for Harry F. Byrd (D, Virginia).

1964	Total number	%
Registered voters	73,715,818	–
Valid votes	70,644,592	95.8
Lyndon B. Johnson (D)	43,129,566	61.1
Barry M. Goldwater (R)	27,178,188	38.5
Eric Hass (Socialist Labor)	45,219	0.1
Clifton DeBerry (Socialist Workers)	32,720	0.0
Others	258,899	0.4

1968	Total number	%
Registered voters	81,658,180	–
Valid votes	73,211,875	89.7
Richard M. Nixon (R)	31,785,480	43.4
Hubert H. Humphrey (D)	31,275,166	42.7
George C. Wallace (American Independent)	9,906,473	13.5
Henning A. Blomen (Socialist Labor)	52,588	0.1
Others	192,168	0.3

1972	Total number	%
Registered voters	97,283,541	–
Valid votes	77,718,554	79.9
Richard M. Nixon (R)	47,169,911	60.7
George S. McGovern (D)	29,170,383	37.5
John G. Schmitz (American)	1,099,482	1.4
Benjamin Spock (People's)	78,756	0.1
Others	200,022	0.3

1976	Total number	%
Registered voters	105,024,916	–
Valid votes	81,555,889	77.6
James E. Carter (D)	40,830,763	50.1
Gerald R. Ford (R)	39,147,793	48.0
Eugene J. McCarthy (Independent)	756,691	0.9
Roger MacBride (Libertarian)	173,011	0.2
Others	647,631	0.8

1980	Total number	%
Registered voters	113,036,958	–
Valid votes	86,515,221	76.5
Ronald W. Reagan (R)	43,904,153	50.7
James E. Carter (D)	35,483,883	41.0
John B. Anderson (Independent)	5,720,060	6.6
Ed Clark (Libertarian)	921,299	1.1
Others	485,826	0.6

1984	Total number	%
Registered voters	124,184,647	–
Valid votes	92,652,842	74.6
Ronald W. Reagan (R)	54,455,075	58.8
Walter F. Mondale (D)	37,577,185	40.6
David Bergland (Libertarian)	228,314	0.2
Lyndon H. LaRouche Jr. (Independent)	78,807	0.1
Others	313,461	0.3

1988	Total number	%
Registered voters	126,381,202	–
Valid votes	91,594,809	72.5
George Bush (R)	48,886,097	53.4
Michael S. Dukakis (D)	41,809,074	45.6
Ron Paul (Libertarian)	432,179	0.5
Lenora B. Fulani (New Alliance)	217,219	0.2
Others	250,240	0.3

1992	Total number	%
Registered voters	133,821,178	–
Valid votes	104,425,014	78.0
William J. Clinton (D)	44,909,326	43.0
George Bush (R)	39,103,882	37.4
Ross Perot (United We Stand, America)	19,741,657	18.9
Andre V. Marrou (Libertarian)	291,627	0.3
Others	378,522	0.4

1996	Total number	%
Registered voters	146,211,960	–
Valid votes	96,277,223	65.8
William J. Clinton (D)	47,402,357	49.2
Bob Dole (R)	39,198,755	40.7
Ross Perot (Independent)	8,085,402	8.4
Ralph Nader (Green)	684,902	0.7
Others	905,807	0.9

2000	Total number	%
Valid votes	105,405,100	–
George W. Bush (R)	50,456,002	47.9
Al Gore (D)	50,999,897	48.4
Ralph Nader (Green)	2,882,955	2.7
Patrick J. Buchanan (Reform)	448,895	0.4
Others	617,351	0.6

2004[a]	Total number	%
Valid votes	119,073,000	–
George W. Bush (R)	60,693,000	51.0
John F. Kerry (D)	57,356,000	48.2
Ralph Nader (Independent/Reform)	406,000	0.3
Michael J. Badnarik (Libertarian)	384,000	0.3
Others	234,000	0.2

[a] Preliminary results.

2.9.2 Presidential Elections, Electoral College Votes 1789–2004

Year	1789	Year	1792
	Votes		Votes
Totals	182[a]	Totals	270[b]
George Washington (F)	69	George Washington (F)	132
John Adams (F)	34	John Adams (F)	77
Others	11	Others	55

[a] Two votes for each elector, 34 electors did not vote.
[b] Two votes for each elector, three electors did not vote.

Year	1796	Year	1800
	Votes		Votes
Totals	276[a]	Totals	276[a]
John Adams (F)	71[b]	Thomas Jefferson (D-R)	73[c]
Thomas Jefferson (D-R)	68[b]	Aaron Burr (D-R)	73[c]
Charles Cotesworth Pinckney (F)	59	John Adams (F)	65
Others	78	Others	65

[a] Two votes for each elector.
[b] One Federalist elector from Pennsylvania voted for Jefferson instead of Adams.
[c] Under the constitution, the tie of the votes in the electoral college had to be resolved by the majority of the representatives of the 16 states. The stalemate in the house lasted through 35 ballots, and not until 17 February 1801 was Jefferson elected president.

Year	1804	Year	1808
	Votes		Votes
Totals	176	Totals	176[a]
Thomas Jefferson (D-R)	162	James Madison (D-R)	122
Charles Cotesworth Pinckney (F)	14	Charles Cotesworth Pinckney (F)	47

[a] One Kentucky elector did not vote.

Year	1812	Year	1816
	Votes		Votes
Totals	218[a]	Totals	221[b]
James Madison (D-R)	128	James Monroe (D-R)	183
George Clinton (F)	89	Rufus King (F)	34

[a] One Ohio elector did not vote.
[b] One Delaware and three Maryland electors did not vote.

718   *United States of America*

Year	1820	Year	1824
	Votes		Votes
Totals	235[a]	Totals	261[c]
James Monroe (D-R)	231	John Q. Adams (D-R)	84
John Q. Adams (D-R)	1[b]	Andrew Jackson (D-R)	99
		William H. Crawford (D-R)	41
		Henry Clay (D-R)	37

[a] One elector each from Mississippi, Pennsylvania and Tennessee did not vote.
[b] One Democratic-Republican elector from New Hampshire voted for Adams instead of the official party nominee Monroe.
[c] As no candidate received a majority of the electoral votes, Adams was elected president upon a decision of the house.

Year	1828	Year	1832
	Votes		Votes
Totals	261	Totals	288[a]
Andrew Jackson (D-R)	178	Andrew Jackson (D-R)	219
John Q. Adams (N-R)	83	Henry Clay (N-R)	49
		Others	18

[a] Two Maryland electors did not vote.

Year	1836	Year	1840
	Votes		Votes
Totals	294	Totals	294
Martin Van Buren (D)	170	William H. Harrison (W)	234
William H. Harrison (W)	73	Martin Van Buren (D)	60
Hugh L. White (W)	26		
Others	25		

Year	1844	Year	1848
	Votes		Votes
Totals	275	Totals	290
James K. Polk (D)	170	Zachary Taylor (W)	163
Henry Clay (W)	105	Lewis Cass (D)	127

Year	1852	Year	1856
	Votes		Votes
Totals	296	Totals	296
Franklin Pierce (D)	254	James Buchanan (D)	174
Winfield Scott (W)	42	John C. Fremont (R)	114
		Millard Fillmore (American)	8

Year	1860 Votes	Year	1864[a] Votes
Totals	303	Totals	234[b]
Abraham Lincoln (R)	180	Abraham Lincoln (R)	212
John C. Breckinridge (Southern Democrat)	72	George B. McClellan (D)	21
John Bell (Constitutional Union)	39		
Stephen A. Douglas (D)	12		

[a] Eleven Southern states (Alabama, Arkansas, Florida, Georgia, Louisiana, Mississippi, North Carolina, South Carolina, Tennessee, Texas, Virginia) had seceded from the Union and did not vote.
[b] One Nevada elector did not vote.

Year	1868 Votes	Year	1872 Votes
Totals	294[a]	Totals	366[b]
Ulysses S. Grant (R)	214	Ulysses S. Grant (R)	289
Horatio Seymour (D)	80	Thomas Hendricks (D)	42[c]
		Others	35

[a] Mississippi, Texas, and Virginia were not yet readmitted to the Union and did not participate in the election.
[b] Congress refused to accept electoral votes of Arkansas (6) and Louisiana (8) because of disruptive conditions during Reconstruction.
[c] Democratic presidential nominee Horace Greely died between the time of the popular vote and the meeting of the electoral college. As the democratic electors had no party nominee to vote for, most of them voted for Hendricks, democratic governor-elect of Indiana. The rest of the electors split their votes among other politicians.

Year	1876 Votes	Year	1880 Votes
Totals	369	Totals	369
Rutherford B. Hayes (R)	185[a]	James A. Garfield (R)	214
Samuel J. Tilden (D)	184	Winfield S. Hancock (D)	155

[a] Initially, Tilden appeared to have won the election. However, the electoral votes of Oregon and three Southern states, which still were under military rule, were in doubt. In order to sort out the matter, congress created a special electoral commission. The so-called Compromise of 1877, which was worked out between party leaders, granted Hayes the presidency. In return, the Republicans agreed to remove federal troops from the South.

Year	1884 Votes	Year	1888 Votes
Totals	401	Totals	401
Grover Cleveland (D)	219	Benjamin Harrison (R)	233
James G. Blaine (R)	182	Grover Cleveland (D)	168

Year	1892 Votes	Year	1896 Votes
Totals	444	Totals	447
Grover Cleveland (D)	277	William McKinley (R)	271
Benjamin Harrison (R)	145	William J. Bryan (Democrat, Populist)	176
James B. Weaver (Populist)	22		

Year	1900 Votes	Year	1904 Votes
Totals	447	Totals	476
William McKinley (R)	292	Theodore Roosevelt (R)	336
William J. Bryan (D)	155	Alton B. Parker (D)	140

Year	1908 Votes	Year	1912 Votes
Totals	483	Totals	531
William H. Taft (R)	321	Woodrow Wilson (D)	435
William J. Bryan (D)	162	Theodore Roosevelt (Progressive)	88
		William H. Taft (R)	8

Year	1916 Votes	Year	1920 Votes
Totals	531	Totals	531
Woodrow Wilson (D)	277	Warren G. Harding (R)	404
Charles E. Hughes (R)	254	James M. Cox (D)	127

Year	1924 Votes	Year	1928 Votes
Totals	531	Totals	531
Calvin Coolidge (R)	382	Herbert C. Hoover (R)	444
John W. Davis (D)	136	Alfred E. Smith (D)	87
Robert M. La Follette (Progressive)	13		

Year	1932 Votes	Year	1936 Votes
Totals	531	Totals	531
Franklin D. Roosevelt (D)	472	Franklin D. Roosevelt (D)	523
Herbert C. Hoover (R)	59	Alfred M. Landon (R)	8

Year	1940 Votes	Year	1944 Votes
Totals	531	Totals	531
Franklin D. Roosevelt (D)	449	Franklin D. Roosevelt (D)	432
Wendell Willkie (R)	82	Thomas E. Dewey (R)	99

Year	1948 Votes	Year	1952 Votes
Totals	531	Totals	531
Harry S. Truman (D)	303[a]	Dwight D. Eisenhower (R)	442
Thomas E. Dewey (R)	189	Adlai E. Stevenson (D)	89
J. Strom Thurmond (States' Rights Democrat)	39[a]		

[a] One democratic elector from Tennessee voted for Thurmond instead of Truman.

Year	1956 Votes	Year	1960 Votes
Totals	531	Totals	537
Dwight D. Eisenhower (R)	457	John F. Kennedy (D)	303
Adlai E. Stevenson (D)	73	Richard M. Nixon (R)	219
Walter B. Jones (D)	1[a]	Harry F. Byrd (D)	15[b]

[a] One Stevenson elector from Alabama cast his vote for Jones.
[b] Eight Mississippi and six Alabama electors, elected as 'unpledged Democrats', cast electoral votes for Byrd. One Nixon elector from Oklahoma voted for Byrd.

Year	1964 Votes	Year	1968 Votes
Totals	538	Totals	538
Lyndon B. Johnson (D)	489	Richard M. Nixon (R)	301[a]
Barry M. Goldwater (R)	52	Hubert H. Humphrey (D)	191
		George C. Wallace (American Independent)	46[a]

[a] One republican elector from North Carolina voted for Wallace instead of Nixon.

Year	1972 Votes	Year	1976 Votes
Totals	538	Totals	538
Richard M. Nixon (R)	520	James E. Carter (D)	297
George C. McGovern (D)	17	Gerald R. Ford (R)	240
John Hospers (Libertarian)	1[a]	Ronald W. Reagan (R)	1[b]

[a] One Nixon elector from Virginia voted for Hospers.
[b] One Ford elector from Washington voted for former governor of California Reagan.

Year	1980 Votes	Year	1984 Votes
Totals	538	Totals	538
Ronald W. Reagan (R)	489	Ronald W. Reagan (R)	525
James E. Carter (D)	49	Walter F. Mondale (D)	13

Year	1988 Votes	Year	1992 Votes
Totals	538	Totals	538
George Bush (R)	426	William J. Clinton (D)	370
Michael S. Dukakis (D)	111	George Bush (R)	168
Lloyd Bentsen (D)	1[a]		

[a] One Dukakis elector from West Virginia voted for Dukakis's running mate Bentsen.

Year	1996 Votes	Year	2000 Votes
Totals	538	Totals	538[a]
William J. Clinton (D)	379	George W. Bush (R)	271
Bob Dole (R)	159	Al Gore (D)	266

[a] One abstention in D.C.

Year	2004 Votes
Totals	538
George W. Bush (R)	286
John F. Kerry (D)	251
John Edwards (D)	1[a]

[a] One Minnesota elector voted for John Edwards for both president and vice president.

2.10 List of Power Holders 1789–2004

Head of State[a]	Years	Remarks
George Washington (F)	1789–1797	Formation of the executive branch; Neutrality Proclamation of 1793 and the beginning of party conflict; the Whiskey Rebellion of 1794. Retirement.
John Adams (F)	1797–1801	Transformation of the presidency from a non-partisan to a partisan institution; diplomatic crisis with France. Vice president from 1789 to 1797.
Thomas Jefferson (D-R)	1801–1809	'Popular' leadership; beginning of realignment in favour of the Democratic-Republicans; era of rapid territorial expansion begins (Louisiana Purchase). Vice president from 1797 to 1801, retirement.

Head of State[a] (cont.)	Years	Remarks
James Madison (D-R)	1809–1817	Decline of the presidency and congressional dominance; war against Britain (from 1812 to 1815). Retirement.
James Monroe (D-R)	1817–1825	Growing split in majority party between 'old' Democratic-Republicans and more nationalistic National-Republicans; status of slavery in newly admitted states becomes political issue (Missouri Compromise of 1820); Monroe Doctrine (1823). Retirement.
John Q. Adams (D-R)	1825–1829	First 'divided government' after midterm elections; Democratic-Republicans split into two factions. Electoral defeat.
Andrew Jackson (D)	1829–1837	'Jacksonian Democracy' ("equal rights for all, special privileges for none"); expansion of popular sovereignty; rise of the party convention in the presidential nominating process. Retirement.
Martin Van Buren (D)	1837–1841	Economic crisis ('The Panic of 1837'). Vice president from 1833 to 1837, electoral defeat.
William H. Harrison (W)	1841	Died a month after inauguration.
John Tyler (W)	1841–1845	Frequent exercise of presidential vetoes and intense conflicts with Whig caucus. Vice president in 1841, no party nomination in 1844.
James K. Polk (D)	1845–1849	Reinforcement of executive functions; forceful performance as commander in chief during the Mexican-American War (1846-1847); territorial expansion and Manifest Destiny; slavery issue divides Democrats. Retirement.
Zachary Taylor (W)	1849–1850	Opposition to 'Compromise of 1850' designed to preserve temporary peace on the slavery issue. Died after 16 months in office.
Millard Fillmore (W)	1850–1853	Aggravation of crisis engendered by slavery question. Vice president from 1849 to 1850, no party nomination in 1852.
Franklin Pierce (D)	1853–1857	Growing polarization on slavery issue ('Bleeding Kansas'); collapse of the Whigs. No party nomination in 1856.
James Buchanan (D)	1857–1861	Failure to end agitation on slavery and outpour of sectional strife further fracturing the Democratic Party. No party nomination in 1860.

Head of State[a] (cont.)	Years	Remarks
Abraham Lincoln (R)	1861–1865	Secession of slave states and Civil War (from 1861 to 1865); wartime measures; Emancipation Proclamation of 1863; three Civil War Amendments. Assassinated in office.
Andrew Johnson (R)	1865–1869	Reconstruction era; congressional resurgence; impeachment in 1868 fails to reach a 2/3 majority in the senate. Vice president in 1865, no party nomination in 1868.
Ulysses S. Grant (R)	1869–1877	Patronage abuses and numerous scandals. Retirement.
Rutherford B. Hayes (R)	1877–1881	'Compromise of 1877' bringing disputed Southern electoral votes to the Republican candidate in exchange for his promise to remove federal troops from the former Confederate states; conflict between president and congress over civil service. Retirement.
James A. Garfield (R)	1881	Party factionalism dominates politics. Assassinated in office.
Chester A. Arthur (R)	1881–1885	Civil service reform. Vice president in 1881, retirement.
Grover Cleveland (D)	1885–1889	Controversies over patronage; prelude to a more active presidency. Electoral defeat.
Benjamin Harrison (R)	1889–1893	Absence of presidential leadership; dominance of congress and party organizations; rise of ideological politics. Electoral defeat.
Grover Cleveland (D)	1893–1897	Economic crisis ('Panic of 1893'); departure from 'hands-off' approach to legislation; federal intervention in the Pullman strike. No party nomination in 1896.
William McKinley (R)	1897–1901	Realignment in favour of the Republicans; presidential leadership in legislation; Spanish-American War of 1898. Assassinated in office.
Theodore Roosevelt (R)	1901–1909	Progressive Era, expansion of executive power and New Nationalism; the beginning of the 'rhetorical presidency'. Vice president in 1901, retirement.
William H. Taft (R)	1909–1913	Passive use of presidential legislative powers; tariff reductions; growing centrifugal tendencies within the Republican Party between conservatives and progressives. Electoral defeat.

Head of State[a] (cont.)	Years	Remarks
Woodrow Wilson (D)	1913–1921	Pronounced executive leadership; reforms of tariff and banking systems ('New Freedom'); U.S. enters World War I in 1917; numerous idealistic diplomatic initiatives (Fourteen Points of 1918). No party nomination in 1920.
Warren G. Harding (R)	1921–1923	Passive presidential leadership; numerous scandals. Died in office.
Calvin Coolidge (R)	1923–1929	'Silent' presidential politics; intensified public relation efforts. Vice president from 1921 to 1923, retirement.
Herbert Hoover (R)	1929–1933	Stock market crash in 1929 and Great Depression; political paralysis. Electoral defeat.
Franklin D. Roosevelt (D)	1933–1945	Institutionalization of the Modern Presidency; New Deal program of Keynesian-style state interventionism and welfare policies (Social Security Act of 1935), New Deal electoral coalition emerges; World War II and war economy. Died in office.
Harry S Truman (D)	1945–1953	Expansion of social security ('Fair Deal'); extensive exercise of presidential vetoes; Truman Doctrine to contain communist expansion, Marshall Plan to rebuild Europe. Vice president in 1945, retirement.
Dwight D. Eisenhower (R)	1953–1961	Presidency of the 'hidden hand'; continuation of internationalist foreign policy; McCarthyism; intensifying conflicts over racial segregation. Reached maximum allowable term.
John F. Kennedy (D)	1961–1963	Personalizing the presidency; 'New Frontier' agenda; civil rights legislation initiatives; confrontation with communist block. Assassinated in office.
Lyndon B. Johnson (D)	1963–1969	'Great Society' agenda and 'presidential government'; Civil Rights Act of 1964; Vietnam War. Vice president 1961–1963, retirement.
Richard Nixon (R)	1969–1974	'New Federalism' agenda; administrative presidency due to divided government; bitter relations with congress; end of Vietnam War. Resigned in order to avoid impeachment after the Watergate scandal.
Gerald R. Ford (R)	1974–1977	Vietnam amnesty program; frequent exercise of presidential vetoes. Vice president in 1974, electoral defeat.
James E. Carter (D)	1977–1981	Tensions with congress; Camp David Accords in 1978; oil price crisis; Iranian seizure of US hostages. Electoral defeat.

Head of State[a] (cont.)	Years	Remarks
Ronald W. Reagan (R)	1981–1989	Neo-conservative welfare state retrenchment and tax reduction; dramatic increase in national debt; end of nuclear arms race. Reached maximum allowable term.
George Bush (R)	1989–1993	End of Cold War; Persian Gulf War of 1991; failures in domestic, mainly economic policy. Vice president 1981–1989, electoral defeat.
William J. Clinton (D)	1993–2001	Balanced budget; NAFTA in 1993; failure to instigate health care reform; prosecutorial investigations into the president's sexual relationship with a former White House intern, impeachment fails to reach a two-thirds majority in the senate. Reached maximum allowable term.
George W. Bush (R)	2001–	'War' on terrorism, invasion of Iraq; tax reductions and massive budget deficits.

[a] The head of state is also head of government.

3. Bibliography

3.1. Official Sources

Federal Election Commission (2004). *Federal Election Campaign Laws*. September 2004. Washington, D.C. <http://www.fec.gov> (as of 05/12/04).

National Archives & Records Administration (2005). *2004 Presidential Election*. Washington, D.C. <http://www.archives.gov/federal_register/ electoral_college/2004/election_results.html> (as of 20/01/05).

United States Bureau of the Census (1975). *The Statistical History of the United States. From Colonial Times to 1970*. Washington, D.C.: U.S. Government Printing Office.

United States Bureau of the Census (various publication dates). *Statistical Abstract of the United States*. Washington, D.C.: U.S. Government Printing Office.

United States Bureau of the Census (2004). *Census Bureau Home Page*. <http://www.census.gov> (as of 05/12/04).

United States Congress (2005). *Office of the Clerk. Election Information*. Washington, D.C. <http://clerk.house.gov/members/electionInfo/index.html> (as of 20/01/05).

3.2. Books, Articles, and Electoral Reports

Adams, W. P. et al. (eds.) (1998). *Länderbericht USA. Geschichte, Politik, Geographie, Wirtschaft, Gesellschaft, Kultur* (3rd edn.). Bonn: Bundeszentrale für politische Bildung.

Berg, M. (2000). *The Ticket to Freedom. Die NAACP und das Wahlrecht der Afro-Amerikaner.* Frankfurt/Main: Campus.

Binning, W. C. et al. (1999). *Encyclopedia of American Parties, Campaigns, and Elections.* Westport, Conn.: Greenwood Press.

Bott, A. J. (1990). *Handbook of United States Election Laws and Practices. Political Rights.* New York: Greenwood Press.

Burnham, W. D. (1955). *Presidential Ballots, 1836–1892.* Baltimore, Md.: Johns Hopkins University Press.

— (1970). *Critical Elections and the Mainsprings of American Politics.* New York: Norton.

— (1982). *The Current Crisis in American Politics.* New York: Oxford University Press.

Chambers, W. N. and Burnham, W. D. (eds.) (1975). *The American Party Systems. Stages of Political Development.* New York: Oxford University Press.

Clubb, J. M. et al. (eds.) (1981). *Analyzing Electoral History. A Guide to the Study of American Voter Behavior.* Beverly Hills and London: Sage.

Congressional Quarterly Inc. (ed.) (1997). *Presidential Elections, 1789–1996.* Washington, D.C.: Congressional Quarterly Inc.

— (1998). *Congressional Elections, 1946–1996.* Washington, D.C.: Congressional Quarterly Inc.

Davies, P. J. (1992). *Elections USA.* Manchester and New York: Manchester University Press.

Dubin, M. J. (1998). *United States Congressional Elections, 1788–1997. The Official Results of the Elections of the 1st through 105th Congresses.* Jefferson, N.C.: McFarland & Co.

Flanigan, W. H. and Zingale, N. H. (2002). *Political Behavior of the American Electorate* (10th edn.). Washington, D.C.: CQ Press.

Fraenkel, E. (1981). *Das Amerikanische Regierungssystem* (4th edn.). Köln: Westdeutscher Verlag.

Heideking, J. (1999). *Geschichte der USA* (2nd edn.). Tübingen: A. Francke.

Jewell, M .E. and Morehouse, S. M. (2001). *Political Parties and Elections in American States* (4th edn.). Washington, D.C.: CQ Press.

Key, V. O. (1955). 'A Theory of Critical Elections'. *Journal of Politics* 17/2: 3–18.

Keyssar, A. (2000). *The Right to Vote. The Contested History of Democracy in the United States.* New York: Basic Books.

Kleppner, P. et al. (eds.) (1981). *The Evolution of American Electoral Systems*. Westport, Conn.: Greenwood Press.

Ladd, C. E. (1994). *The American Ideology. An Exploration of the Origins, Meaning, and Role of American Political Ideas*. Storrs, Conn.: Roper Center for Public Opinion Research.

Lawson, S. F. (1976). *Black Ballots. Voting Rights in the South, 1944–1969*. New York: Columbia University Press.

Lösche, P. (1989). *Amerika in Perspektive. Politik und Gesellschaft der Vereinigten Staaten*. Darmstadt: Wissenschaftliche Buchgesellschaft.

Lowenstein, D. H. (1995). *Election Law. Cases and Materials*. Durham, N.C.: Carolina Academic Press.

McKay, D. (1993). *American Politics & Society* (3rd edn.). Oxford: Blackwell Publishers.

Madison, J. et al. (1987). *The Federalist Papers* (first published 1788). London: Penguin Books.

Maisel, L. S. (ed.) (1991). *Political Parties and Elections in the United States. An Encyclopedia* (2 vols.). New York: Garland Publishing.

Milkis, S. M. and Nelson, M. (1999). *The American Presidency. Origins and Development, 1776–1998*. Washington, D.C.: CQ Press.

Moore, J. L. (ed.) (1994). *Congressional Quarterly's Guide to U.S. Elections* (3rd edn.). Washington, D.C.: Congressional Quarterly.

Peterson, S. (1981). *A Statistical History of the American Presidential Elections* (first published 1968). Westport, Conn.: Greenwood Press.

Rush, M. E. (ed.) (1998). *Voting Rights and Redistricting in the United States*. Westport, Conn.: Greenwood Press.

Rusk, J. G. (2001). *A Statistical History of the American Electorate*. Washington, D.C.: CQ Press.

Scammon, R. M. et al. (ed.). (various publication dates). *America at the Polls: A Handbook of American Presidential Election Statistics*. Washington, D.C.: Elections Research Center.

Scammon, R. M. (ed.). (various publication dates). *America Votes. Biennial 1952–1998*. Washington, D.C.: Elections Research Center (vols. 1–18), Congressional Quarterly Press (vols. 19–23).

Schlesinger Jr., A. M. (ed.) (1973). *History of U.S. Political Parties* (4 vols.). New York: Chelsea House Publishers.

Stonecash, J. M. et al. (2003). *Diverging Parties. Social Change, Realignment, and Party Polarization*. Boulder, Co.: Westview Press.

Sundquist, J. L. (1983). *Dynamics of the Party System. Alignment and Realignment of Political Parties in the U.S.* Washington, D.C.: Brookings Institution.

Tocqueville, A. de (1835). *De la Démocratie en Amérique*. Paris: C. Gosselin.

Verba, S. and Nie, N. H. (1972). *Participation in America. Political Democracy and Social Equality*. New York: Harper and Row.

Wattenberg, M. P. (1990). *The Decline of American Political Parties, 1952–1988*. Cambridge, Mass.: Harvard University Press.

Glossary

The following glossary of key concepts of elections and electoral systems refers to those definitions only that are systematically applied in this handbook.

Absentee voting: Under an absentee voting provision a person entitled to vote and unable or unwilling to go to the assigned polling station on election day may still cast his/ her vote. Voting takes place before election day by mail or before or on election day at a different and sometimes special polling station than the one originally assigned. In the special case of *external* or *overseas voting*, embassies and military bases function also as polling stations for absentees. In most cases there is an application deadline for absentee voting before the elections. In *electoral systems* with more than one *constituency* it deserves special attention to which constituency absentee and especially overseas ballots are added.

Absolute majority system: An *electoral system* in which a candidate becomes elected if he or she has received more than half of the valid *votes*. If no candidate reaches the necessary absolute majority, runoffs usually ensue among only the two candidates with the highest shares of votes. In order to avoid a runoff, in some cases the parliament decides.

Alternative vote (system): An *electoral system* in which voters rank candidates according to their preferences. The decision-rule is the *absolute majority* of first preference votes. If no candidate obtains the necessary absolute majority, the candidate with the lowest number of first preference votes is eliminated, and his/ her votes are redistributed among the remaining candidates on the basis of the voters' second preferences. This procedure is repeated until one candidate obtains an absolute majority.

Binomial system: An *electoral system* in which all MPs are elected in two-member-*constituencies* on a *closed and non-blocked list* of parties or electoral alliances, i.e. each elector has one vote. The decision rule is plurality. This electoral system tends to favor the second largest political forces in a country: only if the winning *list* receives twice as many votes as the list which finishes second, both seats will be given to the winning list (to the candidate with the second largest number of votes on this list).

Blank votes: Blank votes, i.e. leaving the ballot blank, are seen in Latin America as a form of protest against the government and many statistics list blank votes separately from invalid votes.

Candidacy: The form of candidacy is particularly important because the relationship between voter and representative can be influenced by different institutional arrangements. A fundamental distinction must be drawn between individual candidacies and party *lists*, i.e. between voting for certain candidates (in *SMCs* or small *MMCs*), or for lists of parties or independents (in MMCs).

Closed and blocked list: A list system (also referred to as simply *closed list*) which allows the voter to cast his/ her vote only for one fixed list of party candidates, without being it possible for him/ her to express his/ her preferences within this list. See *list*.

Closed and non-blocked list: A list system which allows the voter to decide who should represent the party in Parliament by letting him/ her choose between the candidates of a given list. See *list*.

Combined electoral system: Generalized expression for *electoral systems* in which more than one *principle of decision* is applied (like in *mixed-member proportional systems*, *compensatory systems* or *segmented systems*).

Compensatory system: A *combined electoral system* with more than one tier of seat allocation where the additional tier systematically favors those parties which were disadvantaged in the preceding step of seat allocation. Contrary to the *segmented system*, where the allocation of parliamentary seats takes place separately according to the *majority principle* and to *proportional representation*, the parts of a compensatory system are inter-connected insofar as the unsuccessful votes of the majority part are additionally taken into account in the allocation of the PR-seats. By this hyper-proportional procedure, smaller parties or alliances are partially *compensated* for their disadvantage in the distribution of the majority seats.

Constituency (or *Electoral District*): The territory in which elections are held is divided into constituencies in which candidates are elected. The number of constituencies in an election may range from one—all representatives are elected nationwide—to as many as there are representatives to be elected (i.e. parliamentary seats). *Single-member constituencies* (*SMCs*) where only one candidate is elected can be distinguished from *multi-member constituencies* (*MMCs*) of small size (2– 5 seats), medium size (6–10 seats) and large size (11 or more seats). The district magnitude is hence measured with reference to the number of seats to be distributed in the constituencies. The lower the number of constituencies, and the higher the number of seats awarded in each district, the stronger is the proportional effect of the electoral system.

Decision rule: see *Principle of decision*.

Deposit: Electoral laws frequently provide for candidates to pay a certain amount of money to get on the ballot. As a rule, a candidate will only be refunded after an election, if he has achieved a minimum of the *vote* share or has won a seat. While deposits tend to reduce the number of frivolous *candidacies*, they may also be exclusionary for candidates who cannot pay or raise the money for the deposit. An alternative to the deposit is the requirement of a certain number of certified supporters.

D'Hondt method: A highest average formula with the sequence of divisors 1, 2, 3, 4, 5, etc. Favors larger parties. See *Electoral formulae*.

Droop quota: The total number of valid votes cast (V), divided by the district magnitude (M) plus one (V/[M+1]). Identical to *Hagenbach–Bischoff quota*.

Electoral formulae: Where seats are distributed proportionally, a specific method of calculation has to be used. Although there are manifold methods, most of them can be classified into two basic categories, namely those based on average formula and those based on a quota. The typical feature of the *highest average formula*—the best known examples are the *d'Hondt formula* and the *Saint-Laguë formula*—is as follows: The votes gained by the various political parties are divided by a series of divisors (1, 2, 3, 4, 5, etc. in the case of the *d'Hondt formula*) so that decreasing numerical series result for each party. The seats are allocated to the highest numbers of quotients. The advantages of this method of distribution are its simplicity and the fact that all seats are distributed in just one step. Under quota systems, on the other hand, a quota is calculated. The number of seats the relevant parties will gain will be the same as the number of times their vote total can be divided by the quota. Examples are the *Hare, Droop* or *Hagenbach-Bischoff quota,* calculated by dividing the number of total votes cast by a certain divisor. These formulae do not allow for a one-step seat allocation, so the remaining seats have to be distributed in a second stage, often by the method of *largest remainder of votes* or by the *greatest average* method. The same effect on seat distribution as the *Hare quota* in combination with *largest remainder* has the *Hare-Niemeyer formula.* In comparison to average formula systems, the quota systems normally produce a more proportional outcome, thereby favoring smaller parties.

Electoral system: Set of formal rules according to which voters may express their political preferences in elections and which enables the conversion of votes into parliamentary seats (in the case of parliamentary elections) or into executive positions (in the case of elections for President, governors, mayors, etc.). These rules affect the following spheres: *constituencies, candidacies*, voting procedures, and modes of seat allocation.

External voting (or *overseas voting*): A provision which enables the voting age population living or staying abroad to cast their vote outside their home country. External voting is a special case of *absentee voting*.

First vote: In a *combined electoral system* with two votes to be cast (e.g. *segmented system*), the first vote refers to the candidate vote (usually in *SMCs*) and the *second vote* to the party vote (in *MMCs*).

Gerrymandering: This term refers to the practice of drawing electoral district boundaries to suit the interests of political parties. It entails a deliberate political manipulation and exploits the varying spatial distribution of support for the various political parties. This tactic is named after Elbridge Gerry, a governor from Massachusetts who cut out a safe salamander-shaped district for himself in Boston.

Greatest average: Method for the allocation of remaining seats. The seats that cannot be distributed under the electoral quota are allocated later to those parties with the highest average number of *votes* per seat (parties that have suffered most from the application of the electoral quota benefit most from the additional allocations). See *Electoral formulae.*

Hagenbach-Bischoff quota: The total number of valid votes cast (V), divided by the district magnitude (M) plus one (V/[M+1]). See *Electoral formulae.*

Hare quota: The total number of valid votes cast (V), divided by the district magnitude (M): (V/M). See *Electoral formulae.*

Hare-Niemeyer formula: The number of seats for each party is calculated by dividing the valid votes of each party (PV) by the total number of valid votes (TV), and subsequently multiplying the result by the district magnitude (M): SP (seat portion) = ([PV/TV]*M). The greatest integer (GI) less or equal to the SP determines the number of seats given to each party. Remaining seats are given to the parties according to their largest remaining SP: (SP–GI). Identical with *Hare quota* together with *Largest remainder*. See *Electoral formulae.*

Highest average formula: see *Electoral formulae.*

Largest remainder: Formula used to allocate the remaining seats. The seats that cannot be distributed under the corresponding electoral quota are allocated successively to those parties with the largest remainder (total votes of the respective party minus its successful votes). See *Electoral formulae.*

List, forms of lists: The different forms of party lists influence the relationship between the voter and the candidates or between the candidates and their parties. The strictly *closed and blocked list* permits only voting en bloc for a political party, and does not allow the voter to express his/ her preferences for or rejection of a given candidate. Instead, party committees decide the sequence of the candidates on the lists. Closed and blocked lists thus tend to increase the dependence of the representatives on the political parties. On the other hand, the parties can plan the composition of the party in Parliament (experts, minorities, women, etc.). On the contrary, *preferential voting* within a *closed, (but) non-blocked list* permits voters to decide who should represent the party in Parliament. This decision is only pre-structured by the party committees. A representative therefore feels less dependent on his/ her party. The *open (i.e. non-closed and non-blocked) list* allows voters to cross party lines and enables them to compile their own lists. Consequently, an *open list* may be considered as a mere proposal by the parties.

Majority principle: see *Principle of decision*.

Majority representation: see *Principle of representation*.

Majority system: see *Absolute majority system*.

Mixed-member proportional system: An *electoral system* in which two *votes* are cast. Unlike the *segmented system*, the number of seats per party *list* is determined by the *second vote* according to *proportional representation* in national or regional *MMCs*. Yet, a fixed number of seats (lower than the seat total) is allocated directly to winning candidates according to the *plurality system* in *SMCs* or MMCs determined by the *first vote*. The seats won by candidates—which are usually associated with a party and are also on this party's *list*—are subtracted from the party's seat total. If there are fewer seats per party than seats per (party) candidates, the elected candidates remain in parliament as additional members (surplus seats). Usually, the mixed-member proportional system—also known as the German model—does not cause many of such additional members of parliament and has therefore hardly any effect upon the proportionality of votes and parties: it is in effect a personalized system of *proportional representation*.

MMC, Multi-member constituency: see *Constituency*.

Multiple vote: see *Vote(s)*.

Open (i.e. non-closed and non-blocked) lists: A list system which allows voters to cross party lines and enables them to compile their own list of preferred candidates disregarding their party affiliation. See *List*.

Overseas voting: see *External voting*.

Parallel system: see *Segmented system*.

Plurality system: An *electoral system* in which a candidate (in *SMCs* or *MMCs*) or a party *list* (in *MMCs*) is elected if he/ she/ it receives more valid *votes* than any other candidate or party *list*. Unlike in the *absolute majority system*, the plurality of valid votes—not the majority—is sufficient to get elected.

Preferential voting: see *Alternative vote system*.

Principle of decision: The decision principle is the formula that determines the winners and losers of an election. If the decision principle is the majority formula, it will be the majority of votes cast that will decide who wins and who loses the election (*majority principle*, i.e. either by plurality or by an [absolute] majority). If the proportional formula is the principle of decision, the result of an election is decided according to the proportion of votes cast obtained by each candidate or party (*proportional principle*).

Principle of representation: There are two basic principles to classify *electoral systems* according to their impact they are intended to have upon the *votes*/seats relationship: *majority representation* and *proportional representation*. The objective of majority representation is to produce a parliamentary majority for one party or for a coalition of parties; this is achieved by the disproportion between *votes* and seats inherent in majority electoral systems. *Proportional representation*, on the other hand, aims at reflecting the existing social forces and political groups in a given country as accurately as possible, i.e. a more or less proportional relation between votes and seats.

Proportional principle: see *principle of decision*.

Proportional representation (PR): 1. see *principle of representation*. 2. An *electoral system* in which the share of seats reflects the share of *votes* in a *constituency*. The fewer the number of constituencies, and the larger they are, the more proportional is the overall effect of the system. The size of the constituencies creates natural *thresholds* which infringe proportionality, and legal thresholds have analogous effects. Furthermore, the *electoral formula* applied may have disproportional effects on the votes/seats ratio. An electoral system with only one (national) constituency and without a legal threshold is called *pure PR*. If there is more than one constituency the system is called *PR in multi-member constituencies*. In some countries, a part of Parliament is elected in (regional) MMCs and another part in one national constituency (e.g. in Guatemala): the system is then labeled *PR in multi-member constituencies with an additional national list*. In contrast to the *segmented system*, only one *principle of decision* is applied and the vote counts twice. See also *Combined electoral system*.

PR in multi-member constituencies: see *Proportional representation*.

PR in multi-member constituencies with an additional national list: see *Proportional representation*.

Pure PR: see *proportional representation*.

Quota systems: see *Electoral formulae* and *Droop, Hagenbach-Bischoff* and *Hare quota*.

Runoff: see *Absolute majority system*.

Saint-Laguë formula: A highest average formula with the sequence of divisors 1, 3, 5, 7, 9 etc. In comparison with the d'Hondt formula it tends to favour smaller parties. See *Electoral formulae*.

Second vote: In a *combined electoral system* with two votes to cast (e.g. in a *segmented system*), the second vote refers to the party vote (in *MMC*s) and the *first vote* to the candidate vote (usually in *SMC*s).

Segmented system (or *parallel system*): Two *electoral systems* are used to elect members of a parliamentary chamber separately: for a fixed portion of seats, *proportional representation* in medium- to large-sized (often national) *MMC*s is applied; for another portion of seats, MPs are elected in *SMC*s by *plurality* or *absolute majority*. These two parts of the segmented system are not connected in any way and their respective *electoral formulae* are also applied separately. This is the basic difference to *compensatory systems*, where the different parts of the electoral system are interconnected and the disproportional effect of the initial seat allocation by the *majority principle* is reduced by a hyper-proportional formula that favors smaller parties.

A valuable indicator of the degree of proportionality of a segmented system is the ratio between the number of MPs elected by *majority principle* and the number of MPs elected by *PR*.

SMC, Single-member constituency: see *Constituency*.

SNTV, Single non-transferable vote: A *plurality electoral system* in *MMC*s in which the voter can only cast one *vote*. Seats are distributed by plurality according to the number of votes for the single candidates. The larger the *constituencies*, the more SNTV tends to *proportional representation*. Unlike in *STV*, in SNTV there is no quota, additional preferences cannot be given, and there is only one count of the votes.

STV, Single Transferable Vote (also PR-STV): An *electoral system* in which voters can rank candidates according to their preferences in *MMC*s. In a multiple-round counting process, surplus votes of candidates who have reached the *STV Droop Quota* are transferred to second preference candidates proportionally to all second preferences of the voters of the successful candidate. Likewise, candidates with the lowest share of *votes* are eliminated and the corresponding votes are transferred to the next preference. The counting process continues until all seats of the constituency are filled. STV is also called PR-STV to distinguish it from the *alternative vote*.

STV Droop quota: One plus the greatest integer (GI) less than or equal to the total number of valid votes cast (V), divided by the district magnitude (M) plus one: $1+ (GI \leq V/[M+1])$. See *Electoral formulae*.

Thresholds of representation: A legal threshold (or hurdle) of representation is a certain, legally fixed number of votes or seats that a political party (or candidate) has to reach in order to be allowed to participate in the allocation of seats. Legal (or artificial) thresholds differ from natural thresholds, which may result from districting, i.e. from the size of the *constituencies*.

Vote(s): Depending on the *electoral system*, voters can either cast one, two or a series of votes. If there is one vote, this is usually either for a single candidate, a *closed and blocked list* of a party or a candidate on a *closed and non-blocked list*. If the voter is entitled to two or more votes, he may cast them in favor of one candidate on a *closed and non-blocked list* exclusively (cumulative voting), of more than one candidate on a *closed and non-blocked list* (preference voting) or of candidates on various *lists* (panachage; see *open list*). Two votes are also the rule in *combined electoral systems*, where the *first vote* is to be cast for a candidate and the *second vote* for a party. The term *multiple vote* refers to an *electoral system* in which the voter may cast as many votes as seats are to be filled in the *constituency*.